THE LEGAL HISTORY OF THE EUROPEAN BANKING UNION

How was the Banking Union, the most advanced legal and institutional integration in the single market, created? How does European law impact European integration?

To answer these questions, this book provides a sweeping account of the evolution of European law. It identifies five integration periods of the single financial market, intertwined with the development of global finance, from its origins, through its expansion and crisis, to the Banking Union. Each period is defined by innovations to deepen integration, such as the single passport for financial services, soft governance and comitology, agencies, or a single rulebook.

Providing a far-reaching explanation of the legal and institutional rationality of the European Banking Union, this book demonstrates that the Banking Union is not an accident of history or simply the product of the existential crisis of the Monetary Union. It has deep roots in the evolutionary process of European law and its drive towards supranational integration.

The Legal History of the European Banking Union

How European Law Led to the Supranational Integration of the Single Financial Market

Pedro Gustavo Teixeira

•HART•

OXFORD • LONDON • NEW YORK • NEW DELHI • SYDNEY

HART PUBLISHING

Bloomsbury Publishing Plc

Kemp House, Chawley Park, Cumnor Hill, Oxford, OX2 9PH, UK

1385 Broadway, New York, NY 10018, USA

HART PUBLISHING, the Hart/Stag logo, BLOOMSBURY and the Diana logo are trademarks of Bloomsbury Publishing Plc

First published in Great Britain, 2020

A catalogue record for this book is available from the British Library.

Library of Congress Cataloging-in-Publication data

Names: Teixeira, Pedro Gustavo, author.

Title: The legal history of the European Banking Union : how European law led to the supranational integration of the single financial market / Pedro Gustavo Teixeira.

Description: Oxford, UK ; New York, NY : Hart Publishing, an imprint of Bloomsbury Publishing, 2020. | Includes bibliographical references and index.

Identifiers: LCCN 2020033071 (print) | LCCN 2020033072 (ebook) | ISBN 9781509940622 (hardback) | ISBN 9781509940639 (ePDF) | ISBN 9781509940646 (Epub)

Subjects: LCSH: Banking law—European Union countries—History.

Classification: LCC KJE2188 .T45 2020 (print) | LCC KJE2188 (ebook) | DDC 346.24/082—dc23

LC record available at https://lccn.loc.gov/2020033071

LC ebook record available at https://lccn.loc.gov/2020033072

ISBN: HB: 978-1-50994-062-2
ePDF: 978-1-50994-063-9
ePub: 978-1-50994-064-6

Typeset by Compuscript Ltd, Shannon

This work is dedicated to my family:
Jennie, Emília, Carolina, and Gabriela

O mal verdadeiro, o único mal, são as convenções e as ficções sociais, que se sobrepõem às realidades naturais.

Fernando Pessoa, O Banqueiro Anarquista, 1922

ACKNOWLEDGEMENTS

This book is more than an account of the historical evolution of European law. It is an account of my academic and professional learning since arriving at the European University Institute (EUI), and later engaging in a career at the European Central Bank (ECB), where I was privileged to be involved in the integration processes of both the Monetary Union and the Banking Union.

At the EUI, I would like to thank Karl-Heinz Ladeur for broadening my intellectual horizons, and acknowledge the enduring academic influence of Christian Joerges. In the final stages of the preparation of this work, I would like to express my gratitude for the encouragement of Renaud Dehousse, and the generous availability of Giorgio Monti, Luís Morais, and René Smits to be part of the Examining Board of my doctoral thesis.

At the ECB, I would like to acknowledge those who gave me professional opportunities and the privilege to work with them, since many of their insights on European integration are reflected in this work. Chronologically: in the early days of the ECB, Chiara Zilioli, the late Tommaso Padoa-Schioppa, Mauro Grande, Andrea Enria, Panagiotis Strouzas, Peter Praet, Arnaud Marés and Lars Nyberg; during the financial and sovereign debt crises, Jean-Claude Trichet, Lucas Papademos, and Vítor Constâncio; in the setting-up of the Single Supervisory Mechanism, Ignazio Angeloni, Danièle Nouy, and Sabine Lautenschläger; and, as Secretary of the decision-making bodies of ECB, Mario Draghi.

Many of the arguments in this book were developed in discussions with Stefan Niessner and successive generations of students at the Institute for Law and Finance of the Goethe Universität in Frankfurt. I would like to thank them for the lively exchanges of views. I would like also to express my appreciation to Edoardo Chiti and Agustín José Menéndez for having involved me over the years in some of their research projects, which influenced decisively the direction of this work, and keeping my academic flame alight.

Finally, I would like to thank Roberta Bassi from Hart Publishing for her excellent and patient support for this publication, and an anonymous reviewer for very helpful suggestions. All errors remain mine.

This book reflects legal and policy developments up to May 2020. Opinions expressed are those of the author, and not necessarily those of the European Central Bank.

Frankfurt/M
9 May 2020

TABLE OF CONTENTS

LIST OF TABLES AND FIGURES

TABLE OF CASES

ABBREVIATIONS

BAC	Banking Advisory Committee
BCBS	Basel Committee on Banking Supervision
BIS	Bank for International Settlements
BRRD	Bank Recovery and Resolution Directive
CEBS	Committee of European Banking Supervisors
CEIOPS	Committee of European Insurance and Occupational Pensions Supervisors
CESR	Committee of European Securities Regulators
CPSS	Committee on Payment and Settlement Systems
CRD	Capital Requirements Directive
CRR	Capital Requirements Regulation
DGS	Deposit Guarantee Scheme
DIF	Deposit Insurance Fund
EBA	European Banking Authority
EBC	European Banking Committee
ECB	European Central Bank
ECOFIN	Economic and Financial Affairs Council
ECSC	European Coal and Steel Community
EDIS	European Deposit Insurance Scheme
EDP	Excessive Deficit Procedure
EEC	European Economic Community
EFC	Economic and Financial Committee
EFSF	European Financial Stability Facility
EFSM	European Financial Stabilisation Mechanism
EIOPA	European Insurance and Occupational Pensions Authority

ELA	Emergency Liquidity Assistance
EMS	European Monetary System
EMU	European Monetary Union
ERM	Exchange Rate Mechanism
ESA	European Supervisory Authorities
ERSC	European Systemic Risk Council
ESCB	European System of Central Banks
ESFS	European System of Financial Supervision
ESM	European Stability Mechanism
ESMA	European Securities Markets Authority
ESRB	European Systemic Risk Board
EURATOM	European Atomic Energy Community
FATF	Financial Action Task Force
FCD	Financial Conglomerates Directive
FOLTF	Failing or Likely to Fail
FSAP	Financial Services Action Plan
FSA	Financial Services Authority
FSB	Financial Stability Board
FSF	Financial Stability Forum
GHOS	Group of Governors and Heads of Supervision
IAIS	International Association of Insurance Supervisors
IASC	International Accounting Standards Committee
IFAC	International Federation of Accountants
IIMG	Inter-Institutional Monitoring Group
IMF	International Monetary Fund
IOSCO	International Organisation of Securities Commissions
ISDA	International Swap Dealers Association
ISD	Investment Services Directive
MiFID	Markets in Financial Instruments Directive
MoU	Memorandum of Understanding
MREL	Minimum Requirement for own funds and Eligible Liabilities

NCB	National Central Banks
NCWO	No Creditor Worse Off
NGO	Non-Governmental Organisation
OECD	Organisation for Economic Co-operation and Development
OMT	Outright Monetary Transactions
PSPP	Public Sector Purchases Programme
SEA	Single European Act
SGP	Stability and Growth Pact
SRB	Single Resolution Board
SRM	Single Resolution Mechanism
SRF	Single Resolution Fund
SSM	Single Supervisory Mechanism
TEC	Treaty establishing the European Community
TFEU	Treaty on the Functioning of the European Union
TSCG	Treaty on Stability, Coordination and Governance in the EMU
UCITS	Undertakings for the Collective Investment in Transferable Securities

Introduction

'C'est souligner que, si étendue qu'elle soit, l'intégration économique que réalisera la libre circulation des marchandises, des services, des personnes et des capitaux ne constitue encore qu'une intégration économique partielle, puisquelle ne comporte pas de renonciation à l'autonomie des politiques budgétaires, financières ou sociales, ni la création d'une monnaie unique. Au moins possède-t-elle, en elle-même, une force assez grande pour maintenir le degré utile de convergence entre ces politiques, et assurer que le mouvement lancé ne s'arrêtera pas en chemin.'

Spaak Report, 1956[1]

I. Purpose

Easter 1956, Grand-Hôtel du Cap-Ferrat, South of France. Pierre Uri and Hans von der Groeben finalise the drafting of the report requested from Paul-Henri Spaak by the foreign ministers of the six Member States of the European Coal and Steel Community (ECSC), when meeting at the Messina Conference of June 1955. The draft report was completed in four weeks. It was transmitted without modifications by Spaak to the Conference of Ministers meeting in Venice, at the San Giorgio Monastery, at the end of May 1956. The ministers approved the report in around two hours as the basis for the negotiations of the Intergovernmental Conference on the Common Market and Euratom, which drafted the Treaty establishing the European Economic Community, signed in Rome on 25 March 1957.[2]

The above quote from the Spaak Report is the leitmotif of this book. It is a normative prediction of the future dynamics of economic integration. Once the four freedoms are introduced, they will provide by themselves the engine of integration. Economic integration will, however, always be incomplete until Member States relinquish policies at the core of their sovereignty: budgetary, financial and social policies, as well as

[1] PH Spaak, *Rapport des Chefs de Délégation aux Ministres des Affaires Etrangères*, Comité Intergouvernemental créé par la Conférence de Messine (Brussels, 21 April 1956) 96.

[2] As told by P Uri, *Penser pour l'Action: Un fondateur de l'Europe* (Paris, Odile Jacob, 1991), and H von der Groeben, 'Europäische Integration aus historischer Erfahrung: Ein Zeitzeugengespräch mit Michael Gehler' (2002) C108 *Zentrum für Europäische Integrationsforschung, Discussion Paper* 13. The main drafter of the Spaak Report was the economist Pierre Uri, a close collaborator of Jean Monnet, who participated in the preparation of the Schuman Declaration. He was, at the time, Director of the General Economics Division of the High Authority of the ECSC, and worked together in the final draft with the lawyer Hans von der Groeben, Head of the German Delegation at the Intergovernmental Committee established by the Messina Conference, and later the influential first European Commissioner responsible for Competition Policy.

monetary policy. There is thus an intrinsic conflict between integration and the preservation of national policies. Until this conflict is solved, the four freedoms will compel the convergence of such national policies to the extent required for integration; they will ensure that integration is inevitable and irreversible. The renouncement by Member States of their sovereignty over those policies is then the endpoint of integration, when economic integration will be complete.[3]

The aim of this book is to assess the extent to which this prediction came true in the remarkable evolution of the integration of the single financial market. It culminated in the establishment of the supranational European Banking Union, when Member States renounced banking supervision and resolution policies, almost 60 years after the Spaak Report. This is all the more striking as the Treaty of Rome of 1957 did not include a financial market as one of the components of the common market. The first piece of European legislation on financial services was only introduced in 1973. Contrary to what was foreseen by the Spaak Report, the movement of capital was not a basic freedom until the Single European Act (SEA) entered into force in 1987. The single financial market then expanded significantly when Member States renounced their sovereignty over monetary policy in 1999, with the start of the third stage of European Monetary Union (EMU) and the introduction of the euro.

Most European citizens only became aware of the existence and consequences of a single financial market in October 2008, with the successive bank failures and bail-outs with public funds. The financial crisis was immediately followed by the sovereign debt crisis in the euro area in 2010. It became exacerbated by the vicious circle between the financial deterioration of banks and the deterioration of the public finances of the Member States which rescued them. On 30 June 2012, at the peak of the sovereign debt crisis, the Euro Summit announced the creation of a Single Supervisory Mechanism (SSM) to break this vicious circle. It would become the first pillar of the Banking Union, followed two years later by the Single Resolution Mechanism (SRM). A European Deposit Insurance Scheme, a third pillar of the Banking Union, is still being debated at the time of writing.

The Banking Union then became the most advanced form of supranational legal and institutional integration in the single market, whereby Member States relinquished their sovereignty over the policies regarding the banking sector of the economy. It is a unified system of law on the basis of a 'single rulebook,' which is legislated and defined at the European level. The application and enforcement of this rulebook, in the form of banking supervision and resolution, is under the exclusive competence of European authorities. The acts of these authorities are subject to the judicial review of the Court. They are formally accountable to the Parliament and the Council, while also reporting to national parliaments.

[3] On the concept of the irreversibility of the common market in the Spaak Report, see AS Milward, *The European Rescue of the Nation-State*, 2nd edn (London, Routledge, 1994) 183–184, who considers that it originated in the thinking of the Dutch Finance Minister Johan Willem Beyen – previously an international banker, governor of the Dutch central bank and president of the BIS – that the customs union should be automatic and irrevocable. This was in contrast to the French position that harmonisation of economic and social policies would need to precede the customs union.

The purpose of this book is to verify how prescient the quote of the Spaak Report was: whether the loss of sovereignty of Member States over the banking sector and the creation of the Banking Union was a 'predictable' consequence of the logic of integration or an accident of history. In order to understand why European integration proceeded in the direction of the legal construction of the Banking Union, the narrative of this book will be guided by the following strand of questions: What explains the creation of the Banking Union, and how does legal change happen and impact the European integration process?

II. Explaining the Creation of the Banking Union

What explains the creation of the Banking Union, the most advanced form of legal and institutional integration within the single market? Why did the powers over a vital sector of the economy – the banking sector – close to the core of the sovereignty of the Member States move from the national to the supranational level? And why did such integration happen more rapidly than in other areas of the single market?

The conventional explanations of the origins of the Banking Union focus on two related causes. One causal link was the structural flaw of the Monetary Union, which was established without including within its scope the supervision of the euro area banking sector. As pointed out quite forcibly by Tommaso Padoa-Schioppa at the time, it was unique in history that the central banking jurisdiction – the euro area – did not coincide with the jurisdiction for banking supervision, which remained at the national level. This fact had many implications.[4]

A fragmented banking sector along national lines could not support the smooth transmission of a single monetary policy. For example, if the interest rates set by banks for loans diverged widely across the Member States of the euro area, the single monetary policy would not function properly. Financial integration was also a pre-requisite for Monetary Union. An integrated financial system enables cross-border risk-sharing through the financial markets. In the absence of public risk-sharing among Member States, and also of significant labour mobility within the euro area, private risk-sharing is the only mechanism left to withstand financial shocks. For example, cross-border banks will be more resilient if they diversify their lending, thus compensating losses in a Member State facing a recession with returns in other Member States.[5]

Moreover, the fact that the banking sector remained subject to national jurisdictions meant that despite European harmonisation initiatives, it was still regulated by

[4] See T Padoa-Schioppa, 'EMU and Banking Supervision' (1999) 2 *International Finance*, 295, 303–ff; and *Regulating Finance: Balancing Freedom and Risk* (Oxford, Oxford University Press, 2004) 83–92; J Pisani-Ferry, A Sapir, N Véron, and G Wolff, 'What Kind of European Banking Union' (2012) 2012/12 *Bruegel Policy Contribution*; and, for the historical perspective, H James, *Making the European Monetary Union* (Cambridge, The Belknap Press of Harvard University Press, 2012) 89–107.

[5] On the concept of risk-sharing, see M Draghi, 'Risk-reducing and risk-sharing in our Monetary Union' (2018), Speech at the European University Institute, Florence, at www.ecb.europa.eu/press/key/date/2018/html/ecb.sp180511.en.html. On the implications of the Monetary Union's structural flaw for the financial crisis of 2007/2008 and the sovereign debt crisis, see PR Lane 'The European Sovereign Debt Crisis' (2012) 26 *Journal of Economic Perspectives* 49.

divergent national rules and enforcement practices. Since they were accountable to national political institutions, national authorities had to pursue domestic interests in banking regulation and supervision. This often materialised as protectionism of domestic banking markets and the promotion of 'national champions', given the importance of the banking sector for the economy. Effective banking regulation and supervision was then undermined by being captured by the interests of the financial industry. In turn, there was moral hazard in the risk-taking of the banking sector, given the likelihood of public bail-outs by national governments. In the case of a financial crisis, there would be ring-fencing of domestic banking systems by national authorities to minimise the cost of bail-outs. This would exacerbate sudden stops in capital flows, further destabilising the financial system and national economies. Furthermore, the Monetary Union did not provide crisis management arrangements, as financial stability competences remained at the national level. The assumption was that spontaneous cooperation among national authorities would suffice to contain risks and manage financial crises.[6]

As a consequence, the Monetary Union would never function properly without a 'Banking Union', which would ensure financial integration, private risk-sharing, and a well-regulated and supervised banking system in the European interest.[7]

The implications of this flaw of the Monetary Union crystallised with the financial crisis of 2007/2008 and the ensuing sovereign debt crisis of the euro area. This was the second causal link of the Banking Union. Following successive failures to quell the ever worsening sovereign debt crisis, the euro area Member States announced on 29 June 2012 the intention to establish a 'single supervisory mechanism' involving the ECB. It would enable the ESM to recapitalise banks directly in order to cut the mutual dependence between Member States and banks. It would be the first component of a 'Banking Union'.[8]

The origin of the European Banking Union, in this context, was seen as an emergency response of Member States to the existential crisis of the euro. Facing the prospect of disintegration, Member States decided to move ahead quickly towards the centralisation of banking supervision powers at the ECB. This was considered by many strands of legal doctrine as another manifestation of the circumvention of the established modes of action provided by the Treaty, which was common to other responses to the euro crisis. According to this view, the transfer of powers was decided among Member States through an intergovernmental mode, with recourse to a fragile legal basis, and without consideration of democratic legitimacy concerns related to such a concentration of powers at the European level. The Banking Union would epitomise, in this sense, the

[6] See T Padoa-Schioppa, *Regulating Finance*, (n 4) 83–92; and J Pisani-Ferry et al, 'What Kind of European Banking Union' (n 4).

[7] See eg E Monnet, S Pagliari, and S Vallée, 'Europe between financial repression and regulatory capture' (2014) 2014/08 *Bruegel Working Paper*; and B Eichengreen, 'European Monetary Integration with Benefit of Hindsight' (2012) 50 *Journal of Common Market Studies* 123. See also D Schoenmaker, *Governance of International Banking: The Financial Trilemma* (Oxford, Oxford University Press, 2013), who reformulates this conclusion in the form of a 'financial trilemma' on the impossibility of having simultaneously integrated banking markets, national supervision and financial stability.

[8] For an account of the steps for the creation of the Banking Union during the sovereign debt crisis, see N Véron, 'Europe's Radical Banking Union' (2015) *Bruegel Essay and Lecture Series*, at bruegel.org/wp-content/uploads/imported/publications/essay_NV_CMU.pdf.

supranational executive structures emerging from the euro crisis as the harbinger of future European integration.[9]

Most of these explanations about the Banking Union also relate its creation to the political preferences and interests of Member States. The creation of the Banking Union and the design of its legal and institutional features are depicted as the result of intergovernmental politics. The decision to establish the SSM was taken in the intergovernmental setting of the Euro Summit, in the context of the worsening sovereign debt crisis also affecting larger Member States. The main attributes of the SSM, such as its jurisdiction, governance, and competences, were judged to be the result of political compromises among Member States. A similar reasoning would apply to the European banking resolution regime and the establishment of the SRM. Intergovernmental divergences would also hinder, at the time of writing, a European deposit insurance scheme.[10]

The narrative provided in this book on the creation of the Banking Union looks beyond these conventional explanations. It claims that the causal logic of the Banking Union is in fact entrenched in the evolutionary process, over several decades, of the law and institutions of the European financial market since the Treaty of Rome. It considers such explanations of the Banking Union from a broader perspective. It shows that the Banking Union is more a fundamental outcome of European integration, within the logic of supranational legal integration, rather than an accident of history triggered by a crisis.[11]

III. Explaining Legal Change in European Integration

Tracing back the evolutionary process towards the Banking Union also provides empirical evidence on how legal change occurs in European integration. It should

[9] For an overview of these arguments, see C Joerges, 'Europe's Economic Constitution in Crisis and the Emergence of a New Constitutional Constellation' (2014) 15 *German Law Journal* 985; S Grundmann and HW Micklitz, 'The European Banking Union and Constitution – The Overall Challenge' in S Grundmann and HW Micklitz (eds), *The European Banking Union and Constitution: Beacon for Advanced Integration or Death-Knell for Democracy?* (Oxford, Hart Publishing, 2019); E Chiti and PG Teixeira 'The Constitutional Implications of the European Financial and Public Debt Crisis' (2013) 50 *CML Rev* 683; and, generally on European integration, J Habermas, *The Lure of Technocracy* (Cambridge, Polity, 2015) 56–58.

[10] On the preferences of Member States regarding the establishment of the SSM, see S De Rynck, 'Banking on a union: the politics of changing eurozone banking supervision' (2016) 23 *Journal of European Public Policy* 119. On the argument that European economic governance after the crisis is the result of intergovernmental processes, see S Donnelly, 'Power Politics and the Undersupply of Financial Stability in Europe' (2014) 21 *Review of International Political Economy*, 980; D Howarth and L Quaglia, 'The New Intergovernmentalism in Financial Regulation and Banking Union' in CJ Bickerton, D Hodson and U Puetter (eds), *The New Intergovernmentalism: States and Supranational Actors in the Post-Maastricht Era* (Oxford, Oxford University Press, 2015) 146–162; and also G Maris and P Sklias, 'France, Germany and the New Framework for EMU Governance' (2016) 24 *Journal of Contemporary European Studies* 1. With a different take, arguing for a neofunctionalistic logic that 'a coalition of supranational institutions, member state governments and private actors in the banking sector mobilised behind ever-closer banking union against the opposition of Germany and its allies', see RA Epstein and M Rhodes, 'The political dynamics behind Europe's new banking union' (2016) 39 *West European Politics* 415.

[11] The historical link between the Banking Union and the initial blueprints for banking regulation and supervision made at the early stages of European integration, and in the context of monetary integration, is argued by E Mourlon-Druol, 'Banking union in historical perspective: the initiative of the European Commission in the 1960s-1970s' (2016) 54 *Journal of Common Market Studies* 913, 918–921.

help with understanding how supranational structures like the Banking Union came about. This corresponds to the second contribution of this book, besides explaining the creation of the Banking Union: it also aims at ascertaining how precisely European law and its evolution lead to integration.

This book challenges alternative narratives, which dismiss the relevance of legal change in explaining how Member States transfer their sovereignty towards supranational structures. This relates in particular to those theories claiming that the outcomes in European integration are essentially the result of intergovernmental bargaining, which dominate the explanations on the creation of the Banking Union. Further, it confronts neofunctionalist theories, whereby integration proceeds by functional spillovers from one policy area to another, beyond the control of Member States.[12]

The analytical lens taken in this book is instead closer to narratives stressing European law as the source of integration. Chief among these theories is the one developed under the 'integration through law' moniker, whereby European law has a dual meaning: it is both the object of integration – the creation of a European legal order – and the instrument of integration – the means to steer political, economic, and social dynamics towards European integration. In this account, European law plays a strategic role. It makes integration move forward by framing the actions and relations between European institutions, Member States, national authorities, market players, or citizens. The modus operandi of European law is then to direct those actions and relations towards integration, its own object. Such dual meaning was originally revealed in the 1960s when the Court introduced the doctrines of direct effect and supremacy of European law in the *Van Gend en Loos* and *Costa v ENEL* cases, respectively. The Court made explicit that the sovereignty of Member States is limited in favour of integration, thus confirming the supranational nature of the European legal order, as intended by the Treaty.[13]

[12] The original neofunctionalist argument that European integration moves forward through spillovers from one integration process to another was made by EB Haas, *The Uniting of Europe: Political, Social, and Economic Forces, 1950-1957* (Stanford, Stanford University Press, 1958), especially at 311, predicting that '[t]he spill-over may make a political community of Europe in fact even before the end of the transitional period [in 1969].' For the classic opposing intergovernmentalist view, see S Hoffmann, 'Obstinate or Obsolete? The Fate of the Nation-State and the Case of Western Europe' (1966) 95 *Daedalus, Tradition and Change* 862. See also the overview of the theories on supranational change by M Wind, *Sovereignty and European Integration: Towards a Post-Hobbesian order* (London, Palgrave, 2001).

[13] On the concept of law as both the object and instrument of integration, see R Dehousse and JHH Weiler, 'The Legal Dimension' in W Wallace (ed) *The Dynamics of European Integration* (London, Pinter, 1990) 242–60. On the original source of the 'integration through law' doctrine, see M Cappelletti, M Seccombe and JHH Weiler, 'Integration Through Law: Europe and the American Federal Experience' in M Cappelletti, M Seccombe and JHH Weiler (eds) *Integration Through Law, Vol.1* (Berlin, Walter de Gruyter, 1986) 3-68. For a contemporary overview, see L Azoulai, 'Integration through law and us' (2016) 14 *International Journal of Constitutional Law* 449. See also M Rasmussen, 'Revolutionizing European law: A history of the Van Gend en Loos judgment' (2014) 12 *International Journal of Constitutional Law* 136; and J Baquero Cruz, *What's Left of the Law of Integration? Decay and Resistance in European Union Law* (Oxford, Oxford University Press, 2018), arguing at 17–20 that the principles of direct effect and primacy were contained in the Treaty and were not the outcome of a legal 'revolution' by the Court. On the role of the Court in this process, see also KJ Alter, *Establishing the Supremacy of European law: The Making of an International Rule of Law in Europe* (Oxford, Oxford University Press, 2006).

In this way, the book aims to contribute to European legal scholarship by enquiring how legal change happens and how it impacts the wider European integration process.[14]

The analysis pivots on the sequence of strategies employed by European law to structure the integration process, from starting the development of a single financial market until achieving the Banking Union. These strategies conform largely to well-known paradigms of legal integration, such as the harmonisation of national laws, regulatory competition, multilevel governance, or the centralisation of executive powers. Each of the strategies is dissected so as to expose the underlying legal and institutional innovations, which were introduced to promote integration in a certain period of time. This includes, for example, the single passport in financial services, comitology, or European agencies with ever increasing powers. The reasons for the success or failure – usually failure – of each legal strategy in achieving integration are then assessed, together with what that implies for shaping the successive one. The purpose is to determine whether there is a causal chain in the change from one legal strategy to another, leading ultimately to the creation of the Banking Union.

The book's account also considers the policy preferences and national interests of Member States in shaping legal change in the single financial market. It will be argued that the outcome of legal change in each period of integration also reflects the conflict between the increase in integration and the preservation of the sovereignty of Member States. This finding tallies well with the influential insight of Joseph H.H. Weiler that the engine of European integration is the interplay between supranational law and intergovernmental politics. As will be shown, European law appears to structure intergovernmental dynamics towards integration: to create pressure on Member States to provide more and more authority to the supranational level. For example, the legal and institutional differentiation introduced by the Monetary Union is a potent factor in promoting deeper integration among the Member States of the euro area.[15]

The central thread running through this book, therefore, is that legal change determined the path towards the Banking Union. It provides evidence that European law has its own normative and causal logic towards more and more integration. The precise instruments of change – the legal and institutional innovations – can be determined

[14] On the explanations of legal change in European integration, see the seminal work by AM Burley and W Mattli 'Europe Before the Court: A Political Theory of Legal Integration' (1993) 47 *International Organization* 41, claiming, on the basis of neofunctionalist arguments, that European law leads to transfer of sovereignty to the European level; and G De Búrca, 'Rethinking law in neofunctionalist theory' (2005) 12 *Journal of European Public Policy* 310, arguing that there is no empirical methodology to explain legal change in European integration. For an explanation of legal integration in the context of institutionalist theories, focusing on the role of the Court, see A Stone Sweet, *The Judicial Construction of Europe* (Oxford, Oxford University Press, 2004) 235–244; and A Stone Sweet, W Sandholtz, N Fligstein, 'The Institutionalization of European Space' in A Stone Sweet, W Sandholtz, N Fligstein (eds) *The Institutionalization of Europe* (Oxford, Oxford University Press, 2001). See also the narrative of A Vauchez, *Brokering Europe: Euro-Lawyers and the Making of a Transnational Polity* (Cambridge, Cambridge University Press, 2015) emphasising the historical role of law – and lawyers – in unifying the European polity.

[15] See JHH Weiler, 'The Community System: the Dual Character of Supranationality' (1981) 1 *Yearbook of European Law* 267. For another seminal interpretation of the process of legal integration, see C Joerges, 'Taking the Law Seriously: On Political Science and the Role of Law in the Process of European Integration' (1996) 2 *European Law Journal* 105.

by many factors, including the will of Member States, political and legal doctrines, economic factors, global standards, crisis events, or 'spillovers' from other policy areas of integration. The analysis in this book breaks ground by showing how the evolution of European law, by itself, compelled integration. It posits that legal change operated through a sequence of trial and error strategies, progressively steering the EU institutions, Member States, national authorities, market participants, citizens, and others, into further integration. This helps explain why European integration then proceeded in a certain direction. These successive strategies became interlocked over time to form a continuous strand of legal integration towards a supranational structure, the Banking Union.

IV. Overview

Taking into account the above analytical framework, the narrative of this book reconstructs into five phases of integration the legal evolution of the single financial market from its origins, through its crisis, and to the Banking Union. The distinction between the phases was made by grouping together the legal and institutional innovations, which were introduced to increase financial market integration in a certain historical period. These phases of integration also reflect the milestones in the evolution of the wider single market, such as the 1992 single market programme, as well as the policy thinking and legal doctrines prevalent in each period. Chapters 1 to 5 are devoted to analysing each of these phases, with the respective legal and institutional innovations summarised in a table at the end of each chapter.

Chapter 1 deals with the first phase of integration, from the mid-1970s to the mid-1980s, which is designated as 'integration through harmonisation.' The approach was to pursue the full harmonisation of national laws. It was constrained by capital controls and the need for unanimity voting by Member States for the adoption of harmonisation initiatives. It did not lead to any financial integration. Some building blocks were set up, though, for the future, with innovations such as the harmonisation of basic legal concepts and the first European committees of national authorities, whose set-up also influenced the establishment of standard-setting committees at the global level.

The second phase corresponds to the single market programme, where integration would be achieved through competition in the spirit of Jacques Delors's 1985 White Paper. This related to competition both among market players and regulatory competition among Member States. The key legal innovation for this purpose was the introduction of the single passport for financial services. Chapter 2 explains how the single passport would provide a sort of perpetual motion to market integration: as financial firms competed for market share, there would be more and more regulatory competition between Member States. Together, these dynamics would deliver an integrated market with an optimal regulation. This approach was also not successful. It was constrained by protectionism by Member States, as embodied legally in the general good exception pre-empting mutual recognition.

The third phase of integration starts after the introduction of the euro in 1999, which is characterised by experimental multi-level governance. Comitology became the main regulatory mode of the single financial market as the result of the recommendations of the Report of Alexandre Lamfalussy of 2001. As argued in Chapter 3, this governance period gave rise to the illusion that the single financial market was regulated at the European level, while in reality no national competences had been transferred. In turn, the powers of national authorities became significantly constrained as the financial market gained a European dimension. In this way, the governance period promoted financial integration but, in doing so, it created a void of competences, where neither the European nor the national levels were actually capable of regulating and stabilising the single financial market.

Chapter 4 analyses the unfolding of the great financial crisis of 2007/2008 and its (dis-) integration implications for the single financial market. Member States took discriminatory measures to rescue their domestic banks. Pan-European banking groups were split along national lines. Financial markets were ring-fenced. The single financial market was renationalised, as there were only national responses to the crisis. The only European competence, state aid control, was largely put aside. Following this disintegration, the reaction was to replace committees by European agencies, with reinforced powers over national authorities, as recommended by the report of Jacques de Larosière. However, this did not imply any transfer of competences to the European level. All financial stability functions remained national.

The Banking Union then emerges as a centralisation of powers at the European level. Chapter 5 traces it back to the sovereign debt crisis, which was triggered by the realisation that Member States of the euro area could actually default. It led to the first mutualisation of risks among the euro area Member States in the form of the European Stability Mechanism (ESM). At the peak of the crisis, the Euro Area Summit of 28/29 June 2012 decided to enable the ESM to directly recapitalise banks in order to break the nexus between the finances of Member States and the soundness of banks. There was one condition: banks had to be subject to European supervision. A forgotten clause of the Treaty was then used to entrust the ECB with supervisory powers. The beginning of the Banking Union was thus a consequence of the differentiation of the Monetary Union from the EU. As a result of its legal basis and the compromise made among many objectives, the legal and institutional shape of SSM is complex, as explained in this chapter. Some two years later, and following the actions taken to address the crisis in Cyprus, the Bank Recovery and Resolution Directive introduced a resolution regime based on the mandatory bail-in of banks' liabilities. In the euro area, the Single Resolution Board was established as an agency to exercise resolution competences by stretching the boundaries of Article 114 of the Treaty. The third pillar of the Banking Union, a European Deposit Insurance Scheme, remains on hold at the time of writing, due to concerns about risk-sharing. The remainder of this chapter tackles the democratic legitimacy challenge for the Banking Union and the implications of the legal and institutional differentiation for the EU.

Chapter 6 wraps up this legal history by putting forward the interpretative keys of both the past and future of the Banking Union. It provides answers to the initial questions of what explains the creation of the Banking Union and how legal change led to it. It concludes with what can be drawn from such an interpretation of the Banking Union for the wider process of European integration.

1

Integration through Harmonisation (1973–1984)

Delouvrier speaks about the Spaak intergovernmental committee. He says good work is being done on the Common Market, but is it possible to have a Common Market without federal social, monetary and conjuncture policies? Monnet does not think that this will be possible. Therefore, according to Monnet, it is essential to go into the political side of the thing. Uri defends the possibility [of a Common Market without all this superstructure].

Diary of Max Kohnstamm, entry for end of November 1955[1]

I. Introduction

The legal history of the Banking Union starts when the first generation of the Community law instruments on financial services emerged in the mid-1970s, with the first directive adopted in 1973. This period lasts until 1984, before the 1985 Commission's White Paper on Completing the Internal Market, which announced a new approach to market integration.

The shaping of a European financial market began with the Spaak Report of 1956, which first diagnosed the tension between the integration of finance and national sovereignty persisting until the present day. It also put forward the approach of 'integration through harmonisation', which characterised this period. Ten years later, the Segré Report of 1966 further advocated the full harmonisation of national laws to develop a European financial market. This started to be implemented in 1973 with the first directive on the abolition of restrictions on freedom of establishment of banks. This initiative was made in the context of the increasing internationalisation of finance after the collapse of Bretton Woods in 1973, the steps towards a Monetary Union with the 'currency snake' of 1972, the Paris Summit of October 1972, and the accession of Denmark, Ireland, and the UK in the European Economic Community (EEC) in 1973.

In 1977, the First Banking Directive started the long process of harmonisation of national laws towards a common market in banking services, which would culminate four decades later with the Banking Union. The approach of 'integration through harmonisation' was completed with the establishment of European committees of

[1] Historical Archives of the European Union, INT555.

national authorities. These committees were involved in the first type of comitology procedures and in promoting the convergence of the enforcement of Community law throughout the European financial market. This also inaugurated the institutional evolution of a European financial market, later based on comitology procedures and governance arrangements.

At the end of this period, the legal and institutional foundations for the evolution of the European financial market had been set, but there was limited, if any, progress in financial integration.

II. Origins

A. The Concept of Legal Integration in the Spaak Report

The Spaak Report of 21 April 1956 provided the basis for the discussions at the Intergovernmental Conference on the Common Market and Euratom preparing the Treaties of Rome. It argued for a horizontal and comprehensive common market in Europe. It was part of the strategy for the 'relance européenne' after the first and traumatic crisis of European integration: the failure of the European Defence Community, when the French National Assembly decided not to ratify it on 30 August 1954.[2]

Paul-Henri Spaak believed that European integration should proceed through economic integration and without requiring transfers of political sovereignty from Member States. The priority would be to achieve economic growth in Europe. Market forces would drive integration, while economic and financial policies would remain at the national level. This implied that there was no need for supranational institutions with political powers, as preferred by Jean Monnet. A specialised European administration would suffice to manage integration. Over time, the policies of Member States would then become more and more constrained by economic integration. Political unification would follow as a functional consequence to fulfil the goals of economic integration. In the view of Spaak, this strategy towards integration was the one most likely to be agreed between France and Germany, in the context of the negotiations for the Treaty of Rome. Otherwise, Member States would block any formal attempt to reduce their sovereignty and integration would likely fail, as it happened with the initiative of the European Defence Community. The framework for integration presented in the Spaak Report was thus a rejection of Jean Monnet's original strategy for achieving European political integration one step at a time, with the transfer of national sovereignty from one economic sector to another, starting with the ECSC and moving on to nuclear energy and the European Atomic Energy Community (EURATOM). In sum, the Spaak Report represented the bifurcation into two distinct beliefs in the process of

[2] See the historical overview by Carl Friedrich Ophüls, the head of the German delegation to the intergovernmental conference, at CF Ophüls, 'La Relance Européenne' in B Landheer and WH Carter (eds) Annuaire Européen / European Yearbook (Martinus Nijhoff, The Hague, 1958) 3; and by Robert Marjolin on the negotiations of the Treaty regarding the concept of a 'common market, R Marjolin, *Le travail d'une vie: Mémoires 1911–1986* (Paris, Éditions Robert Laffont, 1986) 282–294.

European integration. Spaak argued for the 'fusion of markets', hoping that this would then bring about future political integration, while Jean Monnet's preference was to integrate each economic sector through the fusion of national political sovereignty into supranational institutions.[3]

Against this background, a 'European capital market' was part of the notion of a horizontal common market put forward by the Spaak Report. Accordingly, the freedom of movement of capital was presented as one of the four economic freedoms. It also already cautioned at the time about the constraints posed to financial integration by the preservation of national sovereignty in the field of finance. It pointed to the nationalism and protectionism underpinning capital controls among the founding Member States and to the progressive irrelevance of such controls in an integrated economic area. At the same time, it acknowledged the need to avoid that unrestrained capital flows would lead to imbalances among Member States, affect their ability to implement monetary policy or to tax capital income, and lead to insufficient or more costly financing of less developed regions. Such risks could only be addressed gradually as economic integration would progress.[4]

The way forward was gradualism: a flexible process, without a precise calendar or milestones, for the progressive liberalisation of capital movements, which would adapt itself to the development of the common market. Each Member State would also follow its own rhythm of liberalisation on the basis of general directives by the Commission. During the transitional period of four years, safeguards would be allowed to prevent speculative capital flows, after which they would lose their effectiveness once the freedoms for the provision of goods and services were fully implemented.[5]

The legal approach advocated by the Spaak Report to underpin economic integration was the general approximation of national laws to the extent necessary to eliminate distortions created by differences among them. It would be crystallised initially in Articles 100 to 102 of the Treaty of Rome, and later encapsulated in the current Article 114 of the Treaty on the Functioning of the European Union (TFEU), which was introduced

[3] See R Marjolin, *Le travail d'une vie*, (n 2) 282–294; and J Monnet, *Mémoires* (Paris, Fayard, 1976) 472–472. For an early account, see Pierre-Henri Laurent, 'Paul-Henri Spaak and the Diplomatic Origins of the Common Market, 1955–1956' (1970) 85 *Political Science Quarterly* 373. On the Christian democratic support for the concept of 'horizontal market integration' see W Kaiser, *Christian Democracy and the Origins of the European Union* (Cambridge, Cambridge University Press, 2007) 253–303. In the context of monetary integration, see I Maes, 'On the Origins of the Franco-German EMU Controversies' (2004) 17 *European Journal of Law and Economics* 21.

[4] For an analysis of the theory of economic integration underpinning the Spaak Report, see J Pelkmans, J, 'Economic Theories of Integration Revisited' (1980) 18 *Journal of Common Market Studies* 333, who argued at the time that the assumptions made by the report were drawn from the US model, which equates the size of markets to efficiency. Pelkmans was sceptical of the ambition of the Spaak Report of achieving economic integration without requiring political integration, since 'only under extreme integrationist assumptions, it can be expected that politicians would permit the core of the mixed economy to be organised outside their electoral reach'.

[5] On the French objections to having the freedom of movement of capital, due to concerns about international speculation, see R Marjolin, *Le travail d'une vie*, (n 2) 297–298. For the explanation of the liberalisation process, see T Padoa-Schioppa, *L'Europa verso l'unione monetaria: Dallo Sme al trattato di Maastricht* (Turin, Einaudi, 1992), 40–41. See also the concept of a 'progressive economic integration', as developed by Pierre Uri in the preparatory work for the Spaak Report, at Historical Archives of the European Union, PU-53. On the ideology behind this concept, see F Denord and A Schwartz, 'L'économie (très) politique du traité de Rome' (2010) 89 *Politix* 35.

by the Single European Act. This harmonisation approach would be also applicable to capital movements, where the Report considers that differences in financial regulation could remain, as long as they would not lead to discrimination among issuers of capital and investors on the grounds of nationality. The legal harmonisation measures would be proposed by the Commission for adoption by unanimity by Member States in the transitional period of four years, followed by qualified majority voting thereafter.[6]

The Spaak Report provided thus the basic framework for the initial development of a European financial market, which would be based on 'integration through harmonisation': the harmonisation of national laws by Community law measures in order to eliminate distortions that would hinder integration. This implied that, ultimately, all divergences among national laws would have to be eliminated over time as the deepening of market integration would require more and more harmonisation to prevent distortions of competition. Accordingly, in the first phase of the evolution of the single financial market, legal integration would be pursued largely through full harmonisation measures. Although it failed in providing an effective legal framework for integration, it put in place the main building-blocks for evolution in the next decades until the Banking Union.[7]

B. The 'Ordoliberal' Influence on Legal Integration

The concept of legal integration through harmonisation advocated by the Spaak Report was influenced by the German 'ordoliberal' thinking of the post-war years. This was justified to have a concept of economic integration, which would be supported by Germany in the Treaty negotiations. It reflected the 'social market economy' promoted by Ludwig Erhard, the German minister of economic affairs, and his adviser Alfred Müller-Armack.[8]

According to 'ordoliberal' principles, the market is created by a legal and institutional order, its economic constitution. The aim of this order is to define and enforce

[6] Spaak Report 60–66. In the negotiations leading to the Treaty of Rome, France argued for extensive harmonisation also with regard to economic and social policies, such as the harmonisation of wage and social security costs, which was rejected by Germany. On the opposition of France to the concept of a common market, see R Marjolin, *Le travail d'une vie*, (n 2) 282–294. See also AS Milward, *The European Rescue of the Nation-State*, 2nd edn (London, Routledge, 1994), 184–189. On Art 100 of the Treaty of Rome, see S Weatherill, *The Internal Market as a Legal Concept*, (Oxford, Oxford University Press, 2017) especially at 18.

[7] For a historical analysis of the development of legal strategies for European integration in this period, and highlighting the role of the first President of the European Commission, Walter Hallstein, in claiming the constitutional character of the Treaty, see A Vauchez, *Brokering Europe: Euro-Lawyers and the Making of a Transnational Polity* (Cambridge, Cambridge University Press, 2015) 19–34; and HJ Küsters, 'Walter Hallstein and the Negotiations on the Treaties of Rome 1955–57' in W Loth, W Wallace, W Wessels (eds) *Walter Hallstein: The Forgotten European?* (London, Palgrave Macmillan, 1998). On the meaning of harmonisation of national laws in the Spaak Report and the Treaty of Rome, see E Stein, 'Assimilation of National Laws as a Function of European Integration' (1964) 58 *American Journal International Law* 1, especially at 7.

[8] The main concern of Hans von der Groeben during the drafting of the Spaak Report was, accordingly, the design of the common market. See interview to Hans von der Groeben, Historical Archives of the European Union, INT501; and P Uri, *Penser pour l'Action: Un fondateur de l'Europe* (Paris, Odile Jacob, 1991) 54–58. As mentioned in the introductory quote to this chapter, Pierre Uri was in agreement with the concept of common market favoured by Germany, as also argued by F Denord and A Schwartz, 'L'économie (très) politique du traité de Rome' (n 5).

a framework of rules to ensure the proper functioning of the market based on free trade and freedom of contract. Rules should be general and limited to prevent market distortions, such as competition rules preventing the abuse of market power against the freedom of contract. This would also mean that the rules should apply equally to all market participants, without any preferential treatment. In turn, market participants should be liable for their actions and not expect government support. This 'unlimited' liability would work as a strong disciplinary device, preventing market participants from moral hazard, ie taking excessive risks counting on external help. The implication is that the regulation of the market should be protected from the political intervention of the government. Pursuing redistributive policies to protect special interests, or allotting rents and wealth among the electorate, would undermine the common interest which should determine economic and market outcomes. These 'ordoliberal' concepts, rejecting the intrusion of governmental politics, reflected the extreme experience of the appropriation by the state of the economy and private property in Nazi Germany and in the centrally planned and nationalised economy of the Soviet Union.[9]

The Spaak Report transposed 'ordoliberal' doctrines to European integration by reasoning that a common market would arise out of the economic freedoms and within a supranational legal order. Legal integration through harmonisation would aim at creating the essential set of rules to enforce such freedoms equally throughout the Member States. The result would be borderless economies and markets, subject to supranational legal rules and insulated from the national political powers. Economic and market integration would require therefore only legal integration, without any need for political integration into a federal state. The European harmonisation of rules would detach the regulation of the economy and the market from the reach of Member States. Supranational rules would prevent protectionist and nationalistic intrusions by their respective governments, which would otherwise distort the functioning of the common market. The assumption was that the pursuance of national interests would disrupt the economic and market order. In this sense, divergent national laws had distortionary implications and had to be harmonised.

The European common market would thus be subject to its own rules, focused on the protection of economic freedoms, and safeguarded from the economic nationalism of Member States. At the same time, the supranational rules would ensure that the cross-border transactions of a common market would be effectively regulated. A supranational legal order would overcome in this way the territorial limitations of national jurisdictions, which could not capture the international dimension of the economy and markets.[10]

[9] For an overview of 'ordoliberal' thinking, see VJ Vanberg, 'The Freiburg School: Walter Eucken and Ordoliberalism' (2004) 04/11 *Freiburg Discussion Papers on Constitutional Economics*. See also the influence of FA Hayek in his conceptualisation of a European federation in, 'The Economic Conditions of Interstate Federalism' in FA Hayek, *Individualism and Economic Order* (Chicago, Chicago University Press, 1948) 255–272. On the ordoliberal influence on the Spaak Report, see F Denord and A Schwartz, 'L'économie (très) politique du traité de Rome' (n 5).

[10] For a critical analysis of the influence of 'ordoliberalism' in European law, see J Hien and C Joerges, 'Dead man walking? Current European interest in the ordoliberal tradition' (2018) 24 *European Law Journal* 142, as well as the contributions in J Hien and C Joerges (eds) *Ordoliberalism, Law and the Rule of Economics* (Oxford, Hart Publishing, 2017).

This conceptualisation of the economic constitution of the common market, underlying the Spaak Report, was explained very clearly by Hans von der Groeben:

> Any distortions of competition which could result from different laws or administrative regulations are to be removed through a harmonisation of laws and administrative practices. The coordination of individual planning decisions through the market occurs therefore in all Member States within the same legally binding framework consisting of far-reaching guarantees of private property, freedom to establish a business, the determination of prices by supply and demand, freedom to exercise a profession, and free access to any market. This market-oriented order is ensured and controlled by the institutions of the community, which have no dirigiste or planning powers beyond these controls.[11]

Under this thinking, European integration would be based on a clear principle: the ordering of the common market should be the exclusive subject of supranational European law and – neutral or bureaucratic – institutions. This ordering should be limited to ensuring market functioning, without any redistributive objectives at European level, and while safeguarding it against the interventionist policies of Member States.

This, however, led to an internal contradiction in the integration process. The pursuance of economic and financial policies remained under the sovereignty of Member States. Unless such national policies were fully aligned with the ordering of the common market, they would undermine the resolution of European problems and, in any case, become powerless to address national problems. For example, free trade with fixed exchange rates would later become incompatible with national monetary policies. It would also mean that, in the case of economic and financial crises, the stabilisation policies would remain national and would be inadequate at the European level. This was why economic integration would not be completed until national sovereignty over economic and financial policies was fully removed, as stated in the quote of the Spaak Report at the introduction of this book. The creation of the Banking Union several decades after would be one of the consequences of this contradiction.[12]

C. Freedom of Capital as a Second Order Objective in the Treaty of Rome

In line with the framework of the Spaak Report, the project of a European financial market started as a second order objective to that of the common market. The original

[11] H von der Groeben, 'The Role of European Integration in the West German Economic Order' (1979) 135 *Zeitschrift Für Die Gesamte Staatswissenschaft* 493, 497. A similar description of the European economic constitution is made by EJ Mestmäcker: 'What is historic about the EEC Treaty is that it integrates the internationality of economic relationships into the internationality of law and political institutions. In this sense, the EEC Treaty includes an economic constitution … Expressed in terms of state and society, the EEC takes as its starting point the law of bourgeois society and its institutions as the first manifestation of the universal in the international realm,' as quoted by C Joerges, 'Europe's Economic Constitution in Crisis and the Emergence of a New Constitutional Constellation' (2014) 15 *German Law Journal* 985.

[12] On the decoupling of the European economic constitution from social policies, see C Joerges, 'What is left of the European Economic Constitution? A Melancholic Eulogy' (2005) 30 *European Law Review* 461. On the claim that the Spaak Report and the Treaty of Rome embodied neoliberal ideals, see especially Q Slobodian, *Globalists: The End of Empire and the Birth of Neoliberalism* (Cambridge MA, Harvard University Press, 2018) 184–193, as well as the review article by W Streeck, 'Fighting the State' (2019) 50 *Development and Change* 836.

version of Article 67 of the EEC Treaty provided that the liberalisation of capital movements would take place in the transitional period of 12 years only 'to the extent necessary to ensure the proper functioning of the common market.' This also implied that, in contrast with the other fundamental freedoms, the freedom of movement of capital did not have direct effect in Member States.[13]

The degree of liberalisation of capital movements needed for the functioning of the common market was thus left to the interpretation of the Member States, with France having the most restrictive approach compared to the Benelux (Belgium, the Netherlands, and Luxembourg) and Germany. As a result, the exercise of the three freedoms – capital, services and establishment – which would provide the basis for a European financial market, were substantially limited.[14]

The freedom of movement of capital was secondary to those relating to the provision of goods and services, as it was subordinated to the development of the common market as a whole, rather than considered as one of its essential components. In turn, the freedom to provide financial services could only be invoked on the basis of capital movements which were expressly liberalised by the Council, in accordance with the original version of Article 61 of the EEC Treaty, and as confirmed by the Court on several occasions. The freedom of establishment was also subject to the provisions on capital movement, in accordance with the original version of Article 52 of the EEC Treaty, thus making it also implicitly dependent on the deregulation of capital movements.[15]

The freedom of movement of capital, as proposed by the Spaak Report, would be realised through Community measures proposed by the Commission to the Council, which were subject to unanimity voting in the first two stages of eight years of the transitional period, and by qualified majority thereafter from 1 January 1966. Regarding banking services, Article 57(2) of the EEC Treaty required the Council to act always by unanimity on measures concerned with the protection of savings, in particular the granting of credit and the exercise of the banking profession.[16]

D. Attempting to Lift Restrictions to Capital Movements

In its 1962 Report on the Execution of the Treaty, the Commission concluded that 'there would have to be the broadest and most rapid liberalization possible' of capital

[13] Judgment of the Court of 23 February 1995, *Bordessa*, Joined cases C-358/93 and C-416/93, EU:C:1995:54, paras 17 and 33 confirming that the direct effect of the freedom of movement capital was only achieved with Council Directive 88/361/EEC of 24 June 1988 for the implementation of Art 67, EEC Treaty, [1988] OJ L178, 5–18. For an analysis of the case law see L Flynn, 'Coming of Age: The Free Movement of Capital Case Law 1993–2002' (2002) 39 *CML Rev* 773, 787–788.

[14] See R Marjolin, *Le travail d'une vie*, (n 2) 297–298.

[15] Art 61, EEC Treaty stated that the freedom of banks and insurance companies to provide the services linked with capital movements was 'to be established in step with the gradual liberalisation of capital movements' The Court confirmed this interpretation in the Judgment of the Court of 11 November 1981, *Casati*, 203/80, EU:C:1981:261, paras 17 to 20; and Judgment of the Court of 21 September 1988, *Van Eycke v ASPA*, 267/86. EU:C:1988:42, para 22. For an overview, see JA Usher, *The Law of Money and Financial Services in the EC* (Oxford, Oxford University Press, 2000) 15–ff.

[16] See AFP Bakker, *The Liberalization of Capital Movements in Europe* (Dordrecht, Kluwer, 1996) 42–44.

movements. Otherwise, the freedoms of movement of persons, goods and services and the right of establishment 'cannot yield the desired results.'[17]

The first move towards lifting restrictions to capital movements between Member States consisted of two Directives, in 1960 and 1962 respectively, which aimed at facilitating the basic freedoms of the common market by deregulating capital transactions associated with commercial transactions, investments, personal capital movements and trade in quoted securities. In order to safeguard the monetary policy of Member States, the deregulation was not extended to short-term capital movements, since such movements were associated with currency speculation.[18]

A decade of inactivity and even reversal followed these first steps towards a European financial market. A succession of international crises from the mid-1960s involving a loss of confidence in the US dollar, which culminated in the collapse of the Bretton-Woods system in 1971 and followed by waves of increases in oil price in the 1970s, resulted in the reintroduction by several Member States of strict controls on capital movement. This also resulted in the failure to implement the plan for economic and monetary union agreed by the Hague Summit in 1969. The plan for an economic and monetary union was subsequently adopted by the Council of Ministers on 22 March 1971.[19]

E. The Segré Report of 1966

If the beginnings in the 1960s towards a European financial market were largely limited in concrete achievements, the design of the legal and institutional framework that would follow was nevertheless ongoing. In 1966, the Commission set-up a *Comité des Sages* chaired by Claudio Segré, at the time Director at the European Commission. The product of this committee, the first of many that would follow on the development of a European financial market was the so-called Segré Report.[20]

Despite its comprehensive diagnosis, the recommendations of the Report failed to provide new impetus to financial integration. The Report was however quite prescient.

[17] European Commission (1962) The first stage of the Common Market: Report on the Execution of the Treaty (January 1958 – January 1962), 41–43, at aei.pitt.edu/1324/1/internal_market_first_stage_memo.pdf.

[18] First Council Directive of 11 May 1960 for the implementation of Art 67 of the Treaty (capital movements), [1960] OJ L43; and Second Council Directive of 18 December 1962 adding to and amending the First Directive for the implementation of Art 67 of the Treaty (capital movements), [1963] OJ L9. For an overview of the measures on the deregulation of capital movements, see European Commission, The European Financial Common Market, Office for Official Publications of the European Communities, Luxembourg (1989) 13–ff. The OECD also agreed in 1961 to a Code of Liberalization of Capital Movements, which however had a limited nature since the obligation to liberalise capital flows was only to the extent necessary to achieve economic cooperation.

[19] On the evolution of capital controls in this period, see AFP Bakker, *The Liberalization of Capital Movements in Europe*, (n 16) 109–140; as well as R Abdelal, *Capital Rules: The Construction of Global Finance* (Cambridge MA, Harvard University Press, 2007), 48–50.

[20] European Commission, The Development of a European Capital Market, Report of a Group of experts appointed by the EEC Commission ('Segré Report') (1966). The Segré Report also presupposed an economic and monetary union, see T Padoa-Schioppa, *L'Europa verso l'unione monetaria*, (n 5) 34–39.

The main recommendation, which would be repeated in several other reports in the next decades, was that:

> Active participation by the various types of financial institutions in the creation of a European capital market may be hampered by the rules under which they operate and the supervisory controls to which they are subjected. The differences in these rules and controls are, moreover, liable to distort competition and therefore constitute an obstacle to the process of integration.[21]

The Segré Report thus elaborated upon the approach to legal integration proposed by the Spaak Report. The differences in national laws created distortions and prevented integration. The only possible way forward would be to embark on a wide-ranging process of full harmonisation of national laws. In this context, the Report drew attention not only to rules but also to the enforcement of rules through national authorities, which enlarged significantly the scope for the harmonisation efforts. 35 years later, in 2001, the Alexandre Lamfalussy Report – whose author was also a member of the committee which prepared the Segré Report – set out a European framework for financial regulation and supervision which still aimed at addressing the same problems. It then culminated in the single rulebook based on a maximum harmonisation process and in the Single Supervisory Mechanism in 2013.[22]

The full harmonisation of national laws recommended by the Segré Report was not successful. The unanimity voting required for financial legislation made it unfeasible. There was also strong opposition from the UK, as a new Member State at the time, due to the fact that its banking law was based on practices and not on written statutes.[23]

III. Starting a European Financial Market

A. The Context in the Early 1970s

The first generation of Community law instruments towards a European financial market can be traced back to the early 1970s, which marked the end of what became known as 'les trente glorieuses', the 30 years of prosperity in Europe since the end of the Second World War. A long period of slowdown in productivity, high inflation, unemployment, and resulting economic recession was then starting, also exacerbated by the oil crises of 1973 and 1979. Given the combination of inflation and economic stagnation, it became known as the period of 'stagflation' in Europe. This period led to a momentous shift in politics and economics. Among others, it provided the ground for the rise of free-market ideologies in Europe, which would play a decisive role in economic and market liberalisation.[24]

[21] See Segré Report 31.

[22] On the importance of the Segré Report for the initial steps towards a European financial market, see E Mourlon-Druol, 'Banking union in historical perspective: the initiative of the European Commission in the 1960s-1970s' (2016) 54 *Journal of Common Market Studies* 913–927.

[23] As argued by E Mourlon-Druol, 'Banking union in historical perspective' (n 23) 916.

[24] See E Helleiner, *States and the Reemergence of Global Finance: From Bretton Woods to the 1990s* (Ithaca, NY, Cornell University Press, 1994) 146–168, and R Abdelal, *Capital Rules*, (n 19) 54–65. For an

One of the more symbolic events of this time was in March 1973. The Bretton Woods system of pegged exchange rates was formally abolished, after the unilateral end to the convertibility of the dollar into gold by the Nixon administration in August 1971. It was replaced by a floating rate system. As largely a consequence of increasing cross-border capital mobility, it represented the move towards market liberalisation and the beginning of the globalisation of finance, also helped by the start of the revolution in personal computing and communications technology. At the same time, the end of Bretton Woods had one major implication for European integration. Since floating exchange rates would hinder intra-European trade, and thus economic integration, a convergence of exchange rates would be required and eventually a monetary union. This led to the European 'currency snake' in 1972 preventing fluctuations of more than 2.25 per cent, and later to the establishment of the European Monetary System (EMS) in 1979.[25]

The period starting in 1973 is also identified with increasing political and legal expansion of the European Community, which included the accession of Denmark, Ireland, and the UK in the EEC in 1973. Although little progress was achieved in these years in the political and market integration of the Community, there were two developments in this period, which set the conditions for the beginning of the construction of the European financial market.

B. The Expansion of Community Competences

The first development was the expansion of the Community competences from the mid-1970s onwards, which culminated in the single market programme of 1985–1992, also following the *Cassis de Dijon* judgment of the Court in 1979. The institutional and legal foundations for the single financial market, as one of sectoral policy objectives of the wider single market of the Community, were thus set in this period.[26]

The Community competences started to expand to policy fields beyond those strictly enumerated in the Treaty. At the historic Paris Summit of October 1972, which included the three new Member States – Denmark, Ireland and the UK – the Heads of State or government declared their intention to expand the range of policies pursued by the Community into areas not explicitly covered by the Treaty, including economic and monetary issues, if required also through the use of Article 235 of the EEC Treaty (Article 352, TFEU). This provided a new dynamic to the expansion of Community competences as it was not constrained to the powers attributed explicitly in the Treaty.[27]

account of the post-war period, see AS Milward, *The European Rescue of the Nation-State*, (n 6) 18–39, and more broadly T Judt, *Postwar* (New York, Penguin, 2005) 453–ff.

[25] See H James, *Making the European Monetary Union* (Cambridge, The Belknap Press of Harvard University Press, 2012) 89–107; and B Eichengreen, *The European Economy since 1945* (Princeton, Princeton University Press, 2007) 246–251.

[26] Judgment of the Court of 20 February 1979, *Rewe-Zentral AG v Bundesmonopolverwaltung für Branntwein (Cassis de Dijon)*, 120/78, EU:C:1979:42.

[27] Statement from the Paris Summit (19 to 21 October 1972), Bulletin of the European Communities, 10 October 1972, Luxembourg, Office for official publications of the European Communities, 14–26. The *ERTA* case of 1971 is also relevant in this context since the Court derived a sort of implied powers doctrine, whereby the Community had also exclusive competences to conclude external agreements in areas of internal policy, such as transport policy in the case, without this being explicitly provided by the Treaty. Judgment of the Court of 31 March 1971, ERTA, 22/70, EU:C:1971:32.

Therefore, from the mid-1970s, the Community started to expand, within its own institutional system, its competence into new policy areas. There were two implications. First, the Community became involved in new policy areas previously reserved to Member States, without having to rely on a revision of the Treaty through the cumbersome procedure of an intergovernmental conference, which would require the agreement of all Member States to the transfer of competences. Second, the progressive nature of the expansion of the Community competences meant that the relationship and the boundaries between supranational policies and national competences were not well-defined. The legal and institutional evolution of Community policies became very much determined by this ambiguous relationship between European and national competences. Among other effects, it led to the combination of supranational and national instruments and procedures, for instance in the form of comitology, in the pursuance of integration policies.[28]

C. The Beginning of the Internationalisation of Finance

The second development was the beginning of the internationalisation of finance in the 1970s and early 1980s. Together with other factors, it challenged the strictly national pursuance of economic and financial policies by Member States, and provided impetus to the development of a European financial market.

Following the collapse of the Bretton Woods system, the volume of international financial flows increased substantially in the 1970s, among others, as the result of the US economic policy and also the recycling of the revenues of oil producing countries. It also led to the significant growth of the so-called 'Euromarkets', which remained largely unregulated since they developed outside the national regulatory systems. The absence of a regulated European financial market was one of the reasons for the development of 'Euromarkets'. This was followed, in the early 1980s, by a new expansion of international finance due to developments in financial innovation, advances in computing and communications technology, and also increasing deregulation.[29]

In the 1970s, the reaction by Member States to the internationalisation of finance was increasing protectionism. In particular, the successive waves of increases in oil prices in 1973 and 1979 led to economic difficulties and balance of payments problems in most Member States. In the context of the Treaty, some Member States resorted to exchange controls, which had to be authorised by the Commission in accordance with

[28] On the expansion of Community competences in this period, see JHH Weiler, *The Constitution of Europe* (Cambridge, Cambridge University Press, 1999) 51–58.

[29] The Euromarkets is the designation given to the markets on assets denominated in foreign currencies – but mostly US dollar – based in European financial centres. The Euromarkets were introduced in the late 1950s by British merchant banks to avoid regulatory restrictions on pound sterling transactions and also to attract assets denominated in US dollars. The Euromarkets increased significantly in volume in the 1970s due the credit restrictions, capital controls and banking regulations imposed by the Member States and the US in that decade (such as the Regulation Q, a rule introduced in the 1930s which restricted the interest rate that US banks could pay on deposits), which led to increased volumes of US dollar assets towards foreign markets. For an overview of the development of Euromarkets in this period, see E Helleiner, *States and the Reemergence of Global Finance*, (n 24) 81–100; and T Padoa-Schioppa, *L'Europa verso l'unione monetaria*, (n 5) 43.

the safeguard clauses provided for in the event of such difficulties, in accordance with Articles 73 and 108 of the EEC Treaty.[30]

The growth in international finance provided, nevertheless, stimulus to the integration of the Member States' financial markets. The exchange controls and restrictions to capital movements kept by Member States did not appear to solve economic problems. The international liberalisation of capital movements, the increasing opportunities provided by international finance, and the increase in international competition, as well as the economic and financial problems faced by Member States, provided the rationale for a larger internal financial market.[31]

D. Re-starting the Project Towards a Monetary Union

The wish for reform was made explicit in 1977 by the then President of the European Commission, Roy Jenkins, when delivering the first Jean Monet lecture at the European University Institute. In his speech, Jenkins put forward a set of arguments for monetary union in order to address, in particular, the Member States' 'apparently intractable problems of unemployment, inflation and international financing.'[32]

This speech triggered the re-start of the process towards monetary union, which had been disrupted by the economic and financial instability of the 1970s. In December 1978, the European Council created the EMS involving the coordination of the Member States' monetary policies in order to prevent large fluctuations between their currencies.[33]

The realisation of the European financial market, as a pre-condition to monetary integration, was also influenced by this. In the period between 1973 and 1984, the first legislative initiatives towards a European financial market were then introduced. The focus of these initiatives was on making effective the freedom of establishment for financial institutions and on the progressive removal of obstacles to cross-border financial services through the harmonisation and co-ordination of national laws and policies. It had a number of building-blocks, which were at the heart of the construction of the single financial market.

[30] The Treaty allowed the possibility of restrictions to capital movements when such movements could lead to disturbances in the functioning of the capital market in a Member State (Art 73, EEC Treaty) or when a Member State is in difficulties or is seriously threatened with difficulties as regards its balance of payments (Art 108, EEC Treaty). The Member States' obligations regarding capital movements were defined in the First and Second Council Directives for the implementation of Art 67, EEC Treaty, [1960] OJ L43/921–932, and [1963] OJ L9/ 62–74, respectively. The use of safeguard clauses included Italy in 1974, which was authorised to reintroduce substantial restrictions on capital movements. When Denmark, Ireland and the UK joined the EC they also brought with them strict controls on capital movements, which they were allowed to maintain by virtue of the transitional provisions of the Treaties of Accession and authorisations granted by the Commission. See AFP Bakker, *The Liberalization of Capital Movements in Europe*, (n 16) 109–140.

[31] See E Helleiner, *States and the Reemergence of Global Finance*, (n 24) 125–145.

[32] R Jenkins, 'Europe's present challenge and future opportunity' (1977) *Jean Monet Lecture, European University Institute, European Archives, Florence*. See also the diagnosis of the obstacles to a monetary union in the Marjolin Report: European Commission, Report of the Study Group 'Economic and Monetary Union 1980,' Brussels, March 1975, at ec.europa.eu/archives/emu_history/documentation/chapter7/19750308en57reportstudygroup.pdf.

[33] The EMS comprised: (i) the European Currency Unit (ECU); (ii) the Exchange Rate Mechanism (ERM); (iii) European credit facilities; and (iv) the European Monetary Cooperation Fund. On the negotiations leading to the EMS, see H James, *Making the European Monetary Union*, (n 25) 163–180.

IV. The Principle of Non-Discrimination and the Harmonisation of National Laws

A. The Freedoms of Establishment and to Provide Services

In the framework of the original version of the EEC Treaty, as described in the previous section, the freedom to provide financial services was particularly constrained: it was dependent on the liberalisation of capital movements, and any measures in this field by the Council would require unanimity. This reflected the core importance of the banking industry for national sovereignty. In this context, the first step towards a European financial market was limited to implementing the principle of non-discrimination, which prohibits discriminatory treatment with regard to establishment and the provision of services, based either on nationality or place of establishment.[34]

Accordingly, the first Directive was only adopted in 1973 after much resistance by Member States. It took eight years of negotiations and 21 meetings to reach unanimous agreement by Member States – as required by Article 57(2) of the EEC Treaty – on a Commission proposal of 1965 on 'the abolition of restrictions on freedom of establishment and freedom to provide services for self-employed activities of banks and other financial institutions.' Due to the resistance of Member States, the Commission gave up the full harmonisation approach recommended by the Segré Report. It decided to move towards a limited and sectoral harmonisation, which could deliver integration through the harmonisation of national laws gradually, over time.[35]

Accordingly, the scope of the 1973 Directive was quite narrow. Under its Article 2, it requested Member States to abolish the restrictions which prevented 'natural persons and companies or firms from establishing themselves or from providing services in the host country under the same conditions and with the same rights as nationals of that country'. The Directive limited itself to facilitating the administrative procedures regarding the freedom of establishment. It did not include any provisions regarding the legislation or regulation of banking activities.[36]

Although the abolishment of national entry-requirements could have fostered cross-border banking activities, it did not lead to noteworthy, if any, progress in the European banking market. The freedoms of establishment and to provide services in the banking sector were subject to the compliance with the laws of the host Member States, which were justified under Article 57(2) of the EEC Treaty by the public interest of consumer

[34] Art 57(2), EEC Treaty required the Council to act by unanimity on measures concerned with the protection of savings, in particular the granting of credit and the exercise of the banking profession. For an analysis of this period, see T Padoa-Schioppa, *L'Europa verso l'unione monetaria*, (n 5) 40–45.

[35] See E Mourlon-Druol, 'Banking union in historical perspective,' (n 23) 917–918.

[36] Council Directive 73/183/EEC of 28 June 1973 on the abolition of restrictions on freedom of establishment and freedom to provide services in respect of self-employed activities of banks and other financial institutions, [1973] OJ L194/1–10. The Directive was part of a series of directives aiming at making effective the freedom of establishment and the freedom to provide services, which had to be fulfilled by 1970. Although all the necessary legislation had not been adopted by then, the Court considered that these two freedoms had direct effect as from 1 January 1970. See Judgment of the Court of 21 June 1974, *Reyners v Belgian State*, 2/74, EU:C:1974:68; and Judgment of the Court of 3 December 1974, *van Binsbergen v Bestuur van de Bedrijfsvereniging voor de Metaalnijverheid*, 33/74, EU:C:1974:13133/74.

protection. Moreover, the significant legal and regulatory differences across Member States constrained the entry into their respective markets and limited the potential economic benefits in the cross-border provision of services. A complete business infrastructure was required to conduct the activities in the host-country, thus preventing any economies of scale. As a result, the fragmentation of the European banking markets was preserved.[37]

B. The Initial Harmonisation Effort in Banking

The freedoms of establishment and to provide services in the banking sector only truly started to be implemented with the First Banking Directive, which entered into force at the end of 1979. This Directive represented the first effort to harmonise the laws of Member States, in order to achieve a European banking market. It focused on implementing the freedom of establishment for banking activities through the harmonisation of the basic legal definitions, principles and rules regarding the authorisation, supervision and withdrawal of the authorisation of a 'credit institution'.

The Directive introduced the first set of definitions of the Community's banking legislation, which largely remain valid to this day. This includes the definitions of a 'credit institution' – an undertaking whose business is to receive deposits or other repayable funds from the public and to grant credits for its own account – as well as 'branch', 'authorisation' and 'own funds'. Regarding the authorisation process, national regulators could only grant a banking licence if a credit institution possessed separate and adequate minimum own funds, was run by at least two persons of good repute and sufficient experience, and had a programme of operations. Regarding supervision, banking regulators could establish ratios between the various assets and liabilities of credit institutions in order to monitor their solvency and liquidity, and with the objective to ensure the protection of savings. Lastly, the authorisation of a credit institution could be withdrawn in several instances, such as not using the authorisation, obtaining the authorisation through irregular means, or not fulfilling obligations towards its creditors.[38]

This level of harmonisation remained basic, but was conceived as a precursor to full harmonisation. Initially, it supported the application of the principle of non-discrimination to branches of a credit institution with the head office in another Member State. Branches – a place of business which forms a legally dependent part of a credit institution and which conducts directly all or some of the operations of credit institutions – may be subject to authorisation in another Member State, but according to

[37] The special nature of the banking sector from the perspective of the public interest has been recognised in several instances by the Court. See Judgment of the Court of 9 July 1997, *Parodi v Banque de Bary*, C-222/95, EU:C:1997:345 at para 22: 'It must be recognised that the banking sector is a particularly sensitive area from the point of view of consumer protection. It is, in particular, necessary to protect the latter against the harm which they could suffer through banking transactions effected by the institutions not complying with the requirements relating to solvency and whose managers do not have the necessary qualifications or integrity.'

[38] Arts 1, 3, 6, and 8 of Council Directive 77/780 of 12 December 1977 on the co-ordination of laws, regulations and administrative provisions relating to the taking up and pursuit of the business of credit institutions, [1977] OJ L322/30 ('First Banking Directive').

the same law and procedure applicable to credit institutions established in its territory. In addition, authorisation could not be refused to a branch of a credit institution on the sole ground that it is established in another Member State in a legal form which is not allowed for a credit institution in the host-Member State. Accordingly, discrimination in favour of nationals was forbidden, but the establishment and the provision of services remained nonetheless subject to the laws of the host-country Member State.[39]

C. Harmonisation in other Financial Sectors

Regarding the other financial sectors, Community legislation also aimed at reducing the scope for restrictive measures to market-entry through harmonisation of national laws, while allowing for the application of stricter local rules by Member States.

The development of a European securities market, where investors can issue and trade securities across the Community, started with the minimum harmonisation of the basic investor protection rules regarding the admission of securities for listing in stock exchanges and the information to be provided to investors. This was because the degree of divergence across national laws regarding the information to be provided to investors was one of the main legal barriers to the European securities market. Ensuring a minimum equal treatment of investors regarding financial information would facilitate both the issuance and the investment in securities across the Community: all investors should receive the same information at the same time regarding the same securities. The Admissions Directive of 1979 was the initial instrument of the first-generation of directives for a European securities market. It intended to limit the scope for discretion in the listing of securities in stock exchanges by harmonising the minimum conditions for such listings.[40]

The integration policies for the European market for insurance services in the period were similar to the other sectors. In the area of property insurance, the 1973 Directive abolishing restrictions on freedom of establishment in the business of direct insurance

[39] The harmonisation efforts initiated by the First Banking Directive were followed by the Consolidated Supervision Directive of 1983, Council Directive 83/350/EEC of 13 June 1983 on the supervision of credit institutions on a consolidated basis, [1983] OJ L193/18–20; and the Consolidated Accounts Directive of 1986, which harmonised the accounting rules for banks, Council Directive 86/635/EEC of 8 December 1986 on the annual accounts and consolidated accounts of banks and other financial institutions, [1986] OJ L372/1–17.

[40] The rationale for a European securities market was put forward by the Schmidt Report: European Commission, The Advantages and disadvantages of an integrated market compared with a fragmented market (on file) (1977). See Council Directive 79/279/EEC of 5 March 1979 coordinating the conditions for the admission of securities to official stock exchange listing, [1979] OJ L66/ 21–32. The Directive sets out the conditions for issues of securities, such as the minimum issue price, free transferability, and provision of information to investors in the markets where the securities were listed by issuers, and in the language of those markets. The Member States could impose stricter requirements. The other directives of this first generation included the 'Listing Particulars Directive' of 1980, which harmonised the main disclosure requirements of a prospectus for the listing of shares and bonds; and the Council Resolution of 1982 on the Directive on information to be published on a regular basis by companies whose shares have been admitted to official stock-exchange listing. On the role of law in the European securities market, see E Ferran, *Building a European Securities Market* (Cambridge, Cambridge University Press, 2000) 25–38.

other than life assurance, provided to insurers in one Member State the right to establish themselves, also through agencies or branches, in another Member State under the same conditions and the same rights as residents of this Member State. The parallel First Non-Life Insurance Directive harmonised basic aspects of insurance regulation, including the definition and legal form of insurance companies, restrictions on their activities, supervision, co-operation between supervisory authorities, technical reserves, and solvency margins. The First Life Insurance Directive of 1979 extended this approach to direct life insurance.[41]

V. The Introduction of the Principle of Home-Country Control

A. The DNA of International Banking Regulation: The 1975 Basel Concordat

The Basel Committee on Banking Supervision (BCBS) was the first standard-setting body for international finance. It was established at the end of 1974, under the aegis of the Bank for International Settlements (BIS), comprising the central banks of the G-10 countries. It emerged in the context of the impact of the failure of the Herstatt-Bank, which was the first materialisation of systemic risk in international finance.[42]

The initial step taken by the BCBS to improve the regulation and supervision of international banking activities was the adoption of the so-called 'Basel Concordat' of 1975. The Concordat was the first international standard, setting out how the responsibilities for the supervision of cross-border banking should be shared between the authorities of

[41] Council Directive 73/240/EEC of 24 July 1973 abolishing restrictions on freedom of establishment in the business of direct insurance other than life assurance, [1973] OJ L228/20–22. First Council Directive 73/239/EEC of 24 July 1973 on the coordination of laws, regulations and administrative provisions relating to the taking-up and pursuit of the business of direct insurance other than life assurance, [1973] OJ L228/3–19. First Council Directive 79/267/EEC of 5 March 1979 on the coordination of laws, regulations and administrative provisions relating to the taking up and pursuit of the business of direct life assurance, [1979] OJ L063/1–18.

[42] The BCBS first took the denomination of the 'Committee on Banking Regulations and Supervisory Practices.' The objectives were to establish communication channels between banking authorities and to co-ordinate joint policy on the supervision of international banking: see BCBS, 'History of the Basel Committee and its membership,' in *Compendium of Documents produced by the BCBS* (Bank for International Settlements, 2000), as well as C Goodhart, *The Basel Committee on Banking Supervision: A History of the Early Years, 1974–1997* (Cambridge, Cambridge University Press, 2011) 10–51. The Herstatt-Bank crisis happened in June 1974, when international payments were disrupted due to the failure of this bank based in Köln. The difference in the time zone between Köln and New York led to a mismatch of payments in Deutschmarks and US dollars. This was a materialisation of settlement risk, in which one party in a foreign exchange transaction pays out the currency it sold but does not receive the currency it bought. This type of risk became known as Herstatt risk and was only eliminated in 2001 with a creation of a global settlement system, the Continuous Linked Settlement (CLS) system. For a detailed historical account, see E Mourlon-Druol, 'Trust is good, control is better: the 1974 Herstatt-Bank crisis and its implications for international regulatory reform' (2015) 57 *Business History* 311.

the home- and host-countries. It provided the basis for the development of international financial regulatory standards in the course of the next three decades.[43]

The Concordat introduced several sets of principles. The first regarded the objectives of international regulatory cooperation. The basic aim of international cooperation between banking regulators was to ensure that the foreign banking establishments of a bank are adequately supervised, as judged by the standards of both home-country and host-country authorities. This implied that home- and host-country authorities should cooperate and share information with regard to the activities of the bank or banking group as a whole. According to the Concordat, national legislation may need to be amended in order to facilitate this cooperation, such as removing obstacles to cross-border sharing of information stemming from banking secrecy laws, or allowing regulators from the home-country to perform inspections of foreign establishments in host-countries.[44]

A second set of principles introduced by the Concordat regarded the distribution of responsibilities between home-country and host-country regulators. The Concordat explicitly established the 'principle of home-country control'. According to this principle, a national authority is not only responsible for the regulation and supervision of a bank licensed and operating in its respective country, but also for its foreign branches with regard to the control of the overall solvency of a bank. Foreign subsidiaries, as independent legal institutions, remained subject to the home-country control of the country where they are licensed.

There were two legal implications from the introduction of the principle of home-country control. First, the regulators accepting this principle were under the obligation to supervise foreign banking subsidiaries in their territory, and also to supervise them adequately. Second, given the extension of the home-country control to foreign banking branches, the host-country authorities could not impose additional regulatory requirements on foreign branches besides those set by the home-country. These implications, in turn, involved the implicit acknowledgement of an additional principle: the 'principle of mutual recognition' between the home-country and host-country's jurisdictions.

The Basel Concordat pioneered these building principles of legal integration of international banking as a statement of best regulatory practices, which it hoped to spread beyond the G-10 countries. Although the objective was to address the challenges from the increasing internationalisation of banking at the time of the collapse of Bretton Woods, the principles of the Concordat also promoted the expansion of cross-border

[43] BCBS, Committee on Banking Regulations and Supervisory Practices, Report to the Governors on Supervision of Banks' Foreign Establishments, dated 26 September 1975, at www.bis.org/publ/bcbs00a.pdf. For an overview of the Basel Concordat, see EB Kapstein, *Governing the Global Economy: International Finance and the State* (Cambridge MA, Harvard University Press, 1996) 103–128; and C Goodhart, *The Basel Committee on Banking Supervision*, (n 42) 96–126.

[44] In accordance with the Concordat, the concept of 'foreign establishments of a bank' includes: (i) branches, which operate in a foreign country with no independent legal personality and are therefore part of the parent bank; and (ii) subsidiaries, which are legally independent banks licensed and incorporated in the country of operation and controlled by a foreign bank. The country of the parent bank is normally called the home-country, while the country where foreign branches and subsidiaries are established is called the host-country.

banking activities. The principle that foreign banks had to be subject to adequate regulation in host-countries reduced the restrictions at the home-country level to the setting-up of foreign establishments, which before could be seen as a source of risks to the parent bank. This also provided part of the basis for the progressive liberalisation of capital controls. The entry-costs into foreign markets were reduced. Banks were able to expand cross-border through the establishment of branches on the basis of the responsibility of the same authorities from the jurisdiction where they are based, and without being subject to additional regulatory burden by host-country authorities. The development of a regulatory framework for international banking would then provide a level-playing field between financial institutions, which fostered competition and increased demand for banking services.[45]

The principle of home-country control introduced by the Concordat did not, however, guarantee the effective supervision of foreign establishments. On the contrary, this principle fostered regulatory competition among countries for international banking business, which leads to a race to the bottom in regulatory standards. The expansion of international banking required cross-border cooperation between regulators, in order to ensure that foreign banks were supervised adequately in accordance with minimum standards. The Concordat was thus subject to subsequent revisions pursuing these twin objectives: first, no foreign banking establishment should escape supervision; and, second, such supervision should be adequate on the basis of minimum standards.[46]

Therefore, the principle of home-country control introduced by the Concordat was not just a 'conflict-of-laws' rule between jurisdictions. It set in motion a process of regulatory integration of global finance. As it developed over the following decades, the principle of home-country control promoted the expansion of international banking, with the following dynamics. First, the presence of international banks in host-countries increased as a result of home-country control. Such presence constrained the jurisdiction of host-countries in favour of the increasing extra-territoriality of the home-country's regulations. Second, over time, it led to increased banking risks in host-countries and competitive inequality among international banks, since their competitiveness depended on the regulations of the home-country. Third, this created the demand for international standards among jurisdictions, so as to reduce the extra-territorial impact of the home-country in the host-country, avoid a regulatory 'race to the bottom', and create a level playing field for international banking. Fourth, in turn, the development of international standards reinforced the principle of home-country control, since differences in national regulations became less and less of an obstacle to market integration. As international banking expanded, it required more and more increasingly detailed international regulatory standards, and so on, in a continuous feedback loop. These dynamics represent the DNA of international banking regulation. Similar processes were later at play in the integration of the European financial market.

[45] See EB Kapstein, *Governing the Global Economy*, (n 43) 103–128.
[46] See C Goodhart, *The Basel Committee on Banking Supervision*, (n 42) 96–126.

Figure 1 The Conceptual Engine of Integration through Home-Country Control

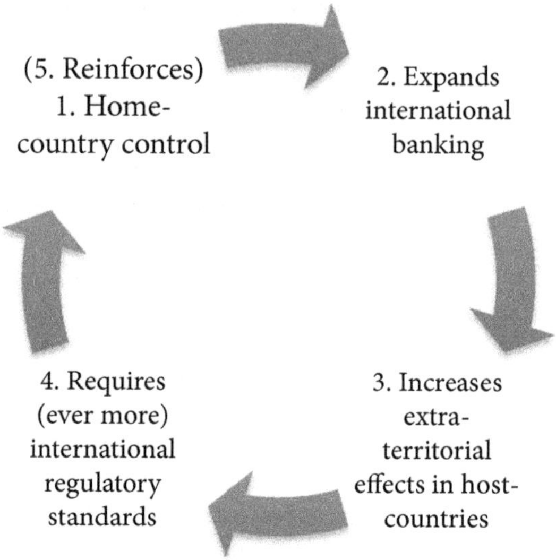

B. The Emergence of Home-Country Control in the First Banking Directive

The First Banking Directive of 1977 stated in the recitals that it was at the initial stage of the process to create a European banking market through the elimination of the most obstructive differences between the laws of Member States regarding credit institutions. The ultimate objective, in line with the Basel Concordat, should be:

> to provide for the overall supervision of a credit institution operating in several Member States by the competent authorities in the Member State where it has its head office, in consultation, as appropriate, with the competent authorities of the other Member States concerned.[47]

Accordingly, the Directive already aimed at the application of the 'principle of home-country control' of the Basel Concordat as a driver of financial market integration. This, in turn, would require a high-level of harmonisation of national laws. Beyond this intention, the First Banking Directive did not implement the home-country control principle. This was due to the differences across national laws, as well as the political difficulties in achieving unanimity among Member States for further harmonisation in a strategic area such as finance.[48]

The approach of the Directive was, in this context, to merely facilitate the establishment of branches as the main instrument to be used by credit institutions for the cross-border provision of financial services. First, the Directive harmonised the main

[47] See Recital 3 of the First Banking Directive.

[48] See also EL Camilli, 'Basel-Brussels One Way? The EU in the Legalization Process of Basel Soft Law' in E Chiti and BG Mattarella (eds) *Global Administrative Law and EU Administrative Law* (Berlin, Springer, 2011) 323, at 344–345.

elements of national banking laws, which could constitute a barrier to entry by credit institutions established in another Member State. Second, it then allowed the application of national law to the authorisation of branches from institutions established in another Member State. Third, it forbade the refusal of authorisation solely on the basis that the credit institution is established in the home-country Member State in a legal form not allowed in the host-country. The Directive thus supported the establishment of branches through the harmonisation of national laws and also by reducing the 'particularly wide discretionary powers' of banking regulators in the authorisation of foreign branches, which could provide the basis for protectionist measures.[49]

This scheme for the authorisation of foreign branches implied that they would remain subject to the law and regulation of the host-country. A credit institution providing cross-border financial services in other Member States would therefore be obliged to comply with both the law and regulation of its home-country, as well as the local rules of the host-countries where it established branches.

This restrictive approach was sanctioned by the Court to the extent justified by the special nature of the banking sector, relating in particular to the regulatory needs of consumer protection. In *Parodi v Banque de Bary*, where the loan at issue had been granted in 1984, the Court concluded that:

> [i]t must therefore be accepted that, [before the entry into force of the Second Banking Directive], there were within the banking sector imperative reasons relating to the public interest capable of justifying the imposition by the Member State of destination of conditions regarding access to the activity of credit institutions and their supervision which could go beyond the minimum conditions required by the First Banking Directive.[50]

Therefore, the realisation of the freedom to provide financial services on the basis of the principle of home-country control could be restricted on the basis of the regulatory interests of Member States. This was a condition which endured throughout the process of leading a single financial market, namely under the concept of 'public good'.[51]

C. Cooperation between Home- and Host-Country Authorities

The First Banking Directive also introduced a legal framework for co-operation between home-country and host-country authorities. The purpose was to support the progressive expansion of the scope of the home-country control principle, in line with the diagnosis by the Segré Report that supervisory controls also play a role in hindering integration. The Directive required the national authorities to collaborate closely in the supervision of credit institutions operating in other Member States than the home-country, eg through branches. This collaboration should involve the exchange of information

[49] See E Lomnicka, 'Home Country Control Principle in the Financial Services Directive and the Case Law' (2000) 11 *European Business Law Review* 324.

[50] *Parodi v Banque de Bary*, para 26. On the implications of this case for the European law of financial services, see JA Usher, *The Law of Money and Financial Services in the EC*, (n 15) 90–ff.

[51] On the application and evolution of the home-country control principle, see E Lomnicka, 'The Home Country Control Principle in the Financial Services Directives and the Case Law' in M Andenas and W Henning-Roth (eds) *Services and Free Movement in EU Law* (Oxford, Oxford University Press, 2002) 295.

across jurisdictions, which would facilitate the supervision by the national authorities. Since most of the regulatory powers could only be exercised with regard to the parent bank, this would support the exercise of supervisory functions by the home-country authorities with regard to their credit institutions' foreign establishments.[52]

After the First Banking Directive, the principle of home-country control in financial services also emerged in the context of the Consolidated Supervision Directive of 1983. This Directive introduced in Community legislation the framework defined in the 1983 revision of the Basel Concordat regarding the supervision of banking groups – comprising a parent bank and foreign branches and subsidiaries controlled by holdings of more than 50 per cent. In particular, the Basel Concordat attributed to the banking regulator of the country where the parent bank was established, the responsibility to oversee the consolidated balance sheet of the banking group as a whole. This was the result of the regulatory lessons learnt from the collapse of Banco Ambrosiano in 1982, which challenged the basic principle of the Basel Concordat that no internationally active bank should escape supervision. The Consolidated Supervision Directive aimed at reinforcing the framework for the operation of banking groups by creating an additional layer of supervision, rather than realising the freedom to provide services through the elimination of barriers to entry. Therefore, it had limited impact in terms of facilitating the cross-border provision of banking services.[53]

VI. The Introduction of Committees of National Authorities

A. The First European Committees

The other building-block of the construction of the single financial market in this period was the introduction of European committees between national regulators as an instrument for pursuing Community objectives.[54]

The first committee created in this period was the so-called 'Groupe de Contact', established in 1972 by national banking supervisory authorities of the Member States.

[52] Art 7(1) of the First Banking Directive. The First Non-Life Insurance Directive and the First Life Insurance Directive contained similar provisions.

[53] Council Directive 83/350/EEC of 13 June 1983 on the supervision of credit institutions on a consolidated basis, [1983] OJ L193/18–20. The collapse of Banco Ambrosiano in 1982 revealed a failure of international supervision. The Italian authorities, together with a consortium of Italian banks, bailed out the creditors of the parent bank. The creditors of the Luxembourg subsidiary were, however, not safeguarded, since this was a holding company not subject to banking supervision. The Luxembourg corporate secrecy laws also protected it from scrutiny by the Italian authorities. The BCBS responded by revising the Concordat in 1983 with the BCBS, Principles for the Supervision of Banks' Foreign Establishments (1983), at www.bis.org/publ/bcbsc312.pdf. The principles introduced the consolidated supervision of international banking groups, which strengthened the home country authority with the oversight of the entire consolidated balance sheet of a parent bank including foreign branches and subsidiaries. For an overview of the implications of this case, see RJ Herring and RE Litan, *Financial Regulation in the Global Economy* (Washington DC, The Brookings Institution, 1995) 102–112.

[54] The first European committee of national authorities in the field of finance was the Conference of European Insurance Supervisors, established in Paris in 1958.

It comprised middle-management representatives of these authorities. Its objective was to promote cooperation and information sharing between supervisors at the practical level. This included methodologies for banking supervision, procedures for cross-border cooperation among the national authorities, and the financial condition of credit institutions operating in more than one Member State, as required by the First Banking Directive, which acknowledged the role of the Groupe de Contact in its recitals.[55]

The First Banking Directive also established an 'Advisory Committee of the Competent Authorities of the Member States,' comprising representatives from both national supervisors and finance ministries. This stemmed from an initial group created by the Commission in 1969 on the 'coordination of banking legislation'. The tasks of the Banking Advisory Committee (BAC), as it was later denominated, included assisting the Commission in the implementation of the banking directives, making suggestions on areas for co-ordination among regulatory authorities, and deciding on the technical content of banking regulations, such as the solvency ratios of credit institutions. It was also tasked to assist the Commission in the preparation of legislative proposals concerning further coordination in the sphere of credit institutions, thus introducing comitology procedures in the field of financial services.[56]

B. The Objectives of the Committees

The First Banking Directive provided, therefore, that the development of a European banking market would rely, together with the full harmonisation of national laws, on the institutional cooperation between national authorities through European committees. This cooperation would pursue at least three objectives.[57]

The first was to support the harmonisation process of national laws. The committees would agree on common approaches to the implementation of Community law into national laws and regulatory practices, thus increasing its effectiveness. The committees would also promote consensus among national authorities regarding the regulatory areas, which could be further harmonised through Community law, thus providing impetus to the legislative initiatives of the Commission. This was the main aim of the BAC.

The second objective was to help lift regulatory barriers to cross-border banking services. Given the highly regulated nature of banking markets, the reduction of such barriers could not operate on the basis of Community legislation alone. The enforcement practices of national authorities were significant barriers, which could only be eased by the authorities themselves through increased convergence of such practices.

[55] The Groupe de Contact lasted until the end of 2010, when the European Banking Authority was established. On the origins of the Groupe de Contact, the initial reluctance to include the European Commission, and its influence on the procedures of the BCBS, see C Goodhart, *The Basel Committee on Banking Supervision*, (n 42) 12–25.

[56] Art 11, First Banking Directive. For an analysis of the relevance of BAC in improving the coordination between national authorities and support harmonisation, see E Mourlon-Druol, 'Banking union in historical perspective' (n 23). Comitology procedures, as a mechanism for monitoring the Commission's delegated powers, were first introduced in the Common Agricultural Policy in 1961, but only formally recognised by the Single European Act. For a history of comitology and its rationale, see CF Bergström, *Comitology, Delegation of Powers in the EU* (Oxford, Oxford University Press, 2005), 43–53.

[57] See Recitals 12 to 15 of the First Banking Directive.

This also included addressing together those regulatory challenges, which required coordination among authorities, such as those relating to the increase in cross-border banking services, or to the supervision of banking institutions providing these services. This was one of the main areas of the work of the Groupe de Contact, which was the European equivalent of the BCBS at the operational level.[58]

Third, the committees would also provide an instrument to start developing among national authorities a European regulatory culture for the single financial market. As stated by the Vice-President of the European Commission, Henri Simonet, in 1974, the aim was to 'harmonise mentalities' of national authorities as a pre-requisite to harmonisation.[59]

VII. The Limited Progress in Financial Integration

This period under analysis concluded with a deadlock in the process of financial integration, as stated by the Commission in its 1983 White Paper on Financial Integration. In contrast to the other freedoms, no progress was made in realising the provisions of the Treaty regarding the freedom of capital movements, which were not directly applicable. The White Paper concluded that 'financial markets are probably even less integrated now [1983] than in the 1960s, since capital movements within the Community are less free and the differences between the Member are more marked', as Member States imposed capital controls under the safeguard clauses of Articles 73 and 108 of the EEC Treaty. These restrictions on capital movements prevented market integration on the basis of the freedoms of establishment and to provide cross-border financial services.[60]

Therefore, between the years of 1973 and 1984, the progress in financial integration was very limited, if any. The European banking markets remained fragmented. The establishment of branches had to be authorised by the host-country authorities and was subject to the laws and regulations of the host-country. Branches often had to comply with the same initial capital requirements as that of new banks. This severely restricted the opportunities for cross-border banking services on the basis of the business infrastructure established in the home-country. The securities markets were likewise lacking in integration, due to the substantial differences among national laws on market disclosure and investor protection. This implied that the issuance and trading of securities had to comply with the local rules of each Member State where services were provided. Insurance was the sector where even less progress was made. The differences across national laws were greater, given the different arrangements for insurance business activities, insurance supervision, and protection of policy holders.[61]

[58] See C Goodhart, *The Basel Committee on Banking Supervision*, (n 42) 12–25.

[59] Quoted from E Mourlon-Druol, 'Banking union in historical perspective,' (n 23) 922.

[60] European Commission, Financial Integration, Communication from the Commission to the Council, COM (1983) 207 final. See also E Mourlon-Druol, 'Banking union in historical perspective' (n 23).

[61] On the legal developments in this period, see E Ferran, *Building a European Securities Market*, (n 40) 8–57. On the evolution of the European market for insurance services, see M Everson *Laws in Conflict – A Rationally Integrated European Insurance Market?* Doctoral Thesis (Florence, European University Institute, 1993).

The White Paper of 1983 concluded that the partition of financial markets in the Community was hampering the reinforcement of the common market as a whole, due to the increased financial costs of doing business, and preventing the efficient investment of savings in the European economy. For the process towards a European financial market to re-start, it would be necessary to remove the restrictions to capital movements and to establish interconnections between capital markets, the provision of financial services, and the gradual establishment of financial unity in Europe vis-à-vis third-countries. This would require many measures: lifting gradually capital controls; coordinating the national regulatory policies in order to achieve common banking, insurance and securities markets; achieving more stable exchange rates and closer convergence in economic and monetary policies; and recognising the ECU as a convertible currency with the same status as all major currencies, while also giving privileged treatment under exchange control rules to transactions in ECU.[62]

VIII. Conclusion: The Beginnings of a 'Banking Union'

The main takeaway from this chapter is that the design of a legal and institutional order for a European financial market started early in the preparatory work of the Treaty of Rome. This was despite the Treaty not having any reference or specific provision for its development. The approach of 'integration through harmonisation' – whereby integration would be achieved through the full harmonisation of national laws – was spelled out originally in the Spaak Report for the common market. It arguably reflected the influence of 'ordoliberal' thinking, according to which European harmonisation of rules would realise the economic freedoms and pre-empt Member States from interfering with market functioning through protectionist measures. The 'integration through harmonisation' strategy would thus aim at detaching a European financial market from the reach of the political interests of Member States, as expressed in their respective national laws.

The strategy for legal integration through harmonisation was later specified by the Segré Report for the European financial market, which argued for the harmonisation of both national laws and enforcement practices by national authorities. The European Commission then attempted in the 1970s to convert it into legislative initiatives, with limited success. This approach already aimed, though, at a legal structure akin to part of the future Banking Union some 50 years later: a 'single rulebook' would give rise to a European financial market.

Furthermore, although there was no intention expressed anywhere to create a European financial authority, there were very early steps towards providing an institutional framework for the integrating banking markets. The creation of committees of national financial authorities was pioneered in Europe and influenced the creation of international standard-setting committees such as the BCBS. The Groupe de Contact was created by the national authorities themselves, while the BAC was created

[62] European Commission, Financial Integration, (n 60) 21–ff.

by European legislation. They were the institutional seed for more elaborate future committees and authorities.

Accordingly, the approach to 'integration through harmonisation' introduced the following legal and institutional innovations.

First, the Community initiated the harmonisation of national laws relating to banking, securities and insurance markets. The implementation of the freedom of establishment in these sectors through the principle of non-discrimination provided the basis for the Community's competences to create a European financial market. This involved the harmonisation of basic legal definitions, the main elements of the licensing process of financial institutions, methods for supervision, and relations with third-countries. It was the foundation for the extensive harmonisation decades later of national laws.

Second, the principle of the home-country control of financial institutions providing cross-border services directly or through branches started to emerge in this period. It reflected the influence of the Basel Concordat of 1975, which was one of first regulatory steps towards the globalisation of finance. The principle would later be at the heart of European financial services law with the concept of the single passport and the extensive harmonisation of the Financial Services Action Plan of 1999.

Third, the Community also introduced, as mentioned, committees of national authorities as instrumental for the harmonisation process, particularly for banking services. This included comitology procedures, where the BAC supported the implementation of Community law and the preparation of Commission legislative proposals for the banking sector. It also included the convergence of enforcement practices in the supervision of financial services. Therefore, Community law initiated in this period the development of a layer of administrative cooperation among national authorities, which reached its most elaborate stage with the Lamfalussy framework in 2001 and provided the basis for European Supervisory Authorities in 2013.[63]

The introduction of European competences for the development of a financial market through these innovations was then constrained by the limits imposed by national sovereignty. The political and economic conditions were more conducive to protectionism of the financial industry, including through capital controls, than to market liberalisation. In this context, an agreement among Member States for a sufficient harmonisation of national laws for a realising a European financial market was hardly achievable. It required harmonising national laws in a core area of national sovereignty. Moreover, in the spirit of the Luxembourg compromise of 1966 to constrain the supranational evolution of the Community, Member States maintained unanimity voting on financial legislation. The principle of home-country control was also made ineffective when host-country Member States safeguarded the application of national law as a matter of public interest. Likewise, the committees of national authorities would tend to be more interested at protecting national interests than expanding European competences. As a result, such first conflict between the expansion of European competences and the safeguarding of national sovereignty enabled little or no progress in the integration of a European financial market.[64]

[63] See, below, ch 3.

[64] On the origins and impact of the Luxembourg compromise, see L Van Middelaar, 'Spanning the River: The Constitutional Crisis of 1965–1966 as the Genesis of Europe's Political Order' (2008) 4 *European Constitutional Law Review* 98.

This chapter thus shows that the initial period of development of a European financial market was largely caused by idealistic policy and legislative initiatives, which aimed at the full harmonisation of national laws as the means of integration. The contextual factors leading to these initiatives were many. They included the common market project, as reflected in the Spaak Report, the related attempt to realise the freedom of capital, the context of the internationalisation of finance, the ambition to achieve monetary integration, the expansion of Community competences beyond the Treaty, or the start of international standard-setting in the area of banking regulation. By contrast, the interests of Member States played a role mainly in resisting and removing the effect of such integrationist initiatives.

This phase of integration provided, however, the above legal and institutional seeds for the future integration of the European financial market. It is a first piece of evidence that the Banking Union is ultimately the product of a legal and institutional construction dating back to the preparatory work of the Treaty of Rome.

Table 1 Legal Change in 'Integration through Harmonisation' (1973–1984)

Legal and institutional innovations to expand European competences		**Market integration policies**	**Constraints to integration by national sovereignty**
1	**Full harmonisation of national laws**	• Support the application of the principles of non-discrimination and home-country control • Development of a European financial market with a uniform law	• Unanimity voting of Member States for Community measures • Harmonising national laws in a core area of national sovereignty
2	**Initial expression of the principle of home-country control**	• Regulation and supervision of a credit institution by the home-country authority throughout the common market	• Application of the national laws of host-countries • Divergence of national laws
3	**European committees of national authorities**	• Implementation of Community law • Support to the preparation of Commission proposals • Cooperation in regulatory and supervisory practices	• Wide divergence of national laws and implementation practices

2

Integration through Competition (1985–1997)

The conclusion that, in a federation, certain economic powers, which are now generally wielded by the national states, could be exercised neither by the federation nor by the individual states, implies that there would have to be less government all round if federation is to be practicable. […] Indeed, this readiness to have no legislation at all on some subjects rather than state legislation will be the acid test of whether we are intellectually mature for the achievement of suprastate organization.

Friedrich A. Hayek, 1939[1]

I. Introduction

The period between 1985 and 1997 corresponds largely to the pursuance of the single market programme, which was triggered by the 1985 White Paper of the Commission and consolidated by the reforms of the Single European Act (SEA).[2]

By the mid-1980s the Member States were only starting to recover from the recessions of the previous decade. There were very high levels of unemployment, accelerating inflation and rising fiscal imbalances. This was largely due to government spending on the welfare state, such as unemployment benefits, as well as loss of international competitiveness to the US and Japan. The heavy state intervention in the economy also gave rise to rigidities, which prevented economic growth. At the same time, Member States were increasingly interdependent as a result of trade linkages, capital flows, and obligations stemming from the European Monetary System (EMS). The remaining barriers to trade and services did not allow the unleashing of the economic potential of market integration in Europe.[3]

This justified the political willingness of Member States to undertake economic reform, namely in the direction of market liberalisation and deregulation. Politically

[1] FA Hayek, 'The Economic Conditions of Interstate Federalism' in FA Hayek, *Individualism and Economic Order* (Chicago, Chicago University Press, 1948) 255, 266.

[2] For a historical overview of the steps towards European integration in this period, see NP Ludlow, 'European Integration in the 1980s: on the Way to Maastricht?' (2013) 19 *Journal of European Integration History* 11.

[3] See B Eichengreen, *The European Economy since 1945* (Princeton, Princeton University Press, 2007) 290–293; and H James, *Making the European Monetary Union* (Cambridge MA, The Belknap Press of Harvard University Press, 2012) 216–226.

and ideologically, regulation became a synonym of protectionism and inefficiency that stymied the economic potential of free market forces. There was a convergence of economic preferences among Member States – Benelux, France, Germany and the UK – to abolish barriers to trade and services. The Community was seen as the platform for reform by deregulating protected sectors of the economy. In some Member States, notably France, the objective was to circumvent domestic resistance to liberalisation. In other Member States, notably the UK, the aim was to expand the scope of domestic reform and benefit from a larger market.[4]

The liberalisation of financial services by the UK since 1979 provided major impetus to a European financial market. The main reform was that of the London Stock Exchange enacted by the Thatcher Government on a single day on 27 October 1986, which became known as the 'Big Bang'. This was a major deregulation move, whereby the stock exchange abolished its restrictive practices, which had previously benefited and protected its membership. It influenced liberalisation measures in other Member States, such as France and Germany, and it justified the support of the UK Government to an integrated European financial market, with the City of London at its core.[5]

This context of market liberalisation and deregulation was conducive to a single market through 'negative integration'. National constraints to free competition had to be removed. In turn, the law and institutions of the Community had to be strengthened to remove them. This provided the political will to Member States to adopt the reforms of the SEA. Market integration would then advance out of the competitive dynamics of free and efficient markets within a reinforced institutional framework. The premise was that this would lead to substantial economic benefits, as quantified by the Cecchini Report in 1988.[6]

The legal approach to integration turned thus from the full harmonisation of national laws of the previous period to the new period of 'integration through competition': competition both among financial institutions for market share and among Member States for attracting financial services to their jurisdiction. The main legal innovation was the concept of a 'single passport': financial institutions would provide services throughout the single financial market with a single licence issued by the

[4] For an account of the national economic preferences underpinning the SEA, see A Moravcsik, *The Choice for Europe: Social Purpose and State Power from Messina to Maastricht* (Ithaca NY, Cornell University Press, 1998) 314–ff. See similar interpretations by L Van Middelaar, *The Passage to Europe* (New Haven, Yale University Press, 2013) Chapter 3; and B Eichengreen, *The European Economy since 1945*, (n 3) 339–340. See also the account of Jacques Delors on the interests of each Member States, J Delors, *Mémoires* (Paris, Plon, 2004) 202–228.

[5] The main changes operated by the 'Big Bang' were that member firms could be owned by an outside company, could operate as both brokers and dealers with no minimum commissions, and trading became electronic. See GA Walker, *International Banking Regulation, Law, Policy and Practice* (The Hague, Kluwer Law International, 2001) 169–170; and C Bellringer and R Michie, 'Big Bang in the City of London: An intentional revolution or an accident?' (2014) 21 *Financial History Review* 111. For France, see PG Cerny, 'The 'little big bang' in Paris: financial market deregulation in a dirigiste system' (1989) 17 *European Journal of Political Research* 169.

[6] European Commission, The Cecchini Report: The Economics of 1992: An assessment of the potential economic effects of completing the internal market of the European Community (1988) 35 *European Economy*. On the impact and controversies of this report, see G Grin, *The Battle of the Single European Market: Achievements and Economic Thought 1985-2000* (London, Routledge, 2003) 235–303.

home-country, subject to mutual recognition and minimum harmonisation of national laws. This avoided the need to harmonise national laws, which had been the main obstacle to market integration. Instead, a 'competition among rules' between Member States would spontaneously lead to the optimal framework of rules for integrating markets. This Hayekian evolutionary process would create a new equilibrium where the exercise of national sovereignty would deliver, rather than constrain, market integration.[7]

II. The Emerging Regulation of International Finance

A. The Internationalisation of Finance

The internationalisation of finance increased in the mid-1980s as the result of the liberalisation of capital controls. This led to an increasing volume of capital flows between industrial countries. Capital flows became less related to development and trade with developing economies and more directed at investment. At the same time, this was accompanied by the evolution of communication technology and the setting-up of market infrastructures for international financial transactions. International finance was concentrated in the financial centres of New York, London, Tokyo and Frankfurt.[8]

The internationalisation of banking, together with the deregulation and market liberalisation in this period, gave rise to concerns about both the risks posed by international banks and fair competition among them. Deregulation meant that banks operated with lower capital levels, while the risk of their activities increased with their internationalisation, the increasing use of innovative financial instruments, and complex transactions. This reflected the experience with the debt crises of developing countries and the spread of insolvencies among savings and loans' institutions in the US in the 1980s. Furthermore, those banks subject to lower capital requirements had a competitive advantage over others, leading to an uneven level playing-field. Higher or lower capital requirements determine the volume and type of banking transactions and thus the risks incurred by banks. The principle of home-country control also supported a 'race to the bottom' among international financial centres to attract banking business on the basis of looser regulatory requirements. Finance could circumvent the stricter regulatory regimes of national jurisdictions by quickly de-localising to those jurisdictions with more favourable, and less costly, regimes. This later created the demand for international regulatory standards to constrain such 'races to the bottom'.[9]

[7] On the free-market liberalism of Hayek, see VJ Vanberg, 'The Freiburg School: Walter Eucken and Ordoliberalism' (2004) 04/11 *Freiburg Discussion Papers on Constitutional Economics*, and also *The Constitution of Markets: Essays in Political Economy* (London, Routledge, 2001) 17–36. The expression 'competition among rules' is drawn from T Padoa-Schioppa, *Efficiency, Stability and Equity, A Strategy for the Evolution of the Economic System of the European Community* (Oxford, Oxford University Press, 1987).

[8] See AM Kose, E Prasad, K Rogoff, and SJ Weil, 'Financial Globalization: A Reappraisal' (2009) 56-1 *IMF Staff Papers* 8–62. For an analysis of the international financial system in the 1970s and 1980s, see S Strange, *Casino Capitalism* (Manchester, Manchester University Press, 1986).

[9] See E Helleiner, *States and the Reemergence of Global Finance: From Bretton Woods to the 1990s* (Ithaca, NY, Cornell University Press, 1994) 146–168.

B. The First International Regulatory Standards: The Basel Accord of 1988

This was the context for the first international regulatory standard for the minimum harmonisation of banking regulations: the Basel Accord on the 'International Convergence of Capital Measurement and Capital Standards' adopted by the BCBS in 1988.[10]

The 1975 Basel Concordat had introduced the principle of home-country control as a jurisdictional rule, which promoted international banking by facilitating the provision of banking services. This, however, increased banking risks and competitive inequality as the home-country jurisdictions imposed different capital requirements for their respective banks. The 1988 Basel Accord then aimed at addressing coordination failures among national authorities in the regulation of international banking and at defining a level playing-field, so as to avoid competitive inequality among international banks. This was achieved through the setting of an 8 per cent ratio, on the basis of risk weighing of assets, as the minimum capital requirement for international banks to address credit risk, which is the proportion of capital needed to balance the risks incurred in financial transactions. In this sense, the harmonisation of international banking regulation was a consequence of the increasing application of the principle of home-country control.[11]

This process of international minimum harmonisation through regulatory standards, which was started by the BCBS, had direct implications for the European financial market. The implementation of the Basel Accord was made through Community law, thus leading also to minimum harmonisation within the internal market.[12]

C. The Expansion of International Standard-Setting Bodies

The period from the mid-1980s to the mid-1990s was also characterised by the exponential growth in the number of international standard-setting bodies for finance.

[10] On the process of achieving agreement for the Basel Accord, see EB Kapstein, 'Supervising international banks: origins and implications of Basel Accord' (1991) 185 *Essays in International Finance, Princeton University* 103–ff and WR White, 'International agreements in the area of banking and finance: accomplishments and outstanding issues' in G von Furstenberg (ed) *Regulation and supervision of financial institutions in NAFTA countries and beyond* (Dordrecht, Springer, 1997) 48.

[11] See the preparatory document for the 1988 Basel Capital Accord, BCBS, Consultative Document – Proposals for International Convergence of capital measurement and standards (1987) at bis.org/publ/bcbs03a.pdf, and the final Basel Accord at bis.org/publ/bcbs04a.pdf. The 8% capital ratio is denominated as the 'Cooke ratio' from the first Chairman of the BCBS, Peter Cooke from the Bank of England. The Cooke ratio calculated the amount of capital which a bank should have as a percentage of its total risk-weighted assets in order to cope with losses. The 8% ratio originated as the compromise in negotiations about the appropriate level-playing field among international banks. It was not based on technical findings about the right level of capital to preserve the soundness of a bank. The ratio achieved nonetheless a regulatory role, since the success of the 1988 Accord made it the benchmark for successive capital regulations. For an overview of the dynamics of banking regulation following the 1988 Basel Accord, see R Dale, *The Regulation of International Banking* (Englewood Cliffs NJ, Prentice Hall, 1986) 172–ff, as well as, RJ Herring and RE Litan, *Financial Regulation in the Global Economy* (Washington DC, The Brookings Institution, 1995) 107–ff.

[12] See also EL Camilli, 'Basel-Brussels One Way? The EU in the Legalization Process of Basel Soft Law' in E Chiti and BG Mattarella (eds) *Global Administrative Law and EU Administrative Law* (Berlin, Springer, 2011) 323 at 345–346.

The development of international regulatory standards was increasingly seen as the instrument to address the internationalisation of finance, also following the model of the BCBS.[13]

The international standard-setting bodies were networks of national authorities. They generated regulatory knowledge – as a sort of 'epistemic communities' – and issued regulatory standards as a result. The soft law nature of standards enabled their implementation without constraining explicitly national sovereignty in such a strategic sector as finance. In most cases, standards were then implemented into national laws through the intermediation of the local legislators. This was thus the answer to the so-called 'globalisation paradox': the need to address collective problems on a global scale, while not being feasible to transfer sovereignty to the supranational level.[14]

The international standard-setting bodies for finance emerged and developed in different ways, but progressively covered all the components of the financial system.[15]

First, there were standard-setters congregating the national authorities for each financial sector. After the BCBS, the International Organisation of Securities Commissions (IOSCO) was established in 1983. It was followed by the International Association of Insurance Supervisors (IAIS) in 1994. In 1996, the BCBS, the IOSCO, and the IAIS created the 'Joint Forum', which aimed at addressing financial conglomerates and the areas of finance which are common to the three sectors of banking, securities, and insurance.[16]

Second, the Committee on Payment and Settlement Systems (CPSS) was created in 1990 as a standard-setting body of the central banks of the G-10 countries for

[13] Standards may be defined as rules whose compliance is voluntary, and which aim at creating homogeneity among those adopting them. The International Organization for Standardization defines a standard as 'A document established by consensus and approved by a recognized body, that provides, for common and repeated use, rules, guidelines or characteristics for activities or their results, aimed at the achievement of the optimum degree of order in a given context' (SS-EN 45020 1999). Quoted from N Brunsson and B Jacobsson, *A World of Standards* (Oxford, Oxford University Press, 2000) 15. See KH Ladeur, *Das Umweltrecht der Wissensgesellschaft* (Berlin, Duncker & Humblot, 1995) 187–ff on the role of standards in facilitating the experimentation of the state's administration in order to address decision-making in conditions of complexity.

[14] On the 'globalisation paradox', see AM Slaughter, *A New World Order* (Princeton, Princeton University Press, 2004) 8. On the role of 'epistemic communities, see PM Haas, 'Epistemic Communities and International Policy Coordination' (1992) 46 *International Organization* 1.

[15] On the emergence of international regulatory standards, see A Hirsch, 'Worldwide Legal Harmonization of Banking Law and Securities Regulation' in R Buxbaum, G Hertig, I Hirsch and KJ Hopt (eds) *European Business Law: Legal and Economic Analyses on Integration and Harmonization* (New York, De Gruyter, 1991) 347, at 349–50; and K Alexander, R Dhumale, and J Eatwell, *Global Governance of Financial Systems: The International Regulation of Systemic Risk* (Oxford, Oxford University Press, 2005) 34–78.

[16] On the role of IOSCO, see GRD Underhill, 'Keeping Governments Out of Politics: Transnational Securities Markets, Regulatory Cooperation, and Political Legitimacy' (1995) 21 *Review of International Studies* 251, 252–ff. On the establishment of the IAIS, see D Masciandaro, 'International Association of Insurance Supervisors' in T Hale and D Held (eds) *Handbook of Transnational Governance: New Institutions and Innovations* (Cambridge, Polity Press, 2011) 71–79. On the transposition of the standards of 'The Joint Forum' in Europe, see M Gruson (2004) 'Supervision of financial conglomerates in the European Union' (2004) 19 *Journal of International Banking Law and Regulation* 363. The definition of financial conglomerates used by the Joint Forum is 'any group of companies under common control whose exclusive or predominant activities consist of providing significant services in at least two different financial sectors (banking, securities, insurance)'.

payment, settlement and clearing systems as well as cross-border and multicurrency settlement systems.[17]

Third, the Financial Action Task Force (FATF) was established in 1989 by a G-7 summit, under the auspices of the OECD, with the objective of combating money laundering, given the threat it poses to the integrity of the financial system.[18]

Lastly, there were also standard-setting bodies set-up by market participants. The most important were the International Accounting Standards Committee (IASC), established in 1973 to develop global accounting standards, the International Federation of Accountants (IFAC) established in 1977, and the International Swap Dealers Association (ISDA) established in 1985 to develop standardised contractual documentation, notably the 'ISDA Master Agreement'.[19]

Despite their differences in composition, working methods, and output, these standard-setting bodies had all three main functions. The first was to provide platforms for information-sharing among its members on regulatory and market developments. On the basis of this knowledge-creation capacity, the second function was to achieve regulation by gathering consensus on international standards, often reflecting the best practices among their members. Such standards would then provide the basis for minimum harmonisation and regulatory convergence among jurisdictions. The objectives were to address the mismatch between the territoriality of national jurisdictions and the internationalisation of finance, to mitigate the extra-territorial spillover of the home-country's regulations on host-countries, and also to liberalise financial markets by reducing barriers to entry. The third function of standard-setting bodies was to enforce their respective standards and to ensure compliance, initially among its members and then worldwide. There were several mechanisms for this purpose, ranging from regular compliance evaluations, peer reviews, technical assistance, or censorship of non-complying jurisdictions.[20]

The increasing number of international standard-setting bodies in this period thus gave rise to extensive information-, regulatory- and enforcement-networks for

[17] The origin of the CPSS is the ad hoc Committee on Interbank Netting Schemes, which led in 1990 to a set of minimum standards for the operation and oversight of bilateral and multilateral netting schemes, also known as 'Lamfalussy Report.' Since 2015, it became the Committee for Payments and Market Infrastructures (CPMI). See BIS Report of the Committee on Interbank Netting Schemes of the central banks of the Group of Ten countries (Lamfalussy Report) (1990) at www.bis.org/cpmi/publ/d04.htm.

[18] The main standard issued by the FATF are its 'Forty Recommendations' against money laundering, first adopted in 1990 and later revised in 2001, in order to also encompass terrorism financing. On the evolution of the FATF standards and its application in Europe, see V Mitsilegas and B Gilmore, 'The EU legislative framework against money laundering and terrorist finance: a critical analysis in the light of evolving global standards' (2007) 56 *International & Comparative Law Quarterly* 119.

[19] The International Accounting Standards Board (IASB) replaced the IASC in 2001. See K Camfferman and S Zeff, *Financial reporting and global capital markets: A history of the international accounting standards committee, 1973-2000* (Oxford, Oxford University Press, 2006). The ISDA subsequently changed its name switching from 'Swap Dealers' to 'Swaps and Derivatives.' The ISDA Master Agreement enables the close out and netting of all transactions under one swap agreement. On the role of swaps in financial innovation, see HTC Hu, 'Swaps, The Modern Process of Financial Innovation and the Vulnerability of a Regulatory Paradigm' (1989) 138 *University of Pennsylvania Law Review* 333, 366–ff.

[20] On the evolution of international regulatory standards from 'soft law' to binding regulation, see K Alexander, R Dhumale, and J Eatwell, *Global Governance of Financial Systems*, (n 15) 134–154.

international finance. The regulation of finance became gradually a sectoral body of rules of the global economy, which was largely autonomous from domestic jurisdictions. This provided later the basis for the regulatory governance of global finance, which gave rise to ever more detailed international standards and convergence among national jurisdictions. It played an important role in the deregulation leading up to the global financial crisis starting in 2007 and also in the reform that followed.[21]

Finally, the expansion of international standard-setting bodies had an influence on the legal and institutional approach to the European financial market, which came to rely more than before on committees and networks of national authorities as tools of market integration.

Table 2 International Standard-Setting Bodies by 1997

<table>
<tr><th>Banking</th><th>Securities</th><th>Insurance</th><th>Anti-money laundering</th><th>Accounting</th><th>Derivative Contracts</th></tr>
<tr><td>BCBS
(1973)</td><td>IOSCO
(1983)</td><td>IAIS
(1994)</td><td rowspan="2">FATF
(1989)</td><td>IASC
(1973)</td><td rowspan="2">ISDA
(1985)</td></tr>
<tr><td colspan="3">Joint Forum on Financial Conglomerates
(1996)</td><td>IFAC
(1977)</td></tr>
</table>

III. The Framework for Completing the Internal Market by 1992

A. The Legal Dynamics of *Dassonville* and *Cassis de Dijon*

The Court's jurisprudence on the freedom of movement of goods of *Dassonville* of 1974 and, in particular, *Cassis de Dijon* of 1979 was exported to the single market programme of the 1985 White Paper and formed the basis for the mutual recognition principle.[22]

In *Dassonville*, the Court considered that:

> [a]ll trading rules enacted by Member States which are capable of hindering, directly or indirectly, actually or potentially, intra-community trade are to be considered as measures having an equivalent effect to quantitative restrictions. (paragraph 5).

[21] The rise of international standard-setting in finance was part of the emerging government networks at the end of the 20th century. AM Slaughter argued that such networks contribute to world order by: (1) creating convergence and informed divergence; (2) improving compliance with international rules; and (3) increasing the scope, nature and quality of international cooperation. See AM Slaughter, *A New World Order*, (n 14) 52–55.

[22] Judgment of the Court of 11 July 1974, *Dassonville*, 8–74, EU:C:1974:82, para 5; and *Cassis de Dijon*, para 14. On the process of translation of this jurisprudence into the single market programme, see K Nicolaïdis, 'Kir Forever? The Journey of a Political Scientist in the Landscape of Mutual Recognition' in M Poiares Maduro and L Azoulai (eds) *The Past and Future of EU Law* (Oxford, Hart Publishing, 2010) 447–455, 451–453; and also K Nicolaïdis and SK Schmidt, 'Mutual Recognition 'On Trial': The Long Road to Services Liberalisation' (2007) 14 *Journal of European Public Policy* 717.

Regulatory measures by the state which may be deemed restrictive trade were therefore inadmissible, unless justified under Community law under Article 30 of the EEC Treaty. *Cassis de Dijon* went further and provided that:

> [o]bstacles to movement within the Community resulting from disparities between the national laws relating to the marketing of the products in question must be accepted in so far as those provisions may be recognised as being necessary in order to satisfy mandatory requirements relating in particular to the effectiveness of fiscal supervision, the protection of public health, the fairness of commercial transactions and the defence of the consumer.' (paragraph 8) and that 'There is therefore no valid reason why, provided that they have been lawfully produced and marketed in one of the Member States, alcoholic beverages should not be introduced into any other Member State. (paragraph 14).

On the one hand, *Cassis de Dijon* allowed Member States to justify restrictive measures on the basis of policies other than those listed in the Treaty. On the other hand, it introduced the principle that the importing Member States must recognise the technical standards under which products are produced and marketed in the Member State of origin, as long as the importing Member State cannot justify the application of its rules under the exceptions listed by the Court. This corresponded to the affirmation of the principle of mutual recognition in the field of the freedom of movement of goods. In the field of services, the mutual recognition principle was first applied in the *Säger* case.[23]

The implication of the Court's jurisprudence for the single market was that integration could be advanced by constraining the regulatory autonomy of Member States in protecting their national markets. Rather than requiring the harmonisation of national laws and regulations, the legal approach to market integration could be limited to setting out the minimum requirements at Community level for the operation of mutual recognition between Member States. Therefore, market integration could be pursued largely through liberalisation and deregulation. This concept of 'negative integration' – the removal of national obstacles rather than 'positive integration' through European regulation of trade – fitted the economic and political needs of both Member States and the Community to build the single market.[24]

B. The 1985 White Paper

The Commission's White Paper on 'Completing the Internal Market' marked the beginning of the new policy and legal approach for the integration of the single financial

[23] Judgment of the Court of 25 July 1991, *Säger*, C-76/90, EU:C:1991:331. See JHH Weiler, 'The Constitution of the Common Market Place: Text and Context in the Evolution of the Free Movement of Goods' in P Craig and G De Burca (eds) *The Evolution of EU Law*, (Oxford, Oxford University Press, 1999) 349, 364. Weiler describes the *Cassis de Dijon* doctrine as one of 'functional parallelism' rather than mutual recognition, since the Court in *Säger*, para 15, required the regulations of Member States to be functionally parallel in achieving the desired result, such as fairness of commercial transactions.

[24] As argued by A Menon and S Weatherill, 'Transnational Legitimacy in a Globalising World: How the European Union Rescues its States' (2008) 31 *West European Politics* 397. On the concept of negative and positive integration in the context of European market integration, see F Scharpf, *Governing in Europe: Effective and Democratic?* (Oxford, Oxford University Press, 2011).

market. It was prepared under the responsibility of the Commissioner for the Internal Market, Lord Cockfield. The White Paper set out the strategy for the removal of physical, technical and fiscal barriers, together with a timetable of specific measures for achieving the objective of completing the internal market by 1992.[25]

The financial integration of the Community was to be achieved through greater liberalisation of capital movements and by facilitating the cross-border provision of financial services. The pursuance of these two objectives were closely interlinked, as the harmonisation of national laws regarding financial services would only fulfil its aim of creating a single financial market if there were no restrictions to capital movements.[26]

Restrictions of capital movements would be progressively lifted by a stricter approach of the Commission to the authorisation of safeguard clauses, which at the time were only applied to measures taken by France, Italy and Ireland. The Commission would also propose to liberalise through directives the capital movements required to make effective the freedom to provide financial services in certain areas, such as units issued by investment funds.[27]

The cross-border provision of financial services would be facilitated essentially through the extension of the *Cassis de Dijon* doctrine from industrial and agricultural products under Article 30 of the EEC Treaty to the free circulation of 'financial products' throughout the Community. This would involve the application of three legal principles.

First, the principle of home-country control: the primary task of regulating a financial institution and its branches would be entrusted to the authorities of the Member State of origin. The financial institution would report to its home-country authorities regarding both domestic and cross-border provision of services directly or through branches. The authorities of the host-country would have a 'complementary role'. This principle had been introduced with regard to international finance by the Basel Concordat of 1975 and mentioned, but not implemented, by the First Banking Directive of 1977.

The second principle was the mutual recognition by Member States and their respective authorities. Financial institutions would be free to provide financial services directly or through branches in the jurisdiction of host Member States, subject to the laws, regulation and supervision of the home-country. For host-countries, this would imply recognising that the safeguard of the public interests underlying financial regulation in their jurisdictions – such as depositor and investor protection, and financial stability – would be adequately pursued by the home-country authorities.[28]

Third, home-country control and mutual recognition would be supported by the minimum harmonisation of national laws, which would set the standards regarding

[25] See J Delors, *Mémoires*, (n 4) 203–207, highlighting the role of Lord Cockfield in producing the White Paper and in addressing objections, including by Margaret Thatcher. European Commission, Completing the Internal Market, White Paper to the European Council of 28/29 June 1985 in Milan, COM (1985) 310 final. On the framework of the White Paper, see, at the time, J Pelkmans and P Robson, 'The aspirations of the White Paper' (1987) 25 *Journal of Common Market Studies* 181; and G Grin, *The Battle of the Single European Market*, (n 8) 111–165.

[26] See T Padoa-Schioppa, *L'Europa verso l'unione monetaria: Dallo Sme al trattato di Maastricht* (Turin, Einaudi, 1992) 156–160.

[27] See AFP Bakker, *The Liberalization of Capital Movements in Europe* (Dordrecht, Kluwer, 1996) 187–217.

[28] For an analysis of the approach of the White Paper to mutual recognition, see G Majone, 'Mutual Recognition in Federal Type Systems' (1993) 1993/01 *EUI SPS Working Papers*.

authorisation, supervision and winding-up of financial institutions. This principle of minimum harmonisation of national laws would replace the approach in the previous period based on full harmonisation as the condition for financial integration.

The development of the European financial market would, therefore, rely on the 'regulatory competition' between Member States which would unfold from the application of the principles of home-country control, mutual recognition, minimum harmonisation of national laws, and freedom to provide cross-border provision of financial services.[29]

The application of these principles would provide a 'single passport' to financial institutions for the provision of services throughout the Community, directly or through branches. A separate licence in the host-countries was not required. As financial institutions would be free to select the Member State of origin, Member States would adapt their laws and regulations to the needs of cross-border business in order to attract and retain it in their jurisdiction. At the same time, the coexistence of several regulatory regimes across the Community for the provision of financial services would set off a dynamic of legal integration, which would lead to the spontaneous harmonisation of national laws on the basis of the most efficient standards. The minimum harmonisation of national laws would prevent a 'race to the bottom' by Member States on regulatory standards, as well as the application by the host-country of the 'public good exception' under Article 56(1) of the EEC Treaty.[30]

The vision of the White Paper was thus that market integration would develop out of the dynamics of competitive market forces, whose interaction with national legal orders would lead to positive spillovers in terms of market regulation. To a large extent, it was faithful to the political context of the time in favour of deregulation and free competition. It is in this sense that it was a period of 'integration through competition'.[31]

C. The Single European Act

The implementation of the White Paper and of its timetable for completing the single market by 1992 – also with regard to financial services – was made possible by the revision of the EEC Treaty on 28 February 1986, which entered into force on 1 July 1987 as the SEA.[32]

[29] On regulatory competition in the field of finance, see also T Padoa-Schioppa, *Regulating Finance: Balancing Freedom and Risk* (Oxford, Oxford University Press, 2004), especially at 40–ff.

[30] See M Poiares Maduro, *We the Court: The European Court of Justice and the European Economic Constitution* (Oxford, Hart Publishing, 1998) 126–142, on the competitive model of the European Economic Constitution.

[31] This was also the vision endorsed by Margaret Thatcher at her Bruges speech of 1988, calling for free movement of capital and the establishment of 'a genuinely free market in financial services in banking, insurance, investment', at www.margaretthatcher.org/document/107332. For some, the 1985 White Paper was thus fulfilling a 'Thatcherite agenda,' see A Moravcsik, *The Choice for Europe: Social Purpose and State Power from Messina to Maastricht*, (n 4) 324–5, and R Dehousse 'Integration v. regulation? On the dynamics of regulation in the European Community' (1992) 30 *Journal of Common Market Studies* 383. See J Delors, *Mémoires*, (n 4) 202–228, on the political achievements of the SEA.

[32] The SEA also added the fulfilment of economic and monetary union to the areas of Community competence. Decisions in this area remained subject to unanimity and ratification by Member States (Art 20, SEA).

The SEA formalised the introduction of the concept of 'internal market' seemingly replacing that of the 'common market'. The distinction between them was, however, not clarified in the Treaty. For commentators like Pierre Pescatore, the definition of the 'internal market' focused on the elimination of barriers to trade. This was reductive of the 'common market', which should be interpreted as a 'full economic union', as intended in the Treaty of Rome. This is why it could be seen that an 'internal market' reflected the UK's push for liberalisation and deregulation, as compared to a 'common market' encompassing common economic policies. Ultimately, there were no discernible legal consequences in this distinction. References to a 'common market' remained in the Treaty, until the Lisbon Treaty changed them all to 'internal market'.[33]

The main innovation of the SEA was to enable a much more flexible and wider process for achieving the harmonisation of national laws. It introduced a new provision in the Treaty – Article 100a of the SEA (Art 114, TFEU) – which enabled the adoption by the Council by qualified majority voting of harmonisation measures for the achievement of the internal market. This addressed the main stumbling block of the previous period, which was the unanimity voting requirement for harmonisation of national laws under Article 100 of the EEC Treaty (Art 115, TFEU). It provided the basis for the development of the single financial market in the next decades, and for large part of the Banking Union.

Furthermore, the SEA also broadened the range of legal acts that the Council could enact for fulfilling the internal market. While Article 100 of the EEC Treaty only contemplated directives as the instrument for the approximation of laws, Article 100a of the SEA referred to 'measures', which may include both directives and regulations. In addition, the SEA also subjected the legislation on internal market to a newly introduced 'co-operation procedure', according to which the Parliament would be consulted by the Council on such legislation.[34]

Lastly, the SEA formally recognised the possibility of comitology procedures as a condition that the Council may set for the exercise by the Commission of delegated powers. The constitutionality of these procedures had been previously challenged before the Court, which confirmed their validity in the *Köster* case. Accordingly, the SEA introduced the possibility that the Council could delegate powers to the Commission subject to conditions, which then provided the basis for comitology procedures.[35]

[33] As explained by S Weatherill, *The Internal Market as a Legal Concept*, (Oxford, Oxford University Press, 2017) 18–21. See also P Pescatore, 'Some Critical Remarks on the "Single European Act"', (1987) 24 *CML Rev* 9, who considered that the SEA was a setback, since, among other problematic issues, it supposedly restarted the process towards an 'internal market', thus dismissing the substantial progress in integration made under the 'common market'.

[34] On the introduction of Art 100a, SEA and its relationship with Art 100, EEC Treaty, see S Weatherill, *The Internal Market as a Legal Concept*, (n 33) 18–21. For the context of the single financial market, see JA Usher, *The Law of Money and Financial Services in the EC* (Oxford, Oxford University Press, 2000) 91.

[35] Judgment of the Court of 17 December 1970, *Köster*, 25/70, EU:C:1970:115. On the evolution of 'comitology procedures' under the Treaty, see P Craig, *The Lisbon Treaty: Law, Politics, and Treaty Reform* (Oxford, Oxford University Press, 2010) 48–66. The Council then specified in its Comitology Decision of 1987 the procedures for the exercise by the Commission of implementing powers conferred by the Council. Three types of committee procedures were foreseen: (1) advisory committee, where the Commission had to take the utmost account of the committee's opinion; (2) management committee, where the application of the Commission's measures not in line with the committee's opinion should be deferred, with the opportunity for the Council to take a different decision within a time limit; and (3) regulatory committee, where

D. The Maastricht Treaty

The Maastricht Treaty – the Treaty on the European Union – was signed on 7 February 1992 and entered into force on 1 November 1993, after two Danish referenda, and in the wake of the EMS crisis, when the UK Government withdrew the pound sterling from the Exchange Rate Mechanism on 16 September 1992 following a speculative attack.[36]

The Maastricht Treaty introduced a number of provisions which provided the framework for the further development of the single financial market.

First, it introduced the co-decision procedure between the Council and the Parliament under Article 251 of the TEC (Art 294, TFEU), which governs the adoption of measures regarding the approximation of national laws under Article 95 of the TEC (Art 114, TFEU), the legal basis for the directives regarding the single financial market.

Second, the principle of subsidiarity, which was first introduced for environmental policy in the SEA, became of general applicability to all Community policies, including therefore the single financial market.[37]

Third, on the basis of the Delors Committee Report on Economic and Monetary Union, the Maastricht Treaty set out the framework and the timetable for the EMU and the creation of the single currency. The Treaty provided for three stages: the first stage, liberalising the movement of capital, from 1 January 1990; the second stage, from 1 January 1994, leading to the convergence of the economic policies of the Member States; and the third stage, from 1 January 1999, with the creation of a single currency and the establishment of the ECB and the ESCB.[38]

At the time, the Maastricht Treaty could have led to a significant institutional move towards the integration of the European financial market. The Committee of Governors proposed to the Intergovernmental conference to also entrust banking supervision tasks to the ECB. The proposal was motivated by the need to improve the arrangements for banking supervision to match the growing integration of the banking markets of

the Commission could only adopt the measures if they were in accordance with the committee's opinion – if not, the Commission would need to submit a proposal to the Council, which could act on the measures by a qualified majority (variant a), also known as 'filet procedure', or could decide against such measures by a simple majority (variant b), also known as 'contrefilet procedure'. In matters relating to the internal market, the Council preferred this last 'contrefilet procedure', which provided less flexibility to the Commission. See Council Decision 87/373/EEC of 13 July laying down the procedures for the exercise of implementing powers conferred on the Commission, [1987] OJ L197/33. See E Vos, 'Fifty Years of European Integration and Forty-Five Years of Comitology' in A Ott and E Vos (eds) *Fifty Years of European Integration: Foundations and Perspectives* (The Hague, T.M.C. Asser Press, 2009) 31–56.

[36] The second Danish referendum was positive after the agreement reached at the Edinburgh European Council of December 1992 to grant Denmark four opt-outs, including on the Monetary Union, see European Council Conclusions, 12 December 1992, at www.consilium.europa.eu/media/20492/1992_december_-_edinburgh__eng_.pdf.

[37] This principle specifies that in areas that are not within its exclusive powers the Community shall only take action where objectives can best be attained by action at Community rather than at national level. Art A provides that the Union shall take decisions as close as possible to the citizen. On the relevance of the principle of subsidiarity for the single financial market, see RM Lastra 'The Governance Structure for Financial Regulation and Supervision in Europe' (2003) 10 *Columbia Journal European Law* 49.

[38] See European Commission, Report on Economic and Monetary Union in the European Community, Committee for the Study of Economic and Monetary Union, (Delors Report) (1988).

Member States. Such integration would further increase with EMU and would give rise to common banking risks, which would need to be addressed by central banks. Moreover, most European central banks had competences for banking supervision and this would be reflected at the European level. Given the divergence of views on whether a central bank should conduct banking supervision, the Treaty of Maastricht included as a compromise an enabling clause in Article 105(6) of the TEC (Art 127(6), TFEU) whereby the Council could decide to entrust banking supervision tasks to the ECB through a specific decision.[39]

The Maastricht Treaty was the subject of a legal case before the German Constitutional Court. The complaints were essentially, first, that the transfer of competences to the EU infringed citizens' rights to democratically legitimate representation in a Parliament and, second, that it corresponded to the surrender by Germany of key areas of sovereignty. The German Constitutional Court ruled that the Treaty was compatible with the German Constitution. The transfer of powers of the Bundesbank to the ECB was deemed in line with constitutional requirements, given that the central banking independence granted to the ECB was 'tested and proven in the German legal system' as appropriate to guarantee the value of the currency compared to state bodies. At the same time, the German Constitutional Court conceptualised the European Community as an 'association of states' ('Staatenverbund'), excluding thus its supranational nature, and expressed the right to review the ultra vires reach of European legal acts beyond the competences transferred under the Treaty. Any further transfer of competences would require the involvement of national parliaments and would not be binding in Germany otherwise. This ruling would later resonate in another decision of the German Constitutional Court, notably in the context of the sovereign debt crisis in the euro area.[40]

E. Towards a European Financial Market

Before the end of the 1980s the main conditions for the development of the European single financial market were largely in place. The economic and political context, marked by growing liberalisation and economic interdependence among Member States, the evolution in technology, as well as the rise of free market doctrines, provided the setting for using market forces themselves as the driver for integration. The developments in Community law, including the Court's jurisprudence following *Dassonville* and *Cassis de Dijon*, not only supported market liberalisation through negative integration but also created the dynamics later on for the expansion of Community law. This was underpinned by the institutional changes of the Single European Act and the Treaty of Maastricht.

[39] For the historical background, see H James, *Making the European Monetary Union*, (n 3) 313–317. For a more detailed analysis, see below ch 5.

[40] Cases 2 BvR 2134/92 and 2159/92 *Brunner v The European Union Treaty* reported in English in [1994] 1 CMLR 57 (Maastricht Decision). For an analysis of the judgment, see JHH Weiler, 'Does Europe Need a Constitution? Demos, Telos and the German Maastricht Decision' (1995) 1 *European Law Journal* 219; and C Joerges, 'States Without a Market? Comments on the German Constitutional Court's Maastricht-Judgement and a Plea for Interdisciplinary Discourses' (1997) 1–20 *European Integration Online Papers* eiop.or.at/eiop/texte/1997-01920htm. For an account of the EMS crisis, see H James, *Making the European Monetary Union*, (n 3) 324–381, and B Eichengreen, *The European Economy since 1945*, (n 3) 357–366.

Internationally, it was the beginning of the globalisation of finance. The development of regulatory standards by the Basel Committee aimed at market liberalisation and a minimum level playing field, as demonstrated by the Basel agreement on an international solvency ratio of banks. This, in turn, would promote the harmonisation of national laws in Europe, which was made easier by the evolving Community law.

The freedom of movement of capital, as analysed in the next section, was the most decisive condition for the European financial market realised in this period. Without it, the freedom to provide financial services remained void of any significant effect. It would represent a catalyst for institutional change, justifying the EMU. Conversely, one of the main arguments for introducing EMU was the completion and development of the single financial market: 'One Market, One Money' was the title of the Commission Report spelling out the benefits of EMU. Later on, the introduction of the euro justified the extensive legislative reform of the Financial Services Action Plan in 1999. And some 20 years later, the provision of the Treaty of Maastricht that allowed the Council to entrust banking supervision tasks to the ECB was activated for the establishment of a Banking Union.[41]

IV. The Liberalisation of Capital Movements

A. The Lifting of Capital Controls until Stage One of EMU

The SEA placed the free movement of capital at the same level as that of goods and services. In accordance with Article 8a of the EEC Treaty as amended by the SEA, the internal market is 'an area without internal frontiers in which the free movement of goods, persons, services and capital is ensured in accordance with the provisions of this Treaty'.[42]

In May 1986, the Commission launched its 'Programme for the liberalisation of capital movements in the Community,' which set out the approach for achieving a single financial market. This involved extending the Community's competences concerning the free movement of capital and also ensuring that liberalisation is accompanied by measures which support the integrity of the European financial area, such as legislation relating to the protection of investors. The Commission's programme led to the adoption of Directive 86/566/EEC, which deregulated the capital transactions necessary for to smooth functioning of the common market and the integration of national securities markets.[43]

[41] See T Padoa-Schioppa, *Efficiency, Stability and Equity*, (n 7) and European Commission, One Market, One Money: An evaluation of the potential benefits and costs of forming an economic and monetary union, 44 *European Economy* (1990).

[42] The liberalisation of capital movements was not directly applicable and would need to be achieved by directives, in accordance with Art 70(1), EEC Treaty, as amended by the SEA. Any measures that would restrict capital movements were subject to unanimity voting.

[43] European Commission, Communication on the programme for the liberalisation of capital movements in the Community, COM (1986) 292 final. Council Directive 86/566/EEC of 17 November 1986 amending the First Directive of 11 May 1960 for the implementation of Art 67 of the Treaty, [1986] OJ L332/22–28.

In November 1987, the Commission presented to the Council a legislative proposal with the aim of removing all controls on capital movements by the middle of 1990. Together with the adoption of the SEA, this provided the basis for Directive 88/361, which established the principle of free movement of capital as directly enforceable as a matter of Community law, both between Member States and with third countries. It became effective from 1 July 1990.[44]

While Directive 88/361 mentioned that monetary policy remained a matter of national competence, the full liberalisation of capital movements required the strengthening of cooperation on monetary policy within the EMS. Such liberalisation would substantially increase monetary flows and reduce the scope for national monetary and exchange rate policy between Member States. This provided the basis for the Delors Committee meeting in Basel on 12 and 13 April 1989 to put forward a three stage plan for the completion of EMU. In accordance with the Delors Report, as reflected in the conclusions of the Madrid European Council of 26 and 27 June 1989, the liberalisation of capital movements from 1 July 1990 corresponded to the first stage of EMU, which should also involve the full implementation of the European financial common market.[45]

B. The Provisions of the Maastricht Treaty

The full freedom of capital movements became a Treaty principle with the entry into force of the Maastricht Treaty on 1 November 1993, which also led to the start of the second stage of EMU from 1 January 1994. In particular, Article 56 of the TEC (Art 63, TFEU) provided for the principle of full freedom of capital movements and payments between Member States. This principle was extended to capital movements between Member States and third countries. Temporary safeguard measures may, however, be taken under Article 59 of the TEC (Art 66, TFEU) where they are justified on serious political grounds or where capital movements to and from third countries cause serious difficulties for the functioning of EMU.

Article 58(1)(b) of the TEC (Art 65(1)(b), TFEU) was particularly relevant for the development of a single financial market as it allowed Member States:

> to take all requisite measures to prevent infringements of national law and regulations, in particular in the field of taxation and the prudential supervision of financial institutions, or to lay down procedures for the declaration of capital movements for purposes of administrative or statistical information, or to take measures which are justified on grounds of public policy or public security.

[44] Proposal for a Council Directive for the Implementation of Art 67 of the EEC Treaty (Liberalization of capital movements) COM (1987) 550 final, [1988] OJ C26/1–11. Transitional arrangements were introduced for Spain, Portugal, Greece and Ireland, which were allowed to maintain restrictions until 31 December 1992. An extension not exceeding three years was granted to Portugal and Greece.

[45] The fact that monetary policy remained a national competence also justified the possibility for Member States to continue to regulate bank liquidity which have an impact on capital transactions. See European Commission, Progress Report on the European Monetary System and the Liberalization of Capital Market, COM (1987) 650 final.

This provision allowed administrative measures by Member States restricting entry into national markets, although in accordance with Article 58(3) of the TEC, 'the measures and procedures referred to in paragraphs 1 [...] shall not constitute a means of arbitrary discrimination or a disguised restriction on the free movement of capital and payments'.

C. The Jurisprudence of the Court Regarding Financial Services

The jurisprudence of the Court on the extent to which the freedom of movement of capital may be restricted by Member States was prolific in the areas of direct taxation and 'golden shares', the special rights of Member States over companies that may deter direct investment.[46]

The concept of restrictions of capital movements in the field of financial services corresponds to that developed by the Court with regard to the other fundamental freedoms, especially the freedom of movement of goods. Accordingly, any measure that makes the cross-border transfer of capital more difficult or less attractive, and is thus liable to deter the investor, constitutes a restriction on the free movement of capital. Regarding the conditions for restrictions, the Court considered that the free movement of capital, as a fundamental principle of the Treaty, may be restricted only by national rules which are justified by overriding public interest grounds. Such national rules must guarantee the attainment of the objective pursued and satisfy the criterion of proportionality. In this context, the free movement of capital and loans should not be restrained by national provisions that are likely to deter the parties concerned from approaching banks established in another Member State. However, the export of important amounts of money may be subjected to a prior declaration, so that the national authorities may exercise effective supervision in order to prevent infringements of their laws and regulations.[47]

The Court also clarified to a certain extent the relationship, as well as the demarcation, between the free movement of capital under Article 56 of the TEC (Art 63, TFEU) and the other Treaty freedoms, notably the freedom to provide services under Article 49 of the TEC (Art 56, TFEU). The distinction between freedoms is important, given that the Treaty provides for more exceptions to the freedom of capital movements than to the other freedoms. There were two main conclusions drawn by the Court. First, the Court considered that the granting of credit constitutes both a service and the exercise of free movement of capital. Second, although closely linked, the different position which the provisions of Articles 49 TEC and 56 TEC occupy in the Treaty suggested that they were designed to regulate different situations and that they each had their own field of application. This was confirmed by Article 51(2) of the TEC (Art 58(2), TFEU), which distinguished between banking and insurance services, and the free movement

[46] See the analysis by L Flynn, 'Coming of Age: The Free Movement of Capital Case Law 1993–2002' (2002) 39 *CML Rev* 773. See also, with regard to direct taxation, JA Usher, 'The Evolution of the Free Movement of Capital' (2008) 31 *Fordham International Law Journal* 1533.

[47] Judgment of the Court of 7 September 2004, *Manninen*, C-319/02, EU:C:2004:484, para 28; Judgment of the Court of 15 January 2002, *Commission v Italy*, C-439/99, EU:C:2002:14, paras 22 and 30; and Judgment of the Court of 9 July 1997, *Parodi v Banque de Bary*, C-222/95, EU:C:1997:345, para 3.

of capital, and which provided that the achievement of those services must be achieved in step with liberalisation of movement of capital.[48]

The Court concluded most clearly in the *Fidium Finanz* case that, in order to determine which freedom should prevail over the other, it is necessary to consider whether, and, if necessary, to what extent, the potentially restrictive national rules affect the exercise of each freedom. The Court determined that the rules on authorisation of credit institutions form part of the banking legislation, which has the purpose of supervising the provision of financial services. In addition, the Court also noted that the Community's legislation regulates the activity of granting loans from the point of view of both the freedom of establishment and the freedom to provide financial services. Accordingly, such rules on authorisation affect primarily the exercise of the freedom to provide financial services, while the potential related restriction to capital movements is an 'unavoidable consequence'.[49]

The Court, therefore, recognised the primacy of financial services legislation over the freedom of movement of capital. This implied that the cross-border provision of financial services, although fostered by the freedom of capital movements from 1 July 1990, remained dependent on the degree to which Community law would realise their liberalisation.

V. The Single Passport for Financial Services

A. The Principles of Home-Country Control and Mutual Recognition

The single passport for the cross-border provision of financial services was the pivotal instrument for the building-up of the single financial market in this period. The Community law framework for the operation of the single passport included several components.

The first component was the combined application of the principles of home-country control and mutual recognition. These principles stemmed from the Court's jurisprudence analysed above, as well as from the framework developed by the international regulatory standards of the BCBS. Essentially, the application of these principles gave the right to financial services providers to operate in all Member States, directly or through a branch, on the basis of the single authorisation, regulation and supervision of one Member State.[50]

[48] Judgment of the Court of 3 October 2006, *Fidium Finanz*, C-452/04, EU:C:2006:631, para 43; Judgment of the Court of 14 November 1995. *Svensson and Gustavsson*, C-484/93, para 11; and *Parodi v Banque de Bary*, (n 47) para 17. For an analysis see M Tison, 'Free movement capital and (financial) services: Moving on separate tracks' (2006) 3 *Euredia* 410.

[49] *Fidium Finanz*, (n 48) para 39.

[50] On the implications of the single passport concept, see G Hertig, 'Regulatory Competition for EU Financial Services' in DC Esty and G Damien (eds) *Regulatory Competition and Economic Integration* (Oxford, Oxford University Press, 2001) 218–240, 221–228.

The cross-border provision of financial services is then facilitated in several ways. In legal terms, the provider is subject to a single national jurisdiction for the provision of services in several Member States. This increases legal certainty and lowers the regulatory burden and costs in cross-border business, which is crucial in a highly regulated sector such as financial services. In economic terms, services may be provided cross-border on the basis of the business infrastructure in one Member State, without involving the investment in setting-up physical and legal structures in other Member States. Moreover, the concept was that home-country control and mutual recognition would foster regulatory competition among Member States for attracting financial services providers to their jurisdictions. In turn, this would lead to a more efficient legal environment for the conduct of cross-border business across Europe.[51]

B. The Second Banking Directive

The Second Banking Directive, adopted by the Council on 15 December 1989, was the instrument for achieving the freedoms of establishment and to provide financial services for credit institutions. It stipulated that the competent authorities of the home Member State, which authorised a credit institution, would have the responsibility for supervising its financial soundness and in particular its solvency. The host Member State's authorities would only retain the responsibility for the supervision of liquidity, given that monetary policy would remain a national competence. Regarding mutual recognition, the credit institutions authorised in one Member State would be able to provide across the Community, directly or through branches, those financial services listed in Annex 1 of the directive. This is still the framework largely in place in the single financial market.[52]

Accordingly, the Member States were under the obligation to ensure that there were no obstacles to the provisions of the services benefiting from mutual recognition. A credit institution wishing to provide services or establish a branch in another Member State would only have to observe a notification procedure by informing its home-country authorities, which in turn would inform the host-country authorities. The regulatory authorities of the host-country would have limited powers over the provision of services or branches of credit institutions authorised in other Member States. Such powers were limited to imposing statistical requirements, enforcing rules relating to liquidity when a credit institution does not comply and after the failure of the home-country authorities to ensure its compliance, and enforcing the host-country's rules relating to the 'general good'. In emergencies, such as financial crisis situations, the host-country authorities were entitled to take precautionary measures to protect the interests of depositors, investors and others to whom services are provided.

[51] See E Lomnicka, 'Home Country Control Principle in the Financial Services Directive and the Case Law' (2000) 11 *European Business Law Review* 324.

[52] Second Council Directive 89/646/EEC of 15 December 1989 on the coordination of laws, regulations and administrative provisions relating to the taking up and pursuit of the business of credit institutions and amending Directive 77/780/EEC, [1989] OJ L386/1–13 ('Second Banking Directive').

C. The Single Passport in Securities and Insurance Markets

The concept of a single passport was first introduced in securities markets in 1985. Investment funds (Undertakings for the Collective Investment in Transferable Securities (UCITS)) were provided with a single passport on the basis of a minimum level of coordination between national laws, mutual recognition, and home-country control by the authorities of the Member State which authorised the investment fund. The single passport was later provided in 1987 to issuers of securities to be listed in stock exchanges: the listing particulars approved in one Member State would be automatically recognised in the stock exchanges of other Member States without additional approval. This was complemented in 1989 by a directive regarding the prospectus to be published when transferable securities are offered to the public.[53]

The 1993 Investment Services Directive (ISD) completed the implementation of the single passport in the securities sector by setting out the conditions under which investment firms and credit institutions could provide investment services with the authorisation and supervision by the home-country. However, the provision of investment services continued to be subject to the host-country's laws, relating for instance to conduct of business rules or advertising, given the need to protect consumers in national markets. The ISD also provided the right of direct or remote access of an investment firm to trading on exchanges or regulated markets in other Member States. The qualification of 'regulated markets' would be granted by the home-country of such markets and mutually recognised by Member States, although the host-country could impose its regulations on market access and organisation.[54]

The single passport was implemented with greater delays and less effectively in the insurance sector, due to the wider differences between national laws regarding the regulation of this sector and the protection of policy-holders. The 1985 White Paper's approach started to be implemented after the series of the so-called 'insurance cases of 1986', where the Court decided on the Commission's legal action against Denmark, France, Germany and Ireland, regarding the restrictions placed by these Member States on the authorisation of insurance companies from other Member States. The Court considered that such restrictions were in principle compatible with the EEC Treaty, provided that they were justified by regulatory concerns related to consumer protection. The development of the single insurance market could only proceed with regard to the

[53] Council Directive 85/611/EEC of 20 December 1985 on the co-ordination of laws, regulations and administrative provisions relating to undertakings for collective investment in transferable securities (UCITS) [1985] OJ L375/3–18. The Directive sets out the minimum harmonisation necessary for equal conditions of competition and protection of investors, including provisions on the information to be supplied to unit-holders, the observance of the laws of the Member State in which the units are marketed, the rights and obligations of the supervisory authorities and the creation of a Contact Committee. See also the 'Prospectus Directive': Council Directive of 22 June 1987 amending Directive 80/390/EEC coordinating the requirements for the drawing up, scrutiny and distribution of the listing particulars to be published for the admission of securities to official stock-exchange listing. Council Directive 89/298/EEC, of 17 April 1989, coordinating the requirements for the drawing-up, scrutiny and distribution of the prospectus to be published when transferable securities are offered to the public, [1989] OJ L124/8–15.

[54] Council Directive 93/22/EEC of 10 May 1993, on investment services in the securities field, [1993] OJ L141/27–46 ('Investment Services Directive'). For an overview, see M Tison, 'The Investment Services Directive and its Implementation in the EU Member States' (1999) 1999/17 *Financial Law Institute Working Paper*.

provision of services where consumer protection was not a main concern. Accordingly, the first initiative in the insurance sector was the Second Non-Life Insurance Directive, which reflected the Court's decisions by only providing the single passport to insurance services related to large industrial risks. The host-country, the Member State where the risks are situated, retained control over the services related to general risks due to the need to safeguard consumer protection.[55]

D. The Jurisprudence of the Court on the Scope of the Single Passport

According to the jurisprudence of the Court, the single passport framework gave rise to a number of obligations between Member States.

First, the host-country must recognise the jurisdiction of the home-country over the cross-border provision of services in its territory. The jurisdiction of the home-country comprised both the regulation of such services and the enforcement of the compliance with regulatory requirements. This implied that the provision of services in one Member State could be regulated by several other national jurisdictions at the same time, depending on the origin of the providers of services. The wide scope of this obligation was confirmed in the *Alpine* case, where a restrictive measure imposed by the home-country to the provision of financial services in the host-country was considered compatible with Article 49 of the TEC (Art 56, TFEU). The Court argued that the home-country's restrictive measure was necessary for investor protection, which could not be fulfilled by the host-country within the framework for the single passport.[56]

Second, it followed that the host-country could not impose requirements, which could constrain or complement the regulation by the home-country. In this context, the principle of mutual recognition in the area of financial services could be conceived as a principle of regulatory equivalence, or 'functional parallelism', among national laws, as argued in relation to the free movement of goods. Given, however, the highly regulated nature of financial services in Member States, it was hard to consider that national

[55] Judgment of the Court of 4 December 1986, *Commission v Germany*, 205/84, EU:C:1986:463. Second Council Directive 88/357/EEC of 22 June 1988 on the coordination of laws, regulations and administrative provisions relating to direct insurance other than life assurance and laying down provisions to facilitate the effective exercise of freedom to provide services and amending Directive 73/239/EEC, [1988] OJ L172/1–14. The approach of this Directive was extended to the life insurance sector by the Second Life Insurance Directive of 1990, which applied home-country control and mutual recognition to those services where the policy-holders took the initiative to contract, thus not requiring special protection. Later, the Third Life Insurance Directive and the Third Non-Life Insurance Directive of 1992 extended home-country control and mutual recognition to all services related to life and non-life insurance.

[56] Judgment of the Court of 10 May 1995, *Alpine*, C-384/93, EU:C:1995:126, para 48. The question was whether a ban imposed by the Netherlands on financial intermediaries regarding the marketing practice of 'cold calling' was a restriction on the freedom to provide services, since it affected offers made to investors in the host-country Member State. The Court considered the restriction justified to protect investors and the good reputation of national markets: 'The Member State from which the telephone call is made is best placed to regulate cold calling. Even if the receiving State wishes to prohibit cold calling or to make it subject to certain conditions, it is not in a position to prevent or control telephone calls from another Member State without the cooperation of the authorities of that State.'

laws in this area were functionally equivalent in the pursuit of regulatory objectives. The challenge of harmonising financial services laws indicated that Member States would not accept that the regulatory objectives pursued by their national laws could be pursued in other ways.[57]

The consequence was that the principle of mutual recognition in the financial services field was more intrusive in the Member States' legal framework than in the freedom of movement of goods. This may also explain why integration in the financial services sector was so difficult to achieve in this period. In the financial services field, the national laws of the home-country should be recognised, even though they may not be functionally equivalent in the pursuit of regulatory objectives such as financial stability or of investor protection.

Ultimately there was a considerable limitation to the exercise of their respective competences by national jurisdictions, since the host-country had to abstain from interfering with the legal and economic implications of the home-country's jurisdiction, both in terms of regulation and enforcement. This was confirmed in *Caixa-Bank France*, where the Court found that the host-country's legislation, which prohibited the payment of interest on current accounts by all banks in France, was incompatible with Community law.[58]

Third, it may be questioned in addition, whether the home-country had an obligation to also safeguard the regulatory interests of the host-country, rather than just considering its domestic interests. In particular, the principle of mutual recognition raised the question of whether it gave rise to a delegation by the host-country to the home-country regarding the fulfilment of regulatory safeguards; or whether, instead, it was limited to the presumption that the jurisdiction of the home-country is equally effective in pursuing such regulatory safeguards and interests as the jurisdiction of the host-country. An obligation of the home-country to safeguard the regulatory interests of the host-country was, however, not construed in either legislation or jurisprudence regarding the financial services sector. In *Germany* v *Parliament and Council*, the Court considered that the principle of home-country supervision was not a principle laid down by the Treaty.[59]

Therefore, the fundamental freedoms and the Treaty did not impose the application of the home-country's legislation. Instead, what the principle of mutual recognition

[57] For an analysis of the distinction of the principles of mutual recognition and functional equivalence in the field of financial services, see M Ortino, 'The role and functioning of mutual recognition in the European market of financial services' (2007) 56 *International Comparative Law Quarterly* 309.

[58] Judgment of the Court of 5 October 2004, *CaixaBank*, C-442/02, EU:C:2004:586. The action was brought by the French subsidiary of a Spanish bank, Caixa Holding, following the decision by the French Committee for Banking and Financial Regulation that Caixa-France was not allowed to offer a 2% interest rate on current account. The Conseil d'État, the French administrative Supreme Court, referred the issue to the Court, which found that the prohibition of interest on current accounts constituted 'a serious obstacle' to the pursuit of the activities of foreign banks operating in France because it deprived them from competing with French banks, which have an extensive network of branches. According to the Court, para 14, 'competing by means of the rate of remuneration paid on [current accounts] constitutes one of the most effective methods to that end'.

[59] Judgment of the Court of 13 May 1997, *Germany* v *Parliament and Council*, C-233/94, EU:C:1997:231, para 12 of the summary. At stake was the application of Art 4(2) of Directive 94/19/EC on deposit-guarantee schemes, which requires Member States to include in their deposit-guarantee schemes the branches of credit institutions authorised in other Member States so that they supplement the guarantee already enjoyed by their depositors in the home-country.

did was to impose the obligation on the host-country not to exercise its jurisdiction – regarding regulation and supervision – on the provision of services subject to the home-country's jurisdiction. This was also confirmed by the Commission's interpretation that the host-country could not question the granting of the single licence, or the conditions under which the licence was granted, to a credit institution intending to provide services directly or through a branch in its territory. The home-country had the exclusive responsibly to grant a single licence. The host-country could only question whether the home-country fulfilled its obligations under the Community legislation, in accordance with Article 227 of the TEC (Art 259, TFEU).[60]

In conclusion, the Court's jurisprudence only recognised a dimension of 'negative integration' to the principle of mutual recognition: limiting the jurisdiction of the host-country vis-à-vis the home-country. However, this principle could not operate only with such a negative dimension. The highly regulated nature of the financial sector, the fact that national laws were not functionally equivalent, together with the requirements of cross-border collaboration between home- and host-country authorities, meant that the operation of mutual recognition depended on the degree of trust that Member States had on each other's ability to safeguard regulatory interests. Therefore, in practice, the operation of the principle of mutual recognition required the home-country to safeguard not only its own regulatory interests but also those of the host-country.

VI. The 'General Good' Exception

A. The Origin of the Exception

The freedom to provide financial services on the basis of the principles of home-country control and mutual recognition could be limited by the application by the host-countries of the general good exception. This exception was based on the jurisprudence developed by the Court initially with regard to the freedom of movement of goods, notably in *Dassonville* and *Cassis de Dijon*, as analysed above: the regulations of a host-country posing restrictions to the free movement of goods may be justified on the basis of the need to safeguard mandatory public policy requirements, subject to the principle of proportionality.[61]

[60] European Commission, Interpretative Communication on the freedom to provide services and the interest of the general good in the Second Banking Directive, SEC (1997) 1193 final, 14–15. The Commission makes this interpretation on the basis of Judgment of the Court of 10 September 1996, *Commission* v *Belgium*, C-11/95, EU:C:1996:316, para 86, where the Court ruled that the receiving Member State was not authorised to monitor the application of the law of the originating Member State applying to television broadcasts.

[61] For an overview, see M Tison, 'What is "General Good" in EU Financial Services Law?' (1997) 24 *Legal Issues of European Integration* 1. See also, on the notion of the general good, W van Gerven and J Wouters 'Free Movement of Financial Services and the European Contracts Convention' in M Andenas and S Kenyon Slade (eds) *EC Financial Market Regulation and Company Law* (London, Sweet & Maxwell, 1993) 43–79, 55–ff. See further SE Katz, 'The Second Banking Directive' (1992) 12 *Yearbook of European Law*, 249; and M Bjorkland, 'The Scope of the General Good Notion in the Second EC Banking Directive According to Recent Case Law' (1998) 9 *European Business Law Review* 227.

This exception was applied by the Court with regard to the freedom to provide services in the German insurance case of 1986 and later in the *French tourist* and the *Säger* cases. Later in the *Gebhard* case, the Court extended its doctrine to all the freedoms. This implied that the concept of general good could justify restrictions on all freedoms, thus requiring its uniform interpretation. Following such jurisprudence, the concept of general good was also applied with regard to the provision of financial services.[62]

B. The Restrictions to the Single Passport

The legislation adopted under the single passport approach explicitly acknowledged the possibility for host-countries to invoke the general good exception against home-country control and mutual recognition. The Second Banking Directive stated this in its recitals and provided that the host-country could impose sanctions on infringements of legal rules adopted in the interest of the general good, apply rules on the form and content of advertising, also in the interest of the general good, and impose conditions for the operation of a branch based on these rules justified by the general good.[63]

The potential application of the general good exception by host-countries, under the Court's jurisprudence and the Community legislation on the provision of financial services, was one of the factors that prevented the single passport from being exploited in this phase of the development of the single financial market.

The legal certainty for the cross-border provision of financial services, particularly with regard to retail banking and investment services, was pre-empted by the unilateral discretion of the host-country to qualify certain legal rules as adopted in the interest of the general good. Moreover, the conditions under which such rules could be invoked were relatively vague and a matter of interpretation by the Court. The highly regulated nature of the financial sector, and the high-degree of regulatory divergence across Member States, also increased the likelihood of the host-country invoking the general good in support of protectionist moves. This defeated, therefore, the purpose of the single passport of increasing legal certainty, reducing the regulatory burden, and reducing the legal and economic costs in the cross-border provision of financial services. Given the legal uncertainty connected to the general good exception, the providers of financial services would end up by complying with host-country regulations in order to avoid regulatory conflicts. Accordingly, the workability of the single passport in financial services was largely constrained.[64]

[62] *Commission v Germany*; Judgment of the Court of 26 February 1991, *Commission v France*, C-154/89, EU:C:1991:76; *Säger*; and Judgment of the Court of 30 November 1995, *Gebhard*, C-55/94, EU:C:1995:411.

[63] For the Second Banking Directive, see Recital (16): 'Whereas the Member States must ensure that there are no obstacles to carrying on activities receiving mutual recognition in the same manner as in the home Member State, as long as the latter do not conflict with legal provisions protecting the general good in the host Member State.' See also Arts 21(5) and (11) of this Directive. Similar provisions were included in the legislation for other financial sectors, namely the Investment Services Directive and the Third Life and Non-Life Insurance Directives.

[64] See G Hertig, 'Imperfect mutual recognition for EC financial services' (1994) 14 *International Review of Law and Economics* 177.

C. The Commission Communication of 1997

The Commission addressed the legal uncertainty on the general good exception in a Communication in 1997. It clarified that the application of national measures restricting the single passport should meet a set of criteria, as defined by the jurisprudence of the Court: (1) the measure must not have been subject to prior Community harmonisation; (2) it must not be discriminatory; (3) it must be justified by a compelling reason of the general good, such as consumer protection, fraud prevention, or cohesion of the tax system; (4) it must not duplicate rules applicable in the home-country; and (5) it must be necessary and proportionate to the objective pursued, in which case the nature of the service and the level of sophistication of investors should be taken into consideration by the host-country. The Communication also clarified that the host-country was not required to communicate its general good rules to credit institutions wishing to open a branch in its territory, and that the principle of mutual recognition should be applied irrespective of whether credit institutions were operating by way of the freedom to provide services or through a branch on the basis of the right of establishment.[65]

In conclusion, the general good exception to the jurisdiction of the home-country remained an important obstacle to the single passport. This was particularly the case for the integration of the market for retail financial services. The general good exception was generally applicable to protect depositors, retail investors regarding conduct of business rules, and policy holders regarding the payment of claims or complex insurance products.[66]

VII. The Minimum Harmonisation of National Laws

A. Harmonisation as a Condition for the Single Passport

The operation of the single passport for financial services was underpinned by the minimum harmonisation of national laws. It corresponded to a level of harmonisation that did not go beyond what was necessary and sufficient to enable the application of the principles of home-country control and mutual recognition. This replaced the approach followed in the previous period of 'integration through harmonisation' until 1984,

[65] See European Commission, Interpretative Communication on the freedom to provide services and the interest of the general good in the Second Banking Directive. The Communication also affirms the precedence of Community law over the application of Arts 5, 7 and 16 of the Rome Convention of 1980, which led to the application in banking contracts of the rules of the country of the consumer if the consumer received the offer and concluded the contract in his/her country, or if the other party received the consumer's order in the same country. Accordingly, the application of the law of the consumer under the Rome Convention may be overruled by Community law if it does not conform to the criteria applicable to the general good exception.

[66] European Commission, Interpretative Communication 2000/C 43/03 on freedom to provide services and the general good in the insurance sector, [2000] OJ C43; and European Commission, Communication on 'The application of conduct of business rules under Art 11 of the Investment Services Directive' (93/22/EEC), COM (2000) 722 final, of 14.11.2000.

according to which complete harmonisation would represent the corollary of integration. Such complete harmonisation would have been, in addition, if not unrealistic, cumbersome and lengthy to achieve with the Community legislative process. Instead, the regulatory competition among Member States triggered by the single passport would lead to an efficient, decentralised but compatible, legal framework for the single financial market.[67]

The minimum harmonisation approach supported the principle of mutual recognition since it only addressed those differences between national laws, which host-countries could invoke under the general good exception to restrict the cross-border provision of services. This was particularly relevant, as financial services are an activity which is highly regulated by comparison to goods, closely related to the development of the national economy, and subject to continuous monitoring and supervision. Therefore, the application of the mutual recognition principle depended to a large extent on the degree to which the host-country trusted that its own regulatory objectives would be safeguarded by the home-country.[68]

This justified minimum harmonisation, since it would aim at defining the minimum common denominator among Member States for safeguarding the regulatory goods underlying the provision of financial services, such as financial stability and consumer protection. The implication, however, was that as the home-country jurisdiction became more intrusive in the host-country due to increasing market integration, more legislative harmonisation was necessary to safeguard the interests of the host-country. Therefore, the application of the principle of mutual recognition justified both the ex ante and the ex post harmonisation of national laws with regard to market integration. Ultimately, and somewhat paradoxically, 'minimum harmonisation' required a considerable convergence of national laws which culminated in the opposite approach of 'maximum harmonisation' introduced later in 2010.

B. The Start of a European Banking Law

The single market in banking was considered to be in place on 1 January 1993, when the Second Banking Directive entered into force, since it introduced the principle of the single licence regarding the banking services listed in its annex. This justified a surge of harmonisation of national banking regulations, which was needed for the functioning of the single banking licence. In addition, such harmonisation was driven by the need to have a uniform transposition in Europe of the regulatory standards issued by the Basel Committee.

The first harmonised rules included the obligation to have a minimum level of capital, disclose the identities of the holders or acquirers of qualifying holdings, maintain own funds at the level of minimum capital, as well as have sound administrative and accounting procedures and adequate internal controls, and limit the qualifying holdings

[67] See T Padoa-Schioppa, *Regulating Finance,* (n 29) especially at 40–ff.
[68] As concluded in *Parodi v Banque de Bary* (n 47) and *Alpine* (n 56).

on non-banking institutions (optionally on insurance companies). This corresponded to the early stages of what would become a European banking law.[69]

Accordingly, the Community banking law expanded through directives in a wide range of matters, including the rules on the preparation and publication of annual and consolidated accounts (1986), own funds (1989), the definition of a solvency ratio (1989), the prevention of the use of the banking system for money laundering (1991), the supervision of credit institutions on a consolidated basis (1992), the monitoring and control of large exposures of credit institutions (1992), and also requiring each Member State and all credit institutions to join deposit guarantee schemes with harmonised minimum features, covering each deposit up to €20,000 in the event of deposit becoming unavailable (1994).[70]

In 1995, the lessons of the crisis of the Bank of Credit and Commerce International (BCCI) led to further regulatory changes. The so-called post-BCCI Directive aimed at preventing the cross-border business of a bank being hidden by requiring national authorities to consider the close links of a bank with other entities in the granting of the single licence, obliging a bank to have its head office in the Member State where it actually carries on its business, and requiring banking supervisors to exchange of information.[71]

[69] Similar developments took place in the insurance and securities, albeit at a later stage, with the completion of the single market in insurance services with the entry into force of the Third Life and Non-Life Insurance Directives in July 1994, and the Investment Services Directive in July 1995. There were also harmonisation efforts in these other sectors, especially regarding securities markets with the UCITS I and II Directives (1985 and 1988, respectively) regarding the conditions for the operation of investment funds; the Public Offer Prospectus Directive (1989) regarding the conditions for securities to be offered to the public; the Insider Dealing Directive (1989) regarding the measures prohibiting the use of inside information; the Investor-Compensation Schemes Directive (1997) regarding the harmonisation of arrangements for compensating investors; and the Settlement Finality Directive (1998) aiming at ensuring the finality of settlement in payment and securities settlement system as well as the enforceability of collateral security.

[70] Respectively, Council Directive 86/635/EEC of 8 December 1986 on the annual accounts and consolidated accounts of banks and other financial institutions, [1986] OJ L372; Council Directive 89/299/EEC of 17 April 1989 on the own funds of credit institutions, [1989] OJ L124; Council Directive 89/647/EEC of 18 December 1989 on a solvency ratio for credit institutions, [1989] OJ L386; Council Directive 91/308/EEC of 10 June 1991 on prevention of the use of the financial system for the purpose of money laundering, [1991] OJ L166; Council Directive 92/30/EEC of 6 April 1992 on the supervision of credit institutions on a consolidated basis, [1992] OJ L110; Council Directive 92/121/EEC of 21 December 1992 on the monitoring and control of large exposures of credit institutions, [1993] OJ L29; Directive 94/19/EC of the European Parliament and of the Council of 30 May 1994 on deposit-guarantee schemes, [1994] OJ L135.

[71] The BCCI was an international bank based in London and operating in Europe on the basis of an authorisation provided in Luxembourg. At its peak, it operated in 78 countries with over 400 branches, and the 7th largest bank in the world. In 1991 it was found by UK and US regulators to be involved in crimes such as money laundering, bribes, terrorism financing, arms trafficking, sale of nuclear materials, and tax evasion. The bank was then closed down. The corporate structure of BCCI aimed at hiding its criminal activities through complex cross-border structures and benefitting from banking secrecy laws. See the post-BCCI Directive: European Parliament and Council Directive 95/26/EC of 29 June 1995 amending Directives 77/780/EEC and 89/646/EEC in the field of credit institutions, Directives 73/239/EEC and 92/49/EEC in the field of non- life insurance, Directives 79/267/EEC and 92/96/EEC in the field of life assurance, Directive 93/22/EEC in the field of investment firms and Directive 85/611/EEC in the field of undertakings for collective investment in transferable securities (UCITS), with a view to reinforcing prudential supervision, [1995] OJ L168. Later, on 26 February 1995, the Barings Bank collapsed, but it did not give rise to specific regulatory action at the Community level. It triggered, however, the transfer of banking supervision from the Bank of England to a single separate authority, the Financial Services Authority, in 1997. See UK (1995) Report on the Inquiry by the Board of Banking Supervision, HMOS.

Finally, in 2000, most of these directives were consolidated in a single text, creating the first European code of banking law.[72]

C. The Failure of Minimum Harmonisation

The minimum harmonisation for the operation of the mutual recognition and home-country control principles between 1985 and 1997 became, in fact, a rather extensive approximation of national laws. The single passport for the provision of financial services ended up by requiring a harmonised regulatory framework across the Community. It did not trigger a regulatory competition among Member States, as initially envisaged for the freedom of movement of goods. As argued above, this was mainly due to the public policy reasons underlying the highly-regulated nature of the financial sector, which prevented the single passport from working without a high-degree of harmonisation of national laws.[73]

As a result, the harmonisation which took place in this period was largely insufficient for the fulfilment of the single financial market, as it did not cover many areas of the law and regulation of financial services.

VIII. The Inclusion of National Authorities in the Single Passport Framework

A. The Introduction of Comitology Procedures

Another prominent feature of this period of integration was the inclusion of national authorities in the framework of the single passport. This was also in the context of the introduction into Community law in 1987 by the Council of the so-called 'comitology procedures': the Commission would exercise implementing powers delegated by the Council and Parliament through the involvement of committees of national authorities.[74]

The first inclusion mechanism was the cooperation between the authorities of Member States through committees to support the single passport.[75]

The main committee was the BAC, which was established in 1977 by the First Banking Directive, comprising representatives of banking regulators, finance ministries, and the Commission. The BAC advised the Commission on updating or amending the

[72] Directive 2000/12/EC of the European Parliament and of the Council relating to the taking up and pursuit of the business of credit institutions, [2000] OJ L126/1.

[73] See G Hertig, 'Imperfect mutual recognition for EC financial services,' (n 64) who concludes that there was an 'imperfect mutual recognition' in the single market for financial services, since it ended up by requiring an extensive harmonisation of national laws.

[74] See Ellen Vos, 'Fifty Years of European Integration and Forty-Five Years of Comitology' (n 35).

[75] The need for cooperation between authorities is explicitly acknowledged in the relevant directives, such as in the recitals of the Second Banking Directive: 'Whereas the smooth operation of the internal banking market will require not only legal rules but also close and regular cooperation between the competent authorities of the Member States.'

Community banking legislation, on the consistency of the implementation by Member States of the banking directives, and on the need for convergence of regulatory practices and new harmonisation proposals. The BAC also had a regulatory function, as certain technical provisions of the banking directives could be amended according to a comitology procedure. In addition, the BAC provided a platform for the exchange of information and joint technical work among banking supervisors and regulators. The Groupe de Contact remained as an operational committee of banking supervisors, reporting to the BAC.[76]

On the basis of this model, an Insurance Committee was set-up in 1992 with similar functions, including a comitology function in the field of direct non-life insurance and direct life assurance. In the securities field, committees had a more limited role, as they were established only with an advisory role to the Commission and for the strict purposes of the Directive which established the committee, rather than a wider horizontal role for the whole sector. Such committees were known as 'Contact Committees,' which were established in 1979 for the Listing Particulars Directive, and in 1985 for the UCITS Directive.[77]

The introduction of committees of national authorities in the management of the single financial market marked, therefore, this period of legal integration. In practice, however, the involvement of committees in 'comitology' procedures remained very limited, due to the narrow scope provided by directives for the amendment or adaptation of their provisions through such procedures.

B. The Harmonisation of the Powers of National Authorities

The second inclusion mechanism was the harmonisation of a minimum set of regulatory and enforcement powers of national authorities, with the justification that such was necessary to allow them to fulfil their responsibilities under Community law. This harmonisation included providing authorities with powers relating to the imposition of sanctions against credit institutions and investment firms or those controlling their business, the ability to request information, and take any measures to ensure that insurance undertakings comply with laws and regulations.[78]

The Community legislation in this period thus required Member States to introduce a layer of harmonised regulatory and administrative powers of national authorities. This was in order to support the consistent implementation of directives and the

[76] The BAC corresponds now to the European Banking Committee. As a follow-up to the strategic programme on making the most of the internal market (see below), the Commission also set up in 1993 a Working Group on the Implementation of the Banking Directives to address the problems of interpretation of such legislation, also known as GTIAD from its French designation.

[77] Council Directive of 19 December 1991 setting up an Insurance Committee (91/675/EEC) [1991] OJ L374. The Investment Services Directive referred in its recitals to the establishment of a securities committee, which however was never set-up. The introduction of comitology procedures in the securities field only took place in 2003 with the adoption of the Directive 2003/6/EC of the European Parliament and of the Council of 28 January 2003 on insider dealing and market manipulation (market abuse) [2003] OJ L96. See N Moloney, *EU Securities and Financial Markets Regulation* (Oxford, Oxford University Press, 2014) at 854–ff.

[78] Art 17, Second Banking Directive, Art 27, Investment Services Directive, Art 10, Third Life Insurance Directive, and Art 8, Second Non-Life Insurance Directive.

operation of the single passport, particularly with regard to the cooperation between home and host-country authorities. It would later be instrumental to the development of governance arrangements in the next period of legal and institutional integration.

C. Obligations of Cooperation and Exchange of Information

The third mechanism for the inclusion of national authorities in the single passport was the obligation under Community law for home- and host-country authorities to cooperate with each other, including sharing information for the exercise of their respective responsibilities. In order to ensure compliance with this obligation, Community law also granted to the home-country authorities the right to carry out themselves on-site verification of information regarding branches in host-countries. This represented a significant extension operated by Community law of the territorial jurisdiction of administrative national authorities, which under public international law could not operate beyond borders.[79]

The sharing of information between home- and host-country authorities was also enabled by exceptions in Community law to the duty of professional secrecy incumbent on national authorities, which prohibits the disclosure of confidential information, except in summary or collective form, such that individual institutions cannot be identified. Such exceptions were in the form of legal gateways in directives for the exchange of information between authorities, which were later expanded by the post-BCCI directive, for example to central banks.[80]

These obligations of cooperation and sharing of information provided the basis for a mesh of bilateral agreements in the form of memoranda of understanding, which governed the relationship between home- and host-country authorities in the supervision of banks and their branches in the single financial market.[81]

IX. The Success and Failure of 'Integration through Competition'

At the end of 1992 – the deadline set for the completion of the internal market – most of the legislative initiatives foreseen in the 1985 White Paper had been adopted, largely through the qualified majority voting rule introduced by the SEA. The development

[79] Arts 15, Second Banking Directive, Art 24, Investment Services Directive, and Art 14, Third Non-Life Insurance Directive.

[80] Art 30, Second Banking Directive, Art 25, Investment Services Directive, Art 19.2, Non-Life Insurance Directive and Art 4, post-BCCI Directive.

[81] Art 7, First Banking Directive, Art 23, Investment Services Directive and Art 28, Second Non-Life Insurance Directive. These provisions require the competent authorities to collaborate closely and to supply one another with all information necessary to facilitate the pursuance of their respective tasks.

of the single financial market was then based on the full liberalisation of capital movements, together with the adoption of a legislative framework to realise the freedoms of establishment and to provide services in the banking, insurance and later, securities markets.

The framework for the legal integration of the single financial market in this period comprised thus the following instruments: (1) home-country control for the issuance of the single licence to provide financial services throughout the Community, as well as for the regulation and supervision of such services; (2) mutual recognition of national competences to enable the home-country control; (3) minimum harmonisation of national laws, to enable in turn mutual recognition; and (4) institutionalised cooperation between national authorities for the enforcement of regulation, notably through committees. Put together, these instruments provided the single passport for the provision of financial services.[82]

The completion of the single financial market was, however, not achieved in practice by 1992. This was due to a number of shortcomings, as diagnosed by the Sutherland Report, which assessed the extent to which the internal market had been completed. These included failures by Member States in transposing Community legislation into national law, as well as failures in the implementation by national authorities, for instance due to different regulatory practices and legal interpretations. In addition, the market participants and the consumers affected by such failures did not have access to effective means of redress.[83]

This legal and institutional approach to the development of the single financial market did not deliver the level of market integration that was expected. The national financial industry remained highly regulated and protected by Member States given its role for the national economies and thus to national sovereignty. Moreover, the principle of minimum harmonisation of national laws did not prove sufficient for the functioning of home-country control and mutual recognition of national laws. As analysed above, the 'general good exception' represented a powerful obstacle, both explicitly through the application of the laws of the host-country and implicitly through the enforcement practices of national authorities. As a result, the cross-border provision of financial services in the single market did not expand out of the use of the single passport, either in the direct provision of services or through branches. Instead, the preferred mode of market entry for financial services remained the acquisitions of local firms, also due

[82] See E Lomnicka (1996) The Single European Passport in Financial Services, in BAK Rider and M Andenas (eds) *Developments in European Company Law, vol.1*, (London, Kluwer Law International, 1997) 181–201.

[83] European Commission, The Internal Market After 1992: Meeting the Challenge, Report to the EEC Commission by the High-Level Group on the Operation of the Internal Market presided by Peter Sutherland, SEC (92) 2044 (1992). The Commission took repressive action under the EC Treaty for prosecuting infringements by the Member States which were delaying transposition of directives, transposing them incorrectly, or implementing them badly. These actions are reported in the series of three reports between 1993 and 1995 by the Commission to the Council on the operation of the single market: European Commission, The Community Internal Market, COM (1994) 55 final; European Commission, The Single Market in 1994, COM (1995) 238 final; and European Commission, The Single Market in 1995, COM (1996) 51 final.

to a number of factors, such as proximity to customers, taxation, labour laws, and also protectionist practices by Member States.[84]

The period of 'integration through competition' from 1985 until 1997 had nonetheless deep implications for European integration. It was successful at placing market integration as the core objective of Community policies, regardless of the level of political and regulatory integration among Member States. The vision first put forward by the 1985 White Paper, and formalised in the SEA, was that of a single market conducive to permanent and unconstrained economic growth accessible to all: the Community and each individual Member State. This provided the main justification for Member States to agree to the institutional changes introduced by the SEA.[85]

Integration would be pursued via deregulation by abolishing barriers to entry and ensuring free competition across the single market. This would expand the single market without explicitly constraining national sovereignty. It reflected the influence of 'ordoliberalism' in the Community legal order, whereby the supranational level should be limited to ensure economic rationality and free competition, while redistributive policies should only take place at national level. From then on, the ever deepening of market integration as the basis for economic growth became a political, economic and legal objective by itself. The logic of integration became the only necessary and sufficient justification for European policies and law.[86]

In financial services, such logic was pursued through the single passport. This legal concept introduced the premise that finance could expand unlimitedly throughout the single market, independently of the Member State of origin, in line with the principles of non-discrimination and equality of Member States enshrined in the Treaty. It also introduced the 'democratisation of capital' across the Community, whereby any investor from any Member State could access financial instruments from other Member States. The European law of the single financial market was the most liberal framework for cross-border finance at the time, which became widespread globally in the course of

[84] The most ambitious Commission initiative after 1992 was the 'Action plan for the single market' of 4 June 1997, which aimed at addressing the shortcomings in the completion of the internal market in Community legislation, as well as the national transposition and implementation of Community law: European Commission, Commission Communication, Action Plan for the Single Market, CSE (1997) 1 final. This action plan included the SLIM methodology, as part of the 'Better law-making' approach, which aimed at simplifying the legislation relating to the internal market.

[85] See AS Milward, *The European Rescue of the Nation-State*, 2nd edn (London, Routledge, 1994) at 379 on the concept of economic growth in the SEA, which in his view aimed at providing a common ideology about integration among Member States at the time.

[86] In this sense, see C Joerges, 'Democracy and European Integration: A Legacy of Tensions, a Re-conceptualisation and Recent True Conflicts' (2007) *EUI Working Paper LAW*, at 6–9. For a critique of the concept of European law dominated by the 'ever closer' integration objective, see A von Bogdandy 'European Law Beyond "Ever Closer Union" Repositioning the Concept, its Thrust and the EJC's Comparative Methodology' (2016) 22 *European Law Journal* 519. See also JHH Weiler, 'The Transformation of Europe' (1991) 100 *Yale Law Journal* 2403, on the impact of the concept of 'a single European market': 'This need for a successful market not only accentuates the pressure for uniformity, but also manifests a social (and hence ideological) choice which prizes market efficiency and European-wide neutrality of competition above other competing values.' at 2478.

the 1990s. Indeed, the rules of global finance first started in the single European financial market.[87]

X. Conclusion: The Perpetual Integration of the European Financial Market

The main implication of the strategy of 'integration through competition' was that everlasting integration became the endpoint of the European financial market. This is the conclusion which is drawn from this chapter.

The legal and institutional innovations introduced in this period would deliver a perpetual motion for the expansion of the European financial market. Drawing on the previous failure of 'integration through harmonisation', the legal concept of the single passport would expand the single financial market without requiring any explicit constraint to national sovereignty as before. Home-country control and mutual recognition operated through national competences, which were in addition safeguarded by the 'general good exception'. The minimum harmonisation of national laws was also not as intrusive as full harmonisation. Progress was then made towards a European banking law through several legislative initiatives widening the scope of harmonisation. The buy-in of national authorities was supported by committees, which were involved in the preparation and updating of Community law through comitology procedures.

The perpetual motion towards integration would then be achieved by the following self-reinforcing dynamics. Once cross-border financial services started to expand, the reach of home-country control and mutual recognition would increase, thus also increasing the interdependence between national authorities. This, in turn, would require more convergence in regulatory enforcement through committees. It would further require more harmonisation of national laws to avoid incompatible national regimes, and also to provide adequate regulation to the growing volume of cross-border financial services. In this way, the preservation of national competences in the expanding single financial market would paradoxically require ever more harmonisation of national laws. This represented the conceptual engine for market integration in this period (Figure 2 below).

This engine of integration was thus a creation of European law, which determined how legal change would come about. The legal integration of the European financial market would no longer happen through the failed strategy of the previous period, whereby full harmonisation would be imposed from the top down. Legal change would instead occur through the combined structural pressure of ever-increasing competition

[87] As argued by R Abdelal, *Capital Rules: The Construction of Global Finance* (Cambridge MA, Harvard University Press, 2007), especially at 218–ff.

among market players and regulatory competition among Member States. The minimum harmonisation of national laws would then suffice as the starting point for legal change, leading to more and more harmonisation through home-country control and mutual recognition. Such structural pressure would then deliver, over time, an optimally regulated financial market at the European level. The premise for this construction to function as intended was, therefore, that the European financial market would be in perpetual integration, adjusting continuously to such competitive dynamics and being more and more subject to European law.

The design of this strategy of 'integration through competition' was due to the many influences referred to above in this chapter, including the political thinking of the time towards market liberalisation and deregulation, the increasing internationalisation of finance, the expanding global standard-setting, and, most importantly, the single market programme. However, as in the previous phase of integration, it failed in delivering a European financial market. National sovereignty prevailed once more against this integration strategy. Member States rejected the single passport framework through protectionist measures, divergences of national laws and enforcement practices, and the use of the 'general good' exception.

This phase had, nonetheless, decisive implications for the future emergence of a Banking Union as an outcome of the evolution of European law. It introduced perpetual integration as the dominant logic for legal change in the European financial market. Within this logic, legal and institutional integration akin to the Banking Union – uniform European law applied by a European authority – would be the optimal regulatory setting and thus the end destination.

Figure 2 The Conceptual Engine of Perpetual Integration through the Single Passport

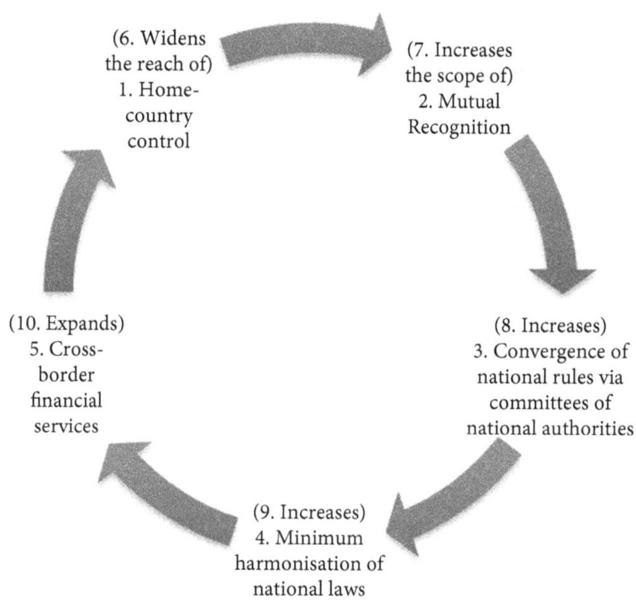

Table 3 Legal Change in 'Integration through Competition' (1985–1997)

<table>
<tr><th colspan="2">Legal and institutional innovations to deepen integration</th><th>Integration policies</th><th>Remaining obstacles to integration</th></tr>
<tr><td>1</td><td>Freedom of movement of capital</td><td>• Provide direct effect to the freedom of capital movements as with the other Treaty freedoms</td><td rowspan="6">• Application of host-country laws on the basis of the 'general good' exception
• Insufficient harmonisation of national laws
• Divergence of enforcement practices by national authorities
• Lack of compliance by Member States with Community law
• Lack of redress mechanisms against non-compliance with Community Law
• Other obstacles such as taxation, labour laws, or lack of physical proximity to the markets</td></tr>
<tr><td>2</td><td>Principle of home-country control</td><td>• Licence, regulation and supervision of a credit institution by the home-country authority throughout the common market</td></tr>
<tr><td>3</td><td>Principle of mutual recognition</td><td>• Enable the operation of home-country control by avoiding the application of the national laws of host-countries</td></tr>
<tr><td>4</td><td>Minimum harmonisation of national laws</td><td>• Support the application of home-country control and mutual recognition
• Provide a uniform law
• Transpose international regulatory standards in a uniform manner</td></tr>
<tr><td>5</td><td>Committees of national authorities</td><td>• Consistent implementation and interpretation of Community law
• Convergence of enforcement practices
• Support the technical preparation of Commission proposals
• Enable 'comitology' procedures</td></tr>
<tr><td>6</td><td>Single passport for the cross-border provision of financial services</td><td>• Provide the right to financial services providers to operate throughout the single market</td></tr>
</table>

3

Integration through Governance (1998–2007)

The right tactics here consist in action to ensure that unification in the monetary field never lags behind and is in fact always slightly ahead, since the policy of ensuring a lead to the monetary field would at least encourage, and perhaps, indeed, provide a commanding inducement to the integration process in other fields.

Hans von der Groeben, 1968[1]

I. Introduction

Following the liberalisation of the 1980s, the globalisation of finance accelerated in this period and created new policy challenges. The reach of national jurisdictions to regulate global financial institutions, markets and market infrastructures was increasingly constrained. Financial innovation increased the complexity and intensity of risks. At the same time, as global finance created more investment opportunities, finance became equated with economic growth. A bigger financial system, with bigger financial institutions, would increase economic wealth. As a result, restrictions to cross-border finance were lifted worldwide.[2]

This called for a new regulatory approach towards global finance. The financial liberalisation and deregulation of the 1980s were not sufficient to ensure well-functioning markets, particularly after the experience of the Latin American and Asian financial crises of the 1990s. These crises, and the resulting lack of economic growth, demonstrated that the institutional framework also mattered to prevent market failures. This would not mean that markets should be constrained or replaced by the government. Instead, the government should follow or be embedded in markets to support its regulation and stability over time. Moving beyond the neoliberal and spontaneous order of the previous period, markets should be subject to 'liberal institutions' in the form

[1] European monetary policy: Towards the gradual establishment of a European monetary system (European Commission, 1968).

[2] On the liberalisation of finance in this period, see R Abdelal, *Capital Rules: The Construction of Global Finance* (Cambridge MA, Harvard University Press, 2007) at 136–161. On the link between finance and growth, see R Levine, 'Finance and Growth: Theory and Evidence' in P Aghion and S Durlauf (eds) *Handbook of Economic Growth* (Amsterdam, Elsevier, 2005) 865–934.

of 'good governance' and 'good policies'. In practice, this would materialise into global governance based on standard-setting bodies, regulatory standards, and requirements for national institutional frameworks.[3]

The development of a European financial market was a major part of the globalisation of finance. The Member States were keen to increase the size of their domestic financial systems and to foster financial institutions as 'national champions' to increase their economic growth. The progress in financial integration was, however, limited at the end of the 1990s, despite the full liberalisation of capital movements and the introduction of the single passport. The introduction of the euro provided the impetus for deepening financial integration beyond the previous period. The single financial market became an explicit objective to support the economy and the Monetary Union, also in the context of the Lisbon Strategy introduced in 2000.[4]

The third period of the legal evolution of the single financial market thus starts with the preparations for the establishment of the European Central Bank (ECB) on 1 June 1998 followed by the introduction of the euro on 1 January 1999. It is defined by the move from the Hayekian world of the previous period, based on the spontaneous evolution of rules, towards a new paradigm for integration based on developing the 'governance' of markets at the European level. Such a move reflected similar approaches to the global governance of finance, such as the introduction of multilevel governance structures. The numerous legal and institutional innovations of this period are identified in this chapter, which concludes with an analysis of its consequences in the run-up to the financial crisis in Europe in 2007–2008.

II. The Governance Model of Regulation

A. The New Governance Doctrine

The 'new governance' doctrine emerged with regard to the role of government in delivering public services in the most efficient manner. This was in the context of liberal public choice theories emphasising the efficiency of free markets and the need to adapt

[3] The origin of 'good governance' may be traced back to new institutional economics, which claimed that institutions played a fundamental role for the functioning of the economy and markets. See D North, *Institutions, Institutional Change and Economic Performance* (Cambridge, Cambridge University Press, 1990) 73–82. See the move towards constitutional liberalism in VJ Vanberg, *The Constitution of Markets: Essays in Political Economy* (London, Routledge, 2001) 17–36. On the role of institutions and rules in managing globalisation, see D Rodrik, *The Globalization Paradox* (Oxford, Oxford University Press, 2011) 233–247.

[4] The 'Lisbon Strategy' was introduced at the Lisbon European Council of 23 and 24 March 2000. See European Council, Presidency Conclusions, at www.consilium.europa.eu/uedocs/cms_data/docs/pressdata/en/ec/00100-r1.en0.htm. The goal was to 'strengthen employment, economic reform and social cohesion as part of a knowledge-based economy'. The Open Method of Coordination, as an instrument of 'new governance' was introduced as part of this strategy. The completion of the internal market for financial services was also part of the Lisbon Strategy and included the implementation of the Financial Services Action Plan. Ultimately, the Lisbon Strategy was deemed a failure ten years later, due also to weak governance structures. See European Commission, Commission Staff Working Document: Lisbon Strategy Evaluation Document, SEC (2010) 114 final, at 6.

public administration to the complexity of economic, social, scientific and technological problems, which were increasingly out of reach of government action. It acknowledged the 'bounded rationality' of the government in decision-making, in problem-solving, and in enforcing rules in a complex world. The main implication was the replacement of the hierarchical and centralised 'command and control' of traditional Weberian public administration by a more cooperative and decentralised administration, which relies on creating and managing networks for the provision of public services.[5]

Regulation and compliance would be achieved through a wide range of indirect policy tools. One of those tools would be 'soft law' or standards produced and enforced among networks of public and private actors, which constantly generate regulatory knowledge and stimulate self-regulation. The focus of public administration changed thus from rule-making to the design of procedures that enabled networks to decide on policies and rules, independently of their outcome.[6]

Political and legal outcomes became linked to the outcomes of technical or scientific processes of deliberation. Traditional boundaries, such as the public and private distinction in politics and law became blurred. This also changed the notion of administrative accountability, which was previously based on the direct accountability to the political institutions. Under 'new governance', accountability is provided by the procedures themselves, such as participation rights in networks, disclosure of information, or transparency of decision-making.[7]

'New governance' gained expression in many fields, ranging from economic and social policies to corporate governance. It was also applied quite prominently in the development of global governance. As globalisation limited the ability of national governments to formulate policy on a territorial basis, 'new governance' provided the strategy of creating global policy and regulatory networks among national agencies, the private sector, and non-governmental organisations (NGOs). These networks would, for example, gather and exchange information, develop regulatory standards and best practices, and ensure cross-border enforcement of such standards. They would enable national governments to retain their role in public policy in a globalised world, as an alternative to a utopian 'world government'. In legal terms, the output of these networks,

[5] On the rise of governance in administrative law, see KH Ladeur, 'The Changing Role of the Private in Public Governance: The Erosion of Hierarchy and the Rise of a New Administrative Law of Cooperation. A Comparative Approach' (2002) 2002/9 *EUI Working Papers Law*.

[6] The focus on the 'search process' originated in the theory of 'bounded rationality' developed by Herbert A Simon, which claims that rational decision-making is subject to cognitive limits derived from the lack of complete information and other factors. Therefore, decision-making should basically consist of a 'search process' assessing different alternatives. This theory was applied in several contexts, including business and public administration. For the original theory, see HA Simon, *Models of Man* (New York, Wiley, 1957).

[7] 'New governance' was also influenced by the search in political theory for democratic legitimisation of supranational processes in the wake of globalisation. See J Habermas, *Between Facts and Norms: Contributions to a Discourse Theory of Law and Democracy* (Cambridge MA, MIT Press, 1996) 400. For an interpretation in the EU context, see JP McCormick, *Weber, Habermas, and Transformations of the European State: Constitutional, Social, and Supranational Democracy* (Cambridge, Cambridge University Press, 2007) 231–ff. This was also reflected in legal theory, particularly in the concept of 'proceduralisation of law', originally by R Wiethölter, 'Materialization and Proceduralization in Modern Law' in G Teubner (ed) *Dilemmas of Law in the Welfare State* (Berlin, Walter de Gruyter, 1986) 221.

such as global standards, became recognised as private sources of law, a new form of *lex mercatoria* challenging the monopoly of the state in the creation and adjudication of law.[8]

Moreover, the emergence of global networks also challenged the concept of representative democracy organised within a sovereign state. These networks typically comprise technocratic groups, which take decisions and solve problems detached from political and democratic deliberation. The state itself became conceptualised as a 'network of networks', whose primary role was to maintain the knowledge-generation and problem-solving capacity of networks. This would lead to a new form of democracy not constrained by its dependence on the centralised sovereign state. Representative democracy would be replaced by direct participation in networks, procedures in the functioning of networks, such as transparency, mutual observation among networks, and accountability obligations.[9]

B. New Governance in European Integration

In Europe, 'new governance' emerged in contrast to the traditional Community method based on the division of competences between the European institutions and on the Community legal instruments, as provided in the Treaty.[10]

The new governance period introduced by the Prodi Commission in 1999 would foster institutional and legal innovations to pursue integration. This included the setting-up of Community agencies, a much wider use and recognition of comitology, the introduction of 'better regulation' practices, the reliance on 'soft law', or the development of the 'Open Method of Coordination' for social policy. These innovations aimed at deepening European integration beyond the framework of the Treaty, while not involving the transfer of national competences. They operated 'outside the Treaty'

[8] Anne-Marie Slaugher described the emergence of global networks and the possible types of regulatory networks. See especially AM Slaughter, *A New World Order* (Princeton, Princeton University Press, 2004) 18–23 and 52–64. This new *lex mercatoria* was conceptualised by G Teubner, '"Global Bukowina': Legal Pluralism in the World Society"' in G Teubner (ed) *Global Law Without the State* (Aldershot, Dartmouth, 1997) 3, especially at 19–21, where he characterises global law as structurally coupled to economic processes, and therefore insulated from national legal orders. It is no longer based on nation-states but on 'invisible social networks', and originates from processes of a highly specialised and technical nature. It is also 'soft law' as it refers more to values and principles than to precise rules. And it is a plural law, with several sources, public and private, national and transnational.

[9] See KH Ladeur, 'Globalization and the Conversion of Democracy to Polycentric Networks: Can Democracy Survive the End of the Nation State?' in KH Ladeur (ed) *Public Governance in the Age of Globalization* (Burlington VT, Ashgate, 2004) 89, at 113–118.

[10] 'New governance' was one of key strategic objectives in the programme of the Prodi Commission, which started its mandate in 1999. The approach was set out in European Commission, European Governance: a White Paper, COM (2001) 428 final; and on the follow-up European Commission, Report from the Commission on European Governance, Office for Official Publications of the European Communities (2003). It was extensively dealt with in academic doctrine. For an overview, see C Joerges, Y Meny and JHH Weiler, 'Symposium: Mountain or molehill? A critical appraisal of the Commission White Paper on Governance' (2001) 6/01 *Jean Monnet Working Paper*, at www.eui.eu/Documents/RSCAS/Research/OnlineSymposia/Joerges.pdf.; and also J Scott and DM Trubek, 'Mind the Gap: Law and New Approaches to Governance in the European Union' (2002) 8 *European Law Journal, Special Issue on Law and the New Approaches to Governance in Europe* 1.

and thus did not interfere with the constitutional principle of supremacy or threaten the institutional balance.[11]

'New governance' was also aimed at counteracting the institutional evolution towards Europe as a centralised and hierarchical 'regulatory state'. This evolution was not only unlikely to be viable, but was also anathema to public and democratic conscience on European integration, as later reflected in the rejection of the Constitutional Treaty in the French and Dutch referenda in 2005. In this context, it was also important to face the challenges of the enlargement of the European Union by 12 new Members in 2004 and 2007.[12]

'New governance' offered thus the promise of fulfilling the seeming paradox of deepening integration, while neither centralising powers at the European level nor decentralising them to the national level. This could be achieved through 'experimental multilevel governance' where European decision-making would rely on non-hierarchical networks comprising both European and national administrations. According to the doctrine developed by Charles Sabel and Jonathan Zeitlin, multilevel governance would deliver a decision-making architecture through four main functions. First, the highest level of governance, which would include both European and national authorities, would design framework goals. These goals would be developed into rules and implemented by lower-levels of national authorities, as the second function. These lower governance levels would have a large degree of autonomy, including the ability to propose changes to the goals and rules. In turn, as the third function, these levels of national authorities would have accountability and reporting obligations to the highest level on their performance. Fourth, the framework goals, rules, and procedures would be revised regularly in light of experience, in order to enhance their functioning and reflect continuous deliberations and inclusion of all views.[13]

This 'networked deliberative decision-making' would overcome the institutional constraints of the Treaty for complex decision-making, such as those constraints

[11] On these innovations, see R Dehousse, 'Regulation by Networks in the European Community: The Role of European Agencies' (1997) 4 *Journal of European Public Policy* 246; KH Ladeur, 'Towards a Legal Theory of Supranationality -The Validity of the Network Concept' (1997) 3 *European Law Journal* 33; C Joerges and E Vos (eds) *EU-Committees: Social Regulation, Law and Politics* (Oxford, Hart Publishing, 1999); and, for an overview of what governance implied for European integration, see P Kjaer, *Between Governing and Governance: On the Emergence, Function and Form of Europe's Post-National Constellation* (Oxford, Hart Publishing, 2010). The vision of a European regulatory state was developed more extensively by G Majone, 'The European Community as a Regulatory State' in *Collected Courses of the Academy of European Law, V-1* (New York, Kluwer Law International, 1996) 321–419; and also G Majone, *Dilemmas of European Integration: The Ambiguities and Pitfalls of Integration by Stealth* (Oxford, Oxford University Press, 2005) 64–ff, on the debate regarding the delegation of regulatory powers within the Community.

[12] For an overview of the challenges of governance to law, see C Joerges, 'Constitutionalism and Transnational Governance: Exploring a Magic Triangle' in C Joerges, I Sand and G Teubner (eds) *Transnational Governance and Constitutionalism* (Oxford, Hart Publishing, 2004) 339, 340–344.

[13] See C Sabel and J Zeitlin, 'Learning from Difference: The New Architecture of Experimentalist Governance in the European Union' in C Sabel and J Zeitlin (eds) *Experimentalist Governance in the European Union: Towards a New Architecture* (Oxford, Oxford University Press, 2010) 1–28, especially 2–3. See also O Gerstenberg and C Sabel, 'Directly-Deliberative Polyarchy: An Institutional Idea for Europe' in R Dehousse and C Joerges (eds) *Good Governance and Administration in Europe's Integrated Market* (Oxford, Oxford University Press, 2002), 289–341.

stemming from the distribution of competences between the EU and Member States and also between the European institutions. It would also address the problem of the European democratic deficit, since the principles and procedures underpinning the functioning of networks would provide new and enhanced forms of democratic accountability. For example, transparency obligations would enable political institutions to scrutinise the working of networks, and to challenge their findings more effectively, than by traditional representative democracy.

As a result, 'new governance' became a new paradigm of European integration. It aimed at delivering a new form of decision-making and regulatory system, which would fulfil three objectives: (1) overcome the limitations of the Community method; (2) develop new European policies and expand existing ones, without an explicit transfer of competences; and (3) address the European democratic deficit. This would be enabled by several means: developing networks of European and national authorities; making a wider use of indirect policy instruments through soft law, while limiting the use of traditional, hard-law instruments; and developing new forms of accountability obligations and transparency practices.[14]

C. New Governance in the Regulation of Finance

'New governance' was implemented in the field of finance in the context of the development of risk-based regulation, which focused on prioritising risks in order to define regulatory activities and allocate resources. It followed the experience with financial crises, such as that of Barings Bank in 1995. It also aimed at tackling the increasing expansion and complexity of finance resulting from globalisation, information technology, and the democratisation of finance, whereby small investors and households had more and more direct access to financial instruments.[15]

This motivated a regulatory shift towards 'principles-based regulation'. It was based on the definition of general objectives and principles, rather than detailed prescriptive rules. The aim was to preserve flexibility and adaptability in addressing ever more complex financial risks, which would not be captured by rigid regulatory frameworks. Moreover, risk-based regulation also attempted to keep pace with the fast-moving developments in financial markets. It would rely on the internal self-regulation and risk management practices of financial institutions, which were assumed to retain the best knowledge on the nature and scope of risks. This implied that, in line with 'new governance', the emphasis was on regulatory outcomes rather than command and control. The

[14] See J Black, 'The rise (and fall?) of principles based regulation' in K Alexander and N Moloney (eds) *Law reform and financial markets* (Cheltenham, Elgar, 2011) 3.

[15] On the role of networks in European law, see KH Ladeur, 'Towards a Legal Theory of Supranationality-The Validity of the Network Concept' (n 11) 155. On soft law as a new means to achieve compliance, in the lack of more effective mechanisms in Community law, see F Snyder, 'The Effectiveness of European Community Law: Institutions, Processes, Tools and Techniques' (1993) 56 *Modern Law Review* 19. For an overview of governance concepts in European integration, see B Kohler-Koch and B Rittberger 'The "Governance Turn" in EU Studies' (2006) 44 *Journal of Common Market Studies* 27.

financial institutions were directed at achieving outcomes such as consumer confidence, while preserving flexibility on the means, as long as the outcomes were achieved.[16]

The principles-based regulation also had implications for the institutional framework. The focus on risks and outcomes, rather than on rules, led to integrating regulation in one single regulatory agency that would cover the full spectrum of financial risks. The zenith of this approach was the establishment of the UK Financial Services Authority (FSA) in 1997 by the Labour Government of Tony Blair, which removed banking supervision from the Bank of England. The FSA heralded the era of principles-based regulation for finance, which spread widely in Europe and across the globe. Many, if not most, countries with important financial centres adopted this new legal and institutional model for financial regulation. The 2008 financial crisis marked later the debacle of principles-based regulation in finance, as it became associated with light touch regulation, which placed excessive reliance on the self-discipline of financial institutions with regard to risk-taking. This then led to a reversal, both in the approach for rule-making and in the institutional models for the regulation of finance.[17]

'New governance' also defined the global governance of finance. This period witnessed a massive increase in the activity of global standard-setting bodies in the field of finance, which functioned as networks exchanging information, generating regulatory knowledge, and developing best practices and rules in the form of global standards. Most of these standards, such as the Basel II Framework, followed new regulatory techniques inspired by principles-based regulation and consultation practices. The enforcement of such standards also relied on new governance approaches, making use of tools such as peer reviews.

III. The Multilevel Governance of Global Finance

A. The Globalisation of Finance

The globalisation of finance accelerated towards the end of the 1990s and this was reflected in the expansion of the single financial market. International finance was no longer concentrated in the major financial centres. The worldwide liberalisation of capital controls, financial market deregulation, together with the rapid expansion of the internet and the World Wide Web, created a global marketplace. In the 1980s, all of the Organisation for Economic Co-operation and Development (OECD) countries constrained the establishment of foreign financial institutions. By the mid-1990s, no such restrictions were in place in industrial countries and in many of the developing economies, particularly as finance became equated to economic development.

[16] See J Black, 'The rise (and fall?) of principles based regulation' (n 14).

[17] On the institutional models for banking supervision, see T Padoa-Schioppa, *Regulating Finance: Balancing Freedom and Risk* (Oxford, Oxford University Press, 2004) 68–74; and C Goodhart et al, *Financial Regulation: Why, How and Where Now?* (London, Routledge, 1998) 142–187.

This reduced the market entry-costs for financial institutions, issuers of capital, investors, and providers of market infrastructures, thus increasing exponentially global market integration. As a result of this integration, global financial transactions were performed – decided, implemented and settled – in the same conditions to those of domestic transactions, such as costs and speed of transactions. Financial assets became subject to the 'law of one price' at the global level, ie traded at the same price independently of their location. Investors became thus less likely to display a 'home-bias' by only investing in domestic financial assets.[18]

The globalisation of finance gave rise to several new regulatory concerns as financial transactions became linked to more than one jurisdiction. In the global financial system, economic and financial shocks would not remain confined within jurisdictions, but would spillover across institutions, markets, and market infrastructures. Moreover, the scope for systemic risk would also be exacerbated by other factors, such as the rapid spread of financial innovation and increasing possibilities for regulatory arbitrage and circumvention.[19]

The experience with the Latin American and Asian financial crises of 1995 and 1997 confirmed the intensity of the transmission of disturbances in global financial markets. The process of globalisation included not only finance but also systemic financial risks. The answer to this challenge, the spreading of risks beyond the confines of national jurisdictions, was the development of a global governance system for finance, which also influenced to a large extent the approach to the governance of the single financial market.[20]

B. The Financial Stability Forum and Global Governance Standards

The first major development in the governance of global finance was the establishment of the Financial Stability Forum (FSF) in April 1999 by the Finance Ministers and Central Bank Governors of the G7 countries. The FSF had three broad objectives: (1) identifying the sources and formulating the policies to mitigate systemic risk; (2) ensuring that regulatory standards are developed by standard-setting bodies and implemented by jurisdictions; and (3) ensuring that such standards apply to all types of significant

[18] On the globalisation of finance in this period, see DB Crane, KA Froot, SP Mason, A Perold, RC Merton, Z Bodie, ER Sirri, and P Tufano, *The global financial system: A functional perspective* (Cambridge MA, Harvard Business School Press, 1995); and AM Kose, E Prasad, K Rogoff, and SJ Weil, 'Financial Globalization: A Reappraisal' (2009) 56-1 *IMF Staff Papers* 8–62.

[19] See WR White, 'Why Financial Stability is Important' (1998) 62/1998 *BIS Review*, 2; A Greenspan, *The Globalization of Finance* (1998) 17 *Cato Journal* 243. See also GJ Schinasi, *Safeguarding Financial Stability: Theory and Practice* (Washington DC, IMF, 2005) 153–ff for a more complete consideration of the challenges of the globalisation of finance.

[20] See E Posner, 'Making rules for global finance: transatlantic regulatory cooperation at the turn of the millennium' (2009) 63 *International Organization* 665.

financial institutions. The FSF was thus conceived as the global standard-setter for all the standard-setting bodies.[21]

The standard-setting bodies developed in the short period of 1997 to 1999 a series of standards, which comprised the principles and institutional features of the framework for regulating and supervising finance in national jurisdictions (see Table 3 below). For example, the 1997 Basel Core Principles required that banking supervision authorities should have clear objectives, independence, transparent processes, powers to ensure compliance with laws, sound governance and adequate resources, and be accountable for the discharge of its duties. They also set minimum requirements regarding the licensing and acquisitions of banks, accounting and disclosure, the methods for the regulation and supervision of banks, as well as for the international cooperation between authorities.[22]

This constituted a new type of standards. They were different from the regulatory standards seeking the harmonisation of financial rules. They were instead 'standards about having something', setting out the best institutional framework that all national jurisdictions should have: global governance standards.[23]

The standards provided a benchmark for the convergence of the governance of regulatory systems, so as to ensure that finance was effectively regulated across jurisdictions. In this context, since they largely reflected the features of the regulatory systems of developed economies, the standards also represented a mechanism of 'regulatory export' to the rest of the world. This was justified to avoid that under-regulated jurisdictions posed threats to finance. Broadly equivalent governance would facilitate the interaction between jurisdictions, which promoted in turn the transposition of the regulatory standards issued by the same standard-setting bodies. Moreover, it would also promote the globalisation of finance, as compatible regulatory regimes would lead to the integration of markets.[24]

These standards provided a layer of the global governance of finance, the minimum common denominator for all jurisdictions. This layer became visible through one of the first initiatives of the FSF in 2000 to identify the 'twelve key standards for sound financial systems'. This codification of standards introduced by the FSF, as any codification of legal norms, had a normative nature. It presented the standards as a coherent whole, in order to reinforce their global validity and promote their compliance.

[21] The FSF was established following the recommendations put forward in the Tietmeyer Report. See H Tietmeyer, 'International Co-operation and Co-ordination in the Area of Financial Market Supervision and Surveillance' (1999) 21/1999 *BIS Review*. The membership of the FSF comprised the national authorities responsible for financial stability in the major developed countries (Australia, Canada, France, Germany, Hong Kong, Italy, Japan, Netherlands, Singapore, Switzerland, the UK and the US), the standard-setting bodies (BCBS, IOSCO, IAIS, IASB, CPSS, Committee on the Global Financial System), and the IMF, World Bank, BIS and the OECD.

[22] See BCBS, Core Principles for Effective Banking Supervision (2006), at www.bis.org/publ/bcbs230.htm.

[23] On the standardisation processes by the end of century, see N Brunsson and B Jacobsson, *A World of Standards* (Oxford, Oxford University Press, 2000) 1–20, who distinguish between standards as 'being something', 'doing something' or 'having something'.

[24] See AM Slaughter, *A New World Order*, (n 8) 173–178, who considers that one of the functions of regulatory networks is 'regulatory export', so that there is sufficient policy convergence to achieve more formal agreements on a common regulatory regime.

Table 4 The Twelve Key Financial Standards of the FSF in 2000[25]

Standards	Standard-Setting bodies
Macroeconomic fundamentals	
Code of Good Practices on Transparency in Monetary and Financial Policies (1999)	IMF
Code of Good Practices on Fiscal Transparency (1998)	IMF
Special Data Dissemination Standard (1996) and General Data Dissemination System (1997)	IMF
Institutional and Market Infrastructure	
Principles of Corporate Governance (1999)	OECD
International Accounting Standards	IASC
International Standards on Auditing	IFAC
Core Principles for Systemically Important Payment Systems (1999, finalised in 2001)	CPSS
Principles and Guidelines on Effective Insolvency Systems (finalised in 2001)	World Bank
The Forty Recommendations against money laundering (1990, revised in 1996) [followed by 9 Special Recommendations against terrorist financing (2001)]	FATF
Financial Regulation and Supervision	
Core Principles for Effective Banking Supervision (1997)	BCBS
Objectives and Principles of Securities Regulation (1998)	IOSCO
Insurance Core Principles (1997)	IAIS

C. Global Rules: The Basel II Framework

In June 1999, the BCBS issued a proposal of almost 300 pages – replacing the 30 pages of the previous 1988 Basel Accord – with more uniform standards for banking regulation. The aim was to address the challenges in the globalisation of finance. Global finance created opportunities for banks to diversify their risks, invent innovative financial instruments such as securitisation of loans and financial derivatives, and, together with the progress in technology, develop ever more complex models to manage their risks. Global banks had also emerged, in the form of banking groups with establishments in several jurisdictions. These developments, which had been promoted by the liberalising framework of the 1988 Accord, went well beyond the reach of its basic rules. The Accord did not take into account the increasing complexity of the risks of banking activities or

[25] See FSF Report of the Follow-Up Group on Incentives to Foster Implementation of Standards (2000), at www.fsb.org/wp-content/uploads/r_0009.pdf. In 2020, the list of the key standards remains largely the same, with the addition of standards on deposit insurance and resolution regimes. See the current list maintained by the FSB at www.fsb.org/what-we-do/about-the-compendium-of-standards/key_standards.

the supervision of a banking group as a whole, thus not fulfilling its objective of requiring banks to set aside sufficient capital to cope with the risks of their transactions. After several consultation rounds, the so-called Basel II Framework was agreed in 2004.[26]

Like the 1988 Accord, the Basel II Framework aimed at the stability of the international banking system, while also setting a level playing-field for competition among banks. These objectives were pursued by a 'three-pillar concept'. Pillar 1 included minimum capital requirements for the major sources of banking risk, namely credit risk, market risk and operational risk. Banks could calculate the degree of their credit risk on the basis of their internal rating models. Pillar 2 corresponded to the review process by supervisors to ensure that banks have adequate capital and manage the whole range of risks, such as liquidity risk, reputational risk or legal risk. Pillar 3 promoted market discipline by setting disclosure requirements to enable market participants to assess and price adequately the risk of a bank.[27]

Furthermore, the Basel II Framework expanded the extra-territorial scope of home-country control to the whole banking group, comprising either subsidiaries or branches, thus not only foreign branches as in the 1975 Basel Concordat. The authority of the home-country would exercise, for the first time, competences over legal entities incorporated in foreign jurisdictions, such as the approval of internal models for the calculation of credit risk. This was in order to reinforce, and also simplify, the supervision of banking groups with operations in multiple jurisdictions. In turn, this would promote larger banking groups.[28]

The Basel II Framework marked a significant change in global standard-setting design and process, very much in line with the 'new governance' approaches. First, the Pillar 2 of Basel II aimed at integrating into regulation the self-assessment by a bank of its own risks and the appropriate capital to cover such risks. Given the complexity of such risks, the concept was that the banks were in the best position to calculate their own capital needs. In turn, Pillar 3 aimed at integrating the market's assessment of such risks, so that the banks had incentives to set aside sufficient capital to cover the risks in order to avoid high funding costs. Therefore, banking regulation under Basel II relied on the internal knowledge of banks and the monitoring by markets, rather than on the traditional 'command and control' approach.[29]

Second, it was a principles-based framework for the regulation of banks, which went beyond the 'minimum harmonisation' of the 1988 Basel Accord. It required an overhaul of the national laws and regulations, as well as of enforcement practices. Moreover, the Basel II rules aimed at being implemented globally for all countries and all banks. While the 1988 Accord addressed potential coordination failures in the regulation of international banks by the G-10, Basel II was an all-encompassing framework providing a uniform regulation for both domestic and international banks.

[26] See BCBS, International Convergence of Capital Measurement and Capital Standards: A Revised Framework (2004), at www.bis.org/publ/bcbs107a.pdf.

[27] This description of the main concepts underlying the Basel II Framework is drawn from BCBS, International Convergence of Capital Measurement and Capital Standards: A Revised Framework. For an academic analysis, see H Benink, J Danielsson and C Goodhart, *The future of banking regulation: the Basel II Accord* (London, Wiley, 2009).

[28] See BCBS, International Convergence of Capital Measurement and Capital Standards: A Revised Framework (n 26).

[29] For a description of the Basel II framework, see HM Schooner and MW Taylor, *Global Bank Regulation: Principles and Policies* (London, Elsevier, 2010).

Third, for the first time, the process for the design of the standards involved an extensive global consultation process. The design of the Basel II rules also relied on a cost-benefit analysis, known as Quantitative Impact Studies (QIS), to assess whether they would meet their objectives with regard to the capture or risks. This inclusive global design process aimed at enhancing the acceptability of Basel II worldwide.[30]

Overall, Basel II promoted the expansion of global banking, in particular of large banking groups, by significantly harmonising banking regulation, relying on internal assessments of risks by banks, and expanding the scope of home-country control.[31]

D. The Multilevel Global Governance System

By the end of the century, a multilevel global governance system for finance was in place. It comprised global standard-setting bodies for all major areas of finance, the FSF, governance standards as framework principles, rules in the form of regulatory standards issued after global public consultation, and a global implementation and enforcement process. All these components were very much in line with the 'new governance' approaches to public policy.[32]

As analysed above, the standard-setting bodies started by issuing global governance standards in the form of 'principles', which set out the minimum requirements for a sound regulatory framework for each financial sector. These 'principles' were codified by the FSF and represented the minimum layer of global governance among national jurisdictions. This, in turn, provided the conditions for the incorporation into national jurisdictions of more developed and detailed regulatory standards, such as the Basel II framework.

The standard-setting bodies then developed 'methodologies' with detailed criteria and requirements for the implementation of the global governance standards by national jurisdictions. Such 'methodologies' were subsequently used by the standard-setting bodies to assess whether the standards had been implemented. In case of non-compliance, there were a number of enforcement instruments. These included peer pressure among jurisdictions, the controversial 'name and shame' lists of non-compliant jurisdictions, and even counter-measures, such as embargoes of institutions originating in such jurisdictions.[33]

[30] See BCBS, Quantitative Impact Studies: QIS 2 and QIS 2.5 history (2001), at www.bis.org/bcbs/qis/qishist.htm.

[31] On the international financial architecture on this period, before the financial crisis, see EB Kapstein, 'Architects of Stability? International Cooperation Among Financial Supervisors' (2006) 199 *BIS Working Papers*.

[32] Almost at the same time as Basel, the US Congress enacted on 12 November 1999 the Gramm–Leach–Bliley Act, which also promoted the expansion of banks by removing the prohibition of the 1933 Glass–Steagall Act that a bank could combine investment banking and commercial banking. Financial Services Modernization Act of 1999, Pub.L. 106–102, 113 Stat. 1338, enacted on 12 November 1999.

[33] See, eg, BCBS, The Core Principles Methodology (1999), at www.bis.org/publ/bcbs61.htm. The first 'name and shame list' was issued in June 2000 by the FATF regarding the Non-Cooperative Countries and Territories (NCCT) in the international fight against money laundering, which included 23 jurisdictions subject to increased scrutiny and the target of counter-measures by the FATF members. See FATF, Annual Report 1999-2000 (2000), at www.fatf-gafi.org/media/fatf/documents/reports/1999%202000%20ENG.pdf.

After the Latin American and Asian financial crises of 1995 and 1997, there was a push for the implementation of standards at the global level, which accelerated towards the end of the 1990s. In 1999, the IMF and World Bank launched their 'standards and codes initiative', which aimed at ensuring financial stability through the dissemination of global standards. The IMF and the World Bank started to assess the compliance with the above '12 key financial standards' as part of their regular Financial Sector Assessment Program (FSAP) of each national jurisdiction. They thus started acting as the global enforcers of standards by certifying their implementation and including them in the conditionality of IMF programmes and within the scope of the World Bank's technical assistance.[34]

The multilevel governance system provided, therefore, a structured approach to global standard-setting and implementation by national jurisdictions. The ultimate aim was to address the scope for financial and systemic risks from under-regulated jurisdictions. At the same time, it also promoted the globalisation of finance by requiring all jurisdictions to incorporate the same global governance and regulatory standards, thus as a consequence of the integration of their national markets into global finance.[35]

Table 5 The Multilevel Global Governance of Finance by the End of the Twentieth Century

	G7 Finance Ministers and Central Bank Governors
Function	Political guidance
	Financial Stability Forum
Function	Policy guidance for standard-setting
	Standard-Setting Bodies (BCBS, IOSCO, IAIS, …)
Function	Issuance of standards and methodologies
	Global Governance Standards (Twelve Key Financial Standards)
Function	Minimum institutional framework of national jurisdictions
	Global Regulatory Standards (Basel III, …)
Function	Global regulation of finance
	National Jurisdictions
Function	Consistent implementation of global standards in line with methodologies
	Standard-Setting Bodies (BCBS, IOSCO, IAIS, …)
Function	Assessment of implementation of global standards and enforcement via peer pressure, name and shame, counter-measures.
	IMF and World Bank
Function	Assessment of implementation of global standards and enforcement via programme conditionality and technical assistance.

[34] The governance of global finance appeared as a model for the concept of global administrative law, which started to be developed in the early 2000s, see MS Barr and GP Miller, 'Global Administrative Law: The View from Basel' (2006) 17 *European Journal of International Law* 15. On the concept of global administrative law, see KH Ladeur, 'The emergence of Global administrative law and transnational regulation' (2012) 3 *Transnational legal theory* 243.

[35] On the emergence of the global governance of finance, see PG Teixeira, 'Public Governance and the Co-operative Law of Transnational Markets: The Case of Financial Regulation' in Karl-Heinz Ladeur (ed) *Public Governance in the Age of Globalization* (Aldershot, Ashgate, 2004) 305–335.

IV. The Economic and Monetary Union

A. The Institutional Framework

The SEA and the objective to complete the single market by 1992 provided the starting point for the setting-up of the Delors Committee by the Hannover European Council of June 1988, and the resulting report issued in 17 April 1989.

The main premise of the Delors Report was that the development of the single market would require close co-ordination of economic policies between Member States. The single market programme would remove the obstacles to the full freedoms of movement of capital, goods and services. It would increase integration but it would result over time in increasing constraints in the conduct of national economic policies. In turn, this would hinder economic development in the Community and undermine the single market. It was thus the same reasoning as originally in the Spaak Report, that economic integration contradicts national economic policies. This contradiction was described by Tommaso Padoa-Schioppa, one of the rapporteurs of the Delors Report, as an 'inconsistent quartet': the impossibility of maintaining simultaneously in the Community: (i) free trade; (ii) full capital movement; (iii) fixed or managed exchange rates; and (iv) independent national monetary policies. Freedom of trade with capital mobility requires exchange rate arrangements between Member States, which cannot be kept permanent with independent national monetary policies.[36]

The institutional framework of Economic and Monetary Union (EMU) comprised, therefore, three components. The first was the single market on the basis of the SEA. The second was monetary union. It involved the conduct of a single monetary policy by a European institution as an exclusive competence. This led to the creation of the ECB and the European System of Central Banks. The third component was the economic union through the coordination of economic policies, notably fiscal and budgetary policies.

The main objective of this third component was ensuring fiscal and budgetary discipline, in order to preserve monetary stability and avoid macroeconomic imbalances, without transferring economic policy to the European level. The set of rules and procedures for this purpose included upper limits on budget deficits by individual Member States. These limits were defined in the 1997 Stability and Growth Pact (SGP), which provided that budget deficits could not exceed 3 per cent of GDP and the public debt could not exceed 60 per cent of GDP. Compliance with these rules was based on monitoring and the application of 'preventive' and 'corrective' procedures by the Commission and the Council.

Other rules for ensuring fiscal and budgetary discipline included the prohibition of monetary financing of governments by central banks, under Article 123 TFEU, and

[36] European Commission, Report on Economic and Monetary Union in the European Community, Committee for the Study of Economic and Monetary Union, (Delors Report) (1988). On the interpretation of the report, see T Padoa-Schioppa, *L'Europa verso l'unione monetaria: Dallo Sme al trattato di Maastricht* (Turin, Einaudi, 1992) at 116–120 and 169–184; 'The Genesis of EMU: A Retrospective View' (1996) *96/40 Jean Monnet Chair Paper RSC, European University Institute*, at 2–3; as well as H James, *Making the European Monetary Union* (Cambridge MA, The Belknap Press of Harvard University Press, 2012) at 236–264.

the no-bail out clause of Article 125 of the TFEU. According to the no-bail out clause, neither the Community nor Member States can be liable or assume the commitments of other Member States. Fiscal liabilities cannot be financed by the central bank or mutualised with the Community or other Member States. This would provide a constraining framework combining both self-discipline and market discipline: Member States would promote sound fiscal policies in accordance with the rule-based framework, while a deviation from such policies would be reflected in higher interest rates of public debt in financial markets.[37]

B. The ECB as the First Independent Regulatory Authority

The framework of the EMU led to a new regulatory system in the Community legal order. The Treaty conferred exclusive central banking competences in the Community to the European System of Central Banks (ESCB), comprising the ECB with its own legal personality and the national central banks (NCBs) of the participating Member States.[38]

These competences, notably the conduct of the monetary policy of the Community, would be exercised on the basis of two legal and institutional innovations.[39]

First, the central banking competences were entrusted by the Treaty to a new type of institutional structure, the ESCB: a system of central banks, including both a European institution and national authorities. The decisions are taken by the decision-making bodies of the ECB: the Governing Council and the Executive Board. The implementation of decisions is carried out by the whole ESCB, since the ECB is obliged to have recourse to the NCBs to carry out operations which form part of the tasks of the ESCB. This provided NCBs with a dual institutional nature as both national authorities, with their own legal personality and tasks, and Community authorities when implementing

[37] On the origins of the monetary financing prohibition and no bail-out principle, see MK Brunnermeier, H James and JP Landau, *The Euro and the Battle of Ideas* (Princeton, Princeton University Press, 2016) 97–100. On the rationale and assumptions underlying economic governance, see F Amtenbrink and Jakob de Haan, 'Economic Governance in the European Union: Fiscal Discipline Versus Flexibility' (2003) 40 *CML Rev* 1075; and K Tuori and K Tuori, *The Eurozone Crisis: A Constitutional Analysis* (Cambridge, Cambridge University Press, 2014) 41–57.

[38] Arts 129(2), TFEU and 9.1 of the Statute of the ESCB and the ECB (Protocol No 4 on the Statute of the European System of Central Banks and of the ECB [2016] OJ C202/230). The Treaty of Lisbon clarified the status of the ECB by elevating it to the level of 'institution' under Art 13, TEU. See the Judgment of the Court of 10 July 2003, *Commission v ECB*, C-11/00, EU:C:2003:395, para 135, where the Court concluded that the ECB's 'independence does not have the consequence of separating it entirely from the Community and exempting it from every rule of Community law'. See also Opinion of AG Jacobs delivered on 3 October 2002, C-11/00, EU:C:2002:556, para 60.

[39] The single monetary policy is carried out through the means foreseen under Arts 17 to 23 of the Statute of the ESCB and ECB, which include opening accounts, conducting open market and credit operations, imposing minimum reserves requirements on credit institutions, and conducting foreign exchange transactions. The competence to issue banknotes in the euro area is attributed only to the ECB, rather than the ESCB. The other basic tasks include conducting foreign-exchange operations; to hold and manage the official foreign reserves of the euro area countries; and to promote the smooth operation of payment systems. The ancillary competences relate to the collection of statistical information either from national authorities or directly from economic agents, and to the contribution to national policies relating to the prudential supervision of credit institutions and the stability of the financial system (Arts 127(5), TFEU and 3.3 of the ESCB and ECB Statute).

the ESCB tasks under the instructions of the ECB. It also implied that the NCBs became involved in the decision-making process of the ESCB through internal committees and through their respective governors as members of the Governing Council, without prejudice to the governors acting in their personal capacity under the principle of independence. The ESCB thus combined the exclusive Community competences of a European institution with the involvement of national authorities in the decision-making and implementation processes.[40]

Second, the ECB was entrusted with independent regulatory powers, including the ability to directly impose sanctions for the enforcement of such powers. It was the first time in Community law that a European institution could exercise such regulatory powers. The ECB may make regulations to implement the tasks entrusted to the ESCB, namely the definition and implementation of monetary policy, minimum reserves requirements on credit institutions, and efficient and sound clearing and payment systems. The ECB regulations, like all European regulations, have general application, are binding in their entirety, and directly applicable in all Member States. However, they are subject to a 'necessity test', since they may only be issued 'to the extent necessary' to implement the tasks of the ESCB.[41]

The regulatory powers of the ECB were strengthened by powers of direct enforcement through sanctions. The effectiveness of the Community system of central banking was the rationale for the direct enforcement powers. It enabled central banking policies to be implemented consistently across Member States, irrespective of the location of undertakings. It also ensured that policy-making was credible, since it could be executed directly without any mediation by other authorities or courts. The range of regulatory sanctions available to the ECB correspond to those for the enforcement of competition law by the Commission, namely the imposition of fines and periodic penalty payments. These sanctions can be imposed on undertakings, including both natural and legal persons, for failure to comply with obligations under ECB regulations or decisions.[42]

[40] The decentralisation of the executive tasks is provided under Art 12.1 of the Statute of the ESCB and the ECB. In accordance with the ECB's rules of procedure, the Governing Council may establish internal ESCB committees in order to assist the decision-making bodies of the ECB, which is akin to 'internal comitology' within the ECB. See Art 9 of the Decision of the ECB of 19 February 2004 adopting the Rules of Procedure of the European Central Bank (ECB/2004/2), (2004/257/EC), L 080/33, 18.03.2004. On the role of national central banks as agents of the ECB, see R Smits, *The European Central Bank: Institutional Aspects* (The Hague, Kluwer Law International, 1997) 94; and C Zilioli and M Selmayr, *The Law of the European Central Bank* (Oxford, Hart Publishing, 2001) 79, on the characterisation of such role as being functionally disconnected from Member States.

[41] Art 132, TFEU and Art 34 of the Statute of the ESCB and the ECB. In addition to regulations, the ECB may issue decisions with binding instructions on its addressees, and guidelines. Guidelines are legal acts of the ESCB, referred to in Art 14.3 of the Statute of the ESCB and ECB, through which the ECB exercises regulatory power over the national central banks. This represented the 'ECB law', as argued by C Zilioli and M Selmayr, 'The European Central Bank: An Independent Specialised Organisation of Community Law' (2000) 37 *CML Rev* 591, 630. See also JV Louis 'A Legal and Institutional Approach for Building a Monetary Union' (1998) 35 *CML Rev* 33.

[42] Art 132(3), TFEU and Art 34.3 of the Statute of the ESCB and the ECB. The direct enforcement model, including the rules of infringement procedures, was not a novelty in the Community legal system, since it existed in the field of competition policy. See JF Martin and PG Teixeira, 'The Imposition of Regulatory Sanctions by the European Central Bank' (2000) 25 *European Law Review* 56. Council Regulation No 2532/98, concerning the powers of the ECB to impose sanctions, has specified the limits and conditions under which

The independent regulatory and enforcement powers of the ECB reflected the degree of constitutionalisation of the central banking law of the Community, which had been crystallised in the Treaty like no other set of competences. This was in order to safeguard the independence of the central banking competences from political institutions. The principle of independence is a constitutional principle that extends to both the ECB and to the NCBs of the ESCB for the performance of their tasks: when exercising central banking powers and carrying out the related tasks and duties, neither the ECB, nor a NCB, nor any member of their decision-making bodies shall seek or take instructions from Community institutions or bodies, from any government of a Member State or from any other body.[43]

The introduction of central banking as an exclusive European competence led to a new regulatory model, which was centred on the ECB as the first independent regulatory authority in Community law. This model combined the transfer of decision-making powers to the European level with the preservation of executive powers of national authorities, which act on behalf of the Community within their respective national jurisdictions. This enabled European and national authorities, and their respective laws, to be combined into a single regulatory system, which would later be at the heart of the Banking Union.[44]

C. A Monetary Union without a Banking Union

The EMU framework did not include financial regulation and supervision as one of its components. This was despite the fact that financial integration was among the main reasons, consequences and indeed requirements for a Monetary Union. The EMU would

these regulatory sanctions may be imposed (Council Regulation (EC) No 2532/98 of 23 November 1998 concerning the powers of the ECB to impose sanctions, [1998] OJ L318/4). The ECB Regulation No 2157/99, on the powers of the ECB to impose sanctions, has further specified certain procedural arrangements (ECB Regulation (EC) No 2157/1999 of 23 September 1999 on the powers of the ECB to impose sanctions (ECB/1999/4), [1999] OJ L264/21.

[43] Art 130, TFEU and Art 7 of the Statute of the ESCB and the ECB. This constitutional protection of the independence of the ECB and NCBs has been considered by the Court as mainly relating to the protection of the pursuance of the functions entrusted to the ESCB. In accordance with the Court, Art 130, TFEU seeks, in essence, to shield the ECB from all political pressure in order to enable it effectively to pursue the objectives attributed to its tasks. See Judgment of the Court of 10 July 2003, *Commission v ECB*, C-11/00, EU:C:2003:395. On the principle of central banking independence, see C Zilioli 'Accountability and Independence: Irreconcilable Values or Complementary Instruments for Democracy? The Specific Case of the European Central Bank' in G Vandersanden (ed) *Mélanges en hommage à Jean-Victor Louis* (Bruxelles, Editions de l'Universite de Bruxelles, 2003) 395–422.

[44] See the Judgment of the Court of 26 February 2019, *Rimšēvičs v Latvia*, C-202/18, EU:C:2019:139, para 48, where the Court annulled directly national measures for the first time ever in European law, which in the case at stake were preventing the member of a decision-making body of a European institution from performing its duties. The Court further stated at para 69, that 'The ESCB represents a novel legal construct in EU law which brings together national institutions, namely the national central banks, and an EU institution, namely the ECB, and causes them to cooperate closely with each other, and within which a different structure and a less marked distinction between the EU legal order and national legal orders prevails.' For an analysis of this case, see R Smits, 'A National Measure Annulled by the European Court of Justice, or: High-level Judicial Protection for Independent Central Bankers' (2020) 16 *European Constitutional Law Review* 1.

lead to standardisation and transparency in pricing mechanisms in financial markets, equalisation of costs of capital, elimination of exchange rate risk, and unification of bank refinancing by the liquidity provided by the ECB. Moreover, the transmission of monetary policy, as well as financial stability, required an integrated and well-functioning single financial market.[45]

However, in the debate leading to the drafting of the EMU provisions in the Maastricht Treaty, several arguments were used against the transfer of regulatory and supervisory competences in the banking sector to the ECB. It was argued that the definition of banking policies was a strategic task linked to the core of national sovereignty. A banking crisis could give rise to fiscal liabilities and therefore it would fall under the prerogative of national governments and parliaments. It was also argued, most prominently by the Bundesbank, that entrusting supervisory tasks to the ECB could lead to moral hazard in the conduct of monetary policy, namely the possibility that the central bank would be prone to support the banking system in order to prevent a supervisory failure. As a result, the policies and rules for preventing and managing financial crises in the Monetary Union remained at the national level within the single market framework of the Treaty. The ECB was only entrusted with a general task to contribute to financial stability and with advisory functions with regard to European and national laws related to financial stability. The conduct of banking supervision tasks by the ECB remained a possibility under a clause of the Treaty upon a unanimous decision by the Council, and also the assent of the Parliament until the Lisbon Treaty abolished this latter requirement.[46]

Therefore, out of the three components of the EMU – single market, economic union, and monetary union – only the third represented a transfer of competences to the European level, while the others remained subject to soft governance arrangements, which were loosely enforced. This eventually contributed to the rise of the financial and economic imbalances that exacerbated the financial and public debt crisis that started in 2007.[47]

[45] On the fact that the need for banking supervision and a crisis management capacity were overlooked in the design of the Monetary Union, see B Eichengreen, 'European Monetary Integration with Benefit of Hindsight' (2012) 50 *Journal of Common Market Studies* 123.

[46] On the debate regarding the attribution of banking supervision tasks to the ECB, see H James, *Making the European Monetary Union*, (n 36) 313–317; and also K Tuori and K Tuori, *The Eurozone Crisis*, (n 37) 54–56.

[47] The loose enforcement of economic governance rules was first made evident in 2002 when the Council rejected the recommendations of the Commission to issue early warnings to Germany and Portugal, taking into account the commitments by these Member States to take corrective measures, in accordance with ECOFIN Council conclusions of 12 February 2002. The most prominent case came in 2003, when the Council failed to adopt a decision by a qualified majority voting to issue notices against France and Germany under the excessive deficit procedure, as recommended by the Commission. Following an appeal by the Commission, the Court stated that the Council could not replace a procedure with political conclusions, in the absence of an appropriate recommendation by the Commission. This led to the first reform of the Stability Growth Pact in 2005. See Commission recommendations of 18 November 2003 for Council decisions giving notice to Germany and France to take measures to correct their excessive deficits; ECOFIN Council conclusions of 25 November 2003; and Judgment of the Court of 13 July 2004, Case C-27/04, *Commission v Council (Stability and Growth Pact)*, EU:C:2004:436. For an analysis, see JV Louis, 'The Review of the Stability and Growth Pact' (2006) 43 *CML Rev* 85.

V. The 1999 Financial Services Action Plan

A. From Negative to Positive Integration

The Financial Services Action Plan (FSAP) was launched in May 1999 and provided the basis for a new Community policy on financial services following the introduction of the euro. It put forward 42 initiatives for harmonising by 2005 the national laws relating to the provision of financial services. The FSAP provided a structured regulatory programme – with a ranking in terms of priorities, objectives, actors, and timeframe – for most of the policy areas related to financial services. It aimed at fulfilling three strategic objectives. First, the completion of a single wholesale market for corporate issuers of capital, investors and financial intermediaries, and investment services providers. Second, the integration of retail markets on the basis of safeguarding consumers in cross-border transactions, such as the FIN-NET network launched in 2001 for out-of-court settlements in the financial field. Third, the enhancement of the regulatory framework for the supervision of banks, securities, insurance companies, and financial conglomerates. The FSAP also had the general objective of supporting the wider conditions for an optimal single financial market, such as addressing disparities in tax treatment and promoting an efficient and transparent corporate governance system.[48]

The FSAP corresponded to a shift from implementing the single passport concept on the basis of minimum harmonisation to an approach based on a wider harmonisation of national laws. The negative integration pursued in the previous period was not successful in dismantling the obstacles to the cross-border provision of financial services. The FSAP approach was the re-regulation of the single financial market through an extensive harmonisation of national laws for addressing such obstacles, and making effective the rights relating to the exercise of the single passport. In turn, it also implied that regulatory policies regarding the provision of financial services would be increasingly defined at the Community level, thus prevailing over the national regulatory frameworks. Therefore, the FSAP marked the move from negative integration to positive integration through the re-regulation of the single financial market by Community law.[49]

B. The Reform of European Financial Services Law

The FSAP operated an extensive reform of European financial services law through several strands of legal and institutional innovations.

The first innovation was a higher degree of harmonisation of national laws compared to the previous period. This included both an extension of the perimeter of European law and a deeper harmonisation in terms of detailed rules. It was reflected in the reform of

[48] European Commission, Financial Services: Implementing the framework for financial markets – Action Plan, COM (1999) 232 final.

[49] On the political factors for the financial services policy in the period of 1999–2004, see L Quaglia, 'The politics of financial services regulation and supervision reform in the European Union' (2007) 46 *European Journal of Political Research*, 269; and E Posner and N Véron, 'The EU and financial regulation: power without purpose?' (2010) 17 *Journal of European Public Policy* 400.

securities regulation by the 2004 Markets in Financial Instruments Directive (MiFID), which replaced the ISD of 1993. It aimed at developing a single European securities rulebook which would lead to a consistent enforcement of the national laws of host-countries to securities transactions, notably standards for consumer protection. This was required for the operation of the single passport in securities markets, where the host-countries remained competent for the application of conduct of business rules.[50]

In the banking sector, the Capital Requirements Directive of 2006 (CRD I) replaced the previous banking directives in order to transpose the Basel II Framework. This provided a body of comprehensive rules for the operation of credit institutions in the single financial market.[51]

The 2009 'Solvency II' Directive introduced a new regime for insurance undertakings, which also removed the obstacles to integration stemming from different national regulatory requirements, including for consumer protection.[52]

The second innovation introduced by the FSAP, which followed the Basel II Framework, was the extension of the home-country principle to financial groups with establishments in several Member States, as will be analysed in the next sections.

The third innovation was the introduction, for the first time in European financial services legislation, of requirements for the enforcement of European law by national authorities. This was particularly evident in the MiFID, which developed a European-wide enforcement system, based on mechanisms for cooperation between national authorities for the passporting procedure and for investigating and prosecuting breaches of the obligations laid out in the directive. In order to enable such enforcement system, the MiFiD also included requirements for institutional convergence, notably a common minimum set of powers that should be attributed to the national authorities. Similar institutional requirements were introduced by the Solvency II Directive. The aim was to achieve an equivalent intensity of enforcement across the single financial market.[53]

[50] Under the ISD, the investment services providers were required to comply with the different conduct of business rules across the host-Member States, which defeated the purpose of the single passport. The MiFID set out a comprehensive set of rules regarding matters under the jurisdiction of host-countries, namely on the conduct of business and trade execution rules required for investor protection, and on requirements that investment firms should meet for safeguarding market transparency and integrity. Directive 2004/39/EC of the European Parliament and of the Council of 21 April 2004 on markets in financial instruments amending Council Directives 85/611/EEC and 93/6/EEC and Directive 2000/12/EC of the European Parliament and of the Council and repealing Council Directive 93/22/EEC, [2004] OJ L145. On the transition from the ISD to the MiFID, see N Moloney, *EU Securities and Financial Markets Regulation* (Oxford, Oxford University Press, 2014) 327–335.

[51] The CRD III transposed the Basel II Framework in Europe and replaced the Codified Banking Directive (2000/12/EC) and the Capital Adequacy Directive (93/6/EEC). It comprised two instruments: Directive 2006/48/EC of the European Parliament and of the Council of 14 June 2006 relating to the taking up and pursuit of the business of credit institutions, and Directive 2006/49/EC of the European Parliament and of the Council of 14 June 2006 on the capital adequacy of investment firms and credit institutions.

[52] This reform was required to adapt EU insurance law, which was first designed in the mid-70s, to the broader range of insurance risks. While the previous directives only required insurance undertakings to hold capital against insurance risk, the Solvency II Directive required capital to also cover market risk, credit risk and operational risk. See Directive 2009/138/EC of the European Parliament and of the Council of 25 November 2009 on the taking-up and pursuit of the business of Insurance and Reinsurance (Solvency II), (recast), [2009] OJ L335/1.

[53] See Arts 5(1), 31 to 32, and 56 to 59 of MiFID on the passporting procedure. Art 50(2) of MiFID required national authorities to have a minimum set of enforcement powers, such as the ability to carry out on-site inspections, require telephone and data records, request the freezing or sequestration of assets, and adopt

The reform of EU financial services law also involved a first enlargement of the perimeter of European financial services law. It included measures in areas beyond the banking, insurance and securities sectors, such as the application of accounting standards, the supervision of financial conglomerates, the harmonisation of company law and the European Company Statute, the framework for anti-money laundering and terrorism financing, retail banking, the single payments market and clearing and settlement.[54]

Finally, the FSAP led to the codification of the scattered pieces of legislation into single legal acts, so as to provide as much as possible a uniform EU rulebook for the provision of financial services. It was also part of the Commission's 'Better Regulation' strategy to simplify the regulatory environment. The codification was made through a 'recasting' technique, which allowed simultaneously making amendments to previous directives, codifying the texts of previous directives, and repealing such directives.[55]

Taking these components of the FSAP together, it marked the shift from the 'minimum harmonisation' and 'regulatory competition' of the previous period, to the re-regulation of the single financial market as a whole. This involved the development of a single European source of law through more extensive harmonisation of financial services law, while relying on national enforcement through the extension of the home-country principle to financial groups, and on committees of national authorities to achieve a consistent enforcement. In other words, the FSAP aimed at centralising the source of the law of the single financial market, while decentralising its enforcement at national level. The workability of this approach required a governance framework, which was provided by the Lamfalussy proposals for the regulation and supervision of the single financial market.

C. The Post-FSAP: Better Regulation and *Peter Paul*

The FSAP was largely completed by mid-2004, with agreement reached on 93 per cent of the 42 initiatives. It was followed by a period of regulatory pause, without major new initiatives, up to the reaction to the financial crisis in 2008. This was the result, not only of the regulatory fatigue that the FSAP had created, but also the active promotion of the 'Better Regulation' approach in Community policies by the Barroso Commission, which started its first mandate later in the same year. It was considered that the completion of the FSAP and the Lamfalussy process had provided the single financial market with a complete governance framework, which did not require many more pieces of

measures to ensure that investment firms and regulated markets continue to comply with legal requirements. Similarly, Arts 30 and 34 of the Solvency II Directive, included, respectively, requirements of transparency and accountability of national authorities, and a minimum set of enforcement powers to ensure that undertakings comply with the obligations provided in the Directive. On MiFID, see N Moloney, *EU Securities and Financial Markets Regulation*, (n 50) 407–414.

[54] The initiatives for the integration of European market infrastructures were based on the so-called Giovannini Report, which identified the obstacles to such integration: European Commission, The Giovanni Report: Cross-border clearing and settlement arrangements in the EU, Economic Papers, 163 (2002).

[55] The 'recasting technique' is set out in the Inter-institutional Agreement of 28 November 2001 on a more structured use of the recasting technique for legal acts (2002/C 77/01).

regulation. The impact of the FSAP had to be allowed to materialise before any new legislative programme.[56]

The 'Better Regulation' approach emerged following the 2001 Commission's White Paper on Governance. It was presented as a means to increase competitiveness in the context of the 'Lisbon Strategy.' This also applied in the financial services field, as put forward in the 2005 Commission's White Paper on Financial Services Policy. It consisted of a strategy placing less emphasis on proposing new legislative measures and more on the transposition and enforcement of existing measures. This included improving the quality of regulation by holding open consultations on whether new regulation was required and preparing impact assessments of Commission proposals. It also involved monitoring and supporting the transposition of Community law, evaluating ex post the impact of rules, simplifying and codifying existing legal instruments, as well as hearing consumers.[57]

The regulatory pause in the post-FSAP period was in line with the spirit of the time of improving competitiveness through market liberalisation and less regulation, as encapsulated in the 2004–2006 debate regarding the 'Bolkestein' Directive on services in the internal market. It also reflected the emergence of the tension within the Treaty framework on the extent to which the expansion of market regulation could be justified by the objective of market integration. More specifically, whether the 'harmonisation clauses' of the Treaty, notably Article 114 of the TFEU, could provide the legal basis for the extensive re-regulation operated by the FSAP, which reduced the scope for divergence in national laws.[58]

This was the context of the 2004 *Peter Paul* case, where the Court was asked to decide on a preliminary ruling on whether the banking and deposit-guarantee Directives would provide direct rights to individuals for claiming compensation for damages resulting from defective banking supervision by national authorities. The Court took the restrictive interpretation that the harmonisation of national laws under the Treaty is limited to the extent necessary to achieve market integration. The Directives at stake introduced the minimum harmonisation of national laws for achieving the internal market in the field of credit institutions, namely for ensuring the functioning of the mutual recognition and home-country control principles. Individuals could not rely directly on their provisions for claiming compensation rights from supervisory authorities. This also

[56] The commitment to conclude the FSAP by mid-2004 was taken by the Lisbon European Council of 23/24 March 2000, and confirmed by the Brussels European Council of 20/21 March 2003. See European Commission, Financial Services: Turning the Corner, Preparing the challenge of the next phase of European capital market integration (2004).

[57] European Commission, Communication on 'European Governance: Better lawmaking,' COM (2002) 275 final; Implementing the Community Lisbon Programme: A strategy for the simplification of the regulatory environment, COM (2005) 535 final; and A Single market for 21st century Europe, COM (2007) 724 final; as well as White Paper on Financial Services Policy (2005–2010), COM (2005) 629 final. For an evaluation of the 'better regulation' strategy in the context of 'new governance', see A Alemanno, 'The Better Regulation Initiative at the Judicial Gate: A Trojan Horse within the Commission's Walls or the Way Forward?' (2009) 15 *European Law Journal* 382. See also S Weatherill, *The Internal Market as a Legal Concept*, (Oxford, Oxford University Press, 2017) 209–222, on the debate on minimum vs maximum harmonisation under Art 114, TFEU.

[58] The main legal concern with the Bolkestein Directive was applying the laws of the home-country of the service provider, which led to deregulation without re-regulation as argued by B de Witte, 'Setting the Scene: How did Services get to Bolkestein and Why?' (2007) 2007/20 *EUI Working Paper*. On the concerns at the time regarding the use of Art 114, TFEU as the legal basis for regulation, see N Moloney, 'New Frontiers in EC Capital Markets Law: from Market Construction to Market Regulation' (2003) 40 *CML Rev* 809, 833–ff.

implied a confirmation of the purely national nature of supervisory competences in the single financial market.[59]

The FSAP represented the first test of the boundaries of the Treaty for regulating directly the single financial market. The harmonisation of national laws went much beyond what was required to achieve market integration under minimum harmonisation. This created resistance by Member States to additional harmonisation measures which replaced their ability to regulate their domestic markets. This endured until the financial crisis in 2007–2008, which then prompted the move towards 'maximum harmonisation'.

Table 6 Key Measures of the FSAP (1999–2005)

Banking Directives	Capital requirements; Re-organisation and winding-up of credit institutions; Prudential supervision of electronic money institutions.
Insurance and occupational pensions Directives	Solvency II; Reinsurance supervision; Insurance mediation; Re-organisation and winding-up of insurance undertakings; Activities and supervision of institutions for occupational retirement provision.
Securities and investment funds Directives	Transparency obligations for securities; MiFID; Prospectus; Insider dealing and market manipulation; Distance marketing of consumer financial services; UCITS.
Financial conglomerates Directives	Supplementary supervision of credit institutions, insurance undertakings and investment firms in a financial conglomerate.
Payments, clearing and settlement Directives	Financial collateral arrangements; Settlement Finality Directive.
Accounting regulation Directive	Application of international accounting standards.
Company law Directives	Cross-border mergers; Cross-border transfer of the registered office of limited companies; Takeover bids; European Company Statute; Statutory audit of annual accounts and consolidated accounts.
Market integrity Directives	Prevention of the use of the financial system for the purpose of money laundering, including terrorist financing.
Taxation Directives	Taxation of savings income in the form of interest payments.

[59] Judgment of the Court of 12 October 2004, *Peter Paul*, C-222/02, EU:C:2004:606, para 36. For an analysis of the implications of this case for the issue of the liability of banking supervisors, see M Tison, 'Do not attack the watchdog! Banking supervisor's liability after Peter Paul' (2005) 42 *CML Rev* 639.

VI. The Multilevel Governance of the European Financial Market: The 'Lamfalussy Framework'

A. The Lamfalussy Report

The FSAP focused initially on securities markets, which was one of the less integrated sectors of the single financial market. The single passport had little expression due both to the lack of harmonisation of securities regulation and to divergent enforcement practices among Member States. This prompted the establishment of a 'Wise Men Committee' by the ECOFIN Council on 17 July 2000, under the chairmanship of Alexandre Lamfalussy. It was mandated to address the shortcomings in the regulation of the EU securities markets, focusing on the national transposition of Community directives and the enforcement of Community rules by national regulators. The Committee worked on the basis of public consultations and released its final report in March 2001.[60]

The diagnosis of the Lamfalussy report was that the Community method was not able to deliver a regulatory system for a single securities market. The co-decision procedure between the Council and the Parliament for the adoption of directives was overly cumbersome. The Commission was slow in delivering its proposals, the Council attempted to fit the features of as many as possible national laws into the draft legislation, and the reading of the proposals by the Parliament was a source of blockage. As a result, legislative proposals aimed at developing the single financial market had taken an average of two and a half years to be adopted, with extremes of 30 years for the European Company Statute and 15 years for the take-over bids Directive. This would prevent the FSAP from achieving its objectives. Moreover, the ambiguity and generality of the provisions arising from the co-decision procedure led to highly divergent interpretations, transposition and enforcement of Community law among Member States.[61]

The recommendations of the Lamfalussy Report comprised two elements. First, the expansion of the use of comitology procedures, in order to enable more flexible and detailed enactment of rules at the Community level. Second, the establishment of committees of national authorities, in order to provide technical advice to the Commission and support the convergence of regulatory practices in the implementation of Community law. This would enable delivering a regulatory system for the single securities market within the existing Community method. The new system would be implemented on a voluntary basis, without a specific legal instrument, by the main institutional players: Council, Parliament, Commission, national authorities and the

[60] Alexandre Lamfalussy was involved in the preparation of the Segré Report of 1966, a member of the Delors Committee, General Manager of the BIS, and the first President of the European Monetary Institute. On his contributions to European integration, see I Maes, 'A Lamfalussy: A Cassandra about Financial Stability' in K Dyson and I Maes (eds) *Architects of the Euro: Intellectuals in the Making of European Monetary Union* (Oxford, Oxford University Press, 2016) 233. EU Council, ECOFIN Council, Terms of reference for the Committee of Wise Men, 10491/00, ECOFIN 213 (2000); and A Lamfalussy, 'Initial report of the Committee of Wise Men' (2000) (on file with the author).

[61] See A Lamfalussy, 'Final Report of the Committee of Wise Men on the Regulation of European Securities Markets' (2001) (on file with the author), at 13–17.

financial services industry and investors. It would not involve any transfer of competences from the national to the Community level, thus not requiring any Treaty change. It would be established on an experimental basis until 2004.

The framework proposed by Lamfalussy was a 'four-level approach' – along the lines of a multilevel governance system – to the regulation and supervision of the single financial market. At Level 1, the adoption of Community legislation under the co-decision procedure by the Council and the Parliament would be limited to the definition of 'framework principles' for the harmonisation of national laws. Community directives, and where possible regulations, would refrain from covering regulatory details. At Level 2, the Commission would issue implementing measures under a comitology procedure complementing or amending the Level 1 legislation, which would include wide delegation clauses to the Commission. These Level 2 acts would provide the regulatory details for the implementation of the Level 1 framework principles. The Commission would prepare the Level 2 acts on the basis of the technical advice provided by a committee of national supervisors. At Level 3, national supervisors would establish committees, independent from the Commission, which would support the convergence of national enforcement practices of both Level 1 and Level 2 acts. Lastly, at Level 4, the monitoring of the compliance of Community law by Member States would be reinforced, also through reporting mechanisms.

The functioning of the Lamfalussy framework would rely on the 'better regulation' approach. For example, the proceedings of the comitology procedures at Level 2 would be published, and the technical advice to the Commission and the standards elaborated by the Level 3 committees would be subject to public consultation.[62]

The Lamfalussy framework for the regulation and supervision of securities markets was endorsed by the European Council in Stockholm on 23 and 24 March 2001. Later, the ECOFIN Council of 3 December 2002 decided to extend it to the banking, insurance and pensions sectors by establishing new sectoral committees at Level 2 and Level 3. This extension only became effective in April 2005, with the delay due to the misgivings of the Parliament in granting wide comitology powers to the Commission.[63]

By mid-2005, a multilevel governance system for the single financial market was in place, comprising several new committees at various levels: the regulatory level

[62] See A Lamfalussy, 'Final Report of the Committee of Wise Men on the Regulation of European Securities Markets' at 19–40, and N Moloney, 'The Lamfalussy Legislative Model: A New Era for the EC Securities And Investment Services Regime' (2003) 52 *International Comparative Law Quarterly* 509.

[63] European Council, Resolution of the European Council on more effective securities market regulation in the European Union, Stockholm, 23 March 2001. The Commission followed up with the establishment of the European Securities Committee and the Committee of European Securities Regulators, which replaced the previous Forum of European Securities Commissions (FESCO) set-up in 1997. See Commission Decision 2001/528/EC of 6 June 2001 establishing the European Securities Committee, [2001] OJ L191/45–46, and Commission Decision 2001/527/EC of 6 June 2001 establishing the Committee of European Securities Regulators, [2001] OJ L191/43–44. The extension of the Lamfalussy framework to all financial sectors was made on the basis of a legislative package comprising the Directive 2005/1/EC of the European Parliament and the Council of 9 March 2005, amending Council Directives 73/239/EEC, 85/611/EEC, 91/675/EEC, 92/49/EEC and 93/6/EEC and Directives 94/19/EC, 98/78/EC, 2000/12/EC, 2001/34/EC, 2002/83/EC and 2002/87/EC in order to establish a new organisational structure for financial services committees, [2005] OJ L79/9–17.

for comitology procedures, the supervisory level for the convergence of enforcement practices, and the policy-making level for providing advice on strategic issues to the Council, namely with the Economic and Financial Committee and its sub-structure, the Financial Services Committee.[64]

Table 7 The Committees of the Single Financial Market by 2005

	Banking	**Insurance and Occupational Pensions**	**Securities**	**Financial conglomerates**
Regulatory Committees (Level 2)	European Banking Committee (EBC)	European Insurance and Occupational Pensions Committee (EIOPC)	European Securities Committee (ESC)	Financial Conglomerates Committee (FCC)
Committees of Supervisors (Level 3)	Committee of European Banking Supervisors (CEBS) (London)	Committee of European Insurance and Occupational Pension Supervisors (CEIOPS) (Frankfurt)	Committee of European Securities Regulators (CESR) (Paris)	Joint Committee on Financial Conglomerates (comprising CEBS, CEIOPS and CESR)
Policy-making Committees (Finance Ministries)	– Economic and Financial Committee (also in the bi-annual format of a 'Financial Stability Table') – Financial Services Committee (replacing the Financial Services Policy Group)			

B. Creating Rules: The Expansion of Comitology Procedures

The underlying concept of the Lamfalussy framework was to replicate at the Community level the distinction between law-making and rule-making. Community legislation often intruded into matters of detail that better suited the regulatory level, while leaving wide scope to national discretion in regulatory matters. The single financial market would require a framework with a coherent distinction between law and regulation to address the complexity and fast pace of finance. This would be achieved by distinguishing between Level 1 and Level 2 acts, which would enable the Commission to develop a rule-making function through implementing measures subject to comitology procedures. The Commission would then become the regulator of the single financial market.

The distinction between law and regulation was however not straightforward in the Community context. The principle of separation of powers does not correspond to a

[64] The Economic and Financial Committee was established by the Treaty under Art 134, TFEU, with the main task of contributing to the preparation of the work of the Council on economic policy.

strict separation between the legislative and the executive. The Commission has the monopoly of the legislative initiative, while executive functions may also be performed by the Council, with Member States having responsibility for the bulk of the implementation of Community policies. The distinction in Community law between essential legislation, to be adopted by the Council and the Parliament, and implementing legislation, that may be delegated to the Commission, is also hard to define. It ultimately depends on the political will of the Council and the Parliament to delegate implementing measures to the Commission. And the role of the Commission in adopting implementing measures is not equivalent to the rule-making role of national regulators, given the differences in mandate, specialisation and expertise.[65]

The implications for the Community's institutional balance of the rule-making role of the Commission led both the Council and the Parliament to set conditions for the expanded use of implementing measures under comitology procedures.

The Council was concerned that the voting rules under the regulatory comitology procedure would enable the Commission to adopt measures against national interests without the assent or veto by the Member States which would be most affected. In order to address such concern, the Commission took the commitment – known as the 'aerosol clause' – that it would avoid going against predominant views within the Council on implementing measures deemed particularly sensitive.[66]

The concern of the Parliament was that comitology procedures could impinge on its prerogatives under the co-decision procedure. The Parliament could only adopt a non-binding resolution stating that implementing measures would go beyond the enabling legislation, while the Council could impose requirements on the Commission and exercise directly implementing powers, the so-called 'call-back clause'.[67]

[65] On the difficulties in distinguishing the scope of implementing measures, see Y Avgerinos, 'Essential and Non-essential Measures: Delegation of Powers in EU Securities Regulation' (2002) 8 *European Law Journal* 269. The Court has also provided little clarification in this respect. In *Köster*, the Court upheld the constitutional validity of the comitology system and distinguished between the basic elements of law, which should be defined by Council, and detailed measures.

[66] In accordance with the regulatory comitology procedure, the implementing measures envisaged by the Commission can only be blocked if there is no qualified majority in the regulatory committee in favour of such measures and subsequently a qualified majority in Council against them. See Art 5 of Council Decision 1999/468/EC of 28 June 1999 laying down the procedures for the exercise of implementing powers conferred on the Commission [1999] OJ L184/23–26. The 'aerosol' method of blocking implementing rules was used for the first time in the 1970s in legislation on chlorofluorocarbon emissions from spray cans. See Resolution of the European Council on more effective securities market regulation in the European Union, para 5.

[67] Comitology has been seen historically by the Parliament as a threat to the institutional balance of powers, as it risks merging legislative and administrative activities into one procedure, thus limiting the possibility of democratic control. As a result of the Parliament's concerns, there were several interinstitutional agreements along the years according to which the Commission committed to keep the Parliament informed of the comitology procedures. Such agreements included the '*Plumb-Delors*' (on forwarding to the Parliament acts of a legislative nature), '*Modus Vivendi*' (on the Council and the Commission consulting the Parliament and taking due account of its opinion), and 'Samland-Williamsen' (on increasing the transparency of management and regulatory committees). On 28 June 1999, the Council adopted a new Comitology Decision, which set out criteria for the choice of comitology procedures, simplified the procedures, increased the involvement of the Parliament, and enhanced their transparency: Council Decision of 28 June 1999 laying down the procedures for the exercise of implementing powers conferred on the Commission [1999] OJ L184/23–26. The Commission's White Paper on Governance then stated that both the Council and the Parliament should control in an equal fashion the exercise of executive functions by the Commission. This was then reflected in the draft Constitutional Treaty and later the Lisbon Treaty.

In order to set-up the Lamfalussy framework, the Council, the Parliament, and the Commission then agreed on a 'sunset clause': the duration of implementing powers conferred on the Commission would be limited to four years from the entry into force of a directive, unless it was prolonged by agreement between the Parliament and the Council, or unless the Treaty was revised accordingly. The Parliament requested a commitment from the Commission that it would ensure a similar treatment to that accorded to the Council.[68]

In 2009, the entry into force of the Lisbon Treaty provided the Parliament with the same institutional position as the Council vis-à-vis the exercise of delegated powers by the Commission. Similar to the provisions envisaged in the European Constitution, Article 290 of the TFEU provides that either the Parliament or the Council may decide to revoke the delegation, and that the delegated act may enter into force only if no objection has been expressed by the Parliament or the Council. The prerogatives of the Council and the Parliament are also safeguarded where the Commission is provided with powers to enact under Article 291 of the TFEU 'implementing acts' for the uniform implementation of European law.[69]

The Lamfalussy framework thus led to a new generation of comitology procedures. It introduced the innovation of involving national authorities in comitology by subjecting the delegated powers of the Commission to the technical advice of the Level 3 committees. In turn, the representatives of Member States in the Level 2 committees ensured that the implementing measures reflected such technical advice. The Lamfalussy framework thus fused together the national regulatory processes with the Community legislative process regarding the delegated powers of the Commission. This aimed at expanding the rule-making process in the single financial market by increasing the delegated powers of the Commission and reducing the potential for regulatory divergence at national level.[70]

[68] The President of the Commission made a solemn declaration on 5 February 2002: (i) accepting the introduction of 'sunset clauses' on financial services directives; (ii) giving the Parliament three months to provide an opinion on draft implementing measures, and agreeing to the 'aerosol clause'; (iii) ensuring transparency of comitology procedures and public consultation on implementing measures; (iv) agreeing to a consultative group of market participants for CESR; (v) committing to take into utmost consideration the opinions of the Parliament and any resolution about implementing measures considered to exceed the scope of implementing powers. See Romano Prodi, Implementation of financial services legislation in the context of the Lamfalussy Report, Intervention at the Parliament's plenary session, 5 February 2002.

[69] The draft European Constitution would have established a system of delegating powers to the Commission under Art I-36 (Delegated European Regulations). Following the failure of its ratification process with the French and Dutch referenda of 2005, the Parliament and the Council reached an agreement in 2006 on modifications to the Comitology Decision to avoid the sunset clauses of the Lamfalussy Directives, with the new 'regulatory procedure with scrutiny'. See Council Decision of 17 July 2006 amending Decision 1999/468/EC laying down the procedures for the exercise of implementing powers conferred on the Commission, [2006] OJ L200/11. Under the Lisbon Treaty, this Decision was replaced by Regulation (EU) No 182/2011 of the European Parliament and of the Council of 16 February 2011 laying down the rules and general principles concerning mechanisms for control by Member States of the Commission's exercise of implementing powers, [2011] OJ L55/13. For an analysis of Arts 290 and 291, TFEU, see J Mendes, 'Delegated and implementing rule making: proceduralisation and constitutional design' (2013) 19 *European Law Journal* 22; and JC Piris, *The Lisbon Treaty: A Legal and Political Analysis* (Cambridge, Cambridge University Press, 2010) 92–103.

[70] The use of implementing measures was previously limited to the technical updating of legislation. For example, close to a third of the MiFID provisions included implementing measures (20 out of 73 Articles), while the previous ISD contained few provisions with implementing measures, which were never used. See JP Casey, and K Lannoo, 'The MiFID implementing measures: excessive detail or level-playing field?' (2006) 1 *ECMI Policy Brief*.

Table 8 The Comitology Procedures under the Lamfalussy Framework

	Decision-making level	Procedural steps
1	**Supranational**	Legislation is adopted by the Council and the Parliament with a distinction between 'framework principles' and 'technical rules' whose definition is delegated to the Commission through implementing measures, subject to comitology.
2	**Infranational**	The Commission requests technical advice on the content of implementing measures from the Level 3 committees of national authorities (CEBS, CESR, CEIOPS).
3	**Infranational**	The Commission submits implementing measures to consideration by the Level 2 comitology committees (EBC, ESC, EIC, FCC).
4	**Supranational**	The implementing measures (directives or regulations) are adopted by the Commission if (i) the Council or the Parliament raises no objections within 3 months, and (ii) the Level 2 committees do not adopt by qualified majority an opinion opposing the implementing measures.

C. Enforcing Rules: The Level 3 Committees

The regulatory system envisaged by the Lamfalussy framework required the uniform enforcement of both Level 1 and Level 2 acts. This would reduce the compliance costs for the cross-border provision of financial services and avoid discrimination or competitive distortions. The approach was to create another governance layer, designated as Level 3, comprising committees of national supervisory authorities: CESR, CEBS, and CEIOPS.

The institutionalisation of the cooperation between national supervisors goes back to the early beginnings of the single financial market with the establishment of the 'Groupe de Contact' of banking supervisors in 1972 and the 'Forum of European Securities Commissions' in 1997. These were informal groupings, with no formal recognition of their role. The Level 3 committees were, instead, established by the Commission and recognised as a component of the regulatory system by Community law. They were not set-up as Community bodies, but as advisory groups to the Commission, which operated on the basis of national legal statutes.[71]

The Level 3 committees had two main functions. The first, as analysed in the previous section, was to provide technical advice into the preparation of Level 2 acts by the Commission. This not only supported rule-making at European level, but also the consistent enforcement of the Level 2 acts by national supervisors as they themselves had provided the content of such measures. This corresponded to the second function,

[71] The Level 3 committees comprised representatives of the supervisory authorities of EU and EEA Member States. The CEBS also included representatives of central banks not involved in banking supervision and the ECB. The CEBS was established as an English company, the CEIOPS as a German foundation, and the CESR as a French association.

the uniform enforcement of Community legislation. For this purpose, the committees could issue guidelines, interpretative recommendations, and standards on how legislation should be applied by national authorities, particularly in those areas of national discretion or not covered by European law.

The aim of Level 3 was thus to deliver a convergence of day-to-day regulatory and supervisory practices. Such uniform enforcement would make the application of national rules undistinguishable across Member States for the cross-border provision of financial services. This would be as close as possible to a single European regulator, without involving a transfer of national competences.[72]

Table 9 The Functions and Instruments of the Level 3 Committees

	Functions	Instruments
1	**Design of European financial legislation**	Technical advice (on its own initiative or on request) to the Commission for the preparation of Level 2 measures
2	**Uniform enforcement and convergence of regulatory and supervisory practices**	Guidelines on best regulatory practices, interpretative recommendations, standards, and opinions on request of national authorities
		Annual review and assessment of convergence of supervisory practices
		Peer reviews
		Mediation among national regulators of supervisory decisions
		Delegation of tasks by host- to home-country regulators
		Promotion of a common supervisory culture

D. The Failures of the Lamfalussy Framework

The Lamfalussy framework was considered from the start as an experimental process. Its workability depended on the willingness of European institutions, national authorities, and market participants, to act in accordance with the levels of governance. The procedures in each Level were interdependent. The Level 2 comitology rules required Level 1 legislation to provide a wide scope of implementing measures. Level 3 should deliver a uniform enforcement of both Level 1 and Level 2 acts. Level 4 should ensure an adequate transposition in national law. If such procedures did not operate in tandem, the whole framework would not function.

The Lamfalussy framework was reviewed at the end of 2007 by an 'Inter-institutional Monitoring Group' (IIMG). Although there was a positive assessment of the increased

[72] On the implication that the Lamfalussy process led to a large body of European law with implementation left to national authorities, see RD Kelemen, *Eurolegalism: The Transformation of Law and Regulation in the European Union* (Cambridge MA, Harvard University Press, 2011) at 93–142.

flexibility provided by the new regulatory processes and of the 'better regulation' practices, there were fundamental shortcomings at all levels.[73]

At Levels 1 and 2, the distinction between 'framework principles' and 'technical details' was not implemented to a large extent. In practice, Level 1 legislation contained excessive detail and provided a limited scope for implementing measures. This resulted from the concerns of the Parliament and Council on the use of comitology procedures. Most of the Level 1 acts also continued to be adopted as directives, instead of directly applicable regulations, as recommended by the Lamfalussy Report. Some Level 2 acts were adopted as Commission regulations, with the justification that this instrument was more appropriate for technical measures, but it then led to a lack of legal coherence between Level 1 and Level 2 rules.[74]

In this context, the Commission was also constrained by the technical advice provided by the Level 3 committees on the content of Level 2 acts. This facilitated the swift adoption of Level 2 acts, but it impinged on the Commission's right of initiative under the Community method. While such advice was not binding, deviating from it defeated its purpose of representing the basis for agreement among Member States in comitology procedures. The Commission committed to 'comply or explain' any deviation from the Level 3 technical advice.

Moreover, the sequencing between Level 1 legislation and Level 2 implementing measures proved problematic. The transposition of Level 1 legislation into national law could only take place after implementing measures had been adopted at Level 2, while, at the same time, Level 2 acts could only be adopted after the enabling of Level 1 acts. This led to a gridlock in regulatory procedures, as there was little time left both for the Commission to adopt Level 2 acts, and for Member States to transpose Community legislation within the period of 18 months. As a result, the transposition period had to be extended in some cases.[75]

At Level 3, the key limitation was the non-binding nature of the committees' instruments, which did not provide legal certainty in the single financial market. Decision-making was also based on consensus, which implied being captured by national interests and leading to guidelines or standards that often represented an amalgamation of the existing national practices, rather than a European benchmark. In addition, the concept of 'supervisory convergence' remained elusive in practice, making it difficult to assess the extent to which it was really achieved. The guidelines

[73] The IIMG was established in October 2002 with the mandate to assess the progress made by the Lamfalussy framework. The review was discussed at the ECOFIN of December 2007. See European Commission, Communication on the 'Review of the Lamfalussy Process: Strengthening supervisory convergence,' COM (2007) 727 final; and, Inter-Institutional Monitoring Group, Final Report Monitoring the Lamfalussy process (on file with the author) (2007); EU Council (2007) 2,836th Council meeting, Employment, Social Policy, Health and Consumer Affairs 15698/07.

[74] Among many examples, see the Commission Regulation of 22 December 2003 implementing Directive 2003/6/EC of the European Parliament and of the Council as regards exemptions for buy-back programmes and stabilisation of financial instruments (EC) No 2273/2003).

[75] The Council requested the Commission to map beforehand the likely outcomes of Level 1 and Level 2 in order to ensure consistency between them and to provide the co-legislators with clarity about the content of Level 2 measures. See 2,836th Council meeting, Employment, Social Policy, Health and Consumer Affairs 15698/07 (2007).

and standards were formulated in a broad manner, which only required minimal adjustments to national supervisory practices. The Level 3 committees were also undermined by their hybrid institutional status as private associations combining national authorities in the pursuance of European interests. Since national authorities remained with a national mandate, the committees could not be accountable for pursuing the European interest. This led to a self-serving bias, according to which the committees would take credit for successful outcomes, but accept little responsibility for unsuccessful ones.[76]

At Level 4, the shortcomings related to the lack of transparency on the transposition of Community law and to the accumulation of national rules beyond the level of harmonisation, the so-called 'gold-platting' practices. This led the Commission to start publishing 'scoreboards' of transposition of Community law and to initiate an approach of maximum harmonisation to address the 'gold-platting', namely by using regulations for Level 2 measures and requiring Member States to justify any regulatory additions.[77]

These failures of the Lamfalussy framework led the Council in December 2007 to decide on a number of improvements. It strengthened the role of the Level 3 committees and its instruments, but without changing their non-binding nature. It included in the mandates of national supervisors the pursuance of European supervisory cooperation and convergence. It expanded the possibilities for the delegation of tasks between national authorities. It harmonised the powers of national supervisors. And it also required common formats to disclose the national transposition of Community law.[78]

In practice, the Level 3 committees had very limited means for achieving convergence of supervisory practices. Their instruments, which included guidelines, recommendations and standards, were not binding on national authorities and had no status under Community law, unless their content would be later transposed by the Commission into implementing measures. The national authorities were free to comply with them on a voluntary basis, similarly to 'club rules', which implied that the committees could not provide any legal certainty on the matters covered by their decision-making. There were only soft compliance mechanisms, such as the regular assessment of the extent of convergence in supervisory practices and peer reviews. The committees could also assume a mediation role in disputes between national supervisors, promote the delegation of tasks between national supervisors, and develop a common supervisory culture among national authorities.[79]

[76] European Commission, Communication on the 'Review of the Lamfalussy Process: Strengthening supervisory convergence', COM (2007) 727 final, at 6–12; and Inter-Institutional Monitoring Group, Final Report Monitoring the Lamfalussy process. In January 2009, the Commission attempted to improve the functioning of the Committees by introducing qualified majority voting, if consensus could not be reached, as well as the 'comply or explain' rule, according to which national authorities should either comply with the Committees' decisions or explain the reasons for non-compliance. See Art 14 of the CEBS Commission Decision, Commission Decision C(2009)177 establishing the Committee of European Banking Supervisors of 23 January 2009.

[77] European Commission, Communication on the 'Review of the Lamfalussy Process: Strengthening supervisory convergence', COM (2007) 727 final at 6.

[78] 2,836th Council meeting, Employment, Social Policy, Health and Consumer Affairs 15698/07 (2007); and European Commission, Europe's financial system: adapting to change, COM (2008) 122 final.

[79] Under Art 144, CRD I, the national authorities were obliged to disclose information with a common format in a single electronic location of the texts of laws, regulations, and administrative rules, so as to enable a meaningful comparison of the enforcement approaches in each Member State. The aim was to achieve supervisory convergence in the same way that the disclosure by financial institutions leads to market discipline. The development of a common supervisory culture was made through training programmes, staff

E. Assessing Multilevel Governance

The innovation of the Lamfalussy framework was to introduce multilevel governance in the single financial market. It combined the traditional Community method with intergovernmental comitology procedures, and with committees of national authorities in the adoption and implementation of Community law. As an institutional experiment, the premise was that the involvement of national authorities in the governance of the single financial market replaced the need for the transfer of competences to the Community.[80]

This experiment in multilevel governance was introduced on a voluntary basis and did not require any changes to the Treaty. The Council and the Parliament committed at Level 1 that co-decision procedures would be limited to framework principles of legal harmonisation. Regulatory details would be delegated extensively, more than ever before, to the Commission on the basis of implementing powers to be exercised through comitology procedures at Level 2. The Commission would become, as a result, the regulator of the single financial market. However, also more than before, the Commission's implementing powers were interwoven with intergovernmental procedures. The Commission was voluntarily bound by the technical advice of the Level 3 committees in implementing measures. The representatives of Member States in comitology procedures, in turn, verified that the technical advice was followed. The national authorities committed, on their part, to the uniform enforcement of Community law through the Level 3 committees. The Lamfalussy framework led thus to a shared Community administration between the EU, the Member States, and national authorities. It also represented a concrete application of the 'co-regulation' concept proposed in the Commission's White Paper on European Governance.[81]

This multilevel governance framework had, however, several drawbacks. It made Community legislation and rule-making heavily dependent on intergovernmental procedures in comitology committees and on infranational supervisory committees, which were insulated from political and democratic control both at the Community and national levels. The format and philosophy of these committees was indeed drawn from the global standard-setting bodies, which also operated outside legal and political orders.

Moreover, national authorities acted on the basis of national mandates, without being accountable for the pursuance of European interests. The introduction of a

exchanges, joint inspection teams, and technical networks. See Art 6 of the Commission Decisions establishing the Level 3 Committees. See CEBS, Assessing CEBS' progress so far Inter-Institutional Monitoring Group, Final Report Monitoring the Lamfalussy process (2007) www.eba.europa.eu/documents/10180/16118/CEBS+assessment+report.pdf.

[80] For an assessment of the Lamfalussy process as multigovernance, see E Posner, 'The Lamfalussy process: polyarchic origins of networked financial rulemaking in the EU' in C Sabel and J Zeitlin (eds) *EU Governance: Towards a New Architecture?* (Oxford, Oxford University Press, 2010) 43; and L Quaglia, 'Financial sector committee governance in the European Union' (2008) 30 *European Integration* 563.

[81] See P Craig, 'Shared Administration and Networks: Global and EU perspectives', in G Anthony, JB Auby, J Morison, and T Zwart (eds) *Values in Global Administrative Law* (Oxford, Hart Publishing, 2011) 81–116. The European Commission, White Paper on European Governance, at 20–23, proposed that implementing measures may be prepared within a framework of co-regulation, combining binding legislative and regulatory action, with actions taken by the actors most concerned. The result would be wider ownership of policy-making by involving those most affected by implementing rules in their preparation and enforcement, which may also facilitate better compliance even where the rules are non-binding.

'European mandate' for national authorities was considered at several stages but it did not materialise. A 'European mandate' was incompatible with national mandates, its observance would have been difficult to assess in practice, and it seemed rather difficult to hold a national authority accountable for European interests. At the same time, the cooperation between national authorities through committees led gradually to a blending of national policies into European policies for the single financial market. This implied that national authorities became less accountable to their domestic constituencies, as policies were justified as a result of the standards elaborated by committees. The multilevel governance arising from the fusion of the Community method with intergovernmental procedures led thus to a neutralisation of both Community and national sources of legitimacy and accountability.[82]

The main objective of the Lamfalussy-type of multi-level governance was to fuse together the supranational, national and local levels and convert them into a European regulatory system. The limitations of the Community method in delivering market regulation led, however, to an excessive reliance on intergovernmental and infra-national networks. This was partly at the origin of the lack of a European regulatory and supervisory system, which amplified, instead of containing the financial crisis in 2007–2008.[83]

Table 10 The Multilevel Governance of the Single Financial Market by 2008

<table>
<tr><th></th><th>Steps</th><th>Level</th><th>Layers</th></tr>
<tr><td>1</td><td>Proposal of the Commission for Level 1 Legislation</td><td rowspan="2">Level 1</td><td rowspan="2">Supranational</td></tr>
<tr><td>2</td><td>Council and Parliament agree under the co-decision procedure on Level 1 legislation (Directive or Regulation) regarding framework principles and scope of implementing measures</td></tr>
<tr><td>3</td><td>Commission requests technical advice on content of implementing measures from supervisory committees (CEBS, CESR, CEIOPS)</td><td rowspan="5">Level 2</td><td rowspan="3">Infranational</td></tr>
<tr><td>4</td><td>Level 3 committees provide technical advice, after consultation of market participants</td></tr>
<tr><td>5</td><td>Commission prepares implementing measures, also on the basis of open consultation and impact analysis and submits them to consideration by comitology committees (EBC, ESC, EIC, FCC)</td></tr>
<tr><td>6</td><td>Commission provides Parliament with draft implementing measures</td><td rowspan="2">Supranational</td></tr>
<tr><td>7</td><td>Implementing measures (Directives and/or Regulations) are adopted by the Commission if (i) Parliament raises no objections within 3 months, and (ii) the comitology committees do not adopt by qualified majority an opinion opposing the measures</td></tr>
</table>

(continued)

[82] On the possible concept of the European mandate, see DCL Hardy, 'A European Mandate for Financial Sector Supervisors in the EU' (2009) 09/5 *IMF Working Paper*.

[83] On the possibilities of regulatory networks as an alternative to centralisation of competences at the European level, see KH Ladeur, 'Towards a Legal Theory of Supranationality' (n 11).

Table 10 ***(Continued)***

	Steps	Level	Layers
8	Level 3 committees promote the convergence of supervisory practices through guidelines, standards, and recommendations	Level 3	Infranational
9	National authorities enforce Community and national legislation in line with the guidance agreed by Level 3 committees		National
10	Member States transpose into national law the provisions in Level 1 or Level 2 legislation	Level 4	National
11	Commission monitors compliance of Member States		Supranational

VII. The Expansion of Home-Country Control to Financial Services Groups

A. The Emergence of Pan-European Financial Services Groups

The single passport introduced in 1985 encompassed the provision of financial services directly or through branches in other Member States. As it happened, the single passport did not become the main mode for market-entry. Financial institutions preferred the indirect provision of services through subsidiaries, either through new companies or the acquisition of existing ones. This was due to several factors, including adapting business activities to national features, taxation regimes, insulation of liability and legal risk, company law constraints regarding the merger of companies from different Member States, as well as the constraints posed by the preference of national authorities to retain their jurisdiction over significant financial activities in their territory. By 2006, also as a result of the introduction of the euro and the accession of ten new Member States in 2004, there were more than 40 major banking groups comprising subsidiaries present on average in more than six Member States and holding 70 per cent of the EU's banking assets. There were similar developments with insurance groups and financial conglomerates, which became significant in the European financial system.[84]

The single passport framework did not capture pan-European financial services groups. The regulation and supervision of the subsidiaries of a group was performed on a national stand-alone basis with overlapping and diverging requirements. This went against the integrated economic and financial structure of the groups, which centralised key business functions such as liquidity and risk management, in order to reap synergies and save costs. It did not also take into account the risks specific to a group, such as the interlinkages between its subsidiaries deriving from intra-group exposures and

[84] See J Dermine, 'Banking in Europe: Past, Present, and Future' in V Gaspar (ed) *The Transformation of the European Financial System* (Frankfurt/M, European Central Bank, 2003) 31; J de Haan, S Osterloo and D Schoenmaker, *European Financial Markets and Institutions* (Cambridge, Cambridge University Press, 2009) 349–357.

common liquidity and risk management, which can spread difficulties at one subsidiary to the rest of the group. Moreover, the increasing size and significance of financial groups, as well as the degree of their involvement in financial markets and market infrastructures, implied that they could pose risks for the stability of the European financial system and national economies. The regulation and supervision of a financial group as a whole was, however, constrained by the territoriality of the jurisdiction of national authorities, which prevented them from imposing requirements over financial institutions licensed in other Member States.[85]

The FSAP included a framework for the supervision of financial services groups. It aimed at expanding the cross-border provision of services by eliminating regulatory barriers, reducing structural, capital, and compliance costs. The legal approach was to widen the scope of the single passport by expanding the principle of home-country control from branches to the subsidiaries comprising a group. This was achieved by entrusting powers and tasks to the home-country authority, normally the authority responsible for the parent company, regarding the subsidiaries of the financial services group located in other Member States, and also the coordination of the national authorities responsible for each of these subsidiaries.

Community law provided thus for the first time extra-territorial powers to national authorities, which represented another component of the governance framework of the single financial market in this period. The home-country authorities of a financial services group would become responsible for the application and enforcement of Community law in several Member States and also for addressing the risks that the group could pose for the single financial market. Similarly to the Lamfalussy framework, the legal strategy was to entrust national authorities with the task of pursuing European interests, thus avoiding any transfer of competences to the European level.

B. The Coordinator, Consolidating and Group Supervisors

The expansion of the home-country control principle was implemented in different shapes and forms with regard to financial conglomerates, banking groups and insurance groups.

Chronologically, it first took place with the adoption of the Financial Conglomerates Directive (FCD) in December 2002. It created the concept of 'supplementary supervision' of the regulated entities from the insurance sector and either banking or securities sectors, which form part of a financial conglomerate. The FCD required the appointment of a 'coordinator supervisor', from among the national authorities from where the financial conglomerate had establishments. The main tasks of the 'coordinator supervisor' were to ensure that the requirements of supplementary supervision are fulfilled by all entities comprising a conglomerate, and to coordinate the national authorities involved to have a consistent supervision of the conglomerate. This implied providing an extra-territorial effect to the national law and powers of the 'coordinator supervisor'

[85] As argued by L Papademos, 'Banking supervision and financial stability in Europe' (2006) 70 *Forum Financier-Revue Bancaire et Financiaire, Bank en Financiewezen* 3.

for the purposes of the supervision of the conglomerate and the coordination of national authorities.[86]

The second expansion of home-country control took place in 2004 with the concept of the consolidating supervisor of banking groups in the Capital Requirements Directives (CRD I), which implemented the Basel II Framework. The consolidating supervisor was as a rule from the Member State where the bank heading the group was based. It coordinated the other national supervisors of the banking group and had specific powers and tasks, such as gathering and disseminating information, coordinating supervisory activities, including those concerning the Pillar II or supervisory review, and liaising with other authorities in crisis situations.[87]

The expansion of the home-country control was later complemented by the CRD II concept of 'college of supervisors', which was chaired by the consolidated supervisor and gathered the national supervisors of the subsidiaries and of the systemic branches of the banking group. The colleges were a formal network of national authorities, without decision-making powers, for supervising a banking group and reaching commonly agreed decisions.

The most significant legal implication of the consolidating supervisor regarded the decision-making procedure for allowing a banking group to use its internal models to measure own risks and the respective capital requirements. The CRD II required all the supervisors in the college to reach a joint decision with six months. In case of disagreement, the CEBS would provide advice within two months. If no consensus were reached, the consolidating supervisor would take a final decision binding all the other supervisors of the banking group. The legal innovations introduced by the CRD II in this respect were, therefore, to oblige national authorities to take joint decisions, and that, in the lack of a joint decision, the home-country supervisor could take unilateral decisions applying to legal entities in other Member States and enforced by the respective national authorities. This lack of a joint decision would imply a surrender of the jurisdiction of the host-country authorities over the subsidiaries of a banking group.[88]

[86] A financial conglomerate is defined as comprising insurance undertakings and either credit institutions or investment firms, on the basis of a number of indicators. The FCD set out regulatory requirements regarding the solvency position and risk concentration, the intra-group transactions, the internal risk management processes, and the fit and proper character of the management of the conglomerate. Directive 2002/87/EC of the European Parliament and of the Council of 16 December 2002 on the supplementary supervision of credit institutions, insurance undertakings and investment firms in a financial conglomerate and amending Council Directives 73/239/EEC, 79/267/EEC, 92/49/EEC, 92/96/EEC, 93/6/EEC and 93/22/EEC, and Directives 98/78/EC and 2000/12/EC of the European Parliament and of the Council. For an analysis of the lead regulation concept for financial conglomerates, see GA Walker, *International Banking Regulation, Law, Policy and Practice* (The Hague, Kluwer Law International, 2001) at 231–267.

[87] The framework of CRD I implied that cross-border consolidated supervision should be carried out only at the top level in the EU, thus preventing any other national authorities but the consolidating supervisor to consider foreign subsidiaries in its regulatory tasks. Host-country supervisors were only allowed to carry out their tasks with regard to the components of the group situated in their respective Member States. This reduced the number of levels of supervision to a maximum of three: EU group, national subgroups, and solo supervision. See Recital 13 and Arts 125 and 126 of the CRD I.

[88] See Art 129(2), as well as Arts 84(1), 87(9) and 105, and Annex III, pt 6 of the CRD I. Under Art 131, the CRD I provided the opportunity for further enlarging the extra-territorial reach of the consolidating supervisor by allowing host-country regulators to delegate to it additional tasks in a written agreement, including delegating the overall responsibility for the supervision of subsidiaries.

The last evolutionary step in the expansion of home-country control was made by the 2009 Solvency II Directive with regard to insurance groups. The innovation was entrusting the group supervisor with a large number of supervisory tasks, which were exercised directly over the whole insurance group and which pre-empted national decisions. It was not limited to supplement solo supervision, as with the financial conglomerates and banking groups. The group supervisor had primary responsibility for all the key aspects of group supervision.[89]

The attribution of extra-territorial decision-making powers to the consolidating banking supervisor and the insurance group supervisor, together with the surrender of sovereignty from the host-countries to the home-country, marked a significant step in the evolution of the law of the single financial market. It further constrained the national jurisdictions of Member States over subsidiaries of a financial services group, which are companies with an independent legal personality. This represented a move towards the horizontal transfer of competences among Member States as an alternative to the vertical transfer of competences to the EU level for the regulation of the single financial market.

Table 11 The Expansion of Home-Country Control to Financial Services Groups

	Coordinator supervisor of financial conglomerates (2003)	**Consolidating supervisor of banking groups (2006 and 2009)**	**Insurance group supervisor (2009)**
Scope	– Supplementary supervision to the solo supervision of the regulated entities comprising the conglomerate	– Supplementary supervision to the solo supervision of the subsidiaries comprising the banking group	– Direct group supervision (not supplementary)
Main tasks	– Supervising compliance by the conglomerate – Coordinating the national supervisors of the regulated entities of the conglomerate	– Supervising compliance by the banking group – Coordinating the national supervisors of the subsidiaries of the banking group – Chairing and coordinating the college of supervisors	– Supervising the insurance group and compliance with prudential rules – Coordinating the national supervisors of the components of the insurance group

(continued)

[89] This regime was justified by the fact that the European insurance market was largely dominated by large insurance groups and that insurance activities, in contrast to banking, are neither as crucial for the economic development of Member States, nor as disruptive to financial stability in the case of a crisis. See J de Haan, S Osterloo and D Schoenmaker, *European Financial Markets and Institutions*, (n 84) at 358–398.

Table 11 ***(Continued)***

	Coordinator supervisor of financial conglomerates (2003)	Consolidating supervisor of banking groups (2006 and 2009)	Insurance group supervisor (2009)
Decision-making process	– Decisions by the coordinator supervisor, after consulting the national supervisors	– Decisions by the consolidating supervisor, after consulting the national supervisors in colleges – Decisions on the internal models by a group is taken by the consolidating supervisor if there is no agreement in the college in 6 months	– Group supervisor should always be consulted in some situations
Enforcement of decisions	– The coordinator enforces decisions with respect to the mixed financial holding company, and the other national authorities with respect to each regulated entity	– The consolidating supervisor enforces its decisions on the financial holding of the group or parent bank – The national supervisors enforce their decisions on the respective subsidiaries	– The group supervisor enforces its decisions on the insurance holding company or parent company – The national supervisors enforce their decisions on the insurance undertakings

C. The Colleges of Supervisors

The colleges of supervisors, informally in place since the 1980s, were decided by the ECOFIN in 2007 and formalised in European law in 2009. The concept related to the expansion of home-country control as an alternative to the centralised supervision of financial groups, and without the transfer of competences to a European authority.[90]

[90] See ECOFIN roadmap of 4 December 2007 in 2,836th Council meeting, Employment, Social Policy, Health and Consumer Affairs 15698/07; and the Council Conclusions on the EU supervisory framework and financial stability arrangements, in 2,866th Council Meeting, Economic and Financial Affairs, 8850/08 (2008). For the historical background to the colleges, see DA Alford, 'Supervisory Colleges: The Global Financial Crisis and Improving International Supervisory Coordination' (2010) 24 *Emory International Law Review* 57, 59.

A college was defined as a grouping of the national supervisors responsible for a cross-border financial group. It provided a platform for cooperation and for reaching common decisions on the supervision of the group. Since all the national supervisors retained their legal authority, the colleges had no decision-making powers. Each supervisor took its own decisions, which did not need to be commonly agreed in the college. The colleges were chaired by the consolidating banking supervisor and the insurance group supervisor. They functioned on the basis of written agreements on the responsibilities of the authorities, information exchange, and crisis management. The colleges also promoted the convergence of supervisory practices vis-à-vis a financial group, such as the coordination of supervisory activities, the risk assessment and supervisory review, determination of capital adequacy, or on-site inspections.[91]

Similar to the shortcomings of the Level 3 committees, the colleges of supervisors provided little more than a network structure for sharing of information on a financial group. The fact that the colleges had no authority over supervisory decisions implied that a national supervisor could always take unilateral decisions not agreed in the college or even against the interests of the other authorities. This was particularly so in a crisis situation, where the national supervisors were not mandated or accountable for pursuing European interests. Accordingly, the national interests of safeguarding the local financial system and taxpayers' funds took precedence over the interests of the financial group, as confirmed in the events of the financial crisis in Europe since 2007–2008. The colleges did not provide, therefore, a credible alternative to the transfer of competences to the European level.[92]

D. The Inadequacy of Absolute Home-Country Control as a Governance Instrument

The expansion of the principle of home-country control from branches to subsidiaries of financial services groups was a key development in the evolution of the law of the single financial market. It implied providing a national authority with extra-territorial jurisdiction over companies licensed in other Member States, and the corresponding surrender by the host-countries of part of their jurisdiction. The objective was to develop a governance framework without the transfer of competences to a European authority. The vertical supremacy of EU law would be replaced by the horizontal supremacy of one Member State over another. It would be a principle of absolute home-country control.[93]

[91] Since the college was required to also function in a financial crisis, it included the supervisors of the subsidiaries and also those of systemically relevant branches, as defined in Art 42(1) of the CRD I, in order that the interests of all potentially affected Member States in a crisis were represented. The decision on whether a branch is systemically relevant should be taken jointly by the home-country and host-country authorities, as well as the consolidating supervisor. See CEBS and CEIOPS, Colleges of Supervisors: 10 Common principles (2009), at eiopa.europa.eu/CEIOPS-Archive/Documents/Standards/CEBS-CEIOPS-IWCFC-10-principles-colleges-of-supervisors.pdf.

[92] See DA Alford, 'Supervisory Colleges,' (n 90) 77–79.

[93] The Court has recognised the application of the home-country control principle to subsidiaries of a banking group in *Caixa Bank*, on the basis of the freedom of establishment. The Court considered that the law of the host-country of a subsidiary of a banking group, which prohibited financial services allowed under the law of the parent company, was a restriction to market access under the meaning of Art 49, TFEU.

Like multilevel governance, this concept of absolute home-country control largely failed in replacing the need for a European authority. Its workability depended on the extent to which a national authority could be entrusted with the performance of EU-wide tasks in other Member States. This proved illusionary. Subsidiaries, in contrast to most branches, may have systemic relevance for the economy and financial system of the Member States of establishment. Decisions of the home-country on subsidiaries could therefore impact on the welfare of host-countries. There was, however, no requirement in EU or national laws for home-country authorities to take the welfare of host-countries into account. In addition, there were no changes to the financial stability framework, which would widen the home-country responsibilities to the safety net of the financial group. The insurance of deposits and the provision of emergency liquidity assistance by central banks remained territorial functions within each Member State.

The concept of a European mandate for national authorities was proposed at a certain stage as the way forward. It would imply that home-country authorities would act in a dual nature, as both European and national agents. This was unworkable since national supervisors would remain accountable to their national political institutions. This, in turn, implied that the home-country could not be made liable for decisions that have a negative impact in host-countries, or held responsible for rescuing the whole financial group in a crisis with national funds.[94]

Furthermore, the extra-territorial reach of home-country control was constrained by the potential conflict with the territoriality of national laws of the subsidiaries, which remained subject to company or bankruptcy law. One example related to the transfer of capital and liquidity between subsidiaries within the financial group: it may be required for the soundness of the group, but it may be in conflict with the national rules preventing transactions detrimental for the creditors and shareholders of a company.[95]

Lastly, the horizontal supremacy of home-country control of financial groups would also lead to a sort of local federalism. Only an oligarchy of national authorities would be entrusted with expanded home-country control over the others, since the major financial groups were headquartered in few Member States. This would reduce the number of national authorities involved in the supervision of financial groups, but it would also lead to the dominance of some Member States over others.

As a result, despite the expansion of home-country control to a financial group, the host-countries preserved de facto and de jure their jurisdiction over subsidiaries. The public interest of host-countries, such as preserving their own financial stability, conflicted with absolute home-country control. This led to a governance framework, which was overly complex and fragmented, comprising: (1) the home-country jurisdiction for the group as a whole; (2) the jurisdiction of host-countries for the subsidiaries

[94] See E Wymeersch, 'The Future of Financial Regulation and Supervision in Europe' (2005) 42 *CML Rev* 987, who argued that home-country control over financial groups would require changes to the deposit protection system and to the lender of last resort functions. See also DCL Hardy, 'A European Mandate for Financial Sector Supervisors in the EU' (n 82).

[95] On the possible tensions between the supervisory framework and general principles of company law, relating in particular to those relating to the group of companies, see E Wymeersch 'Conflicts of interest in financial services groups' (2007) 2007-5 *Working Paper, Ghent University, Financial Law Institute.*

and their financial stability; (3) the colleges of supervisors; and (4) the guidelines of Level 3 committees. The financial crisis in Europe proved how inadequate such governance was for financial groups.[96]

VIII. Competition Policy in the Single Financial Market

A. Competition Policy Until the 1990s

The application of competition policy in financial services was significantly intensified in this period. Until then, it had seldom been relevant either at the European or national level. Although the Commission had stated as early as 1973 that competition rules also apply to the banking sector, the first court case involving the banking sector was *Züchner* in 1980, relating to potential concerted practices in charging cross-border transfers between bank accounts.[97]

The reason for such limited application was that finance was a strictly regulated sector, where the conduct of monetary policy and regulation prevailed over market competition. The assumption was that the behaviour of financial institutions was less likely to influence or be constrained by the markets. Competition policy was thus subsumed to a large extent by financial regulation. This was supported by the 'prudential carve-out' in Article 21.4 of the 'Merger Regulation,' which includes 'prudential rules' as the basis for Member States to take appropriate measures to protect legitimate interests in the application of competition rules. It was also reinforced by the fact that the banking supervisor would also be the competition authority for the banking sector, or be involved in the application of competition rules, in several Member States, such as France, Greece, Italy or the UK.[98]

Competition policy then gained relevance in the wave of banking mergers and acquisitions in the 1990s, both in Europe and the US. This wave of mergers was largely the result of financial globalisation, deregulation, increasing competition for banking services, and also the revolution in digital technology, which enabled efficiency gains in bigger organisations. Most of the banking consolidation was, however, domestic, within the US and individual Member States (eg Belgium, France, Germany, Netherlands, Italy, Spain, and the UK), with few cross-border transactions. This reduced substantially the number of banks. For example, between 1997 and 2003, there was a reduction of 23 per cent in the number of banks in the EU, equivalent to around 2,200 banks. At the

[96] The public interest in the regulation of financial services falls under the exceptions set by the *Cassis de Dijon* jurisprudence for the application of the home-country control principle. See A Menon and S Weatherill, 'Transnational Legitimacy in a Globalising World: How the European Union Rescues its States' (2008) 31 *West European Politics* 397.

[97] See European Commission, Second Report on Competition Policy (1973) at 58; and Judgment of the Court of 14 July 1981, *Züchner*, 172/80, EU:C:1981:178.

[98] The prudential carve-out is contained in Art 21.3 of the Council Regulation (EC) No 139/2004 of 20 January 2004 on the control of concentrations between undertakings (the EC Merger Regulation), [2004] OJ L24/1–22. See E Carletti and X Vives, 'Regulation and Competition Policy in the Banking Sector,' in X Vives (ed) *Competition Policy in Europe, Fifty Years Treaty of Rome* (Oxford, Oxford University Press, 2009) 260, 261–262.

same time, it led to the promotion of large banking organisations as 'national champions', which would support the growth and development of national economies in a globalised environment.[99]

In the single financial market, it was expected that the introduction of the euro, the FSAP, the implementation of the Basel II Framework, the expansion of home-country control for financial groups, as well as the Lamfalussy framework, would promote pan-European banking groups. As demonstrated in a succession of cases, national protectionism remained, however, an obstacle to cross-border transactions. This brought competition policy to the fore in achieving financial integration in this governance period.

B. Competition Policy versus Economic Patriotism

The wave of banking mergers and acquisitions, particularly after the introduction of the euro, was accompanied by increasing expressions of government intervention and protectionism. The aim of governments was twofold. First, discouraging or hindering acquisitions by foreign banks, on the basis that it would make the economy dependent on foreign influence. Second, creating national champions through domestic acquisitions, which could compete with major players in the single financial market. This government behaviour became associated at the time with the term 'economic patriotism'.[100]

The intervention of governments to prevent foreign mergers and acquisitions in order to protect national interests would be contrary to the freedoms of establishment and movement of capital of the Treaty, besides infringing the principle of non-discrimination by reason of nationality. The application of prudential rules could, however, be considered as one of the legitimate interests that Member States could invoke under the prudential carve-out of the Merger Regulation. Starting in 1999, the intervention of governments blocking cross-border transactions was challenged in a succession of cases, which brought into play national protectionism, the scope of prudential rules, and competition policy as a tool of integration.

The first case involved Banco Santander Central Hispano ('BSCH'), from Spain, and Mr António Champalimaud, from Portugal. In June 1999, the Portuguese Government opposed a concentration operation between the two parties, which would have led to their joint control of the banking and insurance group of Mr Champalimaud in Portugal. The motives stated in the decision included the sound and prudent management of the insurance company Mundial Confiança and its appropriate supervision, the

[99] There were several economic and policy studies at the time on the causes and effects of banking consolidation. See BIS, Group of Ten, Report on Consolidation in the Financial Sector (2001) at www.bis.org/publ/gten05.pdf. For the European context, see ECB, Report on EU Banking Structures (2004), at www.ecb.europa.eu/pub/pdf/other/eubankingstructure2004en.pdf.

[100] The term was coined in July 2005 as 'patriotism économique' by the former French Prime Minister Dominique de Villepin, when he expressed himself in favour of protecting French firms against hostile take-over bids, after the attempt of PepsiCo to take-over the French group Danone. *Dominique de Villepin en appelle au 'patriotisme économique'*, Le Monde, 29 July 2005. The framework for cross-border takeovers in the single market was the subject of a long saga, starting with the first Commission proposal for a Directive on Takeover Bids in 1989, revised successively until its final adoption in 2004.

fact that the operation related to strategic sectors essential to the Portuguese economy and financial system, and the lack of compliance with procedural rules. In July 1999, the Commission suspended the decision of the Portuguese Government on the basis that there were considerable doubts that it could be based on prudential rules. The concentration operation was then authorised by the Commission in August 1999. The initial operation was replaced in January 2000 by the acquisition by BSCH of two Portuguese banks belonging to Mr Champalimaud and the sale of the insurance company to the state owned Caixa Geral de Depósitos.[101]

A second case regarded another cross-border concentration where the Italian bank Unicredito Italiano (Unicredit) proposed to acquire the German bank Bayerisch Hypo-und-Vereinsbank (HVB). The operation would lead to significant financial activities in several Member States, in particular in Poland where the merger would create the largest bank in terms of assets. The Commission approved the acquisition in October 2005. In December of the same year, the Polish Government instructed Unicredit to sell its shares in the Polish Bank BPH, which was controlled indirectly by HVB. The reason was that Unicredit had signed a 'non-competition clause' when it bought another Polish bank (Polska Kasa Opieki) in 1999, according to which it could not have invested for ten years in another bank. The Commission opened an infringement procedure against Poland in March 2006 on violation of the Merger Regulation, since the Polish measure represented a competition policy decision against the exclusive competences of the Commission, and also the Treaty freedoms of establishment and capital movement. The dispute was resolved by an agreement between the Polish Government and Unicredit in 2006, whereby Unicredit committed to divest from BPH.[102]

The third case related to a series of takeover bids for Italian banks in 2005. The Spanish Banco de Bilbao Vizcaya Argentaria (BBVA) launched a takeover bid of Banca Nazionale del Lavoro (BNL) on 29 March, followed the day after by a takeover bid by the Dutch bank ABN Amro of Banca Antoniana Popolare Veneta (Antonveneta). They were followed by competing takeover bids by Italian firms: the insurance company Unipol counter-bidding for BNL, and Banca Popolare Italiana (BPI) counter-bidding for Antonveneta. In December 2005, after having approved in April the two initial proposed concentration operations, the Commission opened an infringement procedure against

[101] For an overview of the case, see Commission Decision in Case No IV/M.1616 – BSCH/A. Champalimaud of 20 July 1999, at ec.europa.eu/competition/mergers/ cases/decisions/m1724_19990720_1290_en.pdf; Commission Press Releases, 'Commission approves the acquisition of joint control by BSCH (Spain) over the Champalimaud group (Portugal),' IP/99/610, 3.8.1999, at europa.eu/rapid/press-release_IP-99-610_en.htm; and 'Commission authorises the acquisition by Banco Santander Central Hispano (BSCH) of two Portuguese banks belonging to the Champalimaud Group,' IP/00/21, 12.1. 2000, at europa.eu/rapid/press-release_IP-00-21_en.htm.

[102] For an overview, see Commission Decision in Case No COMP/M.3894 – Unicredit/HVB of 18 October 2005, at ec.europa.eu/competition/mergers/cases/decisions/ m3894_20051018_20310_en.pdf; Commission Press Releases, 'Commission approves acquisition of German bank HVB by Italy's UniCredito,' IP/05/1299, 18.10.2005; 'Commission Opens Infringement Procedure Against Poland in Context of UniCredit/HVB Merger,' IP/06/276, 8.3.2006; and 'Commission Launches Procedure Against Poland for Preventing Unicredit/HVB Merger,' IP/06/277, 8.3.2006; and Unicredit, 'Signing of the Agreement between the Ministry of Treasury and Unicredit,' at www.unicreditgroup.eu/en/pressandmedia/pressreleases/2006/PressRelease0378.html.

Italy on violation of the freedoms of establishment and capital movement. At stake was the lack of transparency of the provisions of the Italian supervisory law dealing with the acquisition of bank holdings. Moreover, the exercise of supervisory authority by Banca d'Italia with regard to the foreign bidders was publicly questioned, also in the context of an Italian judicial enquiry. The Governor of Banca d'Italia resigned in December 2005 and the competence for competition policy in the banking sector was transferred from Banca d'Italia to the antitrust authority. Eventually, ABN Amro gained control of Antonveneta in January 2006 and the French bank BNP Paribas acquired in February the majority of the shares of BNL from both BBVA and Unipol.[103]

The fourth case related to the attempted acquisition of ABN Amro itself by the UK's Barclays Bank in March 2007, which was followed in April by a counterbid by a consortium of banks led by the UK's Royal Bank of Scotland (RBS), and including Belgium's Fortis, and Spain's BSCH. The RBS consortium planned to break-up the ABN Amro group, whose components would then be distributed among the banks of the consortium. The Dutch central bank, as the banking supervisor, stated that it considered from a prudential point of view that the offer by the consortium was a 'risk-increasing and complicating factor'. This led to a public warning by the Commission regarding possible discrimination in the national interest, since the break-up of ABN Amro was not the preferred outcome. The case concluded when, in October 2007, Barclays withdrew its lower priced bid and the RBS consortium acquired control of ABN Amro. The vast amounts involved in acquisition were one of the major causes of the downfall of RBS and Fortis when the financial crisis erupted in Europe in 2007–2008. ABN Amro was later nationalised, together with the component of Fortis bank in the Netherlands, by the Dutch state in October 2008 in the midst of the financial crisis.[104]

C. The Revision of Prudential Rules for Cross-Border Banking Acquisitions

The above succession of cases proved that cross-border banking mergers and acquisitions could be blocked or delayed by government intervention. The instruments for intervention included raising concerns regarding financial stability, possibly misusing supervisory powers, and the opaqueness and complexity of supervisory approval processes. It provided the ground for limiting at the European level the extent to which

[103] For an overview of the operations, see Commission Decision in Cases No COMP/M.3678 – BBVA/BNL and COMP/M.3780 ABN AMRO/Banca Antonveneta, both of 27 April 2005, at ec.europa.eu/competition/mergers/cases/decisions/m3768_20050427_20310_en.pdf and ec.europa.eu/competition/mergers/cases/decisions/m3780_20050427_20310_en.pdf, respectively; Commission Press Release, 'Commission opens an infringement procedure against Italy on the issue of acquisition of stakes in domestic banks,' IP/05/1595, 14.12.2005; and Commission Press Release, 'Commission closes infringement procedure against Italy concerning acquisition of stakes in domestic banks,' IP/07/83, 24.1.2007.

[104] For an overview, see Commission Decision in Cases No COMP/M.4692 BARCLAYS/ABN AMRO of 6 August 2008, and COMP/M.4843 RBS/ABN AMRO Assets, COMP/M.4844 FORTIS/ABN AMRO Assets, and COMP/M.4845 SANTANDER/ ABN AMRO Assets, all of 19 of September 2007. The statement of the Dutch central bank on 18 April 2007 is at www.dnb.nl/en/news/news-and-archive/persberichten-2007/auto125003.jsp. The *Financial Times* reported on the Commission's warning on 19 April 2007, 'McCreevy warns Dutch central bank over ABN.'

prudential rules could be invoked for political reasons. The Informal Ecofin Council of Scheveningen of September 2004, which took place at the time of the initial moves of ABN Amro and BBVA to acquire Antonveneta and BNL, respectively, mandated the Commission to identify the supervisory and other obstacles to mergers and acquisitions.[105]

The result was a directive revising the supervisory assessment procedure for acquisitions in the financial sector, adopted in September 2007. The Directive introduced three new rules in the supervisory assessment process. First, it set a maximum limit of 60 working days for assessing a proposed acquisition of a qualifying holding in the financial sector. Second, it forbade supervisors from considering the economic needs of the market and restricted the assessment to a checklist of five criteria, including the reputation and financial soundness of the acquirer, the management experience, and compliance with prudential rules. It also clarified the 'principle of national treatment', namely that, in the case of competing bids, the proposed acquirers should not be discriminated. The specific reasons for a negative decision may also be published at the request of the prospective acquirer. Third, it required the supervisors of the home and host-countries to consult with each other.[106]

The main legal innovation of the Directive was that it followed the approach of 'maximum harmonisation', which would later be used in the response to the financial crisis: Member States could not transpose the Directive with stricter national rules. However, in practice, it did not have far-reaching implications. Each national supervisor remained exclusively competent for authorising acquisitions in its jurisdiction. There were no responsibilities given to the home-country supervisor of the proposed acquirer and the original proposal to give the Commission the right to verify an assessment process was not adopted. The Directive was limited to introducing transparency and procedural constraints to prevent the potential misuse of prudential rules.[107]

D. The Application of State Aid Rules

The application of state aid rules in the banking and financial sector also intensified in the 1990s. The first major case was the public rescue of Crédit Lyonnais of France

[105] See EU Council, 'Results of the Informal Meeting of Economics and Finance Ministers,' The Hague, 10–11 September 2004, MEMO/04/214. The Commission fulfilled its mandate with the report European Commission, Cross-Border Consolidation in the EU Financial Sector, SEC (2005) 1398 final.

[106] The principle of national treatment in the financial sector already stems from the freedom of movement of capital in the Treaty (Art 63, TFEU). See also Judgment of the Court of 11 October 2007, *Hollmann v Fazenda Pública*, C-443/06, ECLI:EU:C:2007:600, para 29; and Judgment of the Court of 10 January 2006, *Cassa di Risparmio di Firenze*, C-222/04, EU:C:2006:8, para 99. The Commission also stated that nationals of Member States should be free to acquire controlling stakes, exercise voting rights and manage domestic companies under the same conditions in a given Member State for its own nationals. European Commission, Communication on intra-EU investment in the financial services' sector C/2005/4080, [2005] OJ C/293. See Directive 2007/44/EC of the European Parliament and of the Council of 5 September 2007 amending Council Directive 92/49/EEC and Directives 2002/83/EC, 2004/39/EC, 2005/68/EC and 2006/48/EC as regards procedural rules and evaluation criteria for the prudential assessment of acquisitions and increase of holdings in the financial sector, [2007] OJ L247.

[107] For an analysis, see S Kerjean, 'The legal implications of the prudential supervisory assessment of bank mergers and acquisitions under EU law' (2008) 6 *ECB Legal Working Papers*.

in 1995, the biggest European banking group at the time. In its state aid decision, the Commission argued extensively that, notwithstanding the regulated nature of this sector, banking rescues should also be subject to state aid scrutiny and, in particular to the 'private investor principle': there is aid if a private investor would not have invested under normal market conditions. This would also apply when the aid is limited to ensuring the compliance with the regulatory solvency ratio, since such compliance should be ensured by supervision and not public subsidies. There are two exceptions to this principle. Under Article 107.3(b) of the TFEU, the aid to remedy a serious disturbance in the economy of a Member State may be considered compatible with the single market, which could be applicable in a systemic financial crisis. Under Article 107.3(c) of the TFEU, the aid to facilitate the development of certain economic activities could also be considered compatible where it does not affect trading conditions to an extent contrary to the common interest. This exception was applied to Crédit Lyonnais.[108]

Throughout the 1990s and 2000s, the Commission applied a strict interpretation of state aid rules to the banking sector, without providing exceptions to a public subsidy to avoid the failure of a bank. The Commission's 'guidelines on rescue and restructuring aid to companies in financial difficulties' were applied in several cases of aid of both rescue and restructuring of banks, such as Banco di Napoli (Italy), Bankgesellschaft Berlin (Germany), and BAWAG (Austria). This state aid framework was applied to the crisis of individual banks, but it was later challenged by the systemic financial crisis, which erupted in 2007–2008.[109]

E. The Implications of Competition Policy as Governance Tool

The enforcement of competition policy, including state aid rules, by the Commission became one of the tools of the governance framework in this period. The Commission intervened in the increasingly conflicting dynamics between cross-border banking integration and the protectionist moves by Member States. In doing so, it played a role in expanding the cross-border provision of financial services in the single market. Many of the obstacles to integration stemmed from the entry barriers posed by Member States' economic policies.

This period represented the pinnacle of the policy objective of cross-border financial consolidation. The focus on consolidation implied increasing the size and market share of financial institutions. For Member States, it would translate into economic growth,

[108] The Commission approved the rescue of Crédit Lyonnais in 1995 on the basis of Art 107.3(c), TFEU. Commission Decision 95/547/EC of 26 July 1995 giving conditional approval to the aid granted by France to the bank Crédit Lyonnais [1995] OJ L308/92–119.

[109] For an explanation of the Commission's approach to state aid in the banking sector, see A Bomhoff, A Jarosz-Friis, N Pesaresi, 'Restructuring banks in crisis – overview of applicable State aid rules' (2009) 3 *Competition Policy Newsletter* 3. See European Commission, Community guidelines on State aid for rescuing and restructuring firms in difficulty, [2004] OJ C/2442–17. See also Commission Decision 99/288/EC of 29 July 1998 conditionally approving the aid granted by Italy to the Banco di Napoli, [1999] OJ L/11636; Commission Decision of 18 February 2004 on restructuring aid implemented by Germany for Bankgesellschaft Berlin AG, [2005] OJ L116/1; Commission Decision 2008/263/EC of 27 June 2007, State aid C 50/2006 implemented by Austria for BAWAG-PSK, [2008] OJ L/837.

taxation, employment, and increasing economic influence. It provided a framework of incentives for financial institutions and Member States to expand the provision of financial services, both domestically in the form of 'national champions' and across borders to increase competitiveness. As a result, there was a push towards the expansion of financial services in the single market, which involved a looser policy in favour of increasing the size of financial institutions.[110]

At the same time, another implication was that the expansion of financial services in the single market could take place without being constrained by the related financial risks. For example, the size and dimension of a financial institution could not be constrained by the ability of the Member State of origin to support it financially in a crisis. The main assertion of competition policy was that providers of financial services could not be discriminated on the basis of the country of origin. This was confirmed by the Directive on the supervisory assessment of bank acquisitions. It was an inversion of the logic of Article 21.4 of the Mergers Regulation, where prudential rules could prevail over competition policy. Instead, the Directive dictated that prudential interests could not limit free competition and financial integration. For example, the five assessment criteria of the Directive did not include the possibility that the acquisition could lead to financial stability risks in the home or host-country of the acquirer.[111]

Therefore, competition policy contributed to detaching the expansion of the domestic financial systems from the individual capacity of Member States to provide a safety net. This, together with the lack of a European framework for financial stability, was one of the contributing factors for the financial crisis in 2007–2008.[112]

IX. Crisis Prevention in the Single Financial Market

A. The Increase in Systemic Risk

The expansion of the provision of cross-border financial services, particularly after the introduction of the euro in 1999, not only accelerated financial integration, but also increased the likelihood that a financial crisis would spread across Member States. The scope for systemic risk expanded from each Member State to the whole single financial market. This was due to the deeper inter-linkages between national financial systems stemming from common financial institutions, markets and market infrastructures.[113]

[110] See, eg, Hans-Werner Sinn, who describes the period up to the financial crisis as 'competition in laxity' between financial regulators, which applied looser policies to retain financial business and avoid its migration. See HW Sinn, *Casino Capitalism* (Oxford, Oxford University Press, 2010) 157–161.

[111] As acknowledged in the review of the Directive by the European Commission, Application of Directive 2007/44/EC amending Council Directive 92/49/EEC and Directives 2002/83/EC, 2004/39/EC, 2005/68/EC and 2006/48/EC as regards procedural rules and evaluation criteria for the prudential assessment of acquisitions and increase of holdings in the financial sector, COM (2013) 64 final, at 8.

[112] On the role of competition policy in fostering financial integration as a factor in the financial crisis, see N Véron, 'Banking Nationalism and the European Crisis,' (2013) at www.piie.com/publications/papers/veron20130627.pdf.

[113] On the concept and scope of systemic risk in the regulation of finance, see MK Brunnermeier et al, 'The fundamental principles of financial regulation' (2009) 11 *Geneva Reports on the World Economy.*

The most relevant factor for systemic risk was the increasing number of large and complex pan-European financial groups, which emerged out of cross-border mergers and acquisitions of subsidiaries in several Member States. Given their size and relevance, they became systemically significant in the single financial market, with a significant percentage of deposits and market share in several Member States. By 2007, there were 46 systemically important banking groups, which accounted for 68 per cent of EU banking assets. At the same time, there were also increasingly large domestic banks, the 'national champions' that were promoted by Member States. This was also reflected in the high concentration ratios in many Member States, particularly the small and medium-sized ones: eg in Finland, the Netherlands, and Belgium, the concentration ratio of the five largest banks exceeded 80 per cent. This implied that the stability of the financial system in most Member States became dependent on a small number of banks whose size could range from half of their GDP, eg in France and Germany, to one-and-a-half of their GDP, eg in Belgium, Ireland, and Netherlands.[114]

The systemic risk in the single financial market also increased as a result of the enlargement of the EU in May 2004 by ten new Member States. The banking institutions from the 'old' Member States acquired banking assets in the new Member States or created new banks, which increased the ratio of foreign ownership of financial assets. In many cases, this was in excess of 70 per cent, and even 90 per cent in Slovakia and Estonia of the capital of banks, compared to the previous EU average of 30 per cent.[115]

Finally, systemic risk also stemmed from the integration of financial markets, especially those related to the euro, including money markets and government bond markets. The same happened with market infrastructures, notably with the TARGET payment systems operated by the ECB and representing 90 per cent of large-value payments in euros, and with pan-European providers of clearing and settlement services, such as Euroclear and Clearstream.

The scope for systemic risk in the single financial market thus increased significantly since 1999. The potential for financial contagion was much larger, as a crisis could be transmitted and amplified through institutions, markets and market infrastructures in several Member States, as later confirmed by the financial crisis of 2007–2008.

B. The European Financial Stability Framework

A financial stability framework comprises three functions: the prevention of a crisis, the management of a crisis, and crisis resolution.[116]

Crisis prevention starts with the regulation of the financial system to ensure its safety and soundness. This is enforced by supervisory authorities, which are responsible for ensuring compliance by financial institutions. Central banks monitor the

[114] For an overview of the new financial landscape at the time, see ECB, EU Banking Structures (2006) at www.ecb.europa.eu/pub/pdf/other/eubankingstructures2006en.pdf at 9–20; and European Commission, European Financial Integration Report 2007, SEC (2007) 1696 final, at 37–41.

[115] See European Commission, European Financial Integration Report 2007, (n 114) at 39–40.

[116] On the main components of a financial stability framework, see GJ Schinasi, *Safeguarding Financial Stability*, (n 19) at 98–133; and T Padoa-Schioppa, *Regulating Finance*, (n 17) at 40–ff.

financial system in conducting monetary policy and oversee financial markets and market infrastructures.[117]

If a crisis emerges, leading to the lack of liquidity or the risk of insolvency of financial institutions, the authorities may have recourse to several instruments. Supervisors may take corrective measures to manage the crisis, such as requiring more capital, prohibiting the distribution of dividends, or withdrawing the licence of a bank. Central banks may fulfil their lender of last resort function by providing liquidity to the markets or emergency liquidity assistance (ELA) to individual banks.[118]

Ultimately, the insolvency of a bank may be prevented by government intervention, which may include the provision of capital, guarantees, or nationalisation. Finally, if the bank is not able to continue to operate with sufficient liquidity or capital, the bank or financial institution is resolved, restructured or liquidated. The deposits that cannot be repaid by the bank are reimbursed by the deposit guarantee fund up to a certain threshold.[119]

Table 12 The Components of a Financial Stability Framework

	Function	**Authority**
Crisis prevention	Regulation	Government and regulator
	Supervision and enforcement of regulation	Supervisor
	Monitoring financial stability	Central Bank
Crisis Management	Supervisory measures on banks to contain risk of insolvency (eg prohibition of dividends)	Supervisor
	Provision of liquidity to markets or to illiquid but solvent banks (ELA)	Central Bank
	Provision of capital support to banks to prevent insolvency, including guarantees and nationalisation	Government (Finance Ministry)
Crisis Resolution	Resolution, restructuring or liquidation of an illiquid or insolvent bank to compensate creditors	Resolution authority Judicial authority
	Reimbursement of deposits not repaid by banks	Deposit guarantee fund

The EU's legal and institutional framework for financial stability during this period relied solely on the national competences of banking supervisors, central banks, treasuries and deposit insurance schemes. The link between managing a crisis and the potential use of

[117] On the role of central banks in safeguarding financial stability, see T Padoa-Schioppa, *Regulating Finance*, (n 17) at 94–ff.

[118] On the lender of last resort function, see GJ Schinasi and PG Teixeira, 'The Lender of Last Resort in the European Single Financial Market' (2006) *WP/06/127 IMF Working Paper.*

[119] For an assessment of the crisis management instruments in Europe in this period, see European Commission, Report on Financial Crisis Management (2001) 156 *Economic Papers.*

taxpayers' funds meant that national authorities preserved their autonomy and discretion on whether and how to intervene. This implied that national authorities would not commit to collective and coordinated action in a crisis affecting the single financial market. Otherwise, the concern was that national sovereignty would be compromised by a commitment to take a certain action which could lead to a fiscal liability. In addition, the risk of 'moral hazard', ie that the explicit possibility of a bail-out would increase the propensity of banks to engage in risk-taking, often emerged at the time as a justification for not formalising a EU crisis management framework. Crises would be prevented primarily by market discipline and managed by market-led solutions.[120]

The only European authority with competences related to financial stability was the ECB. One of its tasks was to contribute to the national financial stability policies under Article 127(5) of the TFEU, which translated into monitoring and advisory functions. However, the ECB was not responsible for providing ELA in the euro area, since this was a task performed under the responsibility and liability of national central banks. The reason was that the provision of ELA was considered as a financial stability task outside of the ECB mandate. The only possibility for the ECB to intervene was the Governing Council objecting by a majority voting of two thirds to the provision of ELA by an NCB, but only if this was deemed to interfere with the objectives and tasks of the Eurosystem, under Article 14.4 of the ESCB and ECB Statute.[121]

The governance arrangements developed in this period for safeguarding financial stability did not go beyond loose and non-legally binding cooperation agreements between national authorities, which took the form of Memoranda of Understanding (MoU). There were two MoUs agreed on financial crisis management. The first was adopted in 2003 between EU banking supervisors and central banks, the second in 2005 with these authorities and finance ministries, which was updated in June 2008. The MoUs dealt with the responsibilities of authorities and the sharing of information in cross-border crises. The more specific 2008 MoU introduced the concept of a 'cross-border stability group' among the Member States sharing common financial stability concerns, as well as a template for assessing the systemic implications of a financial crisis. The most ambitious provision related to the burden-sharing between Member States of the budgetary costs to resolve a crisis, which would be based on two principles: equity, whereby the costs would be shared depending on the economic impact of the crisis in each of the countries affected; and accountability, whereby the greater responsibility of

[120] The first impetus for the development of arrangements for financial stability in the single financial market was made by EFC, which adopted a first report on financial stability (April 2000) and a second one on financial crisis management (April 2001), also known as the 'Brouwer Reports' from Henk Brouwer, the Dutch central banker who chaired the groups. The reports recommended: (1) the sharing of information among authorities; (2) the convergence of supervisory practices; and (3) the enhancement of crisis management arrangements. In the area of crisis management, the EFC highlighted that the first line of defence should remain within financial institutions themselves. For an analysis of crisis management in this period, see GG Garcia and MJ Nieto, 'Banking crisis management in the European Union: Multiple regulators and resolution authorities' (2005) 6 *Journal of Banking Regulation* 206.

[121] Against this opinion, René Smits considers that the provision of emergency liquidity assistance is a core central banking function linked to its monetary functions. Therefore, he argues that the lender of last resort function is subsumed under Art 18.1 of the Statute and can also be exercised by the ECB. See R Smits, *The European Central Bank*, (n 40) at 269–271. See also GJ Schinasi and PG Teixeira, 'The Lender of Last Resort in the European Single Financial Market' (n 118). The Eurosystem Agreement on ELA is available at www.ecb.europa.eu/pub/pdf/other/Agreement_on_emergency_liquidity_assistance_20170517.en.pdf.

the home- vis-à-vis the host-countries' authorities would also be reflected in the sharing of the costs.[122]

Besides the MoUs, the management of a financial crisis in the single financial market would also involve a number of committees. These included the Economic and Financial Committee (EFC) in providing advice to the ECOFIN Council, assisted by its Financial Services Committee; the Level 3 committees in promoting the cooperation between national supervisors; and the internal committees of the Eurosystem for the cooperation between central banks, including the ESCB Banking Supervision Committee (BSC).[123]

The rules and procedures provided by the MoU were tested at the time in financial crisis simulation exercises, which aimed at assessing how they would work in practice in different crisis scenarios. A first European simulation exercise was organised by the BSC in 2003, and a second in 2006 involving all EU banking supervisors, central banks and finance ministries. The ECB also organised exercises of this type to test its own functions.[124]

Table 13 The EU Committees with a Role in Financial Stability (1999–2008)

Committee	Composition	Mandate
Economic and Financial Committee (including a bi-annual 'Financial Stability Table')	Finance ministries, Commission and ECB, as well as national central banks	Advisory role to the ECOFIN Council and to the Commission on economic and financial matters
Financial Services Committee	Finance ministries, Commission and ECB	Strategic policy on financial services Assisting the EFC
Level 3 Supervisory Committees: CEBS, CESR, CEIOPS	Supervisors	Exchange of supervisory information Supervisory convergence
ESCB Banking Supervision Committee	Central banks, supervisors and ECB	Analysis of the EU financial system

C. Financial Integration without Financial Stability?

The governance approach to market integration in this period assumed that decentralisation of competences, together with voluntary cooperation between national

[122] MoU are administrative agreements, not legally binding under public or private international law, which are designed to provide for flexible international legal and administrative regimes. See BCBS, Essential elements of a statement of cooperation between banking supervisors (2001) at www.bis.org/publ/bcbs83.htm, which sets out the basic and main elements of a MoU in the field of banking supervision. See ECB, Memorandum of Understanding on Cooperation between the Financial Supervisory Authorities, Central Banks, and Finance Ministries of the European Union on Cross-Border Financial Stability (2008) at www.ecb.europa.eu/pub/pdf/other/mou-financialstability2008en.pdf.

[123] For an overview of the crisis arrangements, see European Commission, Report on Financial Crisis Management (n 119).

[124] For a description of the exercise, see ECB, The EU Arrangements for Financial Crisis Management, ECB Monthly Bulletin, February 2007, 73–84.

authorities, would suffice to safeguard financial stability in the single financial market and in the Monetary Union.[125]

Similarly to the economic governance framework, the belief was that the absence of an explicit crisis management framework would foster discipline in financial markets. Each Member State and respective national authorities would not commit to cooperate with each other since this could impinge on national fiscal sovereignty and indirectly on the bail-out prohibition between Member States in Article 125 of the TFEU. Instead, the spontaneous cooperation between national authorities would provide a governance system able to contain systemic risk. This would replace the need for the transfer of competences to the European level to safeguard financial stability. This was also the result of the principle of separation in the Maastricht Treaty, which dictated that the single monetary policy would not be accompanied by European competences in financial stability.[126]

In reality, such an institutional architecture was unlikely to provide an adequate framework to prevent and manage financial crises. The MoUs contained for the most part statements of principles with no binding commitments, and therefore without operational implications. The coordination challenges between national authorities were also immense. The financial stability functions were segmented, with different institutional set-ups across Member States. In some cases, financial supervision was under the responsibility of a single authority, while in most countries it was exercised by several authorities, including the central bank. This was reflected in the 2008 European MoU on financial stability, which was signed by more than 100 national authorities. It was thus difficult to conceive that such institutional complexity could result in unified policy responses in a crisis.[127]

Likewise, the committees could prove unwieldy in a crisis. They had no decision-making powers and, at their best, could only facilitate the pooling of information and the coordination of national decisions. They involved cumbersome procedures and operated with representatives from all Member States, while a crisis would only affect a few of them. This hindered the dissemination of confidential information, as required in a crisis. Moreover, there were various committees involved in a crisis with overlapping areas of competence. Finally, in the absence of an allocation of responsibilities, the committees would also dilute the accountability for decisions in crisis situations.

The implication of this institutional architecture was that the single financial market and the Monetary Union were functioning without an effective European financial

[125] The reliance on national competences and committees for financial stability was reaffirmed in European Commission, Europe's financial system: adapting to change, COM (2008) 122 final. For a criticism of this approach, see A Enria, 'Establishing the Banking Union and repairing the Single Market' in F Allen, E Carletti, and Gray (eds) *Political, Fiscal and Banking Union in the Eurozone?* (Philadelphia PA, FIC Press, 2013), 47, at 48–54.

[126] As also argued by D Schoenmaker, 'Is Burden Sharing Needed for International Financial Stability?' in P Hartmann, H Huang, and D Schoenmaker (eds) *The Changing Fortunes of Central Banking* (Cambridge, Cambridge University Press, 2018) 203–226.

[127] The 'separation doctrine' between monetary policy and banking supervision applied to crisis management was described and criticised at the time by T Padoa-Schioppa, 'EMU and Banking Supervision' (1999) 2 *International Finance*, 295.

stability framework. This corresponded to the materialisation of the 'financial trilemma', according to which European financial integration, financial stability in the single market, and preserving national competences for financial stability were mutually incompatible. National authorities would tend to preserve only domestic stability at the expense of financial integration. The European response to the financial crisis in 2008 confirmed this trilemma.[128]

Table 14 The EU Financial Stability Framework (1999–2008)

Levels	Functions	Decision-Making	Committees
EU	• Legislation • Policy-coordination • State aid control	• ECOFIN Council • European Parliament • European Commission	• Economic and Financial Committee • Financial Services Committee • Level 2 regulatory committees
EMU	• Single monetary policy • Contribution to national financial stability and supervision	• ECB Governing Council	• Eurosystem committees
National	• National legislation • Use of public funds	• Finance ministries • National parliaments	–
	• Banking supervision • Insurance supervision • Securities regulation • Supervision of financial conglomerates	• Central banks • Financial supervisors • Banking supervisors • Insurance and pensions supervisors • Securities regulators	• Level 3 supervisory committees
	• Deposit insurance	• Ca. 37 national schemes	–

X. The Democratic Legitimacy of Governance Structures: Transparency and Accountability

As multilevel governance expanded, with a growing impact of its policy- and rule-making capacity, there were increasing concerns about its democratic legitimacy. First,

[128] The concept of a 'financial trilemma' was defined by D Schoenmaker, *Governance of International Banking: The Financial Trilemma* (Oxford, Oxford University Press, 2013).

governance operated above and across national jurisdictions, precisely to overcome their limitations to regulate integrating markets. This also meant that such governance was outside the reach of national political institutions. Second, multilevel governance included several hierarchical levels – supranational, national, and infranational – with no clear centre of authority and without falling into any system of federalism. Third, governance was largely based on voluntary and informal structures and procedures, such as committees and networks, rather than on legal or constitutional orders. All this made governance structures too complex to be scrutinised by political institutions, citizens, or the courts for judicial review.[129]

As a result, governance largely eluded democratic control, which, in turn, undermined its legitimacy. Securing legitimacy – understood in the Weberian meaning as the ability of an authority to justify its existence as the most appropriate to exercise its powers – was essential for the effectiveness of governance structures, given their 'soft' rule-making and enforcement. In order to address such concerns, there was a gradual emphasis on transparency and accountability as sources of legitimacy. Transparency was expected to gather ex ante 'input' legitimacy, by promoting as much participation in policy- and rule-making procedures as possible. If the governance policies and rules reflected such external input, they would have more legitimacy. Accountability aimed at securing ex post 'output' legitimacy, by enabling democratic institutions to assess whether policy and regulatory objectives had been achieved. If such objectives were achieved, they would justify the existence of governance structures. Both 'input' and 'output' legitimacy would provide predictability to policy and rule-making, which further contributed to their credibility.[130]

In the single market, transparency and accountability arose out of the principles of good governance, as outlined in the Commission's White Paper on European Governance, such as openness and participation in European policies. The post-FSAP better regulation strategy implemented these principles in the form of public consultation practices, impact assessments of draft legislation, transparency of legislative debates, and increased public communication. Later, the Lisbon Treaty in 2007 categorised the openness and transparency of European institutions as democratic principles of the Union under Article 11 of the TEU, together with the obligation for the Commission to conduct public consultations.[131]

[129] In this sense see D Curtin, 'Holding (Quasi-)Autonomous EU Administrative Actors to Public Account' (2007) 13 *European Law Journal* 523, pointing out that the main problem with EU administrative governance, comprising executive agencies and comitology committees, is not so much the absence of accountability but the 'chronic lack of transparency,' which hinders the operation of the checks and balances by the Parliament, especially at 540–541.

[130] On the legitimacy problems in European governance, arguing that it would be sufficient that regulatory policies conducted by agencies are legitimised by results, see G Majone 'Europe's "democratic deficit": The question of standards' (1998) 4 *European Law Journal* 5, 14–28. See also C Joerges, 'Deliberative Political Processes' Revisited: What Have We Learnt About the Legitimacy of Supranational Decision-Making' (2006) 44 *Journal of Common Market Studies* 779. On the concept of accountability, see M Bovens, 'Analysing and Assessing Accountability: A Conceptual Framework' (2007) 13 *European Law Journal* 447.

[131] See European Commission, European Governance: a White Paper, at 10–ff; Interinstitutional Agreement on better law-making between the European Parliament, Council and Commission, [2003] OJ C/321/1; European Commission, Towards a reinforced culture of consultation and dialogue – General principles

Accountability by results was the main legitimacy instrument in the EMU framework. As an independent institution, the ECB could not be subject to ex ante democratic control in carrying out its mandate, since otherwise it would contradict its status. The democratic control is instead exercised ex post, based on the extent to which it fulfils its measurable primary objective of price stability. For this purpose, the accountability mechanisms were the statutory reporting commitments of the ECB: quarterly reports and an annual report, which should be submitted to the Parliament, the Council, the Commission and the European Council. The Parliament provides an ex post assessment of the ECB's policy performance through a resolution on the annual report. The President of the ECB attends regular hearings with the Committee of Economic and Monetary Affairs of the Parliament. The ECB has, in addition, transparency and communication practices, such as the disclosure of its monetary policy framework or the press conferences after monetary policy decisions.[132]

The multilevel governance structures, like the Lamfalussy framework, relied, in turn, more on 'input' legitimacy. First, there was 'internal input' across the governance levels, for example, the advice provided by Level 3 committees to the Commission for the preparation of Level 2 acts. Second, there was 'external input' via public consultations by the Commission regarding draft Level 2 acts, and by the Level 3 committees when preparing technical advice or standards, which also created consultative committees of market participants and consumers. The Level 3 committees developed as well transparency requirements for their own operation and for their members, such as the obligation for supervisory authorities to publish their national transposition of Community law and of Level 3 acts. Regarding accountability, the Level 3 committees only had informal reporting obligations since their institutional status remained unclear. They were required to report their achievements to the Council, the Parliament and the Commission, and also to have regular contacts with the respective Level 2 committees.[133]

The move towards transparency and accountability also took place at the global level. As analysed above, the IMF issued in 1999 the Code on Transparency of Monetary and Financial Policies, which became part of the core set of global standards. The BCBS started to report to the G7 on its activities and introduced increasing transparency and consultation procedures in its standard-setting with non-member authorities and market participants.[134]

and minimum standards for consultation of interested parties by the Commission, COM (2002) 704 final, at 15–16. For an analysis of Art 11, TEU, see J Mendes, 'Participation and the Role of the Law after Lisbon: A Legal View on Article 11 TEU' (2011) 48 *CML Rev* 1849.

[132] See Art 284, TFEU and Art 15 of the ESCB and ECB Statute. In addition to reporting requirements, the ECB is subject to judicial review of its legal acts (Arts 263 to 265, TFEU) and to the Court of Auditors, regarding the operational efficiency of the management of the ECB (Art 27.2 of the Statute). For an analysis of the ECB's accountability, see F Amtenbrink, *The Democratic Accountability of Central Banks* (Oxford, Hart Publishing, 1999); and J de Haan, SCW Eijffinger, S Waller, *The European Central Bank: Credibility, Transparency, and Centralization* (Cambridge MA, MIT Press, 2005), at 110–114; Chiara Zilioli, 'Accountability and Independence,' (n 43) at 400.

[133] See Arts 9 and 13 of the Commission Decisions establishing the Level 3 committees. On the accountability of governance arrangements, see C Harlow, *Accountability in the European Union* (Oxford, Oxford University Press, 2002) at 168.

[134] On the accountability and legitimacy of the BCBS through public consultation practices, see MS Barr and GP Miller, 'Global Administrative Law: The View from Basel' (n 34).

The transparency and accountability practices introduced in this period were far from providing democratic legitimacy to governance structures. Regarding transparency, the multiplication of the number of parties providing input to policy- and rule-making, eg in public consultations, was not sufficient to secure legitimacy. For example, the consultations by Level 3 committees of market participants could help to provide 'technical legitimacy' to the regulatory process. However, such consultations were just practices. They were not part of a constitutional framework for safeguarding the legal rights of the persons affected by policies and rules, namely their right to influence regulatory outcomes.[135]

Regarding accountability, the main challenge related to multilevel governance, where there was no central authority to be called to account and adjust its policies and rules. The Level 3 committees, for example, could not really be held accountable for their European tasks as they represented the sum of their individual members, which remained accountable to their national political institutions. Moreover, the outcomes from multilevel structures could be diffuse and not measurable enough to allow for accountability.[136]

In conclusion, transparency and accountability of governance structures had ambivalent implications. They increased significantly the participation in policy and regulatory processes, as well as their public scrutiny. At the same time, they remained embryonic in this period and did not have the quality to achieve democratic legitimacy: there were no constitutional or legal guarantees ensuring that those affected by the regulatory outcomes of governance structures could influence them through transparency and accountability. This period was nonetheless the starting point for pursuing the democratic legitimacy of regulatory policies, particularly in areas that had been so opaque until then like the regulation of finance.[137]

XI. The Consequences of 'Integration through Governance'

A. A New Financial Landscape …

Financial integration increased significantly in this period. There was considerable integration of money and financial markets, an increasing number of pan-European banking groups and financial conglomerates, and also more cross-border market infrastructures, such as clearing and payment systems. The accession of new Member States to the EU in 2004 also contributed to integration, as their financial institutions were privatised and acquired in many cases by financial groups from other Member States.

[135] As argued by J Mendes, *Participation in EU rule-making: A rights-based approach* (Oxford, Oxford University Press, 2011) at 268–318.

[136] In this sense, see Inter-Institutional Monitoring Group, Final Report Monitoring the Lamfalussy Process, 2007, at 17–18, (on file). See also Y Papadopoulos, 'Problems of Democratic Accountability in Network and Multilevel Governance' (2008) 13 *European Law Journal* 469.

[137] See D Curtin, 'Holding (Quasi-)Autonomous EU Administrative Actors to Public Account,' (n 128) on the fragmentary nature of public accountability of EU administration in this period.

There were two dynamic processes in financial integration. First, an expansion of the financial sector within each Member State. In order to gain competitiveness in the single financial market, and also to protect themselves from foreign take-overs, financial institutions increased their size through domestic mergers and acquisitions, and expanded their business through leverage. In several cases, they achieved a financial dimension beyond what would be proportional to the economy of the respective Member State. Second, an expansion of cross-border finance. As financial institutions gained sufficient size and had no space left to grow domestically, they expanded their cross-border business throughout the single financial market. There was an acceleration of cross-border acquisitions in the single financial market, starting in the early 2000s and culminating in 2007 with the acquisition of ABN-AMRO by RBS, Fortis and Banco Santander. As a result, the European financial landscape in 2007–2008 comprised an increasing number of sizeable domestic banks and pan-European financial groups. It represented the high-point of integration in the single financial market.[138]

This landscape was the deliberate outcome of both EU and national policies to reap the benefits of the expansion of financial services in Europe, financial innovation, such as securitisation, and financial globalisation. The corollary of the policies underpinning the governance period was to enable any financial institution to increase in size and expand its business to compete in the single financial market, regardless of the Member State of origin and the size of its respective economy. This was exacerbated by the interest of Member States to have 'national champions' to prevent dominance by foreign banks and generate income for the national economy. The global governance of finance, notably the Basel II Framework, supported such dynamics by favouring larger financial institutions over smaller ones, relying on internal self-assessment of risk and on market discipline. The outcome, together with other factors, was an unsustainable credit boom and asset price inflation, which was one of the main causes of the financial crisis in 2007–2008. It then led to the debacle of many of the largest financial institutions and pan-European financial groups.[139]

B. … Without a Financial Stability Framework …

The 'integration through governance' period is therefore characterised by creating a legal and institutional framework geared towards a self-reinforcing and irreversible process of financial integration. This provided financial markets and institutions with a clear set of incentives to expand their business throughout the single financial market and reach a size commensurate with their new 'domestic market'.

At the same time, the expansion and integration of finance led to deeper systemic interlinkages, which increased the likelihood that a financial crisis could affect the single

[138] On the financial integration in this period, see European Commission, European Financial Integration Report 2008, SEC (2009) 19 final, at 10–12. See a similar assessment in ECB, Financial Integration in Europe (2008) 17–20, at: www.ecb.europa.eu/pub/pdf/other/ financialintegrationineurope200804en.pdf.

[139] In this sense, see A Turner, 'The Turner Review: a regulatory response to the global banking crisis' (2009) *Financial Services Authority*, 11–49; and HW Sinn, *Casino Capitalism*, (n 110) at 46–66.

financial market. The failure of a pan-European financial group would certainly impact several Member States. However, the governance framework only provided a regime of incentives for financial integration. It did not give rise to any connection between the level of financial integration and European liability for the negative externalities of integration, for example, in a financial crisis. This would require transferring risk-sharing competences to the European level and a change in the EU's constitutional principles, which was not anticipated under the governance approach. Instead, the stability of the single financial market was based on the principle that individual Member States and their authorities would be exclusively responsible for the prevention and management of financial crises. While the benefits of financial integration would be shared by all Member States, its potential costs would not be shared, since this would infringe national fiscal sovereignty. As mentioned before, this reflected 'ordoliberal' principles, according to which redistributive policies should only take place at the national level, while the supranational level should be limited to promote free competition.[140]

This had several consequences. Full national responsibility implied that there could not be any meaningful framework for addressing financial crises. The arrangements for financial stability did not go beyond soft law and non-binding agreements, such as MoUs among national authorities. In a financial crisis, each Member State and their respective authorities would pursue what they would perceive as their national interest, notably to minimise their potential financial liability, even though it could lead to higher costs for other or for all Member States.

The absence of EU financial liability also implied that there were no reasons at the European level to constrain financial integration and the related systemic risk. The Treaty only enabled the pursuance of deeper integration. It did not provide any instruments to put a break on 'excessive integration' that went beyond the ability of the EU and Member States to address potential negative spillovers. For example, there were no measures available – and it would be illegal under the Treaty – to prevent banks originating in smaller Member States from achieving a European dimension beyond the fiscal capacity of their home country.[141]

C. … And with a Fragmented Rulebook

Another consequence of this period was that, despite the elaborate governance structures and the re-regulation operated by the FSAP, the single financial market remained largely subject to national jurisdictions. As a result, multilevel governance led to many more additional legislative and regulatory layers, which did not replace the national jurisdictions. The profusion of governance structures, from supranational to infranational, gave

[140] On the failure of 'ordoliberalism', which 'ignored or underestimated the weight and the dynamics of the new regulatory policies' in the single market, see J Hien and C Joerges, 'Dead man walking? Current European interest in the ordoliberal tradition' (2018) 24 *European Law Journal* 142.

[141] For the global context, S Claessens, R Herring, D Schoenmaker, and KA Summe, 'A safer world financial system: Improving the resolution of systemic institutions' (2010) 12 *Geneva reports on the world economy*, at 7–37.

rise to an overly complex and fragmented rulebook with multiple sources and categories of rules, subject to different forms of enforcement.

The Level 1 and Level 2 legislation could include directives requiring national transposition, directly applicable regulations, or a combination – a directive at Level 1 and a regulation at Level 2 implementing the directive. The transposition of Level 1 and Level 2 rules into national laws could be inconsistent and the enforcement could diverge. The Level 3 instruments, such as guidelines, were not binding on national authorities and could not provide legal certainty. Therefore, despite increasing financial integration, more extensive harmonisation and elaborate governance structures, the rules of the single financial market were loosely and inconsistently enforced.[142]

This period ended thus with largely incompatible regimes: (1) a legal and institutional framework directed at ever more financial integration; (2) with a much more integrated single financial market; but (3) without mechanisms for preventing or managing a financial crisis; and (4) based on a complex and fragmented rulebook. Such incompatibility was exacerbated in the Monetary Union, where a single monetary jurisdiction was combined with multiple national jurisdictions for banking supervision and financial stability.[143]

Table 15 The Layers of the Rulebook of the Single Financial Market

Layer		**Rulebook**
Supranational	Level 1	EU legislation adopted by the Council and the Parliament (Directives or directly applicable Regulations)
Supranational with intergovernmental procedures	Level 2	Implementing measures adopted under comitology procedures by the Commission (Directives or directly applicable Regulations)
National rules		National laws transposing Level 1 or Level 2 legislation
		National laws regulating matters not harmonised by Level 1 or Level 2 legislation
		Regulatory acts and enforcement practices of national authorities
Infranational rules	Level 3	Guidelines, standards, and interpretative recommendations issued by the Level 3 Committees (CEBS, CESR, CEIOPS)

[142] The report of the Commission on the 10 years of EMU, which was published in May 2008, made the diagnosis that EU legislation was applied inconsistently and the harmonisation of supervisory practices was insufficient; and that financial stability arrangements remained national-based, despite the increasing financial integration. See European Commission, EMU@10: successes and challenges after 10 years of Economic and Monetary Union, European Economy 2/2008, at 268–269. For an academic analysis, see E Wymeersch, 'The Future of Financial Regulation and Supervision in Europe' (n 94).

[143] See T Padoa-Schioppa, 'EMU and Banking Supervision,' (n 127) at 303–ff.

XII. Conclusion: Creating the Conditions for a 'Banking Union'

'Integration through governance' corresponds to the period of the largest expansion of the single financial market. The strategy was to pursue legal and institutional integration by combining various policies and instruments derived from 'new governance' thinking. It led to significant legal change and exponential growth in European regulation. The previous failed strategy of relying on minimum harmonisation and competition among national rules was replaced by deepening and widening the scope of harmonisation. A multilevel European regulatory system was then put in place to underpin such harmonisation efforts. As a result of this move, together with the globalisation of finance and the Monetary Union, the provision of cross-border financial services increased in volume and many financial institutions increased in size and attained a European dimension.

Accordingly, there were various legal and institutional innovations in this period to achieve integration. The Lamfalussy framework introduced multilevel governance, also replicating developments in the global governance of finance. Comitology became the regulatory mode for a higher level of harmonisation of national laws. The expansion of home-country control, the setting-up of colleges of supervisors, and the Level 3 committees, led to networks of national authorities to pursue the European interest. Level 3 and MoU instruments reflected the increasing use of soft law. The 'better regulation' approach, as well as the introduction of accountability and transparency obligations, aimed at providing democratic legitimacy to the regulatory process.

The rationale of these innovations was to realise the balancing act of expanding European competences while avoiding a conflict with national sovereignty: regulating the single market at the European level without any transfer of competences or changes to the Treaty. This would be achieved by involving national authorities in European governance. The European policies would then emerge out of the synthesis of national competences. Such strategy reduced considerably the resistance of Member States to the innovations, enabling a wide-ranging harmonisation drive and the setting-up of the Lamfalussy framework. It created an institutional dynamic of progressive regulatory delegation to European structures comprising national authorities, which, in turn, increasingly confined the regulatory autonomy of Member States. It thus provided the bridge between the decentralised approach to market regulation from the previous period and the centralisation that would occur later with the Banking Union.[144]

The apparent equilibrium between European competences and national sovereignty was, however, an illusion. Involving national authorities in European governance

[144] In the single market context, see S Weatherill, 'Pre-emption, harmonisation and the distribution of competence to regulate the internal market' in J Scott and C Barnard (eds) *The Law of the Single European Market* (Oxford, Hart Publishing, 2002) 41.

structures did not necessarily give rise to European policies. Multilevel governance increased complexity without removing national competences since, for example, the Level 3 committees had no binding instruments. At the same time, it was also an illusion that national authorities preserved their competences within governance structures. The increasing harmonisation, governance constraints, and market integration, confined their regulatory autonomy. All of this led to an institutional ambiguity that enabled integration to progress without any explicit transfer of competences from the national to the European level. The governance illusion provided the basis for financial services providers to expand unlimitedly their business throughout the single financial market. As mentioned above, the expansion of finance and the increase in size of domestic and pan-European financial institutions was the result of EU and national policies. These policies created the motion of a self-reinforcing and irreversible financial integration. They gave the perception that there was a European framework to expand and sustain permanently a single financial market, including in the case of financial crises.[145]

The overall illusion was, therefore, expanding the single financial market without transferring competences to the European level. Similarly to a game of 'Pareto improvements' leading to a 'Pareto equilibrium,' the aim was to continuously increase integration without making Member States explicitly worse-off. In other words, the strategy was to maximise the benefits to Member States of participating in European governance without increasing their costs. This would gradually lead to positive spillovers in integration and constrain the regulatory autonomy of Member States within governance structures. Moreover, it represented a strategy to circumvent any form of risk-sharing among Member States for the negative externalities of increased integration. It was implausible that such risk-sharing, which would affect the core of national sovereignty, would ever be politically agreed as a condition for deeper financial integration.

The end-result was to undermine the effectiveness of both European and national competences in regulating and supervising the single financial market. It was not possible to take 'hard' European decisions under the governance arrangements, since otherwise they would impinge on national powers. Conversely, national competences were increasingly constrained by European governance and policies, such as competition law. This led, in practice, to a wide deregulation of the single financial market, whereby both the EU and Member States relinquished regulatory powers for the sake of integration. In turn, the predominance of technocratic governance structures, together with the absence of risk-sharing among Member States, led to a 'depoliticisation' of regulation. Since it did not involve risks, the regulation of finance at the European and global levels became a purely technical policy, which was removed from political debate. This was also supported paradoxically by increasing accountability

[145] See G Majone, *Rethinking the Union of Europe Post-Crisis: Has Integration Gone Too Far?* (Cambridge, Cambridge University Press, 2014) 58–86, who characterises this approach to integration as stemming from a 'political culture of total optimism', which disregards long-term consequences.

and transparency obligations at the European level, which legitimised governance structures.[146]

Governance then failed when 'hard' European decisions were necessary to address the financial crisis. The legal and institutional illusion became obvious: despite an integrated single financial market, there were no European competences for addressing its risks and for preserving its integration. The single financial market quickly entered into disintegration since it was functioning on the basis of a self-referential illusion. As long as all – EU, Member States, authorities, and market participants – believed in the illusion, the governance of the single financial market enabled it to expand and thrive. This ended the institutional ambiguity that dominated the governance period and led to the disintegration of the single financial market. Therefore, the 'integration through governance' period starts to end when the global financial crisis first hit Europe in August 2007.

The underlying logic of 'integration through governance' can thus be related to the creation of the Banking Union. The causal link is that it gave rise to a comprehensive legal and institutional environment, which was effectively conducive to more integration. Such an environment was, however, inherently fragile: it promoted market integration without European competences to safeguard the stability of an integrated market. Therefore, this period of 'integration through governance' created the conditions for the materialisation of the 'financial trilemma' alluded to before: deeper financial integration implied that financial stability could not be achieved with national competences. In the case of financial crises, preserving the integration achieved would require transferring competences to the European level. This period thus paved the ground towards the inevitability of a Banking Union as an outcome of the evolution of European law.[147]

Table 16 Legal Change in 'Integration through Governance' (1998–2007)

Legal and institutional innovations		**Integration policies**	**Remaining obstacles to integration**
1	The ECB as an independent regulatory authority and the ESCB as an institutional system comprising a European and national authorities	• Monetary Union and the conduct of the single monetary policy	• Multiple national supervisory jurisdictions and the absence of a banking union • Inconsistent transposition and enforcement practices of EU law
2	FSAP: (i) extension of the perimeter of European law and (ii) deeper harmonisation	• Re-regulation of the single financial market	

(continued)

[146] For a critique of technocratic regimes under the label of governance and without democratic legitimation, see J Habermas, *The Lure of Technocracy* (Cambridge, Polity, 2015) 56–58.

[147] On the financial trilemma as the justification for a banking union, see V Constâncio, 'Towards a European Banking Union' (2012) at www.ecb.europa.eu/press/key/date/2012/html/sp120907.en.html.

Table 16 ***(Continued)***

<table>
<tr><th colspan="2">Legal and institutional innovations</th><th>Integration policies</th><th>Remaining obstacles to integration</th></tr>
<tr><td>3</td><td>Better regulation</td><td>• Improving transposition and enforcement of EU law</td><td rowspan="6">• Complicated interplay between Levels 1 and 2
• Non-binding nature of Level 3 to achieve convergence of enforcement practices
• Lack of a 'European mandate' for the home-country authorities of financial services groups
• Lack of a European financial stability framework to address systemic risk
• Lack of accountability of national authorities for pursuing European objectives</td></tr>
<tr><td>4</td><td>Lamfalussy framework: multilevel governance, comitology, and supervisory committees</td><td>• Regulation of the single financial market
• Convergence of enforcement practices
• Compliance with EU law</td></tr>
<tr><td>5</td><td>Expansion of home-country control to financial services groups; and colleges of supervisors</td><td>• Supervision of financial services groups without transfer of competences</td></tr>
<tr><td>6</td><td>Application of competition policy to the banking sector</td><td>• Financial integration, against national protectionism</td></tr>
<tr><td>7</td><td>Memoranda of Understanding on financial stability (non-binding)</td><td>• Safeguarding financial stability without transfer of competences</td></tr>
<tr><td>8</td><td>Accountability and transparency obligations at the European level</td><td>• Increasing legitimacy of European governance
• Accountability of national authorities in the pursuance of European objectives</td></tr>
</table>

4

(Dis-)Integration through Crisis (2008–2012)

> Like all crises, they could have been the occasion of progress, by provoking a crystallization of latent wills. Great things are almost always done in crises. Those of recent years could have been the occasion for a leap forward.
>
> Why did they on the contrary cause a step back? The fact is that at no time did the governments really try to face together the difficult circumstances. Their will did not show itself as a European will, but a series of national wills more or less unaware of those of the others, each one doing its best to find its own way out of trouble. Attempts to face up to the different crises through communal action have been timid and short-lived.
>
> Marjolin Report, 1975[1]

I. Introduction

The financial crisis led to the failure of the law and governance of the single financial market. The expansion of finance promoted in the previous period was not matched by a framework for addressing its increased risks. When the full force of the financial crisis hit Europe in September 2008, there were only national responses. Financial institutions could only be rescued with public funds at the national level. This quickly led to the renationalisation of the single financial market, as Member States insulated their domestic markets from contagion. The Paris Euro summit of 12 October 2008, the first summit of the leaders of the euro area, attempted to provide a European coordination framework for national measures, while relaxing at the same time the application of European law.

This chapter analyses the legal and institutional innovations, which were motivated by the rapid disintegration of the single financial market and the need to revert its re-nationalisation. A new 'Comité des Sages' chaired by Jacques de Larosière, one of the many committees created for a European financial market over the years, was mandated to propose reforms. In February 2009, the De Larosière Report recommended the

[1] European Commission, Report of the Study Group 'Economic and Monetary Union 1980,' Brussels, March 1975, at ec.europa.eu/archives/emu_history/documentation/chapter7/19750308en57reportstudygroup.pdf. For the background of this statement, see R Marjolin, *Le travail d'une vie: Mémoires 1911-1986* (Paris, Éditions Robert Laffont, 1986) 356–359.

establishment of a new European System of Financial Supervision (ESFS) comprising three European Supervisory Authorities (ESA) and a European Systemic Risk Board (ESRB). The concept of macroprudential supervision, one of the many regulatory outcomes of the crisis, was also introduced in European law to safeguard financial stability. A new round of legislation was thus initiated – also to implement the new global standards – which widened the scope and depth of EU financial services law. This provided the basis for a 'single financial services rulebook', which would replace the framework of the previous single passport.[2]

At the end of this period, there was a new legal and institutional landscape in the single financial market, all based on the harmonisation clause of Article 114 of the Treaty on the Functioning of the European Union (TFEU), but still without the transfer of competences to the European level or arrangements for crisis management and risk-sharing among Member States.

II. The Financial Crisis Unfolds in Europe

A. The Start of the Financial Crisis in August 2007

The global financial crisis was triggered by the exposure of the banking system to large amounts of financial products originating in the so-called 'sub-prime' mortgage markets in the US: loans for the purchase of a house granted to borrowers with high credit risk at correspondingly high interest rates. The falling US house prices in 2007 then led to uncertainty regarding the magnitude and concentration of exposures of banks to such markets.[3]

In Europe, the sub-prime related losses of European banks first emerged in July 2007. Substantial losses were reported by IKB, a German Landesbank, with regard to one of its special investment vehicles (SIVs), which was then rescued by the German Government. The crisis of confidence in the banking system escalated in the first week of August 2007, as rating agencies downgraded a range of sub-prime related instruments and BNP Paribas froze three investment funds due to sub-prime losses. Lack of confidence on the soundness of counterparties led to the freezing up of interbank money markets and the drying up of liquidity in many markets. The ECB provided €95 billion in liquidity to the euro area banking sector to address the liquidity crisis.[4]

After this liquidity crisis, the first major event was a bank run, which had not taken place in Europe since 1945. On 15 September 2007, customers queued up outside the branches of Northern Rock in the UK. Funds were quickly withdrawn as it was the first

[2] J de Larosière, 'High-Level Group on Financial Supervision in EU' (2009), at ec.europa.eu/internal_market/finances/docs/de_larosiere_report_en.pdf ('de Larosière Report').

[3] For a full chronology and description of the global financial crisis, see BIS, 79th Annual Economic Report (2009) at www.bis.org/publ/arpdf/ar2009e.htm. On the historical background to the subprime crisis, and parallelisms with the 1929 financial crisis, see B Eichengreen, *Hall of Mirrors: The Great Depression, the Great Recession, and the Uses and Misuses of History* (Oxford, Oxford University Press, 2015) 167–212.

[4] See *Financial Times*, 'ECB injects €95bn to help markets,' 10 August 2007.

run where depositors could also use internet banking. Despite assurances from the UK Financial Services Authority (FSA) that Northern Rock was solvent, the bank run did not stop and only started to slow down once the UK Treasury successively guaranteed both existing and future deposits. The ineffectiveness of the deposit guarantee system in this case led later to a reform in Europe and globally.[5]

B. The Fallout in Europe of the Failure of Lehman Brothers

The momentous event of the financial crisis came on 15 September 2008, when the US investment bank Lehman Brothers filed for bankruptcy. The fact that the US authorities allowed a major global bank to fail changed drastically the paradigm under which financial markets operated since then: the 'too big to fail' assumption, namely that authorities would ultimately rescue a major financial institution to avoid its collapse, was no longer valid. It implied that 'counterparty risk' increased substantially: the risk that a market participant would default on its obligations. This further exacerbated the crisis of confidence in financial markets as the extent of exposures to sub-prime instruments among financial institutions, and hence the extent of potential losses, was unknown.[6]

In Europe, concerns about the soundness of major financial institutions precipitated a wave of governmental interventions. The first was Fortis bank, a pan-European banking group, which epitomised the ideal of the single financial market. It operated with a significant market share in the three Benelux countries (Belgium, the Netherlands, and Luxembourg) and across many Member States. It was also a financial conglomerate involved in banking, insurance, and investment management activities. Following growing market concerns as to the ability of Fortis to withstand the crisis, it had to be rescued on the weekend of 27 and 28 September 2008 through a joint operation of the governments of the Benelux countries. As a result, the Fortis Group was split among these countries and partially nationalised. Similarly, other pan-European banking groups also had to be rescued in quick succession. On 29 September 2008, Dexia was bailed out by a capital injection from the Belgian Government and regional governments, was well as by the French and Luxembourg Governments. On the same

[5] Northern Rock was the 5th largest bank in the UK at the time. Its downfall was due to the reliance on capital markets to fund its core activity of mortgage lending, which meant that it could not refinance its maturing liabilities when liquidity dried up in August 2007. On 14 August 2007, the Bank of England provided emergency liquidity assistance (ELA) to Northern Rock, which was authorised by the UK Chancellor. The UK Treasury provided guarantees for retail deposits. On 5 December 2007 the Commission approved the UK rescue aid for Northern Rock and decided that the ELA did not constitute state aid: Commission Decision of 5.12.2007, NN 70/2007, not yet published. The regulatory lessons from Northern Rock included the following. First, the deposit-guarantee scheme was not credible regarding: (i) the amount guaranteed of deposits, (ii) the delay in returning deposits was too long, and (iii) the funding was insufficient. Second, there was no bank resolution regime, which would have allowed an early intervention by regulators. Third, the institutional framework for supervision was questioned, as the supervisory approach of the FSA did not include the assessment of risks for the financial system. See the official report: UK, The run on the rock, Report of the Treasury Committee of the House of Commons, The Stationery Office (2008); and A Turner, 'The Turner Review: a regulatory response to the global banking crisis' (2009) *Financial Services Authority*.

[6] For an account of the collapse of Lehman Brothers, see B Eichengreen, *Hall of Mirrors*, (n 3) 191–202.

day, the German Government announced a rescue of the Hypo Real Estate group, which ended-up by being fully nationalised in October 2009.[7]

On 30 September 2008, the Irish Government announced a two-year blanket guarantee of the liabilities of six Irish banks, in order to stem the loss of confidence over the Irish banking system. This unilateral guarantee led to immediate spillovers across the single financial market. It undermined the principle of non-discrimination: it did not apply to Irish subsidiaries of EU banks, and it provided a competitive advantage to Irish banks, which reportedly benefited from a flow of funds in their subsidiaries in other Member States, such as the UK. This had a domino effect, as other Member States announced guarantees to maintain the confidence in their respective banking systems. This involved Austria, Greece, and Germany, with rumours abound about many other Member States.[8]

On 6 October 2008, all three major banks of Iceland – Landsbanki, Kaupthing Bank and Glitnir – went into administration, as the Icelandic Government had no financial capacity to rescue them. The banks had expanded throughout several Member States benefiting from the single passport provided by Iceland's membership of the EEA. Depositors in these Member States could not be compensated by the Icelandic deposit guarantee scheme, which had insufficient funds. This was later the subject of an EFTA Court ruling.[9]

C. The Beginning of the Sovereign Debt Crisis

The financial crisis in Europe then became a sovereign debt crisis in October 2009, when Greece disclosed a public deficit much beyond what it had previously reported. This marked the beginning of the uncertainty regarding the sustainability of the public debt of several euro area Member States, as a result of the costs of the banking crisis and the lack of soundness of public finances.

The banks became more and more fragile as their soundness also depended on the ability of their respective Member State to provide public support. In turn, several

[7] According to the Commission's State Aid Decisions on Fortis, the difficulties of the bank were the result of several factors: (i) the involvement of Fortis in the acquisition in October 2007 of the bank ABN AMRO by a consortium of banks, whereby Fortis agreed to a purchase price of €24 billion, which required a vast financing plan that proved difficult to implement; (ii) the subprime crisis, which made it difficult to mobilise the funds to pay the purchase price of ABN AMRO and impaired Fortis's investment in structured credits; (iii) the loss of confidence on the part of the financial markets; and (iv) the liquidity crisis. The combination of these factors created the conditions for a bank run. See European Commission, Letter to the Member State regarding State aid NN 42/2008 – Belgium, NN 46/2008 – Luxembourg NN 53/A/2008 – Netherlands, Restructuring aid to Fortis Bank and Fortis Bank Luxembourg, paras 13–18, at ec.europa.eu/competition/state_aid/cases/227768/227768_1027866_42_1.pdf. For analysis of the coordination problems in the Fortis case, see M Dewatripont, JC Rochet, and J Tirole, *Balancing the Banks: Global Lessons from the Financial Crisis* (Princeton, Princeton University Press, 2010) 123–127.

[8] See N Kroes 'Dealing with the current financial crisis' (2008) *Speech 08/498 at the Economic and Monetary Affairs Committee of the European Parliament.*

[9] The question of whether Iceland was under an obligation to compensate depositors for the failure of its banks was the subject of Case E-16/11 EFTA Ct. Rep [2013] p 4, 28.01.2013. The EFTA Court found that Iceland had not failed its obligations under the EEA Agreement and the Directive 94/19/EC on deposit-guarantee schemes.

Member States also depended on the ability of the banks to acquire public debt. This mutual dependence between Member States and banks led to a self-fulfilling downward spiral in market confidence. It resulted in the successive provision of financial assistance by the EU and the IMF to Greece, Ireland, Portugal, Spain and Cyprus between 2010 and 2013. The sovereign debt crisis was also exacerbated by the increasing lack of confidence on the institutional capacity of the EU and euro area to contain it. It led, ultimately, to an existential crisis of the euro area, which only abated when the ECB committed to intervene in public debt markets in the summer of 2012. The implications of the sovereign debt crisis for the single financial market are addressed in Chapter 5.[10]

D. The Impact on the Single Financial Market

The financial crisis involved, therefore, a series of events in Europe, which spread throughout the single financial market with immediate spillovers: a loss of confidence in the soundness of European banks, bank runs, the failure of cross-border and domestic financial institutions, the financial collapse of an entire country – Iceland – which was part of the single financial market as an EEA member, and the ensuing sovereign debt crisis.[11]

The common implication was the disintegration of the single financial market. As mentioned at the end of Chapter 3, the financial crisis made apparent the legal and institutional 'illusion' underpinning the single financial market: an integrated market but without European competences or liability for addressing the risks and costs of integration. In the case of a financial crisis, competences and liability remained national. Financial integration could not be preserved without financial stability.

Once this 'illusion' vanished, there was a quick reversal in financial integration. As banks were forced to deleverage and reduce their size as a result of the crisis, they retrenched into national markets. The national public support provided to banks also implied that cross-border business was not preserved. The priority was to safeguard the impact of the crisis on the national economies. In turn, this also implied that banks and companies in the more affected Member States had difficulty in accessing financing and lending from other Member States. Pricing of finance was no longer uniform in the single financial market. It diverged across Member States depending on the vulnerability of the national financial system, which was interlinked with the soundness of public finances. Therefore, the assessment of financial risk became national rather than related to the single financial market. Later, the fragmentation of the single financial

[10] Before the Greek crisis, Hungary also had to be rescued by the IMF and the EU with the assistance of about $25 billion in October 2008, following a steep decline on its currency, fall in the stock market, increase of interest rates, and shortage of liquidity in financial institutions, Hungary had a significant public deficit and its economy was dependent on foreign capital, since the government had financed itself through loans in foreign currency, namely the euro and Swiss francs. Many retail banking loans in Hungary had also been made in foreign currency. See IMF, EU, and World Bank Line Up $25 Billion for Hungary, 28 October 2008, at www.imf.org/external/pubs/ft/survey/so/2008/car102808b.htm.

[11] For an account of the impact of the financial crisis in Europe, see See B Eichengreen, *Hall of Mirrors*, (n 3) 134–146 and 213–222.

market accelerated when the sovereign debt crisis raised fears of a possible break-up of the euro area, leading to a redenomination risk of the euro.[12]

As financial integration became inextricably linked with financial stability, the evolution of the single financial market in this period largely consisted of an attempt to reform the legal and institutional framework to preserve both integration and stability, while remaining within the boundaries of the Treaty.

III. The Renationalisation of the Single Financial Market

A. The National Responses to the European Financial Crisis

The immediate European response to the financial crisis was the renationalisation of the single financial market. The collapse of Lehman Brothers did not give rise to a European response within the Treaty framework: there were no proposals by the Commission, decisions by the Council, or common measures agreed among Member States. There was instead a succession of national measures in a domino effect, as each Member State took unilateral decisions to safeguard their national financial systems. This included bank rescues in the UK, Germany, Belgium, the Netherlands and Luxembourg, and deposit guarantees in Ireland, Germany, Belgium, Greece, Luxembourg, Netherlands, Portugal and Spain. These measures were uncoordinated and provided in uneven terms and conditions across Member States.

Following this widespread adoption of national measures, which led to a shutdown of the single financial market, there were attempts for putting together a European response. On 6 October 2008, the members of the European Council issued a statement where they pledged to take whatever measures necessary to safeguard the financial system, particularly depositors. They also acknowledged the need for close coordination and cooperation, without specifying how and when this would be accomplished.[13]

The Economic and Financial Affairs Council (ECOFIN) of 7 October 2008 took a number of commitments, including supporting systemic financial institutions through recapitalisation, ensuring the liquidity of the financial system, and protecting retail depositors. In order to contain the impact of Ireland's unilateral guarantee of deposits, the ECOFIN agreed that all Member States would, at least for one year, provide deposit guarantees for an amount of €50,000, while some Member States would raise their minimum to €100,000, up from the EU minimum of €20,000. The ECOFIN also

[12] For an overview of the reversal in financial integration, see European Commission, European Financial Stability and Integration Report 2012 (2013), ec.europa.eu/info/sites/info/files/efsir-2012-25042013_en.pdf; and ECB, Financial Integration in Europe (2013), at www.ecb.europa.eu/pub/pdf/other/financialintegrationineurope201304en.pdf.

[13] Statement of the 27 European Heads of State and Government on the Stability of the Financial System (6 October 2008): 'All the leaders of the EU declare that each of them will take whatever measures are necessary to ensure the stability of the financial system – whether by injecting liquidity from central banks, by measures targeted at certain banks or by enhanced measures to protect deposits. No depositor in the banks of our countries has suffered losses and we will continue to take the necessary measures to protect the system and depositors. In taking these measures, European leaders acknowledge the need for close coordination and cooperation.'

declared that public intervention had to be decided at the national level and set out 'EU common principles' for the coordination of the national responses to the crisis. The principles stated that such responses should take into consideration potential cross-border effects through daily contact with the EFC and through the application of the EU MoU on cross-border financial stability. Finally, the ECOFIN agreed that the application of the Stability and Growth Pact (SGP) should reflect exceptional circumstances.[14]

The agreement made at the ECOFIN aimed at containing the immediate implications of the unilateral decisions of Member States to support their respective financial systems, which threatened to quickly disintegrate the single financial market. In reality, it reflected the Council's lack of realisation of the seriousness of the crisis for the EU. The emphasis remained on national responses and on light coordination. The 'EU common principles' did not recognise the exceptional nature of the crisis. There was no sense of urgency on the need for European measures. This also reflected the fact that the crisis at that stage was affecting mostly a few Member States and not all 27.

B. The Paris Summit of 12 October 2008: The European 'Branding' of National Measures

The first institutional innovation following the start of the financial crisis in Europe was the meeting of the euro area Heads of State and Government in Paris on 12 October 2008. The re-nationalisation of the single financial market was increasingly affecting the integrity of the euro area. At the same time, it was not feasible to have an agreement among all the 27 Member States on European actions to address the crisis. In order to overcome the stalemate, President Sarkozy of France called for this first meeting of the euro area Heads of State and Government. Until then, in almost ten years since the introduction of the euro, there had not been an institutional setting for the European Council to decide on measures regarding the euro area.

The euro area Member States agreed at the summit to take a number of national measures within a coordinated framework. The spectrum of measures aimed at ensuring liquidity for banks, facilitating their funding, providing capital for them to continue to finance the economy, recapitalising distressed banks, applying flexibility in accounting rules, and enhancing cooperation among EU Member States. The European Council of 15 and 16 October 2008 then endorsed the euro area agreement for the EU.[15]

[14] The ECOFIN common principles on the national responses were the following: (1) interventions should be timely and the support should in principle be temporary; (2) the interests of taxpayers should be safeguarded; (3) existing shareholders should bear the due consequences of the intervention; (4) the government should be in a position to bring about a change of a bank's management; (5) the management should not retain undue benefits – governments may have the power to intervene in remuneration; (6) the legitimate interest of competitors must be protected, in particular through the state aids rules; and (7) negative spillover effects should be avoided. See EU Council, ECOFIN Council Conclusions of 7 October 2008: Immediate responses to financial turmoil, 13930/08 (2008).

[15] See Euro Summit, Summit of the euro area countries: declaration on a concerted European action plan of the euro area countries, 12 October 2008, at ec.europa.eu/economy_finance/publications/pages/publication13260_en.pdf. See also European Council, Presidency Conclusions of 15 and 16 October 2008.

In substance, the coordination framework for such measures was open-ended and left a large discretion to national implementation. The stated objective of the euro area Member States was to 'avoid that national measures adversely affect the functioning of the single market and the other Member States'. The aim was not to safeguard the euro area and the single financial market with European measures. Instead, Member States resorted to a 'European branding' of national measures under the aegis of the meeting of the euro area Heads of State and Government. There was no agreement for sharing the costs of the crisis.

Following the Paris declaration, and throughout the remainder of 2008 and in 2009, Member States implemented their national programmes of financial support. The support included government guarantees on the senior debt of banks, the subscription of equity in banks, mostly preferential shares, and the acquisition of toxic assets from banks through asset relief schemes. Member States also undertook a number of nationalisations of failing banks, which could not be recovered through the provision of additional capital. These financial support measures differed very widely among Member States in terms of features and conditions since they were tailored to the needs of their domestic financial institutions. This further reinforced the fragmentation of the single financial market.[16]

In addition to the governments' support to financial institutions, the ECB took several central banking measures. They included the provision of US-dollar liquidity to banks, the conduct of special refinancing operations, the provision of liquidity with full allotment – instead of competitive bidding – at a fixed rate to banks, the expansion of the list of assets eligible as collateral for such operations, the purchase of covered bonds, as well as the provision by national central banks of ELA to individual banks.[17]

Finally, there were measures to provide economic stimulus. The Commission proposed in November 2008 a 'European Economic Recovery Plan' in the form of a coordinated budgetary spending amounting to 1.5 per cent of the EU's GDP, equivalent to €200 billion. Member States were allowed to breach the SGP with regard to the 3 per cent GDP deficit reference value, and the time needed for economic recovery was taken into consideration for the corrective action. The coordinated framework set by the Commission was very broad and in practice Member States diverged considerably in the type and volume of the stimulus.[18]

[16] The total amount of state aid to the banking sector approved by the Commission between October 2008 and mid-July 2009 accounted for approximately 31% of EU GDP. See DG Competition's review of guarantee and recapitalisation schemes in the financial sector, 7 August 2009, at ec.europa.eu/competition/state_aid/legislation/review_of_schemes_en.pdf.

[17] For an overview of all central bank measures to address the financial crisis see ECB, The implementation of monetary policy since August 2007, ECB Monthly Bulletin, July 2009.

[18] See European Commission, A European Economic Recovery Plan, COM (2008) 800 final; and also European Council, Presidency Conclusions of 11 and 12 December 2008. For a comparison showing the substantial diversity among national plans, see D Saha and J von Weizsäcker, 'Estimating the size of the European stimulus packages for 2009: An Update' (2009) 2009/01 Bruegel Policy Contribution.

Table 17 Measures Agreed at the Paris Euro Summit

1	**Liquidity of banks**	The ECB and other central banks had decided on interest rate cuts and measures to improve the access to central bank money, through the expansion of the collateral eligible for monetary policy operations
2	**Funding of banks**	Provision to liquidity constrained, but solvent, banks of government guarantees for new medium term (up to 5 years) bank senior debt issuance until 31 December 2009; the guarantees would be offered to all banks incorporated in Member States and to foreign subsidiaries with substantial operations[19]
3	**Capital for banks**	Provision of Tier 1 capital to banks, eg through preferred shares, with a pricing taking into account the market situation of each bank
4	**Recapitalisation of distressed banks**	Commitment to support the financial system and to avoid the failure of relevant financial institutions
5	**Accounting rules**	Flexible application of accounting rules by allowing financial and non-financial institutions to value assets with assumptions on default risk, rather than their market value, which was not deemed appropriate due to illiquid markets
6	**Cooperation among Member States**	Procedures for the exchange of information between governments, the President of the European Council, the President of the Commission, the President of the ECB and the President of the Eurogroup, namely a EU financial crisis cell, established at the European Council of 15 October 2008

C. The Application of State Aid Rules in the Crisis

State aid policy was one of the few European instruments used to contain discriminatory national measures during the crisis. From the run on Northern Rock until the failure of Lehman Brothers, the Commission did not recognise the systemic nature of the financial crisis as an exceptional situation for the approval of Member States' financial support measures under the Treaty. As a result, the support measures were subject to the application of the Rescue and Restructuring Guidelines. These required the institutions benefiting from aid to restructure and divest. When applied to financial institutions, it could prevent them from resuming the provision of credit to the economy as intended by the Member States' support measures. Therefore, the application of state aid rules was perceived by Member States as an aggravating factor of the crisis rather than a safeguard of the single market.[20]

[19] The ECB issued recommendations on the conditions for the pricing of state guarantees and recapitalisation of financial institutions, which provided a coordination framework among Member States to preserve the level-playing field: ECB, Recommendations on the pricing of guarantees (2008), at www.ecb.europa.eu/pub/pdf/other/recommendations_on_guaranteesen.pdf, and ECB, Recommendations on the pricing of recapitalisation (2008), at www.ecb.europa.eu/pub/pdf/other/recommendations_on_pricing_for_recapitalisationsen.pdf.

[20] The Commission applied in all cases Art 87(3)(c) of the Treaty and the Rescue and Restructuring Guidelines, which are applicable for any firms in difficulty. The Commission stated in its decisions

Accordingly, the Paris Declaration requested the Commission to act quickly and apply flexibility in state aid decisions, providing in practice a wide discretion to Member States. The Commission then changed its state aid policy and approved in quick succession a series of government support measures. The Commission recognised the uniqueness of the crisis and devised a more flexible regime for the application of state aid rules through a series of Banking Communications, which provided a coordination framework for Member States. Under this framework, the Commission approved €4.5 trillion of state aid to financial institutions, between October 2008 and October 2011.[21]

Table 18 Government interventions in the European banking sector in 2008

Member States	Bank failure	Month	Government intervention
AT	*Kommunalkredit*	November	Acquisition of 99.8% of its shares.
BE, LU, FR	*Dexia*	September	Capital injection of €6.4 billion, jointly agreed by the FR, BE and LU Governments.
BE, LU, NL	*Fortis*	October	The NL Government decided to nationalise Fortis Netherlands for €16.8 billion. The components of the bank in BE and LU were sold to BNP Paribas.

(continued)

that the difficulties faced by the banks were due to the pursuance of specific business models, rather than to a generalised disturbance to the economy under Art 87(3)(b) of the Treaty. See European Commission, Community guidelines on State aid for rescuing and restructuring firms in difficulty, [2004] OJ C244. See also the Commission Decision of 2 April 2008 in Case C-14/2008 to open an in-depth investigation; Commission Decision of 4 June 2008 in Case C-9/2008 to approve the aid to Sachsen LB subject to conditions; and Commission Decision of 21 October 2008 in Case C-10/2008 to approve the aid to IKB subject to conditions. For the analysis of the Commission's state aid policy, see C Ahlborn and D Piccinin, 'The Application of the Principles of Restructuring Aid to Banks during the Financial Crisis' (2010) 9 *European State Aid Law Quarterly* 47.

[21] Following the Paris Declaration, the Commission issued a first 'Banking Communication' on 13 October 2008, where it recognised the systemic nature of the financial crisis in Europe and announced that Art 87(3)(b) of the Treaty would provide the legal basis for justifying aid measures in the form of a general scheme available to financial institutions in a Member State, including state guarantees over bank debt and recapitalisation schemes. The Commission distinguished between illiquid but fundamentally sound financial institutions, and financial institutions which have endogenous problems. Aid to the first type of institutions would require less restructuring. Aid to the second type would require a more far-reaching restructuring, as well as compensatory measures to limit distortions of competition. See European Commission, The application of State aid rules to measures taken in relation to financial institutions in the context of the current global financial crisis, [2008] OJ C270/8–14. This was followed by other Commission Communications specifying the conditions for assessing the recapitalisation of financial institutions and schemes to address the problems of banks' impaired assets: European Commission, The recapitalisation of financial institutions in the current financial crisis: limitation of aid to the minimum necessary and safeguards against undue distortions of competition, [2009] OJ C10/2–10; and European Commission, Treatment of Impaired assets in the Community Banking Sector, [2009] OJ C72. Finally, the Commission concluded its state aid policy during the crisis by setting out a framework for the exit from the dependence of financial institutions over aid. This was announced on 22 July 2009 with a new Communication, the so-called Financial Crisis Restructuring Guidelines, which obliged banks to be submitted to stress-tests and evaluated under EU methodologies as to their long-term viability. See European Commission, The return to viability and the assessment of restructuring measures in the financial sector in the current crisis under the State aid rules, [2009] OJ C195/9–20.

Table 18 ***(Continued)***

Member States	Bank failure	Month	Government intervention
DE	*Hypo Real Estate*	September	Provision of €50 billion in emergency liquidity by the government and other commercial banks; HRE was later nationalised.
	BayernLB	October	Provision of €10 billion in public funds.
	Commerzbank	January 2009	After a first capital injection in November 2008, the Government invested €10 billion in exchange for 25% of the bank's capital.
DK	*Roskilde Bank*	August	The Danish central bank provided a DKK4.5 billion (€600 million) bailout.
Iceland	*Glitnir Bank, Landsbanki, Kaupthing Bank*	October	The government seized control of all three banks, which were put in receivership. New banks, owned by the state, took over the banks' domestic assets.
IE	*Bank of Ireland, Allied Irish Bank*	December	Subscription by the government of €2 billion of perpetual preference shares.
	Anglo Irish bank	January 2009	Nationalisation after a collapse of its share price triggered fears of insolvency.
LV	*Parex Banka*	November	Nationalisation of Latvia's second largest bank.
NL	*ING*	October	Purchase of €10 billion worth of shares.
PT	*Banco Português de Negócios*	November	Nationalisation after the bank had accumulated losses of €700 million.
	Banco Privado Português	December	A group of Portuguese banks extended a loan of €450 million on the basis of a government guarantee.
SE	*Carnegie*	November	Nationalisation.
UK	*Northern Rock*	February	Nationalisation.
	Bradford & Bingley (B&B)	September	Nationalisation, after Abbey Santander bought B&B's deposits and branch network. The government declared that all retail deposits would be safeguarded.
	Royal Bank of Scotland	October	The government took a majority stake by injecting €20 billion through preference shares.
	Lloyds TSB – HBOS	October	The government injected close to £17 billion into the merged bank, controlling over 43.4% of the shares.

Sources: Public Information and European Commission State Aid Decisions.

D. The Consequences of the Single Passport for the Crisis

The responses to the financial crisis demonstrated the fallacy of the main assumption underpinning the single financial market. It had been wrongly assumed that the sharing among Member States of the benefits from market integration implied that the costs of such integration would also be shared. Instead, the crisis exposed the asymmetry in the legal DNA of the single financial market: the community of benefits created by law was not matched by a community of risks, where the costs of integration would be shared by all. National fiscal sovereignty would not allow any transfer of powers to the European level that would involve using public funds to address the costs of integration. In addition, the no-bail out clause of Article 125 of the TFEU forbade the EU or a Member State from being liable or assuming the commitments of another Member State, thus prohibiting any mutualisation of costs.[22]

This legal asymmetry was encapsulated in the single passport regime. The single passport aimed at providing all possible incentives for financial institutions to expand their cross-border activities unlimitedly across the single market, independently of any associated risks. Once risks materialised, the single passport framework quickly led to the opposite effect: a rapid renationalisation of the single financial market.[23]

The principles of home-country control and mutual recognition enabled financial institutions to provide cross-border services without essentially any safeguards. Services could be provided with a simple notification to the home-country in the case of branches, and a simple approval process by the host-country in the case of subsidiaries. Host-country authorities could not protect national markets and question the home-country decisions as this could involve discriminatory measures. At the same time, there were no obligations for home-country authorities to support their financial institutions, or safeguard the interest of the host-countries. For example, there were no provisions on how capital and liquidity would be provided to financial institutions in case of need. Financial institutions were, therefore, able to expand beyond the capacity of the home-country to provide liquidity and/or solvency support, as in the case of Iceland, Ireland, and later Spain. The home-country authorities had no incentives,

[22] See MK Brunnermeier, H James and JP Landau, *The Euro and the Battle of Ideas* (Princeton, Princeton University Press, 2016) at 166, arguing that financial stability concerns did not play a role in the design of the Maastricht Treaty, also due to the fact that the financial system was much less integrated at the time than it came to be.

[23] Cross-border mergers and acquisitions and branching of financial institutions were particularly supported in the previous period of integration. This is well illustrated by the troubled acquisition in 2005 of the Italian bank Antonveneta by the Dutch bank ABN AMRO. It was followed in October 2007 by the acquisition of ABN AMRO itself by a consortium comprising Royal Bank of Scotland of the UK, Banco Santander of Spain, and Fortis of Belgium. Another example was the merger in 2005 between the Italian bank Unicredit and the German bank HVB, which led to a banking group with substantial business in several Member States. The Nordea banking group – the result of acquisitions of Swedish, Finnish, Danish and Norwegian banks – announced in 2004 the intention of establishing itself as a European Company and transforming all its subsidiaries into branches in order not to be subject to four different national regulatory systems. The single passport also facilitated the acquisition of the majority of the financial sector of most new Member States by financial groups from other Member States following the EU enlargement process in 2004.

and the host-country authorities had no powers, to constrain the expansion of finance; both benefitted from finance, but none took responsibility for the risks.[24]

In normal times, the operation of home-country control and mutual recognition prevented this vacuum of responsibilities from coming to the fore, as the expansion of finance spread economic benefits across Member States. When the crisis hit, this vacuum implied that economic and financial risks could not be addressed. National authorities were obliged by their mandates to minimise the costs for their own Member State rather than reducing the collective costs for the EU as a whole. Home-country control and mutual recognition then led to outcomes which were opposite to those of integration: it was rational for the home-country to safeguard the banking assets in its Member State to protect domestic creditors and limit any liabilities vis-à-vis host-countries; while the host-country also ring-fenced domestic assets and avoided their repatriation to the home-country. National regulators cannot rely on assets in one Member State to compensate for losses in another, since the location of assets determines the compensation of the domestic creditors under commercial and insolvency laws. In a crisis, the single passport led thus to the perverse effect of a misallocation of risks and an increase in economic and financial costs among Member States.[25]

The limited harmonisation of national laws also contributed to the absence of a legal framework for addressing the risks and costs of a crisis. Harmonisation was focused on lifting the barriers to cross-border financial services. It did not create safeguards against the unlimited expansion of the single financial market or create a framework for the management of crises. As a result, there were no European procedures for bank recovery and resolution, which could have avoided bailouts with public money. Furthermore, the EU financial services directives allowed significant national discretion. This also implied that the powers of national authorities to respond to the crisis were widely diverse among Member States. For example, rather than an EU-wide ban on short-selling practices after the fall of Lehman Brothers, there were several national bans varying in scope and length.[26]

Finally, the governance of the single financial market also reflected the inability to address the crisis. The Level 3 committees had only soft instruments regarding the convergence of supervisory practices. They had no mandate or capacity to take European

[24] The EU framework for deposit-guarantee schemes also undermined the single passport. There was excessive taking of retail deposits by foreign branches, which was not followed by the reinforcement of the capacity of the home-country's deposit guarantee schemes to compensate depositors both of local and foreign branches. The reliance on national DGSs for safeguarding depositors of foreign branches proved to be inadequate due to the mismatch between the significant deposit guarantee liabilities and the funding ability of the home-country's DGS to meet such liabilities. In addition, governments were not financially responsible for the fulfilment of DGS obligations. See J Pisani-Ferry and A Sapir, 'Banking crisis management in the EU: An interim assessment' (2009) 2009/07 *Bruegel Working Paper*.

[25] See A Enria, 'Fragmentation in banking markets: crisis legacy and the challenge of Brexit, Speech at BCBS-FSI High Level Meeting for Europe on Banking Supervision' (2018) eba.europa.eu/documents/10180/2353431/Andrea+Enria+speech+on+Fragmentation+in+banking+at+BCBS-FSI+High+Level+Meeting+170918.pdf.

[26] The UK introduced the short-selling ban on 19 September 2008 until 16 January 2009, Germany from 20 September 2008 until 31 March 2009, and France from 22 September 2008, each ban with different reach in terms of securities, which in turn hindered cross-border trading. For an analysis of the short-selling ban during the financial crisis, see E Avgouleas, 'The Vexed Issue of Short Sales Regulation When Prohibition is Inefficient and Disclosure Insufficient' in K Alexander and N Moloney (eds) *Law Reform and Financial Markets* (Cheltenham, Elgar, 2011) 71–110.

measures, which could be imposed over national authorities. Furthermore, it was hardly conceivable that committees comprising 27 national authorities, which remained only accountable to national governments and taxpayers, could manage a crisis through collective action. Any measure by the Level 3 committees could not override national interests. This was why any crisis would have to be addressed by national competences.

In conclusion, the full implications of the single passport framework only materialised with the financial crisis. In good times, the single passport led to the expansion of the single financial market. In a crisis, it let to its renationalisation. This was confirmed by the reactions to the crisis, which included initiatives to limit the application of the single passport.[27]

E. The Failure of the Law and Governance of the Single Financial Market

The law and governance of the single financial market failed to safeguard the market integration that it had fostered since 1985. Instead, it actually contributed to the exacerbation of the crisis. The single passport provided the framework for the unlimited expansion of the cross-border provision of financial services. However, such expansion was not accompanied by any meaningful rules to tackle the parallel increase of risks for all Member States. When the crisis created systemic risk across the single financial market, the absence of such rules and the primacy of national fiscal sovereignty implied that the only possible response was the renationalisation by Member States of financial markets and institutions.

As the crisis unfolded, the lack of European powers to manage the crisis, and the lack of mutualisation of costs, led to a spiral of market disintegration. There was a domino effect of protectionist measures to insulate domestic markets, which was first triggered by Ireland's unlimited guarantee of the deposits in Irish banks. Therefore, the European response to the financial crisis in 2008 consisted, in fact, of a collection of national protectionist measures. The coordination framework of the Paris Summit was largely a 'European branding' of such measures, which could not conceal the renationalisation of the single financial market.[28]

One of the major implications of such renationalisation related to the cross-border financial groups which ran into difficulties. In the absence of rules on how to share the burden of the financial rescue of cross-border groups, there were two contradictory types of outcomes. In some cases, the home-country Member State took all the financial cost for supporting the cross-border financial group as a whole. In other cases, particularly the banking groups whose balance sheet exceeded the GDP of their

[27] The most explicit call for constraining the single passport was made by the Turner Review, which argued for branches and subsidiaries to maintain stand-alone liquidity, thus ring-fencing their liquidity, the suspension of the home-country principle with direct intervention in branches by host supervisors, and also putting pressure for conversion of branches into subsidiaries. See A Turner, 'The Turner Review' (n 5).

[28] On the dilemmas facing banking supervision during the crisis, see R Smits, 'European supervisors in the credit crisis: issues of competence and competition,' in M Giovanoli and D Devos (eds), *International Monetary an Financial Law in the light of the Global Crisis* (Oxford, Oxford University Press, 2010) 305.

home-countries, the group was split into national components, which were supported separately by each Member State.

These two contradictory outcomes epitomised the failure of the single passport. Market integration could not be sustained if in a crisis either the home-country has to bear all the costs, or cross-border institutions have to be split along national lines. In the first instance, the home-country will aim at constraining cross-border activities, and, in the second instance, it is unlikely that cross-border institutions will be deemed viable. This provided one of the justifications for the Banking Union.[29]

Another major implication of the renationalisation process was that the liabilities of the previously European financial institutions were transferred to the balance sheets of the governments that rescued them. The level of riskiness of financial institutions then became correlated to the budgetary capacity of their respective home-country Member State. This led to adverse selection, where institutions from larger Member States and higher-rated governments were better able to withstand the crisis. Later, the soundness of entire Member States was questioned, as their liabilities for rescuing the financial system reached massive amounts, which laid the seed of the sovereign debt crisis in 2010.

The failure of the law and governance of the single financial market thus led to the primacy of the intergovernmental mode over the Community method in the European response to the crises. The Paris Summit and the following actions throughout the crisis had the common denominator of relaxing the application of EU law, which could pose constraints to national measures. Such constraints ranged from basic Treaty principles, such as non-discrimination, to financial services law, and economic governance, as detailed below in Table 19.

Table 19 EU Law Constraints on National Measures during the Financial Crisis

Source	Constraints on national measures	Application during the crisis
Treaty principles	Measures should be in line with basic Community principles, such as open market economy with free competition, and safeguard the four freedoms.	Discriminatory financial support measures
EU financial services law	Measures require agreement and coordination among home- and host-country authorities.	Ring-fencing of national markets

(continued)

[29] The financial groups rescued by their home-country included Hypo Real Estate (Germany), RBS (UK), Allied Irish Bank (Ireland), ING (Netherlands), and KBC (Belgium). The financial split along national lines included Fortis (Belgium, Luxembourg and Netherlands) and Dexia, which involved state guarantees by Belgium and France. At the peak of the sovereign debt crisis in May 2012, the *Wall Street Journal* reported that 'German banking regulators ordered Italian bank UniCredit SpA to stop borrowing billions of euros from its German subsidiary. They wanted to protect their banking system from being infected by the weaker one to the south.' The dispute was solved after UniCredit promised to significantly reduce the exposures of the German unit to other parts of the financial group. The article also reports on other instances of 'regulatory nationalism' whereby Member States restricted European banks from freely moving funds. See 'Turmoil Frays Ties Across Continent,' *Wall Street Journal*, 31 May 2012. See C Goodhart and D Schoenmaker, 'Fiscal Burden Sharing in Cross-Border Banking Crises' (2009) 5 *International Journal of Central Banking* 141.

Table 19 *(Continued)*

Source	Constraints on national measures	Application during the crisis
State aid law	Measures should be in line with state aid rules or be subject to conditions set by the Commission.	Relaxation of state aid rules
Competition law	Measures, such as mergers and acquisitions, might need to be approved by competition authorities.	Applied more flexibly in some Member States
Budgetary law	Measures should be in line with the Treaty provisions and the SGP.	Relaxation of SGP
No-bail out clause (Art 125 TFEU)	The EU or a Member State shall not be liable or assume the commitments of another Member State.	(It led later to the EFSF/ESM)
Monetary financing prohibition (Art 123 TFEU)	Measures should not involve a credit facility by the central bank to the public sector.	Prohibition questioned in ELA by central banks

IV. The Global Responses to the Financial Crisis

A. The London Summit and the Creation of the Financial Stability Board

Following the failure of Lehman Brothers and the beginning of the European banking crisis, the G-20 met for the first time at the level of country leaders in Washington DC on 14–15 November 2008. They decided to expand the membership of the FSF and global standard-setting bodies to the G-20, thus ending the G-7/G-10 oligarchy in the governance of finance. They also issued an Action Plan to implement the policy recommendations of the Financial Stability Forum (FSF).[30]

The reform of the global financial system started at the London Summit on 1–2 April 2009, which was led by the UK Prime Minister, Gordon Brown. The G-20 Leaders agreed on the following measures.[31]

The first was to establish a 'Financial Stability Board' (FSB) to replace the FSF, with a broader mandate to promote financial stability and a stronger institutional basis. The FSB's mandate had three new components: (1) assessing the vulnerabilities of the

[30] The FSF recommendations were issued after a request of the G7 finance ministers and central banks in October 2007. The recommendations covered capital requirements, liquidity, risk management, derivatives, transparency, credit ratings, and cooperation between authorities. See FSF, Report of the Financial Stability Forum on Enhancing Market and Institutional Resilience (2008), at www.fsb.org/wp-content/uploads/r_0804.pdf. See also G-20, 'Declaration of the Summit on Financial Markets and the World Economy,' Washington DC, 15 November 2008, at www.g20.utoronto.ca/2008/2008declaration1115.html.

[31] G-20 Leaders' Statement: The Global Plan for Recovery and Reform, London, 2 April 2009, at www.g20.utoronto.ca/2009/2009communique0402.html.

global financial system and taking action to address them; (2) coordinating global standard-setting bodies, and evaluating national jurisdictions regarding the compliance with standards; and (3) formulating policies regarding cross-border systemic matters, including the identification of systemically important financial institutions (SIFIs), the establishment of colleges for these SIFIs, and the development of contingency planning for crisis management. With these functions, the FSB became thus an umbrella-organisation at the top of the global governance of finance, directly accountable to the G-20.[32]

The other decisions of the London Summit included the introduction of macro-prudential supervision, both at the national and the global levels, with early warning exercises conducted by both the FSB and the IMF for the latter. The regulatory perimeter of finance was widened to all systemically important financial institutions, including for the first-time hedge funds and credit rating agencies. The aim was to cover all the regulatory gaps, which could give rise to systemic risks. The G-20 also requested a reform of banking regulatory standards to improve the level of capital and prevent excessive leverage, as well as a single set of global accounting standards for a uniform valuation of financial assets. Another novelty was including corporate social responsibility into the regulation of finance, namely by introducing principles on the compensation of employees of financial firms. Lastly, the G-20 moved towards ending banking secrecy and sanctioning non-cooperative jurisdictions.[33]

B. Basel III

Following the commitment of the G-20 Leaders at the Pittsburgh Summit on 24–25 September 2009 to reform banking regulation, the Group of Governors and Heads of Supervision (GHOS) – the governing body of the BCBS, chaired at the time by the ECB President Jean-Claude Trichet – agreed on 12 September 2010 on the so-called 'Basel III' framework, after only two years of work compared to the eight years of Basel II.

Basel III increased the quality of banks' capital by harmonising the definition of Common Equity Tier 1 (CET 1) and only allowing those instruments with the highest loss-absorbing capacity under this definition, ie, those with similar characteristics to common shares, which are available at any time to absorb losses. It also increased the quantity of capital by raising the minimum requirement for CET 1 from 2 per cent

[32] See E Helleiner, 'What Role for the New Financial Stability Board? The Politics of International Standards after the Crisis' (2010) 1 *Global Policy* 282; DW Arner and MW Taylor, 'The global financial crisis and the financial stability board: Hardening the soft law of international financial regulation' (2009) 32 *University of New South Wales Law Journal*, 488; and A Enria and PG Teixeira, 'A New Institutional Framework for Financial Regulation and Supervision' in F Cannata and M Quagliariello (eds) *Basel III and beyond* (London, Riskbooks, 2011) 421–468.

[33] For a review of these decisions and the role of the G-20 in crisis management, see A Elson, *Governing Global Finance: The Evolution and Reform of the International Financial Architecture* (New York, Palgrave, 2011) 164–176.

to 4.5 per cent of risk-weighted assets. This was complemented by a capital conservation buffer of 2.5 per cent CET 1 for banks to withstand periods of stress, and a countercyclical buffer of up to 2.5 per cent CET 1 for banks to accumulate extra capital during an economic expansion, so as to cope later with a recession. Altogether, with Additional Tier 1 and Tier 2 capital, the minimum capital requirements under Basel III became a minimum of 10.5 per cent, out of which a minimum of 7 per cent CET 1, compared to the 8 per cent of lower capital quality under Basel II.[34]

For the first time, banks also became subject to liquidity rules. These consisted of a liquidity coverage ratio (LCR), whereby banks had to hold high-quality liquid assets to cover liquidity for 30 days, and a net stable funding ratio (NSFR), whereby banks had to ensure their stable funding with a minimum horizon of one year. These ratios aimed at making banks more resilient to periods of liquidity stress, as in the 2007–2008 crisis.

Together with these new capital and liquidity requirements, Basel III also included other constraints on banks. They became subject to a leverage ratio of 3 per cent of Tier 1 capital, ie a minimum ratio of capital to total assets, which limits the potential leverage of a bank. There were also specific measures to address 'too-big-to-fail' institutions. The BCBS introduced a methodology to identify 'Global Systemic Important Banks' (G-SIBs) and make them subject to additional capital requirements to reduce their probability of failure.

C. The New Global Regulation of Finance

The new global model for the regulation of finance arising out of the crisis comprised thus the following principles. First, all financial activities, which could pose a threat to financial stability, should be regulated. The perimeter of financial regulation became significantly wider, encompassing the previously unregulated sectors, such as hedge funds, rating agencies, or offshore centres. Second, risk-taking and the size of the balance sheet of financial institutions should be constrained by higher capital requirements and other limits. Third, 'too-big-to-fail' institutions should be subject to a special regulatory treatment due to their systemic relevance. Fourth, systemic risks should be contained by a macro-prudential approach to financial regulation. Fifth, the trust in the financial system should be promoted through rules on market integrity and transparency, such as rules restricting the executive compensation in financial institutions. Lastly, the failure of financial institutions should be feasible without a public bail-out, notably on the basis of a bank resolution regime.[35]

[34] BCBS, Basel III: A global regulatory framework for more resilient banks and banking systems (2010), at www.bis.org/publ/bcbs189_dec2010.pdf. For an evaluation, see A Admati and M Helwig, *The Bankers' New Clothes: What's Wrong with Banking and What to Do about It* (Princeton, Princeton University Press, 2013).

[35] In the US, this was reflected in the adoption in the 2010 'Dodd-Frank Act'. It also broadened the regulatory perimeter and created the Financial Stability Oversight Council to oversee systemic risk, including identifying systemic financial institutions and making them subject to supervision. It established a new Consumer Financial Protection Agency and introduced rules on executive compensation and corporate governance. The 'Dodd-Frank Act' also incorporated the so-called 'Volcker Rule' – after its creator, Paul Volcker, former

The global responses to the financial crisis represented thus a move towards restraining global finance for the first time, instead of expanding it as in the previous period. This represented a new model for the regulation of finance. It was no longer based on the dominance of free, self-equilibrating and ever-expanding markets, which led to the deregulation and liberalisation of finance and ultimately the financial crisis. It was instead based on the premise that financial markets are not always efficient, can generate crises, especially as a result of excessive growth and leverage, and that financial institutions may fail. Regulation should have a stabilising role, promote a sustainable expansion of finance, and create trust in the financial system.

The implementation of this new regulatory model required a stronger global governance framework, particularly since the aim was restraining rather than expanding finance. For this purpose, the direction set by the G-20 Summits was towards a more inclusive and accountable governance. In order to increase both its reach and legitimacy, it comprised at least the G-20 jurisdictions and was politically accountable to the G-20, which was designated by the Pittsburgh Summit as 'the premier forum for international economic cooperation'.[36]

The FSB stood at the top of the governance as the umbrella-organisation of global standard-setting bodies. It monitored and assessed vulnerabilities of the financial system, it adopted standards on transversal regulatory matters, such as resolution regimes, and provided guidance to the standard-setting bodies. In order to increase the degree of global regulatory convergence, the standards became more detailed with less leeway for differences in national implementation. The enforcement process was reinforced by the FSB through disclosures, peer reviews, identification of non-compliant jurisdictions, and also by the IMF's Financial Sector Assessment Programmes' exercises and the World Bank's technical assistance. The new architecture of governance is summarised below in Table 20, which depicts the evolution from the above Table 5.[37]

The outcome of the financial crisis was thus a more inclusive and institutionalised global governance architecture, akin to a global technocracy, accountable to the leaders of the G-20. It reflected the renewed belief on the role of the state in stabilising markets to prevent financial and economic damage. It also echoed the desirability of a 'world political authority' to manage the global economy and ensure compliance with its decisions, as argued at the time in the 2009 encyclical by the Pope Benedict XVI, 'Caritas in Veritate'.[38]

Federal Reserve Chairman – which prohibited banks from investing in hedge funds, private equity funds, or carrying out any proprietary trading operations for their own profit, in order to limit their risk-taking and systemic risk. For an overview, see T Cooley and I Walter, 'The Architecture of Financial Regulation' in V Acharya, T Cooley, M Richardson, I Walter (eds) *Regulating Wall Street: The Dodd-Frank Act and the New Architecture of Global Finance* (London, Wiley, 2011) 33.

[36] On the evolution of the role of the G-20 during the crisis, see A Tooze, *Crashed: How a Decade of Financial Crises Changed the World* (New York, Viking, 2018), at 255–275.

[37] See FSB, Framework for Strengthening Adherence to International Standards (2010), at www.fsb.org/wp-content/uploads/r_100109a.pdf. For an assessment, see E Ferran and K Alexander, 'Can soft law bodies be effective? The Special Case of the European Systemic Risk Board' (2011) 37 *European law review* 751.

[38] See Benedict XVI, *Lettera Enciclica Caritas in Veritate* (Vatican, Libraria Editrice Vaticana, 2009), in particular, ch 5, paras 65–67 on finance.

Table 20 The Global Governance of Finance after the Financial Crisis

	G20 Heads of State and Governments **G20 Finance Ministers and Central Bank Governors**
Function	Political steering and accountability
	Financial Stability Board
Function	Monitoring of financial stability Standard-setting Coordination of global standard-setting
	Standard-Setting Bodies (BCBS, IOSCO, IAIS, …)
Function	Issuance of standards and methodologies Public consultation
	Global Governance Standards (Twelve Key Financial Standards)
Function	Minimum institutional framework of national jurisdictions
	Global Regulatory Standards (Basel III, …)
Function	Global regulation of finance
	National Jurisdictions
Function	Consistent implementation of global standards in line with methodologies
	FSB and Standard-Setting Bodies
Function	Assessment of Implementation and Enforcement via peer pressure, name and shame, counter-measures
	IMF and World Bank
Function	Assessment of implementation and enforcement via programme conditionality and technical assistance

V. Rescuing the Single Financial Market

A. The Trilemma of the Single Financial Market

The financial crisis revealed the legal and institutional 'trilemma' of the single financial market: the impossibility of preserving at the same time: (1) European financial integration, which increases the common risks among Member States; (2) European financial stability in an integrated market; and (3) national competences for addressing such common risks. Only two of these three objectives could ever be achieved, while the remaining one had to be dropped. This was confirmed by the responses to the crisis, where the primacy of national competences led to dropping European integration in favour of national financial stability. The cost of European integration was European financial instability.[39]

[39] See D Schoenmaker, *Governance of international banking: The financial trilemma* (Oxford, Oxford University Press, 2013.

This incompatibility of objectives within the single financial market was similar to the contradiction between the freedom of capital, fixed exchange rates, and autonomous monetary policy, which preceded the federalisation of monetary policy in the euro area. As with monetary policy, the intensification of the common economic risks in the single financial market led to an institutional crossroads. The alternatives were either transferring the competences for the single financial market to the European level, to the extent required to internalise the common benefits and risks of market integration; or a re-nationalisation of the single financial market, to the extent required to safeguard Member States from the risks of market integration. Both would imply a fundamental change to the legal and institutional framework of the single financial market.[40]

B. The Options for Rescuing the Single Financial Market: 'Total' Home-Country Control and European Competences

The Lamfalussy framework combined the traditional Community method with intergovernmental comitology procedures and networks of national authorities in the preparation, adoption and implementation of EU law. This multilevel governance soon found its limits. It did not provide the institutional setting to manage the crisis and prevent the rapid renationalisation of the single financial market. It demonstrated how soft governance, while able to manage integration in good times, turned inadequate in times of stress.[41]

Immediately before the financial crisis, there were several proposals to Europeanise the law and institutions of the single financial market, which could be grouped into two options.

The first option was 'total home-country control'. On the basis of the approach for the supervision of financial groups introduced by the 1999 Financial Services Action Plan (FSAP), it would consist of an expansion of home-country control leading to a horizontal transfer of competences among national authorities. The home supervisor of cross-border financial groups would be responsible for all its subsidiaries and branches across the single market. The national law of the home-country would apply to the whole financial group, including the protection of all the EU depositors of the group. The horizontal transfer of competences could occur through EU legislation or voluntary delegation among authorities. The home-country would also have a European mandate in order to address potential conflicts with its national responsibilities. The main advantage of this option was to make national authorities act as European authorities. They would have to take into account the European interest when exercising their extra-territorial competences. It would promote integration as each financial group would be subject to a single national authority and jurisdiction, rather than several. It could also increase the level of regulatory competition, which would in turn accelerate regulatory convergence.[42]

[40] See the conclusions of the De Larosière Report.

[41] For a critical assessment, see I Begg, 'Regulation and Supervision of Financial Intermediaries in the EU: The Aftermath of the Financial Crisis' (2009) 47 *Journal of Common Market Studies* 1107.

[42] This option could include the creation of a 'European Banking Charter', whereby the supervision of the banks opting for such charter could be carried out by national supervisors with a specific European mandate

This option of 'total home-country control' was however not realistic. First, the compatibility with the Treaty was questionable. It would run counter to the ability of the host-country to safeguard its own jurisdiction in public good matters under Article 36 of the TFEU. Moreover, managing the single market exclusively through extra-territorial principles, of either home or host country control, would not fulfil the Treaty objectives. The harmonisation provision of Article 114 of the TFEU implies that market integration should aim at fulfilling EU objectives, such as a high level of consumer protection, and not only at dismantling barriers through regulatory competition. Second, it was also not realistic to assume that the home-country authorities could act in the interest of host-countries and the whole single market. National authorities are accountable to national political institutions and are not mandated to pursue European interests or the interests of other Member States. This is particularly so, if they conflict with national interests, such as safeguarding taxpayers' funds.[43]

The second option to regulate the single financial market would be a vertical transfer of competences to the European level. There would be a regulatory system modelled on the European System of Central Banks: a 'European System of Financial Supervision' where decision-making would be centralised at the European level, with decentralisation of enforcement at the national level. This option could have several variations, ranging from a complete centralisation of European competences to the establishment of a two-tier system similar to the US model, whereby financial institutions could choose to be licensed and regulated either at European or national levels. Some proposals included the creation of a '28th regulatory regime' similar to the European Company Statute, which would enable financial institutions to opt for a European charter.[44]

This second option would align the single financial market with a single regulatory jurisdiction. The main impediment was that it would require an amendment of the Treaty to introduce financial regulation as an exclusive competence of the Union, and to establish a new European institution to exercise such competence. It would be akin to the single monetary policy, which was exercised by the only existing independent regulatory agency, the ECB. With a European regulator, financial markets and institutions would be Europeanised and no longer safeguarded by national funds. There would be the need to establish a financial safety net, such as a European fund, which would

and accountability to the European Parliament. Moreover, there would be a complete framework for EU-wide financial stability arrangements, ideally providing for harmonised supervisory powers, uniform prudential regulations, a single deposit insurance scheme and a specific European bank insolvency regime. This proposal was elaborated by M Cihak and J Decressin, 'The Case for a European Banking Charter' (2007) 07/173 *IMF Working Paper*.

[43] See A Menon and S Weatherill, 'Transnational Legitimacy in a Globalising World: How the European Union Rescues its States' (2008) 31 *West European Politics* 397, arguing that the 'constitutional collision between home state and host state control needs to be managed in a more sophisticated manner than the selection of an absolute rule at either end of the spectrum'. This relates to one of the Treaty's horizontal clauses of Art 156(2), TFEU requiring a high level of consumer protection as a Union objective.

[44] As proposed by D Schoenmaker and S Oosterloo, 'Financial supervision in Europe: do we need a new architecture?' (2006) 12 *Cahier Comte Boël, European League for Economic Cooperation*; and G Di Giorgio and C Di Noia, 'Financial market regulation and supervision: how many peaks for the euro area?' (2003) 28 *Brooklyn Journal International Law* 463.

intervene if required in a crisis. This, however, could be in contradiction with national fiscal sovereignty and the no-bail out clause of Article 125 of the TFEU.[45]

Without an amendment of the Treaty, the only possibility left would be to transfer supervisory tasks to the ECB on the basis of Article 127(6) of the TFEU, which enabled the Council to confer such tasks through unanimity voting. There would be two limitations: the ECB would not have jurisdiction over the single market, but only over the euro area; and it would not supervise the insurance and securities sectors, but only the banking system. These two limitations, together with the doctrinal debate on whether the ECB should combine monetary policy with banking supervision, prevented Article 127(6) from being considered realistic at the time.[46]

C. Maximising the Harmonisation Competences in the Treaty

When the 2008 crisis led to the failure of the governance of the single financial market, the only feasible option for reform was to explore the boundaries of Article 114 of the TFEU. This provision, on the harmonisation measures for the functioning of the single market, provided the basis for the EU's competences in the single financial market. The EU does not have exclusive competences but rather parallel competences with Member States to regulate the single financial market to the extent required for its functioning. This implied that Member States were pre-empted from regulating matters addressed in EU legislation due to the primacy of EU law. The EU progressively enlarged the scope of its regulation in tandem with the increase in harmonisation, thus assimilating regulation to integration.[47]

The question was therefore the extent to which the law and governance of the single financial market could be enhanced on the basis of the harmonisation powers of Article 114. According to the Court in the *Tobacco Advertising* case law, the EU may rely on this provision when there are divergences across national laws, which create obstacles to the fundamental freedoms or distortions of competition. The EU may then adopt measures to improve the conditions for the establishment and functioning of the internal market by eliminating such divergences through harmonisation. This also includes the competence to impose limits on the basic freedoms. For example, EU law may limit

[45] See MK Brunnermeier, H James and JP Landau, *The Euro and the Battle of Ideas*, (n 22) at 211–212. See also Editorial, 'Executive Agencies within the EC: the ECB as a model?' (2006) 33 *CML Rev* 623. The recourse to reinforced cooperation among Member States to transfer regulatory competences to the European level was also not an option, without amending the Treaty. The mechanism of reinforced cooperation only allows a group of Member States to deepen integration among them within the framework of the Treaty, not beyond it.

[46] See I Begg, 'Regulation and Supervision of Financial Intermediaries in the EU' (n 41).

[47] The Court has stated that 'by the expression "measures for approximation" in Article 114 TFEU, the Treaty intended to confer on the Community legislature a discretion, depending on the general context and the specific circumstances of the matter to be harmonised, as regards the harmonisation technique most appropriate for achieving the desired result, in particular in fields which are characterised by complex technical features'. See Judgment of the Court of 6 December 2005, *Smoke Flavourings*, C-66/04, EU:C:2005:743, para 45. See A von Bogdandy and J Bast, 'European Union's Vertical Order of Competences: The Current Law and Proposals for Its Reform' (2002) 39 *CML Rev* 227, who characterise Art 114, TFEU as a functional competence with a cross-sectoral character.

the freedoms of establishment and capital movement to safeguard financial stability, or another public good, under Article 36.[48]

There were three legal strategies to enlarge to the maximum extent possible the scope of Article 114 to regulate the single financial market after the 2008 financial crisis.

The first strategy was to widen and deepen the harmonisation of national laws: an increase in both the regulatory perimeter and the detail of EU legislation. There were no limitations to the harmonisation capacity of the EU as long as it met the agreement of the Council and the Parliament as co-legislators. In this context, the financial crisis provided a large political consensus for regulatory reform. The Commission then initiated a strategy of 'maximum harmonisation' to realise the 'single financial services rulebook' as proposed by the De Larosière Report. The main elements of this strategy included: (1) the regulation of areas not previously covered by EU legislation; (2) the adoption of detailed legislation reducing the scope for national discretion; and (3) a wider recourse to directly applicable EU regulations, rather than directives as it had been the case since the 1970s.

The second strategy was to enable more and more the delegation of implementing powers to the Commission. This was supported by the introduction in the Lisbon Treaty of the categories of delegated and implementing acts in Articles 290 and 291 of the TFEU, respectively. With regard to delegated acts, EU directives and regulations may provide the power to the Commission to supplement or amend non-essential elements of these laws. Two conditions may be imposed on the Commission. The Parliament or the Council may reserve the right to revoke the delegation – the so-called 'call-back clause' – or establish that the delegated regulation will enter into force only if there is no objection within a set period. Comitology procedures were thus no longer required for the adoption of delegated acts, but remained for implementing acts. The choice between delegated and implementing acts depended on the political choice of the legislators. In practice, due to the more direct control of the Council and the Parliament, delegated acts were used for more fundamental policy issues, while implementing acts related to more routine implementation of EU legislation.[49]

In the area of financial services, the preferred instrument was delegated acts, which allowed the Council and the Parliament to exercise direct oversight. Although

[48] Judgment of the Court of 5 October 2000, *Germany v European Parliament and Council (Tobacco Advertising)*, C-376/98, ECLI:EU:C:2000:544, paras 106 and 107; and Judgment of the Court of 10 December 2002, *British American Tobacco*, C-491/01, EU:C:2002:741, paras 6–ff. For an analysis of the implications, see S Weatherill, 'The Limits of Legislative Harmonization Ten Years after Tobacco Advertising: how the Court's Case Law has become a "Drafting Guide"' (2011) 12 *German Law Journal* 827; and also *The Internal Market as a Legal Concept*, (Oxford, Oxford University Press, 2017) at 212–215.

[49] The category of 'delegated acts' replaced the 'regulatory procedure with scrutiny' introduced in 2006. It largely corresponded to the concept of 'delegated regulations' foreseen in Art I-35 of the draft European Constitution. See the implementation of Art 291, TFEU by Regulation (EU) No 182/2011 of the European Parliament and of the Council of 16 February 2011 laying down the rules and general principles concerning mechanisms for control by Member States of the Commission's exercise of implementing powers, [2011] OJ L55/13–18, [2011] OJ L55/13. The Regulation foresaw comitology in the form of advisory procedures or examination procedures. Examination procedures apply for acts of general scope or dealing with programmes of substantial scope; they require the issuance of opinions by the committee on the draft act with a qualified majority.

Article 290 of the TFEU does not require comitology procedures, Member States made sure that the Commission was obliged to consult their experts also on delegated acts relating to financial services. In addition, adoption of implementing acts concerning financial services always required a positive opinion of the committee, which was not the case for other matters.[50]

The third strategy was to establish European agencies under Article 114 to support the Commission in the exercise of delegated powers and to manage the application of EU legislation across the single financial market.[51]

The effectiveness of such agencies depended on the ability to use Article 114 to provide them with substantial regulatory powers. There were, however, limits to the delegation of autonomous powers to independent bodies in the EU legal order, as developed by the Court under the *Meroni* case law. First, the Court stated that Article 114 allows the creation of a Community body responsible for contributing to the process of harmonisation. This is limited to situations where, in order to facilitate the uniform implementation and application of legal acts, the adoption of non-binding measures seems appropriate. Second, the Court recognised the possibility to delegate powers to independent executive or regulatory bodies, in so far as the delegation relates only to clearly defined executive competences. Agencies cannot be given the power to adopt general regulatory measures. They are limited to taking individual binding decisions where a defined technical expertise is required, without genuine discretionary powers. Such powers must be contained within a precise legal framework and limited in scope. The use of the delegated powers must be subject to strict review in the light of objective criteria determined by the delegating authority. In addition, the agencies cannot be entrusted with powers which may affect the responsibilities which the Treaty has explicitly conferred on the Commission, such as the guardian of EU law.[52]

The reform of the legal and institutional framework of the single financial market could only be based on these strategies to maximise the harmonisation competences conferred by the Treaty. The transfer of competences to the European level was not feasible, at least without exhausting the possibilities of the Treaty. This was the context for the proposals of the De Larosière Report, which explored the boundaries of Article 114.

[50] In accordance with Declaration 39 on Art 290, TFEU, annexed to the Final Act of the Intergovernmental Conference which adopted the Treaty of Lisbon, the Commission should consult experts appointed by the Member States in the preparation of delegated acts on financial services.

[51] See European Commission, European Agencies – The Way Forward, COM (2008) 135 final, which distinguished between executive agencies and regulatory agencies, with the latter defined as independent bodies with their own legal personality.

[52] The Court validated the use of Art 114, TFEU for the creation of a Community body, subject to two conditions: (1) the objectives and tasks of the agency must be closely linked to the subject matter of existing harmonising legislation; and (2) the objectives and tasks of the agency must be 'likely to facilitate' the application of the harmonising legislation by supporting and providing a framework for its implementation. See Judgment of the Court of 2 May 2006, *ENISA*, C-217/04, EU:C:2006:279, paras 42–47. Moreover, the Court also considered that the recourse to Art 114, TFEU is not justified where the measure to be adopted has only the 'incidental effect' of harmonising the market conditions. See Judgment of the Court of 18 November 1999, *Commission v Council*, C-209/97, EU:C:1999:559, para 35.

D. The Legal and Institutional Reform of the Single Financial Market: The 2009 De Larosière Report

For close to a decade before the 2008 financial crisis, there had not been any major EU or national regulatory initiatives. The framework in place largely consisted of the implementation of the measures provided in the 1999 FSAP, which had lasted until 2007. Furthermore, there was little impetus for new regulations due to the culture of 'principles-based regulation', which had taken hold in Europe and globally since 2006: regulation should not be unduly prescriptive and should instead aim at achieving desirable outcomes in close dialogue with financial firms. In practice, this culture was symptomatic of the light-touch regulation that characterised the period immediately before the crisis. It also prevented the expansion of EU regulation as it was seen not flexible enough for the dynamics of finance.[53]

Financial crises have in common the fact that they occur after periods of deregulation and are usually followed by periods of re-regulation. In Europe, experiences with the bank run on Northern Rock on 15 September 2007 and problems in other UK banks, the failures of Icelandic banks, the losses suffered by German banks, and the collapse of pan-European banking groups, provided the basis for reform of national regulatory systems. The proposals for reform were made in reports such as the Turner Review in the UK, the Issing Report in Germany, and the Lamfalussy Report in Belgium.[54]

In October 2008, soon after the Paris Summit, the Commission established a High-Level Group, chaired by Jacques de Larosière, with the mandate to put forward proposals to improve the arrangements for financial supervision in the EU in light of the financial crisis. The De Larosière Report was issued on 25 February 2009. It identified several shortcomings in the governance of the single financial market: (1) regulatory failures with regard to financial institutions; (2) the impossibility of challenging regulatory practices on a cross-border basis; (3) a lack of cooperation between regulators; (4) a lack of consistent powers across regulators; and (5) a lack of means for regulators to take common decisions. The Report had three recommendations to address these shortcomings.[55]

[53] The UK Financial Services Authority defined in 2007 'principles-based regulation' as '[...]moving away from dictating through detailed, prescriptive rules and supervisory actions how firms should operate their business. We want to give firms the responsibility to decide how best to align their business objectives and processes with the regulatory outcomes we have specified. We will increasingly shift the balance of our activity towards setting out desirable regulatory outcomes in principles and outcome-focused rules, enabling our people to engage with firms' senior management in pursuit of these outcomes.' UK, Principles-based regulation: Focusing on the outcomes that matter, April 2007, at webarchive.nationalarchives.gov.uk/*/http:/www.fsa.gov.uk/. For an overview of such regulatory culture, see J Black, 'The rise (and fall?) of principles based regulation' in K Alexander and N Moloney (eds) *Law reform and financial markets* (Cheltenham, Elgar, 2011) 3.

[54] A Turner, 'The Turner Review' (n 5); O Issing, *New Financial Order: Recommendations by the Issing Committee* (Frankfurt/M, Center for Financial Studies, University of Frankfurt, 2008); A Lamfalussy 'High-Level Committee on a New Financial Architecture' (2009), at www.docufin.fgov.be. In addition, the EFC requested in December 2008 a High-Level Working Group, chaired by Lars Nyberg, to draw the lessons for financial crisis management arrangements.

[55] See De Larosière Report, paras 152 to 166; and European Commission, European financial supervision, COM (2009) 0252 final.

The first recommendation was to establish three European Supervisory Authorities (ESA) in the banking, insurance and securities sectors, which would take over the tasks of the Level 3 committees. Therefore, the committees would be replaced by European agencies with enlarged powers. The step forward was to enable the ESA to have as much as possible 'binding' powers: the ESA would be able to adopt binding supervisory standards, exercise binding mediation among supervisors, and issue binding technical decisions on financial institutions. These powers would only be exercised when required for the effective functioning of the single financial market, in line with the principle of subsidiarity, thus preserving a decentralised framework for the conduct of supervision. The ESA were then established on 1 January 2011: the European Banking Authority (EBA), the European Insurance and Occupational Pensions Authority (EIOPA), and the European Securities Markets Authority (ESMA), acting together through a Joint Committee.[56]

The second recommendation was to establish a European Systemic Risk Council (ESRC) to conduct macro-prudential oversight at the European level. The ESA, the ESRC and the national supervisors would form together the European System of Financial Supervision, whose parties were bound by the obligation of sincere cooperation among them.

The third was to develop rules for the single financial market, which should be based on directly applicable EU regulations and on maximum harmonisation whenever directives were used. This became known as the concept of a 'single financial services rulebook'.[57]

The ECOFIN Council put together these proposals for reform on 20 October 2009 in a roadmap for EU financial supervision, stability and regulation. It included the creation of the ESA and the European Systemic Risk Board, as well as legislative initiatives to enlarge the regulatory perimeter of the EU. The new institutional architecture – the European System of Financial Supervision – was largely in place by the beginning of 2011.[58]

[56] The Commission put forward legislative proposals on 23 September 2009, which were then adopted on 24 November 2010: Regulation (EU) No 1093/2010 establishing a European Supervisory Authority (European Banking Authority), [2010] OJ L331/12; Regulation (EU) No 1094/2010 establishing a European Supervisory Authority (European Insurance and Occupational Pensions Authority), OJ L331/, 15.12.2010, p.48; Regulation (EU) No 1095/2010 establishing a European Supervisory Authority (European Securities and Markets Authority), [2010] OJ L331/84 (given the similar provisions between them, references to these legal acts will henceforth be to 'the ESA Regulations').

[57] The De Larosière Report also contains a set of recommendations in other areas, including: (1) financial regulation, with recommendations covering Basel II, accounting rules, credit rating agencies, Solvency 2, hedge funds, securitised products and derivatives, investment funds, corporate governance, internal risk management of financial institutions (Recommendations 1–12); and (2) financial crisis management, on the further harmonisation of deposit-guarantee schemes, and the need for Member States to agree on detailed criteria for burden sharing (Recommendations 13–15).

[58] See EU Council, ECOFIN Council conclusions on strengthening EU financial stability arrangements (2009), at www.consilium.europa.eu/ueDocs/cms_Data/docs/pressdata/en/ecofin/110617.pdf. An account of the new institutional framework for financial supervision is provided by PG Teixeira, 'The Regulation of the European Financial Market after the Crisis' in P della Posta and L Talani (eds) *Europe and the Financial Crisis* (London, Palgrave Macmillan, 2011) 9–27. See also N Moloney, 'EU Financial Market Regulation After the Global Financial Crisis: 'More Europe' or More Risks?' (2010) 47 *CML Rev* 1317.

Table 21 The European System of Financial Supervision in 2011

Micro-prudential supervision	**Macro-prudential supervision**
European Banking Authority	European Systemic Risk Board
European Insurance and Occupational Pensions Authority	*Voting authorities:* ECB, EU national central banks, Commission, ESA *Non-voting authorities:* EU national financial supervisors, President of the Economic and Financial Committee
European Securities and Markets Authority	
Joint Committee of European Supervisory Authorities	
National financial supervisors (including colleges of supervisors for banking and insurance groups)	

VI. Replacing Committees with Agencies: The European Supervisory Authorities

A. Beyond Committees: The Powers of the European Supervisory Authorities

The establishment of the ESA led to the replacement of the Level 3 committees by agencies, which would provide a stronger institutional structure for the single financial market. For this purpose, the ESA represented a number of institutional innovations in the EU framework. They were entrusted with an extensive set of powers and tasks much beyond those previously exercised by the Level 3 committees. They included rule-making and enforcement powers, as well as tasks relating to supervisory convergence, consumer protection, financial stability and crisis management.[59]

The rule-making powers were the most prominent innovation. The ESA can issue non-binding technical standards, which can then become legal acts in the areas of EU financial services law where the Commission exercises implementing powers under Articles 290 and 291 of the TFEU. In such areas, the ESA can issue 'draft regulatory technical standards', which are then submitted to the Commission for adoption so as to provide for binding legal effect across the EU. The standards have to remain technical, not imply strategic decisions or policy choices, with their content delimited by their legal basis.

In order to enable the ESA to perform regulatory tasks as much as possible within the boundaries of Article 114 of the TFEU, the ESA regulations provided for a

[59] There are certain powers, which are specific to each of the ESA, such as the registration and supervision of credit rating agencies by ESMA. See Regulation No 1060/2009 of the European Parliament and the Council of 16 September 2009 on credit rating agencies, [2009] OJ L302/1. In addition, EU legislation may attribute further powers and tasks to the ESA. For a detailed analysis of the powers of the new European Supervisory Authorities, see A Enria, and PG Teixeira, 'A New Institutional Framework for Financial Regulation and Supervision' (n 32).

procedure whereby the Commission cannot deviate from the 'draft regulatory technical standards' when adopting delegated acts. The ESA submits these standards to the Commission, which decides whether to endorse and adopt them as delegated acts. If the Commission does not endorse them, it should send the standards back to the ESA for amendments. Only after this step can the Commission adopt the standards as delegated acts. Therefore, this procedure provided regulatory powers to the ESA by constraining the right of initiative of the Commission, which can only act on the basis of the prior adoption of 'draft regulatory technical standards' by the ESA. The Parliament and the Council monitor the procedure.[60]

In addition to the 'draft regulatory technical standards', the ESA also have soft rule-making powers in the form of guidelines and recommendations to national supervisors and financial institutions. These instruments aim at ensuring consistent supervisory practices and the application of EU law. Compliance is based on 'comply or explain' mechanisms. National supervisors have to provide reasons for non-compliance, and financial institutions have to report on their compliance. Cases of non-compliance have to be published by the ESA and reported to the Parliament, Council and Commission.[61]

Coupled with rule-making, the ESA's enforcement powers were another institutional innovation. The ESA can take legally binding individual decisions addressed to national supervisors or financial institutions, when this is justified by the need to safeguard the single financial market from threats to its functioning, integrity or stability.

The enforcement procedure is initiated when an ESA takes the initiative or is requested by national supervisors, the Parliament, the Council, the Commission or its own stakeholder group, to investigate an alleged breach – a failure to ensure that a financial institution fulfilled the requirements set by EU law – or the non-application of EU law by a national supervisor. If the ESA finds such infringement, it can issue a recommendation to the supervisor setting out the actions for complying with EU law. If there is no compliance, the Commission can then issue a formal opinion requiring the supervisor to take action. When action is nevertheless not taken, the ESA is able to issue a legally binding decision addressed directly to a financial institution to remedy the infringement of EU law. The decision can only be taken to remedy the non-compliance in a timely manner, to maintain or restore competition in the market, or to ensure the orderly functioning of the financial system. Despite being an overly cumbersome and lengthy procedure, it provides ultimately direct enforcement powers to the ESA throughout the single financial market.[62]

This ability of the ESA to take directly applicable decisions was also foreseen for addressing disagreements among national supervisors on matters of cooperation or

[60] This was reflected in Art 7 of the ESA Regulations, which provides for the mandatory submission by the ESA of a draft technical standard to the Commission as the basis for delegated or implementing acts. At the time, the Commission expressed its disagreement by stating in the explanatory memorandum to legislative proposals that '[it] has serious doubts whether the restrictions on its role when adopting delegated acts and implementing measures are in line with Arts 290 and 291 TFEU'. The EU financial services law included many areas where the ESA were requested to prepare technical standards for the Commission to consider adopting as delegated acts, for example, Art 10 of the ESA Regulations, and Arts 461 and 462 of the CRR. For an analysis of these powers, see M Busuioc, 'Rule-Making by the European Financial Supervisory Authorities: Walking a Tight Rope' (2013) 19 *European Law Journal* 111.

[61] Art 16(1), ESA Regulations.

[62] Art 17(1), ESA Regulations.

joint decision-making between home- and host-country authorities, in supervisory colleges, and among supervisors of different financial sectors. The ESA can take a legally binding decision, after an attempt for conciliation, requiring one or more supervisors to take or refrain from taking action. If the supervisors do not comply, the ESA can also address a decision to a financial institution directing it to comply with its obligations under EU law.[63]

A similar framework for decision-making applies in crisis situations. When the Council declares an emergency situation – on a recommendation by the ESRB or an ESA – the ESA can take decisions to coordinate national supervisors to respond to threats to the orderly functioning and integrity of financial markets or the stability of the EU's financial system. In case of non-compliance by supervisors, decisions can be directed at financial institutions.[64]

These institutional innovations represented a step towards the transfer of national competences to European authorities. This was confirmed by the introduction of a safeguard clause in the ESA regulations relating to the fiscal responsibilities of Member States. Where a Member State considers that an ESA decision impinges on its fiscal responsibility, it can notify that the national supervisor will not implement the decision, together with a justification. The ESA then informs the Member State whether it maintains, amends or revokes its decision. When the decision is maintained, the Member State can refer to the Council, leading to the suspension of the ESA decision. Within two months, the Council should decide whether to maintain or revoke the decision. This clause was justified by the concern that the powers of the ESA could infringe on national fiscal sovereignty, namely by giving rise to a fiscal burden on Member States. These could include decisions adopted in emergency situations, settling disagreements among national supervisors, and on the temporary prohibition or restriction of financial activities.[65]

Therefore, the far-reaching rule-making and enforcement powers of the ESA were, in reality, confined to situations of last-resort, after all the non-legally binding alternatives had been exhausted. Moreover, if the ESA would take such legally binding decisions over national authorities or financial institutions, they could always be challenged by Member States. Despite such limitations, these powers represented the first expression of transfer of competences to the European level immediately after the 2008 financial crisis.

The other powers of the ESA represented much less of an institutional innovation. They are softer in nature and provide continuity to the tasks previously performed by the Level 3 committees, although broadened to a wider range of areas. This was the case for the tasks relating to supervisory convergence by promoting a common supervisory culture, facilitating the delegation of tasks among supervisors, and conducting

[63] Art 19(1), ESA Regulations. This ability of the ESA to mediate between home and host-country regulators, and to support as well the delegation of tasks between them, provides a managed application of the principles of home-country control and mutual recognition.

[64] Art 18(3), ESA Regulations.

[65] Art 38, ESA Regulations. The recitals of the ESA Regulations clarify that the safeguard clause should only be invoked when a decision taken by an ESA leads to a significant material fiscal impact, and not in cases such as a reduction of income linked to the temporary prohibition of specific activities or products in order to protect consumers.

peer reviews. The ESA are also responsible for ensuring consistency in the functioning of colleges. The most significant power is to request a college to review a decision leading to an incorrect application of EU law, or not contributing to supervisory convergence. Another set of tasks relate to financial stability, where the ESA are responsible for monitoring systemic risk in cooperation with the ESRB, conducting stress-testing exercises, and identifying possible vulnerabilities such as recapitalisation or restructuring needs. The ESA also promote consumer protection by monitoring new and existing financial activities. They can issue warnings in case a financial activity posed a serious threat to financial stability, take directly applicable decisions to temporarily prohibit or restrict certain financial activities, and then advise the Commission on permanent measures.[66]

B. Beyond European Agencies? Delegation and the *ESMA* Case Law

The concept of European agencies was defined originally as bodies created by secondary law, which supported the policies and decision-making of the Commission. They were first created in the 1970s, but only started to proliferate in the 1990s to support the completion of the single market. They increased exponentially in the 'new governance' period, where European agencies were considered best suited for achieving decentralisation, transparency, and participation in European decision-making.[67]

Despite this evolution, the constitutional limits on the powers of European agencies remained defined by the *Meroni* case law of the Court first set in the 1950s: the delegation of powers to agencies can only be made with regard to 'clearly defined executive powers', which can be subject to 'strict review in the light of criteria determined by the delegating authority'. The delegation of 'a discretionary power, implying a wide margin of discretion' was excluded. This doctrine was justified in order to safeguard the institutional balance in the Treaty, which could not be disturbed by delegation. The delegating authority could not delegate beyond its own powers. The exercise of delegated powers was subject to the same conditions as those of the delegated authority, such as due process and judicial review.[68]

The question was therefore the extent to which the powers entrusted to the ESA went beyond the scope of the delegation of powers permissible under the *Meroni* doctrine.

Regarding the rule-making powers, the adoption of non-binding instruments by the ESA such as technical standards, guidelines and recommendations, did not affect the institutional balance of the Treaty. The Commission preserved its right of initiative and the powers to adopt implementing and delegated acts. However, the procedure for the adoption of 'draft regulatory technical standards' prepared by the ESA constrained to

[66] Arts 9, 20a, and 21 to 32, ESA Regulations.

[67] On the evolution of agencies, see E Chiti, *Le agenzie europee: Unità e decentramento nelle amministrazioni comunitarie* (Padua, Cedam, 2002).

[68] Judgment of the Court of 13 June 1958, *Meroni*, 9/56, EU:C:1958:7, paras 151 and 152. The doctrine was further expanded by Judgment of the Court of 14 May 1981, *Romano*, 98/80, EU:C:1981:104, para 20, which stated that delegation of powers could not include the ability to adopt acts 'having the force of law'.

a large extent the freedom of the Commission to change their content, which required several iterations with the ESA. There was, in this sense, a de facto transfer of regulatory powers from the Commission to the ESA: the role of the Commission was limited to 'rubber-stamping' the standards adopted by the ESA, unless there was a serious divergence between them. This went beyond the *Meroni* doctrine.

With regard to enforcement powers, the ESA Regulations established a system for the consistent application of European rules in the single financial market. The corollary of this system was that the ESA could, at the last instance, address individual and legally binding decisions to financial institutions to restore compliance with European law. Since this decision could only be taken within a precise legal framework under certain conditions, it could be argued that it remained a clearly defined executive power. However, it was also an involvement of the ESA in the competences of the Commission for monitoring compliance with European law. Moreover, the adoption of individual binding decisions on financial institutions corresponds, ultimately, to the direct enforcement of European law in replacement of national authorities.[69]

This was further confirmed by the powers of the ESA to take individual binding decisions on national supervisors and financial institutions in cases of disagreement between supervisors and in emergency situations. In principle, these powers are also exercised within a precise legal framework and not as a general regulatory power. However, when exercising these powers, the ESA have to make assessments and determine the regulatory solutions, which require discretion and policy choices in replacement of national authorities. This fact is confirmed by the fiscal safeguard clause in the ESA Regulations, which enable Member States not to comply with ESA decisions if they are deemed to infringe fiscal sovereignty. Such clause could only be justified if the powers of the ESA would include making policy choices in lieu of national authorities, thus impinging on national sovereignty.

The powers of the ESA represented thus an evolution of the *Meroni* doctrine towards European agencies: the ESA exercised rule-making tasks, which constrained the Commission's implementing powers; and they could take individual binding decisions to enforce European law with discretion and involving policy choices.[70]

This was later confirmed by the Court in 2014 when assessing the powers of the ESMA to take individual binding decisions regarding short-selling. In accordance with Article 28 of Regulation 236/2012 on short selling and credit default swaps, ESMA may intervene in exceptional circumstances in financial markets to prohibit short-selling transactions through an individual binding decision. Two conditions should be fulfilled for this intervention. First, there is a threat to the orderly functioning and integrity of financial markets, or to the stability of financial system in the Union. Second, no national authority has taken adequate measures to address such threat. The UK challenged this

[69] The Treaty establishes a system for infringements by Member States of European law under Arts 258 to 260, TFEU, where the Commission, or a Member State, considers that a Member State has failed to fulfil an obligation under the Treaty. As an exception, Art 126, TFEU has a specific procedure for excessive government deficits, where the Council may adopt measures against a Member State which fails to comply with its recommendations.

[70] See P Van Cleynenbreugel, 'Meroni circumvented? Article 114 TFEU and EU regulatory agencies' (2014) 21 *Maastricht Journal of European and Comparative Law* 64.

provision before the Court on the basis of three main arguments: (1) the violation of the *Meroni* doctrine, since the measures of ESMA involved 'a very large measure of discretion', including economic and financial policy choices, as well as acts of general application; (2) the incompatibility with the delegation of powers to the Commission under Articles 290 and 291 of the TFEU; and (3) a breach of the harmonisation provision of Article 114, which could not have provided the basis for the powers entrusted to ESMA.[71]

The Court considered that the intervention powers of ESMA complied with the *Meroni* doctrine since the exercise of such powers was subject to a number of conditions and criteria, which limited ESMA's discretion to a large extent. Moreover, agencies could adopt acts of general application under Articles 263 and 277 of the TFEU, relating to judicial review, as long as they complied with the *Meroni* doctrine. Regarding the incompatibility with Articles 290 and 291, the Court considered that these provisions are not the only possibility under the Treaty to delegate powers to an agency. These provisions presuppose that there is the possibility to confer powers to agencies, since these powers would be subject to judicial review. Therefore, the Court explicitly acknowledged that the powers of intervention of ESMA could be deemed as conferred powers. This confirmed that the powers of ESA were the result of a transfer of competences from the national to the European level. Finally, the Court also considered that the intervention powers of ESMA were not 'ultra vires' with regard to Article 114. Such powers aimed at the harmonisation of the national laws regarding short-selling, and at improving the conditions for the establishment and functioning of the internal market by avoiding divergent measures by Member States.[72]

In conclusion, the Court expanded in its ESMA judgment the scope of the powers that may be entrusted to agencies under the Treaty: powers can be delegated or conferred directly upon agencies to adopt legal acts of general application within a legal framework that limits the extent of discretion. Most importantly, the Court acknowledged that the powers of agencies may be provided by a delegation of powers of European institutions or by a direct conferral of powers, which then corresponds to a transfer of national competences to a European body. This confirmed the legal and institutional innovations introduced by the ESA Regulations, which aimed at providing the maximum extent of rule-making and enforcement powers to the ESA as European agencies.

[71] Regulation (EU) No 236/2012 of the European Parliament and of the Council of 14 March 2012 on short selling and certain aspects of credit default swaps, [2012] OJ L86/1; and Judgment of the Court of 22 January 2014, ESMA, C-270/12, EU:C:2014:18, paras 28–34, 56–57, 69–70, and 88–90. For an analysis of the impact of this judgment on the *Meroni* doctrine, see M Scholten and M van Rijsbergen, 'The ESMA-Short Selling Case: Erecting a New Delegation Doctrine in the EU upon the Meroni-Romano Remnants' (2014) 41 *Legal Issues of Economic Integration* 389.

[72] See *ESMA*, paras 41–54, 63–67, 77–86, and 97–117. The Treaty of Lisbon introduced for the first time provisions referring directly to European agencies, including Arts 305 and 309, TFEU, which provide that the acts of agencies intended to produce legal effects vis-a-vis third parties and acts of general application adopted by an agency, respectively, are also subject to judicial review by the Court. For a critical analysis of the ESMA judgment, see C Joerges, 'Integration through Law and the Crisis of Law in Europe's Emergency', in D Chalmers, M Jachtenfuchs and C Joerges (eds), *The End of the Eurocrats' Dream: Adjusting to European Diversity* (Cambridge, Cambridge University Press, 2016) 299, who considers that the Court made recourse to an 'emergency doctrine' to justify the ESMA intervention powers.

This would later spillover to the European legal order in the context of the structures created for the Banking Union.[73]

C. The Limitations of the European Supervisory Authorities

Following the above analysis, the ESA were entrusted with a combination of delegated powers and conferred powers. The delegated powers were carved out from competences of the Commission, including the preparation and adoption of implementing and delegated acts, as well as the monitoring of the compliance of European law by Member States. The ability of the ESA to adopt individual binding decisions to enforce European law corresponded to conferred powers, which may be construed as a transfer of powers from the national authorities to the ESA, although constrained, temporary, and exceptional. The remaining conferred powers of the ESA were largely non-binding coordination tasks of national authorities, as well as advisory tasks, which were previously undertaken by the Level 3 committees.

The competences of the ESA may, therefore, be categorised as including: (1) delegated competences from European institutions; (2) limited parallel or shared competences to take individual binding decisions on financial institutions, which, when exercised, pre-empt national decisions; and, (3) coordination and advisory competences, in their respective fields of expertise, to both European institutions and national authorities.[74]

The combination of these competences provided the ESA – in comparison with the previous Level 3 committees – with wide-ranging steering mechanisms to safeguard the single financial market through more integrated regulation, enforcement, and binding coordination of national authorities. Moreover, the ESA exercise such competences with significant independence, particularly vis-à-vis the Commission. This was another innovation for European agencies, which normally did not have their independence explicitly stated.[75]

At the same time, the ESA framework demonstrated the institutional limits for creating European regulatory bodies in the single market. First, the *Meroni* doctrine, although expanded in the *ESMA* case, prevented the creation of independent authorities with autonomous and discretionary regulatory powers. Second, the powers of the ESA remained constrained by national competences. They were subject to the intergovernmental dynamics of the respective Boards of Supervisors, which comprised the national authorities. Ultimately, the effectiveness of the powers of the ESA were more dependent on the aggregation of national interests than on the pursuance of European interest. This reflected the decentralised system of the single financial market, where national authorities remained competent for the application of European law. It remained unlikely that the ESA would exercise their powers so as to impinge on national competences.

[73] See, in this sense, M Scholten and M van Rijsbergen, 'The ESMA-Short Selling Case' (n 71).

[74] For a categorisation of the competences of agencies, see E Chiti, 'European Agencies' Rulemaking: Powers, Procedures and Assessment' (2013) 19 *European Law Journal* 93. For a discussion in the context of ESMA, see P Schammo, 'The European Securities and Markets Authority: Lifting the Veil on the Allocation of Powers' (2011) 48 *CML Rev* 1879.

[75] See, eg, Art 42 of the ESA Regulations regarding the independence of their respective Boards of Supervisors, which is stated in terms similar to the independence of the ECB.

This was confirmed by the 'safeguard clause' in the ESA Regulations preventing them from taking binding decisions which may give rise to a fiscal burden on Member States, for instance, in a financial crisis. The integrity of national fiscal sovereignty was set as an absolute limit to the exercise of European competences.[76]

Therefore, despite some expression of quasi-federal powers, the new system based on the ESA remained a largely decentralised institutional structure, which did not disenfranchise national authorities of their regulatory competences.[77]

Table 22 The Powers and Instruments of the ESA

Tasks	Instruments
1. Rule-making	Drafting regulatory technical standards and implementing standards
	Issuing guidelines and recommendations on supervisory practices and EU law application
2. Enforcement of EU law	Issuing recommendations to national supervisors failing to ensure compliance of financial institutions with EU law
	Issuing last resort binding decisions directed at financial institutions not in compliance
	Mediating disagreements between national supervisors
3. Supervisory convergence	Promoting a common supervisory culture
	Conducting peer review analyses among national authorities
	Participating and contributing to the functioning of colleges
	Facilitating the delegation of tasks among supervisors
	Issuing opinions on prudential assessment of cross-border mergers
4. Consumer protection	Promoting transparency, simplicity and fairness in the market
	Issuing guidelines and recommendations on safety of markets
	Issuing warnings on financial activities
	Temporarily prohibiting or restricting financial activities
5. Financial stability	Following up to ESRB warnings and recommendations
	Monitoring and assessing systemic risk
	Making inquiries and issuing recommendations on institutions or products
	Collecting information and setting-up a central database
	Conducting stress-testing exercises

(continued)

[76] See E Ferran, 'Understanding the new institutional architecture of EU financial market supervision' in G Ferrarini, KJ Hopt and E Wymeersch (eds) *Financial Regulation and Supervision: A post-crisis analysis* (Oxford, Oxford University Press, 2012) 111.

[77] As stated by the De Larosière Report, para 184, the new system is 'a largely decentralised structure, fully respecting the proportionality and subsidiarity principles of the Treaty. So existing national supervisors, who are closest to the markets and institutions they supervise, would continue to carry-out day-to-day supervision and preserve the majority of their present competences.'

Table 22 *(Continued)*

Tasks	Instruments
6. Crisis management	Issuing a confidential recommendation to the Council regarding an emergency
	Coordinating supervisors in crisis situations
	Issuing decisions addressed to supervisors in crisis situations
	Issuing last resort binding decisions directed at individual financial institutions
7.Crisis resolution	Developing and coordinating recovery and resolution plans
	Contributing to strengthening deposit guarantee schemes
	Contributing to a European resolution framework
8. Advisory and international	Issuing opinions to the Parliament, the Council or the Commission
	Developing relations with third-country authorities

VII. Introducing Financial Stability into Integration: The European Systemic Risk Board

A. The Contradiction between Financial Stability and Financial Integration

The financial crisis made obvious the absence of a European financial stability framework in the single financial market. All the main functions were national competences: national authorities monitored the developments in the financial system; national central banks were responsible for providing emergency liquidity assistance in a crisis; national supervisors were responsible for assessing the solvency of financial institutions; deposit guarantee schemes protected national deposits; and there was no European regime for the resolution of financial institutions.

The main reason for the absence of such a framework was twofold. First, in the context of the Treaty, market integration was pursued as an exclusive objective. The law of the single financial market aimed at removing national obstacles to the freedom to provide financial services. On the other hand, safeguarding financial stability implies constraining the activities of financial institutions and markets, which may create risks for the financial system. For example, excessive mortgage lending by banks may give rise to real estate bubbles. This created a contradiction between financial integration and financial stability: since competences remained national, pursuing financial stability in the single financial market implied allowing national authorities to restrain the freedom to provide financial services. In order to address risks, national authorities could set stricter domestic requirements to financial services, which could then pose obstacles to market-entry by competitors of other Member States. At the limit, imposing capital controls could be a measure to safeguard financial stability. The 'trilemma' of the single financial market prevented thus financial stability from overriding financial integration: the exercise of national powers would conflict with financial integration.[78]

Second, national fiscal sovereignty also prevented a European financial stability framework. Safeguarding financial stability implied, ultimately, resorting to public funds to contain a financial crisis, eg to rescue a banking institution as in 2008–2009. The exercise of financial stability powers by national authorities thus reflected in large part the degree of tolerance of the state to use public funds in a crisis. If the state wished to limit the risk of deploying public funds, it would increase the level of prudential requirements – such as capital requirements – to increase the likelihood that a domestic financial institution withstands a crisis and does not need any rescue. At the same time, increasing the level of such requirements may weaken the competitiveness of domestic institutions and increase the cost of credit to the economy, leading to indirect fiscal implications, such as lower tax revenue. Therefore, a financial stability framework reflected the trade-off between exposing the state's coffers to a financial crisis and the competitiveness of its financial industry. Since this is a matter of national fiscal sovereignty, it could not be replicated at the European level, where no public funds were available to address financial instability.

Therefore, both the pursuance of financial integration under the Treaty and the limits posed by national fiscal sovereignty prevented the development of a European framework for financial stability. When the contradiction between financial stability and integration came to the fore in the 2008 crisis, it led to the dominance of the former over the latter. National financial stability prevailed, leading to a retrenchment in financial integration. Member States protected their domestic institutions and ring-fenced their markets. The preservation of the single financial market then required financial stability to be introduced alongside financial integration as twin objectives at the European level. This, however, had to be accomplished within the boundaries of the Treaty and without compromising national fiscal sovereignty. This largely determined the design of the ESRB.[79]

B. The European Framework for Macroprudential Supervision: Managing the Conflict between Stability and Integration

The financial crisis confirmed the increasing systemic risk resulting from financial integration, as well as the increasing links between the financial system and the real economy, both globally and in Europe. The degree of interconnectedness between financial institutions, markets and the economy, led to a new nature and magnitude of systemic risk. For example, excessive mortgage lending by banks may lead to an increase in the vulnerability of households to a worsening of the economy; this, in turn, may lead later to a financial crisis, widespread defaults and major losses for banks; banks may then cut lending to the economy and sell assets at fire-sale prices, affecting markets

[78] See D Schoenmaker, *Governance of international banking: The financial trilemma*, (n 39).

[79] On the consequences of the financial crisis for market integration, see A Enria, 'Fragmentation in banking markets: crisis legacy and the challenge of Brexit' (n 25).

and other institutions, exacerbating further the crisis. This corresponds to the so-called 'pro-cyclicality' of the financial system: the tendency that the financial system amplifies both 'good times', in the form of expansion of finance, and 'bad times', in the form of financial crises. The causes of pro-cyclicality are linked to the shortcomings in the measurement of risk over the long-term by market participants, as well as collective action problems provoked by the 'herd behaviour' in financial markets, both in good and bad times.[80]

The concept of 'macro-prudential supervision' was developed after the crisis to address systemic risk. It was introduced globally following the G-20 London Summit in April 2009 and by numerous reports on regulatory reform. While micro-prudential supervision focuses on the liquidity and solvency of individual financial institutions, macro-prudential supervision aims at addressing the risks to all components of the financial system, including in the interaction with the real economy. This implies taking macro-prudential measures to contain systemic risk, such as introducing capital requirements for systemic risk, setting limits to lending and borrowing, or posing constraints to the size of financial institutions or the financial system. Therefore, safeguarding financial stability through prudential measures implies constraining the provision of financial services.[81]

In Europe, macro-prudential supervision was introduced on 1 January 2014 by the Capital Requirements Directive and the Capital Requirements Regulation – so-called CRD/CRR IV legislative package – which aimed at transposing Basel III in the single financial market.[82]

The CRD IV required each Member State to have its own macro-prudential authority in the form of a 'national designated authority' responsible for the activation of macro-prudential instruments. The macro-prudential instruments included a 'countercyclical buffer' for banks to address the procyclicality of the financial system; a 'systemic risk buffer' for addressing common risks for banks; and a buffer for 'global systemically important institutions'(G-SIIs), and for other systemically important institutions (O-SIIs).[83]

Since macro-prudential measures are adopted at national level to safeguard domestic financial stability, they may conflict with financial integration. This may happen by affecting the level playing field among financial institutions, leading to ring-fencing of domestic markets, as entry becomes more costly, or to regulatory arbitrage, whereby financial institutions reorganise their group structures to contravene requirements in

[80] For an overview of the concept of pro-cyclicality and the instruments to address it, see FSF, Report of the Financial Stability Forum on Addressing Procyclicality in the Financial System (2009), at www.financialstabilityboard.org/wp-content/uploads/r_0904a.pdf.

[81] See C Borio, 'Towards a macroprudential framework for financial supervision and regulation?' (2003) 128 *BIS Working Papers*. Several countries introduced macro-prudential bodies since then, including the Financial Services Oversight Committee in the US and the Financial Policy Committee in the UK.

[82] Directive 2013/36/EU of the European Parliament and of the Council of 26 June 2013 on access to the activity of credit institutions and the prudential supervision of credit institutions and investment firms, amending Directive 2002/87/EC and repealing Directives 2006/48/EC and 2006/49/EC, [2013] OJ L176/338–436 (CRD IV); and Regulation (EU) No 575/2013 of the European Parliament and of the Council of 26 June 2013 on prudential requirements for credit institutions and investment firms and amending Regulation (EU) No 648/2012, [2013] OJ L176/1–337 (CRR IV).

[83] Arts 130 and 135–140, CRD IV.

a Member State. In turn, the territoriality of macro-prudential measures in an integrated market may reduce their effectiveness to safeguard domestic financial stability. Therefore, the introduction of macro-prudential supervision in the single financial market required a framework to manage the conflict between financial stability and financial integration. European law attempted to manage such conflict with several mechanisms.

The first was to require reciprocity among national authorities regarding the imposition of macro-prudential measures. This ensured that the same constraint was imposed on all relevant financial activities in a Member State, independently of the origin of the financial institutions. The main example was the imposition of a counter-cyclical buffer under the CRD IV: when this buffer is activated in any Member State, all Member States are required to apply the same buffer with regard to the exposures of their respective financial institutions to that Member State. In other cases, such as the systemic risk buffer, reciprocity among Member States is voluntary and not mandatory. Another mechanism was fixing upper limits to capital buffers and requiring approval for measures beyond certain thresholds. For example, a Member State must be authorised by the Commission before setting a systemic risk buffer above 3 per cent. This enabled the Commission to play the role of arbitrator between financial stability and financial integration.[84]

The conflict between financial stability and financial integration emerged especially in cases where European law enabled national authorities to impose stricter micro-prudential requirements to address systemic risk. Since these so-called 'national flexibility measures' may also protect domestic markets from competitors, they were subject to a cumbersome approval procedure. The national authority had to notify the Parliament, the Council, the Commission and the ESRB of the proposed measure and its justification regarding financial stability concerns, its appropriateness and proportionality, its positive or negative impact on the internal market, and its suitability, effectiveness and proportionality. If the Commission, on the basis of the ESRB and EBA opinions, considered that the proposed measure would have a negative impact on the single market that outweighs the financial stability benefits, it could propose to the Council an implementing act to reject the draft national measures. The Council would then decide whether to adopt such an act. This procedure thus privileges integration over stability: the adoption of financial stability measures by national authorities can only take place after confirmation that they will not undermine the single financial market.[85]

Lastly, as a last-resort, the conflict between integration and stability may be addressed by macro-prudential measures by the Commission for the whole single financial market. Under the CRR, the Commission may adopt delegated acts to impose, for a maximum period of one year, stricter prudential requirements to address changes in the intensity of prudential risks arising from market developments. This may concern the level of own funds, the requirements for large exposures, or disclosure requirements.

[84] Arts 133(15), 134 and 140, CRD IV.

[85] Art 458, CRR IV. The stricter micro-prudential requirements may refer to a wide range of measures, including the level of own funds, large exposure limits, public disclosure requirements, the level of the capital conservation buffer, liquidity requirements, risk weights for the residential and commercial property sector, and intra-financial sector exposures.

Such delegated acts may only be adopted where the instruments under the CRD/CRR IV are not sufficient to address the risks, upon the recommendation of the ESRB or EBA.

C. The Establishment of the European Systemic Risk Board

The De Larosière Report recommended the establishment of a European Systemic Risk Council, which would have the tasks to 'make recommendations on macro-prudential policy, issue risk warnings, compare observations on macro-economic and prudential developments and give direction on these issues'. The ECOFIN Council of 9 June 2009 renamed it as the European Systemic Risk Board (ESRB) to follow the terminology of the FSB.

The ESRB was established on 1 January 2011. It was mandated to conduct the macro-prudential oversight of the EU's financial system. This was defined as contributing to the prevention or mitigation of systemic risks that arise from developments within the financial system and taking into account macroeconomic developments, so as to avoid periods of widespread financial distress.[86]

The starting point was providing a legal basis for the establishment of the ESRB. As with the ESA, recourse was made to Article 114 of the TFEU. The choice of this legal basis was questioned at the time, since the ESRB had no direct role in pursuing financial integration through the harmonisation of national laws. It had, instead, a monitoring and advisory role on financial stability, which arguably had no immediate impact on the functioning of the single financial market. The alternative to Article 114 would have been the exceptional clause of Article 352, which enables the Council to take action to attain the objectives of the Treaty, without the Treaty having provided the necessary powers. This provision would have required unanimity voting by the Council and the consent of the Parliament. The fact that the activation of Article 352 was even considered confirmed the difficulty in finding a legal basis in the Treaty for introducing financial stability as a concurrent objective to market integration. Eventually, and since the non-binding role of the ESRB in macro-prudential oversight did not represent a transfer of competences to the European level, it was accepted that Article 114 could provide the legal basis.

The choice of this legal basis was extensively justified in the recitals of the ESRB Regulation, which explained the relation between financial stability and financial integration. There could only be confidence in the cross-border provision of financial services with arrangements for monitoring and assessing risks for financial stability. The ESRB contributed directly to financial integration by addressing such risks, which then enabled Member States to take timely and consistent policy responses. This prevented diverging approaches and improved the functioning of the single market. Therefore, by safeguarding financial stability, the ESRB was promoting financial integration.[87]

[86] Regulation (EU) No 1092/2010 of the European Parliament and of the Council of 24 November 2010 on European Union macro-prudential oversight of the financial system and establishing a European Systemic Risk Board, [2010] OJ L331/1 (ESRB Regulation).

[87] Recital (31) of the ESRB Regulation also recalled the *ENISA* case and held that 'nothing in the wording of Art 95 EC [now Art 114, TFEU] implies that the addressees of the measures adopted by the Community legislature on the basis of that provision can only be the individual Member States. The legislature may

The use of Article 114 suggested that the ESRB could be categorised as a European agency, similarly to the ESA. However, while the ESA are European agencies with their own organisational structure, executive powers, and supporting tasks towards the Commission, the ESRB is a sui generis independent European body whose features are closer to that of a committee. The ESRB has no legal personality, organisational structures or autonomous budget. It basically consists of its governance structures, notably its General Board, which deliberates on the adoption of ESRB instruments through formal voting. Its instruments are mainly risk warnings and recommendations, which are directed at national authorities and European institutions.[88]

The functioning of the ESRB also depends on the support and infrastructure provided by ECB. For this purpose, in addition to Article 114, the establishment of the ESRB was based on a Council Regulation conferring tasks to the ECB under Article 127(6). It was the first time that this provision was used. The reason was that it was considered that Article 114 could not assign tasks to the ECB requiring the use of its own resources, even if such tasks were organisational in nature. The activation of Article 127(6) thus required the ECB to provide analytical, logistical, statistical, administrative and financial support to the ESRB. This enabled the ESRB to draw on the expertise of the ECB and take account of the close relationship between macro-prudential policy and monetary policy. Moreover, the effectiveness of the ESRB could benefit from the independence and reputation of the ECB, including by having the ECB President as the Chair of the ESRB.[89]

D. The ESRB Risk Warnings and Recommendations

The starting point of the ESRB's macro-prudential function is the surveillance and monitoring of systemic risks at EU level. The first problem in this context was how to pool at European level all information from the financial system and the economy for detecting and assessing systemic risks. This had not been legally possible until the establishment of the ESRB, particularly with regard to supervisory information which had been considered privileged information. Information about the risks in the single financial market

deem it necessary to provide for the establishment of a Community body responsible for contributing to the implementation of a process of harmonisation in situations where, in order to facilitate the uniform implementation and application of acts based on that provision, the adoption of non-binding supporting and framework measures seems appropriate.'

[88] The General Board of the ESRB has 67 members, out of which 38 are members with a voting right: the President and the Vice-President of the ECB; the Governors of the national central banks; a Member of the Commission; the Chairs of the European Supervisory Authorities; the Chair and the two Vice-Chairs of the Advisory Scientific Committee; and the Chair of the Advisory Technical Committee. The ESRB governance also comprises a Steering Committee, an Advisory Technical Committee and a Scientific Committee comprising mainly academics.

[89] Council Regulation (EU) No 1096/2010 of 17 November 2010 conferring specific tasks upon the European Central Bank concerning the functioning of the European Systemic Risk Board, [2010] OJ L331/162. The relationship between monetary policy and macroprudential policy, as well as the independence of central banks, justify their close involvement in macro-prudential supervision. This also explains the dominance of central banks as voting members of the General Board of the ESRB. For a survey of the role of central banks in macroprudential frameworks, see D Masciandaro and A Volpicella, 'Macro prudential governance and central banks: Facts and drivers' (2016) 61 *Journal of International Money and Finance* 101.

had not been pooled or gathered centrally until then. The ESRB Regulation enabled it to request information from the ESA on financial institutions. If the requested data are not available, the ESRB may address a direct request to supervisors, central banks, statistics authorities, or Member States.[90]

After the pooling of information, the next step in the ESRB's macro-prudential process is the identification of systemic risks. These risks are assessed and ranked in terms of their probability as well as the severity with which they may impact the financial system. For this purpose, the ESRB and the ESA are mandated to develop a 'risk dashboard' and a 'stress-testing regime' to identify and measure systemic risk. This provides the basis for the ESRB to issue risk warnings and recommendations.[91]

A risk warning is one of the instruments of the ESRB. It may be addressed to the EU, to one or more Member States, ESA, or national supervisors. The aim of the warnings is to raise the awareness of authorities to systemic risks, which may warrant a policy response. The ESRB has a colour-coded system distinguishing between different risk levels, which are then applied to warnings and recommendations. The ESRB Regulation also provides that the ESRB can issue a confidential warning to the Council on an emergency situation, which can trigger the use of certain powers by the ESA.

The other instrument of the ESRB is a formal recommendation. Following the identification of systemic risks, the ESRB may issue recommendations on the policies required to address such risks to the same addressees as for the risk warnings and, in addition, the Commission regarding EU legislation. The recommendations should specify which measures are suitable to address a source of systemic risk, which may range from micro-prudential tools, such as capital requirements, to specific tools to address systemic risk, such as countercyclical capital buffers or surcharges on systemically important institutions.[92]

The European macro-prudential policy cycle concludes when the addressees of recommendations communicate to the ESRB their policy response, or explain why they have not acted. This corresponds to a 'comply or explain' mechanism. If the ESRB decides that its recommendations have not been followed and that the addressees have failed to explain their inaction, it shall inform the Council and the ESA concerned. The ESA are then required to use their powers to ensure a follow-up by national supervisors to ESRB recommendations. The ESRB also has the right to publish its warnings and recommendations, which may increase the incentives for compliance.

As the main instruments for European macro-prudential supervision, the effectiveness of the ESRB risk warnings and recommendations will be measured by the extent

[90] See Art 15, ESRB Regulation. A 'global risk map' was proposed to assess mutual exposures among large and complex financial institutions and counterparties. See O Issing, *New Financial Order*, (n 54) and V Constâncio, 'Information requirements for macro-prudential oversight and the role of central banks' (2010) at www.ecb.europa.eu/press/key/date/2010/html/sp101020.en.html.

[91] Art 3(2)(g), ESRB Regulation and Art 23, ESA Regulations.

[92] Art 16, ESRB Regulation. Under the CRD/CRR IV, the ESRB is also responsible for issuing opinions and recommendations regarding the activation by national authorities of systemic risk buffer rates exceeding 5% under Arts 133 and 134, CRD IV. It should also issue an opinion on the activation of national flexibility measures under Art 458, CRR IV, which should cover the justification of effectiveness and proportionality of the measure, why other instruments in the CRD/CRR cannot adequately address the systemic risk, and the likely impact on the internal market. See ESRB, The ESRB Handbook on Operationalising Macro-prudential Policy in the Banking Sector (2014) at www.esrb.europa.eu/pub/pdf/other/140303_esrb_handbook_mp.en.pdf.

to which they are implemented by the addressees, and then contain systemic risk in practice. Since the ESRB has no binding powers to ensure compliance, it relies on the quality and credibility of its macro-prudential analysis and policies, as well as the regular reporting to the Council, cooperation with the ESA, and the 'comply or explain' mechanism.[93]

Table 23 The ESRB Tools for Macroprudential Oversight

1	Issuing warnings on significant risks to financial stability
2	Issuing recommendations with a specified timeline for policy response
3	Publishing risk warnings and recommendations
4	Monitoring the follow-up to the ESRB recommendations on the basis of a comply or explain mechanism
5	Informing the Council and the ESA when the ESRB recommendations have not been followed and the addressees have failed to explain their inaction
6	Requesting information from the ESA, also on individual financial institutions, and from the ESCB, supervisors, statistics authorities, or the Member States
7	Using indicators of systemic risk and conducting stress-testing exercises (with the ESA)
8	Issuing a confidential warning to the Council in an emergency situation
9	Advisory role on the activation of macro-prudential tools provided in EU law

E. Financial Stability versus Financial Integration

The legal and institutional framework for macroprudential supervision, and the institutional design of the ESRB, confirmed the limitations of safeguarding financial stability in the single financial market. With financial stability remaining a national competence, it contradicted European financial integration. Therefore, stability had to be permanently weighted against integration. This was the rationale that defined the governance, instruments, and policy for safeguarding the stability of the single financial market.

The framework for macroprudential supervision consists, therefore, of provisions that enable national authorities to take unilateral measures to safeguard financial stability, subject to several conditions aimed at preserving integration: (1) reciprocity by other Member States; (2) upper limits to quantitative requirements; (3) notification procedures; and (4) approval procedures, which involve the Commission, Council, ESA and the ESRB. The national authorities remain competent for financial stability, but within a framework of constraints. This leads to a constant balancing act between stability and integration.

Similarly, the establishment of the ESRB aimed at pursuing financial stability without affecting national competences. The implication was that the governance of the ESRB was based on committee-type structures –with its General Board reaching

[93] See E Ferran and K Alexander, 'Can soft law bodies be effective? The Special Case of the European Systemic Risk Board,' (n 37) at 775–777, for a comparison between the soft powers of the ESRB and the FSB, arguing that the ESRB was likely to be more effective since it is anchored on a legal system.

67 members – and that its instruments were only advisory and not binding on the addressees. In fulfilling its tasks, the ESRB relied essentially on the credibility and peer pressure resulting from the wide composition of its General Board, as well as on the moral suasion based on the 'comply or explain mechanism' for its warnings and recommendations. The ESRB has thus only an indirect reach as its analysis needs to be translated into concrete measures. It does not represent more than a steering mechanism to address coordination failures of European and national policies to safeguard financial stability.

In conclusion, financial stability was introduced in the single financial market as a result of the crisis, but as a constrained policy objective. Although an improvement, this stopped short from addressing the shortcomings in managing the financial crisis: (1) the absence of a European capacity to contain the systemic risk arising from integration; (2) the deregulation promoted by integration-driven policies; and (3) the absence of European instruments for managing a crisis. Instead, the new framework confirmed the dominance of national competences and national fiscal sovereignty to safeguard the stability of the single financial market.

VIII. From the Single Passport to the Single Rulebook

A. The Shift Towards the Single Rulebook

As argued above, the recourse to Article 114 of the TFEU to regulate the single financial market included the strategy of widening and deepening the harmonisation of national laws, also benefiting from the political consensus for reform emerging from the crisis. It became known as 'maximum harmonisation', thus replacing the previous paradigm of minimum harmonisation and regulatory competition to support the single passport. Maximum harmonisation was the answer to replace the single passport framework, which had largely failed in both regulating the single financial market and in managing the financial crisis.[94]

The maximum harmonisation strategy was put forward by the De Larosière Report in the form of a 'single financial services rulebook', which was a concept first introduced by Tommaso Padoa-Schioppa in the early 2000s. The objective was to move beyond the several layers of regulation of the single financial market, which comprised: (1) European legislation; (2) national laws implementing EU law and adding specific national rules; and (3) administrative rules by national authorities. These layers implied that, although the bulk of financial regulation had an EU source, market participants were in fact subject to local rules. This allowed a diverse and fragmented regulatory environment to flourish, which defeated the purpose of the single financial market. Furthermore, it was a contributing factor to the crisis as national authorities engaged in regulatory competition to attract business and favour national champions. It also prevented pan-European financial groups from being regulated as an entity due to the

[94] See S Weatherill, *The Internal Market as a Legal Concept*, (n 48) 215–222, who argues that the European Commission started to develop its maximum harmonisation strategy in 2001 in the field of contract law.

diversity of national rules. Lastly, it increased the costs of cross-border financial services as EU law did not remove the need to comply with national rules.[95]

As a result, there was no unified and consistent rulebook for the single financial market. The approach proposed by Padoa-Schioppa, and endorsed by the De Larosière Report, was to develop a single European rulebook aimed at ensuring equal treatment, low costs of compliance, and the removal of regulatory arbitrage. This would be achieved, first, by defining, not only general principles of regulation, but also key technical rules at the EU level; second, by incorporating such rules as much as possible into directly applicable EU regulations. This would mean that market participants throughout the single market would be regulated directly by EU law, without national implementation or additional layers of local rules.[96]

Following the proposals of the De Larosière Report, the main components of the single financial services rulebook were the following.

First, EU regulations would replace directives as the main instrument of harmonisation. This applied both to the primary legislation adopted by the co-legislators and also to the delegated and implementing acts of the Commission, which increasingly took the form of regulations. The direct application of regulations replaced the need for national transposition of EU law, thus drastically shortening the period for EU law entering into force. Furthermore, EU legislation started to contain a wider scope for delegated and implementing acts by the Commission on the basis of the technical standards issued by the ESA. This was also the result of the end of comitology procedures.

Second, EU financial regulation would provide little margin for deviation at the national level. The minimum harmonisation principle was replaced by maximum harmonisation, which does not allow Member States to define either looser or stricter requirements. Therefore, the model of regulatory competition as an engine for market integration was no longer applicable. Only in the case of macro-prudential measures to safeguard financial stability, as analysed above, could Member States impose stricter regulatory requirements.

Third, the ESA themselves would contribute to the single rulebook through their rule-making powers, including standards, guidelines, and recommendations. The ESA also had instruments to promote the convergence of supervisory practices. Such convergence was supported by EU law, which included more and more provisions on the harmonisation of the enforcement powers of national authorities.[97]

Lastly, the regulatory perimeter of EU law would be expanded significantly so as to encompass all activities which could have a bearing on financial stability. This allowed

[95] See T Padoa-Schioppa, 'How to deal with emerging pan-European financial institutions?' (2004) www.ecb.europa.eu/press/key/date/2004/html/sp041103.en.html; and 'Europe Needs a Single Financial Rule Book' (2007) *Financial Times*, 11 December.

[96] On the evolution of the concept of the single rulebook, see A Lefterov, 'The single rulebook: legal issues and relevance in the SSM context' (2015) 15 *ECB Legal Working Paper Series*; and, for a comprehensive overview, G Lo Schiavo, *The Role of Financial Stability in EU Law and Policy* (Alphen aan den Rijn, The Netherlands, Wolters Kluwer, 2017) 166–176.

[97] The EBA also introduced a 'single supervisory handbook', which compiles the non-binding best practices for methodologies and processes. For an analysis, see E Ferran, 'The Existential Search of the European Banking Authority' (2016) 17 *European Business Organization Law Review* 285.

EU law to venture into areas, which were previously out of reach. This included crisis management and resolution of financial institutions, which were previously addressed by voluntary non-binding MoUs. In addition, EU law widened into areas not previously regulated at all, including credit rating agencies, OTC derivatives markets, short-selling and credit default swaps, hedge funds and private equity, or the so-called 'shadow banking' sector, the provision of credit involving entities and activities outside the regulated banking system.[98]

The single rulebook represented, therefore, a shift from the single passport. Maximum harmonisation made the principles of minimum harmonisation and mutual recognition obsolete: EU law replaced the layers of national laws and regulations. The principle of home-country control was also constrained. The competences and powers of home-authorities were more and more limited to the application of EU law, rather than their respective national laws. Therefore, the turn from minimum to maximum harmonisation also led to a shift from market integration to market regulation: regulatory authority moved from the national to the European level.[99]

Table 24 The Single Passport versus the Single Rulebook

	Single Passport	**Single Rulebook**
1	Directives requiring national transposition	Regulations which are directly applicable
2	Minimum harmonisation and mutual recognition	Maximum harmonisation
3	Reinforcement of home-country control	Constrained home-country control, limited to the application of EU law
4	Limited delegation of implementing powers to the Commission, subject to comitology procedures	Extensive use of delegated acts by the Commission, without comitology but based on ESA standards
5	Level 3 Committees	ESA
6	Regulatory perimeter limited to what is necessary for market integration	Regulatory perimeter as wide as required to safeguard financial stability

[98] See European Commission, An EU Framework for Cross-Border Crisis Management in the Banking Sector, COM (2009) 561 final. See also Regulation (EC) 1060/2009 of the European Parliament and of the Council of credit rating agencies, [2009] OJ L302/1; and the analysis by F Amtenbrink and J de Haan, 'Regulating Credit Ratings in the European Union: A Critical First Assessment of Regulation 2060/2009 on Credit Rating Agencies' (2009) 46 *CML Rev* 1915.

[99] See S Weatherill, 'Maximum versus Minimum Harmonization: Choosing between Unity and Diversity in the Search for the Soul of the Internal Market' in NN Shuibhne and LW Gormley (eds) *From Single Market to Economic Union* (Oxford, Oxford University Press, 2012) 175–200. Weatherill argues that the debate between minimum and maximum harmonisation in the consumer field demonstrates well that 'there is no sustainable divide between the Union's interest in market integration and the role of Member States in matters of market regulation'. He also argues that this spillover from market integration into market regulation leads to the conduct of an EU policy in areas where the Treaty does not even confer such competences to the Union such as Art 114, TFEU.

B. The Implementation of the Single Rulebook

The practical implementation of the single rulebook met several challenges. The adoption of EU regulations requires a much more precise agreement among the Commission, the Council and the Parliament. The level of regulatory detail and their direct applicability led to a higher degree of scrutiny in law-making, particularly from the Member States and the financial industry. In this sense, the decision-making process leading to the single rulebook was a powerful integrating force as regulatory interests converged at the European level. The extent to which the single rulebook was implemented depended also on providing a wider scope for delegated and implementing acts, thus leading to a greater involvement from the ESA in preparing draft regulatory or draft implementing technical standards.

The CRD/CRR IV was the first EU legislative package to introduce the single rulebook approach. It had an EU Regulation as it main instrument. It provided for the wide use of delegated and implementing acts on the basis of technical standards by the EBA, namely 110 technical standards – 33 implementing and 77 regulatory standards – in comparison to the 34 standards foreseen in the previous CRD III. The provisions of the CRD/CRR IV were also based on maximum harmonisation. Member States and national authorities were not allowed to impose stricter capital requirements than those defined by EU law, unless to address temporary risks with the involvement of the Commission and the ESRB. Finally, the CRD IV also supported the single rulebook in harmonising the enforcement powers of national authorities, including sanctioning powers for breaches of the CRD/CRR IV.[100]

C. The 'Race to the Top' Challenge to the Single Rulebook

The concept of the single rulebook was a return to the model of 'integration through harmonisation', which characterised the first legal period of the single financial market. This 'integration through harmonisation' failed, due to the cumbersome legislative process based on unanimity voting, and the lack of political and technical willingness to engage in a massive harmonisation process of national laws. At the start, the single rulebook was launched to take advantage of the political consensus among Member States around the need for regulatory reform following the financial crisis. It also benefitted from the push for reform launched at the global level, particularly from the depth and level of detail of the regulatory standards of the FSB and BCBS. Soon into the process, however, the single rulebook met significant opposition by Member States.

The main reason for the opposition was the shift from the focus on financial integration to the inclusion of financial stability as one of the objectives in EU legislation. EU financial services law was no longer conceived as an instrument to champion the

[100] See, eg, Recitals (2) and (3), CRR IV and, regarding the harmonisation of national supervisory powers, Arts 64–66. CRD IV.

national financial industry or attract cross-border business through deregulation, which had favoured the minimum harmonisation approach in the past. Instead, the backlash against finance after the crisis meant that regulation became an instrument for safeguarding national economies and taxpayers from the potential costs of a crisis. This implied that Member States wished to preserve the national discretion to impose stricter regulatory standards, depending, for instance, on the weight of the financial industry in the economy, or a specific development such as an asset bubble.

The protection of national taxpayers thus created new dynamics of regulatory competition: a 'race to the top' replaced the previous 'race to the bottom'. The incentives were no longer to have lax regulation but to safeguard financial stability through stricter regulation, in line with the political will of governments and parliaments. At the same time, the new dynamics of a 'race to the top' reflected the lack of confidence in the EU institutional framework to safeguard the stability of the single market.

The single rulebook was therefore opposed with the argument that Member States should be free to impose stricter regulation to safeguard their own jurisdictions from systemic risks, for instance by raising capital requirements above the EU ratios. This would not be in contradiction of the single rulebook as it would not discriminate against financial markets and institutions of other Member States. Furthermore, the functioning of macro-prudential supervision, which takes into account economic and financial cycles, implies that Member States should be able to fine-tune their regulatory requirements to their national cycles, given the degree of economic divergence among Member States.[101]

The opposition of Member States crystallised in the adoption of CRD/CRR IV, which required two devoted ECOFIN meetings on 2 May and 15 May 2011. The compromise agreement was reflected in the framework for macroprudential supervision, which introduced mechanisms for weighing financial stability versus financial integration, as analysed above.

The shift from the single passport's deregulation to the single rulebook's re-regulation met, therefore, the limits imposed by national fiscal sovereignty. It justified a considerable transfer of financial regulation from the national to the European level, while enabling Member States to exercise discretion, even if constrained, in safeguarding financial stability in their respective jurisdiction. In the absence of fiscal mechanisms at the EU level, financial stability could only be fully pursued at the national level where taxpayers' funds can be deployed. It thus confirmed the trilemma that financial stability competences cannot be transferred to the European level without the transfer of regulatory and fiscal competences as well.

This represented a significant shortcoming of the single rulebook. Without the unification of regulation, the single financial market can always be renationalised whenever national authorities deviate from the EU's regulatory standards to address financial risks.

[101] On the implications of macroprudential policies, see MK Brunnermeier, H James and JP Landau, *The Euro and the Battle of Ideas*, (n 22) at 206–209.

IX. The Democratic Legitimacy of Financial Integration

A. The Legitimacy Crisis of the Regulation of Finance

The 2008 financial crisis also gave rise to a legitimacy crisis in the regulation of finance. This resulted from the downfall of the two core assumptions underpinning financial regulation from the 1980s until then: (1) the efficient market hypothesis; and (2) the related belief that financial regulation was expert-driven and did not involve political and redistributive choices.[102]

Under these assumptions, the objective of financial regulation was to remove obstacles to the functioning of efficient and rational markets, which provided the best possible allocation of capital and distribution of risks. This required the liberalisation and deregulation of finance. It would mainly be subject to self-regulation by financial institutions and markets, which were in the best position to assess and manage financial risks. This was because self-interest in the preservation of accumulated wealth provided strong incentives for market participants to restrain their risks. Market discipline would also prevent the build-up of risks, since excessive risk-taking would translate into higher market prices, difficulties to attract capital and access liquidity. Finance was self-stabilising and did not require regulatory intervention.[103]

In turn, this implied that financial regulation would be designed by experts on finance and by market participants themselves, which had the expertise to identify the obstacles to efficient markets and develop mechanisms for self-regulation and market discipline. Examples of these mechanisms included the recognition of the internal risk management models of banks for the calculation of capital requirements under the Basel II framework, accounting rules on the valuation of financial instruments, the recourse to credit rating agencies for determining the risk of financial instruments, and financial innovation such as securitisation. Instead of being effective in containing risks, these mechanisms were among the causes of the 2008 crisis.[104]

The focus of financial regulation on promoting efficient markets, and its basis on technical expertise, created the illusion that it did not include political or redistributive choices. Ensuring the efficient allocation of capital and distribution of risks was

[102] For the evolution of economic theory regarding efficient markets, see J Fox, *The Myth of the Rational Market: A History of Risk, Reward, and Delusion on Wall Street* (New York, Harper Business, 2009); and AW Lo, *Adaptive Markets: Financial Evolution at the Speed of Thought* (Princeton, Princeton University Press, 2017) 20–44.

[103] Alan Greenspan, the Chairman of the Federal Reserve between 1987 and 2006, was one of the most prominent advocates of financial deregulation in the wake of globalisation. For example, in his 2007 book, he wrote that 'The textbook model of market perfection works if its fundamental premises are observed: people must be free to act in their self-interest, unencumbered by external shocks or economic policy.' See A Greenspan, *The Age of Turbulence* (New York, Penguin, 2008) 368.

[104] For an analysis of the implications of these mechanisms, see FSF, Report of the Financial Stability Forum on Enhancing Market and Institutional Resilience, which identified the major weakness of the financial regulatory framework immediately after the market turmoil in 2007. See also S Claessens, R Herring, D Schoenmaker, and KA Summe, 'A safer world financial system: Improving the resolution of systemic institutions' (2010) 12 *Geneva reports on the world economy*, assigning one of the main causes of the crisis to financial liberalisation and deregulation, at 6.

beneficial to all. It provided the best possible use of resources and fostered economic growth. Financial regulation did not represent the outcome of political choices on the distribution of benefits and costs within the economy or the society. It was instead the outcome of the technical expertise of financial regulators – both at the national and global levels, for example, the BCBS – and the self-regulation by market participants, whose sole aim was to increase the efficiency of finance. There were no value judgments in financial regulation. For example, this justified not imposing any limits on the compensation of bankers, which could have been perceived as limiting personal freedom.

Therefore, financial regulation did not require direct democratic legitimacy. It was self-legitimised by being anchored on the efficient market hypothesis and on the expertise of regulators and market participants. It was endorsed as such into law by governments and parliaments without much, if any, political scrutiny. Furthermore, political institutions had vested interests in promoting efficient markets, since this was equivalent to increasing the competitiveness of domestic financial institutions and markets, thus increasing economic growth and the returns of taxation. This was another contributing factor to the global and European expansion of finance.[105]

When the 2008 financial crisis erupted, it exposed the illusion that financial regulation did not involve redistributive choices. The reliance on the efficient market hypothesis provided incentives for the expansion of finance beyond the capacity of the financial system to manage the increase in risks. The reliance on expertise led to regulatory capture, as regulation pursued the interests of the financial industry in expanding itself. Financial institutions and markets had not managed risks and market discipline had not contained excessive risk-taking, as it had been assumed. Financial risks had not been distributed but had instead accumulated as finance expanded. When the risks materialised, society bore the costs of financial losses by bailing out financial institutions and bearing the economic implications.[106]

The consequence was that the democratic legitimacy of financial regulation became increasingly questioned. The crisis made obvious the previously dormant link between the expansion of finance and the potential liabilities of taxpayers' funds as the ultimate backstop, besides the economic and social ramifications. After all, the regulation of finance included political choices and redistributive implications: it reflected the degree of risk-tolerance of the society towards the expansion of finance. The choice between regulation and deregulation translated as a choice between less or more risk-taking in finance. More risk could potentially increase the economic benefits, but could also increase the liabilities of taxpayers if public funds had to be used to contain a crisis. Furthermore, it also became clear that the regulation of finance was not only a matter of technical expertise but also required democratic legitimacy and accountability. Even the most technically obscure matters of financial regulation, such as the accounting of financial instruments, involved political and redistributive choices as to the functioning of finance. However, political choices had been presented as technical choices in

[105] See A Admati and M Helwig, *The Bankers' New Clothes*, (n 34) in particular ch 1 on 'The Politics of Banking.'

[106] See A Turner, 'The Turner Review' (n 5).

pursuance of market efficiency, which led to the removal of regulation from the scope of politics and to its capture by the financial industry itself.[107]

Therefore, the 2008 financial crisis marked the move away from financial regulation based on the efficient markets' hypothesis and on technical expertise. From then on, financial regulation became more and more a matter of political deliberation as to the appropriate degree of societal risk-tolerance regarding the expansion of finance. The previously de-politicised financial regulation became politicised in the aftermath of the crisis.

B. The Politicisation of the Law of the Single Financial Market

The law of the single financial market also suffered a legitimacy crisis. The assumption that financial regulation did not involve political and redistributive choices was even more powerful in the context of the single market. The pursuance of integration as the functional purpose of the law of the single financial market implied that no political choices were seemingly at stake. The harmonisation of national laws could only be justified by increasing financial integration and not by a European policy to regulate finance as such. Moreover, large parts of EU law represented the implementation of global regulatory standards, such as the Basel II framework. This limited the ability to adopt policy choices, which further reinforced expert-driven regulation and its removal from political deliberation.[108]

Following the financial crisis, the law of the single financial market became increasingly subject to political deliberation, as the economic and social impact of financial integration became clear. This meant that the law of the single financial market started to embody more and more the expression of regulatory policy choices, rather than only the pursuance of financial integration. This was supported by the introduction of financial stability in the legal framework and by the concept of the single rulebook, which excluded regulatory competition in favour of a regulatory policy for the single financial market. Moreover, the replacement of the national layers of regulation by the single rulebook increased the accountability at European level, which became more and more the direct source of financial regulation.

The shift towards politics was expressed in the growing activism of the Parliament and the Council in the negotiations of legislation. This constrained the policy role of the Commission since its proposals were substantially modified more often by the co-legislators in comparison to the previous institutional practice. Furthermore, the Parliament and the Council also exercised a tighter political control of the exercise of

[107] On the argument that European integration should focus on technical and complex policy areas, with no redistributive effects, see G Majone, 'The European Community as a Regulatory State' in *Collected Courses of the Academy of European Law, V-1* (New York, Kluwer Law International, 1996) 321; and the counter-argument that most European policies are actually redistributive, see A Follesdal and S Dix, 'Why There is a Democratic Deficit in the EU: A Response to Majone and Moravcsik' (2006) 44 *Journal of Common Market Studies* 533, 542–544.

[108] For an analysis for the single market, see C Joerges (2002) 'The Law's Problems with the Governance of the Single European Market' in C Joerges and R Dehousse (eds) *Good Governance in Europe's Integrated Market* (Oxford, Oxford University Press, 2002) 3.

delegated powers by the Commission. The Parliament and the Council thus became much more prominent as political institutions in the shaping of the law of the single financial market.[109]

The increasing democratic accountability requirements after the crisis were reflected as well in the framework of the ESA and the ESRB. Their founding regulations provide for accountability to the Parliament and the Council. The ESA have several reporting obligations towards these institutions, such as with regard to regulatory technical standards, the compliance of national authorities with guidelines and recommendations, and in emergency situations. There are also due process requirements, such as conducting impact assessments and public consultations before preparing regulatory technical standards. The fiscal safeguard clauses in the ESA Regulations, which enable a Member State not to comply with an ESA decision if it infringes its fiscal sovereignty, also reflected the political dimension of the tasks of the ESA. On the part of the ESRB, its Chair is invited to an annual hearing in the Parliament, and more frequently in the event of financial distress. The Chair of the ESRB also holds confidential discussions twice a year with the Chair and Vice-Chairs of the Economic and Monetary Affairs Committee of the European Parliament.[110]

C. Democracy versus Financial Integration

The legitimacy crisis of financial regulation should be understood in the wider context of the tension between financial integration and democracy, which was exacerbated by the 2008 crisis. There is a contradiction between increasing integration and preserving democracy at the national level. More integration reduces the scope for choice by national political institutions. By definition, political choices that pursue national interests contradict integration. While some sort of democratic legitimacy could have been found previously for integration policies, as argued by the 'new governance' doctrines, the financial crisis demonstrated that ultimately the national political institutions bear the costs of integration. There were no public funds to contain the crisis, either at the European or global levels.[111]

The realisation that integration could not expand in a vacuum outside democratic politics led to the turn from an expert-driven law of integration to a law increasingly determined by political preferences on financial integration. The introduction of macroprudential supervision as a constraint on financial integration was one expression of this turn. The possibility that the law of the single financial market could give rise to

[109] The increasing activism of the Parliament and Council was clear in the main legislative proposals of regulatory reform after the crisis, including the CRR/CRD IV, which included remuneration rules for bankers; the Credit Rating Agencies Regulation; and later the Bank Recovery and Resolution Directive, as well as the discussions relating to a structural separation between trading and deposit-taking activities of banks on the basis of the recommendations of the 'Liikanen Report'. E Liikanen, Report of the European Commission's High-level Expert Group on Bank Structural Reform (2012), at ec.europa.eu/info/system/files/liikanen-report-02102012_en.pdf.

[110] Art 19, ESRB Regulation.

[111] See D Rodrik, *The Globalization Paradox* (Oxford, Oxford University Press, 2011) ch 9, who conceptualised 'the political trilemma of the world economy', according to which democracy, national sovereignty and global economic integration are mutually incompatible.

fiscal liabilities also became a political concern, as demonstrated by the fiscal safeguard clause in the establishment of the ESA. At the same time, this did not imply necessarily a decline in financial integration. It represented instead a turn from a functional law focused solely on integration to a law expressing a regulatory policy for the single financial market.

Therefore, the financial crisis created the need to provide democratic legitimacy to the law of the single financial market for the first time in its history. The assumption that financial integration would only bring benefits and carry no risks was no longer tenable. The law of the single financial market had to increasingly express political preferences as to the degree of societal risk-tolerance regarding finance in Europe. This implied, in turn, that increasing financial regulation at the European level required an increasing capacity for democratic deliberation. The political and distributive choices in European financial regulation required democratic legitimacy. However, Europe's institutional framework was very far from providing a meaningful democratic control.[112]

X. Conclusion: The Legal Causes and Consequences of the Financial Crisis

A. The Causes of the Crisis in European Law

The 2008 financial crisis in Europe had not only financial and economic causes, but also origins in European law, which further amplified the implications of the crisis.[113]

The first legal origin of the crisis was the framework of the single passport, which was designed to promote the unlimited expansion of the provision of financial services in the single market. Any financial institution could provide its services across the single market without being constrained by its origin. This implied that a financial institution could increase its size beyond what would be proportional to the economic and financial size of the home-country Member State. It could also increase its risk-taking independently of the systemic implications for the domestic markets where it operated. This was enabled by the fact that under European law the home-country authorities had no obligations to support their financial institutions or to safeguard the host-countries where they operated, while the host-country authorities had no powers to protect their domestic markets from the risks created by such institutions. This 'vacuum' of responsibilities created by European law enabled the unlimited expansion of finance within the

[112] For an overview of the implications of the financial crisis for democracy at the European level, see E Chiti, AJ Menéndez, and PG Teixeira, 'The European Rescue of the European Union? The Existential Crisis of the European Political Project' (2012) 3/12 *ARENA Report*, 19 *RECON Report*. On the possible conceptual models for democracy in the EU, see JP McCormick, *Weber, Habermas, and Transformations of the European State: Constitutional, Social, and Supranational Democracy* (Cambridge, Cambridge University Press, 2007) at 236–ff. In particular, McCormick envisages the emergence of a 'Sektoralstaat', which corresponds to multiple specialised policymaking within Europe based on comitology and delegated powers. This would enable variation of regulatory levels across different policy areas and among Member States, within acceptable standards of democratic accountability.

[113] See also AJ Menéndez 'The Existential Crisis of the European Union' (2013) 14 *German Law Journal* 453.

single financial market beyond the ability of Member States to contain the related risks. In good times, the economic benefits of finance were shared by all Member States. When the crisis hit, the authorities of each Member State were obliged by their mandates to ring-fence their domestic markets. The single passport framework thus led to the unsustainable expansion of finance. It then amplified the disintegration of the single financial market when the crisis hit.

The second legal origin was that the law of the single financial market was based on the sole purpose of achieving financial integration, which had primacy over financial stability and other regulatory policies. The legal basis for all of the legislation of the single financial market was the harmonisation provision of Article 114 of the TFEU. Therefore, the harmonisation of national laws could only be justified by the purpose of market integration and not by regulatory needs.

Accordingly, the law of the single financial market aimed essentially at removing national obstacles to the freedom to provide financial services. This purpose excluded the pursuance of other policies, notably financial stability. As analysed above, pursuing financial stability on the basis of national competences was even contradictory with integration. On the other hand, it was questionable that Article 114 could provide the basis to introduce financial stability as an objective of European law. Therefore, in addition to the 'vacuum' of responsibilities between home- and host-country authorities created by the single passport, the narrow integration purpose of European law created a 'vacuum' of regulation of the single financial market.[114]

For the same reasons, Article 114 could not provide the basis for the establishment of European authorities with competences to regulate the single financial market, as discussed at the time of the establishment of the ESA and the ESRB. This was why the institutional structure of the single financial market could not go beyond the soft governance arrangements based on committees and instruments such as recommendations. It corresponded to another failure of European law leading to the crisis: the inability to define legitimate European governance in integrated markets.

The exclusive functional purpose of the law of the single financial market to achieve integration was exacerbated by the belief that financial regulation did not involve political or distributive choices, since it was based on the efficient market hypothesis and driven by technical expertise. If there were no political choices, there was also no need for democratic legitimacy. This further enabled the expansion of the law of the single financial market and the deepening of integration without political scrutiny. It then contributed to deregulation and to the expansion of finance unconstrained by financial stability considerations.

The third legal origin of the crisis was the absence of a crisis management framework or safety net in the single financial market, due to the dominance of national fiscal sovereignty. This dominance implied that the law of the single financial market could only promote the benefits of integration and could not impose on Member States any obligation to share the associated risks and costs of a financial crisis. This prevented the establishment of European regulatory authorities, as confirmed by the fiscal safeguard

[114] See G Majone, *Rethinking the Union of Europe Post-Crisis: Has Integration Gone Too Far?* (Cambridge, Cambridge University Press, 2014) 149–178, arguing that the functional nature of European law puts the emphasis on negative integration at the detriment of regulatory policies.

clause imposing a limit on the powers of the ESA to take decisions. It also prevented home- and host-country authorities from having incentives to cooperate and minimise the collective risks of financial integration. The dominance of national fiscal sovereignty meant that national authorities could only pursue national interests. In the absence of a European framework for crisis management, the only possible outcome was the renationalisation of the single financial market to enable each Member State to limit its fiscal liabilities to their domestic markets.[115]

B. The Crisis and Legal Change

A new legal and institutional approach was introduced after the crisis to remedy the failures identified above. It attempted a shift from integration to the regulation of the single financial market by enlarging to the maximum possible extent the scope of Article 114. As analysed in this chapter, the legal strategies included augmenting the perimeter and deepening the detail of EU legislation, increasing the delegation of implementing powers to the Commission, and establishing regulatory agencies. The De Larosière reform in 2009 encapsulated such strategies in the ESA as agencies with unprecedented rule-making and enforcement powers; in the ESRB and the introduction of financial stability in EU legislation as a regulatory objective; and in the concept of a 'single financial services rulebook'. The combination of all these legal strategies aimed at preserving the integration of the single financial market after the crisis by exploring the boundaries of Article 114.

This represented, however, an evolution within the existing framework. The concept of the single rulebook would provide a more unified source of law, but Member States resisted its implementation. Moreover, enforcement remained decentralised with national authorities. The divergences in national enforcement and supervisory practices would still prevent the rulebook from being applied in a uniform manner. The ESA also remained limited by their largely soft, non-binding instruments over national authorities, similarly to the previous Level 3 committees. They were also dependent on the Commission for exercising binding rule-making powers. Their direct decision-making powers could only be exercised as a last resort in a narrow set of circumstances and, in any case, could be blocked by Member States exercising their fiscal safeguard rights. The pursuance of financial stability, through the introduction of macroprudential supervision, was entrusted to national authorities, which acted in a constrained framework retaining the primacy of financial integration. The ESRB was reduced to a steering mechanism on the basis of non-binding warnings and recommendations.

Therefore, the framework emerging from the crisis stopped short of a legal and institutional sea-change. Article 114 could not provide the basis for a transformation of the law of the single financial market. The ambition could only be to contain disintegration. A single financial market with a single set of European policies, rules, and authorities would require a transfer of regulatory competences to the European level and, ultimately, political integration and the sharing of national fiscal sovereignty.

[115] See MK Brunnermeier, H James and JP Landau, *The Euro and the Battle of Ideas*, (n 22) at 173–208, on the absence of a crisis management framework in the Monetary Union.

C. The Dominance of National Sovereignty During and after the Crisis

The main finding of this chapter is that the financial crisis led to the collapse of the governance edifice of the single financial market. National sovereignty dominated over European law, competences, and structures. This became visible with the unilateral responses by Member States to address the crisis. The Paris Summit of October 2008 was the turning point. It legitimised the national responses by branding them as European measures and by relaxing the application of the Treaty and European law. The financial crisis thus confirmed the trilemma that European financial stability could not be safeguarded by national competences, unless the single financial market was renationalised.

The preservation of the integration of the single financial market was then the justification for another set of legal and institutional innovations, as recommended by the De Larosière Report in 2009. The common denominator to these innovations was to overcome the failings of the previous strategy of 'integration through governance' and buttress to the extent possible the existing framework. The way forward was the institutionalisation of European governance, with the transformation of committees into agencies, the introduction of a single rulebook, and the creation of the ESRB, all on the basis of the harmonisation clause of Article 114. This strategy also mirrored the parallel institutionalisation trend of the global responses to crisis, which included the replacement of the FSF by the FSB, the adoption of more extensive global regulatory standards, and the development of a structured global governance of finance.

Despite this legal and institutional change, national sovereignty remained dominant. Member States constrained the reach of the innovations and resisted any transfer of meaningful competences to the European level. The scope of the competences of the ESA and the ESRB was narrow, since they could not act against the will of Member States. Financial stability, including the newly introduced macro-prudential supervision, remained a national competence. Despite the catastrophic implications of the financial crisis, there were still no European arrangements for risk-sharing or crisis management among Member States.

The attempt to institutionalise European governance was accompanied by the politicisation of the law of the single financial market in the form of new democratic accountability requirements, as well as increasing political activism of the Council and the Parliament in the negotiations of financial services legislation. This was another outcome of the crisis, which made apparent that financial integration carried risks and that financial regulation should reflect the degree of societal tolerance as to such risks. Accordingly, the democratic legitimacy of European competences for the single financial market started to emerge in this period, albeit timidly.

Legal change in this period operated thus a move towards the institutionalisation of the single financial market. Despite not being a radical change due to the limitations imposed by national sovereignty, it led to increasing legal and institutional integration in the path towards a Banking Union. The creation of the ESA provided for the first time regulatory institutions to the single financial market. A single rulebook started to replace the single passport framework and would later provide the basis for unifying European banking law. The pursuance of financial stability became part of the integration process, even if constrained.

However, at the end of this period in 2012, the law of the single financial market had reached its limits. The potential of Article 114 was largely exhausted. Renationalisation and disintegration were exacerbated by the sovereign debt crisis in the euro area, as Member States attempted again to insulate their domestic markets. The question was whether integration had gone too far or not far enough to preserve the existence of the euro area and the single financial market. The centralisation of European competences in the Banking Union would then be the next phase in the evolution of European law.[116]

Table 25 Legal Change in '(Dis-)Integration through Crisis' (2008–2012)

<table>
<tr><th colspan="2">Legal and institutional innovations to deepen integration</th><th>Integration policies</th><th>Remaining obstacles to integration</th></tr>
<tr><td>1</td><td>Creating a single financial services rulebook, based on the maximum harmonisation of national laws and the use of directly applicable EU regulations</td><td>• Providing a direct source of uniform law to market participants
• Developing a regulatory policy for the single financial market
• Widening the regulatory perimeter of EU law</td><td rowspan="5">• Limitations of Art 114 TFEU as a legal basis for regulation of the single financial market
• Limitations of European agencies and non-binding instruments
• Decentralised enforcement of European law by national authorities
• Potential contradiction between financial stability and financial integration
• Lack of a European financial stability framework, including crisis management and risk-sharing arrangements
• Dominance of national fiscal sovereignty</td></tr>
<tr><td>2</td><td>Delegating more implementing powers to the Commission</td><td>• Supporting the maximum harmonisation strategy by increasing the level of detail and the flexibility in amending EU legislation</td></tr>
<tr><td>3</td><td>Establishing agencies with extended rule-making and enforcement powers: the European Supervisory Authorities</td><td>• Rule-making at the European level
• Enabling the direct enforcement of European law
• Converging national enforcement practices
• Promoting consumer protection and financial stability, including crisis management and resolution</td></tr>
<tr><td>4</td><td>Introducing financial stability as a regulatory objective: the European Systemic Risk Board and macroprudential supervision</td><td>• Safeguarding financial stability as a condition for financial integration</td></tr>
<tr><td>5</td><td>Increasing accountability and transparency obligations</td><td>• Providing democratic legitimacy to European financial regulation and regulatory structures</td></tr>
</table>

[116] On the 'structural crisis of the law' in this period, see AJ Menéndez, 'The Crisis of Law and the European Crises: From the Social and Democratic Rechtsstaat to the Consolidating State of (Pseudo-) technocratic Governance' (2017) 44 *Journal of Law and Society* 56.

5

Integration through Centralisation: The Banking Union (2013–...)

In short, the outcome was certainly possible, though perhaps rather unlikely; it nonetheless came about. Trying to explain ex post why something happened should never imply that one considers the events and their outcome as having been inevitable.

Tommaso Padoa-Schioppa, 1996[1]

I. Introduction

At the end of the previous chapter, the legal and institutional limits of the single financial market had been reached. The sovereign debt crisis was fuelling more disintegration. The absence of risk-sharing among Member States was questioning the sustainability of the Monetary Union. This chapter starts thus by recalling how Member States tackled the legal constraints on risk-sharing in their successive responses to the sovereign debt crisis since 2010. It culminated with the creation of the European Stability Mechanism (ESM) in July 2011.[2]

Risk-sharing within the Monetary Union would then be at the heart of the decision to create a Banking Union: a transfer of competences to the European level without precedent since the transfer of monetary policy to the ECB. The process started with the Euro summit of June 2012, where leaders decided to establish the Single Supervisory Mechanism (SSM), in order to enable the direct recapitalisation of banks by the ESM. It continued as the sovereign debt crisis put in motion a process of deeper integration in the Monetary Union. Following the development of a global banking resolution regime – and the experience with the bail-in of banks' liabilities in Cyprus – the

[1] 'The Genesis of EMU: A Retrospective View' (1996) *96/40 Jean Monnet Chair Paper RSC, European University Institute.*

[2] For a critical analysis of the responses to the crisis, see E Chiti, AJ Menéndez, and PG Teixeira, 'The European Rescue of the European Union? The Existential Crisis of the European Political Project' (2012) 3/12 *ARENA Report,* 19 *RECON Report*; C Joerges, 'Law and Politics in Europe's Crisis: On the History of the Impact of an Unfortunate Configuration' (2013) 2013/09 *EUI Working Paper Law*; and C Offe, 'Europe Entrapped: Does the EU have the political capacity to overcome its current crisis?' (2013) 19 *European Law Journal* 595.

Single Resolution Mechanism (SRM) became the second pillar of the Banking Union. A European Deposit Insurance Scheme (EDIS) is still being debated at the time of writing.

The creation of the Banking Union was a fundamental legal change in the single financial market. Integration moved from the previous reliance on governance structures, without any transfer of national competences, to the centralisation of exclusive competences at the European level. Moreover, the Banking Union also led to a process of differentiation of the single financial market, which became more deeply integrated within the euro area and more fragmented regarding the Member States not participating in the euro. The legal and institutional innovations, which underpinned this move to centralisation, as well as the related implications for integration, are the focus of this chapter.

It starts with the legal foundations of the Banking Union. The choice to use Article 127.6 of the Treaty on the Functioning of the European Union (TFEU) as the legal basis of the SSM is key for understanding the genetic code of the Banking Union: the unique legal and institutional features of the SSM reflect the tensions of belonging to the framework of both the Monetary Union and the single financial market. This analysis is further elaborated with regard to the use of the single market's harmonisation clause of Article 114 as the legal basis for the SRM, which includes an agency – the Single Resolution Board – with wide discretionary decision-making powers, and a fund – the Single Resolution Fund – which mutualises for the first-time risks related to the banking sector. The same legal basis was used for the Bank Recovery and Resolution Directive (BRRD), and to underpin the Commission's proposal for EDIS.

These foundations determined the legal and institutional constructions of the SSM and the SRM, such as their respective powers and instruments, decision-making processes, or the relations with national authorities. Another implication relates to the differentiation process of the Banking Union, which is analysed extensively in this chapter. It is followed by an assessment of the extent to which the Banking Union is the optimal endpoint of the evolutionary process of integration. It considers, in this context, whether there is continuity or a break with the single financial market. It also points out the limited risk-sharing underpinning the Banking Union, which is one of its main weaknesses.

The conclusion of this chapter deals with the legal change operated by the Banking Union and recollects its numerous legal and institutional innovations.

II. The Sovereign Debt Crisis in the Euro Area

A. A Monetary Union without Risk-Sharing

The origin of the sovereign debt crisis was the realisation that a Member State of the Monetary Union could default. Until then, there had been the unrealistic assumption that the application of the Stability and Growth Pact (SGP), together with market discipline, would provide the incentives for fiscal rectitude and avoid the risk of a sovereign default. This was reinforced by the 'no bail-out principle' of Article 125 of the TFEU, which prevents the Union or any Member State from becoming liable or assume the commitments of another Member State.[3]

There was, therefore, no risk-sharing mechanism in the Monetary Union. Member States were entirely liable for their respective commitments. This was also highlighted by the judgments of the German Constitutional Court regarding the Lisbon and Maastricht Treaties, which placed fiscal sovereignty as a core national competence not transferrable to the European level. The economic governance of the Monetary Union would be based on national competences constrained by a framework of incentives, and by the exclusive national liability. This would replace the need for fiscal integration.[4]

At the same time, and somewhat contradictorily, it had also been assumed by investors that a Member State would not face the risk of a sovereign default, since ultimately it would be supported by the others to safeguard the integrity of the Monetary Union. If not explicit, there would be an implicit risk-sharing mechanism. This assumption was reflected in the narrow spreads of government debt between the euro area Member States. For example, the spreads of the yield of 10-year government bonds vis-à-vis the German Bund averaged 0.18 per cent in the period from 1999 to 2007. This implied that the euro area Member States shared a common sovereign risk for their debt. After mid-2007, the differences in the risk of default of Member States were then priced in by the markets due to the growing public liabilities for rescuing their banking systems. As the sovereign debt crisis intensified after 2010 and the risk of default increased, the same 10-year yield spreads reached a peak of 2.5 per cent in mid-2012.[5]

B. The Greek Crisis and the Principle of No Sovereign Default

On 20 October 2009, the finance minister of Greece disclosed at the Economic and Financial Affairs Council (ECOFIN) that his country's deficit would reach 12.7 per cent of GDP, up from the 6 per cent of GDP reported by the previous government. The rising bond yields and successive rating downgrades led to a rapid deterioration in the ability of the Greek state to fund itself in the markets. Greece was at risk of no longer obtaining financing and then defaulting on its debt.

The no-bail out principle and the lack of a risk-sharing mechanism limited the scope for financial assistance to Greece when it could no longer fund itself. The economic

[3] On the origins of no bail-out principle in the German economic tradition, see MK Brunnermeier, H James and JP Landau, *The Euro and the Battle of Ideas* (Princeton, Princeton University Press, 2016) 97–100, explaining that Member States in the Monetary Union were left with default on their debt as the only instrument in the case of a shock. The effects on the other Member States from such default were underestimated. For a legal perspective, see JV Louis, 'Economic Policy in the Lisbon Treaty' in S Griller and J Ziller (eds) *The Lisbon Treaty: EU Constitutionalism without a Constitutional Treaty?* (New York, Springer, 2008) 285–298.

[4] Judgment of 30 June 2009, Bundesverfassungsgericht, BVerfG, 2 BvE 2/08 (Lisbon judgment); and the Maastricht decision: Cases 2 BvR 2134/92 and 2159/92 *Brunner v The European Union Treaty* reported in English in [1994] 1 CMLR 57. See P Craig, 'The Financial Crisis, the EU Institutional Order and Constitutional Responsibility' in F Fabbrini, EH Ballin and H Somsen (eds) *What Form of Government for the Eurozone* (Oxford, Hart Publishing, 2015) 17.

[5] See MK Brunnermeier, H James and JP Landau, *The Euro and the Battle of Ideas*, (n 3) at 116–123.

governance of the Monetary Union implied that Member States had to be largely left on their own to solve their fiscal problems. This explained the stalemate in addressing the emerging sovereign debt crisis from the moment that the true fiscal situation of Greece became known. In the meantime, the funding difficulties of Greece worsened as it was realised for the first time that a euro area Member State could actually default.[6]

The options for providing financial assistance to Greece were either an internal solution, using the resources of the EU and Member States, or an external one, through recourse to the IMF. This created a dilemma. For some, the internal solution would confirm the assumption that there was an implicit risk-sharing mechanism in the Monetary Union. This would run counter to the no-bail out principle and the exclusive national liability. For others, the external solution could conceivably weaken the integrity of the economic governance of the Monetary Union by subjecting one of its members to the IMF conditionality in the provision of financial assistance.[7]

As it would become the standard approach to the sovereign debt crisis, the solution found was a combination of arrangements. The Euro Summit of 7 May 2010 agreed on a collection of bilateral loans by the euro area Member States to Greece in the amount of €80 billion, complemented by a €30 billion loan by the IMF. The financing thus totalled €110 billion over three years, after which Greece was expected to return to the markets. The loans were conditional upon an adjustment plan, with a quarterly compliance review by the IMF, the Commission, and the ECB, which became known as the 'troika'.[8]

The financial assistance provided to Greece on the basis of bilateral loans by other Member States was considered to be compliant with the no bail-out principle of Article 125. As later formulated by the Court in the *Pringle* case, Article 125 would not prohibit the provision of loans to a Member State, which would remain liable for its commitments. Moreover, the provision of loans against conditions aimed at restoring a sound budgetary policy would be in line with the rationale of the no-bail out principle.[9]

[6] From 10 May 2010 till February 2012, the ECB intervened in debt markets under a Securities Markets Programme (SMP) for the acquisition in open market of government bonds to ensure liquidity in dysfunctional markets. The ECB justified it on the basis of the need to ensure a smooth transmission of monetary policy throughout the euro area; see ECB, The ECB's Non-Standard Measures: Impact and Phasing-Out, Monthly Bulletin, July 2011, 55–69. This was criticised by some as an infringement of the monetary financing prohibition of Art 123, TFEU: see M Ruffert, 'The European Debt Crisis and European Union Law' (2011) 48 *CML Rev* 1769, and the reaction by R Smits, 'The European debt crisis and European Union law: comments and a call for action' (2012) 49 *CML Rev* 827.

[7] The IMF played a major role in providing assistance to Hungary, Latvia, and Romania, when they also entered into crisis between the end of 2008 and early 2009. These countries were beneficiaries of the EU's facility providing financial assistance for Member States' balance payments in the framework of Art 143, TFEU. On the impact of the financial crisis in Eastern Europe as the 'forgotten crisis', see A Tooze, *Crashed: How a Decade of Financial Crises Changed the World* (New York, Viking, 2018) 220–238. See also Z Darvas, 'EU Support to CEE Countries During the Crisis' (2009) 2009/17 *Bruegel Policy Contribution*.

[8] Euro Summit, Statement of the Heads of State or Government of the Euro Area, 7 May 2010, at www.consilium.europa.eu/uedocs/cms_data/docs/pressdata/en/ec/114295.pdf.

[9] Judgment of the Court of 27 November 2012, *Pringle*, C-370/12, EU:C:2012:756, para 137. See P Craig, 'Pringle: Legal Reasoning, Text, Purpose and Teleology' (2013) 20 *Maastricht Journal of European and Comparative Law* 3, especially at 8–9; and B de Witte and T Beukers, 'The Court of Justice approves the creation of the European Stability Mechanism outside the EU legal order: Pringle' (2013) 50 *CML Rev* 805, 847–8.

The Greek sovereign debt crisis demonstrated that the principle of national liability and no-bail out was not realistic within the Monetary Union. The assumption of an implicit risk-sharing mechanism underpinning the Monetary Union had created financial and political interlinkages between Member States. The default of Greece would quickly lead to contagion to the other Member States by undermining market confidence on the sustainability of their respective debt. This, in turn, would question the integrity of the whole euro area. The implication was that Greece could not be allowed to default by the other Member States, since it would lead to greater costs than those supposed to be prevented by the no-bail out principle. The Greek crisis led, de facto, to a new constitutional principle in the Monetary Union: the principle of no-default of the Member States of the euro area.[10]

C. The Mutualisation of Risks in the EFSF and the ESM

After the rescue of Greece, the sustainability of public finances in the euro area continued to be questioned, leading to a rise in the bond yields of Ireland and Portugal. The principles of national liability and no-bail out made it unlikely that vulnerable Member States could finance themselves at sustainable interest rates. Mechanisms for financial assistance started then to be devised.[11]

Facing the escalating sovereign debt crisis, the Euro Summit of 7 May 2010 decided on a 'European stabilisation mechanism to preserve financial stability in Europe.' It comprised a 'temporary special purpose vehicle', which would be guaranteed pro rata by the euro area Member States up to a volume of €440 billion. This became the European Financial Stability Facility (EFSF), which was established as a private company in Luxembourg for three years. All the national parliaments were asked to ratify the EFSF agreement under public international law. The EFSF was complemented by a European Financial Stabilisation Mechanism (EFSM) as a Commission fund authorised to borrow up to €60 billion, drawing on the Treaty's balance of payments' mechanism. The total of up to €500 billion – with the IMF providing an additional amount of €250 billion – would be available for financial assistance to Member States in difficulties, subject to conditionality.[12]

Like the bilateral financial assistance to Greece, the establishment of the EFSF was deemed compliant with the principles of national liability and no-bail out, as later confirmed by the *Pringle* case. The EFSF was a temporary mechanism, limited to the provision of loans to Member States and subject to conditionality. Moreover, it was

[10] See MK Brunnermeier, H James and JP Landau, *The Euro and the Battle of Ideas*, (n 3) 98 to 100. In this context, the potential contagion to other Member States was underestimated in the design of the Maastricht Treaty; see JV Louis, 'Guest Editorial: The no-bail out clause and rescue packages' (2010) 47 *CML Rev* 971.

[11] For an overview, see A de Gregorio Merino, 'Legal Developments in the Economic and Monetary Union During the Debt Crisis: The Mechanisms of Financial Assistance' (2012) 49 *CML Rev* 1613.

[12] Euro Summit, Statement of the Heads of State or Government of the Euro Area, 7 May 2010, at www.consilium.europa.eu/uedocs/cms_data/docs/pressdata/en/ec/114295.pdf; EU Council, Extraordinary ECOFIN Council of 9 and 10 May 2010, at www.consilium.europa.eu/uedocs/cms_data/docs/pressdata/en/ecofin/114324.pdf; and Council Regulation (EU) No 407/2010 of 11 May 2010 establishing a European financial stabilisation mechanism, [2010] OJ L118/1.

established as an intergovernmental body under public international law and thus outside the EU framework.[13]

The EFSF was, however, not sufficient to stem the sovereign debt crisis. On 18 October 2010, Chancellor Merkel of Germany and President Sarkozy of France agreed in Deauville on the need for a permanent crisis resolution mechanism, which would include arrangements for burden-sharing with the private sector. The aim was to reaffirm the principles of national liability and no-bail out in the euro area economic governance as instruments of market discipline. The Deauville declaration was interpreted as signalling the end of the principle of no sovereign default underpinning the rescue of Greece. It meant that a euro area Member State could default and that bondholders could suffer losses, which had not happened in Europe since Italy in 1940. As a result, it further accelerated the sovereign debt crisis, since financial assistance to prevent sovereign defaults in the euro area had been excluded until then. The investment in sovereign debt of the euro area could no longer be considered risk-free. Instead, it entailed an increased default risk than that from other countries due to the combination of: (1) the no bail-out clause in the euro area; and (2) the prohibition of monetary financing of budget deficits of Member States by the central bank under Article 123 of the TFEU, which did not exist elsewhere.[14]

In order to address the acceleration of the sovereign debt crisis created by the Deauville declaration, the European Council of 28–29 October 2010 agreed to set up a permanent crisis mechanism to safeguard the financial stability of the euro area as a whole. This would involve a limited Treaty change, without modifying Article 125 of the TFEU on the no-bail out principle. The European Council of 16–17 December 2010 decided instead on an amendment to Article 136 of the TFEU enabling the euro area Member States to establish a mechanism to safeguard the stability of the euro area by granting financial assistance subject to strict conditionality. This provided the basis for the European Stability Mechanism (ESM). It was established as an intergovernmental organisation under public international law by a treaty among the euro area Member States on 11 July 2011. The ESM replaced the EFSF and the EFSM as from 1 July 2013.[15]

The amendment of Article 136 served two purposes. First, by providing a foundation in the Treaty for the establishment of the ESM, it ensured its compatibility with the bail out prohibition of Article 125. The new Article 136(3) states that the mechanism can only provide assistance to a Member State to safeguard the stability of

[13] For a critical analysis arguing that the rescue of Greece and the other Member States is in breach of Art 125, TFEU, see M Ruffert, 'The European Debt Crisis and European Union Law' (n 6) at 1785–ff, and the reply by R Smits, 'The European debt crisis and European Union law' (n 6); and K Tuori and K Tuori, *The Eurozone Crisis: A Constitutional Analysis* (Cambridge, Cambridge University Press, 2014) 119–ff.

[14] On the implications of the Deauville declaration, see MK Brunnermeier, H James and JP Landau, *The Euro and the Battle of Ideas*, (n 3) at 29–33. For an account of the 'improvisation mode' of the EU towards the sovereign debt crisis, see L van Middelaar, *Quand L'Europe Improvise: Dix ans de crises politiques* (Paris, Gallimard, 2018) 39–102.

[15] Conclusions of the European Council, 28 and 29 October 2010, at www.consilium.europa.eu/uedocs/cms_data/docs/pressdata/en/ec/117496.pdf; Conclusions of the European Council, 16 and 17 December 2010, at www.consilium.europa.eu/uedocs/cms_data/docs/pressdata/en/ec/118578.pdf; and European Council Decision of 25 March 2011 amending Art 136, TFEU with regard to a stability mechanism for Member States whose currency is the euro, [2011] OJ L91/1.

the euro area, and subject to strict conditions. Since this preserves the objective of a sound budgetary policy, the Court considered it in line with Article 125. Second, it legitimised the establishment by euro area Member States of an intergovernmental mechanism for supporting the functioning of the EU, but outside of the Treaty. The Court considered that Article 136(3) did not increase the competences of the Union and did not affect any of its existing competences.[16]

The mutualisation of risks necessary for preserving the euro area was thus introduced as a mechanism outside the EU framework, first with the temporary EFSF, and later with the permanent ESM. This enabled the Member States, instead of the Commission or a new European institution, to control a mechanism directly supported by national fiscal commitments. It prevented a transfer of competences within the EU framework for pooling national resources, thus preserving national fiscal sovereignty.[17]

In other words, the legal construction of Article 136(3), as well as that of the EFSF and ESM Treaties, aimed at creating the perception that: (1) there was no change in the nature of the principles of national liability and no bail-out; and (2) there was no transfer of fiscal competences to the European level, and thus no loss of national fiscal sovereignty. In reality, the EFSF and the ESM were the first mutualisation of risks among Member States in the single financial market: threats to financial stability would be addressed by pooling Member States' resources. The fact that it was limited to the euro area represented also the first manifestation of the detachment of the euro area from the rest of the single financial market, which would later further materialise with the Banking Union.

D. The End of the Principle of No Sovereign Default: The Private Sector Involvement in Greece

After the Deauville declaration, the European sovereign debt crisis further intensified. The EFSF and the EFSM were activated for the first time at the request of Ireland on 28 November 2010 to cover financing needs of up to €85 billion. On 30 March 2011, Portugal also requested financial assistance leading to loans of €78 billion.[18]

The Euro Summit of 21 July 2011 marked a new phase in the crisis. Facing increasing doubts as to the sustainability of the debt of Greece, it decided to support debt restructuring through Private Sector Involvement (PSI). In order to provide debt relief, investors in Greek sovereign debt would suffer losses. This was the end of the principle of no-default of euro area Member States, which had guided the response to the sovereign debt crisis since the start. The statement of the Euro summit insisted, however,

[16] *Pringle*, (n 9) paras 104–107 and 136.

[17] The German Constitutional Court concluded later in its ESM judgment on 18 March 2014 that Art 136(3), TFEU and the establishment of the ESM did not lead to a loss of the budgetary competence of the Bundestag: BVerfG, Order of 18 March 2014, 2 BvR 1390/12.

[18] EU Council, Statement by the Eurogroup and ECOFIN Ministers, 28 November 2010, at www.consilium.europa.eu/media/25727/118051.pdf; and European Commission, The Economic Adjustment Programme for Portugal 2011–2014 (2010) 202 *European Economy*.

that the solution for Greece was exceptional and unique, while all the other euro area Member States reaffirmed their determination to fully honour their debt and fiscal commitments. The principle of no-default would remain valid, while the debt restructuring of Greece was an exception.[19]

The Euro Summit decision proved insufficient to stem contagion. In early August 2011, the spreads of the government debt of Italy and Spain reached levels that put into question their sustainability. The ECB announced on 7 August that it would implement its Securities Markets Programme (SMP): on 8 August it reportedly started purchasing Italian and Spanish Government bonds in secondary markets bringing down their market yields. At the time, the President of the ECB, Jean-Claude Trichet, addressed the Italian and Spanish Governments with letters setting out measures for the sustainability of public finances, as part of the conditionality for the SMP.[20]

Another round of Euro summits then took place on 23 and 26 October 2011, which agreed on: (1) a new financial assistance programme to Greece, depending on the willingness of private investors to take a 50 per cent nominal discount on their Greek Government bonds; (2) leveraging the resources of the EFSF to increase its capacity to support other Member States; and (3) improving the economic governance of the euro area, including through more regular Euro summits. Furthermore, each euro area Member State would introduce rules on a balanced budget at constitutional level or equivalent by the end of 2012.[21]

Once again, the Euro Summit failed to stabilise the markets. On 1 November 2011, the Prime Minister Papandreou announced a referendum in Greece. The following day, at the Cannes G-20 Summit, Chancellor Merkel of Germany and President Sarkozy of France declared that a referendum should then be held on the exit of Greece from the euro area. An exit had been refuted until then, since there are no mechanisms for such action in the Treaty. Papandreou resigned on 11 November to enable a national unity government led by Lucas Papademos, a former ECB Vice-President.[22]

[19] The Summit also decided to: (i) support a new financial assistance programme for Greece through the EFSF with lower interest rates and extended maturities; (ii) enhance the EFSF and the ESM with the possibility of a precautionary programme, recapitalisation of financial institutions through loans to governments, and intervention in the secondary markets of sovereign debt; and (iii) extend to Ireland and Portugal the lending rates and maturities applied to Greece. See Euro Summit, Statement by the Heads of State or Government of the Euro Area and EU Institutions, 21 July 2011, at www.consilium.europa.eu/uedocs/cms_data/docs/pressdata/en/ec/123978.pdf. For a critical analysis of this rescue package, see Editorial (2011) 48 *CML Rev* 1769 at 1772–ff.

[20] ECB, Statement of the President of the ECB on the activation of the Securities Market Programme, 7 August 2011, at www.ecb.europa.eu/press/pr/date/2011/html/pr110807.en.html. See MK Brunnermeier, H James and JP Landau, *The Euro and the Battle of Ideas*, (n 3) at 334–336.

[21] There were two Euro Summits to reach agreement to increase the financial capacity of the EFSF, since Chancellor Merkel needed to obtain in-between prior consent of the Bundestag. The need for prior consent was reinforced by a decision of the German Constitutional Court of 7 September 2011, which considered that the financial assistance to Greece did not infringe the Bundestag's budgetary autonomy: BVerfG, 2 BvR 987/10; 2 BvR 1485/10; 2 BvR 1099/10. See Euro Summit, Statement, 26 October 2011, at www.consilium.europa.eu/uedocs/cms_data/docs/pressdata/en/ec/125644.pdf.

[22] In Italy, the continuing rise of government debt spreads led to the resignation of Silvio Berlusconi on 12 November 2011. The political parties agreed to support a technical government led by Mario Monti.

At this stage, the possibility of sovereign debt restructuring and defaults in the euro area was openly discussed. As part of a 'capital exercise', the EBA issued a recommendation on 8 November 2011 requiring the major EU banks to establish a capital buffer against sovereign debt exposures. This followed the criticism that the first stress-test exercise of the EBA in July 2011 had not taken into account potential losses in such exposures.[23]

This was the background for the PSI transaction that was launched on 21 February and completed by 9 March 2012. It consisted of an offer for a €200 billion voluntary debt exchange, which enabled Greece to obtain a debt relief of around €107 billion in the face value of its debt, corresponding to more than 50 per cent of GDP. This made it the largest ever sovereign debt restructuring. Such debt relief was, however, not sufficient as the economic situation in Greece worsened over 2012, further increasing the debt burden. On 12 December 2012, the EFSF financed a debt buyback operation by Greece, which led to a further reduction of its debt of around 20 per cent in face value.[24]

The debt restructuring of Greece in March 2012 represented, therefore, a reversal of the principle of no sovereign default. This reversal was moderated by the statement that the situation of Greece was exceptional and by the voluntary nature of the transaction, notwithstanding persuasion mechanisms like the enactment of collective action clauses under Greek law. It demonstrated that there could be a debt restructuring of a euro area Member State without major disruptions, but it likely contributed to the acceleration of the sovereign debt crisis in the second quarter of 2012. All in all, the major implication of the Greek debt restructuring, besides the debt relief, was transferring the debt from private investors to the official sector. By the end of 2012, the EFSF, the ECB and the IMF held most of the Greek debt. The European mutualisation of the risks regarding Greece had been largely achieved.[25]

Five countries of the euro area changed government before their respective term as a direct consequence of the sovereign debt crisis: Ireland, Portugal, Greece, Italy, and Spain. Three changed following early elections and two stemmed from parliamentary agreement on technocratic governments.

[23] EBA, Recommendation on the creation and supervisory oversight of temporary capital buffers to restore market confidence (EBA/REC/2011/1), 8 December 2011; and Joint Statement by the Presidency of the ECOFIN and the EBA, 8 December 2011, at eba.europa.eu/documents/10180/26923/2011+12+08-ECOFIN-EBA-Statement+FINALv2.pdf.

[24] For every old bond of Greece, investors would receive 15% in 1- and 2-year EFSF notes, 31.5% in 30-year new English law bonds, and GDP-linked securities offering an increase in the interest rate of up to 1%, depending on real growth and nominal GDP of Greece. 97% of the bondholders participated voluntarily in the debt exchange. This level of participation was due to the collective action clauses introduced by Greece prior to the exchange, and also to the benefits of the exchange vis-à-vis a sovereign default. The ECB was excluded from the offer and its bonds were exchanged for identical bonds in terms of price and maturities. The ECB committed to return any profits of Greek bonds to its shareholders. For an extensive analysis, see J Zettelmeyer, C Trebesch, and M Gulati, 'The Greek Debt Restructuring: An Autopsy' (2013) 28 *Economic Policy* 513, at 542. See also Eurogroup, Statement on Greece, 27 November 2012, at www.consilium.europa.eu/press/press-releases/2012/11/pdf/Eurogroup-statement-on-Greece-27-11; and Eurogroup, Statement on Greece, 13 December 2012, at www.consilium.europa.eu/press/press-releases/2012/12/pdf/Eurogroup-statement-on-Greece.

[25] For the historical background to the decision on the debt restructuring of Greece, see MK Brunnermeier, H James and JP Landau, *The Euro and the Battle of Ideas*, (n 3) 306 to 312.

III. The Build-up to the Banking Union

A. The 28–29 June 2012 Euro Summit and the Contagion to Italy and Spain

The sovereign debt crisis in the euro area reached its peak in June 2012. The interest rates on the sovereign debt of Italy and Spain rose to unsustainable levels, threatening their market access and leading to default fears. Financial assistance would be politically challenging and require vast amounts. This created an existential risk of the euro, the 'convertibility risk' back to national currencies.[26]

The Euro Summit of 28–29 June 2012 was thus confronted with the urgency to take decisions to contain such an existential crisis. The relatively short and convoluted statement in the early hours of 29 June did not do justice to the institutional change that had been agreed among the euro area Member States: the possibility of direct recapitalisation of banks by the ESM and the transfer of competences of banking supervision to the ECB.[27]

The Euro Summit first decided to make the functioning of the ESM more flexible to facilitate the assistance to Italy or Spain. It enabled the ESM to provide assistance without additional conditionality other than that already under the economic governance procedures, such as the European Semester. Second, it allowed the ESM to recapitalise directly euro area banks. This implied that the financial burden of rescuing an undercapitalised bank would no longer fall on national public accounts and increase the debt of a Member State. Instead, a bank rescue would be mutualised among the euro area Member States, which underwrite the ESM. At the same time, it would provide relief to the Member States which seek assistance to recapitalise their banks.

The ability of the ESM to directly recapitalise banks in the euro area was made dependent by the Euro Summit on the establishment of 'a single supervisory mechanism involving the ECB'. The rationale was that the euro area liability also required control at the euro area level. A euro area banking supervisor would have its incentives

[26] On 25 June 2012, Spain requested financial assistance for its banking system up to €100 billion. The adjustment programme was limited to the financial sector and did not encompass economic policy as previous programmes. See European Commission, The Financial Sector Adjustment Programme for Spain (2012) 118 *European Economy.*

[27] For an account of the Euro summit, see *Monti's Uprising: How Italy and Spain Defeated Merkel at EU Summit*, Spiegel Online, 29 June 2012, www.spiegel.de/international/europe/merkel-makes-concessions-at-eu-summit-a-841663.html; and L van Middelaar, *Quand L'Europe Improvise*, (n 14) 88–102. See also the Euro Summit, Statement, 29 June 2012, at www.consilium.europa.eu/uedocs/cms_data/docs/pressdata/en/ec/131359.pdf. The first paragraph of the statement read: 'We affirm that it is imperative to break the vicious circle between banks and sovereigns. The Commission will present Proposals on the basis of Art 127(6) for a single supervisory mechanism shortly. We ask the Council to consider these Proposals as a matter of urgency by the end of 2012. When an effective single supervisory mechanism is established, involving the ECB, for banks in the euro area the ESM could, following a regular decision, have the possibility to recapitalize banks directly. This would rely on appropriate conditionality, including compliance with state aid rules, which should be institution specific, sector-specific or economy-wide and would be formalised in a Memorandum of Understanding.'

aligned with those of the ESM, namely of minimising risks and costs for all the euro area Member States and respective taxpayers. The transfer of banking supervision competences had therefore at its heart a quid pro quo between the mutualisation of banking risks in the euro area and the loss of national sovereignty over banking supervision.[28]

B. The 'Whatever it Takes' Speech and Outright Monetary Transactions

The decisions of the Euro Summit did not stop the intensification of the sovereign debt crisis and the increasing convertibility or redenomination risk.[29]

On 26 July 2012, after having compared the euro to a bumblebee that should not but does fly, the ECB President Mario Draghi stated at a conference in London that 'Within our mandate, the ECB is ready to do whatever it takes to preserve the euro. And believe me, it will be enough.' This speech, spelling out the willingness of the ECB to intervene to address the rise of sovereign bond yields due to the convertibility risk, marked the beginning of the alleviation of the crisis. The prospect that the ECB would buy sovereign debt drove down the bond yields, especially of Italy and Spain.[30]

The statement of the ECB President provided the basis for a new monetary policy instrument, the Outright Monetary Transactions (OMT), which was announced in a press release on 6 September 2012. The ECB would intervene in secondary markets for sovereign bonds in the euro area to address 'unfounded fears on the part of investors of the reversibility of the euro'. The activation of the OMT required that the benefiting Member State was subject to an EFSF/ESM programme with conditionality, and including the possibility of EFSF/ESM primary market purchases. The ECB also announced that there were no quantitative limits to the OMT and that it would accept *pari passu* treatment with other creditors, which it had avoided in the Greek debt restructuring. These were considered important elements of the credibility of OMT towards the markets.[31]

The OMT instrument was later challenged before the German Constitutional Court, which referred to the Court for a preliminary ruling. The main claims by the

[28] See, eg, the speech by Chancellor Merkel to the Bundestag on 27 June 2012 stressing that a joint liability can only occur once a joint control had been established, as reported by *Spiegel*, Merkel Blasts Euro Partners on Eve of Summit, 27 June 2012, at www.spiegel.de/international/europe/chancellor-angela-merkel-outlines-german-stance-ahead-of-eu-summit-a-841267.html. See J Pisani-Ferry and G Wolff, 'The Fiscal Implications of a Banking Union' (2012) 02 *Bruegel Policy Brief*.

[29] On the discussions regarding the redenomination risk, see MK Brunnermeier, H James and JP Landau, *The Euro and the Battle of Ideas*, (n 3) 226–233.

[30] ECB, Verbatim of the remarks made by Mario Draghi, President of the European Central Bank at the Global Investment Conference in London, 26 July 2012, at www.ecb.europa.eu/press/key/date/2012/html/sp120726.en.html. For the market reactions, see *Financial Times*, ECB 'ready to do whatever it takes', 26 July 2012.

[31] ECB, Introductory statement to the press conference, 6 September 2012, at www.ecb.europa.eu/press/pressconf/2012/html/is120906.en.html; and ECB, Technical features of Outright Monetary Transactions (2012), at www.ecb.europa.eu/press/pr/date/2012/html/pr120906_1.en.html.

applicants, largely endorsed by the German Constitutional Court, were that: (1) the OMT would represent an ultra vires act of the ECB, since it related to economic policy and not to monetary policy; and (2) the OMT would infringe the prohibition of monetary financing of Article 123 of the TFEU. The purchase of sovereign bonds would be economic policy since it is not within the ECB's mandate to safeguard the composition of the euro area. The fact that the OMT would be tied to EFSF/ESM financial assistance programmes would confirm that claim. It would also be an act of monetary financing since the ECB would be exposed to potential losses from a debt cut due to the *pari passu* treatment, all the more so as the OMT would target vulnerable Member States. The common denominator to these claims was that, once part of the ECB's balance sheet, the sovereign debt would be effectively mutualised among Member States as the 'owners' of the national central banks which are the shareholders of the ECB. This would be confirmed by the unlimited purchases committed under the OMT and the explicit acceptance by the ECB that it could incur losses. Such losses would then be borne by the taxpayers of the euro area Member States. Accordingly, the argument went, the Treaty principles of national liability and no-bail out would also be infringed, since the ECB would be providing financial assistance to the Member States.[32]

The OMT was thus challenged on the basis that it enabled the ECB to replicate the effects of mutualisation and fiscal integration to preserve the euro area. This would be a responsibility of the Member States and not of the ECB, which does not have democratic legitimacy to take political decisions. Such reasoning also encapsulated the ordoliberal concept that monetary policy should neither interfere with market functioning nor have distributive implications.[33]

In its *Gauweiler* ruling, the Court concluded that the provisions of the Treaty and the Statute must be interpreted as permitting the ECB to adopt the OMT programme. First, it considered, by analogy to the *Pringle* case, that the indirect effects of a monetary policy measure, such as the stability of the euro area, do not imply that it should be treated as equivalent to economic policy. Second, in order to prevent monetary financing, the OMT had to ensure that the ECB's intervention in the secondary markets does not have an equivalent effect to a direct purchase of government bonds on the primary market. The Court considered that the limitations set by the ECB fulfilled this

[32] German Constitutional Court, Order of 14 January 2014–2 BvR 2728/13, at paras 56–94. It also added the concerns regarding the ECB's holding to maturity of purchased government bonds; the interference with the price formation on the market; and the encouragement of market participants to purchase the bonds in question on the primary market. At the time, the TARGET balances were also challenged as giving rise to liabilities. See HW Sinn, *The Euro-Trap* (Oxford, Oxford University Press, 2014) at 176–201, regarding the potential liabilities among Member States arising out of TARGET balances, which however would only materialise if there would be an exit of a Member State from the euro area. For the counter-arguments, see B Cœuré, 'Monetary policy in a fragmented world, Speech at the 41st Economics Conference of the Oesterreichische Nationalbank, Vienna' (2013), at www.ecb.europa.eu/press/key/date/2013/html/sp130610.en.html.

[33] German Constitutional Court, Order of 14 January 2014–2 BvR 2728/13 at para 89. In this context, it considered at para 100 that the OMT could be considered valid if some conditions were fulfilled, including that the possibility of a debt cut must be excluded, that government bonds of selected Member States are not purchased up to unlimited amounts, and that interferences with price formation on the market are to be avoided where possible.

requirement, namely, the Governing Council's independence in deciding the OMT for monetary policy purposes, and the imposition of a minimum period between the issuance of sovereign debt and its purchase in the secondary market, so as not to influence its pricing at issuance. Furthermore, the OMT conditionality linked to the compliance of a Member State with an EFSF/ESM programme confirmed, contrary to the claims made, that the ECB did not provide incentives to Member States to deviate from sound public finances. Member States could not rely with certainty on the ECB purchases and did not have incentives to undermine sound public finances. The ECB was inevitably exposed to losses as a result of the operations permitted by the Treaty, but the conditions imposed on the OMT reduced the risk of such losses.[34]

This debate on the OMT demonstrated that the ordoliberal concept of monetary policy as neutral, with no distributive implications, proved to be an illusion. Monetary policy has, by definition, distributive effects by influencing saving, investment and spending decisions in order to pursue price stability. It is all the more so in a Monetary Union, where a single monetary policy affects differently such decisions across Member States, depending on economic conditions. This only became apparent in the midst of an existential crisis. The crisis led to economic fragmentation among Member States and increased distortions within the euro area, as reflected in the convertibility risk. Monetary policy then aimed at stabilising the sovereign debt to price levels consistent with the macroeconomic fundamentals, as argued by the Court.[35]

C. The Bail-In of Cyprus and the Imposition of Capital Controls

Cyprus joined the euro area on 1 January 2008. In the first decade of the 2000s there had been strong economic growth, massive inflows of foreign capital and deposits, notably from Russia, expansion of credit, and, as a result, a real estate bubble and large private indebtedness. The Cypriot banking sector expanded exponentially, reaching a size of 800 per cent of GDP in 2010, similarly to the proportional size of the banking sector in Ireland. It then entered into crisis due to the exposures to Greece and the worsening quality of the credit provided in the boom years, together with weak banking

[34] Judgment of the Court of 16 June 2015, *Gauweiler*, C-62/14, EU:C:2015:400, paras 32–127. See also the Opinion of Advocate-General Cruz Villálon, EU:C:2015:7, paras 194–202, challenging the ordoliberal concept of monetary policy and arguing that the context of the Treaty had also to be considered when analysing the validity of the OMT. The reasoning of the Court was confirmed later when answering another request for a preliminary ruling from the German Constitutional Court with regard to the public sector asset purchase programme launched by the ECB on 4 March 2015, Judgment of the Court of 11 December 2018, *Weiss and Others*, C-493/17, EU:C:2018:1000, paras 61 to 70. For an interpretation of *Gauweiler*, see C Zilioli, 'The ECB's Powers and Institutional Role in the Financial Crisis: A Confirmation from the Court of Justice of the European Union' (2016) 23 *Maastricht Journal of European and Comparative Law* 171.

[35] For a critique of *Gauweiler*, see C Joerges, 'Pereat Iustitia, Fiat Mundus: What is Left of the European Economic Constitution after the Gauweiler Litigation?' (2016) 23 *Maastricht Journal of European and Comparative Law* 99, who argues that the discretion accorded to the ECB leads to 'an explicit rejection of ordo-liberal project of an "economic constitution" in which the ordering of the economy would be guided by legal rules and justiciable criteria'.

supervision. The crisis reached its peak in 2012, when the three Cypriot banks suffered heavy losses with the Greek PSI, leading to both a liquidity and solvency banking crisis. The 'perfect storm' resulting from the combination of a high public debt and budget deficit, made worse by the recapitalisation needs of the banks, rising yields of its debt, as well as the explosion in a major power plant in 2011, led Cyprus to request financial assistance from the euro area and the IMF on 25 June 2012. Until then, it had avoided this by negotiating a bilateral loan from Russia at the end of 2011. The negotiations for the assistance were frozen until the election in February 2013, when the Cypriots elected a new President, Nicos Anastasiades, replacing the previous, only ever communist head of state in the EU.[36]

The provision of financial assistance to Cyprus was confronted with several challenges. The recapitalisation of the oversized banking system would require an amount – around €10 billion, half of the GDP, which would make it even more difficult for Cyprus to reach debt sustainability. There was political resistance to use European funds to safeguard offshore banking activities and a large volume of foreign deposits, which could have an uncertain origin. After the rescue of banks in 2008 and the several financial assistance programmes to Member States, there was strong resistance to using public funds to bail-out banks.[37]

The financial assistance to Cyprus would then be made conditional on bank resolution and burden-sharing with the private sector. This approach to the Cypriot banking sector had several origins. First, the development of the bank resolution framework at global level, which included the bail-in of creditor claims. Second, the application of state aid rules in the banking sector by the Commission after the 2008 crisis, as spelled out in its Banking Communications. Third, the experience with the sequence of bank restructuring in Ireland, Portugal and Spain, which introduced bail-in provisions in national laws. Fourth, the PSI process in Greece, which led to the conviction that extensive burden-sharing measures would not give rise to contagion. Lastly, the offshore activities of the Cypriot banking sector, which meant that the largest bank liabilities were deposits, with a limited amount of bank equity and debt to cover losses. The recapitalisation with public funds of the Cypriot banks would be otherwise massive and not economically viable relative to Cyprus's GDP and its public finances.[38]

This background explains the complicated sequence of decisions on the financial assistance programme to Cyprus requiring: (i) bank resolution; (ii) burden-sharing

[36] For a detailed overview of the Cyprus crisis, see European Commission, The Economic Adjustment Programme for Cyprus (2013) 149 *European Economy*.

[37] See the comment of N Véron 'Europe's Cyprus Blunder and its consequences' (2013), at www.bruegel.org/nc/blog/detail/article/1048-europes-cyprus-blunder-and-its-consequences.

[38] Bail-in was also imposed in Ireland, Portugal and Spain, which followed diverging approaches. In Ireland, the nationalisation of banks led to burden-sharing with shareholders and the bail-in of banks' junior debtholders, but not senior debtholders, which was controversial at the time. See European Commission, The Economic Adjustment Programme for Ireland (2011) 76 *European Economy*, at 39. Spain required the bail-in of capital and subordinated debtholders of banks benefitting from public funds. See European Commission, Financial Assistance Programme for the recapitalisation of financial institutions in Spain: Third review of the programme (2013) 155 *European Economy*, at 33. In Portugal, a bank resolution law was introduced in February 2012 (Decree-Law No 31-A/2012), but the resolution powers were first exercised with the resolution of Banco Espirito Santo in August 2014, outside the context of the financial assistance programme.

with bank depositors; and (iii) the imposition of capital controls for the first time in the single financial market. The aim was to limit as much as possible the size of the financial assistance by obtaining burden-sharing with the private sector to the largest extent.[39]

The first decision of the Eurogroup was announced in the early morning of 16 March 2013. It required from Cyprus the imposition of a one-off 'stability levy' on resident and non-resident depositors, both on the insured deposits up to €100,000 with a levy of 6.7 per cent and on those uninsured with a levy of 9.9 per cent, as well as a bail-in of junior bank bonds. The banking sector would be downsized to the EU average in 2018. The financial assistance would then be up to €10 billion, around half of the GDP of Cyprus, with €2.5 billion for bank recapitalisation – instead of the estimated €10 billion without burden-sharing.[40]

Following public protests against the deposit levy, the Cypriot Parliament voted on 19 March to reject the agreement with the Eurogroup. The rationale was that the levy was bailing-in insured deposits below €100,000 and that it also affected all deposits, which was less detrimental to offshore banking at the expense of small depositors.[41]

After the rejection of the stability levy, the Eurogroup reached an agreement with Cyprus on 25 March on an alternative approach to burden-sharing to safeguard deposits below €100,000, while keeping the financial assistance to €10 billion. It consisted of the resolution of Cyprus Popular Bank (Laiki) and of the Bank of Cyprus. The insured deposits at Laiki were moved to the Bank of Cyprus, while the uninsured remained with a 'bad bank'. The uninsured deposits at the Bank of Cyprus were subject to a bail-in of 37.5 per cent with another 22.5 per cent frozen. Junior debt was also bailed-in.

[39] The concept of burden-sharing was first spelled-out in the Commission's 'Restructuring Communication': investors in a bank had to absorb losses and pay a remuneration for State interventions; see European Commission, The return to viability and the assessment of restructuring measures in the financial sector in the current crisis under the State aid rules, [2009] OJ C195/5 at para 21. Following the Cypriot bail-in, the burden-sharing requirements were raised in the 'Banking Communication' of July 2013, which required the bail-in of the bank's shareholders and all junior debt before any kind of restructuring aid to any bank regardless of its solvency situation, but subject to safeguarding fundamental rights and financial stability; see European Commission, The application, from 1 August 2013, of State aid rules to support measures in favour of banks in the context of the financial crisis, [2013] OJ C216/1. In the Judgment of the Court of 19 July 2016, C-526/14, *Kotnik*, EU:C:2016:570, the Court found that the Banking Communication was not binding on Member States, since it reflected guidelines whose effect was to limit the Commission in the exercise of its discretion. It also considered that burden-sharing was not a breach of legitimate expectations and the right to property: it did not lead to additional losses other than what shareholders and subordinated creditors would have suffered in insolvency proceedings if state aid had not been granted. For an analysis of the legal implications of bail-in, see KP Wojcik, 'Bail-in in the Banking Union' (2016) 53 *CML Rev* 91, especially 126–137.

[40] Other measures included the increase of the withholding tax on capital income, a restructuring and recapitalisation of the banks, an increase in the corporate income tax rate, and a privatisation plan. Eurogroup, Statement on Cyprus, 16 March 2013, at www.consilium.europa.eu/uedocs/cms_data/docs/pressdata/en/ecofin/136190.pdf.

[41] The Central Bank of Cyprus introduced a bank holiday on 18 March, in order to prevent a bank-run after the announcement of the Eurogroup, and also to pre-empt an ECB decision to stop the provision of ELA if no programme was available. During the bank holiday, all payments and transfers were prohibited, with exemptions for essential payments. Cash withdrawals at ATMs remained free, subject to the normal limits. See also ECB, Press Release, Governing Council decision on Emergency Liquidity Assistance requested by the Central Bank of Cyprus, 21 March 2013, at www.ecb.europa.eu/press/pr/date/2013/html/pr130321.en.html.

The bail-in of shareholders, uninsured depositors and bond holders covered €10 billion of the capital needs for the two banks.[42]

The resolution and bail-in decisions also implied the imposition by the Central Bank of Cyprus of wide-ranging capital controls, including the prohibition of cashless payments or transfers, and a limit to cash withdrawals of €300 a day per person and per bank. The capital controls were in place for two years and were lifted on 6 April 2015.[43]

This was the first time that capital controls were imposed in the single financial market and the Monetary Union. They were justified by the Cypriot authorities to protect public interest, safeguard financial stability, and ensure public order. The Commission considered that the capital controls fell within Article 65(1)(b) of the TFEU, which enables Member States to impose restrictions on capital movements on grounds of public policy and public security. However, capital controls within the euro area were also seen as equivalent to a demotion of the value of money and the removal of the Member State from the Monetary Union.[44]

The solutions found for the Cypriot crisis represented the culmination of the remarkable sequence of European approaches to the management of the sovereign debt crisis. The fact that the bank resolution and bail-in prevented the use of a large amount of public funds through an immediate downsizing of the banking system without dramatic consequences, despite the extensive capital controls, confirmed the validity of this approach. It provided a blueprint for bank resolution in the BRRD and impetus for the creation of the SRM.[45]

[42] Eurogroup, Statement on Cyprus, 25 March 2013, at www.consilium.europa.eu/uedocs/cms_Data/docs/pressdata/en/ecofin/136487.pdf. In *Mallis*, the Court considered that the Eurogroup statement had a 'purely informative nature' for the public of the political agreement reached with the Republic of Cyprus. Accordingly, it did not impose a legal obligation on Cyprus to implement the measures foreseen in the statement. In this context, the Eurogroup was only an informal body and was not among the different configurations of the Council or otherwise a body, office or agency of the EU within the meaning of Art 263, TFEU. See Judgment of the Court of 20 September 2016, *Mallis*, Joined Cases C-105/15 P to C-109/15 P, EU:C:2016:702, paras 58 to 61.

[43] Central Bank of Cyprus, The Enforcement of Restrictive Measures on Transactions in case of Emergency Law of 2013, 28 March 2013, at www.centralbank.cy/en/announcements/28-03-2013.

[44] European Commission, Statement on the capital controls imposed by the Republic of Cyprus, 28 March 2013, at europa.eu/rapid/press-release_IP-13-298_en.htm. See, for example, GB Wolff, 'Capital controls in Cyprus: the end of Target2?' (2013) at www.bruegel.org/nc/blog/detail/article/1054-capital-controls-in-cyprus-the-end-of-target2, arguing that the value of a euro in a Cypriot bank became significantly inferior to the value of a euro in any other bank in the euro area. Iceland was the first country within the EEA to impose capital controls in November 2008 following the collapse of the banking system, which remained in place until 2015. The controls were deemed compatible with Art 43 of the EEA Agreement by the EFTA Court; see Case E-3/11 *Pálmi Sigmarsson v the Central Bank of Iceland* [2011] EFTA Ct. Rep. 430. The Court argued that for a restriction on the free movement of capital to be justified, the national rules adopted must be suitable for securing the objective they pursue and must not exceed what is necessary to achieve it, so as to accord with the principle of proportionality.

[45] The Court confirmed in *Ledra Advertising* that, in line with *Pringle*, the Commission was required to ensure that the memoranda of understanding concluded by the ESM are consistent with EU law, including with the Charter of Fundamental Rights of the European Union. In this context, the Court considered that bail-in did not constitute a 'disproportionate and intolerable interference' impairing the right to property, within the meaning of Art 17(1) of the Charter, in the context of the adoption of the Memorandum of Understanding of 26 April 2013. Bail-in was justified by the objective of ensuring the stability of the banking system in the euro area, and the risk of losses for depositors if the banks had failed. See Judgment of the Court of 20 September 2016, *Ledra Advertising*, Joined Cases C-8/15 P to C-10/15 P, EU:C:2016:701, para 68 to 74.

D. The End of the Economic Adjustment Programmes and the Beginning of the ECB's Quantitative Easing

The sovereign debt crisis started to subside in 2014, when three of the five Member States benefitting from financial assistance regained access to sovereign debt markets at sustainable interest rates. The first was Ireland, which completed its €85 billion programme in December 2013. At the time, there was a debate on whether it could exit the programme without requesting a precautionary programme, which eventually was the case. The second was Spain, which exited in January 2014 after having used around €40 billion for bank recapitalisation and restructuring out of the available €100 billion. Portugal exited its €78 billion programme in June 2014. The programme of Cyprus concluded in later April 2016 and that of Greece in June 2018.[46]

In January 2015, the ECB decided to launch a 'quantitative easing' programme in the form of a 'Public Sector Purchases Programme' (PSPP). The PSPP involved monthly net purchases of public and private sector securities of €60 billion from March 2015 until March 2016, increased to €80 billion until March 2017, then reduced to €60 billion until December 2017, €30 billion until September 2018, and €15 billion until the end of 2018. It was later restarted in November 2019 at a pace of €20 billion, and it is ongoing at the time of writing. The balance sheet of the Eurosystem reached more than €4.5 trillion in 2018, close to a quarter of the euro area GDP.[47]

The combination of the 2008 financial crisis and the sovereign debt crisis had led to a long recession period in the euro area. Unemployment increased, economic recovery and demand remained weak, and the rate of inflation went steadily down until it reached -0.2 per cent by the end of 2014, also due to a decline in oil prices. The ECB had set negative interest rates in June 2014 with its deposit rate at -0.10 per cent, reaching -0.40 per cent in March 2016, and later -0.50 per cent in September 2019. The only effective monetary policy tool left to address the risks of too long a period of low inflation was to initiate purchases of government bonds of the euro area. This would reduce yields on government bonds, which would support the economic recovery and help bring inflation back to its medium-term objective of below, but close to, 2 per cent. It would work through both 'price and quantity effects': since sovereign yields provide the basic benchmark for the financing of the economy, it would lower the pricing of financial instruments; and the additional liquidity introduced by the purchases would enable investors to use funds on assets other than sovereign bonds, thus supporting further the economy through this 'portfolio rebalancing effect'.[48]

[46] Eurogroup, Statement on Ireland, 14 November 2013, expressing support for the exit of Ireland based on the progress made in financial sector repair, market sentiment, and existing cash buffers, at www.consilium.europa.eu/uedocs/cms_Data/docs/pressdata/en/ecofin/139579.pdf. See European Commission, Spain Post Programme Surveillance, Spring 2014 Report, 193 *European Economy*; and European Commission, The Economic Adjustment Programme for Portugal 2011–2014 (2014) 202 *European Economy*.

[47] Decision of the ECB of 14 May 2010 establishing a securities markets programme (ECB/2010/5), [2010] OJ L124/8.

[48] For the ECB's perspective on the rationale of its quantitative easing programme, see ECB, The Governing Council's Expanded Asset Programme, *ECB Economic Bulletin*, 1/2015. For an analysis of the ECB programme, see MK Brunnermeier, H James and JP Landau, *The Euro and the Battle of Ideas*, (n 3) at 359 to 367.

The launch of the 'quantitative easing' programme by the ECB posed similar questions to those regarding the challenge to the OMT: the extent to which it could represent a mutualisation of sovereign debt through a monetary policy instrument, thus contravening the monetary financing prohibition, as well as the principles of national liability and no-bail out of Member States. The explicit acceptance, as with the OMT, that the ECB would accept the same *pari passu* treatment as private investors implied that losses on the sovereign bonds of one Member State would eventually be borne by the taxpayers of the other euro area Member States. In this context, the Court ruling in the OMT case had clearly a bearing in the design of the PSPP. The ECB decision justified the PSPP as a proportionate measure and reaffirmed that it complied with the monetary financing prohibition and included several safeguards in line with the ruling. For example, only government bonds with a minimum rating or otherwise with a financial assistance programme could be purchased; or the ECB would impose a 'black-out' period during which purchases could not be conducted to avoid influencing the price of issuance of the government bonds.[49]

The implication of the concerns regarding monetary financing was reflected in the ECB's decision that only 20 per cent of the PSPP purchases would be subject to risk sharing within the Eurosystem. Each national central bank would buy government bonds from their respective Member State, which would imply that any potential losses would be borne ultimately only by the taxpayers of that Member State. This represented an exception to the principle that the losses incurred by the ECB in the conduct of its tasks are offset against its monetary income in the proportion allocated to each national central bank in the capital key of the ECB. The lack of loss-sharing in the PSPP challenged therefore the singleness of the monetary policy of the euro area and reflected its limits in the lack of fiscal integration.[50]

As with the OMT, the German Constitutional Court requested a preliminary ruling from the Court on the validity of the PSPP Decision. The questions were, first, whether the PSPP Decision infringed the monetary financing prohibition under Article 123 of the TFEU; second, whether the PSPP Decision was an ultra vires act, outside the ECB's mandate, taking into account the economic policy effects stemming from the volume of the purchases and the implementation period of two years, which would also infringe the principle of proportionality; and, third, whether the unlimited sharing of risks between the NCBs of the Eurosystem could lead to the need to recapitalise the NCBs using budgetary funds, in the case of a default of Member States, thus infringing the monetary financing prohibition, the no-bail out clause of Article 125 of the TFEU, and Article 4(2) of the TEU relating to the respect for the national identities of Member States.[51]

[49] See Recitals (4), (5) and (6) as well as Arts 3 and 4 of Decision of the ECB of 14 May 2010 establishing a securities markets programme (ECB/2010/5), [2010] OJ L124/8 (henceforth, PSPP Decision), regarding the eligibility criteria for marketable debt securities and limitations on the execution of purchases, respectively.

[50] Art 33.2 of the ESCB and ECB Statute. See P Praet, Public Sector security purchases and monetary dominance in a monetary union without a fiscal union, Speech at the Conference, The ECB and its Watchers XVI (2015) at www.ecb.europa.eu/press/key/date/2015/html/sp150311_1.en.html.

[51] *Weiss and Others*, (n 34) para 16.

The Court, drawing on *Gauweiler*, considered the PSPP decision valid. The monetary financing prohibition was not infringed, essentially because the safeguards for this purpose required under *Gauweiler* for the OMT were also fulfilled by the PSPP decision. The ECB acted within its monetary policy mandate, since – in line with *Pringle* and *Gauweiler* – 'a monetary policy measure cannot be treated as equivalent to an economic policy measure for the sole reason that it may have indirect effects that can also be sought in the context of economic policy'. The PSPP was also deemed not to infringe the principle of proportionality. The ECB had adopted measures to reduce risks and the sharing of losses among NCBs was limited to securities issued by international organisations. This also answered partly the last question, but the Court abstained from replying since it considered it hypothetical.[52]

The PSPP quickly led to a dramatic fall in the sovereign bond yields of the euro area, thus lowering the interest rates at which governments borrowed in the markets. While this spelled the end of the sovereign debt crisis – aside from the enduring Greek crisis – it also confirmed how risk-sharing among Member States remained the core obstacle to the functioning of the Monetary Union and, by implication, of the single financial market.[53]

E. The Threat of 'Grexit'

The last episode of the sovereign debt crisis was again in Greece, with the SSM already in place. The left-wing Syriza party won the elections on 25 January 2015 and formed a government with the aim of renegotiating the adjustment programme and ending austerity policies. The stance of the government, and the protracted negotiations with the Eurogroup on the reforms needed for the release of €7.2 billion, raised major uncertainty on the ability of Greece to fulfil its debt repayments and ultimately remain a member of the euro area.[54]

[52] *Weiss and Others*, (n 34) especially paras 63 to 69, 97 to 99, 102 to 108, and 166. On 5 May 2020, the German Constitutional Court responded to the preliminary ruling of the Court. While finding that there was no obvious infringement of the prohibition of monetary financing, it considered that the Court failed in assessing the proportionality of the PSPP and disregarded its economic effects. In this sense, it argued that the Court fell short of the standard of judicial review, since it limited itself to the assessment of whether there was a manifest error on the part of the ECB. Accordingly, the German Constitutional Court requested the Bundesbank not to participate in the implementation of the PSSP, and sell the bonds already purchased, unless the Governing Council of the ECB would adopt a new decision in three months demonstrating the proportionality of the PSPP. This judgment of the German Constitutional Court challenged, therefore, the supremacy of EU law and created a jurisdictional conflict, which remains unsolved at the time of writing. This conflicts also relates to the above-mentioned comment by C Joerges, 'Pereat Iustitia, Fiat Mundus' (n 35) that the *Gauweiler* judgment represented a rejection of the ordoliberal concept of the Monetary Union. See the 'PSPP Decision' of the German Constitutional Court, Judgment of 5 May 2020, 2 BvR 859/15, 2 BvR 980/16, 2 BvR 2006/15, 2 BvR 1651/15.

[53] See M Draghi, Risk-reducing and risk-sharing in our Monetary Union, Speech at the European University Institute, Florence, 11 May 2018, at www.ecb.europa.eu/press/key/date/2018/html/ecb.sp180511.en.html.

[54] Eurogroup, Statement on Greece, 20 February 2015, at www.consilium.europa.eu/en/press/press-releases/2015/02/150220-eurogroup-statement-greece. This statement also fulfilled the request of the Greek government to no longer refer to the concept of 'troika', which was replaced by references to 'institutions'.

After months of acrimonious negotiations, including claims by the Greek Government for war reparations from Germany, the crisis intensified on 18 June when talks between Greece and the Eurogroup broke down. An emergency Euro summit took place on 22 June, one week before the Greek programme expired and the deadline to repay €1.6 billion to the IMF. But talks collapsed again at the Eurogroup on 25 June.[55]

There was then a rapid sequence of momentous events. On 27 June, the Prime Minister of Greece, Alexis Tsipras, called a national referendum on the proposals for reforms put forward at the Eurogroup. Two days later, the Greek Government imposed capital controls and a bank holiday to contain the possibility of a bank run due to the referendum. Among other measures, cash withdrawals were limited to €60 a day and banks would not reopen until after the referendum. When the financial assistance programme expired on 30 June, Greece became the first country in the EU to default when it failed to repay €1.5 billion to the IMF.

The referendum of 5 July delivered 61.31 per cent of the vote as a 'no' against austerity measures despite the public warnings by euro area leaders about Greece leaving the euro. The finance minister Yannis Varoufakis resigned the following day. A Euro Summit took place two days later, which set a new deadline of 9 July for the Greek Government to present a reform agenda, ahead of another summit on 12 July. The President of the Council stated that the lack of an agreement would lead to the bankruptcy of Greece and the insolvency of its banking system. This would presumably mean the exit of Greece from the euro area.[56]

Finally, at the Euro Summit on 12 July, Greece committed to a set of immediate measures, including on the tax and pensions system, on the implementation of the Treaty on Stability, Coordination and Governance (TSCG), and on the transposition of the BRRD. Following these measures and the fulfilment of a number of prior commitments, the negotiations could start on a new financial assistance programme. The statement of the Euro Summit concluded with a reference to the possibility of granting debt relief to Greece in the form of longer grace and payment periods, conditional upon full implementation of the new programme, which was eventually only decided by the Eurogroup three years later on 21 June 2018. This episode of the crisis concluded with the agreement of the Eurogroup on 14 August to a third financial assistance programme under the ESM with the provision to Greece of up to €86 billion until 2018, out of which €25 billion was for the recapitalisation of the banking system, as required by the SSM, or to cover bank resolution costs.[57]

The Eurogroup statement also implied that the EFSF funds available for the recapitalisation of the Greek banking sector could only be released at the request of the ECB as banking supervisor of the euro area, in line with the objective of separating the sovereigns from the banking system that led to the establishment of the SSM.

[55] For a personal account, see Y Varoufakis, *Adults in the Room* (London, Bodley Head, 2016).

[56] Euro Summit, Remarks by President Donald Tusk after the Euro Summit of 7 July 2015 on Greece, at www.consilium.europa.eu/en/press/press-releases/2015/07/07/tusk-remarks-euro-summit.

[57] Euro Summit, Statement, 12 July 2015, at www.consilium.europa.eu/media/20353/20150712-eurosummit-statement-greece.pdf.

IV. 'Towards a Genuine Economic and Monetary Union'

A. The Autonomisation of the Monetary Union

The sovereign debt crisis put in motion a process of deeper integration of the Monetary Union, which became differentiated from the EU. Until then, the Monetary Union had functioned solely on the basis of EU law and institutions, without differentiation. The Monetary Union was inclusive of all Member States, which should mandatorily join once they fulfilled the convergence criteria set in the Treaty – with the exception of the Denmark and the UK, which had an opt-out. There were no euro area formats for the Council and the Parliament, while the Commission did not submit policy and legislative proposals specific to the euro area. This, however, changed fundamentally as a result of the crisis.[58]

'Towards a Genuine Economic and Monetary Union' was the title of the 2012 Report by the President Van Rompuy. Its significance arose from the attempt to provide a political and institutional concept for the architecture of the Monetary Union, which was autonomous from the EU. It rationalised ex post the legal and institutional fragments arising out of the piecemeal approach to the management of the sovereign debt crisis. This included a wide range of disparate arrangements and instruments within and outside the Treaty, combining EU law, public international law, and national laws, as well as European and national competences. It was the result of the prominence of the intergovernmental mode to address the sovereign debt crisis, which was coined by the Chancellor Angela Merkel as the 'Union Method'. All these fragments had, however, a common denominator, which was the autonomisation of the Monetary Union from the EU.[59]

The process of legal and institutional autonomisation started on 12 October 2008 with the first Euro Summit. It then intensified in 2010 with the sovereign debt crisis leading to specific decision-making bodies and a long line of new institutional arrangements for achieving deeper integration of the Monetary Union. This included the regular Euro Summits, the Eurogroup, the EFSF and later the ESM, the amendment of Article 136 of the TFEU to legitimise the setting-up of the ESM, and the reform of economic governance with the 'Six-Pack' and 'Two-Pack' proposals to strengthen

[58] For an analysis of the differentiation implications of the euro crisis, see B de Witte, 'Euro Crisis Responses and the EU Legal Order: Increased Institutional Variation or Constitutional Mutation?' (2015) 11 *European Constitutional Law Review* 434. See also the Editorial, (2012) 49 *CML Rev* 1, especially at 11–12, which expresses similar concerns regarding the risk that the EMU distances itself from the rest of the EU.

[59] H Van Rompuy in close collaboration with JM Barroso, JC Juncker and M Draghi, 'Towards a Genuine Economic and Monetary Union' (2012), at www.consilium.europa.eu/uedocs/cms_data/docs/pressdata/en/ec/134069.pdf. See also the parallel initiative of the European Commission, A Blue Print for a Deep and Genuine EMU, Launching A European Debate, COM (2012) 777 final. The term 'Union method' was introduced by Chancellor Merkel in a speech in Bruges on 2 November 2010. She argued that the Community method could only manage EU competences explicitly transferred by Member States, while the intergovernmental mode should be followed for coordinated action of Member States in areas of non-EU competence. See A Merkel, Speech by Federal Chancellor Angela Merkel at the opening ceremony of the 61st academic year of the College of Europe in Bruges on 2 November 2010, at www.coleurope.eu/content/news/Speeches/Europakolleg%20Brugge%20Mitschrift%20englisch.pdf.

the SGP, the 'Euro Plus Pact', and the TSCG. In 2012, the differentiation was extended from EMU policies to the single financial market with the introduction of the Banking Union.[60]

The main argument of the Van Rompuy Report was that the architecture of the Monetary Union should have three building-blocks, where these institutional arrangements and legal instruments would fall into place: (i) an integrated financial framework, which would become the Banking Union; (ii) an integrated budgetary framework; and (iii) an integrated economic policy framework. These building-blocks were put forward as intertwined, which could not be pursued without one another: the Banking Union could not be conceived without fiscal and economic integration, which in turn could not be separated.

This conclusion of the Report was the result of the particular sequence of European and Member States' largely reactive responses to the sovereign debt crisis. The sequence started with a first phase of reform of economic governance to address the shortcomings made obvious by the Greek crisis. It then turned into the development of a 'Fiscal Stability Union' as a pre-condition for any European competences with fiscal implications, notably the provision of financial assistance to Member States. It culminated with the establishment of the Banking Union as a quid pro quo for recapitalising banks at the European level, thus breaking the link between the national banking sectors and Member States.[61]

B. The Reform of Economic Governance

The impetus for the reform of economic governance came from the Greek crisis in 2010, which confirmed the failure of the SGP to ensure fiscal discipline. The soft nature and lack of credibility of the SGP had already been demonstrated when the ECOFIN voted on 25 November 2003 to suspend the Excessive Deficit Procedure (EDP) regarding France and Germany, and against the Commission recommendation for the reduction of their respective structural deficits. At the time, the statement of the President of the Commission, Romano Prodi, that 'the SGP was stupid' due to its rigidity was widely quoted. The SGP proved unable to deliver binding policy coordination and was deemed to have failed.[62]

[60] The most relevant decisions are conveyed in the Statements of the Heads of State or Government of the Euro Area from 25 March 2010 till 29 June 2012, at www.european-council.europa.eu/council-meetings/conclusions. See the analysis in E Chiti and PG Teixeira, 'The Constitutional Implications of the European Financial and Public Debt Crisis' (2013) 50 *CML Rev* 683, especially at 690–ff.

[61] See L van Middelaar, *Quand L'Europe Improvise*, (n 14) 88–102.

[62] See S Collignon, 'The End of the Stability Growth Pact?' (2004) 1 *International Economics and Economic Policy* 15; and J de Haan, H Berger and DJ Jansen, 'Why Did the Stability and Growth Pact Fail?' (2004) 7 *International Finance* 235. Following the action of the Commission against the Council, the Court annulled the Council Conclusions of 25 November 2003 on the basis that it could not deviate from the rules which it set for itself under the SGP, namely to suspend the EDP outside the SGP procedures. See Judgment of the Court of 13 July 2004, *Commission v Council (Stability and Growth Pact)* C-27/04: ECLI:EU:C:2004:436.

The reform of economic governance started with the 'Six-Pack' set of legislative proposals to strengthen the SGP, which was put forward by the Commission on 29 September 2010. Almost at the same time, on 21 October, a Task Force chaired by President Van Rompuy, comprising the EU finance ministers, also set out recommendations for economic governance, which were largely in line with the Commission's proposals. These parallel initiatives were yet another indication of the fragmentary approach to the management of the sovereign debt crisis. The reform of economic governance would rely throughout the years on both the Community method and the intergovernmental mode, which would then lead to a patchwork of institutional arrangements and legal instruments.[63]

The main novelty was the introduction in 2010 of the 'European Semester' as a cycle of economic policy coordination. It required the euro area Member States to submit draft budgetary plans to the Commission, which would assess them and propose country-specific recommendations for adoption by the Council. If Member States failed to comply with these recommendations, they would be subject to sanctions or corrective action plans. These procedures were provided with automaticity and had safeguards from political discretion. This was achieved through a wide use of reverse majority voting for blocking the Commission's economic policy proposals, country-specific recommendations, and financial sanctions.[64]

Economic governance was also expanded in scope with a new Excessive Imbalance Procedure (EIP), which included in multilateral surveillance the developments in the debt of Member States, as well as macroeconomic and competitiveness imbalances. There were, in addition, requirements for the alignment of national budgetary frameworks. This was later reinforced by the 'Two-Pack' Regulations in 2013.[65]

[63] See European Commission, Enhancing economic policy coordination for stability, growth and jobs – Tools for stronger EU economic governance, COM (2010) 367/2 final; and European Council, Strengthening Economic Governance in the EU, Report of the Task Force to the European Council, 21 October 2010, at www.consilium.europa.eu/media/27405/117236.pdf.

[64] The 'European Semester' was introduced by the European Council on 7 September 2010, on the basis of the proposals of the Task Force on Economic Governance chaired by the President Van Rompuy. It was introduced first as a soft arrangement under the Code of Conduct of the SGP and later formalised as part of the 'Six-Pack'. Regulation (EU) No 1175/2011 of the European Parliament and of the Council of 16 November 2011 amending Council Regulation (EC) No 1466/97 on the strengthening of the surveillance of budgetary positions and the surveillance and coordination of economic policies, [2011] OJ L306/12. The 'European Semester' aligned in time the submission by Member States of Stability and Convergence Programmes and National Reform Programmes so as to detect deviations from the SGP or imbalances. The Regulation also required Member States to adhere to medium-term objectives (MTO) for budgetary balance and provided the Commission with a stronger enforcement role through 'enhanced surveillance' of Member States deviating from the MTO. Regulation (EU) No 1173/2011 of the European Parliament and of the Council of 16 November 2011 on the effective enforcement of budgetary surveillance in the euro area, [2011] OJ L306/1. For the Commission's proposals and recommendations, where the reverse majority rule only applies in the event that the Council does not adopt a decision, see Art 6(2), 5th para and Art 10(2), 5th para of Regulation 1466/97 as amended by Regulation 1175/2011.

[65] See Regulation (EU) No 1176/2011 of the European Parliament and of the Council of 16 November 2011 on the prevention and correction of macroeconomic imbalances, [2011] OJ L306/25. The 2013 'Two-Pack' included the following. First, the Commission would provide an opinion on each national budget, and it could request a revised plan if it detected non-compliance. It also obliged the Member States to base their draft budgets on independent macroeconomic forecasts and have independent fiscal councils. Second, it provided the Commission with tools to monitor Member States in an EDP and also those receiving financial assistance,

The reform introduced, therefore, three legal and institutional innovations in economic governance. First, there was a reinforcement of the degree of intrusion by the Council and the Commission into national economic and budgetary planning. The surveillance of the macroeconomic performance of Member States was equally reinforced, particularly of those benefitting from financial assistance. Second, political discretion by the Council was significantly constrained by the use of reverse majority voting regarding the proposals and recommendations of the Commission. Third, as a result, the imposition of sanctions and corrective measures on Member States became quasi-automatic.[66]

Previously, the effectiveness of the SGP was essentially dependent on mutual trust between Member States, which had been undermined by the onset of the sovereign debt crisis. The main aim of this reform was to repair economic governance by introducing an enforceable rules-based regime anchored in European law. In line with the ordoliberal ideal, such a regime could then operate without requiring mutual trust between Member States. This represented a fundamental change in the functioning of the Monetary Union.[67]

C. A 'Fiscal Stability Union'

After the reform of economic governance, the process of deepening the monetary union was no longer aimed at replacing the trust lost between Member States regarding economic and fiscal commitments. The aim became fiscal integration as a pre-condition for European competences with fiscal implications, namely with the ESM and later the Banking Union.

This process started on 9 December 2011, when the Euro Area Heads of Statement of Government announced moving towards a 'genuine fiscal stability Union' through the agreement on a new 'fiscal compact'. They also decided to increase the financial resources of the EFSF and to anticipate to June 2012 the entry into force of the ESM Treaty, so as to make the ESM funds available earlier. In order to address the concerns

thus consolidating in EU law the practice already followed by the Commission. See Regulation (EU) No 473/2013 of the European Parliament and of the Council of 21 May 2013 on common provisions for monitoring and assessing draft budgetary plans and ensuring the correction of excessive deficit of the Member States in the euro area, [2013] OJ L140/11–23; and Regulation (EU) No 472/2013 of the European Parliament and of the Council of 21 May 2013 on the strengthening of economic and budgetary surveillance of Member States in the euro area experiencing or threatened with serious difficulties with respect to their financial stability, [2013] OJ L140/1–10.

[66] See the critique by C Joerges, 'How is a closer union conceivable under conditions of ever more socio-economic and political diversity? Constitutionalising Europe's unitas in pluralitate' (2018) 24 *European Law Journal* 257, who characterizes this new economic governance as 'authoritarian managerialism' since, among other problems, 'the Commission lacks legitimate authority to impose highly intrusive policy choices on Member States.'

[67] The argument that European law was used to compensate the lack of mutual trust between Member States is made by G Majone, *Rethinking the Union of Europe Post-Crisis: Has Integration Gone Too Far?* (Cambridge, Cambridge University Press, 2014) 45. For an analysis of the implications of these developments for European governance, see J Zeitlin, 'EU Experimentalist Governance in Times of Crisis' (2016) 39 *West European Politics* 1072.

raised by the Deauville declaration, the ESM Treaty was modified so as to narrow the scope for private sector involvement in restructuring the debt of Member States in difficulty, and to have more flexible voting rules for the ESM in emergency situations, ie an 85 per cent majority instead of mutual agreement.[68]

The new 'fiscal compact' thus emerged together with the decision to increase the pooling of financial resources at the European level, and to make more favourable the granting of financial assistance to Member States. Initially, the 'fiscal compact' was going to be introduced in the Treaty, which would have been an increase of European competences on fiscal and economic policies. The UK vetoed this possibility, unless the other Member States accepted to change the adoption of financial services legislation to unanimity voting. The euro area Member States, and those others willing to join, decided then to adopt the 'fiscal compact' as an intergovernmental agreement under public international law. This was deemed a temporary solution to go beyond EU law without revising the Treaty, which could involve lengthy and uncertain national ratification procedures and referenda.[69]

The resulting TSCG was concluded at the informal meeting of members of the European Council on 30 January 2012. The main innovation of the TSCG was that the 'balanced budget rule' of the SGP – government budgets should be balanced or in surplus – would be transposed in the national law of Member States through 'provisions of binding force and permanent character, preferably constitutions.' The Court is then given jurisdiction, in line with Article 237 of the TFEU, to assess whether the national provisions are in compliance. In addition, the TSCG required that debt should not be allowed to grow and should be paid back as swiftly as possible. The enforcement of fiscal discipline was also reinforced by enhancing further its automaticity.[70]

The TSCG epitomised the entrenchment of fiscal discipline in the Monetary Union at all levels: the law of the 'Fiscal Stability Union' is contained, not only in the Treaty, but also in the secondary law of the 'Six-Pack' and 'Two-Pack', in the soft law of the 'Euro Plus Pact', and outside the Treaty in the provisions of the TSCG, in national laws, as well as in the ESM Treaty. In such palimpsest of rules, the European institutions take up hybrid roles: the Commission plays a surveillance role in both the Treaty and the TSCG; the Euro Summits mirror the European Council; the jurisdiction of the

[68] See Euro Summit, Statement by the Euro Area Heads of State or Government, 9 December 2011, at www.consilium.europa.eu/uedocs/cms_data/docs/pressdata/en/ec/126658.pdf. The day before, on 8 December 2011, the ECB decided to take additional measures to support bank lending and liquidity in the euro area money market with the conduct of two longer-term refinancing operations (LTROs) of a maturity of 36 months. See ECB, ECB announces measures to support bank lending and money market activity, Press Release (2011) at www.ecb.europa.eu/press/pr/date/2011/html/pr111208_1.en.html. The sovereign debt crisis continued, however, to escalate on Friday, 13 January 2012, when the rating agency Standard & Poors downgraded nine euro-area Member States, with France and Austria removed of their AAA status.

[69] For an analysis of the UK's position, see Editorial, (n 58) at 13–14. On the problems created by the intergovernmental solution, see R Dehousse, 'The Fiscal Compact: Legal Uncertainty and Political Ambiguity' (2012) *Notre Europe Policy Brief* 33.

[70] See Communication by euro area Member States, 30.01.2012 at www.consilium.europa.eu/uedocs/cms_data/docs/pressdata/en/ec/127633.pdf; and Treaty on Stability, Coordination and Governance in the Economic and Monetary Union, at www.consilium.europa.eu/media/20399/st00tscg26_en12.pdf.

TSCG is attributed to the Court; and the Parliament organises with national parliaments conferences to discuss budgetary issues.[71]

The replacement of economic governance by a 'Fiscal Stability Union' implied the removal of national sovereignty over budgetary and economic policies. However, such removal consisted essentially of the replacement of national policies by a harmonised, automatic rules-based framework. It did not involve the transfer of the budgetary competences to European institutions or the creation of new institutions, such as a European fiscal authority. Instead, the 'Fiscal Stability Union' would operate by automatic coordination and convergence of economic policies, subject to the surveillance of the Council and the Commission. Policies which were within the realm of national politics and institutions became subject to automatic rules and procedures enforced by the European institutions.[72]

The 'Fiscal Stability Union' emerged thus as a pre-condition for European competences with fiscal implications. This relationship was made explicit by the rule that the entry into force of the ESM Treaty required the ratification of the TSCG. Member States could not receive financial assistance from the ESM without having ratified the TSCG. The ESM Treaty and the TSCG were complementary in fostering fiscal responsibility and solidarity.[73]

In this context, a 'Fiscal Stability Union' became the political and legal concept against the anathema of a 'transfer union'. The argument was that the pooling of financial resources on a permanent basis at the European level with the ESM could not take place without safeguards. A Member State could not free ride, either by lack of fiscal discipline in good times or misuse of financial assistance when it entered into difficulties. Therefore, the argument went, the pooling of financial resources could only take place with increased European competences controlling national fiscal and economic policies. In other words, there could not be European fiscal liability without European

[71] The 'Euro Plus Pact' is a voluntary and self-binding commitment of Member States to implement reforms in the areas of competitiveness, employment, sustainability of public finances and financial stability. It was not anchored in the Treaty or EU legislation, although it aimed at fulfilling the EU objective to increase competitiveness of Member States. The Euro Plus Pact – 'A Pact for the Euro, Stronger Economic Policy Coordination for Competitiveness and Convergence' – is Annex 1 of Euro Summit, Conclusions of the Heads of State or Government of the Euro Area of 11 March 2011, at www.consilium.europa.eu/media/21423/20110311-conclusions-of-the-heads-of-state-or-government-of-the-euro-area-of-11-march-2011-en.pdf. See E Chiti and PG Teixeira, 'The Constitutional Implications of the European Financial and Public Debt Crisis' (n 60) at 690–692, on the implications of such composite arrangements for European integration.

[72] As argued by Francis Snyder 'EMU also exemplifies the use of much more detailed rules and tighter deadlines. [...] Seen from the standpoint of compliance with law, this can be viewed as an example of harmonisation, not only of legal rules and administrative practice but also of national economic systems, economic ideologies and political cultures.' See F Snyder, 'EMU Revisited: Are We Making a Constitution? What Constitution Are We Making?' in P Craig and G De Burca (eds) *The Evolution of EU Law* (Oxford, Oxford University Press, 1999) 417–473, at 453. For a critical analysis of the relationship between the provisions of the TSCG and EU law, pointing out in particular the problematic legal issues regarding the role of European institutions in ensuring the enforcement of the TSCG, see Editorial, (n 58) at 8–9. See also P Craig, 'The Stability, Coordination and Governance Treaty: Principle, Politics and Pragmatism' (2012) 37 *European Law Review* 231.

[73] Recital (5) of the ESM Treaty states that '[t]his Treaty and the TSCG are complementary in fostering fiscal responsibility and solidarity within the economic and monetary union. It is acknowledged and agreed that the granting of financial assistance in the framework of new programmes under the ESM will be conditional, as of 1 March 2013, on the ratification of the TSCG by the ESM Member concerned and, upon expiration of the transposition period referred to in Art 3(2) TSCG on compliance with the requirements of that article'.

fiscal control over Member States. This increasingly became the quid pro quo between the core and the peripheral Member States of the euro area in the management of the sovereign debt crisis.[74]

D. The Concept of a 'Banking Union'

The concept of a 'Banking Union' first emerged at an informal dinner of the members of the European Council on 23 May 2012. President Van Rompuy reported that they had discussed more integrated banking supervision and resolution, and a common deposit insurance scheme to complete EMU. This was then reasserted in the G20 Leaders Declaration on 19 June 2012. The proposals to that end were put forward in the first draft of the Van Rompuy Report to the Euro Summit of 28 and 29 June 2012. The tone of the Report was aspirational and concluded that further work would be necessary to develop a roadmap.[75]

The main rationale for the 'Banking Union' was to address the main exacerbating factor of the sovereign debt crisis: the link between sovereigns and banks. Following the financial crisis in 2008, the soundness of banks became dependent on the fiscal capacity of their respective Member States to support them with public funds. This led to the rapid renationalisation of the single financial market, as analysed in Chapter 4. Those banks from Member States with a stronger capacity better weathered the crisis, either benefitting from public funds to restore their solvency or from the credibility of the respective Member State that such funds were available, also known as the 'public backstop'. Those banks from Member States with a weaker capacity, or whose size exceeded that capacity, were either broken down along national borders or rescued at the expense of the sustainability of the public finances of their Member State, notably in the case of Ireland.[76]

When the sovereign debt crisis began, there was a growing 'feedback loop' or vicious circle between the soundness of banks and Member States. The potential liabilities of Member States for rescuing their weak banks further weakened their public finances and the ability to serve their debt. This was translated in ever higher costs for issuing public debt in the form of sovereign yields. At the same time, the soundness of banks from weak Member States was also put into question due to the lack of credibility of

[74] This argument was often summarised by the German Finance Minister, Wolfgang Schaeuble, as 'solidarity goes hand in hand with solidity'. See, among several references, W Schaeuble, Building a Sturdier Euro, Wall Street Journal, 12 December 2012.

[75] Herman Van Rompuy, Remarks, 24 May 2012, at europa.eu/rapid/press-release_PRES-12-215_en.htm; G20 Leaders Declaration, Los Cabos, Mexico, 18–19 June 2012, at www.consilium.europa.eu/uedocs/cms_data/docs/pressdata/en/ec/131069.pdf. The designation of 'Banking Union' and a discussion on the alternatives for its institutional framework appeared in a policy paper by Bruegel in June 2012: J Pisani-Ferry, A Sapir, N Véron and GB Wolff, 'What Kind of European Banking Union?' (2012) 2012/12 *Bruegel Policy Contribution*.

[76] On the conflicting national interests in creating a Banking Union, see D Howarth, and L Quaglia, 'Banking union as holy grail: rebuilding the single market in financial services, stabilizing Europe's banks and "completing" economic and monetary union' (2013) 51 *Journal of Common Market Studies* 103; and S De Rynck, 'Banking on a union: the politics of changing eurozone banking supervision' (2016), 23 *Journal of European Public Policy* 119.

their public backstop. The financing costs of these banks increased in tandem with the increase in sovereign yields. This was worsened by the fact that domestic banks were often the only willing buyers of the sovereign debt of their Member States. The holdings of sovereign debt established a direct link between banks and sovereigns. A decrease in the value of sovereign debt aggravated the solvency of the banks, which in turn had less capacity to acquire such debt from its respective Member State, which in turn had greater difficulties to finance itself, and so on. The deterioration of the liquidity and solvency of banks and Member States became mutually reinforcing.[77]

The 'Banking Union' would break this vicious circle by transferring both the competences and the potential liabilities for banks to the European level in the form of integrated banking supervision and resolution, and a common deposit insurance scheme. European banking supervision would mean transferring from the national level the competence to enforce the 'single rulebook'. This would remove the possibility of regulatory laxity or forbearance by national authorities, as well as the risk of political or industry capture, which was one of the contributing factors to the crisis. European banking resolution would mean that bank failures would be managed by a single authority and legal regime, with the costs borne by a single resolution fund funded by banks. This would be in contrast with the previous primacy of national instruments to address a crisis. The resolution of a bank would be centralised, financed with funds from the banks themselves, and no longer driven by national considerations. A common deposit insurance scheme would create certainty about the reimbursement of deposits in banking crises independently of the home-country Member State of a bank. It would also ensure that the worthiness of deposits in euros would not need to be distinguished on the basis of their location in Member States.[78]

With a 'Banking Union', banks would become 'Europeanised' or encapsulated in a European legal order. They would no longer be subject to national authorities or dependent on the fiscal capacity of their Member State to rescue them. Member States would no longer internalise in their finances the potential or actual liabilities for rescuing banks. The national taxpayers would also be relieved of the burden of bank bailouts, which had caused so much public consternation. The liquidity and solvency of banks and sovereigns would therefore stop being correlated. This would be a momentous change, since banks had been traditionally entwined with national sovereignty.[79]

[77] The acquisition of domestic sovereign debt by banks was not only due to a 'home-bias' but also to the fact that the CRD III set a zero-risk weighting to bonds issued by Member States, thus not imposing any capital requirement for the risk of holding sovereign debt. Sovereign debt can also be used as collateral in monetary policy operations and in the interbank markets. For an explanation of the interdependence of sovereigns and banks, see, among others, S Merler and J Pisani-Ferry, 'Hazardous tango: sovereign-bank interdependence and financial stability in the euro area' (2012) *Financial Stability Review, Banque de France* 16; and MK Brunnermeier and Y Sannikov, 'Redistributive Monetary Policy' (2013) *Jackson Hole Symposium 2012*, 331.

[78] On the concept of a Banking Union, see J Pisani-Ferry, A Sapir, N Véron and GB Wolff, 'What Kind of European Banking Union?' (n 75); and R Goyal et al, 'A Banking Union for the Euro Area' (2013) *IMF Staff Discussion Notes 13/1*.

[79] Martin Hellwig expressed skepticism about the Banking Union since 'the symbiosis between banks and treasuries has for centuries been a key element of sovereignty.' See M Hellwig, 'Yes Virginia, There is a European Banking Union! But It May Not Make Your Wishes Come True' (2014) 2014/12 *Max Planck Institute for Research on Collective Goods*, at 16–25.

Another implication of the 'Banking Union' would be to repair the single financial market, which had been renationalised since the 2008 financial crisis. The purely national rescue of banks made them repatriate their assets and activities. The deployment of national taxpayers' funds implied that Member States were not willing to extend their public backstop to banks outside their borders. There was a widespread 'ringfencing' of banking activities within each Member State to limit potential fiscal liabilities. This led to a re-sizing of banks in line with the size of their respective Member State, rather than in proportion to the single financial market as promoted by European law.[80]

The 'Banking Union' was, therefore, a concept that emerged to address the sovereign debt crisis and to restore financial integration, given the failures of the previous phase of 'integration through governance'. These twin objectives were instrumental for the viability of the Monetary Union, which could not function without sustainable public finances and an integrated single financial market. The transfer of competences and liabilities to the European level for the banking system became the condition for such viability.[81]

E. The Future of the Monetary Union

The Van Rompuy Report proposed a sequence of stages for achieving a 'genuine Economic and Monetary Union'. The first stage would take place in 2012 and 2013. It would correspond to the implementation of the framework for fiscal governance, the setting-up of the SSM, the enabling of direct recapitalisation of banks by the ESM, and the harmonisation of national bank resolution laws and deposit guarantee schemes. In 2013, the second stage would comprise the setting-up of a European bank resolution authority, as well as contractual arrangements between Member States and European institutions on structural policies. The last stage, after 2014, would include a fiscal capacity at the European level to absorb country-specific economic shocks. In this stage, there could be an increasing degree of European decision-making on national budgets, and an enhanced coordination of economic policies in taxation and employment.[82]

Independently of whether the vision of the Van Rompuy Report would materialise, it conveyed two political indications regarding the future of the Monetary Union. First, it argued for the progressive autonomisation of the Monetary Union from the EU in order to ensure its preservation. This would include the autonomisation not only of the

[80] While European banks became generally large compared to the GDP of individual Member States, they were relatively proportional to the size of the single financial market. See V Constâncio, Towards the Banking Union, Speech at the 2nd FIN-FSA Conference on EU Regulation and Supervision 'Banking and Supervision under Transformation', Helsinki, 12 February 2013, at www.ecb.europa.eu/press/key/date/2012/html/sp120907.en.html.

[81] See M Hellwig, 'Yes Virginia, There is a European Banking Union!' (n 79). On the weight of 'ordoliberal' arguments in the creation of the Banking Union, see D Schäfer, 'A Banking Union of Ideas? The Impact of Ordoliberalism and the Vicious Circle on the EU Banking Union' (2016) 54 *Journal of Common Market Studies* 961.

[82] H Van Rompuy, 'Remarks, 24 May' (2012) europa.eu/rapid/press-release_PRES-12-215_en.htm.

law and institutions required for financial, budgetary and economic policies, but also of the mechanisms for the democratic legitimacy of the Monetary Union. This would require the involvement of the European Parliament and national parliaments, as well as other arrangements that were not spelled out. Therefore, the envisaged autonomisation of the Monetary Union would be legal, institutional, and also political.[83]

Second, it argued that fiscal integration should be the ultimate objective in the evolution of the Monetary Union, which would culminate with a 'euro area fiscal capacity'. Such capacity would aim at enabling risk-sharing within the Monetary Union. As acknowledged by the Van Rompuy Report, that could involve transfers of funds to Member States under a 'shock absorption function'. Such transfers would be dependent on compliance by the benefitting Member States with the legal and contractual requirements for fiscal and structural policies. Therefore, the Van Rompuy Report pointed towards a Monetary Union where European fiscal and economic competences have distributive implications, albeit to a limited and controlled measure.

The development of a fiscal capacity required financial resources. This raised the question of providing the Monetary Union with the ability to borrow, notably through a common debt issuance as the full mutualisation of fiscal liabilities. The possibility of 'Euro Bonds' was first formally proposed in May 2010 by the Monti Report on the Single Market, which advocated the issuance of 'E-bonds' for increasing financial integration. More concrete proposals were made in March 2014 by an Expert Group on a Debt Redemption Fund and Eurobills, which acknowledged the benefits of joint debt issuance but identified economic, financial and moral hazard risks. There would also be no basis in the Treaty for mutualisation of the related fiscal liabilities and the only alternative for joint debt issuance would be intergovernmental mechanisms, giving rise to democratic legitimacy concerns.[84]

The debate on the future of EMU was then relaunched in June 2015 with the so-called 'Five Presidents' Report.' It advocated two stages to achieve 'a genuine Monetary Union'

[83] See the criticism of A Dashwood, 'Guest editorial: Living with the Eurozone' (2016) 53 *CML Rev* 3, noting that the non-euro area Member States require constitutional recognition as a group vis-à-vis EMU. See also T Beukers and M Van Der Sluis, 'Differentiated Integration from the Perspective of Non-Euro Area Member States' in T Beukers, B de Witte, C Kilpatrick (eds) *Constitutional Change through Euro-Crisis Law* (Cambridge, Cambridge University Press, 2017) 143.

[84] The Commission advocated the establishment of a redemption fund and euro bills to help with debt reduction and stabilise financial markets. The fiscal capacity of the EU would be managed by an EMU Treasury within the Commission. In the longer term, the Commission proposed an autonomous euro-area budget providing for a fiscal capacity to support Member States affected by economic shocks. An integrated economic and fiscal governance would allow for the common issuance of public debt, as the final stage in EMU. See European Commission, A Blue Print for a Deep and Genuine EMU, Launching A European Debate, COM (2012) 777 final; M Monti, A New Strategy for the Single Market: At the Service of Europe's Economy and Society (2010), at 61–ff, at ec.europa.eu/internal_market/strategy/docs/monti_report_final_10_05_2010_en.pdf; European Commission, Report of the Expert Group on a Debt Redemption Fund and Eurobills (2004), at ec.europa.eu/economy_finance/articles/ governance/pdf/20140331_report_en.pdf. Since the start of the sovereign debt crisis, there had been several proposals for mechanisms leading to different types of 'Eurobonds', including MK Brunnermeier, 'European Safe Bonds (ESBies)' (2011) euro-nomics.com/wp-content/uploads/2011/09/ESBiesWEBsept262011.pdf; and the redemption fund proposed by the German Council of Economic Experts, A European redemption pact (2011), at www.sachverstaendigenrat-wirtschaft.de/233.html.

comprising an Economic, Financial – including the Banking Union and the Capital Markets Union, and Fiscal Union. In Stage 1, until 30 June 2017, the efforts would be on increasing economic convergence, completing the Banking Union by creating a European deposit insurance scheme, launching the Capital Markets Union, creating a European Fiscal Board, and enhancing democratic legitimacy involving the European Parliament and national parliaments. In Stage 2, to be completed at the latest by 2025, the economic convergence process would become more binding with legal benchmarks, a macroeconomic stabilisation function would be set-up, together with a euro-area treasury. In the words of the Report, at the end of these stages 'a deep and genuine EMU would provide a stable and prosperous place for all citizens of the EU Member States that share the single currency'.[85]

The debate on the future of the Monetary Union was thus focused on the achievement of fiscal integration as its messianic destiny. This can be summarised as the transition from a 'community of benefits' into a 'community of benefits and risks'. The transfer of competences with fiscal implications to the European level should be matched by the capacity for risk-sharing. This required joint fiscal liabilities and the capacity for distributive policies within the Monetary Union. Ultimately, it required political integration to provide democratic legitimacy. The significance of the Banking Union was that it represented the first step in this direction. The exercise of banking supervision and resolution were thus the first European competences with fiscal and distributive implications.[86]

V. The First Pillar of the Banking Union: The Single Supervisory Mechanism

A. The Transfer of Banking Supervision Competences to the ECB

Following the political agreement at the Euro Summit of 28 and 29 June 2012, the Council decided to transfer to the ECB the direct exercise of a wide range of banking supervision competences in the single financial market. This transfer was operated by a Council Regulation adopted on the basis of Article 127.6 of the TFEU, which entered into force on 3 November 2013. The Regulation also established the SSM, which

[85] JC Juncker, in close cooperation with D Tusk, J Dijsselbloem, M Draghi and M Schulz, 'The Five Presidents' Report: Completing Europe's Economic and Monetary Union' (2015), at ec.europa.eu/priorities/sites/beta-political/files/5-presidents-report_en.pdf. The concrete steps for the implementation of Stage 1 were conveyed in European Commission, On steps towards Completing Economic and Monetary Union, COM (2015) 0600 final. The vision of the Five Presidents' Report was later taken up by European Commission, White Paper on the Future of Europe, COM (2017) 2025 final, at ec.europa.eu/commission/sites/beta-political/files/white_paper_on_the_future_of_europe_en.pdf where the five scenarios for Europe by 2025 included the realisation of the aims of the Report.

[86] On this transformation process, see E Chiti and PG Teixeira, 'The Constitutional Implications of the European Financial and Public Debt Crisis' (n 60) 690–ff.

was defined as a system of financial supervision composed by the ECB and national competent authorities (NCAs).[87]

The choice to use Article 127.6 expressed the will to transfer without delay banking supervision competences to the European level, thus also enabling the direct recapitalisation of banks by the ESM. There would be no need to amend the Treaty or engage in any lengthy legislative procedures with uncertain outcomes. Similar factors were at the heart of the other decisions to address the crisis which did not require a Treaty amendment, namely the ESM Treaty and the TSCG. Transferring competences to the ECB provided credibility as to the immediate start of the SSM, without a long transition period.

There were three main concerns about transferring banking supervision competences to the ECB, which would later be reflected in the design of the core provisions of the SSM Regulation. The first related to whether the ECB could combine banking supervision and central banking tasks, while preserving the primacy of the objective of price stability in the conduct of monetary policy. The argument was that such a combination could lead to a conflict of interests, for instance, in the provision of liquidity to the banking system, if it would take into account supervisory interests and not exclusively monetary policy. The second concern was that entrusting supervision to the ECB would imply confining the jurisdiction of the SSM to the euro area Member States. This would exclude the Member States which have not adopted the euro from a more deeply integrated single financial market. The City of London, as the main financial centre, would also be excluded. The third regarded the democratic accountability of the ECB as a banking supervisor. Entrusting supervision to the ECB would imply that its statutory independence as a central bank would spillover to its supervisory tasks. This was deemed incompatible with the nature of banking supervision, which required closer and deeper accountability to political institutions due to the potential impact on taxpayers' funds. Conversely, the political accountability for banking supervision could undermine the independence of the ECB for the conduct of monetary policy.[88]

At the same time, the transfer of competences to the ECB fit the institutional trend to integrate banking supervision within central banks as a lesson from the financial crisis. The model for the conduct of supervision on the basis of a single authority

[87] The SSM was established on 3 November 2013, on the basis of the Council Regulation (EU) No 1024/2013 of 15 October 2013 conferring specific tasks on the European Central Bank concerning policies relating to the prudential supervision of credit institutions, [2013] OJ L287/63–89 (henceforth, 'the SSM Regulation'). The functioning of the European Banking Authority was adjusted to the establishment of the SSM by Regulation (EU) No 1022/2013 of the European Parliament of the Council of 22 October 2013 amending Regulation (EU) No 1093/2010 establishing a European Supervisory Authority (European Banking Authority) as regards the conferral of specific tasks on the European Central Bank pursuant to Council Regulation (EU) No 1024/2013, [2013] OJ L287/5–14 (henceforth, 'the Regulation amending the EBA Regulation').

[88] In this sense, see S Eijffinger and R Nijskens, 'Monetary Policy and Banking Supervision' (2012) *VOX*, www.voxeu.org/article/monetary-policy-and-banking-supervision. The argument of the conflict of interests was advocated explicitly by the Bundesbank, which questioned whether Art 127.6, TFEU could provide the legal basis for a transfer of supervisory tasks to the ECB, see Deutsche Bundesbank, Financial Stability Review (2012), 82–83. For an early overview of the arguments for entrusting banking supervision to a central bank, see ECB, The Role of Central Banks in Prudential Supervision (2001), at www.ecb.europa.eu/pub/pdf/other/prudentialsupcbrole_en.pdf.

separate from the central bank, which had started with the UK's Financial Services Authority in 1997 and had spread for 10 years in Europe and globally, was deemed largely inadequate to prevent and contain the crisis. This marked the return of supervisory competences to central banks, including in the UK and in the US, where the supervisory responsibilities of the Federal Reserve were reinforced by the Dodd-Frank Act. The fact that the majority of the euro area central banks were also national supervisors would facilitate the setting-up of the SSM on the basis of the infrastructure of the Eurosystem.[89]

B. The Debate on the Legal Foundation: Article 127.6 TFEU

The activation of Article 127.6 was questioned at the time as the appropriate legal basis to transfer banking supervision competences to the ECB. Until then, it had only been used once to entrust the ECB with the support to the ESRB. It reads as follows:

> The Council, acting by means of regulations in accordance with a special legislative procedure, may unanimously, and after consulting the European Parliament and the ECB, confer specific tasks upon the ECB concerning policies relating to the prudential supervision of credit institutions and other financial institutions with the exception of insurance undertakings.

The first question was whether this somewhat convoluted wording could enable the transfer of a wide range of banking supervision tasks. More specifically, whether the reference to 'specific tasks concerning policies relating to prudential supervision' could enable the ECB to replace national authorities as the competent authority for the conduct of banking supervision in accordance with EU law. This was disputed in the preparatory work for the Treaty of Maastricht and the Statute of the ESCB and the ECB in the late 1980s. There were two opposing concepts. Most central bank governors argued that the ECB, in line with the dominant model in Europe at the time, should also exercise banking supervision. This was reflected in the draft text prepared by the Committee of Governors:

> The ECB may formulate, interpret and implement policies relating to the prudential supervision of credit and other financial institutions for which it is designated as competent authority.[90]

[89] The involvement of central banks in banking supervision led to a debate on the extent to which multiple objectives may be pursued simultaneously by a single institution, thus calling into question the well-known 'Tinbergen rule' according to which the pursuance of economic policies requires independent policy instruments for each policy target. For an overview of the arguments, see D Masciandaro and M Quintyn, 'Regulating the Regulators: The Changing Face of Financial Supervision Architectures Before and After the Financial Crisis' in S Eijffinger and D Masciandaro (eds) *Handbook of Central Banking, Financial Regulation and Supervision: After the Financial Crisis* (Cheltenham, Elgar, 2011) 428. See also ECB Recent Developments in Supervisory Structures in the EU Member States (2007–2010) (2010), at www.ecb.europa.eu/pub/pdf/other/ report_on_supervisory_structures2010en.pdf.

[90] Draft text proposed by the Committee of Governors for Art 25 of the Statute, which would replicate Art 127, TFEU, in Europe, Document No 1669/1679, p 9. For an interpretation see R Smits, *The European Central Bank: Institutional Aspects* (The Hague, Kluwer Law International, 1997) 335–346.

This text was contested by governments, some banking supervisors and the Bundesbank, on the basis of concerns as to the combination of central banking and supervision tasks. As a compromise, the Delors Report then proposed that the ECB would exercise coordination tasks of banking supervision.[91]

The outcome of these conflicting positions was a compromise. The final texts of the Treaty and the Statute only provided contributing and advisory roles to the ECB regarding banking supervision. The possibility that the ECB could exercise banking supervision in the future was left open and enabled with the clause of Article 127.6.[92]

The final wording of Article 127.6 drew from the proposal of the Committee of Governors, with two main differences. The first was that it referred to entrusting the ECB with 'specific tasks', instead of formulating, interpreting and implementing supervisory policies. This imposed a procedural condition on the Council to clearly specify the supervisory tasks to be conferred upon the ECB. The second difference was not having an explicit reference to the ECB as a 'competent authority'. This broadened, instead of constrained, the scope of the tasks that could be carried out by the ECB, since they were not limited to those of competent authorities, such as the support to the ESRB by the ECB.[93]

Another question regarding Article 127.6 was whether it was the only available legal basis in the Treaty to transfer supervisory competences to the European level. In this context, only Article 352, which enables the Council to take action to attain the objectives of the Union when the Treaty has not provided the necessary powers, could have presented a competing legal basis.[94]

This raised the issue of the nature of Article 127.6. It was included in the EMU chapter of the Treaty and in the Statute of the ESCB and the ECB. However, at the same

[91] See H James, *Making the European Monetary Union* (Cambridge MA, The Belknap Press of Harvard University Press, 2012) at 313–ff.

[92] The ECB was entrusted with three tasks of different nature relating to supervision. First Art 127.5, TFEU provided the ESCB with the task to contribute to the smooth conduct of policies pursued by the competent authorities relating to the prudential supervision of credit institutions and the stability of the financial system. This task fell short of a coordination task and may be interpreted as a central banking contribution to the conduct of national supervision. Second, Art 25.1 of the Statute provided that the ECB may offer advice to and be consulted by the Council, the Commission, and national supervisors on the scope and implementation of EU law relating to the prudential supervision of credit institutions. This was closer to a coordinating function, since the ECB could play the role of supporting the uniform formulation and implementation of Union law relating to supervision, as proposed by the Committee of Governors. The third task was that of Art 127.6, TFEU. For an analysis of these tasks, see JV Louis, *Vers un système européen de banques centrales – Projet de dispositions organiques* (Bruxelles, Éditions de l'Université Libre de Bruxelles, 1989).

[93] In the interpretation of Jean-Victor Louis of Art 127.6, TFEU, 'this enabling clause makes it possible, albeit with substantial procedural impediments to be overcome, to provide for a form of direct Europe-wide supervision of financial institutions'. Another feature of the final text of Art 127.6, TFEU was that it excluded insurance undertakings from its scope, which was a restriction introduced by the Dutch Presidency, late in the negotiation process. See J-V Louis *Banking Supervision in the European Community: Institutional Aspects* (Bruxelles, Université de Bruxelles, 1995) at 44–ff. This was also the conclusion of E Wymeersch, 'The European Banking Union, a First Analysis' (2012) 2012–07 *Working Paper, Ghent University, Financial Law Institute*, at 6–7.

[94] Art 114, TFEU, together with the *Meroni* case law, would not have provided the basis to delegate to a European agency, such as the EBA, autonomous decision-making and regulatory powers for prudential supervision. This limitation was confirmed later by the SRM's legal framework for decision-making analysed in the next section of this chapter.

time, the conduct of banking supervision refers to competences related to the provision of financial services, which is an area of the single financial market. This implied that Article 127.6 had a double nature: it belonged to the framework of both the EMU and the single market. Another indication in this direction was that, in contrast with most of the EMU provisions, Article 127.6 applied to all Member States, including those with a derogation: all Member States had a vote in the unanimous decision to adopt a Council Regulation. Therefore, Article 127.6 reflected the inclusive framework of EMU with regard to the EU, which assumes a perfect coincidence of the two perimeters over time.

As a result, following the jurisprudence of the Court, Article 352 could not have been invoked to confer tasks to the ECB or to another authority: Article 127.6 already provided the EU with the powers to transfer supervision to the European level both for the Monetary Union and the single financial market. Furthermore, it would be doubtful to use Article 352 to transfer national competences to a new European authority, which would represent a constitutional change. A Treaty amendment was therefore the only alternative to transfer banking supervision to the European level, which was hardly feasible both politically and time wise in the circumstances of the sovereign debt crisis.[95]

Therefore, it was concluded by the Council that Article 127.6 would provide the legal basis for the transfer of banking supervision competences to the ECB. However, the political and institutional concerns about its use remained. This regarded the separation between the conduct of monetary policy and banking supervision within the ECB, the ability of Member States outside the euro area to join the SSM in equal terms as the others to preserve the single financial market, and the democratic accountability of the ECB as a banking supervisor. Eventually, to address these concerns, Member States took the political commitment to 'work constructively' on a proposal for a Treaty change. This could conceivably imply modifying the institutional framework of the ECB with regard to the conduct of supervisory tasks or establishing a new European institution devoted to banking supervision.[96]

Overall, the legal basis provided by Article 127.6 defined the SSM's 'genetic code': the unique legal and institutional features of the SSM reflected the tensions of belonging to the framework of both the EMU and the single financial market. Such unique features, which will be analysed in the next sections, included: the principle of separation from monetary policy in the decision-making process of the SSM, involving both a Supervisory Board and the Governing Council of the ECB; the complex matrix of competences of the SSM; the combination of the ECB and the NCAs in the SSM; and the independence and democratic accountability of the SSM, which involves not only the European Parliament but national parliaments.

[95] The Court stated that '[i]t follows from the very wording of Art 235 TEC [352 TFEU] that its use as the legal basis for a measure is justified only where no other provision of the Treaty gives the Community institutions the necessary power to adopt the measure in question'. See Judgment of the Court of 26 March 1987, *Commission v* Council, 45/86, EU:C:1987:163, para 13.

[96] See Recital (85) of the SSM Regulation. The German Constitutional Court also considered later in its Banking Union judgment that the transfer of supervisory powers to the ECB does not manifestly exceed the competences conferred by Art 127(6), TFEU. See German Constitutional Court, BVerfG, Urteil des Zweiten Senats vom 30 Juli 2019, 2 BvR 1685/14, Rn. (1-320), at www.bverfg.de/e/rs20190730_2bvr168514.html.

C. The Separation between Banking Supervision and Monetary Policy

The provision of Article 127.6 could only provide the basis for conferring supervisory tasks and not for changing the institutional framework of the ECB. This implied that such tasks would be conducted on the basis of the decision-making bodies and instruments of the ECB, as provided by the Treaty and its Statute. For example, Article 132.1 and Article 34.1 of the Statute already enabled the ECB to adopt regulations relating to prudential supervision. Another implication was that the supervisory jurisdiction of the ECB could not extend beyond the euro-area Member States.[97]

These mechanics of Article 127.6 were at the origin of one of the foundational principles of the SSM: the principle of separation within the ECB between the conduct of monetary policy and of banking supervision. The ECB was obliged to only pursue the objectives of the SSM regulation in the performance of supervisory tasks, and to carry out such tasks without prejudice to and separately from monetary policy. This principle required the separation in decision-making, and the organisational separation of the staff involved in supervisory tasks. It was dictated by two concerns: the combination of monetary policy and banking supervision under the same roof; and the limitation of the ECB's jurisdiction to the euro area, thus not matching that of the single financial market.[98]

The main expression of the separation principle was the unique decision-making process set out in the SSM Regulation. First, this Regulation established a 'Supervisory Board' as an internal body of the ECB. It comprises a Chair and a Vice-Chair, four ECB representatives, as well as representatives from each of the national supervisory authorities of the euro area Member States and from those in 'close cooperation'. This enables national supervisors to be involved and provide the expertise for the conduct of supervision by the ECB. The key competence of the Supervisory Board is to 'fully undertake' the planning and execution of the ECB's supervisory tasks, which includes the preparation of 'complete' draft supervisory decisions for final decision by the Governing Council.[99]

Second, the relationship between the Supervisory Board and the Governing Council of the ECB is based on reverse voting, which was drawn from economic governance

[97] Although the Council Regulation activating Art 127.6, TFEU requires unanimity of all Member States, the institutional provisions regarding the powers of the ECB decision-making bodies do not apply to the Member States with a derogation. See Art 139. TFEU and Art 42.1 of the Statute.

[98] See Art 25 of the SSM Regulation. The implementation of this provision was made by the ECB Decision 2014/723/EU: Decision of the European Central Bank of 17 September 2014 on the implementation of separation between the monetary policy and supervision functions of the European Central Bank (ECB/2014/39) [2014] OJ L300/57–62. The separation principle was publicly argued by the Finance Minister of Germany before the Commission proposal for the SSM Regulation, see W Schäuble, 'How to protect EU taxpayers against bank failures' *Financial Times*, 30 August 2012.

[99] See Arts 26.1 and 26.8 of the SSM Regulation. The Supervisory Board acts on the basis of simple majority voting, except when taking decisions on the adoption of regulations, which is subject to qualified majority under Art 26.7, SSM Regulation. In this case, the four ECB representatives have a vote equal to the median vote of the other members, which vote in accordance with the voting weight of their respective Member States.

procedures. The 'complete' draft supervisory decisions prepared by the Supervisory Board are considered adopted by the Governing Council unless it objects within ten working days, or 48 hours in emergencies. If the Governing Council objects to a draft decision, it has to state its reasons in writing. And in case of an objection, a 'Mediation Panel' can be convoked as an additional line of defence for the separation principle, in order to prevent the potential dominance of the Governing Council over the Supervisory Board.[100]

The institutional role of the Supervisory Board is akin to the exclusive power of initiative of the Commission. The Supervisory Board has the exclusive competence to prepare and put forward proposals for decision to the Governing Council. It implies that the Governing Council cannot take supervisory decisions without the procedural step of involving the Supervisory Board in the preparation of draft decisions. Moreover, the reverse voting (non-objection) procedure means that the Governing Council cannot change such draft decisions but only object to them. This was why the SSM Regulation required the Supervisory Board to propose to the Governing Council 'complete' draft decisions, which do not require additions or revisions.

The separation principle was, therefore, implemented by the establishment of the Supervisory Board as a 'quasi decision-making body', and by the introduction of the non-objection procedure for the adoption of supervisory decisions by the Governing Council. This enabled the fulfilment of two seemingly contradictory conditions for entrusting the ECB with supervisory tasks. First, it addressed the conflict of interests between monetary policy and banking supervision by providing the Supervisory Board with the exclusive competence to propose supervisory decisions, to which the Governing Council could only object. Second, it respected the institutional framework of the ECB, since the Governing Council adopts formally the supervisory decisions, although subject to the procedural involvement of the Supervisory Board.[101]

The separation principle also served another purpose. Since the ECB's jurisdiction is limited to the euro area, Member States outside the euro area can request to join the SSM in 'close cooperation' and have their banks subject to the supervision of the ECB. These Member States will need to commit to enforce ECB supervisory decisions in their jurisdictions with equivalent national decisions. In turn, their respective national supervisory authorities would become members of the Supervisory Board in equal terms with those from the euro area. The separation principle thus enabled to include representatives of non-euro-area Member States in the Supervisory Board, and thus in the decision-making process of the SSM. Furthermore, a Member State in 'close cooperation' has special rights: in case of an objection of the Governing Council to a draft decision submitted to the Supervisory Board, it can notify the ECB that it will not be

[100] The panel comprises one representative per participating Member State among the members of the Governing Council and the Supervisory Board. It decides by simple majority. See Art 25.5 of the SSM Regulation and Regulation (EU) No 673/2014 of the European Central Bank of 2 June 2014 concerning the establishment of a Mediation Panel and its Rules of Procedure (ECB/2014/26) [2014] OJ L179/72–76.

[101] The setting of procedural conditions for the exercise of competences by European institutions has been accepted by the Court in previous occasions: Judgment of the Court of 30 September 2003, *Eurocoton*, C-76/01 P, EU:C:2003:511, para 55.

bound by an amended supervisory decision resulting from that objection. This right of non-compliance of Member States in 'close cooperation' aimed at preventing the jurisdiction of the Governing Council over Member States outside the euro area. The ECB can then suspend or terminate the 'close cooperation', but it needs to take into account a large array of considerations, including the SSM integrity, adverse consequences for the fiscal responsibilities of Member States, and whether the supervisor of that Member State has taken measures equally effective as the objection of the Governing Council.[102]

The Supervisory Board also provided the basis for separate accountability arrangements for supervisory tasks. As analysed below, the Chair and the members of the Supervisory Board are those required to fulfil the accountability obligations of the SSM separately from the accountability for monetary policy.[103]

Lastly, another dimension of the separation principle relates to the power of the ECB to impose fees on all credit institutions established in the SSM's jurisdiction to cover its expenditures. It prevents the financing of banking supervision by the income of the ECB arising from the conduct of monetary policy. These 'own taxation powers' also prevented the mutualisation of the costs of supervision among Member States.[104]

Figure 3 The Decision-Making Process of the SSM

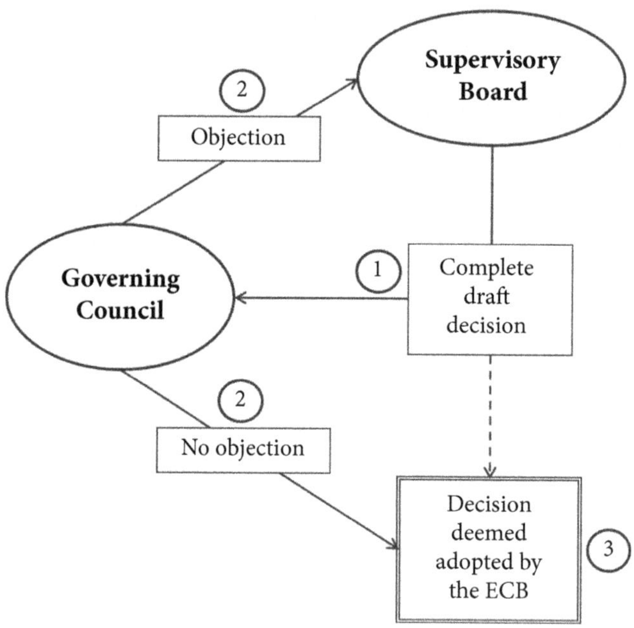

[102] Arts 7.5, 7.6, 7.7. and 7.8 of the SSM Regulation. According to Recital 72 of the SSM Regulation, the Governing Council of the ECB should invite the representatives from non-euro area participating Member States to take part in the discussion, whenever it is contemplated by the Governing Council to object to a draft decision prepared by the Supervisory Board, and when such a decision is addressed to the national authorities in respect of credit institutions from non-euro area participating Member States.

[103] Arts 20 and 21, SSM Regulation.

[104] Art 30, SSM Regulation. The powers of the ECB to levy supervisory fees were specified in Regulation (EU) No 1163/2014 of the European Central Bank of 22 October 2014 on supervisory fees (ECB/2014/41) [2014] OJ L311/23–31

D. The End of the Single Passport: The Exclusive Competences of the ECB

The transfer of exclusive competences in banking supervision to the ECB was at the core of the SSM. The ECB was entrusted with the large part of the supervisory competences provided by EU law to national supervisors as competent authorities. This included, among others, the authorisation of all banks and the withdrawal of their licence in the jurisdiction of the SSM, ensuring compliance of credit institutions with prudential requirements, supervisory review, supervision on a consolidated basis, supervision of branches from credit institutions authorised in the EU, supplementary supervision of a financial conglomerate, early intervention measures, limits to compensation of managers, administrative sanctions, and imposing structural changes in banks. For the exercise of these competences, the ECB had the specific powers provided in the SSM Regulation, as well as all the powers provided by EU banking law – directives or regulations – to national competent authorities. Therefore, the ECB became the competent authority for banking supervision in each Member State of the SSM, thus replacing national supervisors.[105]

The implication of the ECB's exclusive competences for the single financial market was the end of the single passport framework. The principles of home-country control and mutual recognition no longer applied regarding those competences. The credit institutions became subject to the supervision of a single supervisor, independently of the extent of their cross-border business through subsidiaries or branches. The SSM led, in this context, to a substantial unification of banking law through its single interpretation, application, and enforcement, as well as the direct judicial review of the Court. Moreover, besides supervisory decisions, the ECB had the powers to issue guidelines and recommendations, as well as regulations, over both banks and national supervisors, and subject to the full body of the banking law of the single market. This was the first time that a European institution applied such a multi-layered body of law, including European laws, national laws, as well as the non-binding acts of a European agency such as the EBA.[106]

However, this also challenged the principle of the primacy of European law since the ECB's legal acts applied not only European law, but also national law transposing directives, which cannot prevail over acts of a European institution. It led to the situation where the ECB took over the role of the national authorities and had to consider national laws in its decisions and exercise of regulatory powers. In cases where the application of EU banking law would not be sufficient for the ECB to conduct effective

[105] Art 4.1, SSM Regulation. The tasks not transferred to the ECB remained with national competent authorities, including – as recalled by Recital (28) of the SSM Regulation – supervising credit institutions from third countries establishing a branch or providing cross-border services in the EU, supervising payment services, carrying out day to day verifications of credit institutions, and supervise credit institutions in relation to markets in financial instruments, consumer protection and anti-money laundering and terrorism financing.

[106] Art 4.3, SSM Regulation explicitly provided that the ECB should apply Union law, including the national law transposing directives, the national legislation exercising options provided in European regulations, the Commission's delegated and implementing acts under Arts 290 and 291, TFEU, as well as the non-binding EBA's single supervisory handbook.

banking supervision, the ECB could give instructions to national authorities to make use of their powers to support the SSM's tasks.[107]

The exclusive supervisory competences of the ECB led, therefore, to a radical change in the legal regime of the single financial market. The principles of home-country control and mutual recognition, which were at the heart of the framework of the single passport, were no longer applicable. As intended by the Euro Summit, the SSM banks were basically removed of their 'nationality' in order to break the vicious loop between sovereigns and banks. The banks were 'Europeanised' in the sense that the competences for their licensing, for ensuring compliance with EU law in their activities, and for closing them down, became exclusive to a European authority. The judicial review by the Court was substantially expanded as a result. There was a total centralisation of European competences.[108]

E. The Fusion of the Competences of the ECB and National Authorities

The system of competences of the SSM, which combined the competences of the ECB and national authorities in banking supervision, was another institutional innovation.

The starting point for this system was the fact that Article 127.6 of the TFEU could only confer supervisory competences upon the ECB itself. It could not provide the basis for also attributing competences to national supervisors. This represented one important difference with the central banking tasks under Article 127.2, which are to be 'carried out through the ESCB' comprising the ECB and the national central banks. The supervisory tasks are instead 'conferred upon the ECB'. This implied that national supervisors would have been divested of large part of their responsibilities. It also meant that the ECB alone would be exclusively responsible for the supervision of the whole SSM banking system. Such a sudden centralisation of competences previously entrusted in the euro area to more than 20 national authorities regarding around 6,000 banks would have been, in the least, challenging. It would also have been not proportional to dismiss the expertise of national supervisors, as well as their local involvement in the economic and legal context of each Member State.[109]

[107] See Arts 9.1 and 18.5 SSM Regulation. Recital 34 of the SSM Regulation states that the application of national law by the ECB is without prejudice to the principle of the primacy of Union law.

[108] The Court confirmed that the exclusive competences of the ECB – in the case at stake regarding the approval of the acquisition of a qualifying holding in a credit institution – preclude national courts from reviewing the legality not only of EU legal acts, but also of decisions to initiate procedures, preparatory acts or non-binding proposals adopted by national competent authorities. See Judgment of 19 December 2018, *Fininvest*, C-219/17, EU:C:2018:1023, paras 44, 58 and 59.

[109] There were also political preferences for preserving the national supervision of purely domestic institutions. See N Véron, 'Europe's Single Supervisory Mechanism: most small banks are German (and Austrian and Italian)' (2014) *Bruegel Blog Post*, at bruegel.org/2014/09/europes-single-supervisory-mechanism-most-small-banks-are-german-and-austrian-and-italian. For an account of the policy dynamics in the transfer of banking supervision competences, see RA Epstein, and M Rhodes, 'States ceding control: explaining the shift to centralized bank supervision in the eurozone' (2016) 17 *Journal of Banking Regulation* 90.

Conceivably, there were three institutional options for involving national supervisors in the conduct of supervision by the ECB. The first was to follow the model of the ESCB, where decision-making is centralised in the decision-making bodies of the ECB, with executive national decentralisation for the implementation of decisions. This option would still require the ECB to take all supervisory decisions regarding all the euro area banks, but the implementation would be left to national authorities. A second option would be to enable the ECB to delegate the implementation of its supervisory tasks to national authorities, as appropriate. The third option was to adopt a dual banking model, similar to the US system of banking supervision. In this model, there is a coexistence of two regulatory structures: the banks are chartered and regulated either at the national or state level, with corresponding different regulatory authorities, laws and standards. In Europe, this would be translated by a two-tier system, where banks could choose a licence at either the European or national level. Although institutionally feasible, this option could raise questions regarding its compatibility with the framework of the single financial market. The banks in the top tier would benefit from enhanced freedom to provide services, since they would report to a single supervisor, or be perceived as safer than national banks if they would have privileged access to direct recapitalisation by the ESM.[110]

The SSM Regulation combined elements of the above three options. This included decentralisation of operational tasks, preservation of tasks with national authorities within a framework akin to delegation, and aspects resembling a dual banking model. This combination led in practice to a 'fusion' within the SSM of the competences of the ECB and national authorities, thus creating a sui generis institutional system of banking supervision.

The decentralisation mechanism consists of a distinction between 'significant' and 'less significant' banks within the SSM. The purpose was to enable the ECB and the national authorities to have supervisory competences of a different nature with regard to each category of banks. The exclusive competences of the ECB regard the direct supervision of the banks and banking groups, which are considered 'significant'. This includes the banks with total assets above €30 billion, or with a ratio of total assets over the GDP of the domestic economy of above 20 per cent GDP, and also the three largest banks in each Member State. The ECB can add more banks on the basis of their cross-border relevance or domestic significance, in this latter case at the request of a national supervisor. The banks receiving direct or indirect assistance from the EFSF/ESM should also be subject to the ECB supervision.[111]

The scope of 'significant bank' is quite broad. It goes beyond that of 'systemic bank', which is associated with the potential of a bank to cause significant disruption to the financial system. Instead, the criteria set in the SSM Regulation aimed at transferring to the exclusive supervision of the ECB the largest part of the banking sector of the SSM

[110] On the debate on whether the US system of banking regulation should be followed by the EU, see LD Wall, M Nieto, and DG Mayes, 'Creating an EU-level supervisor for cross-border banking groups: Issues raised by the US experience with dual banking' in JR LaBrosse, R Olivares-Caminal and D Singh (eds) *Managing Risk in the Financial System* (Cheltenham, Elgar, 2011) 333.

[111] Art 6.4, SSM Regulation.

jurisdiction, including a proportional share of the banking sector in each Member State. In addition, the inclusion in these criteria of those banks with more than one subsidiary in another SSM Member State, or major cross-border activities, implied that all banks using the single passport to a relevant extent are supervised by the ECB.

The national authorities, on the other hand, supervise the banks considered 'less significant'. Since Article 127.6 of the TFEU could not confer supervisory competences upon national authorities, the SSM Regulation carves out from the exclusive competences of the ECB a list of tasks regarding the day-to-day supervision of less significant banks. These tasks are not transferred to the ECB but remain with the national supervisors. This was a framework akin to a delegation in practice, if not in law.[112]

The national supervisors supervise 'less significant' banks on the basis of the regulations, guidelines or general instructions of the ECB, in order to ensure the consistency of supervisory outcomes within the SSM. The ECB also defines the instances where national supervisors are obliged to notify any material supervisory procedure and draft decisions. Most importantly, the ECB can, at any time, decide to exercise directly itself all the supervisory powers for one or more banks, when it deems it necessary to 'ensure consistent application of high supervisory standards'. This was the most explicit element of delegation, since the ECB, not only defines the manner in which the national tasks are performed, but can also, at any time, take over such tasks as if they were delegated temporarily to national authorities.[113]

Lastly, the ECB can request the assistance of national supervisors for the supervision of 'significant' banks, including that they prepare draft decisions for the Supervisory Board. This enabled some degree of decentralisation for the performance of specific executive tasks, such as implementing a decision of the Supervisory Board. In specific cases, the ECB can also give instructions to national supervisors to make use of their powers under national law, when such powers are not available to the ECB as a competent authority under EU law, for example in the case of the imposition of penalties on natural persons under national law.[114]

The Court, however, challenged this interpretation of the SSM Regulation, namely, that the ECB is competent for the direct supervision of 'significant' banks, while the national authorities remain competent for the direct supervision of 'less significant' banks. The Court concluded that, in accordance with Article 4(1) of the SSM Regulation, the ECB has exclusive competence over the whole banking system, including both 'significant' and 'less significant' institutions. This would mean that the national authorities assist the ECB in implementing its exclusive competences both with regard to 'significant' and 'less significant' institutions. For the reasons mentioned above, the Court's interpretation is hard to conciliate with the legal basis of Article 127.6 of the TFEU, which would not enable to entrust national authorities with decision-making powers on banking supervision, other than administrative assistance to the ECB. The explanation for the ability of national authorities to take supervisory decisions directed

[112] Art 6.5(a), SSM Regulation.
[113] Art 6.5(b), SSM Regulation.
[114] Arts 6.5(a) and 18.5, SSM Regulation.

at 'less significant' institutions is that they remain competent for their direct supervision, albeit under the oversight of the ECB.[115]

Soon after the Court's judgment, the German Constitutional Court also provided its interpretation of the system of competences in the SSM. It argued instead that national authorities exercise their powers of 'less significant' institutions on the basis of their primary competences of national law, not on the basis of powers conferred by the ECB, but subject to the ECB's control. Otherwise, a delegation of powers by the ECB would not be allowed by Article 127(6). Furthermore, the German Constitutional Court also considered that entrusting the ECB with supervision of all banking institutions would exceed the limits of European integration and remove economic governance from Member States.[116]

All in all, this judicial debate reflects the sui generis nature of the system of competences of the SSM regarding the involvement of the ECB and national competences. It is essentially a legal and institutional innovation to enable the creation of the SSM in a proportional manner with the available legal basis. This is why the concept of 'fusion' of European and national competences, but subject to the exclusive control of the ECB as affirmed by the Court, is used here to depict this novel framework.

F. The Parallel Competences of the SSM for European and National Financial Stability

The SSM Regulation also provided a framework of parallel competences whereby both the ECB and the national authorities may exercise macro-prudential tasks and activate the respective instruments provided by European law. This was in order to reflect both the European and national dimensions in financial stability. For example, an asset price bubble may occur either as a European-wide trend or a specific national development. This was the rationale for retaining the competence of national authorities to safeguard financial stability in their respective jurisdiction and for enabling the ECB to safeguard it at the European level.[117]

The macro-prudential competences of the ECB should be exercised at two levels. First, there is an obligation of national authorities to consult the ECB on national macro-prudential decisions based on European law, to which the ECB can object. The national authorities need to consider the objection, but are not pre-empted from proceeding with the decision. Second, the ECB may also apply macro-prudential requirements – for

[115] See Judgment of 8 May 2019, *Landeskreditbank*, C-450/17 P, ECLI:EU:C:2019:372, para 37, confirming the previous Judgment of the General Court of 16 May 2017, *Landeskreditbank*, T-122/15, EU:T:2017:337.

[116] See the Banking Union judgment of the German Constitutional Court, BVerfG, Urteil des Zweiten Senats vom 30 Juli 2019, 2 BvR 1685/14, Rn. (1-320), at www.bverfg.de/e/rs20190730_2bvr168514.html.

[117] At the same time, the macro-prudential competences of the ECB were also justified by the need to coordinate the national activation of macro-prudential instruments, such as the imposition of capital buffers, which often have the same nature as the banking supervision tools of the ECB. The main difference between micro- and macro-prudential instruments is that the former are calibrated to ensure the safety and soundness of each bank, while the latter are mainly set from a systemic perspective. See C Borio, 'Towards a macroprudential framework for financial supervision and regulation?' (2003) 128 *BIS Working Papers*.

all SSM Member States or a specific one – but in an asymmetric manner: it can only set higher requirements than those applied by national authorities. This may be interpreted as including the possibility of setting macro-prudential requirements when the national authorities have not acted and set none.

The ECB can also decide on macro-prudential instruments on its own initiative or at the request of a national authority for its own Member State. When acting on its own initiative, the ECB has to notify the national authorities before the decision and take into account any objection. When acting on request of a national authority, the ECB may consider extending the macro-prudential measure which is proposed for one Member State also for others.[118]

This system of parallel competences operates therefore within a framework based on the mutual consultation of ECB and national authorities. It bears some resemblances to the parallel competences in competition law, with the main difference that the ECB cannot pre-empt, as the Commission can, the actions of national authorities. By contrast, it is a constraining framework to the extent that the ECB may go beyond national authorities, thus preventing any 'race to the bottom' or passivity in macro-prudential supervision.

The SSM Regulation introduced, therefore, two institutional innovations in this context. First, it entrusted explicitly a European institution with financial stability powers. This had been prevented in the past stages of integration by the fact that such powers were hard to justify under Article 114 of the TFEU, and also because they were associated with national fiscal sovereignty. Second, it introduced parallel European and national competences for financial stability, thus also striking an institutional compromise between the centralisation of banking supervision competences at the ECB and the remaining national dimension of financial stability.

G. A Centralised but not Federal System of Competences

The SSM is a multi-layered system of European and national competences, but where national competences are integrated and conducted within a common institutional framework. It may be interpreted, at first sight, as a federal system, with a division of tasks and powers between the centre and the national level. In reality, it is rather a compressed system of competences where the ECB has centralised responsibility and control over all of its parts. It represents, in this sense, a fusion of European and national competences, instead of a two-tier system, such as the dual banking system of the US referred to above.

First, all banks in the jurisdiction of the SSM are subject to the exclusive competence of the ECB regarding the authorisation and withdrawal of their licence. There is no distinction for this purpose between 'significant' and 'less significant' banks, which implies that there are no different banking charters at European or national levels. This brings unity to the system, since all banks are Europeanised. Another important difference is that the banks cannot choose between being considered 'significant' or 'less

[118] Art 5, SSM Regulation.

significant' since this depends on the criteria set out in the SSM Regulation and on the supervisory discretion of the ECB.[119]

Second, the ECB may decide to exercise itself the supervision of 'less significant' banks when necessary to ensure high supervisory standards, thus removing the competence of national authorities regarding specific banks. This sort of 'call-back clause' could appear as an exercise of pre-emption powers, but it is rather a power of European intervention to preserve the unity and integrity of the supervisory system.[120]

Third, all banks are subject to the same law, the European banking law, which is applied by both the ECB and national authorities. This is also one of the areas of innovation stemming from the SSM framework of competences. The SSM, including the ECB and national authorities, will apply the same body of law, albeit with mixed nature, including both directly applicable EU law and national law transposing directives. However, the SSM will be subject to two different judicial jurisdictions: the Court of Justice for decisions taken by the ECB regarding 'significant' banks, and national courts for decisions taken by national supervisors regarding 'less significant' banks.

H. A Complex System of Centralised Competences

The establishment of the SSM marked the start of the Banking Union. It represented the first legal and institutional spillover of the Monetary Union for the single financial market. Its features reflected the compromise made among many objectives.

The SSM was created to address the sovereign debt crisis by separating banks from their respective sovereigns. At the same time, it aimed at addressing the structural flaw of the Monetary Union that banking supervision remained at the national level. Furthermore, the SSM had to be put in place quickly and effectively, which required activating the enabling clause of Article 127.6 to entrust banking supervision powers at the ECB. As the next step, the exercise of such powers by the ECB had to be separated from the conduct of monetary policy, due to moral hazard concerns. Then, once banking supervision powers were exercised by an institution of the Monetary Union, it was also important to preserve the integrity of the single financial market and its single rulebook. This implied devising mechanisms to have an SSM as inclusive as possible and subject to the whole body of European rules. At the same time, the SSM had to take into account that the banking institutions are relevant for financial stability, not only at the European, but also national levels. Lastly, the SSM also had to involve national authorities in the conduct of supervision, in order to have recourse to their local expertise and operational resources.

The result of pursuing at the same time all these objectives was a unique and unprecedented juxtaposition of European and national competences in the SSM, which defies any clear definition or categorisation. The matrix of competences includes, at least, the following layers: (1) the exclusive competences of the ECB regarding the supervision of 'significant' banks; (2) the national competences regarding the supervision of the 'less significant' banks; (3) the possibility for the ECB to take over the supervision of these

[119] Art 6(4), SSM Regulation. See *Landeskreditbank*, (n 115) para 37.
[120] Art 6(5)(b), SSM Regulation.

'less significant' banks from national supervisors; (4) the oversight competences of the ECB over national supervisors, including the powers to give instructions; (5) the parallel competences of the ECB and national authorities regarding financial stability; and (6) also the powers of the ECB to impose directly supervisory fees on banks.[121]

VI. The Second Pillar of the Banking Union: The Single Resolution Mechanism

A. The Emergence of a Global Bank Resolution Regime

The bailout of banks by the state was the default response to the crisis in Europe and globally. There were at least three reasons for this.

First, there was no bank resolution regime, which addressed the functions of banking institutions compared to other commercial companies. This includes the functions that banks play in the economy and the financial system, providing payment services, and other banking services. The disruption in the performance of these functions would, not only affect economic activity, but also give rise to contagion throughout the financial system via interlinkages among banks, markets and market infrastructures. Moreover, banks are especially vulnerable to financial disturbances. Their main function is 'maturity transformation': converting short-term deposits into long-term loans. This implies that banks do not have sufficient funds to repay depositors at all times, for example in the case of a bank-run. In the absence of a framework that addressed these functions, a bail-out with public money would be preferable than the costs of a bank failure for the economy and thus the taxpayers.

Second, there was no resolution regime for dealing with the cross-border implications of a bank failure. This had two aspects. On the one hand, the failure of a bank with significant cross-border operations would lead to disruptions in several jurisdictions, economies and financial systems. Uncoordinated national governments, authorities and insolvency laws could also exacerbate in an unpredictable manner the costs of a bank failure for all affected, which again could exceed the costs of a bailout. On the other hand, it followed that national authorities had incentives to minimise their respective costs in the event of the failure of a cross-border bank. Banking assets would be ring-fenced in a crisis along national borders, so that they would not be used to compensate creditors in other jurisdictions. This could also make the bailout of a bank with cross-border operations the least costly option.[122]

[121] This is why Art 2(9), SSM Regulation defined the SSM as 'the system of financial supervision composed by the ECB and national competent authorities of participating Member States'. In this sense, the SSM goes beyond even the ESCB in integrating national authorities into a European system of competences, which the Court had already considered as a 'novel legal construct in EU law', see Judgment of the Court of 26 February 2019, *Rimšēvičs v Latvia*, C-202/18, EU:C:2019:139, para 69. For a first overview of the SSM, see E Ferran and VSG Babis, 'The European Single Supervisory Mechanism' (2013) 13 *Journal of Corporate Law Studies* 255; and an assessment of the experience with the SSM, see D Schoenmaker D and N Véron, 'European banking supervision: the first eighteen months' (2016) 25 *Bruegel Blueprint Series*.

[122] See D Schoenmaker, 'Banking supervision and resolution: the European dimension' (2012) 6 *Law and Financial Markets Review* 52.

Third, and most importantly, banks were bailed out due to their size and the role they played in national economies and financial systems. This related to the too-big-to-fail problem (TBTF), the fact that banks had reached such a size and complexity that their failure could not be managed without leading to economic, financial and social costs that would far exceed the costs of a bailout. It implied that banks benefited from an implicit public subsidy, which created a 'moral hazard' in the management of risks. It also meant that the public finances of states were made weaker by potential liabilities for the banking sector. This was particularly so in Europe, where the single market framework and Member States promoted cross-border banking and 'national champions', as analysed before. This created a mutual dependence between banks and states, which reached its peak in the sovereign debt crisis.

In 2010, the FSB put forward the objectives of a resolution regime following the financial crisis. First, it would make feasible the resolution of any financial institution, without making taxpayers exposed to losses from solvency support. Second, it would protect vital economic functions. Third, it would include mechanisms to enable shareholders, unsecured and uninsured creditors to absorb losses in their order of seniority. Such 'bail-in' would replace the need for bailouts.[123]

These principles were turned into global regulatory standards by the 2011 FSB 'Key Attributes of Effective Resolution Regimes for Financial Institutions' to be implemented in all jurisdictions. The FSB's Key Attributes had two requirements from jurisdictions. First, to introduce resolution regimes for all financial institutions that may have systemic significance. Second, to create a resolution authority entrusted with a broad range of resolution powers. The resolution process should be initiated when an institution is no longer or likely to be no longer viable, and before it is insolvent and its equity is wiped out. Authorities can then exercise their resolution powers and deploy their tools. These include the ability to operate and resolve the institution to restructure and wind down its operations, such as replacing the management, buying and selling assets, terminating contracts, writing down debt, imposing a moratorium, or transferring assets and liabilities.[124]

The most relevant resolution tools included the ability to set-up a bridge institution to take over the critical functions of a financial institution. This addressed one of the main concerns of a bank failure, the possibility that critical functions are interrupted, with wider damage to the economy and the financial system. The other tool is the power to carry out the bail-in of equity and unsecured and uninsured creditor claims to the extent necessary to absorb the losses of the institution. This replaced the possibility of a bailout with public funds, to the extent that the institution has loss-absorption capacity. For this purpose, the FSB introduced later standards for institutions to maintain the so-called TLAC (Total Loss Absorbing Capacity) in the form of capital requirements. The prevention of bailouts was also achieved by requiring jurisdictions to have privately

[123] See FSB, Reducing the moral hazard posed by systemically important financial institutions (2010), which was endorsed by the G-20 Summit in Seoul, in November 2010, at www.fsb.org/wp-content/uploads/r_101111a.pdf.

[124] See FSB, Key Attributes of Effective Resolution Regimes for Financial Institutions (2011), at www.fsb.org/publications/r_111104cc.pdf, which were endorsed by the G20 Summit in Cannes, November 2011.

financed deposit insurance and resolution funds to provide temporary financing to the resolution of the institution.[125]

The final component of the FSB's resolution framework was the requirement that systemic financial institutions have recovery and resolution plans, also known as 'living wills'. The plans aimed at enabling the resolution of the firm, while protecting critical functions and avoiding a bailout with public funds. The resolution authorities then carry out regular 'resolvability assessments' to ensure that resolution is feasible.[126]

In conclusion, the rationale that underpinned the bank resolution regime, which emerged from the financial crisis, was to minimise the possibility that public funds had to be used to rescue a bank. The aim was to enable a bank failure as close as possible as to any other commercial company. This implied concentrating the costs on the owners and creditors of banks, without creating systemic implications. The resolution of a bank had to be feasible, without implications for financial stability, and without the use of public funds.

The FSB's framework for a global resolution regime was widely implemented. In the US, the Dodd-Frank Act established a resolution framework for systemic financial institutions, with the Federal Deposit Insurance Corporation (FDIC) as the resolution authority. In the EU, the BRRD transposed the framework, with the SRM as the resolution authority of the Banking Union.[127]

B. The Bank Recovery and Resolution Directive: The Resolution Stages

The BRRD was largely based on the FSB's Key Attributes. It reflected in addition the experience with the banking and sovereign debt crises, such as with the burden-sharing requirements in the Commission's state aid decisions, as well as the restructuring of the Cypriot banking sector with the bail-in of bank liabilities as a resolution tool. The BRRD aimed at introducing a regime to resolve banks in a manner that would preserve financial stability and without resorting to public funds. This required creating resolution authorities, equipping them with tools to wind down or restructure a bank, providing them with the powers to bail-in liabilities, and setting up private financing

[125] FSB, Principles on Loss-absorbing and Recapitalisation Capacity of G-SIBs in Resolution (2015), at www.fsb.org/wp-content/uploads/TLAC-Principles-and-Term-Sheet-for-publication-final.pdf.

[126] FSB, Policy Measures to Address Systemically Important Financial Institutions (2011), at www.fsb.org/wp-content/uploads/Policy-Measures-to-Address-Systemically-Important-Financial-Institutions.pdf.

[127] Dodd-Frank Wall Street Reform and Consumer Protection Act 2010, at www.gpo.gov/fdsys/pkg/BILLS-111hr4173enr/pdf/BILLS-111hr4173enr.pdf; Directive 2014/59/EU of the European Parliament and of the Council of 15 May 2014 establishing a framework for the recovery and resolution of credit institutions and investment firms and amending Council Directive 82/891/EEC, and Directives 2001/24/EC, 2002/47/EC, 2004/25/EC, 2005/56/EC, 2007/36/EC, 2011/35/EU, 2012/30/EU and 2013/36/EU, [2014] OJ L173/190–348 (henceforth, BRRD); and Regulation (EU) No 806/2014 of the European Parliament and of the Council of 15 July 2014 establishing uniform rules and a uniform procedure for the resolution of credit institutions and certain investment firms in the framework of a Single Resolution Mechanism and a Single Resolution Fund and amending Regulation (EU) No 1093/2010, [2014] OJ L225/1–90 (henceforth SRM Regulation).

arrangements for resolution. For this purpose, the mechanics of the BRRD were based on the distinction between three stages.[128]

The first stage is preparatory to ensure the 'resolvability' of the credit institution or banking group. This concept is defined as being feasible and credible for the resolution authority to liquidate or resolve an institution or group, while preserving financial stability and ensuring the continuity of critical functions. In line with the FSB framework, the BRRD lists extensively the contents of resolution plans to ensure 'resolvability', such as measures to separate the critical functions of the bank to enable a 'bridge bank', or the minimum required for eligible liabilities subject to the bail-in tool. The plans must be prepared by all supervised institutions and groups and reviewed annually by the resolution authorities. In the case of groups, the BRRD allows the choice between the planning of the resolution at the group level, corresponding to the 'single point of entry' approach, or at the level of each entity, corresponding to the 'multiple point of entry'. If the authorities find that 'resolvability' is not ensured, they have extensive powers to require the institution or group to take measures to restore it, including limiting or ceasing activities, changing corporate structure, or issuing eligible liabilities for the purposes of bail-in.[129]

The second stage is the early intervention in a bank. The BRRD provides a minimum common set of tools to address the deterioration of a bank, including more intrusive powers than foreseen at the level of most Member States. When a bank meets certain triggers, such as reaching a level of capital of only 1.5 per cent above own funds requirements, the supervisory authorities can take early intervention measures to prevent or prepare for resolution. These measures include requiring implementation of the recovery plan, such as negotiating a restructuring of debt, removing the management from the bank, and appointing temporary administrators with powers to restore the financial condition of the bank. The early intervention stage is similar to the concept of 'prompt corrective action' in the US.[130]

The third stage is bank resolution. A bank necessarily enters into resolution if it is determined as 'failing or likely to fail' (FOLTF) by the supervisor or the resolution authority. The FOLTF determination will be made if a bank infringes regulatory requirements leading to a withdrawal of authorisation, including incurred or likely to be incurred losses depleting own funds. It will also happen if the assets of the bank are less than its liabilities, and if the bank is unable to pay its debts or other liabilities as they fall due. Most importantly, a bank will also be determined as FOLTF if it requires extraordinary public financial support.[131]

[128] Art 31, BRRD. See European Commission, Staff Working Document, Impact Assessment, SWD (2012) 166 final, at 12–ff.

[129] Arts 15 to 18, BRRD. The provision of emergency liquidity assistance by the central bank cannot be assumed in the concept of 'resolvability'. Arts 5 and 6 of the BRRD also require the preparation of 'recovery plans', which aim at preventing that institutions and groups fall into resolution by having measures to restore viability in case of financial stress.

[130] Arts 27 to 30 BRRD. The concept of 'prompt corrective action' in the US enables the supervisor to intervene in a bank to minimise the potential loss for the Deposit Insurance Fund once the capitalisation of a bank reaches certain levels. The main difference with 'early intervention' is that 'prompt corrective action' is mandatory when the conditions are fulfilled, rather than discretionary as in the BRRD. See US Code, Title 12, Chapter 6, § 1831o.

[131] Art 32(1) and 4, BRRD.

Once a bank is determined FOLTF, the resolution process starts. In this context, the BRRD opted for a 'mixed resolution model'. The resolution authorities may exercise their powers through either 'executive orders' or 'special management' of the bank. Under the former, the resolution authority adopts executive orders addressed to the bank. At the limit, this may lead to the expropriation of shareholders and creditors without their approval. Under the latter, the resolution authority appoints a special manager of the bank, which assumes all the powers of the shareholders and the management body. The special manager takes the resolution measures, as decided by the resolution authority. This is akin to the 'receivership model' in the US, whereby the FDIC takes control of an institution.[132]

The resolution tools provided by the BRRD, in addition to bail-in analysed below, include the following. First, the sale of the business or shares of the institution under resolution. The resolution authority has the power to transfer the ownership of the institution and any of its assets, rights, or liabilities, to a purchaser, without the consent of the owners or any other party. The transfer should be made on commercial terms, subject to state aid rules. The proceeds revert to the owners or to the institution in the case of sale of assets or liabilities. It is the closest tool to that most commonly used in the US, namely 'purchase and assumption', which enables the FDIC to arrange the sale of a failed bank to another institution. The second resolution tool is the setting-up of a bridge institution. The ownership of the institution under resolution and any of its assets, rights or liabilities is transferred to a new legal entity, which is under the control of the resolution authority and under public ownership. This enables part of the institution to remain under 'going concern', instead of 'gone concern', and critical functions to continue to be performed by the bridge institution. It provides time to sell the institution under resolution, but it cannot exceed two years. The third is the asset separation tool. It enables the transfer of assets from an institution under resolution or from a bridge institution to a 'bad bank'. This tool does not aim at maintaining critical functions, but to dispose of assets later in time if their immediate liquidation, for example, would have an adverse effect on financial markets or lead to lower prices.[133]

The first resolution decision within the framework of the BRRD was taken by the Banco de Portugal on 3 August 2014 regarding the Banco Espírito Santo, which provided the basis for a bridge institution denominated as 'Novo Banco'.[134]

[132] Art 35, BRRD. For a comparison of models of resolution, see European Commission, Staff Working Document, Impact Assessment, SWD (2012) 166 final, at 79.

[133] See Arts 38 to 41 BRRD on the resolution tools. See Title II ('Orderly Liquidation Authority'), Sections 201 to 217, Dodd-Frank Wall Street Reform and Consumer Protection Act, Pub. L. 111–203 (2010). For an analysis, see JN Gordon and WG Ringe, 'Bank Resolution in the European Banking Union: A Transatlantic Perspective on What it Would Take' (2014) 115 *Columbia Law Review* 1297; and for an overview of the resolution toolbox, see JH Binder, 'The Relevance of the Resolution Tools within the Single Resolution Mechanism' in MP Chiti and V Santoro (eds) *The Palgrave Handbook of European Banking Union Law* (Cham, Palgrave Macmillan, 2019) 299–320.

[134] Banco de Portugal, Comunicado do Banco de Portugal sobre a aplicação de medida de resolução ao Banco Espírito Santo, S.A. (2014) at www.bportugal.pt/comunicado/comunicado-do-banco-de-portugal-sobre-aplicacao-de-medida-de-resolucao-ao-banco-espirito. For an analysis of this resolution case, see LS Morais, 'Lessons from the First Resolution Experiences in the Context of Bank Recovery and Resolution Directive' in MP Chiti and V Santoro (eds) *The Palgrave Handbook of European Banking Union Law* (Cham, Palgrave Macmillan, 2019) 371.

C. The Prohibition of Bank Bailouts and Mandatory Bail-In

The wide definition of FOLTF is instrumental for achieving the aims of the BRRD, notably preventing the use of public funds to rescue a bank in difficulties. The fact that a bank will enter into resolution if public financial support is ever required, implies a prohibition of resorting to public funds. Any bank that cannot restore its financial condition, without its own means or private financial sources, will enter into resolution or be liquidated.

There is a very strict exception, whereby the FOLTF can be avoided if the public support provided to a bank is necessary to remedy a serious disturbance in the economy of a Member State and preserve financial stability. However, in order to avoid the determination of FOLTF, such public support has to fulfil a long sequence of conditions: (i) it can only be provided to solvent banks; (ii) it has to be approved by the Commission under the state aid framework; (iii) it has to be precautionary and temporary in nature; (iv) proportionate; and (v) cannot be used to offset losses that the institution has incurred or is likely to incur in the near future. Moreover, public support in the form of capital injections can only be provided to address capital shortfalls identified in stress tests or asset quality reviews conducted by the ECB, EBA or national authorities.[135]

Therefore, capital support, which was the most widely used instrument to address the banking crisis in 2008, cannot be provided to banks in financial difficulties, but only as a precautionary measure to solvent banks and not to offset real financial losses. This is why the FOLTF concept is decisive to introduce the bailout prohibition, thus turning resolution and bail-in as the rule.[136]

The bail-in of shareholders and creditors of the failing institution is the core resolution instrument introduced by the BRRD, which precludes the bailout with public funds. It is not an alternative to the other resolution tools. It is mandatory to recapitalise the institution under resolution, in order to restore its viability and capital requirements, or to provide capital to a bridge institution, support the sale of the business, or the asset separation. The bail-in tool is implemented by the powers of the resolution authority to reduce to zero eligible liabilities or convert them into shares, to cancel debt instruments, and to reduce to zero and to cancel shares or other instruments of ownership of institutions under resolution.[137]

The starting point for bail-in is to determine the amount of eligible liabilities that need to be written down or converted into shares to achieve its purpose. This amount is then allocated to shareholders and creditors on the basis of a sequence, or 'liability cascade', which matches the degree of risk and liability of investors. This is based

[135] On this concept, see N Véron 'Precautionary recapitalisation: time for a review?' (2017) 21 *Bruegel Policy Contribution*.

[136] Art 32, BRRD. The application of state aid rules remained relevant in the Banking Union despite the prohibition of bailout in the BRRD: even if there is an exception under the BRRD allowing precautionary public support of a bank, the state aid rules lead to restructuring and burden-sharing requirements in the form of bail-in of shareholders and subordinated creditors, in line with the Commission's Banking Communication (n 39), but not as extensive as under the BRRD. For a critical analysis, see C Hadjiemmanuil, 'Bank Resolution Financing in the Banking Union' (2015) 6/2015 LSE Legal Studies Working Paper.

[137] See Arts 43 and 44 as well as Art 63(1)(e), (f), (g) and (h), BRRD. For an analysis of these provisions see KP Wojcik, 'Bail-in in the Banking Union' (n 39).

on the *pari passu* treatment of creditors and the statutory ranking of claims under insolvency law. The sequence starts with writing down shares and other Common Equity Tier 1 items. If insufficient, it is followed by writing down or converting into equity Additional Tier 1 and then Tier 2 instruments, subordinated liabilities, other eligible liabilities, including uninsured deposits from large corporates, up to uninsured deposits of SMEs and natural persons. The insured deposits are the last in the sequence, but they are exempted from bail-in. The deposit guarantee schemes have, however, to make a contribution to resolution in the amount of the deposits which otherwise would have been written down as a result of the bail-in.[138]

The effectiveness of the bail-in tool is supported by a minimum requirement for own funds and eligible liabilities (MREL). Banks are obliged to maintain a certain amount of capital and debt instruments, which will be subject to bail-in in case of resolution. The resolution authorities determine the MREL for each institution as a percentage of its total liabilities and own funds, based on several criteria, including its resolvability, size, business model, and risk profile. As a result, the costs of banks in obtaining capital and issuing debt will increase given the risk of bail-in. Before the BRRD regime, banks benefitted from an implicit public subsidy based on the assumption of a public bailout.[139]

The main safeguard of shareholders and creditors against bail-in is the 'no creditor worse off' principle (NCWO): the value of their property rights over the bank in resolution should not fall below the amount, which would have been reached if the bank had been subject to insolvency proceedings. Therefore, the permissible bail-in should be calculated ex ante by resolution authorities on the basis of the hypothetical outcome of an insolvency. If an ex post independent valuation finds that the NCWO principle has not been respected, the shareholders and creditors should be compensated for the difference. Accordingly, the NCWO principle is the main justification for the legitimacy of bail-in vis-à-vis the constitutional protection of property rights.[140]

The key objective of the BRRD was, therefore, to prohibit the use of public funds to bailout a bank. The recapitalisation or the absorption of losses should be relying to the

[138] Arts 46(1) and 48(1), BRRD. According to Art 44(3) and (4), BRRD, the resolution authority may, on an exceptional basis, exclude bail-in regarding specific liabilities, for example, when bailing in deposits of natural persons or SMEs would disrupt financial markets or cause a serious disturbance to the economy of a Member State. In these cases, the losses born by the liabilities excluded are passed on to other creditors or covered by resolution funds. See also Art 109, BRRD on the use of deposit guarantee schemes.

[139] Art 45, BRRD. The revision of the BRRD and the SRM Regulation in 2019 – the so-called BRRD 2 and the SRM Regulation 2 – implemented the FSB's TLAC standards in Europe by imposing a minimum MREL on the European 'G-SIIs' (global systemically important banks), in order to ensure that they are resolvable despite their size and complexity. For this purpose, this legislation introduced a new category of 'top-tier' banks, which are subject to the same requirement as G-SIIs as long as they have more than €100 billion in total assets or are considered by the SRB to pose a systemic risk in case of failure. Directive (EU) 2019/879 of the European Parliament and of the Council of 20 May 2019 amending Directive 2014/59/EU as regards the loss-absorbing and recapitalisation capacity of credit institutions and investment firms and Directive 98/26/EC, [2019] OJ L 150/296–344; and Regulation (EU) 2019/877 of the European Parliament and of the Council of 20 May 2019 amending Regulation (EU) No 806/2014 as regards the loss-absorbing and recapitalisation capacity of credit institutions and investment firms [2019] OJ L 150/226–252.

[140] Arts 73 to 75, BRRD. On the NCWO principle, see C Goodhart and E Avgouleas, 'A Critical Evaluation of Bail-ins as Bank Recapitalisation Mechanisms' (2014) *Centre for Economic Policy Research, Discussion Paper 10065*; and J Zhou, V Rutledge, W Bossu, M Dobler, N Jassaud, and M Moore, 'From Bail-out to Bail-in: Mandatory Debt Restructuring of Systemic Financial Institutions' (2012) SDN/12/03 *IMF Staff Discussion Note.*

largest extent possible on private investors. The use of public funds is permitted before an institution enters into resolution within the above mentioned concept of 'precautionary recapitalisation', but only when it is necessary to preserve financial stability, and limited to covering capital shortfalls resulting from stress tests. Another possibility is the provision of 'extraordinary public support' to an institution already under resolution through government financial stabilisation tools. The support in the form of an injection of capital or temporary nationalisation is allowed, subject to state aid rules, to avoid the liquidation of a bank, and when the resolution tools would not suffice to safeguard financial stability.[141]

In conclusion, the innovation of the BRRD was to introduce a new regulatory function in the single financial market: banking resolution. For this purpose, it was the first time that European law provided for instruments to affect the private property of shareholders and creditors, up to the expropriation and write down of their claims over a bank. Moreover, it provided a wide degree of discretion to the resolution authorities to affect property rights, depending on their assessment, for example, of the implications for financial stability and the economy of a Member State. This is subject to a number of safeguards to preserve fundamental rights, notably the NCWO principle. However, it certainly represented a much more intrusive legal regime than ever before in the single financial market.[142]

D. Overcoming 'Meroni'? The Single Resolution Board

The SRM provided the institutional framework to apply the BRRD in the jurisdiction of the Banking Union. It comprised a Single Resolution Board (SRB) for centralised decision-making and a Single Resolution Fund (SRF) for financing resolution, which is owned by the SRB.[143]

The SRB is the resolution authority of the Banking Union, which was established as an EU agency with legal personality. It adopts the resolution plans and takes all decisions on resolution regarding the 'significant' banks supervised directly by the SSM as well as the 'less significant' banks when the resolution decision requires the use of the SRF.

The SRB decisions take the form of a 'resolution scheme', which places the bank into resolution. There are three conditions for resolution: (1) the bank should be considered

[141] Arts 56 to 58, BRRD. The US also introduced via the Dodd-Frank Act a prohibition of bailouts of investment banks, see 15 US Code § 8305 – Prohibition against Federal Government bailouts of swaps entities. The Dodd-Frank Act prevented the Federal Reserve as well from providing emergency lending to individual banks and to insolvent banks. Emergency lending has to be authorised by the Treasury and should be limited to the provision of liquidity and programmes and facilities to relieve liquidity pressures in financial markets. See s 13(3) of the Federal Reserve Act.

[142] After the entry into force of the BRRD, the management of the problems in the banking sector had to be made on the basis of private liability. One of the main examples was the establishment in June 2016 by Italian banks of the 'Atlante' fund to finance the non-performing loans of the Italian banking system. See M Lamandini, G Lusignani, D Ramos Munoz, 'Does Europe Have What It Takes to Finish the Banking Union?' (2017) 24 *Columbia Journal of European Law* 233.

[143] See GS Zavvos and S Kaltsouni, 'The Single Resolution Mechanism in the European Banking Union: Legal Foundation, Governance Structure and Financing' in M Haentjens and B Wessels (eds) *Research Handbook on Crisis Management in the Banking Sector* (Cheltenham, Elgar, 2015) 117–149.

as FOLTF on the basis of an assessment by the ECB or by the SRB if the ECB does not act; (2) no prospect of a private sector solution; and (3) the resolution should be necessary in the public interest, otherwise it should be liquidated. The 'resolution scheme' also determines the specific resolution tools and the use of the SRF. The national resolution authorities are then required to implement the resolution tools in accordance with the national laws transposing the BRRD in their jurisdiction.[144]

The establishment of the SRM raised several legal and institutional questions relating to its legal basis, decision-making powers, and the financing of the SRF.[145]

The first question was, yet again, whether Article 114 of the TFEU could provide the legal basis for the establishment of the SRM and, within it, the SRB. As analysed extensively until now, Article 114 is a 'harmonisation clause', which does not provide the legal basis for the regulation as such of the single financial market. Instead, as stated by the Court in several instances, it can only provide the basis for the process of harmonisation of national laws for the completion of the single market. Therefore, the establishment of the SRM and the SRB had to be justified as a harmonisation technique of the single financial market.[146]

The SRM Regulation provided three arguments for being based on Article 114. First, the SRM was introduced as part of the harmonisation process of the single financial market in the field of banking resolution, together with the BRRD. The decisions of the SRB were harmonising measures, since the uniform application of resolution rules in the Banking Union requires a central authority. Second, the SSM is only effective if complemented by the SRM, in order to avoid divergent implications of supervisory rules in case of resolution. Third, uniform resolution rules, as well as equal conditions of resolution financing, supports financial stability. This, in turn, facilitated the functioning of the single financial market.[147]

The second question was whether Art 114 provided the legal basis to circumscribe the jurisdiction of the SRM to that of the Banking Union, ie the euro-area Member States and those in close cooperation with the SSM. While the boundaries of the Banking Union stemmed from the Monetary Union, Article 114 applies to all Member States, as well as under Article 52 of the TEU, whereby EU law applies uniformly in the Union. The legal technique used by the SRM Regulation was to define its scope of application, not in relation to Member States, but largely with regard to the significant banks subject to the jurisdiction of the SSM. This avoided the need for any derogation of a

[144] Arts 18(6) and 23, SRM Regulation.

[145] The legal basis of the SRM was so controversial at the time that two opinions of the Council Legal Services dealing with such question were disclosed by the *Financial Times*. See *Financial Times*, 'Blow to German banking union plan,' 12 September 2013; and 'Setback for Brussels as lawyers warn on banking union plans,' 8 October 2013.

[146] See Judgment of the Court of 2 May 2006, *ENISA*, C-217/04, EU:C:2006:279, at para 42; and Judgment of 10 December 2002, *British American Tobacco*, C-491/01, EU:C:2002:741, para 60. Furthermore, in Judgment of the Court of 6 December 2005, *Smoke Flavourings*, C-66/04, EU:C:2005:743, para 41, the Court considered that Art 114, TFEU also confers discretion to the legislature as to the most appropriate harmonisation technique.

[147] The German Constitutional Court in its Banking Union Judgment also concluded that the establishment and the competences entrusted to the SRB fall sufficiently within the scope of Art 114, TFEU in line with the European Court of Justice's case law. See the Banking Union judgment of the German Constitutional Court, BVerfG, Urteil des Zweiten Senats vom 30 Juli 2019, 2 BvR 1685/14, Rn. (1-320), at www.bverfg.de/e/rs20190730_2bvr168514.html.

Member State from the SRM Regulation. Instead, the SRM Regulation was designed as complementing the framework of the SSM, which remained as the institutional anchor of the Banking Union. The banks subject to the SSM became a specific legal category for the purposes of the SRM Regulation, independently of the Member State where they were located.[148]

The third question was whether the SRB, which had been established as an agency, could be entrusted with decision-making powers on bank resolution, which are wide-ranging in nature. They include drawing up the resolution plans of banks and setting the MREL in the preventive phase. In the resolution phase, they include assessing whether the conditions for resolution are met regarding a specific bank, placing a bank under resolution, and selecting the resolution tools and the extent of their application, notably in the case of the bail-in. There are also sanctioning powers, in the form of pecuniary sanctions.

These powers involve a wide margin of discretion and judgement, depending on the circumstances surrounding the resolution cases. They go beyond the clearly defined executive powers underpinning the *Meroni* doctrine. First, resolution decisions can have distributive implications, since they may affect property rights. For example, deciding on the extent of bail-in, such as excluding certain liabilities to preserve financial stability, implies safeguarding the property rights of some to the detriment of others. Second, given the discretion involved, the sequence of decisions leads to the definition of a resolution policy at the European level. The principle of equal treatment implies that each resolution decision will create a precedent and define the policy for successive cases across banks and Member States. Third, the resolution decisions will have implications for financial stability and economic policy in Member States, thus potentially on fiscal sovereignty.[149]

The nature and range of bank resolution powers implied, therefore, that they could not be vested as such on the SRB as a European agency, which was not grounded in the Treaty like the ECB. They required the involvement of the European institutions which may exercise implementing powers, in accordance with Article 291 of the TFEU. This led to a convoluted decision-making process involving the SRB, the Commission and the Council. When the conditions for resolution are met, the SRB should adopt a resolution scheme. However, the Commission has 24 hours to endorse or object to the discretionary aspects of the resolution scheme. Alternatively, the Commission has 12 hours to propose to the Council to object on the basis that the public interest criterion for resolution is not fulfilled. The SRB has then eight hours to modify the scheme accordingly.[150]

In order to address the limits imposed by the *Meroni* doctrine, the SRM Regulation thus introduced a decision-making system involving the Commission and the Council in the areas outside the scope of delegation of powers. The Commission assesses and controls the discretionary aspects of the resolution decisions taken by the SRB.

[148] See Recital (18) and Art 2, SRM Regulation.

[149] On the view that the powers of the SRB infringe the *Meroni* doctrine, see P Lintner, 'De-centralised decision making under the European Resolution Framework: does Meroni hamper the creation of a European Resolution Authority?' (2017) 18 *European Business Organization Law Review* 591.

[150] Recital (24) and Art 18(7), SRM Regulation. On the negotiations between Member States leading to this decision-making process, see P Schlosser, *Europe's Fiscal Union* (Palgrave, 2019), at 133–165, highlighting the reluctance of Germany to transfer to the European level competences with fiscal implications.

The Council, upon proposal by the Commission, controls whether the public interest criterion for resolution is fulfilled in SRB decisions. This was justified by the fact that resolution decisions may impinge on financial stability, which in turn may also lead to fiscal consequences.[151]

Finally, the need to exercise resolution powers in a swift and unconstrained manner justified that resolution decisions were taken by executive session of the SRB – comprising the Chair and four full-time members as well as the Commission and the ECB as observers – rather than the plenary session with representatives from national resolution authorities. The SRB was therefore established as a unique European agency, which was empowered to take discretionary decisions, with a potential fiscal impact, and without depending on a decision-making body comprising representatives from national authorities.[152]

The first resolution decision of the SRB regarded Banco Popular on 7 June 2017, following a FOLTF decision by the ECB. The decision involved the bail-in and sale of the business to Banco Santander, since this was considered in the public interest to protect depositors and ensure financial stability.[153]

Figure 4 The Decision-Making Process of the SRB

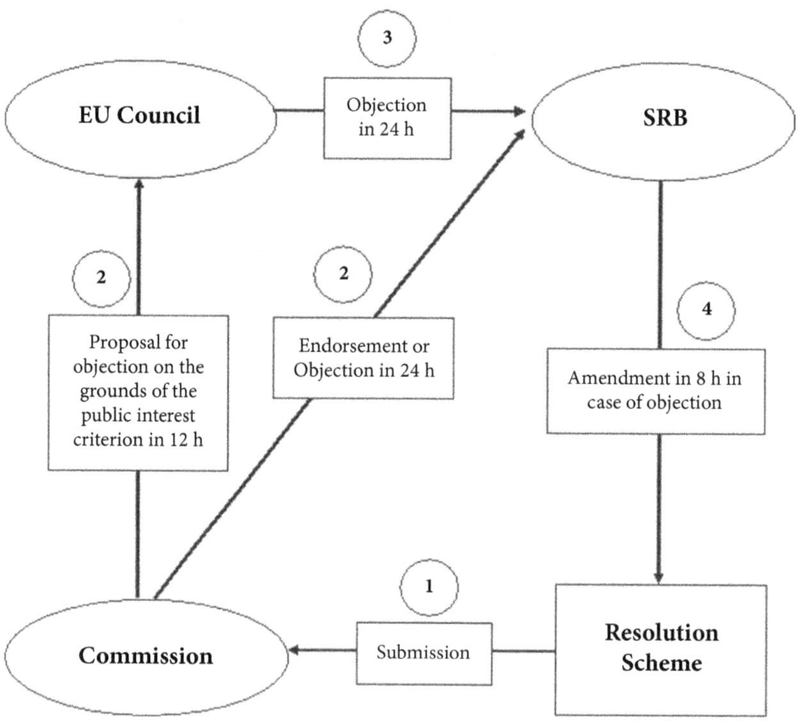

[151] The decision-making powers of the SRB were further constrained by the criteria and conditions that the Commission may set through delegated acts under Art 93, SRM Regulation.

[152] These include the approval of resolution plans, the determination of the MREL obligations, and the preparation of resolution schemes. See Arts 50 1(c) and 54, SRM Regulation.

[153] SRB Decision to take resolution action in respect of Banco Popular Español, S.A. (2017/C 222/05), [2017] OJ C 222/3; and Commission Decision (EU) 2017/1246 of 7 June 2017 endorsing the resolution scheme

E. The Start of the Mutualisation of Risks: The Single Resolution Fund

The SRF is the other component of the SRM. It replaced the national resolution funds of the Members States of the Banking Union and is owned and managed by the SRB. It aims at financing the resolution actions taken by the SRB, including providing loans and guarantees, and to cover losses or recapitalise a bank under resolution or a bridge bank. It is supported by annual levies on the banks subject to the SRM, which are raised by national resolution authorities and are calculated on the basis of their respective size of liabilities and risk-profile. The SRF should reach by 2024 a target level of financial means amounting to 1 per cent of the covered deposits of all banks in the Banking Union (around €55 billion).[154]

The SRF operated the first mutualisation of risks in the Banking Union: funds collected on a mandatory basis from banks located in each Member State were pooled together in a European fund in order to finance the resolution of banks located in any of the Member States of the Banking Union. Member States also agreed to transfer their existing resolution funds and the levies raised from banks in their jurisdictions to the SRF.

In this context, at the time of the negotiations of the SRM Regulation, it was discussed whether the establishment of the SRF would constitute the exercise of budgetary powers. If so, Article 114 of the TFEU could not provide the legal basis. Instead, the establishment of the SRF would require the unanimity of Member States to allocate the SRF to the Union under Article 311 of the TFEU on the 'own resources of Union'. In order to address these concerns and establish the SRF on the basis of Article 114, without impinging on the integrity of national fiscal sovereignty, the SRM Regulation included a number of safeguards.

First, the SRM Regulation started by introducing the general principle that decisions or actions of the SRB, the Council or the Commission shall neither require Member States to provide extraordinary public financial support nor impinge on the budgetary sovereignty and fiscal responsibilities of the Member States. This aimed at insulating the functioning of the SRB, including the use of the SRF, from fiscal liabilities. If the SRF ever required additional financial means, it should obtain them from the banks via extraordinary contributions, or borrow at commercial terms from financial institutions or other parties. At the limit, Member States or the ESM may provide bridge financing to the SRF against repayment by the banking sector. However, the SRM Regulation explicitly forbids any expenses to be borne by the budgets of the Union or Member States.[155]

for Banco Popular Español S.A. (notified under document (2017/C 4038), [2017] OJ L178/15. The previous decisions of the SRB regarding FOLTF declared by the ECB did not lead to resolution, since this was not considered to be in the public interest. See SRB Decision concerning the assessment of the conditions for resolution in respect of Veneto Banca SpA (2017/C 242/02); and Decision concerning the assessment of the conditions for resolution in respect of Banca Popolare di Vicenza SpA (2017/C 242/03), [2017] OJ 242/2 and 242/3, respectively. See also SRB, Press Release, 'The Single Resolution Board does not take resolution action in relation to ABLV Bank, AS and its subsidiary ABLV Bank Luxembourg S.A.,' 24 February 2018, at srb.europa.eu/en/node/495.

[154] Art 67, SRM Regulation.

[155] Art 6(6) and Art 73(3), SRM Regulation, and also Recital (13) of EU Council, Agreement on the transfer and mutualisation of contributions to the Single Resolution Fund (2014) at register.consilium.europa.eu/doc/srv?l=EN&f=ST%208457%202014%20INIT.

Second, the SRF can only be deployed when at least 8 per cent of a bank's total assets is bailed-in. Even in such cases, the SRF contribution cannot exceed 5 per cent of the total liabilities of the bank under resolution. This ensures that the SRF is only used at the last instance, after the claims of shareholders and creditors have been exhausted. In other words, the bailout prohibition of the BRRD was extended to the use of the SRF.

Third, there is a set of procedural safeguards in the decision-making process leading to the use of the SRF. The Council can object to the use of the SRF or to certain amounts, and the plenary session of the SRB has to approve the use of the SRF with a majority including national members representing at least 30 per cent of the contributions to the SRF.

Finally, the use of the SRF is subject to 'fund aid' control by the Commission. While the use of the SRF does not qualify as state aid as such, since no public funds are involved, the Commission is able to control – on the basis of the same criteria as for state aid – whether the use of the SRF is incompatible with the internal market by benefitting an undertaking and distorting competition. The use of the SRF has to be notified to the Commission, which can decide to impose conditions or oppose the use of the SRF. This decision can, in turn, be pre-empted by the Council if, upon application by a Member State, it votes by unanimity that the use of the SRF is, after all, compatible with the internal market.

All these safeguards as to the use of the SRF demonstrate how far-reaching the bailout prohibition is interpreted and implemented in the Banking Union. It encompasses the SRF, which pools the funds raised from bank levies and not from taxpayers. And it includes the control of the SRB decisions on the use of the SRF, despite being a European authority. This aims at dispelling any concern that the use of the SRF can ever evade the spirit of the bailout prohibition. It reflects the reluctance of Member States to transfer to the European level powers to allocate the distribution of funds of any semblance to public funds.[156]

These safeguards helped to justify the SRF as part of the harmonisation process for bank resolution, in order to establish it on the basis of Article 114. The SRF was presented as an essential element of the SRM, since a centralised system of resolution requires a single funding system. Otherwise, the coexistence of national resolution funds would distort competition in the internal market. This also safeguards financial stability in the single market, which is a condition for market integration.[157]

The use of Article 114 was also challenged as the basis for the bank levies raised at the national level for the SRF. The question was whether such levies corresponded to the exercise of taxation powers. It was argued that the banks were financing a service provided to themselves, namely, the resolution actions that safeguard financial stability as a collective good. The bank levies were therefore more akin to insurance premiums

[156] The levy imposed on banks for funding the SRF was challenged before the German Constitutional Court, which considered in its Banking Union Judgment that such levy falls within the scope of Art 114, TFEU and does not impinge on the budgetary responsibility of German Parliament. See the Banking Union judgment of the German Constitutional Court, BVerfG, Urteil des Zweiten Senats vom 30 Juli 2019, 2 BvR 1685/14, Rn. (1-320), at www.bverfg.de/e/rs20190730_2bvr168514.html.

[157] Recital (19), SRM Regulation.

pooled in the SRF as an insurance fund. This was not unprecedented in European law, considering the supervisory fees as a payment for the services provided by the SSM, and the cases where some agencies are financed by the fees of the users.[158]

Ultimately, Article 114 provided the legal basis for the imposition of the bank levies. However, as a harmonisation clause, Article 114 could not impose on Member States the obligation to transfer and mutualise bank levies at the European level. The solution found, similarly to the mutualisation of funds in the EFSF and the ESM, was the adoption of an intergovernmental agreement. The Member States of the Banking Union committed to a progressive mutualisation of the national resolution funds and bank levies. The amounts raised in each Member State would first be allocated to 'national compartments'. The funds in each compartment would then be used to finance the resolution of a bank located in the corresponding Member State, before other compartments could be used, and up to a certain percentage. Every year, the amounts to be used from other national compartments would increase until their complete mutualisation in 2024.[159]

The progressive mutualisation of the 'national compartments' in the SRF was introduced in order to prevent funds collected from the banks in one Member State from being used immediately to finance the resolution of banks in other Member States. The mutualisation of funds had to progress in tandem with the development of the Banking Union, ie with the gradual 'Europeanisation' of banks. Until then, the link of banks with their respective sovereign had to be further severed. Otherwise, the argument went, the SRF could create moral hazard for Member States and their banks not to reduce risks in banking activity in the expectation of benefitting from a fully mutualised SRF.[160]

In conclusion, the SRF was created to further reinforce the bail-out prohibition introduced by the BRRD. It guaranteed that bank resolution did not give rise to budgetary liabilities of Member States, since it was financed by the banks themselves. In turn, this provided a collective good to the financial system in the form of financial stability. Moreover, there were a number of safeguards to ensure that the SRF could only be used at the last instance: the decision-making process of the SRB, the involvement of the Commission and the Council in this process, and culminating in the 'fund aid' control.

F. The Direct Recapitalisation of European Banks

The rationale of the Banking Union was to break the link between banks and sovereigns. The first step to break that link was the decision at the Euro Summit of 29 June 2012

[158] For example, the Office for the Harmonisation of the Internal Market. See Art 139 of Council Regulation 207/2009 on the Community trademark ([2009] OJ L78/1).

[159] Arts 70 and 71 SRM Regulation. See Recital (7) of the EU Council, Agreement on the transfer and mutualisation of contributions to the Single Resolution Fund. See F Fabbrini, 'On banks, courts and international law: the intergovernmental agreement on the Single resolution fund in context' (2014) 21 *Maastricht Journal of European and Comparative Law* 444.

[160] See D Howarth and L Quaglia, 'The Steep Road to European banking union: Constructing the Single Resolution Mechanism' (2014) 52 *Journal of Common Market Studies*, 52, 125, 128–132.

to enable the ESM to recapitalise directly banks in the euro area. As analysed above, this decision was conditional on the establishment of the SSM, in order to match the European banking liability with the European banking supervision.

One year later in 2013, the Eurogroup announced the conditions for the direct recapitalisation of euro area banks: it should be indispensable to safeguard the stability of the euro area or the Member State, with specific conditions for the bank receiving and the Member State requesting the recapitalisation.[161]

The bank would need to be systemic, in breach of capital requirements, and without being able to attract private capital, while remaining viable on the basis of an economic valuation. The Commission would need to approve the assistance and impose conditionality under state aid rules. The ESM could also impose additional conditions on the bank, such as restrictions on the remuneration of the management and bonuses. The bank would be supervised by the ECB, as provided by the SSM Regulation. The Member State requesting the assistance would need to be unable to provide it itself without endangering fiscal sustainability or the access to the market for public debt. It would also need to agree on a MoU, which would include, not only the conditionality on the bank, but also on the economic policies of the Member State. Furthermore, the Eurogroup introduced a burden-sharing scheme between the ESM and the Member State. The Member State had to make a capital contribution of 20 per cent of the capitalisation requested from the ESM, which would go down to 10 per cent after two years of the entry into force of the new ESM financial instrument. The justification was the existence of legacy assets from the financial and sovereign debt crises, which had to be covered in a proportionate manner by the Member State concerned. Over time, this burden-sharing scheme would be reviewed, as the progress in the Banking Union would allow matching European control and liability for banks.[162]

These Eurogroup conditions were further reinforced more than another year later in 2014, in an ESM Guideline on direct recapitalisation. It provided that the financial assistance would require an MoU detailing the policy conditions applicable to the requesting Member State, which could relate to its financial sector and to its general economic policy. Such conditionality would then be monitored by the Commission, in liaison with the ECB, the ESM, and the IMF. The requesting Member State would also be considered as experiencing or threatened by serious difficulties regarding financial stability under the SGP, and thus subject to enhanced surveillance by the Commission. Furthermore, the ESM Guideline also incorporated the bail-in regime under the BRRD and the SRM Regulation: direct recapitalisation could only be provided to a bank under resolution, and it could only be used after the bail-in of 8 per cent of the total liabilities

[161] Eurogroup, ESM Direct Bank Recapitalisation Instrument: Main features of the Operational framework and way forward, Luxembourg, 20 June 2013, at www.consilium.europa.eu/uedocs/cms_data/docs/pressdata/en/ecofin/137569.pdf. The statement set an initial limit of €60 billion and required the ESM to set-up a subsidiary and sub-subsidiary structures for recapitalisation in order to provide transparency on the specific risk-taking regarding each Member State and each bank in case of direct recapitalisation.

[162] In all circumstances, the Member State had to cover fully the capital required for the bank to reach the legal minimum of 4.5% of Common Equity Tier 1 (CET1) under a stress-test, if necessary. After this step, the Member State would have to cover the difference to reach the 20% or 10% of the overall required recapitalisation of the bank. See Eurogroup, ESM Direct Bank Recapitalisation Instrument: Main features of the Operational framework and way forward (n 161).

of the bank, a contribution of the SRF in the amount of 5 per cent of the total liabilities, and a further bail-in of all unsecured liabilities.[163]

The decision to enable the direct recapitalisation of banks that stood at the origin of the Banking Union was thus ultimately reversed a year later by this series of conditions. Direct recapitalisation became the last resort measure, in the very unlikely case of returning a bank under resolution to viability after an extensive bail-in of liabilities and the maximum contribution of the SRF. Direct recapitalisation would also not exempt the Member State where the bank was based from being subject to policy conditionality and enhanced surveillance. While the direct recapitalisation would prevent a transfer of banking liabilities into national finances, it would still impose strict macroeconomic policy conditions on a Member State. This aimed at addressing any possible moral hazard that a Member State could have in free-riding the European liability for bank recapitalisation. These conditions reduced considerably the scope for such direct recapitalisation to be ever requested at all.

The possibility of direct banking recapitalisation by the ESM was then later formally revoked by the agreement at the Euro Summit of 14 December 2018 to provide a common backstop to the SRF in form of a revolving credit line by the ESM.[164]

G. The Privatisation of Risks in the Banking Union

The Banking Union was originally founded on the transfer to the European level of the safety net provided by the state to the banking sector in the form of solvency support. The national liability would be replaced by the joint liability of Member States underpinning the direct recapitalisation by the ESM. This was justified by safeguarding economic and financial stability, which had become a European collective good as a result of the financial and sovereign debt crises. Together with the establishment of the SSM, this would Europeanise the banking sector by disconnecting it from both the liability and control of Member States.

Ultimately, with the BRRD and the SRM, there was no transition from national liability to the joint liability of Member States. The public safety net for the banking sector was removed, rather than transferred to the European level. Rather than a mutualisation of the risks in the Banking Union, there was a privatisation of such risks. Bail-in of shareholders, creditors and depositors became mandatory. It was the first time that European law introduced a regime that had such a direct bearing on property rights. The SRB could decide on the extent to which such rights could be written down or converted in order to resolve a bank. The privatisation of risks was further implemented

[163] ESM Guideline on Financial Assistance for the Direct Recapitalisation of Institutions, 8 December 2014, at www.esm.europa.eu/about/legal-documents/index.htm. See also Regulation (EU) No 472/2013 of the European Parliament and the Council of 21 May 2013 on the strengthening of economic and budgetary surveillance of Member States in the euro area experiencing or threatened with serious difficulties with respect to their financial stability, [2013] OJ L140/1.

[164] The ESM would provide a backstop to all possible uses of the SRF, including liquidity provision. See Statement of the Euro Summit, 14 December 2018, and ESM, Draft Board of Governors Resolution for Annulment of the Direct Recapitalisation Instrument, all at www.consilium.europa.eu/media/41671/20191206-draft-bog-resolution-3-annulment-of-the-dri.pdf.

with the establishment of the SRF, which is funded by bank levies. Any remaining risks of losses after bail-in should be borne by the banks themselves. The involvement of the SRF is subject to a mandatory percentage of bail-in and 'fund aid' control. And the mutualisation of national resolution funds and bank levies is made only gradually over eight years.[165]

The main drivers for this move towards the privatisation of risks in the Banking Union were threefold. First, the global and European political will to prevent bailouts of banks. Second, the urgency in managing the sovereign debt crisis by breaking the link between the euro area Member States and their banks. Third, the political resistance to transfer national competences which could impinge on fiscal sovereignty, including any joint liability of Member States. This resistance was compounded by national constitutional constraints, particularly in Germany, and the absence of a legal basis in the Treaty to mutualise funds.

Therefore, the banking risks were not mutualised in the Banking Union but privatised. European control of the banks did not translate into European liability but into private liability. This also justified the introduction of the bail-in rules under European law interfering with private property. This was a Copernican move compared to the generalised recourse to taxpayer funds to address the 2008 financial crisis. Instead of transferring fiscal sovereignty to the European level to address banking risks, the Member States preferred to remove fiscal sovereignty from the equation altogether. It implied also removing one of the previous instruments available to the state to stabilise markets – the use of budgetary funds. This was formalised by the decision of the Euro Summit to replace the possibility of direct recapitalisation by the provision of a backstop to the SRF by the ESM. It was another step in detaching the Banking Union from Member States.[166]

VII. The Third Pillar of the Banking Union: A European Deposit Insurance Scheme

A. The Rationale for EDIS

In November 2015, the Commission put forward a proposal for a European Deposit Insurance Scheme (EDIS), the third pillar of the Banking Union. It was presented as one of the measures for completing the Banking Union, together with the implementation of the BRRD, the common backstop for the SRF, and further risk reduction

[165] The Court clarified in *Kotnik* (n 39) that the burden-sharing requirements under state aid rules – albeit not specifically under the BRRD and SRM Regulation – could not be considered as infringing property rights. For an analysis, see KP Wojcik, 'Bail-in in the Banking Union' (n 39) at 116–ff, who argues that the principle of no creditor worse off is fundamental to justify bail-in, but points to the legal and practical difficulties of operationalising such principle.

[166] As predicted by Christian Joerges, the construction of the single market tended towards its de-linking from the state functions, see C Joerges, 'The Market Without the State? The "Economic Constitution" of the European Community and the Rebirth of Regulatory Politics' (1997) 1–19 *European Integration online Papers*, at eiop.or.at/eiop/pdf/1997-019.pdf.

in the banking sector, notably with the introduction of limits to banks' exposures to sovereigns.[167]

The aim of EDIS would be to ensure equal treatment among depositors throughout the Banking Union, independently of the national location of banks and deposits. The fact that the national deposit-guarantee schemes (DGS) diverged in their features and funding, had several consequences. First, the DGS would not be able to ensure the same extent of coverage of deposits in the case of large shocks. This increased the likelihood of financial instability and bank-runs in those Member States with weaker DGS, which could then propagate to others. Second, such divergences posed obstacles to market integration. The banks whose home-countries had stronger DGS could choose to expand cross-border on the basis of branches, which would remain protected by the DGS of the home-country. Conversely, the banks based on home-countries with weaker DGS would likely need to establish subsidiaries in other Member States in order to provide the same degree of coverage of deposits as local banks, thus being subject to higher entry costs. This undermined competition among banks and gave rise to unequal treatment of depositors within and across Member States. Third, different levels of deposit protection meant that the value of deposited euros varied across Member States. It ran against Monetary Union and the confidence in the single currency, as demonstrated by the Greek banking crisis in July 2015.[168]

The establishment of the SSM and SRM also led to a mismatch of competences with the DGS. The activation of the DGS remained a national responsibility but became largely dependent on decisions exercised at the European level by the SSM and SRM on supervision. In turn, the SSM and SRM could be constrained in their decisions by the weakness of a DGS in covering deposits, since this led to a higher probability of financial instability.

Therefore, EDIS would be instrumental for completing the Banking Union. The divergence among DGS implied that their soundness remained correlated to the sovereign where the bank or the deposits were based, also depending on whether the bank had established cross-border branches or subsidiaries. EDIS would sever this remaining link of the banking sector with Member States by replacing it with a risk-sharing mechanism.[169]

B. The Mechanics of EDIS

The first question regarding the establishment of EDIS was its legal basis. As with the SRF, it was argued by some that a mutualisation of DGS and the imposition of

[167] European Commission, Proposal for a Regulation of the European Parliament and of the Council amending Regulation (EU) 806/2014 in order to establish a European Deposit Insurance Scheme, COM (2015) 0586 final 2015/0270, (henceforth 'Commission proposal on EDIS'); and European Commission, Towards the completion of the Banking Union, COM (2015) 0587 final.

[168] For an early proposal for EDIS, see D Gros and D Schoenmaker, 'European Deposit Insurance and Resolution in the Banking Union' (2014) 52 *Journal of Common Market Studies* 529.

[169] The DGS Directive of 2014 had only reduced pay-out periods and provided for voluntary borrowing between national DGS, instead of mandatory as initially proposed in 2012. See Directive 2014/49/EU of the European Parliament and of the Council of 16 April 2014 on deposit guarantee schemes, [2014] OJ L173/149–178.

levies on banks to finance EDIS would amount to the exercise of fiscal powers. Protecting depositors is a public policy function for safeguarding taxpayers and financial stability. It is not a private insurance arrangement for the benefit of the banks covered by the DGS. According to this line of argument, the harmonisation clause of Article 114 of the TFEU could not again provide the legal basis. Instead, the unanimity of the Member States was required to establish EDIS, possibly on the basis of Article 352 of the TFEU.[170]

The Commission proposed that EDIS would be established nevertheless on the basis of Article 114. EDIS was presented as a central authority, which would ensure the uniform application of the deposit guarantee requirements in Member States. This, in turn, would facilitate the harmonisation process in the single financial market. Furthermore, in the context of the Banking Union, the Commission argued that EDIS was complementary to the supervision by the SSM and the resolution actions by the SRM. There was a mutual dependence between the centralised application of supervision rules, resolution rules, and deposit guarantee requirements. European supervision requires European resolution, and both require a European DGS as part of the harmonisation process of the Banking Union. Moreover, EDIS would provide an insurance mechanism and would not replace national DGS, or require the transfer of national resources.[171]

EDIS would be established under the SRB and supported by a Deposit Insurance Fund (DIF) owned by the SRB. The SRB would combine the functions of banking resolution and deposit insurance in the Banking Union, similarly to the Federal Deposit Insurance Corporate in the US. This would enable synergies between the two functions, which interact in the case of a bank failure. The DIF would insure the DGS and not deposits directly. Similar to the SRF, it would be filled by contributions from banks collected by the national DGS.

The establishment of EDIS would be based on a progressive mutualisation of the insurance of DGS. The first stage was reinsurance and would last for three years. The DGS could have recourse to EDIS once its funds were exhausted. Then, EDIS would cover up to 20 per cent of the liquidity shortfall and absorb part of the final loss of the DGS. The second stage was co-insurance and would last for four years. In this stage, EDIS would cover an increasing share of the liquidity and losses, ranging from 20 per cent in the first year to 80 per cent in the last year. In the final stage of full insurance in 2025, EDIS would cover the liquidity needs and losses of the DGS without limitations. In all stages, the DGS would have to repay to EDIS any funding received, while any excess losses of the DGS would be absorbed by EDIS.[172]

Rather than insuring directly individual deposits, EDIS was, therefore, designed as an insurance scheme to ensure that all DGS would be able to fulfil its commitments to cover deposits up to €100,000. For this purpose, EDIS included a number of safeguards

[170] This line of arguments was first put forward by D Schoenmaker, 'Banking supervision and resolution: the European dimension' (n 122).

[171] Commission Proposal on EDIS, at 8–12. See C Brescia Morra, 'The Third Pillar of the Banking Union and its Troubled Implementation' in MP Chiti and V Santoro (eds) *The Palgrave Handbook of European Banking Union Law* (Cham, Palgrave Macmillan, 2019) 393.

[172] Commission Proposal on EDIS, at 8–12.

to avoid any free-riding, namely that DGS would be underfunded and rely on EDIS rather than on the contributions from its banks.

First, the DGS would have to comply with the DGS Directive, including raising the ex-ante contributions from banks without any reduction in their yearly targets. Second, during the reinsurance and co-insurance stages, the DGS would have to bear part of the costs and potential losses. Third, in the case of pay-out, the DGS would have to maximise the proceeds from an insolvency procedure of the bank in order to repay back to EDIS. If the DGS would not comply with the provisions of the DGS Directive or with EDIS decisions and thus disregard the principle of sincere cooperation, the DGS could be disqualified and no longer be covered by EDIS, upon initiative by the Commission.

The DIF would also be subject to safeguards regarding its use, like the SRF, in order to prevent the circumvention of the bail-out prohibition. Accordingly, the DIF could not give rise to budgetary liability of the Member States and its expenses and losses could not be covered by the Union budget or national budgets. It could only have recourse to contributions from banks via the DGS or borrowings at commercial terms. If the DIF were to be used for bank resolution purposes in line with the SRM Regulation, the Commission had to be notified for 'fund aid' control purposes.[173]

C. Mutualisation of Risks versus Risk Reduction

The proposal for the establishment of EDIS envisaged, therefore, a gradual European insurance mechanism of national DGS, which would ensure equal protection of depositors in the Banking Union. This would match the transfer of banking supervision and resolution competences to the European level. EDIS would then complete the separation between banks and the Member States, which was the objective originally at the heart of the Banking Union.

At the same time, however, EDIS represented another risk-sharing mechanism in the form of the DIF. It aimed at the mutualisation of risks in the Banking Union, in particular, the risks related to the coverage of bank deposits. As with the SRF, there were concerns that EDIS could create moral hazard. Funds originating from banks located in Member States with sound banking systems could end up by being used to cover deposits from weak banks in other Member States. This would reduce the incentives for weak banks to improve their soundness and reduce their risk-taking. For this reason, the Commission proposed the establishment of EDIS together with measures for 'risk reduction', which would limit the scope for moral hazard. This related to the legacy problems lingering from the financial and sovereign debt crises, including the holdings of national sovereign debt by banks.[174]

[173] Art 74a, Commission Proposal on EDIS.
[174] For an overview of the main arguments, see L Schuknecht, 'An insurance scheme that only ensures problems' (2016), at blogs.faz.net/fazit/2016/02/08/an-insurance-scheme-that-only-ensures-problems-7298; and N Véron, 'A Response to Ludger Schuknecht' (2016), at bruegel.org/2016/02/european-deposit-insurance-a-response-to-ludger-schuknecht.

For this reason, the debate about further mutualisation of risks in the Banking Union revolved around the need for further measures for 'risk reduction' in the banking sector. These measures would include reducing the banks' exposures to the public debt of the Member State where they are located, limiting bank leverage, reducing non-performing loans, and further reinforcing the loss absorption capacity of banks. Therefore, the proposal for the establishment of EDIS further confirmed the far-reaching interpretation of the bailout prohibition in the Banking Union. Any form of mutualisation of risks which could entail the distribution of funds across Member States, even with private funding by the banks themselves, and even with regard to deposits and not to the banks, had to be subject to strict safeguards. Risks had to be reduced before being mutualised.[175]

VIII. The Democratic Legitimacy of the Banking Union

A. The Democratic Challenge

Before the Banking Union, in the previous phases of the evolution of the single financial market, there was a very gradually increasing concern about the democratic accountability of increasingly autonomous administrative bodies, particularly after the introduction of the 'Lamfalussy' committees in 2003. Until the financial crisis, accountability was very much limited to reporting official information, such as annual reports to the political institutions, the Parliament and the Council. After the crisis, the establishment of the ESA and the ESRB in 2010 led to a change of gear in the accountability regime. This included the introduction of wider reporting obligations, due process requirements, and a more extensive involvement of the Parliament in overseeing these bodies, including in the appointment of chairpersons.[176]

Democratic accountability became one of the main challenges in establishing the Banking Union. It was the first time that competences so close to national sovereignty were transferred to the European level and out of the reach of national political institutions. This was all the more so, given the role of the banking sector in financing the economy, and as a major source of employment and tax revenue at national level. Before the crisis, the expansion of the banking sector had been equated to economic growth and actively promoted by Member States as a matter of national policy, for example, in the form of 'national champions'. After the crisis, the rescue of banks gave rise to extensive fiscal liabilities and became a threat to national economic and financial stability.

[175] See V Constâncio, Completing the Odyssean journey of the European Monetary Union, Speech at the ECB Colloquium on 'The Future of Central Banking' (2018) at www.ecb.europa.eu/press/key/date/2018/html/ecb.sp180517.en.html. See also O Scholz, 'Germany will consider EU-wide bank deposit reinsurance,' *Financial Times*, 5 November 2019.

[176] See E Wymeersch, 'The European Financial Supervisory Authorities or ESA' in E Wymmeersch, KJ Hopt, G Ferrarini (eds) *Financial Regulation and Supervision: A Post-Crisis Analysis* (Oxford, Oxford University Press, 2012) 232; and, more generally, E Vos, 'Independence, Accountability and Transparency of European Regulatory Agencies' in D Geradin, R Muñoz, and N Petit (eds) *Regulation through agencies: A new Paradigm of European Governance* (Cheltenham, Elgar, 2005) 120–137.

The banking sector had been, therefore, a source of both major benefits and costs for Member States. This is why the conduct of banking supervision often reflected a political preference as to the degree of risk tolerance of a Member State: stricter supervision, with higher capital requirements, would limit the size of the banking sector at the expense of economic growth, but would reduce the probability of bank failures; lighter supervision would support the expansion of the sector, but could give rise to fiscal costs beyond the capacity of the state.[177]

With the Banking Union, national institutions would no longer define the political preferences for the banking sector, either to expand or contain its size. Such preferences would be defined instead by the outcome of the European legislative process and, more importantly, by the day-to-day policy decisions made in the SSM and SRM. This could have significant distributive implications in terms of benefits and costs among Member States, as well as within the single market, particularly in the first years of the Banking Union. For example, stricter supervisory requirements could affect some banks more than others, and hence the national economies where they operate. The prohibition of bailouts by public funds introduced by the BRRD mitigated the extent to which national fiscal sovereignty could be compromised directly by the failure of a bank. However, the resolution of banks, including the use of tools such as bail-in, could impact more on some national economies than others, depending on the structure of the respective banking system. And the management of a banking crisis could also disrupt more the economy of some Member States than others, relative to their degree of dependence on the banking sector. In addition, with single banking supervision and without reliance on national fiscal backstops, banks could have incentives to move location in the single market based on factors such as tax regimes, and thus benefit more or less some national economies.

The Banking Union would, therefore, imply entrusting distributive choices to the European level of the SSM and SRM to an extent without precedent in European law. Competition policy and monetary policy have distributive effects, but they aim at achieving relatively narrow and measurable outcomes defined by the Treaty. At the limit, if there are no distortions of competition in the single market, and if there is price stability in the euro area, no policy measures are needed to achieve such outcomes. The SSM and the SRM would be responsible instead for policy making regarding a whole market, which requires making choices with distributive effects to pursue broad objectives, such as financial stability, albeit within the boundaries of a legislative framework.[178]

Another related challenge was that the SSM and the SRM would be endowed with unprecedented institutional independence. This was justified by the need to insulate

[177] On this trade-off in financial regulation, see C Goodhart et al, *Financial Regulation: Why, How and Where Now?* (London, Routledge, 1998) at 1–38.

[178] On the distributive implications of EU policies and their relevance for the democratic deficit in the EU, see A Follesdal and S Dix, 'Why There is a Democratic Deficit in the EU: A Response to Majone and Moravcsik' (2006) 44 *Journal of Common Market Studies* 533, 542–544. Follesdal and Dix challenge the distinction put forward by Giandomenico Majone between EU policies on the basis of whether they are Pareto-improving or distributive. They argue instead that there is a continuum between policies that are predominantly efficient, such as court decisions, those that are delegated to independent institutions due to the time inconsistency of preferences, such as monetary and competition policies, and the EU policies regulating the single market, which have distributive consequences.

the SSM and the SRM from national political preferences, and also by the fact that the prohibition of the bailout of banks with public funds no longer posed risks to taxpayers' funds. However, in the extreme case of a systemic financial crisis, there would be considerable implications for the financial system and the economy, which would then impact on citizens and taxpayers. This argued for increased democratic control of the Banking Union.[179]

Lastly, the SSM and the SRM would be responsible for managing public funds collected at the European level, namely the fees to finance their own functioning as well as the contributions of banks to the SRF. As discussed, these funds were considered akin to taxes, which would underpin the mutualisation of risks in the Banking Union.

The Banking Union required therefore a new regime of democratic accountability of European policy functions. The question was how to ensure democratic control and provide democratic legitimacy to independent policy functions, which had significant distributive effects both at the national and European levels.[180]

B. Granting Independence to Banking Supervision and Resolution

Monetary policy was already largely an independent function at the national level before EMU. With the establishment of the ECB, central banking independence was elevated to a constitutional principle under the Treaty. Beyond the original reasons for such independence, the justification was to ensure that the ECB would be insulated from national interests. Otherwise, this could undermine the credibility of the ECB in conducting monetary policy in the interest of the euro area as whole, and not of individual Member States.[181]

The transfer of competences from the national to the European level, as monetary policy has shown, is, in itself, the reason for the supranational independence of a policy function. This is particularly so with regard to policies which have distributive effects: if supranational powers are exercised to the benefit of some political units and to the detriment of others, not only do they lose credibility but may also give rise to political disintegration.[182]

[179] See, eg, the arguments made by M Hellwig, 'Financial Stability, Monetary Policy, Banking Supervision, and Central Banking' (2014) *Max Planck Institute for Research on Collective Goods 2014/9*.

[180] See K Nicolaïdis and M Watson, 'Sharing the Eurocrats' dream: a demoicratic approach to EMU governance in the post-crisis era' in D Chalmers, M Jachtenfuchs and C Joerges (eds) *The End of the Eurocrats' Dream: Adjusting to European Diversity* (Cambridge, Cambridge University Press, 2016) 50–77. They conclude that there are two alternatives for the future EMU governance, either a centralised union with constrained political discretion of Member States, or a 'demoicracy' respecting the integrity of national democracies, while enhancing transnational democracy.

[181] Central banking independence was originally justified in the post-war period by the need to avoid political pressures to increase monetary growth or finance governments, which in turn could lead to the type of hyper-inflation of the 1920s. It was also meant to prevent financial and business interests from compelling central banks to provide credit at low interest rates. Later in the 1980s, independence also became associated with the conditions for good economic performance as a pre-requisite for the credibility of central banks in pursuing their inflation objectives. See H James, *Making the European Monetary Union*, (n 91) 271–ff.

[182] Harold James quotes the historical examples of hyper-inflation in Germany in the early 1920s, which promoted separatism in the Rhineland, Bavaria, and Saxony, as these states believed that this was the result of

This rationale applied even more with regard to banking supervision, which, in contrast to monetary policy, was not a fully independent function before the Banking Union. In many countries, it was a function close to or integrated in finance ministries for the reasons mentioned above related to the role of the banking sector in the economy.[183]

With the establishment of the SSM and the SRM, banking supervision and resolution gained an independent status equivalent to that of central banking. The SSM and the SRM Regulations define independence in terms similar to the independence of the ECB under the Treaty. The only distinguishing feature of the SRM is that the members of the executive session of the SRB are required to comply with the decisions of the Council and the Commission, given their involvement in the decision-making process of the SRB.[184]

The transfer itself of banking supervision and resolution to the European level was, therefore, the cause of their broad institutional independence. The distributive effects of these policies required, before the Banking Union, a proximity to the national political institutions. The Banking Union then led to the exact opposite: the insulation of banking supervision and resolution from both national and European politics.

C. A Multilevel and Polycentric Democratic Accountability

The main innovation in the democratic accountability regime of the Banking Union is its multi-level and polycentric nature: for the first time in European law both the Parliament and national parliaments play a role in the accountability of European institutions and bodies.

At the European level, the SSM and the SRB are primarily accountable for the conduct of their tasks to the Parliament and the Council, in line with the principle that accountability for the exercise of European competences is at the level of the EU institutions. The SRB is also accountable to the Commission, given its involvement in the decision-making process.[185]

The accountability to the Parliament includes the appearance of the Chairs of the Supervisory Board and the SRB in hearings and in confidential discussions with the

political pressure from Berlin; as well as Yugoslavia in the 1980s and in the Soviet Union in the early 1990s, where inflation was a factor for demands for regional independence and autonomy. See H James, 'Central banks: between internationalisation and domestic political control' (2010) 327 *BIS Working Papers*, at 15.

[183] Eg, Principle 2 of the Basel Core Principles only required the 'operational independence' of supervision: BCBS, Core Principles for Effective Banking Supervision (2012) at www.bis.org/publ/bcbs230.pdf. On the concept of supervisory independence, see MG Quintyn, S Ramirez, and MW Taylor, 'The Fear of Freedom: Politicians and the Independence and Accountability of Financial Sector Supervisors' (2007) WP/07/25 *IMF Working Paper*, at 34–ff.

[184] Art 19, SSM Regulation, Art 47(1), (2) and (3), SRM Regulation, and, with regard to the ECB's central banking independence, Art 130, TFEU and Art 7 of the ESCB and ECB Statute. See C Zilioli, 'The Independence of the European Central Bank and Its New Banking Supervisory Competences' in D Ritleng (ed) *Independence and Legitimacy in the Institutional System of the European Union* (Oxford, Oxford University Press, 2016) 125.

[185] Art 20(1), SSM Regulation and Art 45(1), SRM Regulation, respectively. See G Ter Kuile, L Wissink and W Bovenschen, 'Tailor-Made Accountability within the Single Supervisory Mechanism' (2015) 52 *CML Rev* 155.

competent Parliament committee. Under Article 226 of the TFEU, the Parliament may set-up committees of inquiry to investigate alleged contraventions or maladministration of the SSM and SRM. The Parliament is also entitled to access confidential information, subject to professional secrecy requirements. The interaction between the Parliament and the SSM and SRB is detailed in two interinstitutional agreements.[186]

The accountability to the Council includes reporting, hearings, and answering questions. The SSM is accountable to the Eurogroup, which should include the Member States outside the euro area in 'close cooperation'. This specific configuration thus gives rise to a new form of political accountability in the shape of the Eurogroup, as an informal body, and in extended composition. This is not explicitly provided with regard to the SRB, which is accountable to the Council. The reason for this difference is likely related to the formal involvement of the Council as an institution in the decision-making of the SRB.[187]

The SSM and the SRB are also required to report to national parliaments of the participating Member States, starting by transmitting annual reports to them. In turn, the national parliaments may ask questions and invite the Chairs of the Supervisory Board or the SRB for hearings, together with the national authority of the Member State in question. The involvement of national parliaments does not correspond to a formal relationship of accountability but more to the provision of information along the lines of Protocol No 1 of the TFEU on the role of national parliaments in the Union. However, it does involve national parliaments in the regular monitoring of the functioning of the SSM and the SRM, thus providing another layer of democratic scrutiny. This reflects the distributive implications of the powers transferred to the SSM and SRM on individual Member States, as acknowledged in the recitals of both the SSM and SRM regulations. The recitals justify the role of national parliaments due to the potential impact that supervision and resolution decisions may have on public finances, institutions, and the markets in participating Member States. At the same time, national supervisory and resolution authorities remain accountable to national parliaments, not only for those tasks not transferred to the SSM and the SRB, such as the supervision and resolution of less significant institutions, but also for those within the SSM and SRM frameworks, including the assistance to the SSM and the SRB.[188]

This multi-level and polycentric accountability framework of the Banking Union thus reflects the unique matrix of competences of the SSM and SRM, which combines

[186] The interinstitutional agreements cover the content of annual reports, organisation of hearings and confidential meetings, access to information, Codes of Conduct, selection procedures of the Chair, investigation procedures, and information to the Parliament on SSM and SRB decisions. See European Parliament, Agreement between the European Parliament and the ECB on the practical modalities of the exercise of democratic accountability and oversight over the exercise of the tasks conferred on the ECB within the framework of the SSM, [2013] OJ L320; and European Parliament, Agreement between the European Parliament and the SRB on the practical modalities of the exercise of democratic accountability and oversight over the exercise of the tasks conferred on the SRB within the framework of the SRM, [2015] OJ L339.

[187] Art 20(3), 20(4) and 20(6), SSM Regulation. See also EU Council, Memorandum of Understanding between the Council of the European Union and the ECB on the cooperation on procedures related to the SSM 11 December 2013, at www.ecb.europa.eu/ecb/legal/pdf/mou_between_eucouncil_ecb.pdf.

[188] Recital (56) and Art 21(3), SSM Regulation, and Recital (43) and Art 46(3), SRM Regulation.

the exercise of European, euro area, and national competences, at various levels and with variable configurations. The framework includes accountability towards a special format of the Eurogroup in the case of the SSM, the Council, the Commission in the case of the SRB, the Parliament, and also national parliaments for the SSM, SRB and national authorities. This is consistent with the variable geographical jurisdiction of the SSM and its various levels of competences. It is also motivated by the distributive effects of banking supervision and resolution in individual Member States. Such effects justify a closer connection than before between the exercise of European competences and national political institutions. This was similar to the economic governance of the euro area, for example, the conference between the Parliament and national parliaments on budgetary issues under Article 13 of the TSCG.[189]

D. A Diffuse Democratic Legitimacy

Without democratic legitimacy, the Banking Union would be based on technocratic governance pursuing market integration purposes, without the control and backing of political institutions. The legitimacy of such governance would be limited to its legal legitimacy, deriving from the legal foundations of the Banking Union, and to its technical or output legitimacy, deriving from the technical expertise and specialisation of the SSM and SRB.[190]

The SSM and SRM regulations addressed this democratic challenge by introducing a framework of multi-level and polycentric accountability. In other words, the answer to provide democratic legitimacy to the Banking Union was to include in the accountability framework all possible political actors, both European and national. This would enable such actors to obtain information from the SSM and the SRB in order to exercise political oversight. This, in turn, would raise the political costs of policy actions by the SSM and SRB, and contain such actions within a democratic framework.[191]

While this approach reflects the complex institutional structure of the Banking Union, it also leads to a diffuse democratic accountability and hence legitimacy. If the policies of the SSM and SRB have to be justified to a multiplicity of European and national political actors, it is hardly conceivable that this will translate into strong democratic legitimacy. The difficult choices made by the SSM and the SRB, for example, in a crisis situation, would likely not be validated democratically by the combination of all

[189] In this sense, see RM Lastra, 'Accountability and Governance: Banking Union Proposals' (2012) 30 *DSF Policy Paper*, at 8–9; and M Everson, 'Banking on Union: EU Governance between Risk and Uncertainty' in M Dawson, H Enderlein, and C Joerges (eds) *Beyond the Crisis: The Governance of Europe's Economic, Political and Legal Transformation* (Oxford, Oxford University Press, 2015) 137, at 154.

[190] See G Majone, '"Europe's 'democratic deficit'": The question of standards' (1998) 4 *European Law Journal* 5, who argues that regulatory policies at the European level can only be legitimised by results, subject to an accountability framework, due to the lack of political integration.

[191] On the logic of accountability related to a system of 'resistance-norms' providing soft limits to public administration, see PL Lindseth, *Power and Legitimacy: Reconciling Europe and the Nation-State* (Oxford, Oxford University Press, 2010) at 22.

these actors. Instead, the legal and technical legitimacy of the institutions of the Banking Union will likely remain its primary source, trumping its democratic legitimacy.[192]

Legal and technical legitimacy would, however, not be sufficient to sustain the Banking Union over time. Democratic legitimacy will be needed for competences leading to significant distributive implications, both at the national and European levels. For example, decisions such as those of the SSM on the failure of a bank, or of the SRB on the bail-in of banks' liabilities, will impose burdens and costs on some and not on others. At the limit, there could be political disintegration if the policies of the Banking Union are not perceived as democratically legitimate and fair.[193]

In this context, the democratic accountability of the SSM was also addressed by the German Constitutional Court. It found that the independence of the ECB and the national supervisory authorities in banking supervision reduces the level of democratic legitimacy, but that this is compensated by the requirements for democratic accountability to both the Parliament and the national parliaments as well as by the constraints posed by the Treaty and the SSM Regulation. This Court also valued the fact that independence would enhance the effectiveness of supervision and protect it against political and corporate interests. Therefore, the German Constitutional Court acknowledged the, arguably, ordoliberal thinking that the supranational market order should be safeguarded from political interference, thus accepting the trade-off between independence and democratic accountability.[194]

Despite the transfer of distributive competences, the Banking Union has thus not provided an answer to democratic legitimacy beyond the recourse to multiple European and national sources of accountability. This confirms that European institutions cannot yet provide the sole basis for democratic legitimacy, which still emanates to a large extent from national political institutions. The lack of a better answer remains the main obstacle for further transferring distributive competences, such as fiscal competences and the issuance of European public debt.[195]

[192] On the weaknesses of the democratic legitimacy of the Banking Union and arguing that accountability cannot compensate for the lack of democratic legitimacy, see C Möllers, 'Some Reflections on the State of European Democracy with Regard to the Banking Union and the ECB' in S Grundmann and HW Micklitz (eds) *The European Banking Union and Constitution: Beacon for Advanced Integration or Death-Knell for Democracy?* (Oxford, Hart Publishing, 2019) 205–218, at 213–218; and D Curtin, 'Accountable Independence' of the European Central Bank: Seeing the Logics of Transparency' (2017) 23 *European Law Journal* 28, at 38–39.

[193] Habermas warns about delaying the democratisation of the EU in order to give precedence to technocratic solutions to sustain the euro: 'This approach harbours the danger of the gap between a consolidation of regulatory competences, on the one hand, and the need to legitimize these increased powers in a democratic manner, on the other, becoming still larger.' See J Habermas, *The Lure of Technocracy* (Cambridge, Polity, 2015) at 12–ff.

[194] See the Banking Union judgment of the German Constitutional Court, BVerfG, Urteil des Zweiten Senats vom 30 Juli 2019, 2 BvR 1685/14, Rn. (1–320), at www.bverfg.de/e/rs20190730_2bvr168514.html.

[195] Peter Lindseth argues that the national legitimation of European public law safeguards key aspects of national legal orders, while nevertheless allowing integration to proceed. Therefore, this may be conceived as a factor for 'integration's longer-term durability and success'. See PL Lindseth, *Power and Legitimacy*, (n 191) at 280. Democratic legitimacy was one of the conditions discussed by an Expert Group for a European public debt redemption fund and eurobills, but could not also offer a better solution than involving both the European Parliament and national parliaments. See G Tumpel-Gugerell, Report of the Expert Group on a Debt Redemption Fund and Eurobills (2014), at ec.europa.eu/economy_finance/articles/governance/pdf/20140331_report_en.pdf, at 69–ff.

IX. The Differentiation Process of the Banking Union

A. The Implications of the Banking Union for the Single Financial Market

The Banking Union abolished large parts of the framework of the single financial market, notably the single passport, since the principles of home-country control and mutual recognition are no longer relevant within it. Harmonisation of national laws is being progressively replaced by directly applicable European law. The legally binding decisions and acts of the ECB/SSM and SRB replace those of national authorities. The role of the EBA, as an agency of the single financial market, is reduced as a result.[196]

The jurisdictional mismatch of the Banking Union divides the single financial market into two blocks. This mismatch was caused by the original legal basis under Article 127.6 of the TFEU, which is a provision relating both to the Monetary Union and the single market. Its activation presupposed the day when the euro area would coincide with the single market. Therefore, without the fulfilment of this condition, the Banking Union was bound to undermine the single financial market, despite the mitigating mechanism of 'close cooperation'. In this context, the Banking Union had a paradoxical effect on the single financial market: it became at the same time more integrated and more fragmented.

First, the banks within the Banking Union were 'Europeanised' in the sense that the competences for licensing, enforcement, and resolution, became exclusive to European authorities. The banks became subject to a single supervisor and a single resolution authority, independently of the extent of their cross-border business. The single passport framework no longer applies, therefore, within the Banking Union.

Second, the Banking Union gave rise to a two-speed single financial market: an inner core subject to a unified system of European law and a single legal authority within the Banking Union; and an outer core comprising those Member States, which remained subject to the single passport framework in the relations between them and with the Banking Union. Market integration will then deepen within the Banking Union, as the provision of banking services faces lower costs and fewer obstacles. Conversely, integration will stabilise or slow down outside the Banking Union, as national authorities and laws still give rise to attrition in the cross-border provision of services. This undermines the unity and inclusiveness of the single financial market, which is no longer single but contains instead a more integrated market within it.[197]

[196] For a comparison between the framework of the single market and that emerging in the Banking Union, which puts emphasis on rule-making, institution building and centralised enforcement, see HW Micklitz, 'The Internal Market and the Banking Union' in S Grundmann and HW Micklitz (eds) *The European Banking Union and Constitution: Beacon for Advanced Integration or Death-Knell for Democracy?* (Oxford, Hart Publishing, 2019) 85–120.

[197] The Banking Union remains, nonetheless, a complex institutional system with juxtaposed European, intergovernmental, and national laws, a multi-layered single rulebook, as well as comprising the action of both European and national authorities. Over time, the sequence of banking supervision and resolution decisions will necessarily increase uniformity and simplify the system. On the risks of this construction for the single market, see N Moloney, 'European Banking Union: assessing its risks and resilience' (2014) 51 *CML Rev* 1609.

The introduction of the Banking Union led, therefore, to legal and institutional differentiation within the single financial market. It includes a variable composition of Member States subject to different legal regimes, a unified legal system, its own European authorities, and the splitting of existing institutions. In this context, the 'Brexit' process can also be partly interpreted as an extreme consequence of the increasing differentiation process within the European Union, of which the Banking Union is one of the main expressions.[198]

B. The Variable Membership of the Banking Union: The 'Close Cooperation' with Member States Outside the Euro Area

The origin of the differentiation created by the Banking Union is the Monetary Union: the perimeter of the jurisdiction of the Banking Union corresponded to the euro area, since its legal basis was the activation of Article 127.6 of the TFEU. The jurisdiction of the SRM then followed that of the SSM. This legal basis gave rise, therefore, to a mismatch between the jurisdiction of the Banking Union and that of the single financial market. The SSM Regulation aimed at mitigating the implications of this mismatch for the integrity of the single market. The solution found was to introduce a new institutional concept in the European law of the single market: the possibility of 'close cooperation' between the national authorities of Member States outside the euro area and the ECB. This would enable the voluntary participation of Member States outside the euro area in the SSM and the SRM.[199]

According to the 'close cooperation' provisions of the SSM and SRM regulations, the Member States from outside the euro area may request to join the SSM and have their banks subject to the supervision of the ECB. The jurisdiction of the SSM and, as a consequence, the SRM, is amplified by the commitment of the Member States that their respective national supervisors will follow the instructions of the ECB. In turn, the national supervisors become members of the Supervisory Board of the SSM in equal terms with those from the euro area. The commitment is, however, purely contractual and not a legal obligation. If a Member State does not comply with the conditions for close cooperation, the ECB may suspend or terminate it. A Member State may also request the ECB to terminate it at any time after three years of its establishment. It leads to the exceptional case that a Member State may opt-in and opt-out, even repeatedly, from a European system of competences.[200]

[198] On the original differentiation created by the Monetary Union and its implications, as materialised under the Banking Union, see JV Louis 'Differentiation and the EMU' in B de Witte, D Hanf, and E Vos (eds) *The Many Faces of Differentiation in EU Law* (Oxford, Intersentia, 2001) 43; and G Majone, 'One market, one law, one money? Unintended consequences of EMU, enlargement, and eurocentricity' (2007) 1/2007 *LSE Law, Society and Economy Working Papers*. On the differentiation of the Banking Union, see T Tridimas, 'The Constitutional Dimension of Banking Union' in S Grundmann and HW Micklitz (eds) *The European Banking Union and Constitution: Beacon for Advanced Integration or Death-Knell for Democracy?* (Oxford, Hart Publishing, 2019) 25.

[199] The 'close cooperation' mechanism is regulated in Art 7, SSM Regulation and Art 4, SRM Regulation.

[200] For a critical analysis, see G Ferrarini, 'Single Supervision and the Governance of Banking Markets: Will the SSM Deliver the Expected Benefits?' (2015) 16 *European Business Organization Law Review* 513.

The separation principle within the ECB between monetary policy and banking supervision was, in this context, part of the institutional guarantees for Member States in 'close cooperation'. It ensured that the Governing Council, as a decision-making body of the euro area, would not dominate the Supervisory Board. This provided special rights to a Member State in 'close cooperation' with regard to the involvement of the Governing Council. At the limit, in case of an objection of the Governing Council to a draft decision submitted by the Supervisory Board, a Member State could notify the ECB that it would not be bound by the amended supervisory decision resulting from that objection.[201]

The legal basis of Article 127.6 could not provide any other solution than a voluntary arrangement for the participation of Member States outside the euro area in the Banking Union. This solution led, however, to the coexistence of two legal frameworks. First, the Member States of the euro area participate in the Banking Union as an obligation under the Treaty, with a permanent and irrevocable nature. The powers of the ECB/SSM and SRB are exercised on the basis of the supremacy of EU law. Second, the Member States outside the euro area can participate voluntarily in the Banking Union on the basis of a temporary arrangement similar to that of a 'free trade area', which may be suspended or terminated at any time. The acts of the SSM and SRM require a voluntary transposition by national authorities in their Member States, instead of being directly applicable as in the euro area.

C. The Legal Differentiation Process of the Banking Union: The Unification of the 'Single Rulebook'

The process of differentiation of the Banking Union from the single financial market also involved European law. The exclusive competences for banking supervision and resolution of the ECB and the SRB, respectively, led to the single interpretation and enforcement of European law, subject to the single judicial review of the Court. Moreover, the ECB and the SRB have the power to issue guidelines and general instructions to national authorities, in order to achieve consistency in their decisions. The ECB has, in addition, the power to adopt directly applicable regulations. The divergences across Member States arising from the mediation of European law by national authorities and courts were thus removed to a large extent. European law became unified within the Banking Union.[202]

[201] Arts 7.5, 7.6, 7.7. and 7.8 of the SSM Regulation. The representatives of national authorities in 'close cooperation' with the SSM have full membership and voting rights in the Supervisory Board without any distinction from the euro area members.

[202] Art 4.3, SSM Regulation. The ECB can only exercise its regulatory powers to the extent necessary to organise or specify the arrangements for carrying out its supervisory tasks, since otherwise it could interfere with the functions of the EBA. The main example of the exercise of these powers is the so-called 'Framework Regulation' regulating the cooperation between the ECB and national authorities. See Regulation (EU) No 468/2014 of the European Central Bank of 16 April 2014 establishing the framework for cooperation within the Single Supervisory Mechanism between the European Central Bank and national competent authorities and with national designated authorities (ECB/2014/17), [2014] OJ L141.

This unification of European law faced several challenges. In order to safeguard the integrity of the single financial market, the Banking Union had to be subject to the full body of the 'single rulebook', which remained fragmented after being developed over decades. The challenge was how to ensure that the legal acts emanating from the ECB and the SRB, such as decisions, regulations, or guidelines, would comply with such a multi-layered law including EU law, national laws, and the non-legally binding acts of the EBA as a European agency. A number of legal innovations were introduced in order to achieve this effect.[203]

The first innovation was that the ECB and the SRB would be required to apply, not only directly applicable European law, but also the national laws transposing directives. For this purpose, the ECB and the SRB are considered as national authorities under the terms of directives. This is seemingly at odds with the principle of the primacy of European law, since it implies that national laws prevail over legal acts of European authorities. The ECB and the SRB need to apply potentially different national laws via their legal acts, for example when options have been exercised differently, thus also leading to divergent outcomes among Member States. The question is then whether the ECB and the SRB are also required to enforce the national transposition of directives, even if such transposition is incorrect or inconsistent with the directives. This would seemingly run counter the principle of primary of European law and would thus represent a challenge to the Court in reviewing the ECB and SRB legal acts and their compliance with national laws.[204]

The second innovation was to provide the ECB and the SRB with the powers to issue instructions requiring national authorities to take actions under their respective national laws. In the case of the ECB, it relates to those situations where the SSM Regulation does not confer the powers necessary for the ECB to carry out its supervisory tasks. This includes early intervention and precautionary powers regarding banks. A specific instance foreseen in the SSM Regulation is the imposition of sanctions for breaches of national laws transposing directives, for which the ECB is not empowered. In the case of the SRB, it relates to the implementation of a resolution scheme by national resolution authorities under the national laws transposing the BRRD. This legal innovation thus enabled the extension of the jurisdictional reach of the ECB and the SRB, so as to encompass those matters covered by national law, and for which only national authorities are empowered to act.[205]

The third innovation related to whether the ECB and the SRB could also be addressees of the acts of the EBA. Otherwise, the role of the EBA would become void within the Banking Union. The answer was to subject the ECB and the SRB to the full range of

[203] Art 4.3 SSM Regulation and Art 5.2, SRM Regulation provide that the ECB and SRB should apply EU law, including the national law transposing directives and the national legislation exercising options provided in European regulations. These provisions recall that the ECB and SRB should comply with the Commission's delegated and implementing acts under Arts 290 and 291, TFEU, and also subject the ECB and the SRB to the EBA's single supervisory handbook.

[204] Art 9.1, SSM Regulation and Art 5.1, SRM Regulation. Recital (34) of the SSM Regulation states that the application of national law by the ECB is without prejudice to the principle of the primacy of Union law. On the vertical direct effect of directives, see Judgment of the Court of 26 February 1986, *Marshall*, 152/84, EU:C:1986:84, para 48, and Judgment of the Court of 14 July 1994, *Dori*, C-91/92, EU:C:1994:292, para 20.

[205] Arts 9.1 and 18.5, SSM Regulation and Arts 18.9 and 29.1, SRM Regulation.

acts of the EBA, including its non-binding acts. This implies that the ECB and the SRB are assimilated to national authorities for the purposes of the tasks of the EBA. Like national authorities, they are required to 'comply or explain' with regard to guidelines and recommendations of the EBA. In the case of the SRM, this requirement includes the Council and the Commission. The ECB is also subject to individual binding decisions addressed to it by the EBA. This innovation was therefore twofold. First, the SSM and SRM Regulations required European institutions – the ECB and the SRB, as an agency – to comply with the acts of a European agency, the EBA. It seemingly inverted the institutional hierarchy of the EU to ensure that the 'single rulebook' would apply in the Banking Union. Second, the compliance with the acts of the EBA was extended to non-binding acts, such as guidelines and recommendations, based on 'comply or explain'. All efforts were made to ensure that the Banking Union would remain subject to the full body of the 'single rulebook'.[206]

Despite these efforts, the end-result was the co-existence of two regimes of European law in the single financial market: a unified system of European law and legal authority within the Banking Union, and a decentralised system of national jurisdictions elsewhere. This differentiation will likely be exacerbated over time by the centripetal effect of the Banking Union. In this context, directly applicable regulations, which are more appropriate for the Banking Union, are replacing directives as the preferred mode of harmonisation of the single financial market. The EBA will likewise be mindful of the Banking Union when developing its standards. And the Court will gradually develop a jurisprudence on banking supervision and resolution, which will further unify the law within the Banking Union.[207]

D. The Institutional Differentiation Process

Besides legal differentiation, the Banking Union also led to institutional differentiation within the single financial market. The Banking Union has its own decision-making institutions, including the ECB and the SRB. They are subject to a specific accountability framework, which is discharged to the Eurogroup and to the Parliament, with reporting duties also for national parliaments. They also have their own autonomous financing, with the levy of fees for the SSM and SRM as well as the SRF for resolution funding.

Furthermore, the Banking Union has its own political institutions. The Euro Summit created the Banking Union and the Eurogroup is its main political body.

[206] Recital (32) of the SSM Regulation clarifies that '[t]he ECB should carry out its tasks subject to and in compliance with relevant Union law including the whole of primary and secondary Union law, Commission decisions in the area of State aid, competition rules and merger control and the single rulebook applying to all Member States'. This is provided under Art 4.3, SSM Regulation and, for the SRB, Art 5.2, SRM Regulation.

[207] The jurisdiction of the Court only relates to decisions taken by the ECB/SSM and the SRB regarding 'significant' banks. The national courts remain competent for decisions taken by national authorities regarding 'less significant' banks. The Banking Union will therefore be subject to two different judicial jurisdictions: the Court of Justice and national courts. On the jurisdiction of the Court over the exclusive competences of the ECB, see *Fininvest*, (n 108) para 44. On the impact of the Banking Union in rule-setting and adjudication of European law, also drawing the comparison with the impact of EU competition law, see S Grundmann, 'The European Banking Union and Integration' in S Grundmann and HW Micklitz (eds) *The European Banking Union and Constitution: Beacon for Advanced Integration or Death-Knell for Democracy?* (Oxford, Hart Publishing, 2019) 85–120, at 112–115.

The differentiation also applies to the Council in the only case where it needs to take a formal decision in the Banking Union, which is on a resolution scheme proposed by the SRB. In such a situation, the non-participating Member States committed not to prevent the adoption of a decision by the majority of the Member States participating in the Banking Union. This emulates the regime for enhanced cooperation, whereby only the participating Member States take part in a vote under Article 330 of the TFEU.[208]

The institutional differentiation of the Banking Union would be complete if a specialised court were created for the judicial review of the ECB and SRB acts.[209]

Alongside its specific institutions, the Banking Union is also subject to those of the single financial market, in particular, to the ESA and the ESRB. As mentioned above, there were a series of innovations to ensure that the ECB and the SRB would apply the 'single rulebook' in its entirety. In addition to this, the SSM and the SRM Regulations also required the ECB and the SRB to carry out their tasks without prejudice to the competences of the ESA and the ESRB, and to cooperate closely with them.[210]

Despite these attempts to protect the institutional framework of the single financial market, the Banking Union has a number of consequences for its functioning. A first consequence relates to the EBA. Although its role is maintained, the scope for convergence of supervisory practices is significantly reduced: it does not relate anymore to the national authorities of all Member States, but instead to the SSM and the national authorities from the Member States not participating in the Banking Union. Likewise, its mediation task is only relevant for disagreements between the ECB and national authorities from outside the Banking Union. This implies that the functions of the EBA became mainly relevant for the SSM and the SRB, as the authorities responsible for the largest part of the single financial market. The EBA standards will then have the most impact in the Banking Union, since they will be implemented directly by a single authority. As a result, there is a paradoxical impact on the EBA: it became less relevant to the extent that the number of authorities decreased substantially; but it also becomes more significant as the regulator of the Banking Union.[211]

[208] See EU Council, Declaration of 18 December 2013 of the Representatives of the 28 Member States meeting within the Council, 18137/13.

[209] Art 257, TFEU provides for the possibility that the Parliament and the Council establish specialised courts attached to the General Court. Such a specialised court could be justified due to the technical specificity of banking supervision and resolution, the potential volume of acts in these areas, and the need for a timely review of such acts. Art 24, SSM Regulation partly addressed such concerns by introducing an internal administrative board of review of the ECB (ABOR), which provides an appeal mechanism leading to a new supervisory decision within a relatively short period of time. In this context, the General Court considered that a supervisory decision in conformity with an Opinion of the ABOR 'is an extension of that opinion and the explanations contained therein may be taken into account for the purpose of determining whether the contested decision contains a sufficient statement of reasons'. See *Landeskreditbank*, (n 115) para 127, and judgment of 13 December 2017, *Crédit Mutuel Arkéa*, T-712/15 ECLI:EU:T:2017:900, para 51. Similarly, the SRM Regulation introduced an Appeal Panel for bank resolution decisions of the SRB, under Art 45, SRM Regulation. For an overview, see C Brescia Morra, R Smits and A Magliari, 'The Administrative Board of Review of the European Central Bank: Experience After 2 Years' (2017) 18 *European Business Organization Law Review* 567.

[210] Art 4.2(i) and (iv), EBA Regulation for the ECB and the SRB, respectively.

[211] For an overview of the role of the EBA in the Banking Union, see S Cappiello, 'The Interplay between the EBA and the Banking Union' (2015) 2015/77 *EUI Working Papers RSCAS*, especially at 10–ff; and N Moloney, 'International Financial Governance, the EU, and Brexit: The "Agencification" of EU Financial Governance and the Implications' (2016) 17 *European Business Organization Law Review* 451.

This tension was reflected in the internal differentiation within the EBA. There was the concern, particularly from the UK, that the authorities belonging to the SSM would vote in a coordinated way and supress the interests of the single market in favour of those of the Banking Union. The answer was adopting a double-voting system for the Board of Supervisors, grouping the members of the SSM and the others into separate voting constituencies for the most relevant decisions of the EBA, such as those regarding draft guidelines or actions in emergency situations. In these cases, the decisions should be adopted either by qualified majority or simple majority by the Board of Supervisors but always including a simple majority of its members from the SSM and a simple majority of its members from the other authorities.[212]

Another consequence related to the role of ESRB. The ECB was entrusted with macroprudential competences in the Banking Union, including being consulted on national measures and imposing higher requirements to address systemic risks. The scope of the role of the ESRB was reduced accordingly. Within the Banking Union, the ECB has greater macroprudential powers than the ESRB and overlaps with its coordination tasks. By exclusion, the functions of the ESRB thus became mainly relevant for the authorities outside the Banking Union and for addressing systemic risks in other financial sectors.[213]

The Banking Union, therefore, led to institutional differentiation within the single financial market in two ways. First, it has its own institutions, which deepen integration compared to the rest of the single financial market. Second, it affects the institutions of the single financial market, either by leading to an internal institutional split, as with the EBA, or by absorbing large part of their functions.[214]

E. 'Brexit' and the Consequences of Differentiation

On 23 June 2016, 51.9 per cent of UK voters voted for the UK to leave the EU in a national referendum. Following this result, the UK notified the European Council on 29 March 2017 of its intention to withdraw from the EU on the basis of Article 50 of the TEU.[215]

Before the referendum, the European Council had agreed on 'A New Settlement for the UK within the EU', which included a number of principles regarding the consequences of the Banking Union. It acknowledged the need for further deepening of integration in the EMU without discriminating against non-participating Member States. It confirmed that the 'single rulebook' would apply throughout the single financial market, but it left open the possibility that there could be more uniform provisions

[212] In accordance with Art 44.1, EBA Regulation, these voting arrangements cease to apply once there are four or fewer Member States outside the euro area.

[213] See ESRB, The consequences of the single supervisory mechanism for Europe's macro-prudential policy framework, Report of the Advisory Scientific Committee (2013) at www.esrb.europa.eu/pub/pdf/sac/Reports_ASC_3_1309.pdf at 5–6.

[214] See N Moloney, 'International Financial Governance, the EU, and Brexit' (n 211).

[215] European Council, Statement on the UK notification (Art 50), 29 March 2017, at www.consilium.europa.eu/en/press/press-releases/2017/03/29-euco-50-statement-uk-notification. For a first overview of the consequences of Brexit for the EU, see K Nicolaïdis, 'The Political Mantra: Brexit, Control and the Transformation of the European Order' in F Fabbrini (ed) *The Law & Politics of Brexit* (Oxford, Oxford University Press, 2017) 25.

in EU law for the Banking Union than for the other Member States. Lastly, it safeguarded Member States outside the euro area from any budgetary responsibility for the management of financial crises in the euro area. The Council also committed to adopt a Decision, which would have granted the possibility for a non-participating Member State to oppose a legislative act on economic governance to be adopted under qualified majority voting, on the basis that the act would infringe such principles. It was a mechanism following the line of the previous UK demands for safeguards regarding EU financial services legislation at the time of the discussions on the TSCG.[216]

The 'Settlement of the UK' aimed, therefore, at mitigating the impact of the legal and institutional differentiation of the Banking Union by committing to non-discrimination and equality among all Member States, safeguarding the jurisdiction and budgetary responsibility of the outside Member States, and providing a special right to these Member States to oppose legislation on the Banking Union infringing such principles.

The settlement ceased to exist with the outcome of the referendum to leave the EU. After the notification of the UK Government triggering Article 50, the European Council adopted a set of guidelines for the exit negotiations. In what related to the single financial market, the guidelines restated the indivisibility of the four freedoms, which pre-empted the participation of the UK only in parts of the single market, such as financial services. For the future relationship, a free trade agreement with the UK had to safeguard financial stability in the EU, respect its regulatory and supervisory regimes, and avoid unfair competitive advantages through regulatory measures. Any UK access to the single financial market would thus require compliance with EU law and avoidance of regulatory arbitrage.[217]

In this context, the 'Brexit' process should also be interpreted as an extreme consequence of the differentiation dynamics of the EU, particularly after the financial and sovereign debt crises and culminating thus far with the Banking Union. The initiative of a group of Member States to deepen their integration may provide a justification for the other Member States to disengage in the opposite direction towards lower integration. The benefits of participating in the single financial market at the outer boundaries of the Banking Union diminish over time. This is particularly so as the legal and institutional framework of the Banking Union progressively dominates the rest of the single financial market.[218]

F. The New Logic of Integration through Differentiation: Inclusion or Exclusion of the Single Financial Market?

The differentiation introduced by the Banking Union created a new logic of integration. The single market was split into two blocks: an inner core of deep integration and an outer core of looser integration with a differentiated membership, law, and institutional

[216] European Council, A New Settlement for the United Kingdom within the European Union, Extract of the conclusions of the European Council of 18–19 February 2016, [2016] OJ C69 I/1.

[217] European Council, Guidelines following the UK's notification under Art 50, TEU, 29 April 2017, at www.consilium.europa.eu/en/press/press-releases/2017/04/29-euco-brexit-guidelines.

[218] On the options for differentiation in European integration, see JC Piris, *The Future of Europe: Towards a Two-Speed EU?* (Cambridge, Cambridge University Press, 2012).

framework. The question was whether this new logic of integration would lead over time to the inclusion of the whole single financial market into the Banking Union, or end up with the exclusion of those parts of the single financial market remaining in national jurisdictions.[219]

The framework of the Banking Union attempted to prevent exclusion by including provisions prohibiting discrimination, enabling the participation of non-euro area Member States through voluntary arrangements, ensuring the application of the 'single rulebook', and safeguarding the functioning of the EBA and ESRB. Despite the good intentions, such provisions ended up by achieving the opposite effect of reinforcing differentiation. The Member States in 'close cooperation' participate in the Banking Union outside the Treaty, which implies that they have more rights and fewer obligations that those in the euro area. Likewise, the double-voting system in the EBA gives rise to a disproportional voting weight in favour of the not participating Member States. Therefore, it is very unlikely that a workable compromise may be found between participating or not in the Banking Union.

Differentiation will instead intensify over time rather than stabilise: as integration deepens within the Banking Union, the distance to the other parts of the single financial market will necessarily increase. Like the Monetary Union, the evolution and functioning of the Banking Union will warrant ever more integration in the form of more policy coordination, legal harmonisation, and political integration, so as to provide it with a stronger democratic legitimacy. All of this will increase such a distance. As a large group of Member States reinforce their integration, the commitment of the other Member States to maintain lower levels of integration will decrease, as in the extreme case of 'Brexit.' It is thus likely that the Banking Union will exercise a centripetal force for the single financial market until it fully replaces it. So, the choice will be either to join the Banking Union or leave the single financial market.[220]

X. Conclusion: The Completion of Legal Integration?

A. The Legal Change of the Banking Union

The conclusion of this chapter is that the Banking Union is the culmination of the evolutionary process of legal change in the single financial market. It led to the apex of legal and institutional integration with the full centralisation of the competences regarding the banking sector in European authorities. The ECB and the SRB apply and enforce directly a unified body of European banking law, the 'single rulebook'. The acts of these authorities are subject to the judicial review of the Court. They are accountable to the European Parliament and the Council.

[219] See RM Lastra 'Banking Union and Single Market: Conflict or Companionship?' (2013) 36 *Fordham International Law Journal* 1189.

[220] For a more positive assessment of the consequences for the single financial market, see E Ferran, 'European Banking Union and the EU Single Financial Market: More Differentiated Integration, or Disintegration?' in B de Witte, A Ott, and E Vos (eds) *Between Flexibility and Disintegration: The Trajectory of Differentiation in EU Law*' (Cheltenham, Elgar, 2017) 252.

The fundamental legal change operated by the Banking Union was to replace the soft governance of the previous period with centralised, legally binding, enforcement of unified European law, without a distinction between federal and local levels. This was achieved by the combination of a wide-ranging set of legal and institutional innovations, which were identified and analysed in this chapter, as summarised in the table below. The common denominator to the innovations was to generate, essentially through secondary law, a centralised construction by putting together very diverse elements of European law. The purpose was to overcome the absence of a foundation in the Treaty for a Banking Union, which existed by contrast for the Monetary Union.

The legal and institutional innovations of the Banking Union were manifold: the transfer of supervisory powers to the ECB; the distinction between 'significant' and 'less significant' banks; the establishment of the SRB as an agency with unprecedented powers; the application of the unified but multi-layered 'single rulebook' by the ECB and the SRB; the subjection of national authorities to these European authorities; the independence of banking supervision and resolution; and an accountability regime involving both the European Parliament and the national parliaments.

As a result of these innovations, the Banking Union is a centralised system of European law and institutions, but it remains complex and imperfect due to the many compromises made to achieve such centralisation, and also to achieve it through secondary law. It combines European competences and national competences in different and, arguably, non seamless ways. The decision-making processes for banking supervision and resolution are convoluted. The unified banking law stems from several European and national sources that are not always well-knit. The 'close cooperation' mechanisms give rise to a potentially unstable and unequal membership. The differentiation process of the Banking Union threatens the framework of the single financial market. Such complexity and imperfections will certainly become less striking as the Banking Union evolves over time into more centralisation and uniformity of rules and practices, in tandem with increased market integration. Ultimately, a Treaty change will however be required to crystallise the legal change of the Banking Union into a fully coherent model of supranational integration.

B. The Rationale for Legal Change

The rationale for this legal change of the Banking Union was to safeguard the existence of both the single financial market and the Monetary Union. It was to a large extent the unavoidable consequence of prior failings in the integration process. The major failure was the reliance on the soft governance of multiple national jurisdictions by European agencies and committees. It enabled the expansion of the single financial market, but without credible enforcement of rules, and without crisis management or burden-sharing capacity at the European level. As argued before, the evolution of the single financial market had been based solely on increasing the benefits of market integration, without contemplating any risk-sharing mechanism: no European competences, no European liabilities. This promoted integration in good times but it soon reverted into disintegration with the financial and sovereign debt crises. The way forward to preserve the benefits of integration was to transfer banking supervision competences to the ECB as a quid pro quo for the mutualisation of risks in the form of the direct recapitalisation of banks by the ESM.

Originally, the Banking Union aimed at matching European competences with European liabilities. This would be achieved by a permanent and complete transfer to the European level of national competences for banking supervision and resolution, which had been previously closely related to national fiscal sovereignty. These competences would be then underpinned by European liabilities for the materialisation of risks in the form of the facilities provided by the ESM, SRF, and EDIS. The transfer of exclusive competences for the banking sector to European authorities would solve the 'financial trilemma', whereby financial stability and financial integration were not compatible with national competences.

Like in the previous phases of integration, the expansion of European competences under the Banking Union was, however, constrained by the boundaries of the Treaty and the preservation of national fiscal sovereignty. Such constraints were clearly reflected in the safeguards imposed on the functioning of the Banking Union. These included the convoluted decision-making process of the SRB, which involves the Commission and the Council to protect their prerogatives under the Treaty, as well as the fiscal sovereignty of Member States. Another was the mandatory bail-in in resolution cases to prevent the use of public funds, which was the first time that European law affected explicitly property rights. In the same way, there were initially strict conditions for the direct recapitalisation of banks by the ESM, which was later revoked in favour of a backstop to the SRF. Likewise, there are strict conditions for the intervention of the SRF to protect public funds. The preservation of national fiscal sovereignty also meant that a large part of financial stability competences remained at the national level, including the imposition of macroprudential measures and the lender-of-last-resort function by national central banks.

C. The Incomplete Banking Union

The above constraints imply that the regime shift intended with the Banking Union is incomplete: the full transfer of competences is accompanied only by a limited transfer of liabilities to the European level. The risk-sharing within the Banking Union remained constrained by national fiscal sovereignty and by the absence of fiscal capacity at the European level to assume public liabilities. This means that part of the risks generated by market integration within the Banking Union remains either covered by national public funds, with all the constraints arising from the prohibition of public bailouts, or not covered at all. The materialisation of risks will then lead to private losses through financial markets, bail-in and bank resolution or liquidation.

Accordingly, instead of leading to a mutualisation among Member States of the public risks of market integration, the Banking Union ended-up by operating largely on the basis of private risk-sharing. The implication of this full reliance on private risk-sharing is that it amplifies the distributive consequences of the transfer of competences to the European level. Before the Banking Union, the close nexus between banks and their respective sovereigns provided the justification for public intervention, which would alter the composition of the distributive implications of a financial crisis.

For example, a public bailout would safeguard investors to contain systemic risk, while shifting the burden of losses to taxpayers. With the Banking Union being based on private risk-sharing, financial and economic shocks could provoke sudden and severe distributive effects. In the absence of stabilisation and redistribution mechanisms, this, in turn, could lead to fragmentation within the Banking Union. In the extreme, there could be political disintegration, if the policies of the Banking Union are not perceived as democratically legitimate and fair across Member States. Therefore, these limits on the Banking Union, which are set by the dominance of national fiscal sovereignty combined with the absence of stabilisation mechanisms, represent the main threat to its sustainability. The question is then whether the medium- to long-term sustainability of the Banking Union requires achieving yet another functional step, with further fiscal integration in the form of a Fiscal Union.[221]

Following-up on the 'Five Presidents' Report' of June 2015, the Commission proposed further steps for deepening the Monetary Union. The Banking Union would be completed through a common backstop for the SRF and the establishment of EDIS. This would be complemented by a Capital Markets Union, as initially launched in September 2015. The Banking and the Capital Markets Union would form a 'Financial Union.' An 'Economic and Fiscal Union' would include after 2020 a macroeconomic stabilisation function with the aim of protecting the euro area from asymmetric shocks. A European 'safe asset', akin to a 'Euro bond', would be considered to reinforce integration and financial stability. Finally, the Commission proposed a new architecture for the governance and democratic accountability in the Monetary Union. It would include a euro-area Treasury and a European Monetary Fund, built on the ESM, to provide liquidity assistance to the Member States and act as a public backstop of last resort to the Banking Union.[222]

In conclusion, compared to the previous phases, which aimed at deepening integration while avoiding transferring competences to the European level, the Banking Union is a radical step in integration. It goes far beyond the previous harmonisation approaches by creating a unified system of law, legal authority, and judicial review. This may well represent the purest form of supranational legal and institutional integration achieved thus far within the single market, and largely on the basis of secondary law. The Banking Union remains, however, incomplete, and does not conclude the process of integration. Without stabilisation mechanisms, which are democratically legitimate, it will likely not be self-sustaining.

[221] See N Véron, 'Europe's radical Banking Union' (2015) *Bruegel Essay and Lecture Series*, at bruegel.org/wp-content/uploads/imported/publications/essay_NV_CMU.pdf.

[222] European Commission, Reflection Paper on the Deepening of the Economic and Monetary Union (2017) at ec.europa.eu/commission/sites/beta-political/files/reflection-paper-emu_en.pdf. See also European Commission, Action Plan on Building a Capital Markets Union, COM (2015) 468 final; and European Commission, Proposal for a Regulation of the European Parliament and of the Council on sovereign bond-backed securities, COM (2018) 339 final. The proposal was based on Art 114, TFEU and aimed at creating a framework for the private issuance of a sovereign bond backed security, ie a financial instrument whose credit risk is associated to exposures to sovereign bonds of the euro area. This was supported by a report of the ESRB advocating the need for a euro-area-wide, low risk asset from a financial stability perspective: ESRB, Sovereign bond-backed securities: a feasibility study (2018) at www.esrb.europa.eu/pub/task_force_safe_assets/shared/pdf/esrb.report290118_sbbs_volume_I_mainfindings.en.pdf.

Table 26 Legal Change in 'Integration through Centralisation' (2013–...)

<table>
<tr><th></th><th>Legal and institutional innovations to deepen integration</th><th>Integration policies</th><th>Remaining obstacles to integration</th></tr>
<tr><td>1</td><td>• Transfer of exclusive competences to the ECB, relating to both the single financial market and the Monetary Union, and replacing the 'single passport' framework</td><td>• Removing the nexus between banks and sovereigns through banking supervision at the European level, without amending the Treaty</td><td rowspan="4">• Fragmentation of the single financial market due to the legal and institutional differentiation of the Banking Union
• Dominance of the banking sector in the integration of the single financial market
• Reliance on national authorities for the enforcement of some supervisory actions by the ECB or for the transposition of directives
• Convoluted decision-making by the SRB as an agency, which may hinder decisions with an impact on fiscal sovereignty and distributive implications
• Diffuse democratic legitimacy of the Banking Union
• Prevalence of national competences for financial stability, including macroprudential measures, lender of last resort, and use of public funds</td></tr>
<tr><td>2</td><td>• Principle of separation between monetary policy and banking supervision within the ECB, including a Supervisory Board and non-objection procedures for supervisory decision-making</td><td>• Enabling banking supervision decision-making within the ECB through a separate body to the Governing Council, while safeguarding monetary policy</td></tr>
<tr><td>3</td><td>• Establishment of the SSM, based on the distinction between 'significant' and 'less significant' banks, and including ECB power to take over supervision of 'less significant' banks</td><td>• Distinguishing between the banks that justify or not supervision at the European level
• Integrating national authorities into a European enforcement system
• Ensuring consistent standards of supervision for all banks</td></tr>
<tr><td>4</td><td>• Introduction of European parallel competences for macroprudential measures</td><td>• Safeguarding European financial stability, while preserving national competences for local risks
• Preventing national 'inaction bias' in addressing systemic risks</td></tr>
</table>

(continued)

Table 26 ***(Continued)***

	Legal and institutional innovations to deepen integration	Integration policies	Remaining obstacles to integration
5	• Introduction of 'close cooperation' arrangements with the SSM for Member States outside the euro area	• Preserving the integrity of the single financial market by matching its membership with the Banking Union	• Absence of a European Deposit Insurance Scheme • Absence of a Capital Markets Union • Insufficient economic governance arrangements for addressing the distributive implications of the Banking Union, such as a European fiscal capacity • Dominance of national fiscal sovereignty as a limit to further integration
6	• Establishment of the Single Resolution Board as an agency with wide-ranging bank resolution powers, subject to the control of the Commission and Council	• Removing the nexus between banks and sovereigns through banking resolution at the European level, without changing the Treaty	
7	• Introduction of bail-in powers to be exercised by the SRB	• Removing the nexus between banks and sovereigns with the prohibition of bail-out of banks	
8	• Establishment of a Single Resolution Fund	• Mutualisation of the risk of financing banking resolution through bank levies	
9	• Introduction of fund aid control by the Commission	• Prevent distortions of competition or circumvention of state aid rules through the SRF	
10	• Enabling the direct recapitalisation of European banks by the ESM, later replaced by an ESM backstop to the SRF	• Removing the nexus between banks and sovereigns	
11	• Unification of the 'single rulebook' through the single interpretation, application and enforcement of European law	• Ensuring that the Banking Union would remain within the single financial market	

(continued)

Table 26 *(Continued)*

	Legal and institutional innovations to deepen integration	**Integration policies**	**Remaining obstacles to integration**
12	• Introduction of institutional independence for banking supervision and resolution	• Providing credibility to policies with potential distributive implications at both the European and national levels	
13	• Democratic accountability to European Parliament and reporting to national Parliaments	• Providing democratic legitimacy to policies with potential distributive implications at both the European and national levels	
14	• Proposal for a European Deposit Insurance Scheme	• Removing the nexus between banks and sovereigns • Provide equal protection of deposits in euro • Mutualisation of the risk of insuring deposits through mandatory contributions by banks	

6

Unlocking the Past and Future of the Banking Union

Marché unique – monnaie unique – fédération.

Jean Monnet, 1952[1]

I. Introduction

This book has traced back the legal and institutional evolution of the single financial market, since the initial framework set out in the Spaak Report of 1956 and up to the supranational integration of the Banking Union starting in 2013. It has identified five historical phases of legal and institutional change, each of which are distinguished by the strategy for integration: (1) integration through harmonisation (1973–1984); (2) integration through competition (1985–1997); (3) integration through governance (1998–2007); (4) (dis-) integration through crisis (2008–2012); and (5) integration through centralisation of European competences, in the form of the Banking Union (from 2013 onwards).

The purpose of this book, as presented in its introduction, is twofold. The first is to explain the creation of the Banking Union, a supranational legal and institutional construction at the forefront of European integration. The second, reviewing the evidence provided by the emergence of the Banking Union, is to understand how legal and institutional change happens, and how it impacts the European integration process. The review of these decades of legal and institutional evolution provides several findings to answer these questions. These findings not only unlock the past of the Banking Union, but also provide insights into its future, and how sustainable it will be over time.

[1] Quote from 'Note de réflexion de Jean Monnet', USA, avril/mai 1952, FJME, AMM 3/3/6, in G Grin, 'Shaping Europe: The Path to European Integration according to Jean Monnet' (2017) *Jean Monnet Foundation for Europe, Debates and Documents Collection, 7* at 27.

II. Explaining the Creation of the Banking Union: The Endpoint of Supranational Integration through Law

The answer to the question of what explains the creation of the Banking Union is that it is the outcome of an incremental supranational process of legal integration towards a single financial market. Its legal history reveals that its creation was not spontaneous. Banking Union was the 'predictable' result of successive deliberate choices to achieve a legal and institutional order for a market integrated as a domestic market. With the centralisation of law and institutions for a European banking market, the Banking Union is very much the logical endpoint of supranational legal integration.

The process towards the Banking Union started with the original concept of the horizontal common market, as first sketched out in the Spaak Report. As part of the common market, a European financial market would be created and developed through legal integration. The focus would be the full realisation of the economic freedoms, notably the freedoms of movement of capital, establishment, and to provide financial services. A European financial market would then emerge out of European law, which would provide its exclusive legal order. This order would be limited to ensuring market functioning, without regulatory or distributive policies. It would thus not require the transfer of such policy competences to the European level. In turn, Member States would be prevented from creating market distortions through divergent national laws and protectionist measures. This is why the legal integration of the European financial market – and, for the most part, of the Banking Union – was based on the harmonisation clause of the Treaty, now Article 114 of the Treaty on the Functioning of the European Union (TFEU), enabling the adoption of measures for the approximation of national laws, which have as their object the establishment and functioning of the internal market.[2]

The implication of such a concept of legal integration was that throughout its history, the functional purpose of the law of the European financial market was to achieve seamless integration. This was pursued through legal and institutional innovations from one phase of integration to the next. All such innovations were geared towards creating an exclusive legal order for a European financial market, pre-empting interference from Member States in its functioning, and not requiring the transfer of national competences. Yet this created an internal contradiction: as integration progressed, there would be no competences at either the European or national levels to manage the risks of an integrated market. A single financial market ultimately required the transfer of stabilisation competences for preserving its integration against the materialisation of risks, such as a financial crisis. This logic is confirmed by the evidence of the legal history leading to the Banking Union, as follows.

The first legal strategy towards a European financial market was the full harmonisation of national laws, so that they would not constitute an obstacle to the basic freedoms. It was not successful in delivering legal integration due to the unanimity voting required for legislation and the protectionism of Member States. Some building blocks for a

[2] See ch 1 on the concept of legal integration underpinning the Spaak Report.

future legal and institutional order were nonetheless introduced, such as the harmonisation of basic concepts of banking law, as well as the setting up of the first committees of national authorities.[3]

Following this initial failure, another legal strategy was introduced in 1985. 'Integration through competition' relied on the combination of competitive market forces and regulatory competition among Member States. The strategy pivoted on the innovation of the single passport for financial services. This European law mechanism granted directly to market participants the freedom to conduct their business throughout the single market, independently of the Member State of origin. The Member States would then compete for such business by adjusting dynamically their laws and regulations. This would create centripetal forces towards both legal and market integration, leading eventually to an optimally integrated and regulated market. In this way, the single passport promoted the unlimited expansion of a European financial market, but without the capacity to contain the related risks at the European level. Market participants could expand their business beyond what would be proportional to the economic size of the home-country and to the risks for the host-countries. This was because the framework created a vacuum of responsibilities: under European law, the home-country authorities were not liable for the risks of their financial institutions, and the host-country authorities had no powers to protect their markets from such risks. In good times, the economic benefits of an integrated financial market would be shared by all Member States, but the risks would remain with each of them. This legal strategy also failed. Member States did not engage in regulatory competition, as envisaged. They remained able to interfere with the process of creating a European legal and institutional order by preserving their divergences in national laws and protecting their domestic markets.[4]

Along with the start of the Monetary Union and the increasing globalisation of finance, a new strategy was launched, which was influenced by the contemporary doctrine of 'new governance'. It entailed a wider and deeper harmonisation effort of national laws, which would be supported by multi-level governance structures. One of the main innovations was to embed the national authorities in extended comitology procedures, so that they would define together the European regulatory interests. The aim was to detach national authorities from the perspective of their respective Member States, so as to mitigate their divergences. This governance strategy would thus provide the closest approximation possible to legal integration, while not requiring any transfer of national powers. As argued before, this created the 'illusion' that the single financial market was being governed. In reality there was a void of competences at both the European and the national levels: there were no European powers to take binding decisions, and national authorities could only pursue their mandates to safeguard their domestic jurisdictions. The amalgamation of national interests did not, therefore, translate into European governance. In this period, the single financial market expanded significantly, with deepening integration and financial institutions increasing in size and pan-European reach, but without a European safety net.[5]

[3] See ch 1.
[4] See ch 2.
[5] See ch 3.

The financial crisis of 2007–2008 laid bare this internal contradiction of the legal order of the single financial market: despite the deeper integration, there were no stabilisation powers to safeguard it. The immediate consequence of this contradiction coming to the fore was the disintegration and the renationalisation of the single financial market. Member States rescued their domestic banks with public funds and ring-fenced their markets. National interests prevailed and led to a retrenchment in European market integration. It then triggered another phase of legal and institutional innovations to preserve the integration that had been achieved. This phase consisted of more harmonisation in the form of a 'single rulebook', the transformation of committees into European agencies with extended tasks in the shape of the ESA, and the introduction of financial stability into the framework, also through the creation of the ESRB. The soft nature of the overall framework remained nonetheless unchanged: Member States resisted any transfer of national powers to the European level which could impinge on their national fiscal sovereignty.[6]

The sovereign debt crisis of the euro area ensued. The economic constitution of the Monetary Union determined that solely the Member States were responsible for their finances as a disciplinary device, which was reflected in the Treaty principles of 'no bailout' and prohibition of monetary financing by the ECB. The preservation of the euro area eventually required European solutions to the crisis. Member States established the EFSF and the ESM as intergovernmental bodies outside the Treaty to enable risk-sharing, without leading to a transfer of competences to the EU. The ECB decided on the possibility of OMT for sovereign bonds, linked to the activation of the EFSF/ESM.

The Banking Union emerged out of this existential need for risk-sharing among Member States. The combination of the financial and sovereign debt crises had led to a mutual dependence between the soundness of banks and the finances of Member States: the liabilities of banks became the liabilities of the Member States. The way forward to break this nexus was to enable the ESM to directly recapitalise banks. The assumption of European liability then required European control: the banking sector had to be separated from Member States, since national policies could not be trusted to minimise European liabilities. It led to the centralisation of competences for banking supervision and resolution, respectively in the SSM and SRM.[7]

The rationale behind the Banking Union was to overcome the previous internal contradiction in legal integration, which had created a single financial market without mechanisms to address risks and share them among Member States. This contradiction had then been compounded by the framework of the Monetary Union, which further increased integration, but without risk-sharing or European competences to safeguard its stability. In turn, the economic and financial policies remaining under the sovereignty of Member States were inadequate for coping with the implications of integration. As a result, there was a vacuum of responsibilities, with no stabilisation capacity at the European or national levels.

The change operated by the Banking Union involved enclosing the banking sector within a European legal and institutional order and detaching it from Member States.

[6] See ch 4.

[7] See ch 5.

This was achieved through the supranational structure of the Banking Union, which was made autonomous from Member States: the law of the Banking Union was unified under the 'single rulebook' concept, which was enforced directly by the ECB and SRB, and on the basis of extensive institutional independence.

Furthermore, the possibility of Member States intervening to stabilise markets was replaced by making market participants liable for the risks of an integrated market. The mandatory bail-in of banks' liabilities in resolution, and the prohibition of public bailouts, removed the mutual dependence between banks and Member States. The same motivation applies to the establishment of the SRF, which is funded by levies on the banking industry, and to a possible EDIS, which would cut the link with national deposit-guarantee schemes. The original quid pro quo in the foundation of the Banking Union did not thus materialise: there was no transition from national public liabilities to a European public liability for the banking sector. Instead, the risks were transferred to the private liability of market participants. For this purpose, it was the first time that European law provided instruments to a European authority to affect private property rights by enforcing mandatory bail-in and imposing levies directly on market participants.

The Banking Union was therefore the consequence of the logic of legal integration, in line with the blueprint of the Spaak Report: creating through European law an integrated market, which is then subject exclusively to its own rules and institutions. This would be achieved by eliminating progressively the obstacles posed by national laws and constraining the intervention of Member States. While this logic did not require the transfer of national powers to the European level, it assumed that this would be the endpoint of supranational integration as the result of European law and market forces. This logic was the common denominator to all the legal and institutional innovations in the development of the single financial market and the Banking Union, which were based on the harmonisation clause of Article 114 of the TFEU.

The underlying intuition was that, sooner or later, an autonomous European legal order would give rise to an integrated market, insulated from Member States. With the Banking Union, this intuition was to a large extent confirmed. At the Euro Summit of 28–29 June 2012, the Heads of State or government from the euro-area Member States confronted an existential crisis, which stemmed from the market reaction to the flaws of the Monetary Union. As Luuk van Middelaar put it, they then attempted to overcome the crisis by coupling a decision to address the crisis in the short-term, via the direct recapitalisation of banks by the ESM, with the long-term commitment to European integration – the creation of the Banking Union to repair one of the flaws of the Monetary Union.[8]

[8] See L van Middelaar, *Quand L'Europe Improvise: Dix ans de crises politiques* (Paris, Gallimard, 2018) 96–100, who also argues that the creation of the Banking Union was the result of a link made among Member States between solidarity and responsibility, or, as argued somewhat differently in this book, a quid pro quo between European liability and European control.

III. Explaining the Legal Change Leading to the Banking Union

The legal history of the Banking Union also gives an insight into the question of how legal change happens within the integration process. Briefly, the continuum of legal change, from the start of a European financial market to the Banking Union, evolved through cycles which correspond to the transition between each of the five phases of integration identified in this work. The transition was accomplished through various legal and institutional innovations, as summarised at the end of each chapter.

The five phases of integration correspond to the legal strategies generally employed in specific historical periods to pursue the integration of the single financial market. They represent paradigms of legal integration, such as the harmonisation of national laws, regulatory competition, experimental multilevel governance and comitology, agencification, and the centralisation of competences. The phases occurred as a succession of trial and error strategies. Each phase drew on the legal and institutional building-blocks introduced by the previous one and aimed at overcoming their failings in delivering market integration. The trigger for the change from one paradigm to another was the political and economic momentum reached at a particular time. Such momentum coincided largely with either milestones of European integration or crises: the economic slowdown of the 1970s accompanied by the expansion of Community competences, the 1985 White Paper and the Single European Act, the start of Monetary Union, the financial crisis, and finally the sovereign debt crisis for the change to the Banking Union.

The shift to a new phase of integration was then propelled by legal and institutional innovations. The legal design of these innovations was very diverse and influenced by the many factors mentioned previously, including developments in European law, notably the Court's jurisprudence; the legal doctrines of the time, such as 'new governance'; the policy goals of the Commission; the constraints posed in political and legislative processes by Member States; the institutional demands of the Parliament, for example, for democratic accountability; or the transposition of global regulatory standards. However, regardless of their shape or form, most of the innovations relied on the same legal basis: the progressive widening of the scope of the harmonisation clause of Article 114 of the TFEU. For instance, this was the case when the 'Level 3' committees of national authorities were transformed into the ESA, as a European agency with more extensive powers than ever before. The Court then largely validated the innovations, such as the *ESMA* case confirming the appropriateness of the powers of the ESA.[9]

Legal change in the single financial market until the Banking Union happened in cycles: as a repeated pattern of integration dynamics, as depicted in Figure 5 below. The cycles of legal change broadly conformed with the following iterative sequence: (1) a trigger or momentum for change emerges, as mentioned above; (2) this leads to proposals for innovations by the Commission to increase legal and institutional integration, often first put forward in technical reports of '*Comités des Sages*'; (3) Member

[9] On the transformation of committees into European agencies, see ch 4.

States negotiate at the level of the Council to prevent threats to their sovereignty; (4) the resulting innovations lead to another layer of legal and institutional integration, but falls short of transferring competences to the European level; and (5) market integration increases, together with increased risks of integration, but again falling short of its potential.

The process of legal change was gradual, but steady over time. From one phase of integration to another, new layers of legal and institutional integration were placed on top of each other. With this progressive layering, national laws were increasingly harmonised and replaced by directly applicable European laws. National regulatory systems converged and became increasingly interdependent within European governance structures. As this legal and institutional 'glue' became denser, national financial markets also became more deeply integrated. The choices taken in each phase became increasingly path-dependent to the point of making market integration largely irreversible. National sovereignty over economic and financial policies was eroded but remained dominant since there were no competences transferred to the European level.

The additional insight provided by the legal history of the Banking Union is that the continuum of legal change through cycles exacerbated over time the internal contradiction of the integration process. All the innovations aimed at creating a European legal order, while removing the distortions created by national competences. As the single financial market expanded exponentially with 'no stop rule', it also led to a build-up of risks. In this sense, legal change intensified the implications of the financial and sovereign debt crises: without the transfer of stabilisation functions to the European level, disintegration became inevitable. Until then, integration evolved by cycles of European legal and institutional change approximating ever closer, but never replacing, such stabilisation functions, for example, through harmonisation, committees, multi-level governance, agencies, and the other innovations identified previously.

Drawing on the institutionalist theories of political science concerning European integration, the cycles of legal change of the single financial market can be understood as 'cycles of institutionalisation'. These theories emphasise the neofunctional dynamics of supranational governance. As conceptualised by Wayne Sandholtz and Alec Stone Sweet, 'institutionalisation' is defined as 'the process by which rules are created, applied, and interpreted by those who live under them'. Integration would then happen through 'cycles of institutionalisation' or feedback loops connecting together 'transnational activity, the capacity to govern of supranational organisations, and EC law and procedures'.[10]

In other words, the legal change leading to the Banking Union operated through repetitive cycles, which each reinforced the other, leading towards creating ever more European rules and resilient institutional structures, and thereby increasing the structural pressure for market integration. The cycles form a single strand of supranational legal integration towards the Banking Union. These dynamics provide evidence that the evolution of European law, by itself, compels integration.

[10] W Sandholtz and A Stone Sweet, 'Neo-Functionalism and Supranational Governance' in E Jones, A Menon, and S Weatherill (eds) *The Oxford Handbook of the European Union* (Oxford, Oxford University Press, 2012) 18–33.

Figure 5 The Cycles of Legal and Institutional Change

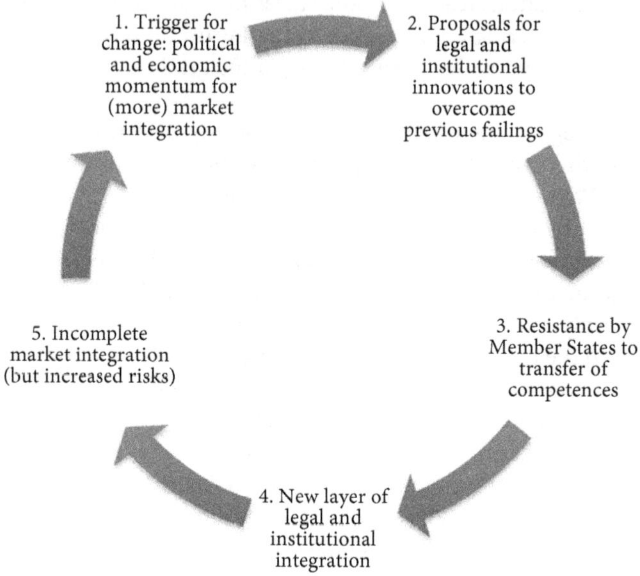

IV. Explaining the Acceleration of Integration Towards the Banking Union: The Spillover of the Monetary Union

The legal integration of the single financial market lasted for four decades, from the initial harmonisation efforts until the supranational structure of the Banking Union was reached. It was a relatively fast-paced integration. Each phase lasted roughly ten years, but there was a clear acceleration of integration after the start of the Monetary Union. This acceleration can be explained by the 'spillover' effects of the Monetary Union on the legal and institutional change towards the Banking Union.

The notion of 'spillover' is drawn from neofunctionalist theories on how Member States transfer their sovereignty towards supranational structures. They claim that integration is not determined by the preferences of Member States, as argued by intergovernmental theories. Instead, it proceeds essentially by unintended functional spillovers: once there is a step towards European integration in one policy area, the fulfilment of the original integration goals will sooner or later 'spillover' by also requiring integration in related policy areas. This happens in succession from one policy area to another and so on, leading to a self-sustaining expansion of integration. Such a spillover-driven process means that Member States are bound to provide more and more authority to the supranational level, and to such an extent that they are no longer in control of European integration. Political integration of Member States becomes, then, the ultimate spillover. The main critique of neofunctionalism is that it ignores the preferences of Member States and the relevance of democratic politics in steering the integration process. The automaticity claimed by neofunctionalism fails to account for either the historical periods of stalemate, or those of major progress towards the milestones of European integration, where the political will of Member States was decisive, such as the SEA or the Maastricht Treaty.[11]

For the purposes of explaining the creation of the Banking Union, the 'spillover' concept is helpful to convey the implications of the differentiation process of the Monetary Union for the single financial market. Regardless of the universal validity of such a concept, referring to 'spillover' dynamics captures well how the Monetary Union set in motion a fundamental structural change in European integration. This change had multiple dimensions, which both accelerated the creation of the Banking Union, and ultimately determined its shape.

First of all, financial integration was largely contained until the introduction of the euro. The Monetary Union then provided a major impetus for a European financial market. Whole components of the financial markets, such as the money market and wholesale payment systems, became integrated with the euro. Cross-border financial flows increased exponentially within the euro area, thanks to the removal of exchange rate risk and the transparency of prices. In order to reap the benefits of the euro and an integrated market, financial institutions increased their size, going beyond what would be proportional to their Member State of origin, and expanded their business throughout several Member States. These developments in financial integration subsequently led to a substantial increase of the scope of risks within the euro area: it became much more likely that a financial crisis would affect several Member States due to the increasingly intense financial interlinkages.[12]

As analysed above in Chapter 3, despite financial integration and a well-regulated financial system being a requisite for its functioning, the framework of the Monetary Union did not include any transfer of competences regarding the single financial market. Banking regulation and supervision, together with financial stability competences, all remained at the national level. Risk-sharing arrangements were excluded. This constituted an institutional flaw of the Monetary Union. It was the first time in history that there was such a mismatch between the monetary and the regulatory jurisdictions. The 'integration through governance' approach attempted to address this mismatch with various legal and institutional innovations. In line with the in-built rationality of European law explained previously, this approach promoted the expansion of the single financial market, but without the provision of a stabilisation capacity at the European level. It implied that the Monetary Union would be vulnerable to financial crises.[13]

The rapid increase in financial integration, compounded by the preservation of national competences for the single financial market and the absence of risk-sharing in

[11] On the concept of 'spillover' in the context of European legal integration see AM Burley and W Mattli 'Europe Before the Court: A Political Theory of Legal Integration' (1993) 47 *International Organization* 41. For the intergovernmental narrative of European integration, see A Moravcsik, *The Choice for Europe: Social Purpose and State Power from Messina to Maastricht* (Ithaca NY, Cornell University Press, 1998).

[12] See, eg, A Sapir and G Wolff, 'The neglected side of banking union: reshaping Europe's financial system,' note presented at the Informal ECOFIN on 14 September 2013, Vilnius, Bruegel, at www.bruegel.org/wp-content/uploads/imported/publications/20130913SapirWolff_final_.pdf.

[13] See T Padoa-Schioppa, *Regulating Finance, Balancing Freedom and Risk* (Oxford, Oxford University Press, 2004) 83–92.

the Monetary Union, exacerbated the consequences of the 2007–2008 financial crisis, and of the sovereign debt crisis a few years later. It gave rise to an existential threat to both the Monetary Union and the single financial market, as the soundness of Member States and their banks became entangled in a vicious circle. In line with the 'spillover' concept, the preservation of monetary integration also necessarily required the integration of the banking sector. European risk-sharing through the ESM, in order to cut the link between the banks and Member States, implied European control through banking supervision. This 'spillover' thus led to a crossroads between reversing monetary integration – if at all possible – and removing the national sovereignty over the banking sector. The 'inevitable' choice to preserve the Monetary Union was to centralise European competences within a Banking Union.[14]

In this way, the legal and institutional differentiation of the Monetary Union from the EU shaped the Banking Union. Given the urgency in tackling the crisis through the intervention of the ESM, the only legal basis available was the activation of Article 127.6 of the TFEU, enabling the transfer of banking supervision competences to the ECB. This is a provision from the EMU chapter of the Treaty, but with a double nature relating both to the functioning of the Monetary Union and the single financial market. Its activation had far-reaching consequences. It built the SSM – the first pillar of the Banking Union – on the legal and institutional framework of the Monetary Union, without requiring any Treaty change. It meant that the jurisdiction and membership of the Banking Union could not go beyond that of the euro area, thus not encompassing the single financial market. Together with other implications, Member States would be detached from the functioning of the Banking Union, also because the independence of the ECB spilled over into banking supervision and resolution. Using the framework of Monetary Union therefore accelerated the supranational integration of the single financial market. With the initial foundation of Article 127.6, the other components of the Banking Union, the 'single rulebook' and the SRM, could then be developed rapidly through secondary law, yet again on the basis of the harmonisation clause of Article 114 used for the single financial market.[15]

Another related factor for the acceleration of integration within the Banking Union was the need arising from the management of the sovereign debt crisis afflicting the euro area. For example, Chapter 5 shows how the rapid introduction of the banking resolution regime through the BRRD and the SRM Regulation was influenced by the experience of restructuring the banking sector in the Member States requiring financial assistance. It would provide the blueprint for the management of any subsequent banking crisis through mandatory bail-in and the prohibition of public bailouts, thus pre-empting any future dependence between banks and Member States. Once in place, the Banking Union then supported the management of the sovereign debt crisis, notably, in the 'Grexit' crisis in June–July 2015.

[14] On the impact of the framework of the Monetary Union on the intensity of the sovereign debt crisis, see PR Lane, 'The European Sovereign Debt Crisis' (2012) 26 *Journal of Economic Perspectives* 49.

[15] For all the implications of the differentiation process of the Monetary Union, see ch 5. See also T Tridimas, 'The Constitutional Dimension of Banking Union' in S Grundmann and HW Micklitz (eds) *The European Banking Union and Constitution: Beacon for Advanced Integration or Death-Knell for Democracy?* (Oxford, Hart Publishing, 2019) 25.

While the Banking Union is the outcome of the legal and institutional evolution of the single financial market, the 'spillover' effect of the Monetary Union accelerated its creation. In sum, the acceleration was propelled by the combination of: (1) increased financial integration; (2) the structural flaw of a Monetary Union without stabilisation functions or risk-sharing; and (3) the amplification of the financial and sovereign debt crises by this flaw and by the governance of the single financial market. All these factors conspired to provoke an existential crisis for both the Monetary Union and the single financial market, leading to a binary choice between supranational integration and disintegration. The interests and preferences of Member States certainly played a role, but they were arguably compelled by such a binary choice. The emergency provoked by this 'spillover' then determined that the law and institutions of the Monetary Union provided the foundation for the Banking Union and its development detached from Member States. An autonomous legal and institutional order then emerged for the Banking Union.

V. Uncovering the Parallel Evolution of Global Standard-Setting

The logic of the legal and institutional evolution of the single financial market was not an isolated phenomenon. It was mirrored right from the start and throughout by the parallel evolution of standard-setting for international and then global finance. The logic of standard-setting was to create a borderless financial market with its own rules. The rules were developed and administered by international and global committees, which had the dual function of bringing together national regulatory authorities and detaching them as much as possible from the pursuance of their domestic interests. This logic reflected the ultimate ambition of 'ordoliberalism': creating a worldwide market with an autonomous legal and institutional order, protected from the interference of nation states. It followed that, as for the single financial market, the global market order did not require any transfer of stabilisation functions to a world authority. As subsequently occurred in the responses to the great financial crisis of 2007–2008, national governments stabilised their respective markets through protectionist measures, which led to the retrenchment of the globalisation of finance.[16]

The law and institutions of the single financial market evolved, therefore, in tandem with the internationalisation and subsequent globalisation of finance. Each phase of European integration largely coincided with the evolution of standard setting.

First, the implementation of international and then global regulatory standards in Member States often provided the rationale for harmonisation proposals by the Commission. The need for consistency in such implementation in the single market

[16] On the 'universalist' ambitions of ordoliberalism, see Q Slobodian, *Globalists: The End of Empire and the Birth of Neoliberalism* (Cambridge MA, Harvard University Press, 2018) especially at 184–193. In the European context, see C Joerges, 'Europe's Economic Constitution in Crisis and the Emergence of a New Constitutional Constellation' (2014) 15 *German Law Journal* 985.

was easily justifiable. The agreement on harmonisation proposals was facilitated by the fact that many Member States comprised the G-10 group of countries at the core of most international standard-setting bodies. This process started concurrently with the development of the single financial market. The foundational principle of home-country control of the Basel Concordat of 1975 was already the aim of the First Banking Directive of 1977, even if it did not implement it due to the resistance of Member States at the time. It then continued with the implementation of the Basel Accord of 1988 in the Second Banking Directive, the Basel II Framework of 1999, and many other regulatory standards as global standard-setting expanded at the beginning of the twenty-first century. The fact that global standards were implemented through European law in turn supported the development of standard-setting, given the importance of European financial markets.[17]

Second, there were parallel developments in the institutional structure of standard-setting bodies and the single financial market. The Groupe de Contact established in 1972 had an influence in the shaping of the BCBS, which was created two years later. The BCBS was largely dominated by European central banks and supervisory authorities, implying an overlapping membership between standard-setting bodies and European committees. This facilitated agreement both at the international and European levels. The parallelism continued in the expansion of international standard-setting bodies from the mid-1980s to the 1990s, which was reflected in the establishment of European committees for each financial sector in roughly the same period. This was due to the need to implement the growing number of international regulatory standards for all sectors of the financial system. It also marked the beginning of comitology procedures in the single financial market to cater for the increasing level of regulatory detail, also stemming from international standards.

By the end of the twentieth century, multi-level governance had been introduced both at the global and European levels. Globally, the new FSF provided an umbrella organisation to provide policy steering to the major standard-setting bodies, which then trickled down to implementation of standards by national jurisdictions, enforcement by the same standard-setting bodies, as well as by the IMF and the World Bank. This provided a model for the concept of 'global administrative law' introduced at the time. In the single financial market, multi-level governance emerged out of the 'new governance' doctrines and replicated the global system with the introduction of the Lamfalussy framework in 2001.[18]

Third, the liberalisation and deregulation operated by the global governance of finance created the conditions for the 2007–2008 financial crisis. The global regulatory responses after the 2007–2008 financial crisis had, then, a direct influence on the law and institutions of the single financial market. The strengthening of the institutional structure of the global governance of finance was reflected in the creation in Europe of the ESA and the ESRB, with the latter as a parallel body to the new FSB. Likewise, the

[17] For an overview of such parallel developments, see also EL Camilli, 'Basel-Brussels One Way? The EU in the Legalization Process of Basel Soft Law' in E Chiti and BG Mattarella (eds) *Global Administrative Law and EU Administrative Law* (Berlin, Springer, 2011) 323, at 344–349.

[18] See ch 3.

introduction of financial stability as a key regulatory objective at the global level, and of macroprudential supervision as a new regulatory function, were incorporated into the EU framework. The greater level of detail of global standards also contributed to the development of a European 'single rulebook', for example, by justifying the use of EU regulations over directives, as it happened with the CRD Regulation of 2013. In this context, global standard-setting gave an impetus for the creation of the Banking Union. The banking resolution regime introduced by the FSB provided the blueprint for the BRRD and the SRM, which in turn represented the most comprehensive legal transposition of such a regime worldwide.

In conclusion, the legal and institutional integration of the single financial market and that of global finance were mutually reinforcing due to their shared logic, with an 'ordoliberal' tone, as argued above. The standards created at the international and global level acted as catalysts for the harmonisation of national laws in Europe via their transposition by European law into Member States. The EU became one of the most faithful jurisdictions in transposing global regulatory standards, which in turn further validated them and stimulated their development. Moreover, the rules of the single financial market were exported to global finance. The freedom of capital, the key condition for globalisation, emerged first in the single financial market. Accordingly, the creation of the Banking Union was also a by-product of such mutually reinforcing dynamics, which further amplified the thrust of European law towards supranational integration.

VI. Understanding the Democratic Legitimacy Problem

The conceptual logic of the legal evolution of the single financial market was creating an integrated market subject to its own rules and institutions and detached from Member States. Arguably, this reflected the 'ordoliberal' influence since the Spaak Report, according to which the functioning of the market should be subject to a 'neutral' order as to its distributive consequences. This implied that the market order should be protected from the intrusion of government. The aim was to avoid governments intervening to pursue distributive objectives to benefit their electorate and special groups. In other words, market order should be insulated from democratic politics. If not, the economic outcomes of a free market would be distorted, thus undermining its existence.[19]

The integration of the single financial market accordingly followed this logic. The European legal order of the single financial market would not have any distributive implications leading to a transfer of wealth among Member States and their citizens. It would be 'neutral' with regard to market forces. It would a 'technical' order, reflecting the best knowledge of financial regulation, including that stemming from global standards. There were no value choices expressed in European law, for example as to the ideal organisation of banking, securities or insurance markets. The only functional purpose was to achieve integration, understood as borderless competitive markets subject to

[19] See VJ Vanberg, 'The Freiburg School: Walter Eucken and Ordoliberalism' (2004) 04/11 *Freiburg Discussion Papers on Constitutional Economics.*

European law. At the same time, this meant that Member States would not be able to interfere with market integration with distributive choices to protect their national interests, such as protectionist measures through national laws. The logic of legal integration of the single financial market was, therefore, always to remain shielded from democratic politics, both at the European and national levels. As claimed by Joseph H.H. Weiler referring to the Schuman declaration: 'democracy was not part of the original DNA of European integration'.[20]

As a result, the legal integration of the single financial market was largely driven by technocratic processes. For example, most proposals for legal and institutional innovations were made by the Comités des Sages and then taken up by the Commission. Committees of national authorities played a prominent role in integration since the start. The scope of comitology procedures for the adoption of European rules was steadily widened throughout the phases of integration. Global standard-setting was often the motivation for further harmonisation of national laws.

The legal history of the Banking Union consisted, therefore, largely of depoliticised technocratic processes, which dismissed the distributive consequences of integration. This, in turn, limited the scope for the democratic control of such processes at the European and national levels. This was one of the reasons for the steady expansion of European law and institutions without much disruption under the so-called 'permissive consensus', which in turn led to the well-known democratic deficit.[21]

Until the 2007–2008 financial crisis, the regulation of finance was perceived to be the outcome of technical choices based on the efficient market hypothesis, and driven by technical expertise to ensure a well-functioning financial system. When risks materialised with the crisis, society bore the costs by bailing out financial institutions and enduring the economic implications. The crisis thus exposed the illusion that financial regulation had no distributive implications. Instead, financial regulation reflects the degree of societal tolerance to the risks of finance. Greater tolerance of risks translates into the increased likelihood that taxpayers' funds will be used as the ultimate backstop.

The same occurred with the expansion of the single financial market. The exclusive functional purpose of the law of the single financial market to achieve integration was exacerbated by the belief that financial regulation did not involve political choices. The single passport, the harmonisation of national laws, and of governance arrangements, were largely perceived as technocratic choices to ensure the good functioning of the single financial market and without distributive consequences. Moreover, the fact that there was no risk-sharing among Member States meant that there was no particular need for democratic control at the national level, also because national fiscal sovereignty was always safeguarded in market integration. The expansion of the single financial

[20] See JHH Weiler, 'In the Face of Crisis – Input Legitimacy, Output Legitimacy and the Political Messianism of European Integration' (2012) 34 *Journal of European Integration* 825. On the consequences of supranational powers without democratic legitimacy, see J Habermas, *The Lure of Technocracy*, (Cambridge, Polity, 2015) at 9–16. For a critique, see W Streeck 'What about capitalism? Jürgen Habermas's project of a European democracy' (2017) 16 *European Political Science* 246, 246–253.

[21] See M Poiares Maduro, 'A New Governance for the European Union and the Euro: Democracy and Justice' (2012) 2012/11 *RSCAS Policy Paper*; and A Moravcsik, 'In Defence of the "Democratic Deficit": Reassessing Legitimacy in the European Union' (2002) 40 *Journal of Common Market Studies* 603.

market was a positive sum game, where only benefits were shared and all Member States were winners.

At the European level, incipient steps in transparency and accountability practices were taken. They were, however, largely ineffective with regard to governance structures consisting of committees, where national authorities had no mandate to pursue the European interest. The absence of meaningful democratic control thus further contributed to the unconstrained deepening of integration. Only when the 2007–2008 crisis hit European shores did it become clear that the single financial market had major distributive implications for Member States, their citizens, depositors, the economy, and fiscal resources, and much more so than in other sectors of the single market.

The Banking Union, then, implied the transfer to European authorities of banking supervision and resolution competences, which were previously close to national fiscal sovereignty and subject to democratic accountability. Unlike the previous phases of the single financial market, where distributive effects could not be traced back to a European authority, the day-to-day decisions of the ECB/SSM and the SRB impact directly the functioning of the banking sector, its financing of the economy, and its stability, both across the single jurisdiction of the Banking Union and in each Member State. The European supervision and resolution of banks impact on Member States, and more on some Member States than others, depending on the circumstances of a financial shock.

The question in the design of the Banking Union was therefore how to make it democratically legitimate, given its significant distributive implications at both the European and national levels. The answer provided by the SSM and SRM Regulations to address this legitimacy problem was a combination of mechanisms, including: (1) legal safeguards obliging the ECB/SSM and the SRM to take into account both European and national interests, and preventing them from taking decisions directly affecting national fiscal sovereignty; (2) the institutional independence of the ECB/SSM and the SRB, so that decisions are based on their technical expertise, in line with the Treaty and secondary law, and not reflecting political and distributive choices; and (3) multi-level accountability to the European Parliament and national Parliaments, so as to contain the distributive implications of supervision and resolution decisions through democratic oversight.[22]

Together, these mechanisms aim at mitigating democratic concerns about the distributive implications of ECB/SSM and SRB decisions at both the European and national levels. The legal safeguards replace, to some extent, political control by judicial review: the ECB/SSM and SRB decisions can be legally challenged before the court if they go beyond such safeguards. The institutional independence ensures that the ECB/SSM and the SRB do not exercise their powers to the benefit of any political actor. In addition, multi-level accountability enables the European Parliament and national Parliaments to scrutinise the impact of the Banking Union policies in their jurisdictions, but without providing ex ante political guidance other than in legislative processes. Therefore, the distributive effects of supervision and resolution policies, which previously entailed a proximity to the national political institutions, led instead in the Banking Union to the

[22] See ch 5.

opposite: insulation from political interference. The legal and institutional framework, and the judicial review of compliance within such a framework, is the main source of its legitimacy.[23]

VII. The End of the Legal History of the Single Market? Determining the Future of the Banking Union

Does the Banking Union correspond to the final stage of integration in the single market? The Banking Union emerged as the purest form of legal and institutional integration thus far in the single market, which can be derived from the Treaty, and developed on the basis of secondary European law: a unified system of law, institutions with exclusive competences and enforcement authority, subject to judicial review by the Court. It is hard to conceive that it could evolve much beyond this framework within the Treaty. In this sense, is the Banking Union the perfect integration model, which all sectors of the single market will ultimately reach in their evolution? Is this the end of the legal history of the single market?

The Banking Union is the corollary of four decades of legal and institutional evolution of the single market in financial services. Its creation was accelerated by the Monetary Union and the succession of the 2007–2008 financial and sovereign debt crises from 2010 onwards. But the Banking Union was an evolutionary – and not a revolutionary – stage of integration within the single market. It was based on the Treaty, notably the harmonisation clause of Article 114 of the TFEU, even if stretched its boundaries. It followed the same logic of legal and institutional integration since the Treaty of Rome.

The question is then how sustainable the Banking Union is over time. The answer, as provided by the above findings, is that it will very much depend on the extent to which the prevailing logic of legal and institutional integration will be overcome. In other words, the internal contradiction of the integration process would need to be untangled before a stable state is achieved. A regime geared towards ever more integration with distributive consequences, but without stabilisation capacity in the form of risk-sharing among Member States, and largely insulated from democratic politics, will likely not be sustainable. It will be especially so, if there is another crisis with far-reaching consequences, when decisions should be perceived as fair and legitimate across Member States. This is confirmed by the debate, at the time of writing, about the degree of solidarity among Member States in the response to the pandemic crisis.

Therefore, two conditions will need to be fulfilled in the Banking Union to safeguard its future: risk-sharing and democratic legitimacy. The Banking Union will likely disintegrate – similarly to the single financial market during the 2007–2008 financial crisis – if its distributive impact is neither fairly shared nor perceived as democratically legitimate at the European level and among Member States. The fulfilment of these

[23] As also concluded by the German Constitutional Court in its Banking Union judgment, BVerfG, Urteil des Zweiten Senats vom 30 Juli 2019, 2 BvR 1685/14, Rn. (1-320).

conditions, however, goes beyond the reach of the framework of the existing Treaty. As illustrated by the cover of this book, the Banking Union is a new building, but still based on an old architectural style.

First, there is no basis in the Treaty to mutualise risks through public funds at the European level. Risk-sharing can only take place through the ESM, as originally envisaged by the Euro Summit of 30 June 2012. The ESM is, however, an intergovernmental organisation outside the Treaty. As occurred in the responses to the 2007–2008 financial crisis, the combination of national interests required for ESM decisions would not safeguard the supranational nature of the Banking Union.

Second, the Treaty cannot really offer much more than legal and technical output legitimacy to the Banking Union. The SSM and the SRM Regulations aimed at broadening such legitimacy by introducing a system of multi-level accountability. If the Banking Union policies have to be justified to a multiplicity of European and national political institutions, it would hardly legitimise the outcome of distributive conflicts at the European level and among Member States in a systemic crisis.

The sustainability of the Banking Union will depend on future treaty-based arrangements, which enable risk-sharing and democratic legitimacy. However, these two conditions are interlocked. Fiscal competences with distributive implications, such as the creation of a euro bond, cannot be transferred from Member States because there is no political integration providing a foundation for democratic legitimacy at the European level. Conversely, there is no justification to achieve political integration because there are no European fiscal competences. This interlocking perpetuates the dominance of national political and fiscal sovereignty, which reduces the Banking Union to a technocratic project and threatens its existence in the case of major shocks.

The Banking Union is thus not the end of the legal history of the single market. Legal and institutional integration with distributive implications, but short of stabilisation capacity and meaningful democratic legitimacy, is not self-sustainable. The law and institutions of the Banking Union will ultimately need to be underpinned by political and fiscal integration between Member States and new sources of democratic legitimacy. A new chapter of integration, likely on 'integration through politics', will be required to secure its future.[24]

VIII. Conclusion: The Banking Union and European Integration

The purpose of this book is to verify the extent to which the supranational integration of the single financial market into the Banking Union was a consequence of European law. The focus has been on the process of legal change, which was reconstructed into

[24] See S Grundmann and HW Micklitz, 'The European Banking Union and Constitution – The Overall Challenge' in S Grundmann and HW Micklitz (eds), *The European Banking Union and Constitution: Beacon for Advanced Integration or Death-Knell for Democracy?* (Oxford, Hart Publishing, 2019) 1.

five historical phases of integration. In summary, this history of European law gives the following insights into the process of integration.

1. The creation of the supranational Banking Union can be ascribed to the deep-rooted logic of integration through European law, which dominated the evolution of the single financial market: a supranational legal order would give rise to a market as integrated as a domestic market, whose functioning would be insulated from Member States. The development of such a supranational order did not require the transfer of national sovereignty, but it gradually contradicted national economic and regulatory policies in an ever integrating financial market.
2. The process of integration leading to the Banking Union operated through successive cycles of change in European law. They correspond to the waves of legal and institutional innovations, which made the transition from one phase of integration to another. Together, these cycles formed a strand of supranational integration: they built on each other to form layer upon layer of European rules and institutional structures. These dynamics steered EU institutions, Member States, market participants, and others, towards ever more integration.
3. The Banking Union was accelerated by the 'spillover' effect of the Monetary Union: preserving monetary integration required the integration of the banking sector. Such an effect emerged out of the combination of: (1) increased financial integration; (2) a Monetary Union without stabilisation functions or risk-sharing; and (3) the amplification of the financial and sovereign debt crises. The Banking Union was then founded on the law and institutions of the Monetary Union.
4. The creation of the Banking Union was also related to global standard setting. The law of the single financial market and the standard setting for global finance shared the same logic: creating an integrated market with an autonomous order. This generated mutually reinforcing dynamics between them in the creation of rules and institutions at the European and global levels. The global response to the great financial crisis then provided further impetus to a Banking Union.
5. The logic of European law is that the functioning of an integrated market should be 'neutral' as to its distributive implications. It should also be safeguarded from the intervention of Member States to pursue distributive objectives. This meant that legal integration was largely detached from democratic politics.
6. The Banking Union is not the end of the legal history of the single market. Its preservation ultimately requires risk sharing among Member States, as well as democratic legitimacy at the European level. Otherwise, its existence may be threatened if the distributive implications are not considered fair and legitimate.

What do these findings from the legal history of the Banking Union bring to the understanding of the wider European integration process?

The Banking Union matches the perfect 'fusion of markets', as heralded by the Spaak Report, where market participants are indistinguishable by their origin and subject equally and exclusively to European law. Such a 'fusion' was achieved over four decades, through successive cycles of legal and institutional innovations towards the supranational integration of the single financial market. This is unique in European integration. In contrast to the other treaty-based supranational systems of competition law and the Monetary Union, the supranational integration of the single financial market largely materialised through secondary law, out of the harmonisation clause of Article 114 of the TFEU.[25]

The original motivation of the Spaak Report also defined the strategy of legal integration leading to the Banking Union: avoiding a traumatic failure like the European Defence Community in 1954 by promoting a 'common market' – as equivalent as possible to an economic union – without requiring the transfer of national powers to the European level. This strategy of the '*relance européenne*' towards the Treaty of Rome in 1957, would lead, however, to an internal contradiction in the integration process. Successive cycles of legal and institutional change cause unstable equilibria between increasing integration, the build-up of common risks, and the preservation of national competences. Over time, and without a stop rule, these feedback loops grow exponentially until a shock happens, such as the financial and sovereign debt crises.

It is in this sense that European integration is inherently 'crisis-prone'. There is an accumulation of risks in an integrated market, which largely takes place by stealth, since risks are not as observable or quantifiable as the benefits of integration. When a shock materialises, there is no stabilisation capacity in the form of direct enforcement of European law or use of fiscal funds. Integration is thus always bound to fail until the capacity to stabilise markets is transferred to the European level. The more Member States resist such transfer, the more likely it becomes, as the magnitude of the shock is exacerbated by the lack of actions to preserve integration. For example, the Deauville declaration exacerbated the sovereign debt crisis and arguably led to the establishment of the ESM. Further delay in controlling the sovereign debt crisis arguably led to the creation of the SSM. At the time of finalising this book, similar dynamics are unfolding in the European response to the pandemic crisis. In the European integration process, a crisis can only be overcome through additional commitments by Member States towards more integration.[26]

Until then, integration evolves during cycles of legal and institutional change approximating European competences closer and closer to such stabilisation functions, including through harmonisation, committees, multi-level governance, agencies, intergovernmental arrangements outside the Treaty, and others identified in this book. These are intermediate outcomes, which are largely transitory and not sustainable when a European stabilisation function is required. They are trial and error 'approximations', which create the utopia that soft governance is sufficient to manage European integration. When risks materialise and have distributive implications, the utopia becomes a dystopia and there is a binary outcome: drastic disintegration or acceleration of

[25] European law was thus both the object and the instrument of supranational integration. See R Dehousse and JHH Weiler, 'The Legal Dimension' in W Wallace (ed) *The Dynamics of European Integration* (London, Pinter, 1990) 242–60.

[26] On the 'improvisation' mode towards the management of crises, see L Van Middelaar, *Quand L'Europe Improvise*, (n 8) especially 88–102. There were similar dynamics in the beginning of the political history of the US, when Alexander Hamilton proposed in 1790 the establishment of a national bank to stabilise a national currency. This would also enable the federal government to assume responsibility for the debts of the states. On this 'Hamiltonian moment', see R Chernow, *Alexander Hamilton* (New York, Penguin, 2004) at 298–99.

integration through the transfer of stabilisation competences. Soft governance is then replaced by supranational powers.[27]

In the flow of this narrative, intergovernmental bargaining, and the need to create rules and institutions at the European level to reinforce the commitments of Member States, have certainly played a role. The political and economic interests of Member States determined the milestones in integration and shaped European law instruments. However, as shown so far, the logic of the process of legal change framed progressively the choices of Member States towards supranational integration.[28]

Legal integration is also not an automatic process, out of the control of Member States, as in neofunctionalist theories. Some concepts related to these theories are nonetheless helpful to convey the compelling nature of legal integration. The definition of 'spillover' is useful to explain the acceleration of integration in a certain direction, as argued above regarding the impact of the Monetary Union. Similarly, the meaning of 'cycles of institutionalisation' characterise well the dynamics of legal change, even though institutionalist theories link supranational integration more to the growth of cross-border transactions and to the pressure by interest groups than to legal change.[29]

The narrative depicted in this book is thus the gradual but continuous change operated by European law over decades, steering political, economic and social dynamics towards supranational integration. Along the way, this legal change leads to more and more intermeshing between European rules and institutions, national sovereignty, market participants, global governance, and citizens. This makes integration compelling and irreversible.[30]

The legal history of the Banking Union confirms, therefore, the supranational nature of European integration, whose direction is towards the full centralisation of European law and institutions. As Jean Monnet expressed it, 'to adopt common rules which our nations and their citizens pledge themselves to follow, and to set up common institutions to ensure their application'. It reflects the suspicion about the nation-state after the horrors of the World War Two era and the idealism that 'perpetual peace' would be achieved in the European continent by supranational government. There are no

[27] In this sense, on 'the rise of executive power and the strengthening of the technocratic rule' following the failure of governance arrangements, see C Joerges, 'Integration through Law and the Crisis of Law in Europe's Emergency, in Chalmers' in M Jachtenfuchs and C Joerges (eds) *The End of the Eurocrats' Dream: Adjusting to European Diversity* (Cambridge, Cambridge University Press, 2016) 299–338, at 308–309. See also R Dehousse, 'Why has EU macroeconomic governance become more supranational?' (2016) 38 *Journal of European Integration* 617, who emphasises in this new stage of European integration, rather than the rise in intergovernmentalism, the reinforcement of the role of supranational actors, like the Commission and the ECB, in the form of new powers and strengthened autonomy.

[28] As first analysed by JHH Weiler, supranational integration is dependent on intergovernmental processes supporting European integration, see JHH Weiler, 'The Community System: the Dual Character of Supranationalism' (1981) 1 *Yearbook of European Law* 267.

[29] AS Sweet, W Sandholtz, N Fligstein, 'The Institutionalization of European Space' in AS Sweet, W Sandholtz, N Fligstein (eds) *The Institutionalization of Europe* (Oxford, Oxford University Press, 2001).

[30] On the dynamics of supranational legal integration, C Joerges, 'Taking the Law Seriously: On Political Science and the Role of Law in the Process of European Integration' (1996) 2 *European Law Journal* 105; and JP McCormick, *Weber, Habermas, and Transformations of the European State: Constitutional, Social, and Supranational Democracy* (Cambridge, Cambridge University Press, 2007), 236–245.

unintended consequences in European integration: the supranational path was clear from its early beginnings.[31]

In conclusion, the answer to the questions posed in the introduction is that the supranational Banking Union was not an accident of history. It was the 'predictable' outcome of the deliberate choices made in integration through European law. The quote of the Spaak Report in the introduction depicts a deterministic framework: if the Treaty freedoms are enforced to the maximum extent by a supranational legal order, Member States will surrender their sovereignty over time. A 'common market' meant a 'full economic union'. Although arguably made under an ordoliberal influence, the assumption that economic integration could preserve itself without a stabilisation capacity and disconnected from democratic checks and balances, was a flaw.[32]

In this sense, the Banking Union also corresponds to the gradual transformation of the European Union from a community of benefits to a community of risk sharing, where Member States not only share the benefits from integration but also start sharing the risks and potential costs. This is a profound transformation that presupposes not only political integration between Member States, but also new sources of supranational democratic legitimacy. It would imply in reality the return to the original concept of Jean Monnet, which was dismissed in the Spaak Report: a 'common market' based on supranational institutions with political powers, including the federalisation of social, economic and fiscal policies. The next question is whether political integration and a supranational democracy are inevitable. There is, however, no historical inevitability in integration; the alternative is disintegration. The choice between the two is beyond the predictable rationality of European law within the current Treaty.[33]

PS 1: As suggested by the cover of this book – 'The Nostalgia of the Infinite' by Giorgio de Chirico – European integration reflects the human yearning for a perpetual and just legal order beyond the confines of the nation-state, even if, as in the opening quote of Fernando Pessoa, European law is a social fiction which is bound not to be eternal.

PS 2: Integration in the time of a pandemic. At the time that I am finalising this book in June 2020, the global spread of the coronavirus is at its peak. It is leading to a standstill in

[31] Excerpt from a quote from Jean Monnet of the Joint declaration adopted by the Action Committee for the United States of Europe, Bonn, 1st and 2nd June 1964, FJME, AMK 16/6/210, in G Grin, 'Shaping Europe: The Path to European Integration according to Jean Monnet' (n 1) at 12. On the original supranational intentions in the drafting of the Treaty of Rome, see JB Cruz, *What's Left of the Law of Integration? Decay and Resistance in European Union Law* (Oxford, Oxford University Press, 2018), ch 2 on 'Law after Auschwitz, especially 13–14. For a critique of this supranational narrative, arguing that Europe should not be seen as a revival of the European nation-state, see KH Ladeur, '"We, the European People …" – Relâche?' (2008) 14 *European Law Journal* 147. See also G Majone, *Europe as the Would-Be World Power: The EU at 50* (Cambridge, Cambridge University Press, 2009) at 72–98, who characterises the supranational process as 'crypto-federalism' since it focus exclusively on the means to achieve integration, without making the ultimate ends explicit.

[32] See P Pescatore, 'Some Critical Remarks on the "Single European Act"', (1987) 24 *CML Rev* 9, who argued at the time, when criticising the concept of an 'internal market' in the SEA, that the notion of 'common market' in the Treaty Rome meant a 'full economic union'.

[33] On this process of transformation of European integration, see E Chiti and PG Teixeira, 'The Constitutional Implications of the European Financial and Public Debt Crisis' (2013) 50 *CML Rev* 683, at 707–708. On Jean Monnet's concept for a 'common market', see above ch 1 on the origins of the single financial market.

the life of Europeans and an unprecedented collapse in economic activity with widespread loss of employment. The first European response was the launch by the ECB of a €750 billion pandemic emergency purchase programme on 18 March, which was increased by €600 billion to a total of €1,350 billion on 4 June. This was accompanied by banking supervision measures providing capital and operational relief to the banks subject to the SSM jurisdiction, while prohibiting the distribution of dividends. The Commission proposed the activation of the escape clause of the SGP and adopted a temporary framework enabling state aid to address the crisis. The European fiscal response consisted of the deployment of resources through the EU budget, the EIB, the ESM, as well as a European recovery fund. It is already being claimed by Heads of State of the euro area that the absence of fiscal solidarity among Member States may pose yet another existential threat to the European project. The way forward would be the assumption at the European level of the debt incurred by Member States to address the economic fall-out of the pandemic crisis. Such sharing of costs and risks would be made in the form of a Euro bond. This would prevent any Member State being left behind due to the economic and social consequences of the pandemic. This potential 'Hamiltonian moment,' stemming from a public health crisis instead of a war, would be the start of yet another phase in European integration.

BIBLIOGRAPHY

Primary Sources

Banco de Portugal, Comunicado do Banco de Portugal sobre a aplicação de medida de resolução ao Banco Espírito Santo, S.A. (2014) www.bportugal.pt/comunicado/comunicado-do-banco-de-portugal-sobre-aplicacao-de-medida-de-resolucao-ao-banco-espirito.

BCBS, Core Principles for Effective Banking Supervision (2012), at www.bis.org/publ/bcbs230.pdf.

—— Basel III: A global regulatory framework for more resilient banks and banking systems (2010), at www.bis.org/publ/bcbs189_dec2010.pdf.

—— Core Principles for Effective Banking Supervision (2006), at www.bis.org/publ/bcbs230.htm.

—— International Convergence of Capital Measurement and Capital Standards: A Revised Framework (2004), at www.bis.org/publ/bcbs107a.pdf.

—— Essential elements of a statement of cooperation between banking supervisors (2001), at www.bis.org/publ/bcbs83.htm.

—— Quantitative Impact Studies: QIS 2 and QIS 2.5 history (2001), at www.bis.org/bcbs/qis/qishist.htm.

—— 'History of the Basel Committee and its membership,' in *Compendium of Documents produced by the BCBS* (Bank for International Settlements, 2000).

—— The Core Principles Methodology (1999), at www.bis.org/publ/bcbs61.htm.

—— Consultative Document - Proposals for International Convergence of capital measurement and standards (1987), at www.bis.org/publ/bcbs03a.pdf.

—— Principles for the Supervision of Banks' Foreign Establishments (1983), at www.bis.org/publ/bcbsc312.pdf.

—— Committee on Banking Regulations and Supervisory Practices, Report to the Governors on Supervision of Banks' Foreign Establishments, 26 September 1975, at www.bis.org/publ/bcbs00a.pdf.

BIS, 79th Annual Economic Report (2009), at www.bis.org/publ/arpdf/ar2009e.htm.

—— Group of Ten, Report on Consolidation in the Financial Sector (2001), at www.bis.org/publ/gten05.pdf.

—— Report of the Committee on Interbank Netting Schemes of the central banks of the Group of Ten countries (Lamfalussy Report) (1990), at www.bis.org/cpmi/publ/d04.htm.

CEBS, Assessing CEBS' progress so far (2007), at www.eba.europa.eu/documents/10180/16118/CEBS+assessment+report.pdf.

CEBS and CEIOPS, Colleges of Supervisors: 10 Common principles' (2009), at eiopa.europa.eu/CEIOPS-Archive/Documents/Standards/CEBS-CEIOPS-IWCFC-10-principles-colleges-of-supervisors.pdf.

Central Bank of Cyprus, 'The Enforcement of Restrictive Measures on Transactions in case of Emergency Law of 2013, 28 March 2013, at www.centralbank.cy/en/announcements/28-03-2013.

Committee of Governors, Letter from the Chairman of the Committee of Governors to the President of the Council of the European Communities enclosing an explanatory note on certain articles contained in the proposed Statute of the ESCB and ECB, 2 September 1991, at www.ecb.europa.eu/ecb/access_to_documents/document/cog_pubaccess/shared/data/ecb.dr.parcg2019_0041letterandnote.en.pdf?0e104201bd6f5922536750454ad7ad73.

Deutsche Bundesbank, Financial Stability Review (2014).

—— Financial Stability Review (2012). Eurogroup, Statement on Greece, 20 February 2015, at www.consilium.europa.eu/en/press/press-releases/2015/02/150220-eurogroup-statement-greece/.

—— ESM Direct Bank Recapitalisation Instrument: Main features of the Operational framework and way forward, Luxembourg, 20 June 2013, at www.consilium.europa.eu/uedocs/cms_data/docs/pressdata/en/ecofin/137569.pdf.

—— Statement on Ireland, 14 November 2013, at www.consilium.europa.eu/uedocs/cms_Data/docs/pressdata/en/ecofin/139579.pdf.
—— Statement on Cyprus, 25 March 2013, at www.consilium.europa.eu/uedocs/cms_Data/docs/pressdata/en/ecofin/136487.pdf.
—— Statement on Cyprus, 16 March 2013, at www.consilium.europa.eu/uedocs/cms_data/docs/pressdata/en/ecofin/136190.pdf.
—— Statement on Greece, 13 December 2012, at www.consilium.europa.eu/press/press-releases/2012/12/pdf/Eurogroup-statement-on-Greece.
—— Statement on Greece, 27 November 2012, at www.consilium.europa.eu/press/press-releases/2012/11/pdf/Eurogroup-statement-on-Greece-27-11.
EBA, Recommendation on the creation and supervisory oversight of temporary capital buffers to restore market confidence (EBA/REC/2011/1), 8 December 2011, at eba.europa.eu/documents/10180/26923/2011+12+08-ECOFIN-EBA-Statement+FINALv2.pdf.
—— Joint Statement by the Presidency of the ECOFIN and the EBA, 8 December 2011, at eba.europa.eu/documents/10180/26923/2011+12+08-ECOFIN-EBA-Statement+FINALv2.pdf.
ECB, The Governing Council's Expanded Asset Programme, ECB Economic Bulletin, 1/2015 (2015).
—— Financial Integration in Europe (2013), at www.ecb.europa.eu/pub/pdf/other/financialintegration ineurope201304en.pdf.
—— Press Release, Governing Council decision on Emergency Liquidity Assistance requested by the Central Bank of Cyprus, 21 March (2013), at www.ecb.europa.eu/press/pr/date/2013/html/pr130321.en.html.
—— Technical features of Outright Monetary Transactions (2012), at www.ecb.europa.eu/press/pr/date/2012/html/pr120906_1.en.html.
—— Introductory statement to the press conference, 6 September (2012), at www.ecb.europa.eu/press/pressconf/2012/html/is120906.en.html.
—— Verbatim of the remarks made by Mario Draghi, President of the European Central Bank at the Global Investment Conference in London, 26 July (2012) at www.ecb.europa.eu/press/key/date/2012/html/sp120726.en.html.
—— The ECB's Non-Standard Measures: Impact and Phasing-Out, ECB Monthly Bulletin, July 2011, 55–69.
—— Statement of the President of the ECB on the activation of the Securities Market Programme, 7 August 2011, at www.ecb.europa.eu/press/pr/date/2011/html/pr110807.en.html.
—— ECB announces measures to support bank lending and money market activity, Press Release, (2011) at www.ecb.europa.eu/press/pr/date/2011/html/pr111208_1.en.html.
—— Recent Developments in Supervisory Structures in the EU Member States (2007–2010) (2010), at www.ecb.europa.eu/pub/pdf/other/report_on_supervisory_structures2010en.pdf.
—— The implementation of monetary policy since August 2007, ECB Monthly Bulletin, July 2009.
—— Memorandum of Understanding on Cooperation between the Financial Supervisory Authorities, Central Banks, and Finance Ministries of the European Union on Cross-Border Financial Stability (2008), at www.ecb.europa.eu/pub/pdf/other/mou-financialstability2008en.pdf.
—— Financial Integration in Europe (2008), at www.ecb.europa.eu/pub/pdf/other/financialintegration ineurope200804en.pdf.
—— Recommendations on the pricing of guarantees (2008), at www.ecb.europa.eu/pub/pdf/other/recommendations_on_guaranteesen.pdf.
—— Recommendations on the pricing of recapitalisation (2008), at www.ecb.europa.eu/pub/pdf/other/recommendations_on_pricing_for_recapitalisationsen.pdf.
—— The EU Arrangements for Financial Crisis Management, ECB Monthly Bulletin, February 2007, 73–84.
—— EU Banking Structures (2006), at www.ecb.europa.eu/pub/pdf/other/eubankingstructures2006en.pdf.
—— Report on EU Banking Structures (2004), at www.ecb.europa.eu/pub/pdf/other/eubankingstructure 2004en.pdf.
—— The Role of Central Banks in Prudential Supervision (2001), at www.ecb.europa.eu/pub/pdf/other/prudentialsupcbrole_en.pdf.
European Commission, Proposal for a Regulation of the European Parliament and of the Council on sovereign bond-backed securities, COM (2018) 339 final.
—— White Paper on the Future of Europe, COM (2017) 2025 final, at ec.europa.eu/commission/sites/beta-political/files/white_paper_on_the_future_of_europe_en.pdf.

—— Reflection Paper on the Deepening of the Economic and Monetary Union (2017), at ec.europa.eu/commission/sites/beta-political/files/reflection-paper-emu_en.pdf.
—— On steps towards Completing Economic and Monetary Union, COM (2015) 0600 final.
—— Proposal for a Regulation of the European Parliament and of the Council amending Regulation (EU) 806/2014 in order to establish a European Deposit Insurance Scheme, COM (2015) 0586 final, (2015) 0270 final.
—— Towards the completion of the Banking Union, COM (2015) 0587 final.
—— Action Plan on Building a Capital Markets Union, COM (2015) 468 final.
—— The Economic Adjustment Programme for Portugal 2011–2014, European Economy 202 (2014).
—— Spain Post Programme Surveillance, Spring 2014 Report, European Economy 193 (2014).
—— Report of the Expert Group on a Debt Redemption Fund and Eurobills (2014), at ec.europa.eu/economy_finance/articles/ governance/pdf/20140331_report_en.pdf.
—— Financial Assistance Programme for the recapitalisation of financial institutions in Spain: Third review of the programme, European Economy 155 (2013).
—— The Economic Adjustment Programme for Cyprus, European Economy 149 (2013).
—— The application, from 1 August 2013, of State aid rules to support measures in favour of banks in the context of the financial crisis', [2013] OJ C216/1.
—— Statement on the capital controls imposed by the Republic of Cyprus, 28 March, at europa.eu/rapid/press-release_IP-13-298_en.htm (2013).
—— European Financial Stability and Integration Report 2012 (2013), ec.europa.eu/info/sites/info/files/efsir-2012-25042013_en.pdf.
—— Application of Directive 2007/44/EC amending Council Directive 92/49/EEC and Directives 2002/83/EC, 2004/39/EC, 2005/68/EC and 2006/48/EC as regards procedural rules and evaluation criteria for the prudential assessment of acquisitions and increase of holdings in the financial sector, COM (2013) 64 final (2013).
—— The Financial Sector Adjustment Programme for Spain, European Economy 118 (2012).
—— A Blue Print for a Deep and Genuine EMU, Launching A European Debate, COM (2012) 777 final.
—— Staff Working Document, Impact Assessment, SWD (2012) 166 final.
—— The Economic Adjustment Programme for Ireland, European Economy 76 (2011).
—— Commission Staff Working Document: Lisbon Strategy Evaluation Document, SEC (2010) 114 final.
—— Enhancing economic policy coordination for stability, growth and jobs – Tools for stronger EU economic governance, COM (2010) 367/2.
—— DG Competition's review of guarantee and recapitalisation schemes in the financial sector, 7 August 2009, at ec.europa.eu/competition/state_aid/legislation/review_of_schemes_en.pdf.
—— The return to viability and the assessment of restructuring measures in the financial sector in the current crisis under the State aid rules, [2009] OJ C195/9–20.
—— Treatment of Impaired assets in the Community Banking Sector, [2009] OJ72/1–22.
—— The recapitalisation of financial institutions in the current financial crisis: limitation of aid to the minimum necessary and safeguards against undue distortions of competition, [2009] OJ C10/2–10.
—— European financial supervision, COM (2009) 0252 final.
—— An EU Framework for Cross-Border Crisis Management in the Banking Sector, COM (2009) 561 final (2009).
—— European Financial Integration Report 2008, SEC (2009) 19 final.
—— Europe's financial system: adapting to change, COM (2008) 122 final.
—— EMU@10: successes and challenges after 10 years of Economic and Monetary Union, European Economy 2/2008 (2008).
—— A European Economic Recovery Plan, COM (2008) 800 final.
—— The application of State aid rules to measures taken in relation to financial institutions in the context of the current global financial crisis, [2008] OJ C270/8–14.
—— European Agencies – The Way Forward, COM (2008) 135 final.
—— A Single market for 21st century Europe, COM (2007) 724 final.
—— Communication on the 'Review of the Lamfalussy Process: Strengthening supervisory convergence,' COM (2007) 727 final.
—— Inter-Institutional Monitoring Group, Final Report Monitoring the Lamfalussy process, Brussels, 15 October 2007 (on file).

—— European Financial Integration Report 2007, SEC (2007) 1696.
—— Implementing the Community Lisbon Programme: A strategy for the simplification of the regulatory environment, COM (2005) 535 final.
—— White Paper on Financial Services Policy (2005–2010), COM (2005) 629 final.
—— Cross-Border Consolidation in the EU Financial Sector, SEC (2005) 1398.
—— Communication on intra-EU investment in the financial services' sector C/2005/4080, [2005] OJ C293/2.
—— Financial Services: Turning the Corner, Preparing the challenge of the next phase of European capital market integration (on file) (2004).
—— Community guidelines on State aid for rescuing and restructuring firms in difficulty, [2004] OJ C244/2–17.
—— Report from the Commission on European Governance, Office for Official Publications of the European Communities, (2003).
—— The Giovanni Report: Cross-border clearing and settlement arrangements in the EU, Economic Papers, 163, (2002).
—— Communication on 'European Governance: Better lawmaking', COM (2002) 275 final.
—— Towards a reinforced culture of consultation and dialogue – General principles and minimum standards for consultation of interested parties by the Commission, COM (2002) 704 final.
—— European Governance: a White Paper, COM (2001) 428 final.
—— Report on Financial Crisis Management, 156 *Economic Papers* (2001).
—— Communication on 'The application of conduct of business rules under Article 11 of the Investment Services Directive' (93/22/EEC), COM (2000) 722 final.
—— Interpretative Communication 2000/C 43/03 on freedom to provide services and the general good in the insurance sector, [2000] OJ C43.
—— Financial Services: Implementing the framework for financial markets – Action Plan, COM (1999) 232.
—— Commission Communication, Action Plan for the Single Market, CSE (1997) 1 final.
—— Interpretative Communication on the freedom to provide services and the interest of the general good in the second banking directive, SEC (1997) 1193 final.
—— The Single Market in 1995, COM (1996) 51 final.
—— The Single Market in 1994, COM (1995) 238 final.
—— The Community Internal Market, COM (1994) 55 final.
—— The Internal Market After 1992: Meeting the Challenge, Report to the EEC Commission by the High-Level Group on the Operation of the Internal Market presided by Peter Sutherland, SEC (1992) 2044.
—— One Market, One Money: An evaluation of the potential benefits and costs of forming an economic and monetary union, European Economy, 44, (1990).
—— The European Financial Common Market, Office for Official Publications of the European Communities, Luxembourg, (1989).
—— The Cecchini Report: The Economics of 1992: An assessment of the potential economic effects of completing the internal market of the European Community, European Economy 35, (1988).
—— Report on Economic and Monetary Union in the European Community, Committee for the Study of Economic and Monetary Union, (Delors Report) (1988).
—— Progress Report on the European Monetary System and the Liberalization of Capital Market, COM (1987) 650 final.
—— Communication on the programme for the liberalisation of capital movements in the Community, COM (1986) 292 final.
—— Completing the Internal Market, White Paper to the European Council of 28–29 June 1985 in Milan, COM (1985) 310 final.
—— Financial Integration, Communication from the Commission to the Council, COM (1983) 207 final.
—— The Advantages and disadvantages of an integrated market compared with a fragmented market (1977) (on file).
—— Report of the Study Group 'Economic and Monetary Union 1980,' Brussels, March 1975, at ec.europa.eu/archives/emu_history/documentation/chapter7/19750308en57reportstudygroup.pdf.
—— Second Report on Competition Policy (1973).
—— The Development of a European Capital Market, Report of a Group of experts appointed by the EEC Commission, (Segré Report), November 1966.

—— The first stage of the Common Market: Report on the Execution of the Treaty (January 1958-January 1962), (1962) at aei.pitt.edu/1324/1/internal_market_first_stage_memo.pdf.
European Council, Guidelines following the UK's notification under Article 50, TEU, 29 April 2017, at www.consilium.europa.eu/en/press/press-releases/2017/04/29-euco-brexit-guidelines.
—— Statement on the UK notification (Art 50), 29 March 2017, at www.consilium.europa.eu/en/press/press-releases/2017/03/29-euco-50-statement-uk-notification.
—— A New Settlement for the United Kingdom within the European Union, Extract of the conclusions of the European Council of 18–19 February 2016, [2016] OJ C69 I/1.
—— Conclusions of the European Council, 16 and 17 December 2010, www.consilium.europa.eu/uedocs/cms_data/docs/pressdata/en/ec/118578.pdf.
—— Conclusions of the European Council, 28 and 29 October 2010, at www.consilium.europa.eu/uedocs/cms_data/docs/pressdata/en/ec/117496.pdf.
—— Strengthening Economic Governance in the EU, Report of the Task Force to the European Council, 21 October 2010, at www.consilium.europa.eu/media/27405/117236.pdf.
—— Presidency Conclusions of 11 and 12 December 2008, www.consilium.europa.eu/ueDocs/cms_Data/docs/pressData/en/ec/104692.pdf.
—— Presidency Conclusions of 15 and 16 October 2008, at data.consilium.europa.eu/doc/document/ST-14368-2008-INIT/en/pdf.
—— Resolution of the European Council on more effective securities market regulation in the European Union, Stockholm, 23 March 2001, at www.esma.europa.eu/sites/default/files/library/2015/11/resolutionstockholm.pdf.
—— Presidency Conclusions (2000), at www.consilium.europa.eu/uedocs/cms_data/docs/pressdata/en/ec/00100-r1.en0.htm.
EU Council, Agreement on the transfer and mutualisation of contributions to the Single Resolution Fund (2014), at register.consilium.europa.eu/doc/srv?l=EN&f=ST%208457%202014%20INIT.
—— Memorandum of Understanding between the Council of the European Union and the ECB on the cooperation on procedures related to the SSM 11 December 2013, at www.ecb.europa.eu/ecb/legal/pdf/mou_between_eucouncil_ecb.pdf.
—— Declaration of 18 December 2013 of the Representatives of the 28 Member States meeting within the Council, 18137/13.
—— Extraordinary ECOFIN Council of 9 and 10 May 2010, at www.consilium.europa.eu/uedocs/cms_data/docs/pressdata/en/ecofin/114324.pdf.
—— Statement by the Eurogroup and ECOFIN Ministers, 28 November 2010, at www.consilium.europa.eu/uedocs/cms_data/docs/pressdata/en/ecofin/118051.pdf.
—— ECOFIN Council conclusions on strengthening EU financial stability arrangements (2009), at www.consilium.europa.eu/ueDocs/cms_Data/docs/pressdata/en/ecofin/110617.pdf.
—— 2,866th Council Meeting, Economic and Financial Affairs, 8850/08 (2008).
—— ECOFIN Council Conclusions of 7 October 2008: Immediate responses to financial turmoil, 13930/08).
—— 2,836th Council meeting, Employment, Social Policy, Health and Consumer Affairs 15698/07 (2007).
—— Results of the Informal Meeting of Economics and Finance Ministers, The Hague, 10–11 September 2004, MEMO/04/214.
—— ECOFIN Council, Terms of reference for the Committee of Wise Men, 10491/00, ECOFIN 213 (2000).
European Parliament, Agreement between the European Parliament and the SRB on the practical modalities of the exercise of democratic accountability and oversight over the exercise of the tasks conferred on the SRB within the framework of the SRM, [2015] OJ L339/58.
—— Agreement between the European Parliament and the ECB on the practical modalities of the exercise of democratic accountability and oversight over the exercise of the tasks conferred on the ECB within the framework of the SSM, [2013] OJ L320/2.
ESM, Guideline on Financial Assistance for the Direct Recapitalisation of Institutions, 8 December 2014, at www.esm.europa.eu/about/legal-documents/index.htm.
ESRB, Sovereign bond-backed securities: a feasibility study (2018), at www.esrb.europa.eu/pub/task_force_safe_assets/shared/pdf/esrb.report290118_sbbs_volume_I_mainfindings.en.pdf.
—— The ESRB Handbook on Operationalising Macro-prudential Policy in the Banking Sector (2014), at www.esrb.europa.eu/pub/pdf/other/140303_esrb_handbook_mp.en.pdf

—— The consequences of the single supervisory mechanism for Europe's macro-prudential policy framework, Report of the Advisory Scientific Committee, (2013), at www.esrb.europa.eu/pub/pdf/sac/Reports_ASC_3_1309.pdf.

Euro Summit, Statement, 12 July 2015, at www.consilium.europa.eu/media/20353/20150712-eurosummit-statement-greece.pdf.

—— Remarks by President Donald Tusk after the Euro Summit of 7 July 2015 on Greece, at www.consilium.europa.eu/en/press/press-releases/2015/07/07/tusk-remarks-euro-summit.

—— Statement, 29 June 2012, at www.consilium.europa.eu/uedocs/cms_data/docs/pressdata/en/ec/131359.pdf.

—— Statement by the Euro Area Heads of State or Government, 9 December 2011, at www.consilium.europa.eu/uedocs/cms_data/docs/pressdata/en/ec/126658.pdf.

—— Statement, 26 October 2011, at www.consilium.europa.eu/uedocs/cms_data/docs/pressdata/en/ec/125644.pdf.

—— Statement by the Heads of State or Government of the Euro Area and EU Institutions, 21 July 2011, at www.consilium.europa.eu/uedocs/cms_data/docs/pressdata/en/ec/123978.pdf.

—— Conclusions of the Heads of State or Government of the Euro Area of 11 March 2011, at www.consilium.europa.eu/media/21423/20110311-conclusions-of-the-heads-of-state-or-government-of-the-euro-area-of-11-march-2011-en.pdf.

—— Statement of the Heads of State or Government of the Euro Area, 7 May 2010, at www.consilium.europa.eu/uedocs/cms_data/docs/pressdata/en/ec/114295.pdf.

—— Summit of the euro area countries: declaration on a concerted European action plan of the euro area countries, 12 October 2008, at ec.europa.eu/economy_finance/publications/pages/publication13260_en.pdf.

FATF, Annual Report 1999–2000 (2000), at www.fatf-gafi.org/media/fatf/documents/reports/1999%20 2000%20ENG.pdf.

FSB, Principles on Loss-absorbing and Recapitalisation Capacity of G-SIBs in Resolution (2015), at www.fsb.org/wp-content/uploads/TLAC-Principles-and-Term-Sheet-for-publication-final.pdf.

—— Policy Measures to Address Systemically Important Financial Institutions (2011), at www.fsb.org/wp-content/uploads/Policy-Measures-to-Address-Systemically-Important-Financial-Institutions.pdf.

—— Key Attributes of Effective Resolution Regimes for Financial Institutions (2011), at www.fsb.org/publications/r_111104cc.pdf.

—— Framework for Strengthening Adherence to International Standards (2010), at www.fsb.org/wp-content/uploads/r_100109a.pdf.

—— Reducing the moral hazard posed by systemically important financial institutions (2010), at www.fsb.org/wp-content/uploads/r_101111a.pdf.

FSF, Report of the Financial Stability Forum on Addressing Procyclicality in the Financial System (2009), at www.financialstabilityboard.org/wp-content/uploads/r_0904a.pdf.

—— Report of the Financial Stability Forum on Enhancing Market and Institutional Resilience (2008), at www.fsb.org/wp-content/uploads/r_0804.pdf.

—— Report of the Follow-Up Group on Incentives to Foster Implementation of Standards (2000), at www.fsb.org/wp-content/uploads/r_0009.pdf.

G-20, G20 Leaders Declaration, Los Cabos, Mexico, 18–19 June 2012, at www.consilium.europa.eu/uedocs/cms_data/docs/pressdata/en/ec/131069.pdf.

—— Leaders Statement: The Global Plan for Recovery and Reform, London, 2 April 2009, at www.g20.utoronto.ca/2009/2009communique0402.html.

—— Declaration of the Summit on Financial Markets and the World Economy, Washington DC, 15 November 2008, at www.g20.utoronto.ca/2008/2008declaration1115.html.

German Council of Economic Experts, A European redemption pact (2011) at www.sachverstaendigenrat-wirtschaft.de/233.html?&L=1.

UK, The run on the rock, Report of the Treasury Committee of the House of Commons, The Stationery Office (2008).

—— Principles-based regulation: Focusing on the outcomes that matter (2007), at webarchive.nationalarchives.gov.uk/*/http:/www.fsa.gov.uk/.

—— Report on the Inquiry by the Board of Banking Supervision, HMOS, (1995).

Secondary Sources

Abdelal R, *Capital Rules: The Construction of Global Finance* (Cambridge MA, Harvard University Press, 2007).

Ahlborn C and D Piccinin, 'The Application of the Principles of Restructuring Aid to Banks during the Financial Crisis' (2010) 9 *European State Aid Law Quarterly* 47.

Alemanno A, 'The Better Regulation Initiative at the Judicial Gate: A Trojan Horse within the Commission's Walls or the Way Forward?' (2009) 15 *European Law Journal* 382.

Alexander K, R Dhumale, and J Eatwell, *Global Governance of Financial Systems: The International Regulation of Systemic Risk* (Oxford, Oxford University Press, 2005).

Alford DA, 'Supervisory Colleges: The Global Financial Crisis and Improving International Supervisory Coordination' (2010) 24 *Emory International Law Review* 57.

Admati A and M Helwig, *The Bankers' New Clothes: What's Wrong with Banking and What to Do about It* (Princeton, Princeton University Press, 2013).

Alter KJ, *Establishing the Supremacy of European law: The Making of an International Rule of Law in Europe* (Oxford, Oxford University Press, 2006).

Amtenbrink F, *The Democratic Accountability of Central Banks* (Oxford, Hart Publishing, 1999).

Amtenbrink F and J de Haan, 'Regulating Credit Ratings in the European Union: A Critical First Assessment of Regulation 2060/2009 on Credit Rating Agencies' (2009) 46 *CML Rev* 1915.

—— 'Economic Governance in the European Union: Fiscal Discipline Versus Flexibility' (2003) 40 *CML Rev* 1075.

Arner DW and MW Taylor, 'The global financial crisis and the financial stability board: Hardening the soft law of international financial regulation' (2009) 32 *University of New South Wales Law Journal*, 488.

Avgerinos Y, 'Essential and Non-essential Measures: Delegation of Powers in EU Securities Regulation' (2002) 8 *European Law Journal* 269.

Avgouleas E, 'The Vexed Issue of Short Sales Regulation When Prohibition is Inefficient and Disclosure Insufficient' in K Alexander and N Moloney (eds) *Law Reform and Financial Markets* (Cheltenham, Elgar, 2011) 71–110.

Azoulai L, 'Integration through law and us' (2016) 14 *International Journal of Constitutional Law* 449.

Bakker AFP, *The Liberalization of Capital Movements in Europe* (Dordrecht, Kluwer, 1996).

Baquero Cruz J, *What's Left of the Law of Integration? Decay and Resistance in European Union Law* (Oxford, Oxford University Press, 2018).

Barr MS and GP Miller, 'Global Administrative Law: The View from Basel' (2006) 17 *European Journal of International Law* 15.

Bellringer C and R Michie, 'Big Bang in the City of London: An intentional revolution or an accident?' (2014) 21 Financial History Review 111.

Benedict XVI, *Lettera Enciclica Caritas in Veritate* (Vatican, Libraria Editrice Vaticana, 2009).

Begg I, 'Regulation and Supervision of Financial Intermediaries in the EU: The Aftermath of the Financial Crisis' (2009) 47 *Journal of Common Market Studies* 1107.

Benink H, J Danielsson and C Goodhart, *The future of banking regulation: the Basel II Accord* (London, Wiley, 2009).

Bergström CF, *Comitology, Delegation of Powers in the EU* (Oxford, Oxford University Press, 2005).

Beukers T and M Van Der Sluis, 'Differentiated Integration from the Perspective of Non-Euro Area Member States' in T Beukers, B de Witte, C Kilpatrick (eds) *Constitutional Change through Euro-Crisis Law* (Cambridge, Cambridge University Press, 2017) 143–174.

Binder JH, 'The Relevance of the Resolution Tools within the Single Resolution Mechanism' in MP Chiti and V Santoro (eds) *The Palgrave Handbook of European Banking Union Law* (Cham, Palgrave Macmillan, 2019) 299–320.

Bjorkland M, 'The Scope of the General Good Notion in the Second EC Banking Directive According to Recent Case Law' (1998) 9 *European Business Law Review* 227.

Black J, 'The rise (and fall?) of principles based regulation' in K Alexander and N Moloney (eds) *Law reform and financial markets* (Cheltenham, Elgar, 2011) 3–34.

Bogdandy A von, 'European Law Beyond "Ever Closer Union" Repositioning the Concept, its Thrust and the EJC's Comparative Methodology' (2016) 22 *European Law Journal* 519.

Bogdandy A von, and J Bast, 'European Union's Vertical Order of Competences: The Current Law and Proposals for Its Reform' (2002) 39 *CML Rev* 227.

Bomhoff A, A Jarosz-Friis, N Pesaresi, *Restructuring banks in crisis – overview of applicable State aid rules* (2009) 3 *Competition Policy Newsletter* 3.

Borio C, 'Towards a macroprudential framework for financial supervision and regulation?' (2003) 128 *BIS Working Papers*.

Bovens M, 'Analysing and Assessing Accountability: A Conceptual Framework' (2007) 13 *European Law Journal* 447.

Brescia Morra C, 'The Third Pillar of the Banking Union and its Troubled Implementation' in MP Chiti and V Santoro (eds) *The Palgrave Handbook of European Banking Union Law* (Cham, Palgrave Macmillan, 2019) 393–407.

Brescia Morra C, R Smits and A Magliari, 'The Administrative Board of Review of the European Central Bank: Experience After 2 Years' (2017) 18 *European Business Organization Law Review* 567.

Brunnermeier MK, H James and JP Landau, *The Euro and the Battle of Ideas* (Princeton, Princeton University Press, 2016).

Brunnermeier MK and Y Sannikov, 'Redistributive Monetary Policy' (2013) *Jackson Hole Symposium 2012*, 331.

Brunnermeier MK et al, 'European Safe Bonds (ESBies)' (2011) euro-nomics.com/wp-content/uploads/2011/09/ESBiesWEBsept262011.pdf.

Brunnermeier MK et al, 'The fundamental principles of financial regulation' (2009) 11 *Geneva Reports on the World Economy*.

Brunsson N and B Jacobsson, *A World of Standards* (Oxford, Oxford University Press, 2000).

Burley AM and W Mattli 'Europe Before the Court: A Political Theory of Legal Integration' (1993) 47 *International Organization* 41.

Busuioc M, 'Rule-Making by the European Financial Supervisory Authorities: Walking a Tight Rope' (2013) 19 *European Law Journal* 111.

Camfferman K and S Zeff, *Financial reporting and global capital markets: A history of the international accounting standards committee, 1973–2000* (Oxford, Oxford University Press, 2006).

Camilli EL, 'Basel-Brussels One Way? The EU in the Legalization Process of Basel Soft Law' in E Chiti and BG Mattarella (eds) *Global Administrative Law and EU Administrative Law* (Berlin, Springer, 2011) 323–358.

Cappelletti M, M Seccombe and JHH Weiler, 'Integration Through Law: Europe and the American Federal Experience' in M Cappelletti, M Seccombe and JHH Weiler (eds) *Integration Through Law, Vol.1* (Berlin, Walter de Gruyter, 1986) 3–68.

Cappiello S, 'The Interplay between the EBA and the Banking Union' (2015) 2015/77 *EUI Working Papers RSCAS*.

Carletti E and X Vives, 'Regulation and Competition Policy in the Banking Sector', in X Vives (ed) *Competition Policy in Europe, Fifty Years Treaty of Rome* (Oxford, Oxford University Press, 2009) 260–283.

Casey JP and K Lannoo, 'The MiFID implementing measures: excessive detail or level-playing field?' (2006) 1 *ECMI Policy Brief*.

Cerny PG, 'The "little big bang" in Paris: financial market deregulation in a dirigiste system' (1989) 17 *European Journal of Political Research* 169.

Chiti E, *Le agenzie europee: Unità e decentramento nelle amministrazioni comunitarie* (Padua, Cedam, 2002).

—— 'European Agencies' Rulemaking: Powers, Procedures and Assessment' (2013) 19 *European Law Journal* 93.

Chiti E and PG Teixeira, 'The Constitutional Implications of the European Financial and Public Debt Crisis' (2013) 50 *CML Rev* 683.

Chiti E, AJ Menéndez, and PG Teixeira, 'The European Rescue of the European Union? The Existential Crisis of the European Political Project' (2012) 3/12 *ARENA Report*, 19 *RECON Report*.

Chernow R, *Alexander Hamilton* (New York, Penguin, 2004).

Cihak M and J Decressin, 'The Case for a European Banking Charter' (2007) 07/173 *IMF Working Paper*.

Claessens S, R Herring, D Schoenmaker, and KA Summe, 'A safer world financial system: Improving the resolution of systemic institutions' (2010) 12 *Geneva reports on the world economy*.

Claessens S and L Kodres, 'The Regulatory Responses to the Global Financial Crisis: Some Uncomfortable Questions' (2014) WP/14/46 *IMF Working Paper*.

Cœuré B, 'Monetary policy in a fragmented world, Speech at the 41st Economics Conference of the Oesterreichische Nationalbank, Vienna' (2013), at www.ecb.europa.eu/press/key/date/2013/html/sp130610.en.html.
Collignon S, 'The End of the Stability Growth Pact?' (2004) 1 *International Economics and Economic Policy* 15.
Constâncio V, 'Completing the Odyssean journey of the European Monetary Union, Speech at the ECB Colloquium on "The Future of Central Banking"' (2018), at www.ecb.europa.eu/press/key/date/2018/html/ecb.sp180517.en.html.
—— 'Towards the Banking Union, Speech at the 2nd FIN-FSA Conference on EU Regulation and Supervision "Banking and Supervision under Transformation"' (2013), at www.ecb.europa.eu/press/key/date/2012/html/sp120907.en.html.
—— 'Towards a European Banking Union' (2012) at www.ecb.europa.eu/press/key/date/2012/html/sp120907.en.html.
—— 'Information requirements for macro-prudential oversight and the role of central banks' (2010), at www.ecb.europa.eu/press/key/date/2010/html/sp101020.en.html.
Cooley T and I Walter, 'The Architecture of Financial Regulation' in V Acharya, T Cooley, M Richardson, I Walter (eds) *Regulating Wall Street: The Dodd-Frank Act and the New Architecture of Global Finance* (London, Wiley, 2011) 33–50.
Craig P, 'The Financial Crisis, the EU Institutional Order and Constitutional Responsibility' in F Fabbrini, EH Ballin and H Somsen (eds) *What Form of Government for the Eurozone* (Oxford, Hart Publishing, 2015) 17–36.
—— 'Pringle: Legal Reasoning, Text, Purpose and Teleology' (2013) 20 *Maastricht Journal of European and Comparative Law* 3.
—— 'The Stability, Coordination and Governance Treaty: Principle, Politics and Pragmatism' (2012) 37 *European Law Review* 231.
—— 'Shared Administration and Networks: Global and EU perspectives', in G Anthony, JB Auby, J Morison, and T Zwart (eds) *Values in Global Administrative Law* (Oxford, Hart Publishing, 2011) 81–116.
—— *The Lisbon Treaty: Law, Politics, and Treaty Reform* (Oxford, Oxford University Press, 2010).
Crane DB, KA Froot, SP Mason, A Perold, RC Merton, Z Bodie, ER Sirri, and P Tufano, *The global financial system: A functional perspective* (Cambridge MA, Harvard Business School Press, 1995).
Curtin D, 'Accountable Independence' of the European Central Bank: Seeing the Logics of Transparency' (2017) 23 *European Law Journal* 28.
—— 'Holding (Quasi-)Autonomous EU Administrative Actors to Public Account' (2007) 13 *European Law Journal* 523.
Dale R, *The Regulation of International Banking* (Englewood Cliffs NJ, Prentice Hall, 1986).
Darvas Z, 'EU Support to CEE Countries During the Crisis' (2009) 2009/17 *Bruegel Policy Contribution.*
Dashwood A, 'Guest editorial: Living with the Eurozone' (2016) 53 *CML Rev* 3.
De Búrca G, 'Rethinking law in neofunctionalist theory' (2005) 12 *Journal of European Public Policy* 310.
De Rynck S, 'Banking on a union: the politics of changing eurozone banking supervision' (2016), 23 *Journal of European Public Policy* 119.
Dehousse R, 'Why has EU macroeconomic governance become more supranational?' (2016) 38 *Journal of European Integration* 617.
—— 'The Fiscal Compact: Legal Uncertainty and Political Ambiguity' (2012) *Notre Europe Policy Brief 33.*
—— 'Regulation by Networks in the European Community: The Role of European Agencies' (1997) 4 *Journal of European Public Policy* 246.
—— 'Integration v. regulation? On the dynamics of regulation in the European Community' (1992) 30 *Journal of Common Market Studies* 383.
Dehousse R and JHH Weiler, 'The Legal Dimension' in W Wallace (ed) *The Dynamics of European Integration* (London, Pinter, 1990) 242–60.
Delors J, *Mémoires* (Paris, Plon, 2004).
Denord F and A Schwartz, 'L'économie (très) politique du traité de Rome' (2010) 89 *Politix* 35.
Dermine J, 'Banking in Europe: Past, Present, and Future' in V Gaspar (ed) *The Transformation of the European Financial System* (Frankfurt/M, European Central Bank, 2003), 31–95.
Dewatripont M, JC Rochet, and J Tirole, *Balancing the Banks: Global Lessons from the Financial Crisis* (Princeton, Princeton University Press, 2010).

Di Giorgio G and C Di Noia, 'Financial market regulation and supervision: how many peaks for the euro area?' (2003) 28 *Brooklyn Journal International Law* 463.
Donnelly S, 'Power Politics and the Undersupply of Financial Stability in Europe' (2014) 21 *Review of International Political Economy*, 980.
Draghi M, 'Risk-reducing and risk-sharing in our Monetary Union, Speech at the European University Institute, Florence' (2018), at www.ecb.europa.eu/press/key/date/2018/html/ecb.sp180511.en.html.
Editorial (2012) 49 *CML Rev* 1.
—— (2011) 48 *CML Rev* 1769.
—— 'Executive Agencies within the EC: the ECB as a model?' (2006) 33 *CML Rev* 623.
Eijffinger S and R Nijskens, 'Monetary Policy and Banking Supervision' (2012) *VOX*, www.voxeu.org/article/monetary-policy-and-banking-supervision.
Eichengreen B, *Hall of Mirrors: The Great Depression, the Great Recession, and the Uses and Misuses of History* (Oxford, Oxford University Press, 2015).
—— 'European Monetary Integration with Benefit of Hindsight' (2012) 50 *Journal of Common Market Studies* 123.
—— *The European Economy since 1945* (Princeton, Princeton University Press, 2007).
Elson A, *Governing Global Finance: The Evolution and Reform of the International Financial Architecture* (New York, Palgrave, 2011).
Enria A, 'Fragmentation in banking markets: crisis legacy and the challenge of Brexit, Speech at BCBS-FSI High Level Meeting for Europe on Banking Supervision' (2018) eba.europa.eu/documents/10180/2353431/Andrea+Enria+speech+on+Fragmentation+in+banking+at+BCBS-FSI+High+Level+Meeting+170918.pdf.
—— 'Establishing the Banking Union and repairing the Single Market' in F Allen, E Carletti, and Gray (eds) *Political, Fiscal and Banking Union in the Eurozone?* (Philadelphia PA, FIC Press, 2013), 47–63.
Enria A and PG Teixeira, 'A New Institutional Framework for Financial Regulation and Supervision' in F Cannata and M Quagliariello (eds) *Basel III and beyond* (London, Riskbooks, 2011) 421–468.
Epstein RA and M Rhodes, 'States ceding control: explaining the shift to centralized bank supervision in the eurozone' (2016) 17 *Journal of Banking Regulation* 90.
—— 'The political dynamics behind Europe's new banking union' (2016) 39 *West European Politics* 415.
Everson M, 'Banking on Union: EU Governance between Risk and Uncertainty' in M Dawson, H Enderlein, and C Joerges (eds) *Beyond the Crisis: The Governance of Europe's Economic, Political and Legal Transformation* (Oxford, Oxford University Press, 2015) 137–163.
—— *Laws in Conflict – A Rationally Integrated European Insurance Market?*, Doctoral Thesis (Florence, European University Institute, 1993).
Fabbrini F, 'On banks, courts and international law: the intergovernmental agreement on the Single resolution fund in context' (2014) 21 *Maastricht Journal of European and Comparative Law* 444.
Ferran E, 'European Banking Union and the EU Single Financial Market: More Differentiated Integration, or Disintegration?' in B de Witte, A Ott, and E Vos (eds) *Between Flexibility and Disintegration: The Trajectory of Differentiation in EU Law*' (Cheltenham, Elgar, 2017) 252–281.
—— 'The Existential Search of the European Banking Authority' (2016) 17 *European Business Organization Law Review* 285.
—— 'Understanding the new institutional architecture of EU financial market supervision' in G Ferrarini, KJ Hopt and E Wymeersch (eds) *Financial Regulation and Supervision: A post-crisis analysis* (Oxford, Oxford University Press, 2012) 111–158.
—— *Building a European Securities Market* (Cambridge, Cambridge University Press, 2000).
Ferran E and VSG Babis, 'The European Single Supervisory Mechanism' (2013) 13 *Journal of Corporate Law Studies* 255.
Ferran E and K Alexander, 'Can soft law bodies be effective? The Special Case of the European Systemic Risk Board' (2011) 37 *European law review* 751.
Ferrarini G, 'Single Supervision and the Governance of Banking Markets: Will the SSM Deliver the Expected Benefits?' (2015) 16 *European Business Organization Law Review* 513.
Flynn L, 'Coming of Age: The Free Movement of Capital Case Law 1993–2002' (2002) 39 *CML Rev* 773.
Follesdal A and S Dix, 'Why There is a Democratic Deficit in the EU: A Response to Majone and Moravcsik' (2006) 44 *Journal of Common Market Studies* 533.

Fox J, *The Myth of the Rational Market: A History of Risk, Reward, and Delusion on Wall Street* (New York, Harper Business, 2009).

Garcia GG and MJ Nieto, 'Banking crisis management in the European Union: Multiple regulators and resolution authorities' (2005) 6 *Journal of Banking Regulation* 206.

Gerstenberg O and C Sabel, 'Directly-Deliberative Polyarchy: An Institutional Idea for Europe' in R Dehousse and C Joerges (eds) *Good Governance and Administration in Europe's Integrated Market* (Oxford, Oxford University Press, 2002), 289–341.

Gerven W van and J Wouters 'Free Movement of Financial Services and the European Contracts Convention' in M Andenas and S Kenyon Slade (eds) *EC Financial Market Regulation and Company Law* (London, Sweet & Maxwell, 1993) 43–79.

Goodhart C, *The Basel Committee on Banking Supervision: A History of the Early Years, 1974–1997* (Cambridge, Cambridge University Press, 2011).

Goodhart C et al, *Financial Regulation: Why, How and Where Now?* (London, Routledge, 1998).

Goodhart C and E Avgouleas, 'A Critical Evaluation of Bail-ins as Bank Recapitalisation Mechanisms' (2014) *Centre for Economic Policy Research, Discussion Paper 10065.*

Goodhart C and D Schoenmaker, 'Fiscal Burden Sharing in Cross-Border Banking Crises' (2009) 5 *International Journal of Central Banking* 141.

Gordon JN and WG Ringe, 'Bank Resolution in the European Banking Union: A Transatlantic Perspective on What it Would Take' (2014) 115 *Columbia Law Review* 1297.

Goyal R et al, 'A Banking Union for the Euro Area' (2013) *IMF Staff Discussion Notes 13/1.*

Greenspan A, *The Age of Turbulence* (New York, Penguin, 2008).

—— *The Globalization of Finance* (1998) 17 *Cato Journal* 243.

Gregorio Merino A de, 'Legal Developments in the Economic and Monetary Union During the Debt Crisis: The Mechanisms of Financial Assistance' (2012) 49 *CML Rev* 1613.

Grin G, 'Shaping Europe: The Path to European Integration according to Jean Monnet' (2017) *Jean Monnet Foundation for Europe, Debates and Documents Collection, 7.*

—— *The Battle of the Single European Market: Achievements and Economic Thought 1985–2000* (London, Routledge, 2003).

Groeben H von der, 'Europäische Integration aus historischer Erfahrung: Ein Zeitzeugengespräch mit Michael Gehler' (2002), *Zentrum für Europäische Integrationsforschung* C108 *Discussion Paper.*

—— 'The Role of European Integration in the West German Economic Order' (1979) 135 *Zeitschrift Für Die Gesamte Staatswissenschaft* 493.

Gros D and D Schoenmaker, 'European Deposit Insurance and Resolution in the Banking Union' (2014) 52 *Journal of Common Market Studies* 529.

Grundmann S, 'The European Banking Union and Integration' in S Grundmann and HW Micklitz (eds) *The European Banking Union and Constitution: Beacon for Advanced Integration or Death-Knell for Democracy?* (Oxford, Hart Publishing, 2019) 85–120.

Grundmann S and HW Micklitz, 'The European Banking Union and Constitution – The Overall Challenge' in S Grundmann and HW Micklitz (eds), *The European Banking Union and Constitution: Beacon for Advanced Integration or Death-Knell for Democracy?* (Oxford, Hart Publishing, 2019) 1–21.

Gruson M, 'Supervision of financial conglomerates in the European Union' (2004) 19 *Journal of International Banking Law and Regulation* 363.

Haas PM, 'Epistemic Communities and International Policy Coordination' (1992) 46 *International Organization* 1.

Haan J de, S Osterloo and D Schoenmaker, *European Financial Markets and Institutions* (Cambridge, Cambridge University Press, 2009).

Haan J de, SCW Eijffinger, S Waller, *The European Central Bank: Credibility, Transparency, and Centralization* (Cambridge MA, MIT Press, 2005).

Haan J de, H Berger and DJ Jansen, 'Why Did the Stability and Growth Pact Fail?' (2004) 7 *International Finance* 235.

Haas EB, *The Uniting of Europe: Political, Social, and Economic Forces, 1950–1957* (Stanford, Stanford University Press, 1958.

Habermas J, *The Lure of Technocracy* (Cambridge, Polity, 2015).

—— *Between Facts and Norms: Contributions to a Discourse Theory of Law and Democracy* (Cambridge MA, MIT Press, 1996).

Hadjiemmanuil C, 'Bank Resolution Financing in the Banking Union' (2015) 6/2015 *LSE Legal Studies Working Paper.*

Hardy DCL, 'A European Mandate for Financial Sector Supervisors in the EU' (2009) 09/5 *IMF Working Paper.*

Harlow C, *Accountability in the European Union* (Oxford, Oxford University Press, 2002).

Hayek FA, 'The Economic Conditions of Interstate Federalism' in FA Hayek, *Individualism and Economic Order* (Chicago, Chicago University Press, 1948) 255–272.

Helleiner E, *States and the Reemergence of Global Finance: From Bretton Woods to the 1990s* (Ithaca, NY, Cornell University Press, 1994).

—— 'What Role for the New Financial Stability Board? The Politics of International Standards after the Crisis' (2010) 1 *Global Policy* 282.

Hellwig M, 'Yes Virginia, There is a European Banking Union! But It May Not Make Your Wishes Come True' (2014) 2014/12 *Max Planck Institute for Research on Collective Goods.*

—— 'Financial Stability, Monetary Policy, Banking Supervision, and Central Banking' (2014) *Max Planck Institute for Research on Collective Goods 2014/9.*

Herring RJ and RE Litan, *Financial Regulation in the Global Economy* (Washington DC, The Brookings Institution, 1995).

Hertig G, 'Regulatory Competition for EU Financial Services' in DC Esty and G Damien (eds) *Regulatory Competition and Economic Integration* (Oxford, Oxford University Press, 2001) 218–240.

—— 'Imperfect mutual recognition for EC financial services' (1994) 14 *International Review of Law and Economics* 177.

Hien J and C Joerges, 'Dead man walking? Current European interest in the ordoliberal tradition' (2018) 24 *European Law Journal* 142.

—— (eds) *Ordoliberalism, Law and the Rule of Economics* (Oxford, Hart Publishing, 2017).

Hirsch A, 'Worldwide Legal Harmonization of Banking Law and Securities Regulation' in R Buxbaum, G Hertig, I Hirsch and KJ Hopt (eds) *European Business Law: Legal and Economic Analyses on Integration and Harmonization* (New York, De Gruyter, 1991) 347–372.

Hoffmann S, 'Obstinate or Obsolete? The Fate of the Nation-State and the Case of Western Europe' (1966) 95 *Daedalus, Tradition and Change* 862.

Howarth D and L Quaglia, 'The New Intergovernmentalism in Financial Regulation and Banking Union' in CJ Bickerton, D Hodson and U Puetter (eds), *The New Intergovernmentalism: States and Supranational Actors in the Post-Maastricht Era* (Oxford, Oxford University Press, 2015) 146–162.

—— 'The Steep Road to European banking union: Constructing the Single Resolution Mechanism' (2014) 52 *Journal of Common Market Studies*, 52, 125.

—— 'Banking union as holy grail: rebuilding the single market in financial services, stabilizing Europe's banks and "completing" economic and monetary union' (2013) 51 *Journal of Common Market Studies* 103.

Hu HTC, 'Swaps, The Modern Process of Financial Innovation and the Vulnerability of a Regulatory Paradigm' (1989) 138 *University of Pennsylvania Law Review* 333.

Issing O, *New Financial Order: Recommendations by the Issing Committee* (Frankfurt/M, Center for Financial Studies, University of Frankfurt, 2008).

James H, 'Central banks: between internationalisation and domestic political control' (2010) 327 *BIS Working Papers.*

—— *Making the European Monetary Union* (Cambridge MA, The Belknap Press of Harvard University Press, 2012).

Jenkins R, 'Europe's present challenge and future opportunity' (1977) *Jean Monet Lecture, European University Institute, European Archives, Florence.*

Joerges C, 'How is a closer union conceivable under conditions of ever more socio-economic and political diversity? Constitutionalising Europe's unitas in pluralitate' (2018) 24 *European Law Journal* 257.

—— 'Integration through Law and the Crisis of Law in Europe's Emergency, in Chalmers' in M Jachtenfuchs and C Joerges (eds) *The End of the Eurocrats' Dream: Adjusting to European Diversity* (Cambridge, Cambridge University Press, 2016) 299–338.

—— 'Pereat Iustitia, Fiat Mundus: What is Left of the European Economic Constitution after the Gauweiler Litigation?' (2016) 23 *Maastricht Journal of European and Comparative Law* 99.

—— 'Europe's Economic Constitution in Crisis and the Emergence of a New Constitutional Constellation' (2014) 15 *German Law Journal* 985.

—— 'Law and Politics in Europe's Crisis: On the History of the Impact of an Unfortunate Configuration' (2013) 2013/09 *EUI Working Paper Law.*
—— 'Democracy and European Integration: A Legacy of Tensions, a Re-conceptualisation and Recent True Conflicts' (2007) *EUI Working Paper LAW.*
—— 'Deliberative Political Processes' Revisited: What Have We Learnt About the Legitimacy of Supranational Decision-Making' (2006) 44 *Journal of Common Market Studies* 779.
—— 'What is left of the European Economic Constitution? A Melancholic Eulogy' (2005) 30 *European Law Review* 461.
—— 'Constitutionalism and Transnational Governance: Exploring a Magic Triangle' in C Joerges, I Sand and G Teubner (eds) *Transnational Governance and Constitutionalism* (Oxford, Hart Publishing, 2004) 339–375.
—— 'The Law's Problems with the Governance of the Single European Market' in C Joerges and R Dehousse (eds) *Good Governance in Europe's Integrated Market* (Oxford, Oxford University Press, 2002) 3–32.
—— 'States Without a Market? Comments on the German Constitutional Court's Maastricht-Judgement and a Plea for Interdisciplinary Discourses' (1997) 1–20 *European Integration Online Papers* eiop.or.at/eiop/texte/1997-01920htm.
—— 'The Market Without the State? The "Economic Constitution" of the European Community and the Rebirth of Regulatory Politics' (1997) 1–19 *European Integration online Papers*, at eiop.or.at/eiop/pdf/1997-019.pdf.
—— 'Taking the Law Seriously: On Political Science and the Role of Law in the Process of European Integration' (1996) 2 *European Law Journal* 105.
Joerges C, and Y Meny and JHH Weiler, 'Symposium: Mountain or molehill? A critical appraisal of the Commission White Paper on Governance' (2001) 6/01 *Jean Monnet Working Paper*, at www.eui.eu/Documents/RSCAS/Research/OnlineSymposia/Joerges.pdf.
Joerges C, and E Vos (eds) *EU-Committees: Social Regulation, Law and Politics* (Oxford, Hart Publishing, 1999).
Judt T, *Postwar* (New York, Penguin, 2005).
Juncker JC in close cooperation with D Tusk, J Dijsselbloem, M Draghi and M Schulz, 'The Five Presidents' Report: Completing Europe's Economic and Monetary Union' (2015), at ec.europa.eu/priorities/sites/beta-political/files/5-presidents-report_en.pdf.
Kaiser W, *Christian Democracy and the Origins of the European Union* (Cambridge, Cambridge University Press, 2007).
Kapstein EB, 'Architects of Stability? International Cooperation Among Financial Supervisors' (2006) 199 *BIS Working Papers.*
—— *Governing the Global Economy: International Finance and the State* (Cambridge MA, Harvard University Press, 1996).
—— 'Supervising international banks: origins and implications of Basel Accord' (1991) 185 *Essays in International Finance, Princeton University.*
Katz SE, 'The Second Banking Directive' (1992) 12 *Yearbook of European Law*, 249.
Kelemen RD, *Eurolegalism: The Transformation of Law and Regulation in the European Union* (Cambridge MA, Harvard University Press, 2011).
Kerjean S, 'The legal implications of the prudential supervisory assessment of bank mergers and acquisitions under EU law' (2008) 6 *ECB Legal Working Papers.*
Kjaer P, *Between Governing and Governance: On the Emergence, Function and Form of Europe's Post-National Constellation* (Oxford, Hart Publishing, 2010).
Kohler-Koch B and B Rittberger, 'The "Governance Turn" in EU Studies' (2006) 44 *Journal of Common Market Studies* 27.
Kose AM, E Prasad, K Rogoff, and SJ Weil, 'Financial Globalization: A Reappraisal' (2009) 56-1 *IMF Staff Papers.*
Kroes N, 'Dealing with the current financial crisis' (2008) *Speech 08/498 at the Economic and Monetary Affairs Committee of the European Parliament.*
Küsters HJ, 'Walter Hallstein and the Negotiations on the Treaties of Rome 1955–57' in W Loth, W Wallace, W Wessels (eds) Walter Hallstein: *The Forgotten European?* (London, Palgrave Macmillan, 1998).
Ladeur KH, 'The emergence of Global administrative law and transnational regulation' (2012) 3 *Transnational legal theory* 243.

—— '"We, the European People …" – Relâche?' (2008) 14 *European Law Journal* 147.
—— 'Towards a Legal Theory of Supranationality-The Validity of the Network Concept' (1997) 3 *European Law Journal* 33.
—— 'Towards a Legal Concept of the Network in European Standard-Setting' in C Joerges and E Vos (eds) *EU-Committees: Social Regulation, Law and Politics* (Oxford, Hart Publishing, 1999) 151–171.
—— 'The Changing Role of the Private in Public Governance: The Erosion of Hierarchy and the Rise of a New Administrative Law of Cooperation. A Comparative Approach' (2002) 2002/9 *EUI Working Papers Law.*
—— 'Globalization and the Conversion of Democracy to Polycentric Networks: Can Democracy Survive the End of the Nation State?' in KH Ladeur (ed) *Public Governance in the Age of Globalization* (Burlington VT, Ashgate, 2004) 89–118.
—— *Das Umweltrecht der Wissensgesellschaft* (Berlin, Duncker & Humblot, 1995).
Lamandini M, G Lusignani, D Ramos Munoz, 'Does Europe Have What It Takes to Finish the Banking Union?' (2017) 24 *Columbia Journal of European Law* 233.
Lamfalussy A, 'High-Level Committee on a New Financial Architecture' (2009), at www.docufin.fgov.be.
—— 'Final Report of the Committee of Wise Men on the Regulation of European Securities Markets' (2001) (on file with the author).
—— 'Initial report of the Committee of Wise Men' (2000) (on file with the author).
Lane PR, 'The European Sovereign Debt Crisis' (2012) 26 *Journal of Economic Perspectives* 49.
Larosière J de, 'High-Level Group on Financial Supervision in EU' (2009), at ec.europa.eu/internal_market/finances/docs/de_larosiere_report_en.pdf.
Lastra RM, 'Banking Union and Single Market: Conflict or Companionship?' (2013) 36 *Fordham International Law Journal* 1189.
—— 'Accountability and Governance: Banking Union Proposals' (2012) 30 *DSF Policy Paper.*
—— 'The Governance Structure for Financial Regulation and Supervision in Europe' (2003) 10 *Columbia Journal European Law* 49.
Laurent PH, 'Paul-Henri Spaak and the Diplomatic Origins of the Common Market, 1955–1956,' (1970) 85 *Political Science Quarterly* 373.
Lefterov A, 'The single rulebook: legal issues and relevance in the SSM context' (2015) 15 *ECB Legal Working Paper Series.*
Levine R, 'Finance and Growth: Theory and Evidence' in P Aghion and S Durlauf (eds) *Handbook of Economic Growth* (Amsterdam, Elsevier, 2005) 865–934.
Liikanen E, 'Report of the European Commission's High-level Expert Group on Bank Structural Reform' (2012) ec.europa.eu/info/system/files/liikanen-report-02102012_en.pdf.
Lindseth PL, *Power and Legitimacy: Reconciling Europe and the Nation-State* (Oxford, Oxford University Press, 2010).
Lintner P, 'De-centralised decision making under the European Resolution Framework: does Meroni hamper the creation of a European Resolution Authority?' (2017) 18 *European Business Organization Law Review* 591.
Lo AW, *Adaptive Markets: Financial Evolution at the Speed of Thought* (Princeton, Princeton University Press, 2017).
Lo Schiavo G, *The Role of Financial Stability in EU Law and Policy* (Alphen aan den Rijn, The Netherlands, Wolters Kluwer, 2017).
Lomnicka E, 'The Home Country Control Principle in the Financial Services Directives and the Case Law' in M Andenas and W Henning-Roth (eds) *Services and Free Movement in EU Law* (Oxford, Oxford University Press, 2002) 295–319.
—— 'Home Country Control Principle in the Financial Services Directive and the Case Law' (2000) 11 *European Business Law Review* 324.
—— 'The Single European Passport in Financial Services' in BAK Rider and M Andenas (eds) *Developments in European Company Law Vol. 1* (London: Kluwer Law International, 1997) 181–201.
Louis JV, 'The EMU after the Gauweiler Judgment and the Juncker Report' (2016) 23 *Maastricht Journal of European and Comparative Law* 55.
—— 'Guest Editorial: The no-bailout clause and rescue packages' (2010) 47 *CML Rev* 971.
—— 'Economic Policy in the Lisbon Treaty' in S Griller and J Ziller (eds) *The Lisbon Treaty: EU Constitutionalism without a Constitutional Treaty?* (New York, Springer, 2008) 285–298.
—— 'The Review of the Stability and Growth Pact' (2006) 43 *CML Rev* 85.

—— 'Differentiation and the EMU' in B de Witte, D Hanf, and E Vos (eds) *The Many Faces of Differentiation in EU Law* (Oxford, Intersentia, 2001) 43–64.

—— 'A Legal and Institutional Approach for Building a Monetary Union' (1998) 35 *CML Rev* 33.

—— *Banking Supervision in the European Community: Institutional Aspects* (Bruxelles, Université de Bruxelles, 1995).

—— *Vers un système européen de banques centrales – Projet de dispositions organiques* (Bruxelles, Éditions de l'Université Libre de Bruxelles, 1989).

Ludlow NP, 'European Integration in the 1980s: on the Way to Maastricht?' (2013) 19 *Journal of European Integration History* 11.

Masciandaro D, 'International Association of Insurance Supervisors' in T Hale and D Held (eds) *Handbook of Transnational Governance: New Institutions and Innovations* (Cambridge, Polity Press, 2011) 71–79.

Masciandaro D and M Quintyn, 'Regulating the Regulators: The Changing Face of Financial Supervision Architectures Before and After the Financial Crisis' in S Eijffinger and D Masciandaro (eds) *Handbook of Central Banking, Financial Regulation and Supervision: After the Financial Crisis* (Cheltenham, Elgar, 2011) 428–484.

Masciandaro D and A Volpicella, 'Macro prudential governance and central banks: Facts and drivers' (2016) 61 *Journal of International Money and Finance* 101.

Maes I, 'A Lamfalussy: A Cassandra about Financial Stability' in K Dyson and I Maes (eds) *Architects of the Euro: Intellectuals in the Making of European Monetary Union* (Oxford, Oxford University Press, 2016) 233–253.

—— 'On the Origins of the Franco-German EMU Controversies' 17 (2004) *European Journal of Law and Economics* 21.

Majone G, *Rethinking the Union of Europe Post-Crisis: Has Integration Gone Too Far?* (Cambridge, Cambridge University Press, 2014).

—— *Europe as the Would-Be World Power: The EU at 50* (Cambridge, Cambridge University Press, 2009).

—— 'One market, one law, one money? Unintended consequences of EMU, enlargement, and eurocentricity' (2007) 1/2007 *LSE Law, Society and Economy Working Papers.*

—— *Dilemmas of European Integration: The Ambiguities and Pitfalls of Integration by Stealth* (Oxford, Oxford University Press, 2005).

—— 'Europe's "democratic deficit": The question of standards' (1998) 4 *European Law Journal* 5.

—— 'The European Community as a Regulatory State' in *Collected Courses of the Academy of European Law, V-1* (New York, Kluwer Law International, 1996) 321–419.

—— 'Mutual Recognition in Federal Type Systems' (1993) 1993/01 *EUI SPS Working Papers.*

Maris G and P Sklias, 'France, Germany and the New Framework for EMU Governance' (2016) 24 *Journal of Contemporary European Studies* 1.

Marjolin R, *Le travail d'une vie: Mémoires 1911-1986* (Paris, Éditions Robert Laffont, 1986).

Martin JF and PG Teixeira, 'The Imposition of Regulatory Sanctions by the European Central Bank' (2000) 25 *European Law Review* 56.

McCormick JP, *Weber, Habermas, and Transformations of the European State: Constitutional, Social, and Supranational Democracy* (Cambridge, Cambridge University Press, 2007).

Mendes J, 'Delegated and implementing rule making: proceduralisation and constitutional design' (2013) 19 *European Law Journal* 22.

—— 'Participation and the Role of the Law after Lisbon: A Legal View on Article 11 TEU' (2011) 48 *CML Rev* 1849.

—— *Participation in EU rule-making: A rights-based approach* (Oxford, Oxford University Press, 2011).

Menéndez AJ, 'The Crisis of Law and the European Crises: From the Social and Democratic Rechtsstaat to the Consolidating State of (Pseudo-) technocratic Governance' (2017) 44 *Journal of Law and Society* 56.

—— 'The Existential Crisis of the European Union' (2013) 14 *German Law Journal* 453.

Menon A and S Weatherill, 'Transnational Legitimacy in a Globalising World: How the European Union Rescues its States' (2008) 31 *West European Politics* 397.

Merkel A, 'Speech by Federal Chancellor Angela Merkel at the opening ceremony of the 61st academic year of the College of Europe in Bruges' (2010), at www.coleurope.eu/content/news/Speeches/Europakolleg%20Brugge%20Mitschrift%20englisch.pdf.

Merler S and J Pisani-Ferry, 'Hazardous tango: sovereign-bank interdependence and financial stability in the euro area' (2012) *Financial Stability Review, Banque de France* 16.

Micklitz HW, 'The Internal Market and the Banking Union' in S Grundmann and HW Micklitz (eds) *The European Banking Union and Constitution: Beacon for Advanced Integration or Death-Knell for Democracy?* (Oxford, Hart Publishing, 2019) 85–120.

Middelaar L Van, *Quand L'Europe Improvise: Dix ans de crises politiques* (Paris, Gallimard, 2018).

—— *The Passage to Europe* (New Haven, Yale University Press, 2013).

—— 'Spanning the River: The Constitutional Crisis of 1965–1966 as the Genesis of Europe's Political Order' (2008) 4 *European Constitutional Law Review* 98.

Milward AS, *The European Rescue of the Nation-State*, 2nd edition (London, Routledge, 1994).

Mitsilegas V and B Gilmore, 'The EU legislative framework against money laundering and terrorist finance: a critical analysis in the light of evolving global standards' (2007) 56 *International & Comparative Law Quarterly* 119.

Moloney N, 'International Financial Governance, the EU, and Brexit: The "Agencification" of EU Financial Governance and the Implications' (2016) 17 *European Business Organization Law Review* 451.

—— *EU Securities and Financial Markets Regulation* (Oxford, Oxford University Press, 2014).

—— 'European Banking Union: assessing its risks and resilience' (2014) 51 *CML Rev* 1609.

—— 'EU Financial Market Regulation After the Global Financial Crisis: "More Europe" or More Risks?' (2010) 47 *CML Rev* 1317.

—— 'New Frontiers in EC Capital Markets Law: from Market Construction to Market Regulation' (2003) 40 *CML Rev* 809.

—— 'The Lamfalussy Legislative Model: A New Era for the EC Securities And Investment Services Regime' (2003) 52 *International Comparative Law Quarterly* 509.

Möllers C, 'Some Reflections on the State of European Democracy with Regard to the Banking Union and the ECB' in S Grundmann and HW Micklitz (eds) *The European Banking Union and Constitution: Beacon for Advanced Integration or Death-Knell for Democracy?* (Oxford, Hart Publishing, 2019) 205–218.

Monnet E, S Pagliari, and S Vallée, 'Europe between financial repression and regulatory capture' (2014) *Bruegel Working Paper* 2014/08.

Monnet J, *Mémoires* (Paris, Fayard, 1976).

Monti M, 'New Strategy for the Single Market: At the Service of Europe's Economy and Society' (2010), at ec.europa.eu/internal_market/strategy/docs/monti_report_final_10_05_2010_en.pdf.

Mourlon-Druol E, 'Banking union in historical perspective: the initiative of the European Commission in the 1960s-1970s' (2016) 54 *Journal of Common Market Studies* 913.

—— 'Trust is good, control is better: the 1974 Herstatt-Bank crisis and its implications for international regulatory reform' (2015) 57 *Business History* 311.

Morais LS, 'Lessons from the First Resolution Experiences in the Context of Bank Recovery and Resolution Directive' in MP Chiti and V Santoro (eds) *The Palgrave Handbook of European Banking Union Law* (Cham, Palgrave Macmillan, 2019) 371–390.

Moravcsik A, 'In Defence of the 'Democratic Deficit': Reassessing Legitimacy in the European Union' (2002) 40 *Journal of Common Market Studies* 603.

—— *The Choice for Europe: Social Purpose and State Power from Messina to Maastricht* (Ithaca NY, Cornell University Press, 1998).

Nicolaïdis K, 'The Political Mantra: Brexit, Control and the Transformation of the European Order' in F Fabbrini (ed) *The Law & Politics of Brexit* (Oxford, Oxford University Press, 2017) 25–48.

—— 'Kir Forever? The Journey of a Political Scientist in the Landscape of Mutual Recognition' in M Poiares Maduro and L Azoulai (eds) *The Past and Future of EU Law* (Oxford, Hart Publishing, 2010) 447–455.

Nicolaïdis K and SK Schmidt, 'Mutual Recognition "On Trial": The Long Road to Services Liberalisation' (2007) 14 *Journal of European Public Policy* 717.

Nicolaïdis K and M Watson, 'Sharing the Eurocrats' dream: a demoicratic approach to EMU governance in the post-crisis era' in D Chalmers, M Jachtenfuchs and C Joerges (eds) *The End of the Eurocrats' Dream: Adjusting to European Diversity* (Cambridge, Cambridge University Press, 2016) 50–77.

North D, *Institutions, Institutional Change and Economic Performance* (Cambridge, Cambridge University Press, 1990).

Offe C, 'Europe Entrapped: Does the EU have the political capacity to overcome its current crisis?' (2013) 19 *European Law Journal* 595.

Ophüls CF, 'La Relance Européenne' in B Landheer and WH Carter (eds) Annuaire Européen / European Yearbook (Martinus Nijhoff, The Hague, 1958) 3–20.

Ortino M, 'The role and functioning of mutual recognition in the European market of financial services' (2007) 56 International Comparative Law Quarterly 309.
Padoa-Schioppa T, 'Europe Needs a Single Financial Rule Book' (2007) *Financial Times, 11 December.*
—— 'How to deal with emerging pan-European financial institutions?' (2004) www.ecb.europa.eu/press/key/date/2004/html/sp041103.en.html.
—— *Regulating Finance, Balancing Freedom and Risk* (Oxford, Oxford University Press, 2004).
—— 'EMU and Banking Supervision' (1999) 2 *International Finance*, 295.
—— 'The Genesis of EMU: A Retrospective View' (1996) *96/40 Jean Monnet Chair Paper RSC, European University Institute.*
—— *L'Europa verso l'unione monetaria: Dallo Sme al trattato di Maastricht* (Turin, Einaudi, 1992).
—— *Efficiency, Stability and Equity, A Strategy for the Evolution of the Economic System of the European Community* (Oxford, Oxford University Press, 1987).
Papademos L, 'Banking supervision and financial stability in Europe' (2006) 70 *Forum Financier-Revue Bancaire et Financiaire, Bank en Financiewezen* 3.
Papadopoulos Y, 'Problems of Democratic Accountability in Network and Multilevel Governance' (2008) 13 *European Law Journal* 469.
Pelkmans J, 'Economic Theories of Integration Revisited' (1980) 18 *Journal of Common Market Studies* 333.
Pelkmans J and P Robson, 'The aspirations of the White Paper' (1987) 25 *Journal of Common Market Studies* 181.
Pescatore P, 'Some Critical Remarks on the "Single European Act"', (1987) 24 *CML Rev* 9.
Piris JC, *The Future of Europe: Towards a Two-Speed EU?* (Cambridge, Cambridge University Press, 2012).
—— *The Lisbon Treaty: A Legal and Political Analysis* (Cambridge, Cambridge University Press, 2010).
Pisani-Ferry J and A Sapir, 'Banking crisis management in the EU: An interim assessment' (2009) 2009/07 *Bruegel Working Paper.*
Pisani-Ferry J and G Wolff, 'The Fiscal Implications of a Banking Union' (2012) 2012/02 *Bruegel Policy Brief.*
Pisani-Ferry J, A Sapir, N Véron and GB Wolff, 'What Kind of European Banking Union?' (2012) 2012/12 *Bruegel Policy Contribution.*
Poiares Maduro M, 'A New Governance for the European Union and the Euro: Democracy and Justice' (2012) 2012/11 *RSCAS Policy Paper.*
—— *We the Court: The European Court of Justice and the European Economic Constitution* (Oxford, Hart Publishing, 1998).
Posner E, 'Making rules for global finance: transatlantic regulatory cooperation at the turn of the millennium' (2009) 63 *International Organization* 665.
—— 'The Lamfalussy process: polyarchic origins of networked financial rulemaking in the EU' in C Sabel and J Zeitlin (eds) *EU Governance: Towards a New Architecture?* (Oxford, Oxford University Press, 2010) 43–60.
Posner E and N Véron, 'The EU and financial regulation: power without purpose?' (2010) 17 *Journal of European Public Policy* 400.
Praet P, 'Public Sector security purchases and monetary dominance in a monetary union without a fiscal union, Speech at the Conference, The ECB and its Watchers XVI' (2015), at www.ecb.europa.eu/press/key/date/2015/html/sp150311_1.en.html.
Quaglia L, 'Financial sector committee governance in the European Union' (2008) 30 *European Integration* 563.
—— 'The politics of financial services regulation and supervision reform in the European Union' (2007) 46 *European Journal of Political Research* 269.
Quintyn MG, S Ramirez, and MW Taylor, 'The Fear of Freedom: Politicians and the Independence and Accountability of Financial Sector Supervisors' (2007) WP/07/25 *IMF Working Paper.*
Rasmussen M, 'Revolutionizing European law: A history of the Van Gend en Loos judgment' (2014) 12 *International Journal of Constitutional Law* 136.
Rodrik D, *The Globalization Paradox* (Oxford, Oxford University Press, 2011).
Ruffert M, 'The European Debt Crisis and European Union Law' (2011) 48 *CML Rev* 1769.
Sabel C and J Zeitlin, 'Learning from Difference: The New Architecture of Experimentalist Governance in the European Union' in C Sabel and J Zeitlin (eds) *Experimentalist Governance in the European Union: Towards a New Architecture* (Oxford, Oxford University Press, 2010) 1–28.

Saha D and J von Weizsäcker, 'Estimating the size of the European stimulus packages for 2009: An Update' (2009) 2009/01 *Bruegel Policy Contribution.*

Sandholtz W and A Stone Sweet, 'Neo-Functionalism and Supranational Governance' in E Jones, A Menon, and S Weatherill (eds) *The Oxford Handbook of the European Union* (Oxford, Oxford University Press, 2012) 18–33.

Sapir A and G Wolff, 'The neglected side of banking union: reshaping Europe's financial system,' note presented at the Informal ECOFIN on 14 September 2013, Vilnius, Bruegel, at www.bruegel.org/wp-content/uploads/imported/publications/20130913SapirWolff_final_.pdf.

Schäfer D, 'A Banking Union of Ideas? The Impact of Ordoliberalism and the Vicious Circle on the EU Banking Union' (2016) 54 *Journal of Common Market Studies* 961.

Schammo P, 'The European Securities and Markets Authority: Lifting the Veil on the Allocation of Powers' (2011) 48 *CML Rev* 1879.

Scharpf F, *Governing in Europe: Effective and Democratic?* (Oxford, Oxford University Press, 2011).

Schaeuble W, 'How to protect EU taxpayers against bank failures (2012) *Financial Times, 30 August.*

—— 'Building a Sturdier Euro' (2012) *Wall Street Journal,* 12 December.

Schinasi GJ, *Safeguarding Financial Stability: Theory and Practice* (Washington DC, IMF, 2005).

Schinasi GJ and PG Teixeira, 'The Lender of Last Resort in the European Single Financial Market' (2006) *WP/06/127 IMF Working Paper.*

Schlosser P, *Europe's Fiscal Union* (Palgrave, 2019).

Schoenmaker D, 'Is Burden Sharing Needed for International Financial Stability?' in P Hartmann, H Huang, and D Schoenmaker (eds) *The Changing Fortunes of Central Banking* (Cambridge, Cambridge University Press, 2018) 203–226.

—— *Governance of international banking: The financial trilemma* (Oxford, Oxford University Press, 2013.

—— 'Banking supervision and resolution: the European dimension' (2012) 6 *Law and Financial Markets Review* 52.

Schoenmaker D and N Véron, 'European banking supervision: the first eighteen months' (2016) 25 *Bruegel Blueprint Series.*

Schoenmaker D and S Oosterloo, 'Financial supervision in Europe: do we need a new architecture?' (2006) 12 *Cahier Comte Boël, European League for Economic Cooperation.*

Scholten M and M van Rijsbergen, 'The ESMA-Short Selling Case: Erecting a New Delegation Doctrine in the EU upon the Meroni-Romano Remnants' (2014) 41 *Legal Issues of Economic Integration* 389.

Scholz O, 'Germany will consider EU-wide bank deposit reinsurance' (2019) *Financial Times,* 5 November.

Schooner HM and MW Taylor, *Global Bank Regulation: Principles and Policies* (London, Elsevier, 2010).

Schuknecht L, 'An insurance scheme that only ensures problems' (2016), at blogs.faz.net/fazit/2016/02/08/an-insurance-scheme-that-only-ensures-problems-7298.

Scott J and DM Trubek, 'Mind the Gap: Law and New Approaches to Governance in the European Union' (2002) 8 *European Law Journal, Special Issue on Law and the New Approaches to Governance in Europe* 1.

Simon HA, *Models of Man* (New York, Wiley, 1957).

Sinn HW, *The Euro-Trap* (Oxford, Oxford University Press, 2014).

—— *Casino Capitalism* (Oxford, Oxford University Press, 2010).

Slaughter AM, *A New World Order* (Princeton, Princeton University Press, 2004).

Slobodian Q, *Globalists: The End of Empire and the Birth of Neoliberalism* (Cambridge MA, Harvard University Press, 2018).

Smits R, 'A National Measure Annulled by the European Court of Justice, or: High-level Judicial Protection for Independent Central Bankers' (2020) 16 *European Constitutional Law Review* 1.

—— 'The European debt crisis and European Union law: comments and a call for action – A reply to the article of Matthias Ruffert, The European debt crisis and European Union law' (2012) 49 *CML Rev* 827.

—— 'European supervisors in the credit crisis: issues of competence and competition,' in M Giovanoli and D Devos (eds), *International Monetary and Financial Law in the light of the Global Crisis* (Oxford, Oxford University Press, 2010) 305–327.

—— *The European Central Bank: Institutional Aspects* (The Hague, Kluwer Law International, 1997).

Snyder F, 'EMU Revisited: Are We Making a Constitution? What Constitution Are We Making?' in P Craig and G De Burca (eds) *The Evolution of EU Law* (Oxford, Oxford University Press, 1999) 417–473.

—— 'The Effectiveness of European Community Law: Institutions, Processes, Tools and Techniques' (1993) 56 *Modern Law Review* 19.

Spaak PH, 'Rapport des Chefs de Délégation aux Ministres des Affaires Etrangères' ('Spaak Report') (1956) *Comité Intergouvernemental créé par la Conférence de Messine, Brussels, 21 avril.*

Stein E, 'Assimilation of National Laws as a Function of European Integration' (1964) 58 *American Journal International Law* 1.

Stone Sweet A, *The Judicial Construction of Europe* (Oxford, Oxford University Press, 2004).

Stone Sweet A, W Sandholtz, N Fligstein, 'The Institutionalization of European Space' in A Stone Sweet, W Sandholtz, N Fligstein (eds) *The Institutionalization of Europe* (Oxford, Oxford University Press, 2001).

Strange S, *Casino Capitalism* (Manchester, Manchester University Press, 1986).

Streeck W, 'Fighting the State' (2019) 50 *Development and Change* 836.

—— 'What about capitalism? Jürgen Habermas's project of a European democracy' (2017) 16 *European Political Science* 246.

Teixeira PG, 'The Regulation of the European Financial Market after the Crisis' in P della Posta and L Talani (eds) *Europe and the Financial Crisis* (London, Palgrave Macmillan, 2011) 9–27.

—— 'Public Governance and the Co-operative Law of Transnational Markets: The Case of Financial Regulation' in KH Ladeur (ed) *Public Governance in the Age of Globalization* (Aldershot, Ashgate, 2004) 305–335.

Ter Kuile G, L Wissink and W Bovenschen, 'Tailor-Made Accountability within the Single Supervisory Mechanism' (2015) 52 *CML Rev* 155.

Teubner G, '"Global Bukowina": Legal Pluralism in the World Society' in G Teubner (ed) *Global Law Without the State* (Aldershot, Dartmouth, 1997) 3–28.

Thatcher M, 'Speech to the College of Europe ('The Bruges Speech')' (1988) www.margaretthatcher.org/document/107332.

Tietmeyer H, 'International Co-operation and Co-ordination in the Area of Financial Market Supervision and Surveillance' (1999) 21/1999 *BIS Review.*

Tison M, 'Free movement capital and (financial) services: Moving on separate tracks' (2006) 3 *Euredia* 410.

—— 'Do not attack the watchdog! Banking supervisor's liability after Peter Paul' (2005) 42 *CML Rev* 639.

—— 'The Investment Services Directive and its Implementation in the EU Member States' (1999) 1999/17 *Financial Law Institute Working Paper.*

—— 'What is "General Good" in EU Financial Services Law?' (1997) 24 *Legal Issues of European Integration* 1.

Tridimas T, 'The Constitutional Dimension of Banking Union' in S Grundmann and HW Micklitz (eds) *The European Banking Union and Constitution: Beacon for Advanced Integration or Death-Knell for Democracy?* (Oxford, Hart Publishing, 2019) 25–48.

Tooze A, *Crashed: How a Decade of Financial Crises Changed the World* (New York, Viking, 2018).

Tumpel-Gugerell G, Report of the Expert Group on a Debt Redemption Fund and Eurobills, (2014), at ec.europa.eu/economy_finance/articles/governance/pdf/20140331_report_en.pdf.

Tuori K and K Tuori, *The Eurozone Crisis: A Constitutional Analysis* (Cambridge, Cambridge University Press, 2014).

Turner A, 'The Turner Review: a regulatory response to the global banking crisis' (2009) *Financial Services Authority.*

Underhill GRD, 'Keeping Governments Out of Politics: Transnational Securities Markets, Regulatory Cooperation, and Political Legitimacy' (1995) 21 *Review of International Studies* 251.

Uri P, *Penser pour l'Action: Un fondateur de l'Europe* (Paris, Odile Jacob, 1991).

—— Historical Archives of the European Union, PU-53.

Usher JA, 'The Evolution of the Free Movement of Capital' (2008) 31 *Fordham International Law Journal* 1533.

—— *The Law of Money and Financial Services in the EC* (Oxford, Oxford University Press, 2000).

Van Cleynenbreugel P, 'Meroni circumvented? Article 114 TFEU and EU regulatory agencies' (2014) 21 *Maastricht Journal of European and Comparative Law* 64.

Van Rompuy H in close collaboration with JM Barroso, JC Juncker and M Draghi, 'Towards a Genuine Economic and Monetary Union' (2012), at www.consilium.europa.eu/uedocs/cms_data/docs/pressdata/en/ec/134069.pdf.

Van Rompuy H, 'Remarks, 24 May' (2012) europa.eu/rapid/press-release_PRES-12-215_en.htm.

Vanberg VJ, 'The Freiburg School: Walter Eucken and Ordoliberalism' (2004) 04/11 *Freiburg Discussion Papers on Constitutional Economics.*

—— *The Constitution of Markets: Essays in Political Economy* (London, Routledge, 2001).

Varoufakis Y, *Adults in the Room* (London, Bodley Head, 2016).

Vauchez A, *Brokering Europe: Euro-Lawyers and the Making of a Transnational Polity* (Cambridge, Cambridge University Press, 2015).
Véron N, 'Precautionary recapitalisation: time for a review?' (2017) 21 *Bruegel Policy Contribution.*
—— 'A Response to Ludger Schuknecht' (2016), at bruegel.org/2016/02/european-deposit-insurance-a-response-to-ludger-schuknecht.
—— 'Europe's radical Banking Union' (2015) *Bruegel Essay and Lecture Series,* at bruegel.org/wp-content/uploads/imported/publications/essay_NV_CMU.pdf.
—— 'Europe's Single Supervisory Mechanism: most small banks are German (and Austrian and Italian)' (2014) *Bruegel Blog Post,* at bruegel.org/2014/09/europes-single-supervisory-mechanism-most-small-banks-are-german-and-austrian-and-italian.
—— 'Banking Nationalism and the European Crisis' (2013), at www.piie.com/publications/papers/veron20130627.pdf
—— 'Europe's Cyprus Blunder and its consequences' (2013), at www.bruegel.org/nc/blog/detail/article/1048-europes-cyprus-blunder-and-its-consequences.
Vos E, 'Fifty Years of European Integration and Forty-Five Years of Comitology' in A Ott and E Vos (eds) *Fifty Years of European Integration: Foundations and Perspectives* (The Hague, T.M.C. Asser Press, 2009) 31–56.
—— 'Independence, Accountability and Transparency of European Regulatory Agencies' in D Geradin, R Muñoz, and N Petit (eds) *Regulation through agencies: A new Paradigm of European Governance* (Cheltenham, Elgar, 2005) 120–137.
Walker GA, *International Banking Regulation, Law, Policy and Practice* (The Hague, Kluwer Law International, 2001).
Wall LD, M Nieto, and DG Mayes, 'Creating an EU-level supervisor for cross-border banking groups: Issues raised by the US experience with dual banking' in JR LaBrosse, R Olivares-Caminal and D Singh (eds) *Managing Risk in the Financial System* (Cheltenham, Elgar, 2011) 333–349.
Weatherill S, *The Internal Market as a Legal Concept,* (Oxford, Oxford University Press, 2017).
—— 'Maximum versus Minimum Harmonization: Choosing between Unity and Diversity in the Search for the Soul of the Internal Market' in NN Shuibhne and LW Gormley (eds) *From Single Market to Economic Union* (Oxford, Oxford University Press, 2012) 175–200.
—— 'The Limits of Legislative Harmonization Ten Years after Tobacco Advertising: how the Court's Case Law has become a "Drafting Guide"' (2011) 12 *German Law Journal* 827.
—— 'Pre-emption, harmonisation and the distribution of competence to regulate the internal market' in J Scott and C Barnard (eds) *The Law of the Single European Market* (Oxford, Hart Publishing, 2002) 41–73.
Weiler JHH, 'In the Face of Crisis – Input Legitimacy, Output Legitimacy and the Political Messianism of European Integration' (2012) 34 *Journal of European Integration* 825.
—— 'The Constitution of the Common Market Place: Text and Context in the Evolution of the Free Movement of Goods' in P Craig and G De Burca (eds) *The Evolution of EU Law,* (Oxford, Oxford University Press, 1999) 349–376.
—— *The Constitution of Europe* (Cambridge, Cambridge University Press, 1999).
—— 'Does Europe Need a Constitution? Demos, Telos and the German Maastricht Decision' (1995) 1 *European Law Journal* 219.
—— 'The Transformation of Europe' (1991) 100 *Yale Law Journal* 2403.
—— 'The Community System: the Dual Character of Supranationalism' (1981) 1 *Yearbook of European Law* 267.
White WR, 'Why Financial Stability is Important' (1998) 62/1998 *BIS Review.*
—— 'International agreements in the area of banking and finance: accomplishments and outstanding issues' in G von Furstenberg (ed) *Regulation and supervision of financial institutions in NAFTA countries and beyond* (Dordrecht, Springer, 1997) 48–81.
Wiethölter R, 'Materialization and Proceduralization in Modern Law' in G Teubner (ed) *Dilemmas of Law in the Welfare State* (Berlin, Walter de Gruyter, 1986) 221–249.
Wind M, *Sovereignty and European Integration: Towards a Post-Hobbesian order* (Loslaughterndon, Palgrave, 2001).
Witte B de, 'Euro Crisis Responses and the EU Legal Order: Increased Institutional Variation or Constitutional Mutation?' (2015) 11 *European Constitutional Law Review* 434.

—— 'Setting the Scene: How did Services get to Bolkestein and Why?' (2007) 2007/20 *EUI Working Paper*.

Witte B de and T Beukers, 'The Court of Justice approves the creation of the European Stability Mechanism outside the EU legal order: Pringle' (2013) 50 *CML Rev* 805.

Wojcik KP, 'Bail-in in the Banking Union' (2016) 53 *CML Rev* 91.

Wolff GB, 'Capital controls in Cyprus: the end of Target2?' (2013) at www.bruegel.org/nc/blog/detail/article/1054-capital-controls-in-cyprus-the-end-of-target2/.

Wymeersch E, 'The European Banking Union, a First Analysis' (2012) 2012-07 *Working Paper, Ghent University, Financial Law Institute*.

—— 'The European Financial Supervisory Authorities or ESA' in E Wymmeersch, KJ Hopt, G Ferrarini (eds) *Financial Regulation and Supervision: A Post-Crisis Analysis* (Oxford, Oxford University Press, 2012), 232–317.

—— 'Conflicts of interest in financial services groups' (2007) 2007-5 *Working Paper, Ghent University, Financial Law Institute*.

—— 'The Future of Financial Regulation and Supervision in Europe' (2005) 42 *CML Rev* 987.

Zavvos GS and S Kaltsouni, 'The Single Resolution Mechanism in the European Banking Union: Legal Foundation, Governance Structure and Financing' in M Haentjens and B Wessels (eds) *Research Handbook on Crisis Management in the Banking Sector* (Cheltenham, Elgar, 2015) 117–149.

Zeitlin J, 'EU Experimentalist Governance in Times of Crisis' (2016) 39 *West European Politics* 1072.

Zettelmeyer J, C Trebesch, and M Gulati, 'The Greek Debt Restructuring: An Autopsy' (2013) 28 *Economic Policy* 513.

Zhou J, V Rutledge, W Bossu, M Dobler, N Jassaud, and M Moore, 'From Bail-out to Bail-in: Mandatory Debt Restructuring of Systemic Financial Institutions' (2012) SDN/12/03 *IMF Staff Discussion Note*.

Zilioli C, 'The Independence of the European Central Bank and Its New Banking Supervisory Competences' in D Ritleng (ed) *Independence and Legitimacy in the Institutional System of the European Union* (Oxford, Oxford University Press, 2016) 125–179.

—— 'The ECB's Powers and Institutional Role in the Financial Crisis: A Confirmation from the Court of Justice of the European Union' (2016) 23 *Maastricht Journal of European and Comparative Law* 171.

—— 'Accountability and Independence: Irreconcilable Values or Complementary Instruments for Democracy? The Specific Case of the European Central Bank' in G Vandersanden (ed) *Mélanges en hommage à Jean-Victor Louis* (Bruxelles, Editions de l'Universite de Bruxelles, 2003) 395–422.

Zilioli C and M Selmayr, *The Law of the European Central Bank* (Oxford, Hart Publishing, 2001).

—— 'The European Central Bank: An Independent Specialised Organisation of Community Law' (2000) 37 *CML Rev* 591.

INDEX

www.ingramcontent.com/pod-product-compliance
Lightning Source LLC
Chambersburg PA
CBHW071305180926
51613CB00001B/125
9781509940622